International Criminal Justice Series

Volume 33

The *International Criminal Justice Series* aims to create a platform for publications covering the entire field of international criminal justice. It, therefore, deals with issues relating, among others, to:

- the work of international criminal courts and tribunals;
- transitional justice approaches in different countries;
- international anti-corruption and anti-money laundering initiatives;
- the history of international criminal law.

It is peer-reviewed and seeks to publish high-quality works emanating from excellent scholars.

Editorial Office

Prof. Dr. Moritz Vormbaum
University of Münster
Faculty of Law
Bispinghof 24-25
48143 Münster, Germany
vormbaum@uni-muenster.de

Johannes Block

Reconciling Responsibility with Reality

A Comparative Analysis of Modes of Active Leadership Liability in International Criminal Law

ASSER PRESS

Springer

Johannes Block
Bonn, Germany

ISSN 2352-6718 ISSN 2352-6726 (electronic)
International Criminal Justice Series
ISBN 978-94-6265-606-2 ISBN 978-94-6265-607-9 (eBook)
https://doi.org/10.1007/978-94-6265-607-9

Published by T.M.C. ASSER PRESS, The Hague, The Netherlands www.asserpress.nl
Produced and distributed for T.M.C. ASSER PRESS by Springer-Verlag Berlin Heidelberg

This T.M.C. ASSER PRESS imprint is published by the registered company Springer-Verlag GmbH, DE, part of Springer Nature.
The registered company address is: Heidelberger Platz 3, 14197 Berlin, Germany

Acknowledgements

This book is based on my thesis (Dr. iur.), which was accepted by the University of Cologne in June 2021 and which I defended in December of the same year. The thesis was awarded the *Promotionspreis der Rechtswissenschaftlichen Fakultät* of the University of Cologne and the *Ernst-Rabel-Preis* of the *Gesellschaft für Rechtsvergleichung e.V.*

I would like to express my deepest gratitude to Prof. Dr. Bettina Weisser, whose invaluable advice guided me through the research process, who encouraged me to look sceptically at established doctrine and allowed me considerable freedom to pursue my research while simultaneously working and teaching at the University of Cologne.

I am also indebted to Prof. Dr. Thomas Weigend, who was always available to discuss the many different aspects of the topic of this work and who provided the second report on my thesis.

I am furthermore grateful to Prof. Dr. Gerhard Werle, Prof. Dr. Moritz Vormbaum and Frank Bakker LL.M. for accepting my manuscript for publication in the *International Criminal Justice* Series and to Kiki van Gurp for her experienced and reliable guidance through the publication process.

The Faculty of Law at the University of Cologne generously supported the language editing of my thesis.

I also wish to thank the many colleagues and friends who have supported and encouraged me over the years of my research: Prof. Dr. Elies van Sliedregt for welcoming me as a visiting scholar at the University of Leeds and for sharing enriching insights into the topic of this work; Sir Howard Morrison QC for sharing his unparalleled expertise as a practitioner; Anna Seyfert for reviewing and discussing several chapters of the thesis; Julia Martens for her incredibly accurate and fast language editing; the team of the *Institut für ausländisches und internationales Strafrecht* at the University of Cologne, especially Kirsten Kindler, Dr. Sandra Petry, Christine Untch, Friederike Klimek, Yara Bröcker and Max Wrobel for great spirit and fruitful discussions; Dr. Jana Berberich and Kirsten Watson Weis for all the serious and not so serious conversations; Falko, Gabriel, Marvin and Lukas for real talk and fantastic encounters.

My mother, father and sister have encouraged and supported me in various ways throughout my years of study and research. Knowing that I will always have a home with them is one of the greatest gifts.

Finally, I am forever grateful to Jana, who has accepted and endured so much and without whose unrivalled positivity, good humour and loving support, I would not have been able to complete this work.

Cologne, Germany
April 2023

Johannes Block

Contents

Part II Responsibility for Ordering a Crime

Abbreviations

Art.	Article
BGH	*Bundesgerichtshof* (German Federal Court of Justice)
CCL 10	Control Council Law 10
e.g.	*Exempli gratia*
ECCC	Extraordinary Chambers in the Courts of Cambodia
et seq.	Et sequence
FDS	*Forces de Défence et de Sécurité* (Ivorian Defense Forces)
fn.	Footnote
FPLC	*Front Patriotique pour la Libération du Congo*
GCC	German Criminal Code
GCCov	German Criminal Code old version
GDR	German Democratic Republic
Gestapo	*Geheime Staatspolizei* (Secret State Police)
HVO	Croatian Defence Council
i.e.	*id est*
ICC	International Criminal Court
ICTR	International Criminal Tribunal for Rwanda
ICTY	International Criminal Tribunal for the Former Yugoslavia
ILC	International Law Commission
IMT	International Military Tribunal (Nuremberg)
IMTFE	International Military Tribunal for the Far East
JCE	Joint Criminal Enterprise
Lit.	*littera/e*
LRA	Lord's Resistance Army
MICT	International Residual Mechanism for Criminal Tribunals
MLC/ALC	*Mouvement de libération du Congo/Armée de libération du Congo*
mn.	Margin number
NJW	Neue Juristische Wochenschrift
NStZ	Neue Zeitschrift für Strafrecht
NVA	*Nationale Volksarmee* (National People's Army)
OKW	*Oberkommando Wehrmacht* (High Command of the Wehrmacht)

OTP	Office of the Prosecutor (of the International Criminal Court)
PNU	Party of National Unity (Kenya)
PTC	Pre-Trial Chamber (of the ICC)
RKFDV	*Reichskommissar für die Festigung des deutschen Volkstums* (Reich Commissioner for the Strengthening of Germanism)
RSHA	*Reichssicherheitshauptamt* (Reich Security Main Office)
RuSHA	*Rasse- und Siedlungshauptamt* (Race and Settlement Main Office)
SCSL	Special Court for Sierra Leone
SD	*Sicherheitsdienst* (Security Service of the SS)
SED	*Sozialistische Einheitspartei Deutschlands* (Socialist Unity Party of Germany)
SS	*Schutzstaffel* (Paramilitary party organisation of the National Socialist Party)
UPC	*Union Patriotique du Congo*
VCLT	Vienna Convention on the Law of the Treaties
WVHA	*Wirtschafts- und Verwaltungshauptamt* (Main Economic and Administrative Office of the SS)

Chapter 1
Introduction

Contents

Abstract How to properly attribute individual criminal responsibility to persons in leadership positions remains one of the most discussed questions of International Criminal Law. This introductory chapter explains the approach taken and method applied to produce an innovative answer to this question in this book. It is argued that applying responsibility for ordering a crime to some or all masterminds of international crimes seems an obvious solution, albeit one often ignored by international criminal tribunals. The reason for this is seen in the application of doctrines such as indirect (co-)perpetration. Therefore, the chapter argues to analyse these two forms of responsibility and compare them in detail. Thus, it may be found out, whether they can be meaningfully distinguished from each other and if not, whether there are any compelling reasons to prefer one over the other. The definitions and terms used in this book are explained with a view to the plethora of legal technical terms that are applied during the course of it.

Keywords Indirect (co-)perpetration · Ordering · *Organisationsherrschaft* · Rome Statute · Adolf Eichmann · Perpetration · Participation

1.1 Topic and Method of this Book

Criminal responsibility of persons in leadership positions is one of the core topics of criminal law whenever mass atrocities are concerned. In the trial against the Holocaust organiser Adolf Eichmann, the Jerusalem District Court famously stated that,

> [i]n such an enormous and complicated crime as the one we are now considering, wherein many people participated at various levels and in various modes of activity—the planners, the organizers and those executing the acts, according to their various ranks—there is not much point in using the ordinary concepts of counselling and soliciting to commit a crime.

J. Block, *Reconciling Responsibility with Reality*, International Criminal Justice Series 33, https://doi.org/10.1007/978-94-6265-607-9_1

> For these crimes were committed en masse, not only in regard of the number of victims, but also in regard to the numbers of those who perpetrated the crime, and the extent to which any one of the many criminals were close to, or remote from, the actual killer of the victim, means nothing as far as the measure of his responsibility is concerned.
>
> On the Contrary, in general, the degree of responsibility increases as we draw further away from the man who uses the fatal instrument with his own hands and reach the higher ranks of command...[1]

The conviction that the responsibility of leading figures, who act as the masterminds behind international crimes, is greater than that of the actual executioners lies at the heart of international criminal justice. But how and under which head of responsibility can the people who bear the most responsibility for mass atrocities be tried?

The Jerusalem District Court convicted Adolf Eichmann as a perpetrator, i.e., a person who committed the crime, for the reasons stated above. Inspired by the *Eichmann* trial, the German legal scholar Claus Roxin developed a doctrine under which a person in a leadership position can be attributed liability held liable for committing the crimes perpetrated under their command, instead of viewing them as an instigator. In the same vein as the Court in *Eichmann,* Roxin observed that mass atrocities would defy the recognized categories of perpetration and participation, and therefore developed his own approach: The *Mittelbare Täterschaft kraft Organisationsherrschaft* was born.

Decades later, the International Criminal Court (ICC) moved to adopt the theory of *Mittelbare Täterschaft kraft Organisationsherrschaft* which had emerged in Germany from the debate which Roxin had initiated.

The doctrine that the ICC embraced was dubbed "indirect perpetration through an organisation" in an approximately direct translation of its German role model. It is based on and read into Art. 25 (3) (a) Rome Statute and, just as its German predecessor, allows for the conviction of leaders behind international crimes for "committing" the crime. Although the term cannot be found in the statute, this is known as perpetrator liability and is considered by many to be the most useful approach to the issue. The theory rests on a specific interpretation of the overall system of Art. 25 (3) Rome Statute. Many believe that the provisions distinguish between the more blameworthy "commission" of a crime in *littera* (a) and the less serious forms of participation in *litterae* (b) to (d). But is this interpretation convincing and is it even necessary?

As an international treaty, the Rome Statute is based on compromises between the delegations of many states. Consequently, Art. 25 (3) does not resemble one national legal system and cannot be said to be based on a coherent legal grounding.[2] Whilst some of the article's features seem to imply a basis in German legal theory, serious doubts surrounding the intended or "correct" form of leadership responsibility arise when considering the following.

---

[1] District Court of Jerusalem, *Judgment Against Karl Adolf Eichmann—Unofficial Translation*, 40/61, No. 197.

[2] Ohlin et al. 2013, p 744.

Art. 25 (3) (b) Rome Statute criminalizes the "ordering" of crimes. When read without the bias of any national legal system, the simple wording of this provision instantly raises the question of the meaning behind this form of responsibility. Where did this mode originate from and, more importantly, if leaders who determine the commission of crimes are perpetrators under *lit.* (a), then who is to fall under ordering pursuant to *lit.* (b)? In the quest to adjudicate the masterminds behind international crimes, an unbiased reading of the two *litterae* of Art. 25 (3), would seemingly assign an important role to ordering. After all, is this not the most important aspect of leadership criminality, where a person gives an order that makes others commit crimes, where a leader cries 'Havoc!' and lets slip the dogs of war?[3]

From a technical viewpoint the question arises: If the path to conviction, which is presented by Art. 25 (3) (b) (ordering) is ignored, as done by the ICC and a widely held opinion in academia, is there any way to meaningfully distinguish indirect perpetration through an organisation from ordering a crime and thus meaningfully apply the latter?[4]

From this perspective, the necessity of the doctrine of indirect perpetration through an organisation, which can but must not necessarily be read into Art. 25 (3) (a) Rome Statute, becomes questionable.

Scholars have repeatedly called for the development of an international doctrine of perpetration and participation in crime.[5] However, the aforementioned issues raise doubts as to whether the application of a doctrine, imported from national criminal law is the best way of doing so. The book focuses on this question.

This book assesses whether the import of indirect perpetration through an organisation into the jurisprudence of the ICC is necessary and convincing or whether the Rome Statute provides for another, better approach to the issue of leadership participation in mass atrocities. The answer to this question is sought through a comparative analysis of forms of responsibility.

Indirect perpetration through an organisation is first displayed in the forms in which the doctrine exists in German scholarly writing and jurisprudence (Chap. 2). The chapter paves the way for the following comparison and illustrates that explanations of the doctrine are often one-sided and less compelling than one might think.

---

[3] "Cry 'Havoc!' and let slip the dogs of war" is a phrase spoken by Mark Antony in William Shakespeare's play Julius Caesar. It implies the triggering of violence and crimes through a superior authority on whose command the "dogs of war" act. In medieval England, the order of "Havoc" had to be given by a high commander and gave the signal to soldiers to start pillaging (see Keen 1989, p 43; see also https://www.oxfordlearnersdictionaries.com/definition/english/havoc?q=havoc. Accessed 6 April 2023).

[4] Manacorda and Meloni 2011, pp 171–2; Vest 2014, pp 303–4; Vogel 2002, p 427 with fn. 112; Weigend 2011, p 105; Yanev 2018, pp 468–70. See also ICC, *The Prosecutor v. Bosco Ntaganda*, Appeals Judgment, 30 March 2021, ICC-01/04-02/06-A A2, Separate opinion of Judge Howard Morrison on Mr. Ntaganda's appeal, paras 7, 42.

[5] See e.g. Stewart 2014, pp 334–5 who calls for the development of an international concept of individual criminal responsibility; see also Jessberger and Geneuss 2008, p 867.

In a second step, the doctrine in the form applied by the ICC is explored through an analysis of relevant jurisprudence. The ICC's approach is then compared to the different German models or versions of the doctrine. Finally, and based on the outcome of this comparison, the ICC's doctrine is confronted with criticism (Chap. 3).

Part II of this book concerns the responsibility for ordering a crime. The historic development of this mode of liability is explored by analysing its role in Post-World War II Jurisprudence, i.e., primarily the Nuremberg Subsequent Trials (Chap. 4), and in the practice of the *ad hoc* tribunals for the former Yugoslavia and Rwanda (Chap. 5). The second part of the book concludes with an assessment and evaluation of the current application of "ordering a crime" by the ICC (Chap. 6). Finally, the outcome of the two parts is compared (Chap. 7). This chapter will evaluate to what extent the two forms of liability in Art. 25 (3) Rome Statute overlap. It will further explore which form should be applied and which should be dispensed with. Finally, the outcome of the comparison leads to an opinion on the preferable form of responsibility to address leadership participation in mass atrocities under the current regulation and to further thoughts on the necessities of future models of imputation (Chap. 8).

The book in its entirety takes different aspects into account to enable a full picture of the issue. The forms of responsibility are compared with respect to their legal requirements and certain features within their respective system of perpetration and participation. Therefore, the chapters will also discuss whether the forms are categorized as principal or secondary liability, whether their attempt is criminalized and in how far they are seen as more or less serious than other forms of responsibility. Furthermore, the theoretical applicability and actual application of forms of responsibility to relevant cases of mass atrocities are explored and compared wherever case material exists. This will enable a second, more intuitive and historical view on the matter: To which extent were the forms of responsibility actually applied to cases which they seem to grasp in theory? And if they were not applied, could they have been used and why were they not?

Finally, during the course of the book, the notion of "appropriateness" of forms of responsibility is first discussed within the German approach to the issue and is subsequently considered as what is recognized as the principles of fair labelling and expressive justice in international criminal law.

By considering these aspects, the book strives to provide a comprehensive picture of the necessity and suitability of indirect perpetration through an organisation and ordering a crime for the adjudication of leaders behind mass atrocities.

Through this comparison, the book aims to contribute to the development of an international model of attribution of responsibility for mass atrocities.

1.2 Limits of and Definitions Used in this Book

Some remarks must be made concerning the scope, terminology, and methodology of this book.[6]

The question of leadership liability in international criminal law is understood here in a narrow sense. This means that the focus will be the active conduct of persons in leadership positions. Instead of using the term mastermind, these persons are described as decision makers and architects of crimes. These terms refer to the actor's respective conduct. Persons who make the decision whether crimes will be committed are considered decision makers. Where the decisions of leaders do not directly concern the commission of crimes but are of a planning or organisational nature, the book will speak of architects of crimes. Both types of conduct can be fulfilled by the same person and can be equally closely connected to a person's role or rank.

The book compares the forms of indirect perpetration through an organisation as a form of commission through another under Art. 25 (3) (a) and the mode of ordering a crime pursuant to Art. 25 (3) (b) Rome Statute. Other forms of responsibility, regardless of their practical role in adjudicating persons in leadership positions are not taken into account. Superior Responsibility under Art. 28 Rome Statute is not part of the comparison as it primarily applies to wrongful omissions of the superior. The combined mode of indirect co-perpetration which has mostly been used in practice by the ICC is also excluded from the analysis. This doctrine is primarily based on co-perpetration but uses indirect perpetration to establish the link between the co-perpetrators and the committed crimes.[7] Due to its reference to co-perpetration, its analysis would overburden this book. Simultaneously, any criticism of indirect perpetration mentioned in this book equally applies to the combined doctrine. If indirect perpetration through an organisation should be found to represent an unnecessary and unconvincing approach to leadership liability, the doctrine of indirect co-perpetration would be equally questionable.

As far as indirect commission is concerned, the point of reference for the exploration and comparison will be German academic literature and jurisprudence. The resemblance and differences between the ICC's approach and the German theories will shed light on the scope and potential criticism of the doctrine. Similar doctrines from other countries cannot be taken into account.

---

[6] For a book with a similar topic see: Lanza 2021. Lanza's book was published after the submission of the work underlying this monography and is therefore only referenced sporadically.

[7] See for explanations of the doctrine of indirect co-perpetration: Ohlin et al. 2013, pp 734–5; Ohlin 2012, pp 777–82. Note especially the explanation of "L-shaped" indirect co-perpetration The possibility of such a form has been confirmed by the ICC (see ICC, *The Prosecutor v. Laurent Gbagbo and Charles Blé Goudé*, Reasons for oral decision of 15 January 2019 on the Requête de la Défense de Laurent Gbagbo afin qu'un jugement d'acquittement portant sur toutes les charges soit prononcé en faveur de Laurent Gbagbo et que sa mise en liberté immédiate soit ordonnée, and on the Blé Goudé Defence no case to answer motion, 16 July 2019, ICC-02/11-01/15, Annex B, para 1922).

As for the methodology, parts of this book rely on the analysis of judgments primarily concerning international law as discussed in Chaps. 3 through 6. The selection made, analysis undertaken and conclusions drawn were made in good conscience and consider vast parts of the relevant jurisprudence. However, this book is not an empirical study and does not claim to be one.

Finally, terminology is an important factor where different legal concepts are closely interlinked with their respective denominations. These, in turn, can vary from one (inter)national legal system to another.

This book uses the following terms within the respective definition provided alongside them:

- "Modes of liability", "forms of responsibility" and every combination of the two elements of these terms describe one or more legal concepts that, under certain requirements, trigger individual responsibility for a crime. Doctrines that are based on interpretations of provisions and usually constitute a sub-category of the explicitly mentioned concepts of liability attribution are equally referred to by these terms (e.g., the abovementioned indirect perpetration through an organisation).
- "Principal" or "primary responsibility", as well as being a "principal" or "perpetrator" describe forms of responsibility that lead to original, non-derivative liability. This means, a principal's or perpetrator's liability does not depend legally on the commission of the crime by another person. It therefore arises irrespectively and independently of the responsibility of other persons. Of course, if the perpetrator or principal does not physically fulfil the elements of the crime, someone else must still physically do so. The term perpetrator will therefore not only be used for persons who fulfil the definitional elements of a crime. Such actors will be called "physical" or "hands-on perpetrators".
- "Secondary" or "accessory responsibility", as well as being an "accessory" are used to describe forms of responsibility that lead to derivative liability. This means that, in one form or another, they hinge on the commission of the crime by a principal/perpetrator. The accessorial object defines to which degree the crime must be committed in the legally relevant sense by the principal to enable accessory or secondary liability.
- "Participation in" and "being a participant" in a crime are used as the overarching terms for principal and accessory forms of liability. A perpetrator and an accessory are "participants in the crime".
- As an exception to the aforementioned, where a system is explicitly described as "consisting of forms of perpetration and participation", the term "participation" refers to accessorial/secondary forms of liability only. Where the term "participation" is used outside of this context, the abovementioned definition is used.
- The terms "complicity" and "accomplice" are avoided as far as possible. If they are used, they refer to secondary/accessory liability in the sense defined above.
- The terms "differentiated/differentiating", "distinction/distinguishing" and "unitary" or "monistic" "model" or "system" refer to the distinction or lack thereof made by a criminal law system between principals and accessories. A system

that uses such a distinction, i.e., recognizes derivative liability, is a "differentiated/differentiating" and "distinction/distinguishing" system, whilst systems that operate without and rely solely on notions of original, i.e., principal/primary liability are called "unitary" or "monistic". The terms imply no hierarchy of blameworthiness between the forms of responsibility within either system.

References

Jessberger F, Geneuss J (2008) On the Application of a Theory of Indirect Perpetration in *Al Bashir*. Journal of International Criminal Justice 6:853–869

Keen M (1989) Richard II's Ordinances of War 1385. In: Archer R, Walker S (eds) Rulers and Ruled in Late Medieval England: Essays presented to Gerald Harriss. London Hambledon Press, London, 33–49

Lanza G (2021) Indirect Perpetration and Organisationsherrschaftslehre. Duncker & Humblot, Berlin

Manacorda S, Meloni C (2011) Indirect Perpetration versus Joint Criminal Enterprise. Journal of International Criminal Justice 9:159–178

Ohlin JD (2012) Second-Order Linking Principles: Combining Vertical and Horizontal Modes of Liability. Leiden Journal of International Law 25:771–797

Ohlin JD, van Sliedregt E, Weigend T (2013) Assessing the Control–Theory. Leiden Journal of International Law 26:725–746

Stewart JG (2014) Ten Reasons for Adopting a Universal Concept of Participation. In: van Sliedregt E, Vasiliev S (eds) Pluralism in International Criminal Law. Oxford University Press, Oxford, 320–341

Vest H (2014) Problems of Participation—Unitarian, Differentiated Approach, or Something Else? Journal of International Criminal Justice 12:295–309

Vogel J (2002) Individuelle Verantwortlichkeit im Völkerstrafrecht. Zeitschrift für die gesamte Strafrechtswissenschaft 114:403–436

Weigend T (2011) Perpetration through an Organization—The Unexpected Career of a German Legal Concept. Journal of International Criminal Justice 9:91–111

Yanev L (2018) Theories of Co-Perpetration in International Criminal law. Brill Nijhoff, Leiden

Part I
Indirect Perpetration Through an Organisation

The doctrine of indirect perpetration through an organisation as applied by the ICC is based on Art. 25 (3) (a) Rome Statute, more precisely on the wording of the commission of a crime "through another". This doctrine was first outlined by Claus Roxin in 1963 as a way to attribute liability under German criminal law to leaders behind crimes committed through members of an organisation.

Chapter 2 explores the development of and different views on the doctrine as well as its underlying theory of perpetration and participation, the theory of domination of the crime in German academic literature and the relevant jurisprudence. Chapter 3 explores the way the doctrine is applied by the ICC, compares this with the German theories and offers criticisms.

Part I sheds light on the current approach as practised by the ICC and advocated for by many scholars. By comparing the ICC's version to the various German approaches, similarities and differences between the theories can be identified. This enables the transference of certain points of criticism known from the German debate. The comparison also widens the perspective by highlighting different approaches to the issue in German national law.

Through the exploration of these topics, a comprehensive picture of the ICC's version of indirect perpetration through an organisation and of this doctrine's issues and shortcomings can be drawn. This in turn will enable a comparison with the form of ordering a crime (Part II).

Chapter 2
The German Origins of Indirect Perpetration Through an Organised Apparatus of Power

Contents

Abstract The question of how to attribute individual criminal responsibility to leaders who plan, organise and instruct the commission of mass atrocity crimes is decades old and has received considerable attention in German academia and practice. The theory today applied by the International Criminal Court (ICC) is largely based on the writings of German scholars and jurisprudence of the German Federal Court of Justice. This chapter therefore explains and analyses German academic writing and jurisprudence on the theory of indirect perpetration through an organisation and its underlying theory of domination of the crime. By shedding light on

J. Block, *Reconciling Responsibility with Reality*, International Criminal Justice Series 33, https://doi.org/10.1007/978-94-6265-607-9_2

these German origins of the doctrine the chapter lays the basis to analyse the theories as applied by the ICC, to critically review the doctrine and to explore whether liability for indirect perpetration through an organisation can be meaningfully distinguished from ordering a crime. This chapter explains three approaches to the theory of indirect perpetration through an organisation which can be distinguished in the German debate: A traditional doctrine, based on the writing of Claus Roxin and other scholars, the approach taken by the jurisprudence and a systemic-functional view. This chapter explores these different approaches and their catalyst case: The trial against Adolf Eichmann.

Keywords Indirect (co)perpetration · Indirect perpetration through an organisation · Adolf Eichmann · *Tatherrschaft* · *Tatherrschaftslehre* · Organised apparatus of power · Domination of the crime

2.1 The Case of Adolf Eichmann—A Catalyst for the Development of a Doctrine

In 1960, a team of Israeli agents captured a man who was living under the name of Ricardo Klement in Buenos Aires, Argentina. After double-checking their detainee's identity, the team smuggled the man out of the country, to bring him before a court in Israel.[1]

His real name was Otto Adolf Eichmann, born in the German Rhineland in 1906. He would eventually be tried, convicted, and executed as one of the persons bearing the main responsibility for the Holocaust.[2]

Eichmann had held a position within the Nazi's *Reichssicherheitshauptamt* (*RSHA*, Reich Security Main Office). In his earlier years in the "third Reich's" bureaucracy, he rose through the ranks of the *Schutzstaffel* (SS) and through positions within Nazi agencies. *Inter alia,* he was tasked with the "emigration" of European Jews from annexed Austria.[3]

Eichmann eventually became head of a department within the *RSHA*. This department was first tasked with the organisation and coordination of trains to deport Jews from occupied and annexed Poland to the General Government and to the city of Łódź in occupied Poland.[4]

In March 1941, Eichmann's department was renamed into "Judenangelegenheiten—Räumungsangelegenheiten" (*Jewish Affairs—Evacuations).*[5] Eichmann participated in the notorious Wannsee Conference in January 1942, albeit "only" as the aide of Reinhard Heydrich, the chief of the *RSHA*. At the Wannsee Conference

---

[1] Cesarani 2004, pp 324–30.

[2] On Eichmann's personal history, see von Lang 1982, p 10 et seq.

[3] Cesarani 2004, p 89 et seq.

[4] Arendt 2018, p 329; Cesarani 2004, pp 118–21.

[5] Cesarani 2004, p 133.

the participants from various agencies of the Nazi state were confronted with the plans for the so-called *Endlösung*, the Final Solution; the plan for the murder of European Jews. From then on, Eichmann knew the true meaning of the forthcoming deportations.[6] When circulating the protocol of the Wannsee Conference, Heydrich designated Eichmann as the specialist for deportations and the point of contact to whom officials of others agencies should turn.[7] Consequently, Eichmann and his department became the central point for all deportations into concentration camps.[8]

The decision as to whether a specific deportation would take place, however, was not Eichmann's to make. Such decisions were made by Heinrich Himmler. The chain of command then went through Reinhard Heydrich and Ernst Kaltenbrunner (who succeeded Heydrich after the Heydrich's death) and Eichmann's immediate superior Heinrich Müller.[9] The latter passed on the orders orally to Eichmann.[10]

As a *Referent* (senior desk officer), Adolf Eichmann was mainly tasked with day-to-day business, after the political decisions had already been made. He himself had no power or authority of command. Provided their knowledge of and consent to the instructions issued by him, he could, however, act on behalf of his superiors.[11]

The political decisions made on and general instructions given by higher levels had to be translated into specific directives and orders by Eichmann and his department. Such orders would, for example, concern the *RSHA*'s officials in occupied territories who were then tasked with gathering information about the local Jewish communities, especially their numbers and their wealth.[12]

The department, headed by Eichmann, could also give orders to the branches of the *Sicherheitspolizei* (Security Police) that would execute the deportations by dispatching the necessary guards for arrest and transport. These guards also received detailed instructions to keep lists on the arrested and deported persons, their baggage and the deaths that occurred during the deportation process.[13]

Additionally, Eichmann and his department determined the train schedules for the deportations throughout Nazi-Germany, as well as the occupied and annexed territories.[14]

Finally, the department designed the mechanisms for the seizure of the deported Jews' property. It prepared documents in which the persons who were to be deported had to list the entirety of their wealth and belongings. During the deportation itself, a bailiff supervised the transfer of assets which was affected by the deported signing another document.[15]

---

[6] Ibid., p 160 et seq.

[7] Ibid., p 170.

[8] Ibid., p 172; Arendt 2018, p 250.

[9] Arendt 2018, p 251; Cesarani 2004, p 173.

[10] Arendt 2018, p 251.

[11] Cesarani 2004, pp 172–3.

[12] Ibid., p 175.

[13] Ibid., p 175.

[14] Arendt 2018, pp 250–1.

[15] Cesarani 2004, p 175.

Eichmann's department was also tasked with the negotiation and conclusion of agreements with other agencies of the Nazi state apparatus, which were also involved in the deportations.

The destination to which the cattle wagons in which Jews would be deported were headed, was not determined by Eichmann's department. Instead, one of his subordinates, upon receiving notice that a deportation was to take place, contacted a department within the *Wirtschafts- und Verwaltungshauptamt* (*WVHA*, the vast economic agency of the SS, which was *inter alia* responsible for running the concentration and extermination camps).[16] A contact person would then name the destination, which had been decided by the responsible officials within his agency.[17] Contact also had to be maintained to the *WVHA* to stay informed about the available "capacities" (i.e., to murder) of the designated extermination camps, as this would influence the final, designated number of deported persons.[18]

Eichmann's department furthermore had to reach out to the Ministry of Traffic, as once a deportation had been ordered from above, the necessary trains had to be acquired; a task, which apparently required a lot of negotiation and convincing.[19]

As deportations could concern Jewish residents with foreign nationalities, further discussions were held with the Ministry of Foreign Affairs. In such cases, the latter often objected to their deportation, necessitating extensive discussions with Eichmann.[20]

Finally, if deportations were to take place outside of the territory of Nazi Germany in its affiliated axis states, such as in Vichy France, Italy and Hungary, Eichmann's tasks included conferring with the local authorities which would have to execute the arrests.[21]

Eichmann's role was therefore not a political one *per se* but rather organisational or executive in nature. This, however, did not mean that his decisions had no influence

---

[16] Ibid., p 176.

[17] Ibid., p 176; The competent person at the *WVHA* was probably informed beforehand as well. When giving the order for a specific deportation, Himmler did not only confer with Heydrich/Kaltenbrunner but also with Oswald Pohl, the head of the *WVHA,* whom he told how many of the deported Jews would be murdered right away and which percentage had to be "spared" for forced labour. Whether Himmler directly instructed the commanders of extermination camps to murder Jews, or whether such orders were passed down through Pohl's *WVHA* seems difficult to determine. According to Hannah Arendt's account, Himmler tasked Pohl with relaying the numbers of the Jews who would be murdered and those who would be used for slave labour, see Arendt 2018, p 251. However, the Nuremberg military tribunal, that sentenced Oswald Pohl to death for running the *WVHA*, believed that he had not been responsible for such direct killing instructions. Instead, the tribunal found that Himmler contacted the secret state police directly for this matter, see Trials of War Criminals Before the Nuernberg Military Tribunals Under Control Council Law No. 10, Vol. V, U.S. Government Printing Service 1950, 981.

[18] Arendt 2018, p 252.

[19] Ibid., p 252; Cesarani 2004, p 176.

[20] Cesarani 2004, pp 177–8.

[21] Arendt 2018, p 252; for details see e.g. ibid., p 263 et seq. on the organisation of deportations from western Europe; see especially 270 on negotiations with the higher leaders of SS and Police, who were directly subordinate to Himmler.

on the fate of the Jewish victims of the deportations. It was *inter alia* up to Eichmann to define the criteria according to which the Jewish target group of a deportation would be selected.[22] Although he could neither decide where the trains would go nor whether they would go at all, every final confirmation of a deportation had to pass through his office, due to its decisive role in the organisation of the complex operations.[23]

In March 1944 Eichmann and a part of his department moved to Budapest, Hungary to be closer to the deportation which was to be executed there.[24] The steps undertaken by him and his group mostly resembled their mode of operation during the earlier Holocaust, with the major difference being that the department was now on site. They set up a Jewish council which would assist them in instructing the Jewish population.[25] Subsequently, negotiations with railroad authorities were held to enable the transport of Hungarian Jews to Auschwitz.[26] At the same time, Rudolf Höß—commander of Auschwitz—was informed of the plan by his superior Glücks. Consequently, Höß had additional railways constructed which ended only a few hundred meters from the crematories of Auschwitz. The potential to murder was consequently increased from 6,000 to 12,000 persons per day.[27] Even after the Hungarian government bent to the massive international pressure and declared an end to deportations, Eichmann was able to organise and channel at least one more deportation train past the Hungarian authorities.[28] After the campaign in Hungary, only 160,000 of formerly 800,000 Jews of the Budapest ghetto were still alive.[29]

The description of Eichmann's department as a "central point" in the organisation of the Holocaust seems to accurately describe the responsibility of the men in this unit. They were not in charge of deciding whether and where Jews would be killed. These decisions were made by Himmler and channelled through the *WVHA* or passed on directly to the camp commanders.[30] However, by large extent due to its organisational and coordinating functions, Eichmann's department was the one group that made the

[22] Cesarani 2004, p 173; the lists of persons who would be deported from a certain region were consequently drawn up by the Jewish Councils or the Police (see Arendt 2018, pp 325–6), but most certainly based on the mentioned criteria which were determined by Eichmann.

[23] Arendt 2018, p 252.

[24] Ibid., p 303.

[25] Ibid., p 303.

[26] Ibid., p 308.

[27] Ibid., p 308.

[28] Ibid., p 309.

[29] Ibid., p 310.

[30] The *WVHA* was the main operator of the Nazi concentration camps and of the extermination camps at Auschwitz-Birkenau and Majdanek. Orders concerning the murder of Jewish people in these and other camps were issued by Himmler through the *WVHA* chain of command or directly to the commanders of the respective camps, e.g., Rudolf Höß in Auschwitz. See Erdmann 1983, pp 532–3; Orth 1999, pp 137–41 (on the first murders in gas chambers of Auschwitz), 200–2 (on the communication between Himmler and Höß in the expansion of Auschwitz into an extermination camp), 203–4 (on further restructuring of Auschwitz under Oswald Pohl's supervision), 255–60 (on Oswald Pohl's and Rudolf Höß' direct decisions concerning the fate of Jewish inmates in Auschwitz and the further expansion of Auschwitz-Birkenau for the murder of Jews from Hungary). Note,

subsequent killings possible. Deportation meant certain death, whether it came about during the round ups, due to the conditions during transport or at the extermination camps. Therefore, Eichmann's contribution to every single murder committed in their wake is beyond question.

However, it is the details of Eichmann's contributions to the murders, which will be of further interest.

Eichmann enjoyed considerable freedom and exercised a lot of personal initiative in effecting the orders that he received from above.

When contemplating the fate of individuals, the tasks carried out by Eichmann's department contributed to the murder of millions of Jews to different degrees. When determining the criteria based on which the target groups for the deportations were defined, Eichmann obviously made (abstract) decisions regarding who would live and who would die.[31] When orders were given to the police to round up and deport, they were Eichmann's instructions, albeit only given as the representative of his superiors. One could say that Eichmann did not determine whether a deportation would take place, but how.[32] Other actions undertaken by Eichmann and his department did not rest on actual decision-making powers but their persuasion and coordination of others. This concerned the necessary negotiations with other Ministries. Such negotiations would result in certain persons being spared or in the operation of the necessary trains by the railroad authorities. In these instances, it was not Eichmann making the relevant organisational decisions, however, he facilitated their execution by making the actions of others align with the plans of his department.

Eichmann's conduct can therefore, be described as organising, coordinating and supervising the deportation of Jews from everywhere within the sphere of power of the "Third Reich". Even though some organisational steps were more directly under Eichmann's control than others, he had a role to play in all of them. His influence only ended, when his victims reached the Nazi's extermination camps; that is, right before they were murdered.

---

however, that a U.S. military tribunal found that Oswald Pohl had no saying in the extermination orders, which seems contradictory to the foregoing findings.

[31] This rather direct connection seemingly escaped Eichmann when he stated that he had never killed anybody. However, the fact that decisions like the one concerning the criteria had an immediate effect on the life and death of individuals, was perhaps overlooked by others as well. Hannah Arendt's famous account of the trial contains a similar statement in which she states that Eichmann and his men indeed lacked the power to decide whom would die and whom would live, see Arendt 2018, pp 325–6.

[32] Note in this regard the description by the District Court of Jerusalem stating that "every trainload of 'Transport Jews' reached the Auschwitz camp with its passengers condemned to death by a general decree given in respect of the transport as a whole by the Accused's section"; District Court of Jerusalem, *Judgment Against Karl Adolf Eichmann—Unofficial Translation*, 40/61, No. 145. This, however, seems like an oversimplification because the decision that the people who would be deported would be murdered was made even before Eichmann's department began organising the deportation.

About two decades after Eichmann's career within the Nazi murder machinery, he was brought before the Jerusalem District Court to answer for the crimes that he had made possible.[33]

2.2 The Traditional Concept of Indirect Perpetration Through an Organisation

But how would a person like Adolf Eichmann answer for his participation in the murder of millions of people and his role in the Holocaust?

The Jerusalem District Court convicted Eichmann as a "perpetrator", a principal, to the crimes.[34] It did so fully aware that the common denomination of someone who did not kill anybody with their own hands would be that of an accessory: an instigator, aider, or abettor. The court, however, discarded this assessment. Finding instead that the influential participation in the unprecedented horrors of the Holocaust defied the classic forms of responsibility as known by most criminal legal systems.[35]

2.2.1 Eichmann as a Perpetrator

With a view to the court in Jerusalem, in 1963 German scholar Claus Roxin, first engaged with the question of how such a case could and would be treated under German law. German jurisprudence at the time would have allowed for the conviction of a person operating in the background, an architect or decision maker of a crime, as a perpetrator.[36]

Claus Roxin, however, rejected this doctrinal approach of the courts. Instead, he developed another theory taking objective and subjective factors into account to convict "masterminds" of crimes as perpetrators.

---

[33] The trial began on 11 April 1961 (Cesarani 2004, p 361), Eichmann was convicted on 11 December 1961 (ibid., p 433) and hanged on the night from 31 May to 1 June 1962 (ibid., pp 451–4) after the judgment was upheld in appeal and his request for pardon denied (see ibid., pp 448–9 (appeal), 450–1 (pardon)).

[34] See the list of convictions and acquittals in *Judgment Against Adolf Eichmann*, No. 244.

[35] Ibid., No. 197.

[36] At the time, German courts distinguished between perpetrators and accessories based on a purely subjective theory. This means, if the courts would have affirmed the necessary *mens rea* of commission in the case of an organiser of a crime, they could have convicted him as a perpetrator of that crime. For details on jurisprudence see below at Sect. 2.3.

He termed this concept "indirect perpetration through an organised apparatus of power".[37] It is founded on Roxin's wider theory of perpetration and participation and was ground-breaking at its time.

With it, Roxin strived to provide convincing answers to the paradox which had been described by the Jerusalem District Court. The judges had elaborated that, in large-scale organised crimes, such as the Holocaust, responsibility would often increase not decrease with growing distance from the crime.[38] Roxin agreed that instigation would not be considered a suitable solution in such cases. Describing an influential character such as Eichmann, or Heinrich Himmler, as someone who had "merely instigated" the crime would not do the true nature of their involvement justice.[39] But if instigation—the prompting of another's decision to commit a crime—was unfit to appropriately describe the responsibility of "masterminds" of mass atrocities, how could such a person's responsibility as a perpetrator be construed?

Roxin turned to the bureaucratic, well organised Nazi state, with its plethora of ministries and agencies, clear hierarchies, and high degree of division of labour to develop his answer.

It was recognized at the time in Germany, albeit not yet in written law,[40] that one could commit a crime "through another", by using this other person to carry out the relevant acts. Usually, this would require coercing or deceiving someone into committing a crime, i.e., it would require the use of an innocent agent. However, as Roxin explained, such a form of indirect perpetration, could also arise, where someone relies on the structures of an organised apparatus of power, within which a multitude of potential perpetrators could be used to carry out the crime. Within this apparatus, these perpetrators would have to be replaceable, or in Roxin's words "fungible", so as not to have the commission of the crime depend on an individual perpetrator's decision. The organisation would have to operate detached from the law, as the necessary structures, the mechanisms of the apparatus would otherwise not work to the benefit of the mastermind. Finally, the mastermind would have to have the power to issue instructions within the organisation.[41]

Thus, Roxin developed an intriguing theory that would satisfy several needs which had become apparent through the case of Adolf Eichmann. A person who was part of an organised power structure and never got their hands dirty, could now be convicted as a perpetrator of the crimes committed far removed from them, but which they nevertheless enabled. A person such as Adolf Eichmann, Heinrich Himmler, or Adolf Hitler, would not have to be deemed an instigator. Finally, the theory neatly mirrors the organisational mechanisms used by the mastermind to realise the crime.

---

[37] Roxin first laid out his influential theory on indirect perpetration in organisations in Roxin 1963, pp 193–207. This work will mostly refer to the article's English translation in Roxin 2011, pp 193–205.

[38] *Judgment Against Adolf Eichmann*, No. 197.

[39] Roxin 2011, p 198.

[40] See below, at Sect. 2.2.2.

[41] Roxin 2011, pp 201–2; see in more detail below at Sect. 2.2.3.3.

2.2.2 Tatherrschaft—*Domination of the Crime: Methodology*

Indirect perpetration through an organisation, however, was not devised as a standalone theory. Instead, it was embedded in Roxin's broader approach to the distinction between perpetration and participation: The *Tatherrschaftslehre* (theory of domination of the crime).[42]

The connection between the notion of indirect perpetration through an organisation and the theory of domination of the crime means, that the requirements which shape the former construct are founded on the basis of the latter. More specifically, Roxin's explanation of Eichmann being a perpetrator singles out certain criteria (for indirect perpetration through an organisation) which, in his view, lead to a person like Eichmann having domination of the crime.

Domination of the crime as a central term to distinguish perpetrators from participants in German criminal law can be found in scholarly literature as early as the 1930s.[43] Claus Roxin,[44] however, is said to have transformed the concept into one cohesive theory, which until then had varied greatly between different authors.[45] It soon became the "leading approach" to distinguish perpetration from participation in German scholarly literature.[46] Nowadays, the doctrine of domination of the crime is the majority opinion in German academia.[47]

As a methodological starting point or formal criterion to determine whether a person has domination of a crime, Roxin uses the term of the *Zentralgestalt des Geschehens* (central figure of the action).[48]

---

[42] The term *Tatherrschaft* has been translated differently into the English language. George P. Fletcher chose the term "hegemony and control over the execution of the criminal act" in Fletcher 2000, pp 655–6. The ICC translates it as "control over the crime", see ICC, *The Prosecutor v. Thomas Lubanga*, Confirmation of Charges, 29 January 2007, ICC-01/04-01/06, paras 322, 326–38. Some authors have also used the term "domination of the act", see e.g. Weigend 2011a, p 95; see also Roxin himself with translator Belinda Cooper in the translation in Roxin 2011, p 196. Kai Ambos chooses "control or domination of the act", see Ambos 2009, p 142. All these terms—hegemony, control, domination, dominance—are suitable translations of the German "*Herrschaft*". "*Tat*" may refer to the natural act or its legal contours as a crime. For the purposes of this work, the term of *Tatherrschaft* will be translated as "domination of the crime" as long as it refers to the concept in German literature and its role in German jurisprudence.

[43] For individual authors see Schünemann 2007, § 25 mn. 7–10. According to Schünemann the first mention of the concept of *Tatherrschaft* goes back to Lobe in the 5th edition of the *Leipziger Kommentar zum Strafgesetzbuch* in 1933.

[44] Roxin's seminal work on perpetration and domination of the crime was published in its 10th edition in 2019. Its content remains largely unchanged in comparison to the 1st edition, but Chapter 12 has been constantly amended, taking up developments in jurisprudence and scholarly literature. This work will refer to the latest edition of Roxin's work: Roxin 2019. Roxin's second relevant book in this regard is volume two of his criminal law textbook: Roxin 2003.

[45] See only Schünemann 2007, § 25 mn. 10.

[46] Werle and Burghardt 2011, p 191.

[47] Heine and Weisser 2019a, Vor §§ 25ff. mn. 57; Heine and Weisser 2019b, § 25 mn. 7, 11.

[48] Roxin 2019, p 29.

Roxin derives the central figure as the decisive criterion from the German Criminal Code's formulations on forms of responsibility in its version of 1963 (GCCov). In his view, the term *ausführen* (to perform, to carry out) in Section 47 GCCov described a person in a central or key position in relation to the criminal conduct. Other forms of responsibility were shaped by the words *bestimmen* (to designate someone to commit a crime, Section 48 GCCov) and *Hilfe leisten* (to provide assistance to the crime, Section 49 GCCov). These can be readily translated to instigating and aiding. According to Roxin, they describe the acts of persons who are, metaphorically speaking, standing somewhat farther away from this central or key position. A perpetrator, indirect perpetrator, or co-perpetrator would therefore be seen as the protagonist of a crime, whilst instigators, as well as aiders and abettors would be those, standing at the side-lines.[49]

Following Roxin, a common contemporary definition describes the perpetrator as the person who dominates a crime. This individual holds the criminal action in their hands and decides whether and how the crime will be committed.[50] It is worth mentioning that Roxin does not explicitly rely on this definition in his seminal work. However, his descriptions of the central figure do not, in substance, differ from this and he does acknowledge without criticism that "holding the criminal action in hands" is the guiding principle of domination of the crime.[51] The description of domination is sometimes amended by the formula that a perpetrator can decide to either let the crime unfold as planned or frustrate its commission.[52]

---

[49] Ibid., p 29. The provisions on perpetration and participation of the German Criminal Code in 1963 read:

Section 47

If several persons who jointly carry out an offence, anyone of them is punished as a perpetrator.

Section 48

(1) As an instigator will be punished who intentionally designates another to carry out a punishable act through presents or promises, threat, misuse of reputation or through violence, or through intentionally creating or supporting a misconception or through other means.

Section 49

(1) As an assistant will be punished who intentionally provides assistance through counsel or deed to the perpetrator of an act which is punishable as a felony or misdemeanour.

Translation provided by the author.

[50] Heine and Weisser 2019a, Vor §§ 25ff. mn. 57; Hoyer 2017, § 25 mn. 13; Maurach et al. 2014, § 47 mn. 87; Rengier 2019, § 42 mn. 11; Wessels et al. 2019, mn. 806. For examples of the English wording, see Weigend 2011b, p 266: "perpetrators are those who 'dominate' the commission of the offence… those who have control over whether and how the offense is carried out", Werle and Burghardt 2011, p 191: "A perpetrator…is a person who 'dominates' the commission of the criminal offence in that he or she has the power to determine whether or not the relevant acts are carried out" and van Sliedregt 2012, p 82: "dominating over the act, … having 'control over the act'".

[51] See in this regard the descriptions in Roxin 2019, p 141 (stipulating that hands-on commission is the prototype of domination because this is the closest to holding a crime in ones hands); see also Roxin's descriptions of indirect perpetrators at Roxin 2011, p 196: "a person is a perpetrator if he controls the course of events".

[52] See e.g. Rengier 2019, § 41 mn. 11; Wessels et al. 2019, mn. 806.

A central feature of Roxin's concept of domination of the crime is the openness of the term. He asserts that although domination of the crime is shaped by the connecting concept of the central figure, it relies on description, rather than definition.[53] Essentially, this means that the range of situations in which a person holds domination of the crime is not definitively defined in Roxin's view. Instead, the notion of domination can be amended to include new modalities should a yet unknown type of central figure surface.[54]

However, the concept of the central figure cannot be supplemented with meaning without exploring the different types of domination, which the law recognizes by enumerating different forms of commission ("*begehen*" of a crime).[55]

German legislation rules out the commission with one's own hands as a possible criterion for delineation between perpetration and participation because the law recognizes different forms of commission (commission through another, commission of an offence jointly with another).[56]

Based on this observation, Roxin explores the different forms of perpetration as laid out in the German Criminal Code to describe the various possible versions of domination. In his view, these forms of domination are perpetration by own action (*Handlungsherrschaft*, domination of the act or, in Roxin's own translation "action control"[57]), perpetration without being involved in the physical execution (*Willensherrschaft*, domination by will) and perpetration by working together with others (*Funktionelle Tatherrschaft*, functional domination of the crime).[58]

This threefold approach to the description of domination of the crime shapes the whole doctrine because, despite the common denominator of the central figure, this means that the doctrine operates with somewhat differing standards of "domination".

Roxin himself describes the concept as relying on a "valuing standard of differentiation" (*wertender Differenzierungsmaßstab*).[59] In other words, Roxin's theory is a normative theory of attribution in which the determination of a person as a central figure—based on the whether and how formula—leads to the categorization as a perpetrator of the crime. This normative evaluation is guided by the three different forms of domination that have been depicted above.

This method of relying on different, open descriptions of a perpetrator has been described as the reason for the doctrine's enormous value but also for the limited possibilities of theoretical recognition that the theory provides. If a description of *three different types* of domination of the crime is the core of the doctrine (rather than one definition), the theory does not enable a deductive answer to all issues of perpetration and participation.[60] Following this approach, means that one must still

[53] Roxin 2019, pp 136–7.

[54] Ibid., pp 137–8.

[55] Ibid., p 140.

[56] Heine and Weisser 2019a, Vor §§ 25ff. mn. 58.

[57] See Roxin 2011, p 201.

[58] Roxin 2019, p 140; Roxin 2003, § 25 mn. 28.

[59] Roxin 2003, § 25 mn. 12.

[60] Heine and Weisser 2019a, Vor §§ 25ff. mn. 59.

identify the various criteria under which one of the forms of domination of the crime will be applicable. That means, exploring and evaluating what circumstances turn a person into a central figure. In the case of Eichmann this question translates to: Under which requirements would Roxin see a person like Eichmann as a central figure? Which criteria would Roxin identify that would allow Eichmann to have domination by will over the Nazi crimes and would therefore make him an indirect perpetrator?

The following sections will explore Roxin's concept of indirect perpetration (in general and through organisations) as the relevant form of commission for the German majority approach on the issue of architects and decision makers behind mass atrocities and as a basis of the ICC's doctrine.

2.2.3 Mittelbare Täterschaft Kraft Organisationsherrschaft—*Indirect Perpetration Through an Organisation*

Indirect perpetration, the commission of a crime through another person, was not yet explicitly embodied in statutory criminal law, when Roxin first elaborated on the *Eichmann* case and his doctrinal proposals. Yet, the commission of a crime through another had been recognized by the jurisprudence and academia for a long time.[61] With the reform of the German Criminal Code it was also introduced as one of three different forms of commission within the new Section 25 GCC.[62]

---

[61] Schünemann 2007, § 25 mn. 1, 60.

[62] The current regulations in the GCC are the sections 25 to 27 and read as follows:

Section 25: Commission of Offence

(1) Whoever commits an offence themselves or through another incurs a penalty as an offender.
(2) If several persons commit an offence jointly, each person incurs a penalty as an offender (joint offenders).

Section 26: Instigation

Whoever intentionally induces another to intentionally commit an unlawful act (instigator) incurs the same penalty as an offender.

Section 27: Aiding and Abetting

(1) Whoever intentionally assists another in the intentional commission of an unlawful act incurs a penalty as an aider or abettor.
(2) The penalty for the aider or abettor is determined in accordance with the penalty threatened for the offender. It must be mitigated pursuant to section 49 (1).

Note that German translations often use the term "abetting" for Section 26 and only use "aiding" for Section 27 (e.g. Weigend 2011b, p 267). As Section 27, however, punishes the physical and psychological assistance in crime, including mere encouragement through words, *Beihilfe* in the sense of Section 27 GCC will be referred to as "aiding and abetting" due to the corresponding use of terms in common law; see Simester et al. 2019, pp 231–3.

It has been asserted that the current regulations as depicted above are oriented towards Roxin's concept of domination of the crime; see Weigend 2011a, p 95; Werle and Burghardt 2011, p 193.

Roxin identified the form of domination of the crime in indirect perpetration as *Willensherrschaft* (domination by will).[63] In his view, domination by will includes three sub-categories: (1) exerting considerable psychological pressure on the physical actor; (2) using a person who acts under the influence of a mistake and finally (3) by using superior power of an organisational apparatus through which a person dominates the action.[64]

These options are condensed by Roxin as the three ways to steer another person to commit a crime.[65]

For the *Eichmann* case and the vast majority of mass atrocities, Roxin had to work with the latter of the three above mentioned manifestations: the use of a superior power over conveyed through an organised apparatus. It was clear from the beginning that the Nazi myrmidons who had operated the gas chambers of the extermination camps—to name only the most prominent of the manifold crimes of the third Reich—were seldom threatened and most certainly never deceived about the circumstances or consequences of their actions.[66]

However, this approach faced an initial hurdle on its way to provide perpetration liability for decision makers and architects of crimes.

A common doctrine, which is still held by multiple German scholars,[67] is the so-called autonomy principle. This strict view bases indirect perpetration on the lack of criminal responsibility of the physical actor. Only if the physical actor is not criminally liable—due to the objective or subjective requirements of the crime not being fulfilled, or the act being justified or excused—can the person in the background dominate the crime. In other words, domination of the crime in indirect perpetration only means the use of an innocent agent.[68] The precision of this doctrine is seen as a major point in its favour. It is precise because it determines domination dependent on the physical perpetrator's liability. Where the physical perpetrator is criminally liable, which—after establishing the facts—is a legal question, the person in the background will not be an indirect perpetrator. In contrast to normative considerations regarding domination, the concept then becomes more of a consequence of the physical actor's liability. Under this approach indirect perpetration is a type of reserve liability.[69]

---

[63] Roxin 2019, pp 140, 157.

[64] Ibid., p 158. Note that Roxin also recognizes a combination of psychological pressure and deception, which he sees in cases where one uses a child or mentally handicapped person to have a crime committed. This combination however is not an own category of domination by will.

[65] Ibid., pp 272–3.

[66] Ibid., pp 270–1; Roxin 2011, p 197. A mistake of fact which would rule out the direct perpetrator's *mens rea* in German criminal law, rendering him a potential "human tool" can be ruled out for mass atrocities committed by members of the Nazi state apparatus.

[67] See e.g. Herzberg 2000, pp 47–8; Krey and Nuys 2009, pp 214, 222–3; Renzikowski 1997, p 89.

[68] See Schünemann 2007, § 25 mn. 62; Weigend 2011b, p 266.

[69] See only Renzikowski 1997, pp 89–91 and Schünemann, who, as an opponent of the principle concedes this advantage in Schünemann 2007, § 25 mn. 62.

Despite its precision, however, the autonomy principle is mostly rejected by German academia.[70]

It is criticised, for example, that the autonomy of the physical perpetrator cannot define the degree of domination over a crime by an indirect perpetrator. Supposedly, it is the other way round: The degree of domination by the indirect perpetrator determines to which extent the direct perpetrator acts autonomously.[71]

The rejection of the autonomy principle can lead to the acknowledgment of a range of cases in which indirect perpetration is affirmed, despite the physical actor being criminally responsible. These cases are however contentious.[72]

Among these discussed cases of the perpetrator behind the perpetrator are:

- The gradual mistake of fact: The physical actor intentionally fulfils the objective requirement but errs about the scope of his action. Consider the case of A, who tells B to smash an expensive Ming vase but credibly asserts that the vase is a cheap replica. A knows the true, enormous value of the vase.
- Causing or using a mistake of the victim's identity: A knows that B wants to kill X. To achieve his own goal, A manoeuvres Y into a situation where B mistakes Y for X and thus kills Y. B is still liable for murder because he knowingly killed a person, but A is also an indirect perpetrator, because ultimately, he decided who would be killed.
- Causing a mistake as to which statutory crime is fulfilled: A credibly but incorrectly tells B that the building, which B is about to set on fire, does not serve a residential purpose. A knows of the actual residential purpose of the building. B will only be liable for arson, while A will be an indirect perpetrator of aggravated arson.[73]
- Relying on an organised power structure to have a crime committed.

For those who acknowledge indirect perpetration, domination therefore does not necessarily presuppose the innocence of the person physically committing the crime. It is rather the imbalance between the knowledge or oversight of the person in the background and the physical perpetrator which demands the conviction of the former as an indirect perpetrator, regardless of the latter's liability.

[70] See e.g. Heine and Weisser 2019b, § 25 mn. 6; Roxin 2019, Chapter 12 mn. 302–3; Schünemann 2007, § 25 mn. 65.

[71] Schünemann 2007, § 25 mn. 65.

[72] Heine and Weisser 2019b, § 25 mn. 22.

[73] It is highly contentious in all these cases whether indirect perpetration is possible. For a list of authors in favour and against see ibid., mn. 23 (gradual mistake of fact) mn. 24 (mistake of the victim's identity) mn. 25 (mistake of the fulfilled crime).

Roxin acknowledged the four aforementioned scenarios as possible cases of indirect perpetration.[74] The requirements under which the latter case would be recognized as such by Roxin and other supporters of this theory, are laid out in the following.

In his first article on the issue, Roxin observed that a single-handed perpetrator would be a rare phenomenon in mass atrocities and that most of those responsible would act as initiators, intermediaries, planners, or advisers in various gradations of function. He posed the question who of these participants would be perpetrators, who would be instigators and who would be aiders and abettors.[75]

With the theory of indirect perpetration through an organisation, Roxin strived to answer this question.

In his theory, domination by will through an organised apparatus of power (*Willensherrschaft kraft organisatorischen Machtapparates)*, materializes as one of the different forms of domination by will which lead to indirect perpetration.[76]

As such, the theory stands equally and independently beside the two other original forms of domination by will; through coercion or through deception.[77] Roxin even uses this distinction to call to attention that not a single case of actual coercion between commanders and rank and file within the Nazi murder machinery has been proven.[78] This categorisation of different forms of dominance by will demonstrates that, in Roxin's conception, the only will that matters to define dominance is that of the (potential) indirect perpetrator. Domination by will through an organisation is not based on the coercive, conjugating power of an organisational structure over its members but on their replaceability (fungibility, "*Fungibilität*" in Roxin's words) within the apparatus.[79]

In developing his theory, i.e., describing instances of indirect perpetration as perceived by him, Roxin relies on two cases; one being the *Eichmann* trial before

[74] For the three scenarios next to indirect perpetration through an organisation see Roxin 2003, § 25 mn. 96, 99, 102. Note that all three other cases, although not involving an innocent agent, rely on mistakes of fact by the direct perpetrator. Roxin categorizes all three of these cases of the perpetrator behind the perpetrator as categories of domination by will by using a person who acts in mistake (see ibid., mn. 95).

[75] Roxin 2011, p 195.

[76] This theory was first published in Roxin 1963, pp 193–207; for a translation see Roxin 2011 with Introductory Notes by Gerhardt Werle and Boris Burghardt (p 191–193), which opts for a translation of the core concept as "control based on organized power structures", see p 198. The following citations of Roxin's theory will refer to the English translation in Roxin 2011, pp 193–207; Roxin has since described the theory in various books and articles such as his two standard textbooks which have been mentioned above (see fn. 50). The theory has however not been fundamentally changed or altered by Roxin since its original conception in 1963, see Herzberg 2000, p 34.

[77] Roxin 2019, pp 269–70, 272; see especially 272: "third form of will dominance"; see also Joecks 2017, § 25 mn. 141.

[78] Roxin 2011, p 197; Roxin 2019, pp 270–1.

[79] See also Schünemann 2007, § 25 mn. 122.

the District Court of Jerusalem, the other being the *Stashynsky* case which was tried before the German Federal Court of Justice (*Bundesgerichtshof*—BGH).[80]

The case of Adolf Eichmann has been discussed above.

The second case involved Bogdan Stashynsky, a KGB agent living in the Federal Republic of Germany. By orders of his superiors, he killed two Ukrainian opposition politicians who had gone into exile in West Germany.[81]

Roxin takes the view that "nobody would hesitate" to describe a high-ranking Nazi official, tasked with the extermination of Jewish people, as having some form of domination over the criminal consequence and being a key figure of the overall event.[82] He describes what he identifies as the reason for this perception as the functioning—the "specific effect"—of the apparatus which stands at the ready for the actor's decisions.[83] To have domination by will through an organised power apparatus, Roxin originally describes four requirements. The organised apparatus of power is the basis for the theory, the hierarchical position of the actor, the fungibility of the physical perpetrators and the apparatus' detachment from the law characterize the specific functioning of the organisation and the actor's role in it.

2.2.3.1 Organised Apparatus of Power

Roxin identifies the organised apparatus of power as the basis for his perception of desk-perpetrators, such as Eichmann and the superiors of Stashynsky, as central figures.[84] It is said that the organisations involved—the Nazi murder machinery and, here specifically, the *RSHA* and a soviet foreign secret service—develop a life of their own, independent from their changing members. This leads to the organisation working "automatically". Consequently, the person in the background, sitting in the "control room" of the organisation, can hit the button[85] to have a murder carried

[80] Roxin 2011, pp 193–4; Roxin 2019, pp 269–70, 271, the *Stashynsky* case concerned an official of the soviet secret service tasked with political assassinations, but Roxin concedes that the national-socialist rule of terror in general was the historic example for his deliberations, see Roxin 2003, § 25 mn. 106.

[81] Roxin 2011, p 194 with fn. ** by the editors; Weisser 2011, pp 29–30.

[82] Roxin 2011, p 198; Roxin 2019, pp 271–2.

[83] Roxin 2019, p 272.

[84] Ibid., p 272; Roxin speaks of organised power structures, see Roxin 2011, p 193; the original German term is *organisatorischer Machtapparat* (Roxin 1963, p 193). In the following, the terms "organised apparatus of power", "organised power structures" and "organisation(s)" will be used equally and synonymously.

[85] It must be remarked that despite the degree and type of Adolf Eichmann's involvement as described above, Roxin's writings treat all potential indirect perpetrators under this doctrine the same. In this, Roxin usually speaks of more direct orders to carry out crimes, see e.g. Roxin 2003, § 25 mn. 106, "When Hitler or Himmler or Eichmann… gave an order to kill" ("*Wenn Hitler oder Himmler oder Eichmann… einen Tötungsbefehl gaben…*", translation by the author); Roxin 2019, p 272, "If … the person in a control room of an organisation hits the button and voices an instruction to kill…" ("*Wenn…der an einer Schaltstelle in einem Organisationsgefüge sitzende Hintermann auf den Knopf drückt und eine Tötungsaufforderung ausspricht…*", translation by the author), 248,

out and rely on the execution of this instruction without even knowing the physical perpetrator.[86] Such organisations require stable organisational structures.[87]

This is thought to be possible within two different types of organisations. The more obvious one is criminal state organisations in which the state itself, or at least the relevant part of its apparatus, is used to have crimes carried out. This would apply to both Eichmann's and Stashynsky's organisation. The other type consists of underground movements, secret organisations, and criminal gangs as long as they possess a tightly knit hierarchy, are unconstrained by changes in individual membership and fulfil the other necessary structural requirements of the organisation (see below).[88] These latter organisations can be referred to as a "state within a state". Roxin, in his original article refers to "underground movements, secret organisations, gangs and similar associations". Examples include the Mafia, the Ku Klux Klan, and two underground organisations from the Algerian War. He envisions political assassinations (*feme murders*) and vendettas as the typical crimes carried out by these organisations.[89]

However, Roxin asserts that criminal gangs aimed at the commission of property crimes and extortion may well fall into this category as well.[90] More recently, he added that the concept also applies to groups, such as terror militias, civil war parties, and groups involved in "tribal wars" and "ethnic cleansings".[91]

2.2.3.2 Fungibility of the Physical Perpetrator

Perhaps the most central or most characterising requirement in Roxin's theory is that of "fungibility", meaning the interchangeability or replaceability, of the physical perpetrator. When outlining how the organisation would work "automatically",

---

"Who has a position at any point in an organisation which enables him to issue instructions to subordinates, is ... an indirect perpetrator, if he uses his competence for criminal conduct" ("*Wer in einen Organisationsapparat an irgendeiner Stelle in der Weise eingeschaltet ist, dass er ihm untergebenen Personen Befehle erteilen kann, ist... mittelbarer Täter, wenn er seine Befugnisse zur Durchführung strafbarer Handlungen einsetzt*", translation by the author); Roxin 2011, p 201, "But one who, in an organizational apparatus, is involved in such a way that he can give orders to subordinates is also a perpetrator if he uses his powers to carry out criminal acts", 201–2, "All that determines his perpetration is the fact that he can direct the part of the organization that is subordinate to him, without having to leave the execution of the offence to the decision of the agent...". This focus is underlined by the following. Despite the fact that Eichmann (as far as his official functions are concerned) had probably never directly told or asked anyone to commit the crime of murder, Roxin constantly compares indirect perpetrators with instigators (of the Holocaust), see e.g. at Roxin 2019, p 274; Roxin 2011, p 205. This comparison has to a certain extent been pre-shaped by the District Court of Jerusalem that employed it as well, see *Judgment Against Adolf Eichmann*, No. 197.

[86] Roxin 2003, § 25, mn 106; Roxin 2011, p 198; Roxin 2019, p 272.

[87] Heine and Weisser 2019b, § 25 mn. 27.

[88] Roxin 2011, p 203.

[89] Ibid., pp 203–4; Roxin 2019, p 278.

[90] Roxin 2011, p 204; Roxin 2019, p 278.

[91] Roxin 2019, Chapter 12 mn. 370.

Roxin does not primarily refer to the "stable structures" (see above at Sect. 2.2.3.1), but first and foremost to this criterion of fungibility. He describes how the person in the background would know that, if the responsible organ evades its task, another organ would immediately take its place without endangering the execution of the overall plan.[92] The physical perpetrator is therefore "a cog in the machine" which is replaceable "at any moment".[93] In Roxin's view, this distinguishes indirect perpetration from instigation.[94] His perception of the functioning of a power structure is that:

> Such organizations must always expect losses and failures, without the mechanism of the apparatus being seriously harmed as a result.[95]

Herein lies the core of Roxin's concept of the three previously mentioned forms of domination by will. Criminal consequences for acting through another thereby arise where another person's actions are steered through (1) coercion, (2) mistake or by (3) ensuring that the criminal executioner can be randomly replaced.[96] It is not coercion or deception within the apparatus, but the simple interchangeability of its executing members that leads to domination of the crime by virtue of this theory.[97]

In Roxin's view, this interchangeability leads to the exceptional effect that even the potential autonomous decision of the physical perpetrator to not execute the instruction would not prevent the crime's commission. Consequently, this autonomous choice of the executioner does not "push the instructing person to the margin of the action", as it would usually do, but instead the interchangeability supposedly enables domination and thus perpetration of the crime.[98] Roxin characterizes this with the term *Einsatz* (deployment), which is developed from German organizational vocabulary reflecting the conception of organisations as he perceives them to be: If someone is deployed (*eingesetzt*), they are in a literal sense only a functional part of a larger, pre-existing whole.[99]

Thus, pursuant to the theory, domination of the crime is the consequence of fungibility because the enterprise set into motion by the person in the background will be realised irrespectively of the executing agent.

Roxin describes this by stating:

> If an assassination that has failed three times succeeds the fourth time, the crime is to be ascribed to the head of the underground movement, as his act. He can from the start plan as many repetitions of the attempt as he wishes, without any individual's authoritative decision

[92] Roxin 2011, p 198; Roxin 2019, p 272; Roxin goes so far as to speak of an "unlimited replaceability" of the direct perpetrator, see Roxin 2003, § 25 mn. 107.

[93] Roxin 2011, p 198; Schünemann 2007, § 25, mn 122.

[94] Roxin 2003, § 25 mn. 107.

[95] Roxin 2011, p 201.

[96] Ibid., p 199; Roxin 2019, p 272, see also Chapter 12 mn. 374, where he currently endorses this view.

[97] Schünemann 2007, § 25 mn. 122.

[98] Roxin 2011, p 199; Schünemann 2007, § 25, mn 122.

[99] Roxin 2011, p 204.

standing between his will and the success of the crime. The individual can at most withdraw from his role, but cannot stop the course of events.[100]

Obviously, such a rational would apply even more so where the potential victims are held captive in a concentration camp or prison and a killing order is given. Even if a whole squad of *SS* myrmidons rejected the order, any higher-ranking official could have easily replaced them.[101] For the victims, it would have presumably made little to no difference.

The fungibility of the executing physical perpetrator is therefore a vital part of Roxin's theory. It describes the mechanism to establish domination by will. The following requirements further describe the necessary role of the indirect perpetrator and of the apparatus itself.

2.2.3.3 Power to Issue Instructions within the Apparatus

To distinguish between perpetrators and participants within the organised apparatus of power, Roxin focuses on the power to issue instructions.[102] Only a person with the authority to give orders within the apparatus is capable of steering its actions and can thus be a perpetrator.[103] As a consequence, the signing of a document or making of a phone call "can be murder".[104]

The capacity to steer the actions of only a part of the organisation is considered to be sufficient.[105] A mid-level official like Eichmann fulfils this requirement of the doctrine. Consequently, there can be a longer chain of perpetrators behind perpetrators going through the hierarchy of an organisation.[106]

Conduct, which does not steer the organisation's actions into any given direction by its own accord will be considered a form of secondary participation under this theory. A person consulting or drafting plans without the power of command or supplying the means for the crime will be an aider or abettor. A denunciator can only be an instigator as he may prompt the organisation to decide to act but cannot steer its actions.[107]

---

100 Ibid., p 204; same in Roxin 2019, p 278. In this regard, Roxin also underlines that the number of victims is irrelevant and that fungibility of the executing perpetrator conveys domination of the crime, even if there is only one victim. Thus, in the case of *Stashynsky* where two persons were assassinated, domination through an organisation would be affirmed, see ibid., p 275.

101 On this case, see Schünemann 2007, § 25 mn. 122.

102 Note that Roxin and some other authors deal with this requirement together with the requirement of an "organised apparatus of power". It is then regarded as one criterion. For a better overview and due to the relevance of both aspects, the power to issue instructions and the organisational character of the apparatus of power, these criteria are treated separately here.

103 Roxin 2019, pp 275–6.

104 Roxin 2011, p 202; Roxin 2019, p 276.

105 Roxin 2011, p 201–2; Roxin 2019, pp 275–6.

106 Roxin 2011, p 202; Roxin 2019, p 276.

107 Roxin 2011, p 202; Roxin 2019, p 276; Schünemann 2007, § 25 mn. 122.

The reference to the *Eichmann* case in Roxin's theory reveals an issue, which has been given astonishingly little attention. This construct of indirect perpetration through an organisation requires the indirect perpetrator to have the authority to issue instructions. However, it remains unclear, whether the position must enable the indirect perpetrator to instruct "the commission of the crime" in the sense of telling the physical perpetrator (directly or through a chain of command) to act accordingly. The *Stashynsky* case provides little guidance in this regard; the agent's superiors are clearly described by Roxin as persons with the power to order Bogdan Stashynsky to commit the political assassinations. Adolf Eichmann, however, had no authority over the officers or rank and file of *SS* myrmidons in the extermination camps. The persons he "commanded" through the *RSHA's* hierarchy—and who were closest to the actual murders—were the guards of the deportation trains. However, they were not the physical perpetrators of the crimes.[108] Given Roxin's necessary familiarity with the case on which he based his ground-breaking idea, one would assume that Eichmann's position would satisfy this requirement. Consequently, the power to issue instructions within an organisation would suffice as long as any part of it is individually steered into action. This capacity to steer the organisation seemingly does not have to extend to the physical perpetrators of the crime. Despite his visible consideration of the *Eichmann* case, it must be noted, however, that Roxin examines persons who do have some direct power of command over the executioners more intensely. This becomes apparent with his assertion that the theory may be applied to smaller organisations which usually lack the highly specialised division of labour that is typical for cases in Nazi Germany. [109] It is also somewhat visible in the concept of fungibility where the requirements of fungibility and power to issue instructions together seemingly imply that the indirect perpetrator himself has some say in replacing the failing direct perpetrators, should this be necessary. Finally, it is discernible how the metaphor of a decision maker who "hits a button" to trigger the commission of crimes is the prevalent description of the actor's conduct.[110] These

[108] One may think about qualifying the guards as co-perpetrators of the murders. In this case, Eichmann's power to issue instructions would have extended over "perpetrators" of the crimes. However, to classify the guards of the deportation trains as co-perpetrators would overextend the concept of joint perpetration in German criminal law. More recent German jurisprudence has established some principles on the liability of low-level supporters of Nazi crimes. Persons who were not involved in the physical commission of the crimes but supported them by contributions in low-level positions have usually been treated as aiders and abettors to the crimes. For an overview, see Weisser 2019, p 252. The BGH treats both, the guard duty during the arrival of Jews in extermination camps and supportive conduct such as the registration of confiscated money as aiding the murders, see German Federal Court of Justice, Decision, 20.09.2016, in: Neue Juristische Wochenschrift (NJW), 2017, 498; Weisser 2019, p 246. According to Weisser, on the execution level, those persons who shape the commission of the crime by throwing the poisoned rags into the gas chambers or selecting those to be killed immediately upon arrival in the camp would be (co-)perpetrators, see ibid., p 255.

[109] Cp. above at Sect. 2.2.3.1.

[110] The example here can be found in Roxin 2019, p 272, "If … the person in a control room of an organisation hits the button and voices an instruction to kill…" ("*Wenn…der an einer Schaltstelle in einem Organisationsgefüge sitzende Hintermann auf den Knopf drückt und eine Tötungsaufforderung ausspricht…*", translation by the author).

factors would not be present in a case in which the indirect perpetrator has no influence whatsoever over the direct perpetrators.

2.2.3.4 Detachedness from the Law

The original theory of indirect perpetration through an organisation limits its applicability to such organisations that operate detached from or outside of the law.[111] Generally speaking, an organisation that acts detached from or unbound by the law, has aims and goals that run counter to the law and the pursuance of which will involve the commission of crimes.[112] The opposite of such an organisation would be one that adheres to the law and does not strive to accomplish its goals through the commission of crimes.

In Roxin's view, this is essential because the law usually holds a higher rank than intraorganisational orders and a subordinate may well choose to obey the law rather than orders.[113]

Thus, if the head of a public authority that works in accordance with the rule of law, wants a crime to be committed and issues the order to do so, it can usually not be said that they dominate the crime. They will therefore be classified as an instigator instead of a perpetrator if the crime is in fact committed. This is due to the fact that they do not use the structures of the organisation to achieve their goal. Instead of being able to rely on these structures, they have to work against them and actively win the physical perpetrator over to their side.[114]

The opposite is believed to be true within structures which operate detached from the legal order. This is the case where the state itself erects criminal organizations—such as Nazi authorities[115] or the Soviet KGB[116]—or where the organisation exists and operates contrary to the law by merit of its goals alone. Underground organisations, mafia-type structures and terror groups are typical examples of this second category,[117] although a "common" criminal gang, specialized on property crimes and extortion may fulfil this requirement as well.[118] According to the theory, in such organisations the law has no higher ranking than orders given by superiors. Consequently, there is no incentive to abide by the law and the instructing person does not have to fear any interference with their orders.[119] In other words, the rank and file,

[111] Ibid., p 277; the German *Rechtsgelöstheit* is also often translated as the requirement that an organisation would have to operate "outside the legal order" (Roxin 2011, p 202; van Sliedregt 2012, p 83) or "outside the bounds of the law" (Weigend 2011a, p 97).

[112] Roxin 2019, Chapter 12 mn. 372, 385; see also Heine and Weisser 2019b, § 25 mn. 27.

[113] Roxin 2011, pp 202–3; Roxin 2019, p 277; Schünemann 2007, § 25 mn. 123.

[114] Roxin 2011, p 203; Roxin 2019, p 277.

[115] Roxin 2011, p 203; Weigend 2011a, p 97.

[116] Roxin 2011, p 203.

[117] Roxin 2019, p 278; Schünemann 2007, § 25 mn. 123.

[118] Roxin 2019, p Roxin, 278.

[119] Ibid., pp 277–8; Weigend 2011a, p 97.

relevant for the execution of the crime, do not expect to be prosecuted or punished for their conduct and are therefore thought to be more likely to comply with (criminal) orders.[120]

The details of this criterion have undergone certain changes in Roxin's portrayal of the doctrine. In his initial writings, he stated that the goals of an organisation would have to run counter to those of a domestic legal order. This was further specified with his catch phrase of a "state within a state" which must have emancipated itself from the communal order in general or in specific regards.[121] This requirement has later been specified by Roxin. He asserts that the apparatus must only detach itself from the adherence to criminal law when acting against specific groups of people (ethnic minorities etc.).[122]

2.2.3.5 Schroeder's "*Tatbereitschaft*"—The Physical Perpetrator's Readiness to Commit the Crime

Aside from the manifold comments and proposed alternatives which amassed over the years, the theory has been shaped significantly by another German scholar as well. Friedrich-Christian Schroeder published his solution to the issue in 1965. He favours another approach to domination of the crime in indirect perpetration, which would be able to *inter alia* explain the type of domination of the crime exerted by a decision maker or architect in a large criminal organisation.[123]

Schroeder's work emerged briefly after the publication of Roxin's seminal piece. Schroeder proposed an alternative to the criteria of fungibility and detachedness from law with what he calls *Tatbereitschaft*, a term that can be translated into the perpetrator's pre-existing "readiness to commit the crime".[124]

Schroeder believes that fungibility is not a typical characteristic of organised systemic crime. One of the reasons being the necessity of specialists. Schroeder asserts that a highly trained spy such as the accused in the *Stashynsky* case cannot be easily replaced.[125]

Additionally, Schroeder argues that the fungibility of physical perpetrators is not decisive because a replacement could also fail to execute the crime.

Schroeder criticises the criterion of an organisation detached from law as vague and therefore, rejects it as well.[126]

---

[120] Roxin 2019, Chapter 12 mn. 386; see also Heine and Weisser 2019b, § 25 mn. 27.

[121] Roxin 2011, p 203; Roxin 2019, p 278.

[122] Roxin 2019, Chapter 12 mn. 386.

[123] Schroeder 1965, p 168; Schroeder 2009, p 569.

[124] Schroeder 1965, p 168; Schroeder 2009, p 569; a similar concept has been developed by Heinrich, called *organisationstypische Tatgeneigheit* (predisposition to commit the crime based on the typical functioning of the organisation), see Heinrich 2002, p 273.

[125] Schroeder 1965, p 168.

[126] Ibid., pp 168–9.

Instead of Roxin's requirements, Schroeder proposes the physical perpetrator's readiness to commit the crime as the criterion that would bestow domination of the crime upon the person in the background. This criterion examines the subjective state of mind of physical perpetrators, i.e., their pre-existing mental willingness to commit a crime, regardless of whether they have already been instructed to do so. Fungibility, Schroeder explains, would be a means to organising a potentially high number of willing actors.[127] Thus, readiness to commit the crime should be the necessary requirement for perpetration through an organisation as the leadership's domination of the crime is defined by the supply of such actors, which stand at the ready for the commission of the offence.[128] In Schroeder's view, this was the typical characteristic of the Nazi state in which members of the numerous organisations would commit "any crime that was ordered".[129] He believes that this is the difference with instigation, because instigators are usually "uncertain" if their instigation will be successful.[130]

The criterion was briefly acknowledged by Roxin as an additional requirement in addition to fungibility.[131] However, Roxin soon drew back his approval and now sees the executioners' readiness to act as a result of the criteria of his original theory, not as an independent requirement. Roxin elaborates that all of "his" requirements lead to the readiness of the perpetrator to act. He portrays how the organisational structures and the hierarchy of command create pressure on the actor, the detachedness from law lowers the threshold to commit the crime and the fungibility leads to the actor's conclusion that defecting would make no difference regarding the eventual crime. With this, Roxin returns to his initial rejection of the criterion.[132]

This notwithstanding, Schroeder's alternative requirement remains one of the most prominent in academic literature.[133]

The dispute over the most suitable requirements of the theory has not been settled in German academic debate, thus, this requirement poses an alternative to fungibility and detachment from law. However, Schroeder and Roxin share the same approach in their general description of the indirect perpetrator's influence over the crime: They dominate the crime, because (based on the respective requirements) they can be certain, that the crime will be committed.

---

127 Ibid., p 169; Schroeder 2009, pp 569–70.

128 Schroeder 2009, p 569.

129 Ibid., p 569.

130 Ibid., p 569.

131 Roxin 2006, p 397.

132 Roxin 2012, p 412; Roxin 2019, Chapter 12 mn. 375–6. On Roxin's initial rejection of the criterion, see Roxin 1995, p 51.

133 See only Schroeder's own comment on the recurrence of the Peruvian jurisprudence in the *Fujimori* case, Schroeder 2009, p 569 et seq. See Heinrich's similar approach in Heinrich 2002, pp 271–85; Heinrich 2010, p 163, but note that Heinrich sees his own concept as "incompatible" with Schroeder's.

2.2.3.6 Certainty of the Commission of the Crime—the Non-requirement

Despite not being mentioned as a requirement, certainty of success or certainty of the commission of the crime, which is supposedly inherent to indirect perpetration through an organisation, plays a vital role for the theory.[134] It is a highly relevant factor in the theoretical groundwork of the doctrine and as such serves as an important argument in favour of the theory.

The argument reasons that the way in which an organised power structure functions leads to the person in the background being certain that the instructed crime will be committed. One might say that the "certainty of success establishes domination of the crime".[135]

This concept can be found in one way or the other in Roxin's[136] and other authors' writings, including those of Schroeder.[137]

Supporters of the theory suggest that such certainty of success follows from the respective requirements which they propose for indirect perpetration through an organisation. They believe that, if such requirements are given, the criminal success of the crime will be certain. For Roxin, fungibility is the central criterion which leads to this certainty, for Schroeder it is the reliance on an actor who is already willing or ready to commit the crime.[138]

Concerning its function, this "non-requirement" could be described as an implied consequence of the theory's criteria,[139] or as an intermediate step between establishing the requirements and the consequent domination of the crime. In other words, it is Roxin's and other supporters' conviction that the criteria of indirect perpetration through an organisation lead to certainty that the crime will be committed. This, in

[134] On its significance for the theory see also Orozco López and Silva Santaularia 2022, p 659; Orozco López 2021, p 234.

[135] Roxin 2007, p 11, "*Erfolgssicherheit begründet die Tatherrschaft*", translation by the author. See also Schroeder 2009, p 569.

[136] Roxin 2007, p 10 ("The persons who work together in the structures of the organisations as a whole assure the success of the person in the background"; "The fact that the apparatus with its particular mode of action guarantees the success…"), 11 ("The apparatus can lead to the commission of the crime with greater certainty than coercion or deception"); Roxin 2003, § 25 mn. 105 ("…apparatus of power that secures the execution of orders…because the apparatus ensures the execution"), 106 ("When Hitler or Himmler or Eichmann…gave an order, they could be certain of its execution"), 107 ("it is therefore fungibility…that guarantees the commission of the crime…"). All translations by the author, emphases omitted.

[137] Ambos 2011, p 840 ("Domination of the crime as certainty of success through domination of the organisation"); Schroeder 2009, p 569 ("Here, the uncertainty of success, which is typical for instigation, is missing", "*Es fehle die für die Anstiftung übliche Erfolgsunsicherheit*"), again at 570; Schünemann 2007, § 25 mn. 122 ("Who…gives an instruction…has domination of the crime, because the structure of the apparatus guarantees the commission of the crime irrespectively of the individual of the physical actor"), all translations by the author.

[138] Roxin 2003, § 25 mn. 107; Schroeder 2009, p 569.

[139] For Roxin, certainty is very much connected with fungibility (see Roxin 2003, § 25 mn. 107), but, as an intermediate step, is not solely dependent on the one but rather on the affirmation of all four requirements.

turn, speaks in favour of domination of the crime through the person in the background. Certainty of success thus becomes an important, if not to say necessary, aspect to rely on in indirect perpetration through an organisation. One author even suspects that the concept of domination is replaced by or defined solely by the thought of certainty. He thus speaks of the "domination of success".[140]

2.2.3.7 Summary and Remark on Further Alternative Proposals

In summary, it becomes clear that the doctrine of *Mittelbare Täterschaft kraft Organisationsherrschaft* requires an organisation with a certain number of members and stable organisational structures. The person in the background giving an instruction can be an indirect perpetrator if further requirements are met. According to Roxin's view, the perpetrators must be fungible (replaceable), because their potential rejection to commit the crime only becomes meaningless under this condition. The person in the background must have the power to issue instructions within the organisation and said organisation must operate detached from the law. Under Schroeder's deviating approach, the organisation must be comprised of perpetrators who are already willing, i.e., ready to commit any crime which is ordered.

What remains dubious in this context is, whether the indirect perpetrator must be able to issue instructions to the physical perpetrators and to replace them, or whether it suffices if they can give instructions to any other part of the organisation. Given that the notion of certainty implies a close connection between the indirect perpetrator and the immediate causes of his domination—fungibility or readiness to commit the crime—one must question whether steering a part of an apparatus which is not tasked with the immediate commission of crimes would suffice. Which role does fungibility of physical perpetrators play, if the leader in the background does not exploit it because his or her orders are directed at members of the organisation who are not directly tasked with the commission of the crime? In other words: If a person steers a part of an organisation that is not concerned with the commission of crimes, why would the fungibility or readiness of killers who are not part of this branch, lead to certainty that crimes will be committed? Would this not only be applicable to those leaders whose subordinates are directly involved in the commission of crimes, and who can therefore make direct use of their supposed fungibility or readiness?

According to this line of thought, Adolf Eichmann would no longer qualify as an indirect perpetrator under the doctrine. Considering the significant role the case had in the development of the doctrine, this would be a curious result. This aspect of the theory remains unclear and somewhat contradictory.

A central point in Roxin's description which is related to the whole theory, rather than an individual requirement, is that it is not decisive whether circumstances from outside of the organisation can hinder the commission of the crime, although the plan as such can naturally fail due to such circumstances. What is essential instead, is that the apparatus' members will not act on their own behalf and contrary to the

---

[140] In this vein: Rotsch 2005, p 16.

group's goals. They will act as organs of the group's leadership whose authority they recognize.[141]

Roxin describes the types of crimes targeted by his doctrine as "not being singular occurrences but crimes which are based on repeating, similar circumstances and which can be carried out through fungible persons". According to Roxin, examples of this can not only be found in the murder of Jews in concentration camps, but also in the shooting of fugitives fleeing East Germany committed by the border troops of the German Democratic Republic (GDR).[142]

Consequently, Roxin describes the concept as applying to an exceptional phenomenon, which he does not believe is usually encountered within a "stable polity regulated by law".[143] Simultaneously, supporters of the theory frequently underline that it would be equally applicable to any type of organisation through which any kind of crime may be committed, provided the necessary requirements are given.[144]

Over the years, a plethora of alternatives and alterations to this concept have been proposed. Based on their respective potential relevance for the upcoming comparison with international criminal law theory, only some will be discussed below.

Schünemann argues that the organised apparatus must be embedded in a system of violence, which he affirms for cases of unjust regimes and mafia-type organizations.[145] His approach thus deviates from Roxin's and Schroeder's in that he explicitly recognizes the necessity of a certain level of psychological pressure on the perpetrator.

In a somewhat similar vein, Schlösser proposes to redefine domination of the crime in indirect perpetration. Domination should be seen as social domination of the physical actor. Social domination, in Schlösser's view, is the product of authority (the central criterion of social power relations) exercised within an organisation.[146] The combination of social power, i.e. authority, and an organisation lead to a domination which outweighs personal autonomy.[147] Through this redefinition of domination, in which the authority of the person in the background is seen as a reason for a limited freedom of the physical actor, Schlösser attempts to credibly explain indirect perpetration through an organisation.[148]

As a consequence, Schlösser also stipulates somewhat differing criteria for indirect perpetration through an organisation: The necessary pre-condition is an organisation (state, enterprise etc.) which aims at certain goals and has formalized structures and a hierarchy.[149] The latter means that a superior-subordinate relationship

---

[141] Roxin 2011, p 204; Roxin 2019, p 278; this comment refers directly to the second, i.e. non-state, category of organisations, but the thought is true for the whole theory.

[142] Roxin 2003, § 25 mn. 119.

[143] Roxin 2011, p 205; Roxin 2019, pp 279–80.

[144] Roxin 2011, p 203; Roxin 2019, p 278 (referring to extortion and crimes against property).

[145] Schünemann 2006, p 412.

[146] Schlösser 2004, pp 206–8.

[147] Ibid., p 208.

[148] Ibid., p 212; he states that the other approaches usually fail to explain while domination of the crime in indirect perpetration would usually, but not always be barred by the autonomy principle.

[149] Ibid., p 332.

must exist in which instructions are—if necessary—enforced through authority. The possibility of enforcement, Schlösser states, will rise with conformity within the organisation and with discipline.[150]

In these proposals it becomes even more obvious that Roxin's fungibility criterion is, despite the frequent consensus with his general theory, not always endorsed. Instead, factors that are perceived as leading to psychological or social pressure on the immediate perpetrators are often singled out as requirements for the theory and are *inter alia* described as a "system of violence" or the "authority" of the leader over the executioners.

Another amendment to the theory has been suggested by Schmidhäuser. He proposes to add "handing over [a victim] to a resolute perpetrator"[151] as an alternative option aside from the organised power structure. He asserts that handing over a potential victim to one, or rather a group of already resolute perpetrators should equally lead to indirect perpetration, irrespectively of the existence of an organisation. He drew this statement from his observation that such situations would be equally possible and frequent "in civil war situations".[152] This quote illustrates that this proposal is more inspired by somewhat chaotic situations and less by neatly organised mass atrocities, but nevertheless hints at another important situation in which a person in the background may enjoy great influence over the commission of crimes.

2.2.4 Domination of the Crime in the Traditional Approach to Indirect Perpetration Through an Organisation

It is at this point, that the notion of domination of the crime as embodied in this traditional approach to indirect perpetration through an organisation deserves a closer look.

It has been stated initially that domination means holding the occurrence of events in one's hands and deciding whether and how a crime is committed.[153]

As has been expounded, for Roxin, domination is based on the fungibility of the physical perpetrators within an organisation that operates outside legal boundaries. Schroeder instead underlines the executioner's readiness to commit the crime, whilst Schünemann and Schlösser suggest basing the theory on requirements which they deem relevant for the pressure to act which is exerted on the perpetrators.

---

150 Ibid., p 332.

151 Schmidhäuser 1982, Chapter 10 mn. 95, "*Auslieferung an einen Tatentschlossenen*", translation by the author, specification in square brackets added.

152 Ibid., Chapter 10 mn. 95.

153 See above at Sect. 2.2.2.

Based on Roxin's requirements especially, one may conclude that domination of the crime is not domination of the individual physical perpetrator, but instead dominance over the organisation and thus, the eventual occurrence of the criminal result.[154] Roxin sometimes calls this the domination of surrogate causes (*Ersatzursachenherrschaft*), to stress the importance of fungibility.[155] By doing so, he recognizes that domination rather occurs through the potential of replacement than through domination of the specific physical perpetrator. This notwithstanding, the base concept remains that the indirect perpetrator dominates the commission of one specific crime through their power over a part of, or an entire organisation.

The same holds true for the alternative requirements described above. Each single out prerequisites which are either believed to create a relevant pressure on the acting physical perpetrator or stress his or her pre-existing willingness. The notion of domination under these approaches seems even more focused on the individual who commits the crime.

Furthermore, all supporters of this theory more or less outspokenly invoke the notion of certainty to complement or back their findings of domination. The described requirements, allegedly result in certainty that the crime will be committed where instructed.

This again leads to the earlier criticism regarding the lack of contour of Roxin's requirement of power to issue instructions within the organisation. All requirements must ultimately be connected to the perceived consequence, the ability of the indirect perpetrator to dominate the crime and the certainty of success. The interrelation of these requirements under Roxin's theory does not necessarily support accepting any kind of position of power within the apparatus. Instead, the logical assumption would be that the indirect perpetrator must be able to assert their power to actively influence whether and how the crime will be committed by ordering the replacement of failing executors when necessary.[156]

These points lead to two important observations regarding the underlying notion of domination of the crime under this theory.

First, it is the individual, specific crime, which supporters of the theory see as the object of the domination of the indirect perpetrator. The position within the organisation and the apparatus' features are stable and independent of the specific crime. However, the attribution of criminal responsibility requires an almost direct connection between the indirect perpetrator and the crime. This can be deduced from the overall picture of the various criteria. This connection can be found in the indirect perpetrator's suggested certainty that the crime will be committed. This certainty is in turn based on the requirements of the doctrine. These requirements are oriented towards specific crimes. Indirect perpetrators can be certain of the commission of

[154] Roxin 2006, p 396 (the apparatus itself is the guarantor of success); see also Bloy 1996, p 441; Heine and Weisser 2019b, § 25 mn. 27.

[155] Roxin 2003, § 25 mn. 117.

[156] This issue has apparently received no attention so far in the scholarly debate. The paradox that casts a doubt over this interpretation and which has been mentioned above in Sect. 2.2.3.7 also remains: it would rule out Adolf Eichmann as an indirect perpetrator and yet it remains the more coherent view on the requirements outlined by Roxin.

crimes, as they are in a position to issue instructions within an organisation. These instructions will lead to the commission of crimes, because of the fungibility of the physical perpetrators or their pre-existing willingness to commit the crimes. The indirect perpetrator therefore dominates the specific crime because the subordinates actually carrying out this crime are either replaceable (Roxin) or already willing ("ready") to commit it (Schroeder).

In other words, despite its reference to organisational structures, the concept of indirect perpetration through an organisation determines who qualifies as an indirect perpetrator based on whether the individual can decide whether and how a specific crime will be committed.[157]

A further implication of such a notion of domination is, that only leaders who actually instruct the physical perpetrators can "dominate" the crimes. Other persons who fulfil important but purely organisational and planning roles cannot exercise such influence. One could say that under this concept of domination only decision makers dominate the crime, whilst architects do not.

The second observation is based on the first: The notion of domination of the crime in such cases is essentially based on factual, not normative, considerations. Of course, it is normative in the sense that there is no natural way to commit a crime "through another person". From this perspective, the concept of domination in all its facets is normative because it does not require a hands-on commission. However, the factors and considerations that carry the notion of domination by will through an organised power structure are based on factual ideas. That is, ideas that a person within an organisation would be able to dominate the specific crimes, i.e., decide whether and how they are committed, when they are committed by subordinates.[158] This evaluation which is inherent to the doctrine has limited normative content for the notion of domination of the crime. For one, it observes certain factual circumstances and dynamics which are found to establish a notion of control. These factors (according to Roxin) are the existence of a lawless organisation, the authority to make decisions within it and the fungibility or crime-readiness of its members. These aspects are factual, rather than normative because they can theoretically be proven through inquiries into the functioning of the organisation, the rank of the accused and the number and general motivation of the members. Only the selection of the relevant factors is a normative decision as the respective scholar decides under which factual circumstances, perpetration liability should arise.

This leads to the next issue, which is inherently connected to this doctrine, and which can be tackled by asking: Why should it be necessary to outline such specific requirements for the attribution of perpetrator liability?

---

[157] This has been identified by Herzberg 2000, pp 47–8, whose criticism on that factualist approach on domination will be discussed in Chap. 3, Sect. 3.3.3.

[158] Cp. also Orozco López 2021, pp 235, 236, who describes this using the term of *Handlungsherrschaft* (domination of the act). This means domination of the crime in indirect perpetration through an organisation is still domination over the specific criminal act of the physical perpetrator.

2.2.5 A Hierarchy of Blameworthiness

Roxin has been quoted above stating that persons like Adolf Eichmann, but also higher Nazi leaders such as Heinrich Himmler and of course Adolf Hitler, should not be found responsible as "mere" instigators.[159] This leads us to an issue which is closely linked to the question of leadership responsibility and is discussed as such in German legal academia: Whether the GCC's rules on perpetration and participation establish a hierarchy of blameworthiness, i.e. whether a perpetrator is—all other things being equal—always more blameworthy than an accessory. The relevance with regard to leadership liability is obvious: If such a distinction exists, attribution of lower forms of responsibility to an architect or decision maker behind a mass atrocity will evidently not reflect their real influence over the crime. They should be classified as responsible under the most serious forms of criminal participation. On the other hand, if no such distinction exists, a striking argument in favour of convicting a decision maker as a (more blameworthy) principal falls apart. If an accessorial form of liability best describes the leader's responsibility and they are considered just as blameworthy and can be punished just as harshly as a principal, a form of accessorial liability may well be used. There is then less reason to develop a notion of principal liability that fits such types of high-level criminal participation.

It would be wrong to state that the system of perpetration and participation in the GCC clearly establishes such a hierarchy of blameworthiness.

The reception of legal concepts in other legal systems can be one-sided and lead to over-simplifications. Describing the German system of perpetration and participation as being a clearly and undisputedly normative differentiation model would be such a misunderstanding or simplification.[160]

The question is whether supporters of the theory of indirect perpetration through an organisation interpret the system as a normative one that differentiates in blameworthiness between perpetrators and accessories.

In his opening words on indirect perpetration through an organised apparatus of power, Roxin states that it is obvious that an official tasked with organising the murder of Jews or with political assassinations carried out by the members of a secret service will dominate the criminal consequence differently than an "ordinary instigator".[161]

In Roxin's statements, especially those referring to the newer version of the German Criminal Code, it becomes evident that he in fact sees a three-tier hierarchy of blameworthiness in German criminal law.

---

[159] Roxin 2011, p 198. See already at Sect. 2.1. Stewart describes this perceived problem in the vivid term of "Hitler as accomplice dilemma", see Stewart 2012, p 173 (or "Hitler as accessory dilemma" e.g. at 168).

[160] This however, seems to be the tendency in certain comparative law text books, see e.g. Keiler 2019, pp 290–1.

[161] Roxin 2019, pp 271–2; see also Roxin 2011, p 198. This tendency can also be seen by the way in which Roxin quotes the District Court of Jerusalem that states that "the magnitude of responsibility instead grows…the more one distances oneself from the one who operates the murder weapon with his own hands and rises to a higher level of command…", *Judgment Against Adolf Eichmann*, No. 197, quoted by Roxin 2011, p 200.

At different points he elaborates on the role and relation of the forms of responsibility in Sections 25 et seq. GCC. He emphasises that less intensive contributions, removed from the centre of the crime are punished less heavily according to their growing distance from it. Therefore, he states, Section 27 para. 2 GCC contains a mandatory mitigation of punishment.[162] He asserts that this mandatory mitigation is due to the lower importance of the aider's or abettor's contribution in comparison to the "executor" and the "trigger" (the latter referring to the instigator).[163]

With regard to instigation according to Section 26 GCC, Roxin recognizes the equal punishment of perpetrators and instigators. He points out that this does not rule out a harsher punishment for perpetrators in comparison to instigators or vice versa.[164]

However, his stance on the matter is shaped by the conviction that instigation is in no way equally blameworthy as perpetration, which he underlines at various points.

He points to the fact that the attempt to instigate is punishable only for felonies and also incurs a mandatory mitigation of sentence (Section 30 para. 1 GCC), which is not the case with the attempted perpetration of a crime.[165] For Roxin, this is the reason why perpetration must be the weightier form of responsibility that takes precedence over instigation where these arise concurrently.[166] In his view, an instigator is an influential character at the margin of the scene. This leads Roxin and others to believe that indirect perpetration would be better suited to convict influential persons who conceived and ordered crimes.[167] This becomes especially apparent in the criticism that "mere" instigation does not reflect the "weight" of the contributions by such persons.[168]

This perception is further substantiated by certain protocols on the legislative procedures on Art. 25 et seq. GCC. These reveal that at least some legislators were of the opinion that in certain cases the instigator's distance from the crime could not be counterbalanced by their "corruption of the perpetrator" and thus that a mitigation of sentence would be appropriate. The legislators, however, believed that this could be achieved within the scope of punishment without having to include a rule for an optional mitigation of punishment for instigators.[169] In this regard, Roxin concedes

162 Roxin 2019, Chapter 12 mn. 213.

163 Roxin 2003, § 26 mn. 287.

164 Ibid., § 26 mn. 179.

165 Ibid., § 26 mn. 180; Roxin is convinced of the appropriateness of this rule as can be seen in ibid., § 25 mn. 3.

166 Ibid., § 26 mn. 180. Note that the precedence of completed indirect perpetration over completed instigation is not laid down in rules, different to the rules on attempt in sections 23 (1), (2), 30 (1) GCC. It is however affirmed by the majority of scholars and the courts; see Heine and Weisser 2019a, Vor §§ 25ff. mn. 47; Sternberg-Lieben and Bosch 2019, Vor §§ 52 ff., Vor §§ 52 ff. mn. 120. This however can also be seen as the logical consequence of the majority opinion on a hierarchy of blameworthiness and not so much as an argument in favour of it.

167 Roxin 1995, p; Roxin 2006, p 391; see also Ambos 1998, p 232, stating that indirect perpetration grasps the blameworthiness of the acts of masterminds of crimes more appropriately.

168 Roxin 2007, p 5; Roxin 2006, p 391.

169 Roxin 2019, Chapter 12 mn. 213, with further sources.

that there is no evidence that there is a general difference in blameworthiness between instigators and perpetrators from the legislator's perspective.[170]

Notwithstanding the aforementioned, Roxin believes that a facultative mitigation of punishment would have been appropriate for instigation.[171] In his view, such a mitigation is desirable and feasible within his desired three tier system.[172]

When explaining his theory of indirect perpetration through organised power structures, Roxin also explains the perceived shortcomings of earlier theories of domination of the crime, where indirect perpetration through an autonomous tool was "unthinkable". Roxin states "in this view, therefore, in our cases those working behind the scenes could *only* be instigators or abettors but never perpetrators".[173]

These considerations demonstrate how the feature of a "central figure" and the notion of domination are normative criteria, in the sense that the weight or importance of someone's actions with respect to the crime determine whether they are a perpetrator or participant. The respective forms of liability with their consequences on punishment (which Roxin would like to see even more graduated) are thought to mirror this normative evaluation.

It is for this reason that Roxin argues that his "open concept" approach to domination is valuable. In his view, the known arsenal of categories of responsibility frequently proves inadequate for the description of extreme forms of delinquency and an open concept of perpetration is a handy tool in such cases.[174] In a more critical vein, such an open concept approach to the more serious form of perpetration allows convictions under this head of liability, even if a specific type of conduct was previously unknown but is considered to be highly blameworthy upon discovery.

Consequently, Roxin's open, "descriptive" approach serves as a normative, if not to say, imprecise, categorisation of forms of conduct for which Roxin either affirms or rejects a form of domination of the crime, based on the viewer's personal evaluation.[175] This categorisation then implies a certain position—as a central figure—and carries a mark of blameworthiness, different from and higher than that of a participant.

2.2.6 Summary and Conclusions

Under the theory of domination of the crime, a perpetrator who dominates the crime holds the "criminal action" in his or her hands, makes a relevant decision "whether and

[170] Roxin 2003, § 26, mn 182.

[171] Ibid., § 25 mn. 3, § 26 mn. 182. The facultative mitigation of punishment for instigators as supported by Roxin has never been incorporated into German criminal law, and there are currently no initiatives to change the GCC's rules on modes of liability.

[172] Ibid., § 25 mn. 3.

[173] Roxin 2011, p 198, emphasis added.

[174] Roxin 2019, pp 279–80.

[175] See only Roxin's view that a Nazi official tasked with the extermination of Jewish people would be "obviously" regarded as a central figure, Roxin 2011, p 198.

how" the crime will be committed and is therefore the central figure of the realisation of it.[176] Today, this theory is the majority opinion on the distinction between perpetration and participation in German literature, but not all details of it are unanimously shared by its supporters.[177]

As has been shown, the theory relies on a certain implied interpretation of the German system of perpetration and participation.[178] Many arguments in favour of that interpretation, including the reliance on different forms of "central figures", are shaped and influenced by the pre-requisites of the GCC's regulations on modes of liability.

In light of this, two remarks on the theory must be made:

First, the doctrine is deeply entrenched in German criminal law and heavily relies on a limited number of statutory provisions that do not exist in other legal systems. Consequently, it is important to recognize that the theory and its differing forms of domination of the crime are closely connected to these specific provisions of the German Criminal Code.

Second, this section shows that, despite the claim of general applicability of the doctrine to criminal organisations, its requirements—especially in Roxin's version—are strongly influenced by the underlying *Eichmann* case. Especially the fungibility requirement seems to be tailored around a large, state-like apparatus supplying an indefinite number of direct perpetrators.[179] The alternative suggestions by Schroeder and others show that this first and ground-breaking approach to indirect perpetration has never been undisputed in German scholarly debate. Instead, a broad range of suggested alternative requirements emerged, mirroring the opinion of different scholars as to which factual dynamic would be decisive to establish domination of the crime through an organisation.

What these approaches share however, apart from their aim to convict leaders behind mass atrocities as perpetrators, is a common understanding of domination of the crime through another person. A narrow, factualist understanding, according to which the indirect perpetrator decides whether and how a specific crime is committed, despite their distance to the crime in time and space.

---

[176] Heine and Weisser 2019a, Vor §§ 25ff. mn. 57; see above Sect. 2.2.2.

[177] See the description in ibid., mn. 57, 61; an overview over different views concerning the theory in general and details of it can be found with Roxin 2019, Chapter 12 mn. 219 et seq.

[178] As has been briefly mentioned before, Roxin's theory is older than the current statutory regulation in Sections 25–27 GCC. However, the current Sections 25–27 clarify the forms of responsibility previously recognized by academia and jurisprudence and therefore no need for change or adaptation of Roxin's theory arose with the change in provisions. It has even been asserted that, to a certain extent, the current provisions were inspired by Roxin's work, see Werle and Burghardt 2011, p 193; Schünemann 2007, § 25 mn. 2.

[179] See in this vein e.g. Weisser 2019, pp 246–7.

2.3 The German Federal Court of Justice and Indirect Perpetration Through an Organisation

Claus Roxin and Friedrich-Christian Schroeder were not the first German jurists who dealt with the criminal liability of former Nazis under the German criminal legal system. However, they were certainly among the more eager to properly highlight the grave responsibility of participation in the "third Reich's" monstrous crimes.

2.3.1 The German Courts' Subjective Theory and Their Failure to Adjudicate Former Nazis

The prosecution of former Nazis through the authorities and courts of West Germany ended in a complete failure. This was made possible, *inter alia*, through the courts' theory on perpetration and participation.

The Imperial Court of Justice (*Reichsgericht*, the precursor of the Federal Court of Justice) had established a form of a subjective theory to distinguish between perpetrators and accessories.[180] Pursuant to this doctrine, all objective contributions would be equally causal for the crime's occurrence, regardless of their significance for the crime as a whole. Therefore, a difference between perpetrators and participants could only be made by looking at the actor's intent or will. A perpetrator was therefore someone who had the mind of a perpetrator (*animus auctoris*, *Täterwille*), i.e., who wanted the crime as their own. Whoever wanted the crime to be that of another person, had the mind of a participant (*animus socii*, *Teilnehmerwille*). Consequently, the will, intent, motives, and interest in the criminal result were the determining factors between perpetration and participation.[181] One indicator for this delineation could be whether the actor acted in their own interest or in the interest of another person when committing the crime. Another important point could be whether a person subordinated their will to the decision of another, leaving the final decision whether to commit the crime up to that other person.[182]

The subjective theory reigned on within the distinction of perpetration from participation in the jurisprudence of the BGH.[183]

Due to the subjective theory, a leader of a criminal organisation such as those found among the authorities of Nazi Germany, could be convicted as a perpetrator because he would certainly have *animus auctoris*. Developing a material or objective theory of attribution of responsibility was therefore unnecessary.[184] Or rather, it would have been unnecessary, if German authorities and courts had shown any will to prosecute

[180] Schünemann 2007, § 25 mn. 17–8.

[181] Heine and Weisser 2019a, Vor §§ 25ff. mn. 52; Weigend 2011b, p 265.

[182] Weisser 2011, p 27.

[183] For the history, see ibid., pp 27–32.

[184] Roxin 2011, p 196; Roxin 2019, p 271.

and adjudicate the crimes that were ordered, planned and organised by Nazi officials. Instead, the theory was used to enable and solidify the complete failure of the German judiciary to prosecute Nazi criminals in the first decades of existence of the Federal Republic of Germany.[185] Based on the subjective theory, courts denied perpetration responsibility in many cases brought against former lower and mid-level Nazi soldiers and officials by asserting, for example, that they had had no "personal interest" in the crime and thus no *animus auctoris*.[186] As a consequence, the defendants in the Frankfurt *Auschwitz* trials, many of whom had been concentration camp staff with active roles in the murdering, were convicted only as aiders.[187]

This approach was congruent with the general view that Hitler, Himmler and the other top-level personalities of the Regime were to blame, while prosecuting the lower ranks—many of whom were still alive in contrast to the leadership level—would unnecessarily "stir up things".[188]

This lack of political will led Fritz Bauer, the Attorney General of the Federal State of Hesse, to inform Israeli authorities about the whereabouts of Adolf Eichmann in Argentina, instead of seeking his arrest through German authorities.[189]

Curiously enough, the case that would consequently give rise to one of the most long-lasting discussions in German criminal law literature and jurisprudence was thus not tried before German courts, which evaded their historic responsibility, but before the District Court of Jerusalem.

2.3.2 *The BGH's Approach on Indirect Perpetration Through an Organisation*

In the following years, however, the Court's approach to distinguishing between perpetrators and accessories changed into what is now referred to as the normative combination theory.[190]

---

185 In detail, see Weisser 2011, p 30–1. See already Arendt 2018, p 290 comparing the contemporary leniency of West Germany's courts towards former Nazis with the failure of the courts in the Weimar Republic in dealing with right-wing extremist murderers.

186 Schünemann 2007, § 25 mn. 124; Werle and Burghardt 2011, pp 192–3.

187 Richter 2020, p 169.

188 Werle and Burghardt 2011, pp 192–3.

189 Bauer suspected that German authorities might warn Eichmann instead of arresting him (see Cesarani 2004, p 314). His concerns were proved correct decades later when it turned out that German authorities had known about Eichmann's place of hiding for years without taking action; see Werle and Burghardt 2011, p 192. Fritz Bauer's own view on individual liability for participating in Nazi crimes has been outlined by Richter 2020, pp 169–73.

190 The BGH's general theory is usually described as an evaluative overall approach, taking objective and subjective factors into account to determine perpetration, see Heine and Weisser 2019a, Vor §§ 25ff. mn. 63–4. The approach of the BGH to the distinction of perpetration and participation slowly changed after the adoption of the new regulations in Sections 25–27 GCC (see above fn. 68). On the development of the jurisprudence in general, see Weisser 2011, pp 32–4.

In 1988, the BGH had to adjudicate the well-known *Katzenkönig* (Cat King) case. In it, a man had tried to kill a woman in the profound belief that this "sacrifice" would stop the mighty Cat King from taking the lives of millions of people upon his return to Earth. The attacker lived in a relationship "shaped by mysticism" with a woman and a man who made him believe in the Cat King. The female's former partner had recently re-married. Coincidentally, the "sacrifice" for the Cat King happened to be this man's newlywed wife. Although the attacker was convicted for attempted murder, the BGH found the other two responsible as indirect perpetrators, for instilling this world vision in the attacker's mind. In the court's view, they were perpetrators because—through the mistake of their executioner—they had willingly triggered and controlled his action. A strict reliance on the autonomy principle, or so the court found, could not serve as a useful distinction criterion between instigation and indirect perpetration in this case. The court also used this opportunity to elaborate on indirect perpetration through other autonomously acting tools. It stated in an *obiter dictum* that the leader of an organisation using its members to commit a crime would serve as another example.[191]

In 1994, the court seized the chance to adopt the theory as mentioned in the previous *obiter*: It used a version of indirect perpetration for actors within organisations to convict high-ranking officials of the former German Democratic Republic.[192]

2.3.2.1 The *Mauerschützen* Cases—The Adoption of Indirect Perpetration Through an Organisation by the BGH

Beginning in the mid-1990s, the BGH found itself confronted with cases concerning persons who—in one way or another—had been involved in the issuance, implementation or execution of the shooting orders for border guards of the former German Democratic Republic. These cases became collectively known as the *Mauerschützen* ("wall shooters" in reference to the Berlin Wall) cases.

It is estimated that hundreds of people died during their attempt to flee from the GDR territory during the separation of Germany.[193] Between 1961 and 1989 alone, around 109 persons died during their attempt to flee from East to West Berlin.[194]

---

[191] German Federal Court of Justice, Judgment, 15.09.1988, in: NJW, 1989, 912–4; see also Roxin 2003, § 25 mn. 110; for an early description of the case in English see also Fletcher 1998, p 198–9 (who erroneously speaks of two women as the controlling power behind the attacker).

[192] Schroeder 2009, p 569.

[193] Due to mostly regional studies on the issue, the numbers remain unclear. The studies furthermore vary depending on the *modus operandi* and time frames of killings taken into account, see the description in Schroeder and Staadt 2018, pp 13–8. One estimate speaks of 421 victims, see ibid., p 17 with fn. 21.

[194] Ibid., p 17.

After the unification, German courts confirmed the principal responsibility of border guards, primarily young men who had been drawn from the National Peoples' Army (*Nationale Volksarmee—NVA*), for a number of these killings.[195]

The judgments by the BGH concerned actors on different levels of the state and military hierarchy. These included members of the political bureau of the GDR (the top-level political entity, the "*Politbüro*"), members of the national defence council (the next lower entity responsible for defence matters, part of which consisted of the border protection), a regiment commander with command over a section of the Berlin Wall, deputy regiment commanders of the border troops and an *Oberleutnant* (equivalent to a senior lieutenant) who had led a guard briefing.[196]

The judgments, if read collectively, draw a comprehensive picture of the course of action, including everything from the decisions made by the political bureau to the killings at the inner-German border.

The political bureau of the centralist committee of the *SED* (*Sozialistische Einheitspartei Deutschlands,* Socialist Unity Party of Germany) was the most powerful entity within the GDR apparatus, its decisions being practically binding for any state authority.[197] By endorsing the decisions of the central committee and preparing resolutions for the party congress, the political bureau maintained the GDR's border regime. As all members of the bureau were aware, an aspect of this regime was to stop people fleeing the GDR, even killing them when necessary.[198] These instructions then made their way down through the different bureaucratic layers of the GDR's state apparatus.[199] The National Defence Council (*Nationaler Verteidigungsrat*) was the central state organ, responsible for the defence and security measures of the GDR. The interdependence of party and state in the GDR resulted in the National Defence Council being closely connected to the political bureau, despite being a state and not a party organ. This proximity even resulted in personal union, the

---

195 See e.g. German Federal Court of Justice, Judgment, 25.03.1993, in: NJW, 1993, 1932; German Federal Court of Justice, Decision, 07.07.2001, in: NJW, 2001, 3060.

196 Cp. German Federal Court of Justice, Judgment, 26.7.1994, in: NJW, 1994, 2703 (Members of the National Defence Council); German Federal Court of Justice, Judgment, 04.03.1996, in: NJW, 1996, 2042 (Regiment commander); German Federal Court of Justice, Judgment, 08.11.1999, in: NJW, 2000, 443 (Members of the GDR's Political Bureau); German Federal Court of Justice, Judgment, 08.03.2001, in: NJW, 2001, 2409 (Deputy Regiment Commanders); German Federal Court of Justice, Decision, 07.07.2001, above n 195 (*Oberleutnant,* senior lieutenant); German Federal Court of Justice, Judgment, 06.11.2002, in: NJW, 2003, 522 (Members of the Political Bureau as indirect perpetrators through omission); for an early and brief description in English, see Fletcher 1998, p 199. For judgments against soldiers who shot the victims as physical perpetrators, see e.g. German Federal Court of Justice, Judgment, 03.11.1992, in: NJW, 1993, 141; German Federal Court of Justice, Judgment, 25.03.1993, above n 195; German Federal Court of Justice, Judgment, 20.10.1993, in: NJW, 1994, 267; German Federal Court of Justice, Judgment, 18.01.1994, in: NJW, 1994, 2237; German Federal Court of Justice, Judgment, 19.04.1994, in: NJW, 1994, 2240; German Federal Court of Justice, Judgment, 26.07.1994, in: NJW, 1994, 2708.

197 German Federal Court of Justice, Judgment, 08.11.1999, above n 196, 445.

198 Ibid., p 444.

199 Ibid., pp 444–5.

membership of Erich Honecker in both bodies being but one example.[200] The decisions of both the political bureau and the national defence council served as the basis for the annual orders (*Jahresbefehle*) of the ministry of defence, which relied on them explicitly when ordering the use of lethal force against people fleeing the GDR.[201] The annual orders were then reissued by the commanders of the following levels of hierarchy.[202] They finally reached the respective lowest organisational sectors of the border troops, where the border guards were briefed accordingly.[203] As a consequence of these orders, people trying to flee the GDR were shot by border guards and, in other instances, killed by spring guns which had been mounted to the border fences.[204]

The BGH convicted the members of the political bureau and the national defence council as perpetrators of these killings. In the first of the respective judgments (concerning members of the national defence council), the BGH discussed Roxin's theory, as well as the support it garnered from others. The court concluded that each individual within a hierarchy with the power of command would be considered a perpetrator because the fungibility of the physical actor would give the desk perpetrator domination of the crime.[205] The BGH cited its earlier judgments on indirect perpetration, where the physical actor had been acting more or less autonomously.[206] It went on to explain its findings:

> There are cases where the contribution by a person in the background almost automatically leads to the commission of the crime which he aimed at. This can be the case where the person in the background uses a certain framework, established by organisational structures, in which his contribution sets off standardized procedures. Such a framework with standardized procedures can exist in state, corporate or business-like organisational structures and within chains of command. If the person in the back acts in awareness of these circumstances and especially uses the unconditional readiness of the direct actor to commit the crime, and if the person in the back also wants the consequence as the result of his own act, he is a perpetrator in the form of an indirect perpetrator.[207]

This wording can be found again in the second judgment on the matter which referred to the members of the political bureau.[208]

The court also adopted a familiar description of responsibility in such cases:

200 German Federal Court of Justice, Judgment, 26.7.1994, above n 196.

201 Ibid.; German Federal Court of Justice, Judgment, 08.11.1999, above n 196.

202 German Federal Court of Justice, Judgment, 08.11.1999, above n 196, p 444.

203 Ibid., p 444; German Federal Court of Justice, Decision, 07.07.2001, above n 195, pp 3060–1.

204 German Federal Court of Justice, Judgment, 08.11.1999, above n 196, p 444.

205 German Federal Court of Justice, Judgment, 26.7.1994, above n 196, p 2706.

206 Ibid., p 2706; among others: the Cat King Case.

207 Ibid., p 2706; translation and emphasis by the author; for another comprehensive account of the jurisprudence in English, see Weigend 2011a, pp 98–9.

208 German Federal Court of Justice, Judgment, 08.11.1999, above n 196, p 448.

> To not treat the person in the background as a perpetrator in these cases would not reflect the objective weight of his contribution, especially because often times responsibility grows but does not lessen with increasing distance from the crime scene.[209]

Based on these ponderations, the BGH convicted the defendants, i.e., members of both the political bureau and the national defence council, as perpetrators of the killings at the inner German border.[210]

The court determined that the defendants were members of the respective committees[211] who were present at and participated in making the respective decisions.[212] Their knowledge regarding the use of lethal force at the border and the effect their decisions had on said use of force was affirmed as well.[213] The accused in the *Politbüro* case were also found not to have played "completely minor roles" in comparison to Erich Honecker.[214] In the view of the court, the apparatus of the GDR qualified as an organisation which provided the necessary framework in which the actor triggers standardized procedures.[215] When negating indirect perpetration for a low-level officer in a later judgment, the BGH asserted that in these cases, the "responsible designing of the relevant orders" would have been necessary.[216]

Most interesting is the BGH's focus on the mental element of the actors. The court established that the person in the background has the intent for the crime if he *knows* that the physical perpetrator will eventually decide to commit the crime based on the framework created by and within the criminal organisation. Based on this, the BGH stated that the actor had the "comprehensive will to have domination of the crime".[217]

Indirect perpetration was also touched upon, although somewhat briefly, in the 1996 judgment concerning the commander of a border regiment.[218] The trial judgment had not addressed his responsibility for issuing the instructions because he was

---

[209] German Federal Court of Justice, Judgment, 26.7.1994, above n 196, p 2706. The court explicitly quotes Schroeder 1965, p 166 there. As illustrated earlier, the wording can be found in the Jerusalem District Court's Eichmann judgment as well and was also relied on by Roxin in his writings on the matter, see Sect. 2.2.

[210] German Federal Court of Justice, Judgment, 26.7.1994, above n 196, p 2705; German Federal Court of Justice, Judgment, 08.11.1999, above n 196, p 445.

[211] German Federal Court of Justice, Judgment, 26.7.1994, above n 196, p 2707; German Federal Court of Justice, Judgment, 08.11.1999, above n 196, pp 443–4.

[212] German Federal Court of Justice, Judgment, 26.7.1994, above n 196; German Federal Court of Justice, Judgment, 08.11.1999, above n 196, 444.

[213] German Federal Court of Justice, Judgment, 26.7.1994, above n 196, p 2707; German Federal Court of Justice, Judgment, 08.11.1999, above n 196, p 445.

[214] German Federal Court of Justice, Judgment, 26.7.1994, above n 196, p 2707.

[215] Ibid., p 2707; German Federal Court of Justice, Judgment, 08.11.1999, above n 196, pp 444–5, 448.

[216] German Federal Court of Justice, Decision, 07.07.2001, above n 195, 3061. One has to remark here that such a technical influence on orders is not required in the earlier decisions on the members of the national defence council and the political bureau.

[217] German Federal Court of Justice, Judgment, 26.7.1994, above n 196, p 2706.

[218] German Federal Court of Justice, Judgment, 04.03.1996, above n 196.

present at the crime scene and further involved in bringing about the death of the victim. However, the BGH briefly mentioned that it was obvious that he could be responsible as an indirect perpetrator. He had been a link in a chain of command through which he received instructions from higher up the hierarchy. He would then pass on these orders to lower levels, using standardized procedures through his power of command.[219]

Two further cases were tried in this context, albeit without convictions for perpetration. Nevertheless, they enable a complete picture of the scope of the BGH's version of indirect perpetration through an organisation.

One case concerned an *Oberleutnant* (senior lieutenant) of the National People's Army who had been responsible for the briefing of the border guards before their respective shifts. He had held, or ordered a substitute to hold, such a briefing for a shift during which a man trying to flee the GDR was shot by guards.[220] During these briefings, the orders to shoot were reiterated by the respective duty officers.[221] The officer was convicted as an instigator in first instance, but the BGH revoked this conviction and replaced it with a conviction for aiding and abetting the killings.[222] The court determined that the shooters were aware of the content of the respective briefings—*inter alia* to shoot fugitives—beforehand. Therefore, their willingness to shoot, should the situation arise, already existed before the specific briefing of their shift. Consequently, the briefing had not generated the shooters' intent to commit the crime.[223] Whist this seems convincing at first, it must be seen in conjunction with the court's determination on indirect perpetration, where the actions of the officer in question were directly contrasted with the conduct of indirect perpetrators. The court states that only those who had taken on a responsible part of the designing of the shooting orders would be found to be indirect perpetrators.[224] In other words, a low-level officer, responsible for the organisation of shifts and respective briefing of his subordinates could not be an indirect perpetrator when merely reiterating the order to shoot fugitives at the border.

In another trial, the BGH upheld the acquittal of two former deputy commanders of a GDR "*Grenzkommando*" (border command).[225] Both of the defendants had contributed to the writing of orders for the border regime, one being responsible for training of troops, the other for maintenance of motorized vehicles and tanks. Their contributions were then aggregated and passed on by the commander of the

[219] Ibid., p 2403.

[220] German Federal Court of Justice, Decision, 07.07.2001, above n 195.

[221] Ibid., p 3060.

[222] Ibid., p 3061.

[223] Ibid., p 3061.

[224] Ibid., p 3061.

[225] GDR border protection was implemented through three regional border commands which received the annual orders from the chief of border troops (who in turn had been ordered to do so by the minister of defence). The border commands wrote their own, more specific orders and passed them down to the border regiments of their command; see German Federal Court of Justice, Judgment, 08.03.2001, above n 196, p 2410.

border command.[226] Both had been accused of participating in killings through anti-personnel mines at the inner-German border, which had been planted by troops of their border command. However, neither had been concerned with the planting and maintenance of these mines in their respective parts of the orders.[227] The BGH therefore denied their aiding and abetting the killings through these mines.[228] A potential responsibility as indirect perpetrators was not discussed at all.

In summary, the BGH used what it called indirect perpetration through an organisation to convict former high-level GDR officials from two different state committees. It also stated that commanders of border regiments could have been convicted under the same form of liability. The obvious deduction would be that the minister of defence and the commander of border commands (highest regional level and superior to border regiments) could also be found responsible as indirect perpetrators. For individuals on lower levels or in organisational positions not directly involved in the killing process, indirect perpetration through an organisation was apparently not even considered. Low-level officers who reiterated the orders were not convicted as indirect perpetrators or instigators. The writing of parts of an order that did not concern acts in connection with crimes was not even found to fulfil the requirements of aiding and abetting.

2.3.2.2 The Career of the Theory at the BGH

With the *Mauerschützen* cases, the theory of indirect perpetration through an organisation began a remarkable career in German jurisprudence.[229] A development, which is of little surprise, given the BGH's own comment on this doctrine in its first decision on the matter:

> The issue of responsibility in an economic enterprise can be solved through this too.[230]

---

[226] Ibid., p 2410.

[227] Ibid., p 2410. Note: It is at least conceivable that the judgment in the specific case would have looked different if persons had been shot by guards under the respective orders (instead of being killed by mines). In this (hypothetical) case, the defendant responsible for the training of troops could have at least been convicted for aiding and abetting such crimes. After all, the order to shoot was part of the training regime.

[228] Ibid., pp 2409–10. In contrast to the District Court, the BGH did not believe that the writing of parts of a more general order could not constitute aiding and abetting *per se*. Such contributions could constitute aiding and abetting through a neutral act. However, as the contributions of the defendants did not solely aim at supporting the commission of such crimes, but had independent (and lawful) aims, they would not classify as such a kind of aiding and abetting (through a neutral act); ibid., p 2410.

[229] Weisser 2012, p 248.

[230] German Federal Court of Justice, Judgment, 26.7.1994, above n 196, p 2706; translation provided by the author. The original in German reads: "*Auch das Problem der Verantwortlichkeit beim Betrieb von wirtschaftlichen Unternehmen läßt sich so lösen*".

One of the judges later explained openly that this idea was the main reason for adopting the theory.[231]

The BGH's version of the theory thus developed, stretching over a multitude of businesses and corporations and their respective leadership positions.[232] The broadening of the scope in this way is possible within the theory as applied by the BGH, as it openly renounces both the fungibility and the detachedness from law criterion.[233]

The BGH later abandoned the label of indirect perpetration through an organisation in some decisions, instead adopting the designation "*Organisationsdelikt*" (organisation offence) when referring to this kind of responsibility.[234] The BGH now describes its version of the organisation offence as follows:

> The jurisprudence has captured certain forms of indirect perpetration under the term of organisation offence. … In such cases, the person in the background uses state, corporation, or business-like structures in which his contribution sets standardized procedures in motion. If the person in the background acts in knowledge of these circumstances and uses the unconditional willingness of the direct actor to commit the crime and if he also wants the result as a consequence of his actions, he has domination of the crime and is an indirect perpetrator.[235]

This description has been referred to by the court in other decisions which all concerned cases of organised fraud.[236]

Furthermore, based on the criterion "using of standardized procedures", the BGH has even convicted an outsider as an indirect perpetrator through an organisation that he was not a part of. It found that a denunciator, who had revealed another person's plans to flee the GDR to the Ministry of State Security, was an indirect perpetrator. The victim had been arrested and sentenced to a prison sentence in the GDR because of the denunciation. By consciously using an illegal apparatus for his own goals, the denunciator had committed deprivation of liberty as an indirect perpetrator, or so the court asserted.[237]

---

[231] Nack 2006, pp 344–5.

[232] See e.g. German Federal Court of Justice, Judgment, 06.06.1997, in: Neue Zeitschrift für Strafrecht (NStZ), 1997, 544 (managing director of waste disposal company); German Federal Court of Justice, Judgment, 11.12.1997, in: NJW, 1998, 767 (Managers of a wood processing company, fraud); German Federal Court of Justice, Decision, 26.08.2003, in: NJW, 2004, 375 (Fraud); see also German Federal Court of Justice, Judgment, 03.11.1994, in: NJW, 1995, 1564 (SED district functionaries, electoral fraud); see Weisser 2012, p 248.

[233] Weisser 2012, p 249; Nack 2006, p 344.

[234] German Federal Court of Justice, Decision, 02.11.2007, in: NStZ, 2008, 89, 90; Weisser 2012, pp 248–9. The different wording is perhaps more striking in German. "*Mittelbare Täterschaft kraft organisatorischen Machtapparates*" and "*Organisationsdelikt*" can be read as implying different foci of the theory. The first indicates acting *through* an organisation. The second may, by a critical reader, be read as simply indicating that an organisation plays any kind of role in the crime, without restrictions as to the role of the indirect perpetrator or the features of the organisation.

[235] German Federal Court of Justice, Decision, 02.11.2007, above n 234, 90.

[236] See German Federal Court of Justice, Decision, 29.07.2009, in: NStZ, 2010, 103, 104; German Federal Court of Justice, Judgment, 22.04.2014, in: NStZ, 2014, 459, 460.

[237] German Federal Court of Justice, Judgment, 23.10.1996, in: NJW, 1997, 951–2; Weisser 2012, p 249.

2.3.2.3 Comparison and Evaluation: The Court's Implementation of a Broader "Organisational Responsibility"

Initially, the application of "the" theory was welcomed in German literature. In 1995, Roxin believed that this marked the final turn of the BGH's jurisprudence toward the domination of the crime theory when distinguishing between (indirect) perpetrators and accessories.[238] Due to their conviction of its suitability, proponents of the doctrine naturally welcomed this development in general.[239] Beyond this, Roxin and others additionally greeted the adoption from the viewpoint of legal policy because it allowed the conviction of political leaders as perpetrators.[240] Other commentators rejected the apparent political dimension of the choice of forms of responsibility in the decisions.[241]

The theory, as applied by the BGH, is shaped quite differently to the one proposed by Roxin. From the beginning, the BGH neither required the organisation to operate detached from the law, nor did it require the fungibility of the perpetrator.[242] Exclusively from the perspective of Roxin's theory, the BGH eliminated two out of four requirements and the two "shaping" ones at that.[243] *En lieu* of these criteria, the BGH relies on the "setting in motion of standardized procedures"[244] and the exploitation of the "unconditional will of the physical perpetrator".[245] However, only the former of these has continuously played a role since the BGH's conception of its own version of the theory.[246]

---

[238] Roxin 1995, p 50; see also Rotsch 1998, p 492.

[239] See Roxin 1995, pp 49–50, reiterating the well-known arguments in favour of the theory and applying it to the *Mauerschützen* cases. See also Bloy 1996, pp 440–2; Gropp 1996, pp 16, 18 (differentiating between the "usual" cases and the "excessive" execution of wounded fugitives, who, in his view, were not dominated by the persons in the background); Küpper 1998, pp 523–4.

[240] Roxin 1995, p 49; Murmann 1996, p 272.

[241] Noltenius 2003, p 319; Rotsch 2000, p 561; Schild 2017, § 25 mn. 41.

[242] Nack 2006, pp 344-5; Morozinis 2010, pp 404–5; Schroeder 2009, pp 569–70; Weisser 2012, p 247; see also Roxin 2007, pp 18, 20 (who does not criticise the BGH's version in general, but limits his findings to the statement that two/three out of four requirements were not fulfilled in certain ordinary crime cases). Note that in general, Roxin takes the view that the BGH has taken up his fungibility criterion, see Roxin 2019, Chpter 12 mn. 389 ("German jurisprudence … regard[s] it as a relevant point", translation by the author); Roxin 1995, p 50. Differently see Rotsch 1998, p 492, who speaks of the mingling of two approaches by the BGH, referring to Roxin and Schroeder's view; this view has been taken up by Jain 2014, p 128 as well.

[243] Roxin 2007, pp 18, 20; Weisser 2012, p 248. Note that Weisser speaks of "two out of three requirements", this is due to the common depiction of "command power in an organized power structure" as one requirement for the original theory; see already above fn. 108.

[244] See alone the title of the article by Nack 2006 ("Indirect perpetration through the use of standardized procedures", translation by the author). Nack was one of the deciding judges in the first *Mauerschützen* case; see ibid., p 343. See also Schroeder 1995, p; Weisser 2012, pp 247–8.

[245] See Schroeder 1995, p 179; Schroeder 2009, pp 569–70, who points out that the BGH essentially took up his criterion (see above Sect. 2.2.3.5); see also Rotsch 1998, p 492; Urban 2004, p 129.

[246] Weisser 2012, pp 247–8 (concluding that the setting in motion of standardized procedures is the "only objective requirement").

The BGH also underlines how the crime will be committed "almost automatically" under these circumstances.[247] This last aspect, however, is rather a consequence of the "setting in motion of standardized procedures" and does not serve as an individual requirement.

Roxin has critically remarked that, based on the change in requirements, the court's theory could not convey domination of the crime. In his view, the two missing requirements are precisely what shapes the original theory. As described above, Roxin would affirm domination of the crime only where physical perpetrators are fungible within an apparatus in which the legal order does not restrain them because it operates detached from the law.[248] However, it is important to recognize that—at least initially—the BGH did demand other objective requirements. It frequently mentioned the unconditional readiness of the physical perpetrator as a requirement for indirect perpetration through an organisation[249]—a tendency which was welcomed by Schroeder.[250]

From a case-analysis viewpoint, the question arises whether the application of the BGH's theory to lower ranking officers produces unintuitive results. As discussed, a low-ranking officer was even acquitted of the charge of instigating the killings at the border, whilst responsibility for indirect perpetration was not even considered by the lower court. Whether this jurisprudence is in line with the theoretical groundwork of the traditional approach is questionable. After all, even a low-ranking *NVA* officer commanded a specific group of soldiers, equipping him with the power to issue orders within the organisation.

With the ever-broader application of the theory to business enterprises in later years, these different perspectives regarding the BGH's objective requirements have lost importance.[251] It has therefore been alleged that the BGH's approach reduces domination of the crime to the causal act.[252]

Additionally, the court places a stark emphasis on the mental element[253]—a focal point foreign to the original theory. The BGH's central phrase stating that the "perpetrator wants the consequence as the result of their own actions" is based on the older subjective theory, leading Roxin to state that the BGH's concept is irreconcilable with the theory of domination of the crime. In his view, saying that "the leadership personnel in a corporation had wanted the crimes, committed by their employees, as consequences of their own acts" is "nothing but a hollow phrase".[254] In the same

---

[247] German Federal Court of Justice, Judgment, 26.7.1994, above n 196, p 2706.

[248] Roxin 2003, § 25 mn. 130; Roxin 2019, Chapter 12 mn. 414 et seq.

[249] German Federal Court of Justice, Judgment, 26.7.1994, above n 196, p 2706; German Federal Court of Justice, Decision, 02.11.2007, above n 234, 90; Schroeder 2009, pp 569-70; Joecks 2017, § 25 mn. 145.

[250] Schroeder 2009, p 569 et seq.

[251] Weisser 2012, pp 248–9.

[252] Rotsch 2009, pp 280–1, 422.

[253] See the definition by the BGH above, stating that if the perpetrator "also wants the result as a consequence of his or her actions...". Description by Schünemann 2007, § 25 mn. 131.

[254] Roxin 2003, § 25 mn. 135.

manner, he believes that the fact that the background actor knows he is independent from the physical perpetrator's decision to act because he can simply turn to somebody else does not make him an indirect perpetrator.[255] As a consequence of the BGH's heavy reliance on the subjective element, it has been suspected that the court's jurisprudence is only an alleged approximation of the theory of domination of the crime.[256]

Based on the aforementioned, it is important to note that the application of "the" doctrine by the BGH never quite corresponded to Roxin's theory as far as certain requirements and the underlying doctrine of domination of the crime are concerned.[257]

Little attention has been paid thus far to the fact that the *Mauerschützen* cases concerned the joint contributions of several members of political and military committees who collectively made decisions to uphold annual shooting orders. This does not correspond to the ideal-typical case of a linear hierarchy with individual decision makers on every level that served as a model for the theory of indirect perpetration through an organisation. The figure as applied by the BGH has therefore occasionally been called *mittäterschaftliche mittelbare Täterschaft* (joint indirect perpetration).[258] In such cases, it has been explained, the necessary domination of the crime through the organisation can only be exercised by a group of people together. Therefore, only when acting in unison, i.e., according to the requirements of joint perpetration, are the requirements of indirect perpetration fulfilled. This unified action can be determined by requiring each individual to act based on a common plan or decision and to contribute their necessary part to the whole, e.g., by voting.[259] The amended—and only roughly outlined—parameters of this notwithstanding, Roxin and others voiced support for this model.[260] It has been described as its own form of perpetration next to single, indirect and joint perpetration.[261]

It is worth noting that the BGH's approach, just as Roxin's, is shaped by the underlying conception of a higher blameworthiness of perpetration vis-à-vis instigation. This is highlighted by the court asserting that not treating the actor as a perpetrator would not do the weight of his objective contribution justice.[262]

In spite of the above-mentioned differences, Roxin essentially endorses the adoption of the theory by the BGH and emphasises how, in his view, the court took up his

---

[255] See already Roxin 2019, p 271.

[256] Rotsch 2000, p 561; See also Heine and Weisser 2019b, § 25 mn. 29 et seq. questioning the BGH's actual reliance on domination of the crime, despite its frequent mentioning of it.

[257] This is often overlooked in the discussion about the doctrine in the ambit of international criminal law, see e.g. ICC, *The Prosecutor v. Bosco Ntaganda*, Appeals Judgment, 30 March 2021, ICC-01/04-02/06-A A2, Separate Opinion of Judge Luz del Carmen Ibáñez Carranza, para 239.

[258] Gropp 1996, p 16; Roxin 1995, p 52; Roxin 2012, pp 414–5; Werle and Burghardt 2010, pp 862–3; the English translation used here is proposed by Ambos, see Ambos 2016, Art. 25 mn. 14.

[259] Werle and Burghardt 2010, pp 862–3.

[260] Gropp 1996, p 16; Roxin 1995, p 52; Werle and Burghardt 2010, pp 862–3.

[261] Heine and Weisser 2019b, § 25 mn. 1.

[262] German Federal Court of Justice, Judgment, 26.7.1994, above n 196, p 2706.

essential thoughts.[263] Whilst it is—unsurprisingly—disputed whose influence on the court's version has been biggest,[264] the effective broadening of the theory to encapsulate the managers and executives of business enterprises has triggered massive criticism in German academic literature.[265]

Based on the foregoing one may summarise the general difference between the BGH's approach and the traditional view on indirect perpetration through an organisation as follows: The theory was conceived by Roxin and endorsed by others as an instrument for exceptional cases of systemic criminality.[266] This limited scope has been broadened significantly by the BGH by erasing two central requirements of Roxin's original theory and eventually also abandoning its Schroeder-inspired criterion. Nowadays, it applies the theory to practically any person who uses standardized procedures in the framework of an organisation.[267] This broadening of the theory and especially its application to business enterprises has been criticised by many commentators.[268]

2.3.3 Summary and Conclusion

After failing miserably in the adequate prosecution of former Nazis German jurisprudence with regards to decision makers on higher levels only changed in the 1990s when former high-ranking members of the GDR's state apparatus had to stand trial.

As summarized in this section, the BGH's current jurisprudence on indirect perpetration through an organisation differs significantly from its academic role model. Apart from its core purpose—to convict leaders and other influential persons in organisations as indirect perpetrators—there is not much similarity between the original concept, and the construct as applied by German courts today.[269] Despite repeatedly stressing the objective weight of the actors' contributions, the court actually opened

[263] See Roxin 2003, § 25 mn. 111–2.

[264] See only Roxin 2019, Chapter 12 mn. 361 et seq.; Schroeder 2009, pp 569–70.

[265] On the reasoning behind capturing business-related crime through this theory, see Nack 2006, p 344; for criticism see Schünemann 2007, § 25 mn. 125; Weisser 2012, p 249 fn. 58–9, both with further references.

[266] On the exceptional nature, see Roxin 2011, p 205; Roxin 2019, pp 279–80; see also Roxin 2003, § 25 mn. 13; Weisser 2012, p 249.

[267] Weisser 2012, pp 248–9.

[268] Ambos 1998, pp 239–40; Heine and Weisser 2019b, § 25 mn. 30; Joecks 2017, § 25 mn. 152 et seq.; Otto 2001, p 759; Roxin 1995, p 51; Roxin 2003, § 25 mn. 129–30; Roxin 2007, pp 18–9 (denying that the limited set of requirements used by the BGH would enable domination of the crime); Roxin 2019, Chapter 12 mn. 414 et seq.; Schünemann 2007, § 25 mn. 130; Weigend 2011a, p 99.

[269] Rotsch 2000, p 561; Weisser 2012, pp 249–50.

possibilities to adjudicate leaders of (really any kind of) an organisation as indirect perpetrators. It turned the (once restrictive) doctrine into an all-purpose weapon.[270]

The jurisprudence is based on rather shapeless objective requirements and relies on the possibility of reverting back to the subjective formula of "wanting the crime as an own". The initial belief that the adoption of the theory led the German jurisprudence to accept the doctrine of domination of the crime[271] has proven to have been wrong. Instead, the BGH's approach is described as an independent, separate form of responsibility.[272] The court is criticized as having completely alienated itself from the domination of the crime doctrine in favour of a subjective approach once again.[273] One commentator goes further still, even seeing the tendency towards a unitary system through this jurisprudence.[274]

The application of the theory to ordinary crimes, committed through and by members of economic enterprises has been heavily criticised in academic literature.[275]

All in all, the doctrine, as applied by the BGH, can be described as a purely normative or evaluative one. Domination of a crime is replaced by a normative ascription of perpetration responsibility that is based on the actor's position within the organisation.[276] The consequence of this is an unrestricted broadening of indirect perpetration.[277]

Notwithstanding these differences, the traditional doctrine as supported by Roxin, Schroeder and others and the BGH's theory have something in common: They rely on

---

[270] Weisser 2012, p 249. The discussion about who had the larger impact on the theory as used by the BGH thus seems to be best answered by stating that both Roxin's and Schroeder's thoughts influenced it (see already Otto 2001, 759). Focus should be laid, however, on the lacking outlines of the theory as applied today, instead of the objective requirements which seem to play a minor role for the BGH.

[271] Roxin 1995, p 50.

[272] Heine and Weisser 2019a, Vor §§ 25ff. mn. 66; Heine and Weisser 2019b, § 25 mn. 29; Reichenbach 2016, p 144; Morozinis 2010, p 405. See also Schild 2017, § 25 mn. 44, who criticises the dissociation of the theory in the BGH's version from the necessary conduct fulfilling the objective elements of the crime; Heine 2000, pp 923-4, speaks of a form of "functional systemic domination of the crime".

[273] Rotsch 2000, p 561; Schild 2017, § 25 mn. 39; Zazcyk 1996, p 414. See in stark contrast: the initial belief that the BGH had completely taken on the domination of the crime theory, Roxin 1995, p 50.

[274] Rotsch 2009, p 417.

[275] See Herzberg 2000, p 33; Küpper 1998, p 523; Murmann 1996, p 275; Otto 2001, p 759; Rotsch 1998, p 493; Roxin 1995, p 51; Roxin 2007, pp 17–20; Schünemann 2006, p 412.

[276] Heine and Weisser 2019b, § 25 mn. 30; Weisser 2012, p 248 with fn. 44, who speaks of a "diagnosis of perpetration via valuation" (*Täterschaftsdiagnose qua Wertung*); see also Weisser 2011, pp 294, 458–9.

[277] Hoyer 2008, p 386; Roxin 2003, § 25 mn. 129; Roxin 2007, p 20; Weisser 2012, p 250 with further sources in fn. 59; see also Rotsch 2009, p 329. For a critical overview in English, see Weigend 2014, p 258.

the perception that the important role of certain actors connected to the commission of a crime can only be properly described by a conviction as perpetrators.[278]

Under this premise, it may strike a reader as interesting that it was not the political explosiveness of former high-level government officials that shaped this development, but rather the ordinary forms of economic crimes.[279]

2.4 The Systemic-Functional Approach to Indirect Perpetration Through an Organisation

The BGH's adoption of the theory in the 1990s brought new momentum to the debate and led certain scholars to question not only the way in which the jurisprudence treated the issue, but also the underlying theoretical notions of domination of the crime. In 2000, Heine examined the jurisprudence and which specific notion of domination of the crime could be the foundation of it. He focused on the *Mauerschützen* cases instead of the burgeoning application to business enterprises, exploring what "domination of the crime" would look like in these cases. Realizing that domination would be "very abstract" in such cases, Heine described the jurisprudence as an approximation of a model of collective liability (*Kollektivverantwortung*).[280]

The BGH's adoption of the theory of indirect perpetration through an organisation and the following momentum of the discussion produced a third major view on the basis and the consequently necessary features of the theory.[281]

This "systemic-functional" view on indirect perpetration through an organisation underlines the normative weight that a position of power within an apparatus carries. It is not so much a form of domination over the direct perpetrator which makes the leader an indirect perpetrator. Rather, it is the responsibility for establishing, maintaining, and/or steering the apparatus as a whole towards its criminal goals which justifies the

[278] See Roxin's approval of the BGH's application of the (or rather its own version of the) theory in Roxin 1995, p 49. See also the description by Fletcher 1998, p 199: "The symbolic point was important, those who direct the killings are still killers, even if the actions are carried out by responsible agents".

[279] The former was understandably suspected as a reason for the jurisprudence in its early days, for example, by Rotsch 2000, p 562.

[280] Heine 2000, pp 925, 926. For a similar analysis in English see Jain 2014, pp 128, 140. Jain does not call this collective liability but underlines how the BGH would recognize the role of the perpetrator in establishing and maintaining the "basic framework conditions" of the organisation (see at 140).

[281] Note that a part of the observations and suggestions governing this approach have been drawn with a view to the more recent development of international criminal law. This is especially true for Kai Ambos' writings. However, as the groundwork for this view developed within the German debate, informed by trials such as those of the *Mauerschützen* cases, the approach is discussed in this chapter. This structure also facilitates the assessment of the ICC's approach in Chap. 3.

attribution of perpetrator liability.[282] The instrument used by the indirect perpetrator is therefore not the immediate physical perpetrator, but the apparatus itself.[283]

The approach was shaped by two factors. Firstly, a fundamental essay by Ernst-Joachim Lampe, which provided a theoretical description of the underlying wrongdoing in collective crime. Secondly, the assessment by various authors, first by Günter Heine, that the approach taken by the BGH in the 1990s already (but covertly) relied on considerations that alienated indirect perpetration through an organisation from its original concept.

Observing the BGH's approach, several authors comment on the "abstract" domination[284] or hypothetical fungibility of the physical perpetrators.[285] These doubts surrounding the notion of domination of the crime arose upon closer inspection of the conduct of potential indirect perpetrators under the approaches pioneered by Roxin, Schroeder and the BGH. It was remarked that, in such cases, the influence exerted by the indirect perpetrator of higher rank within an organisation, would hardly amount to their power to actually influence the specific crime, e.g., the shooting of a person trying to cross the inner-German border.[286]

This criticism, whilst leading some to endorse instigation as an alternative mode of liability for these cases,[287] lead other scholars to advocate for another, normatively backed notion of perpetration through an organisation.

The theoretical groundwork for the approach was first laid down by Lampe in 1996 when he explored a second level of wrongdoing, which he established above the familiar one of individual crimes. This second level is called "systemic wrongdoing" ("*Systemunrecht*") and Lampe underlined that it would usually be enabled and facilitated through a system of wrongdoing ("*Unrechtssystem*").[288] His theory thus establishes two kinds of legal "wrongs" which exist separately but connectedly, *inter*

---

[282] Lampe 1996, pp 743, 745.

[283] Heine and Weisser 2019b, § 25 mn. 27; Weisser 2019, pp 248–9.

[284] Heine 2000, p 925.

[285] Ambos 2018, § 7 mn. 27; Ambos 2013, p 159. Ambos also speaks of "post-factual" fungibility, referring to the fact that a defecting or inactive physical executioner can often only be replaced after he or she has failed to carry out a crime, which questions the validity of the fungibility requirement.

[286] See Herzberg 2000, pp 37–8, who outlines how the final decision whether a certain refugee would be shot at the border rested with the guards on duty and, had they decided not to shoot, the crime would not have been committed because the refugee would have made it over the wall. This is what Heine refers to with the term of "abstract" domination in Heine 2000, p 925. We will come back to this point in Chap. 3.

[287] This so-called "*Anstiftungslösung*" ("instigation solution") is frequently endorsed by scholars from Germany and other countries, see Díaz y García Conlledo 2017, p 720; Herzberg 2000, p 48 et seq.; Herzberg 2009, p 579; Hruschka 1998, p 606; Noltenius 2003, p 322; Renzikowski 1997, p 91; Rotsch 2000, pp 561–2; Zazcyk 1996, p 414; for a summary of the common arguments from German criminal law in English, see Weigend 2011a, pp 102, 105. The line of reasoning of this approach partially appears in Chap. 7, Sect. 7.2.3.5.

[288] Lampe 1996, p 683 et seq. Lampe believes that indirect perpetration through an organisation would be best suited for the responsibility for systemic wrongdoing (p 743), but does not elaborate on any necessary alterations to the theories requirements based on his observations on systemic wrong.

alia in cases of mass atrocities. The "individual wrong" involves the commission of specific crimes by members of an organisation or system.[289] The other "wrong" is comprised of the existence and maintenance of the system of wrongdoing.[290] The individual crimes are complemented by the system of systemic wrong. A rogue state or organisation is one of Lampe's examples of such a system of wrongdoing.[291] The systemic wrongdoing is connected to the individual level because both are dependent on each other. The individual wrongdoings together constitute the systemic wrongdoing. Simultaneously, the system is also determinative for the individual wrongdoings which are committed only because of the existence of the system.[292] One might also say that the systemic wrong encompasses all individual wrongs.[293] Members of such a system can be said to bear responsibility for both the individual wrongs and the systemic wrong. For the latter, responsibility arises for conceiving the system's criminal goals and planning and preparing its crimes.[294] Responsibility for the systemic wrong is therefore closely connected to the position of the person within the system.[295]

Based on these considerations, another reading of perpetration through an organisation emerged in the German debate. Its denomination varies and it is not always clearly distinguished from the more traditional concept of indirect perpetration through an organisation which has been described above. Heine's term of a "systemic-functional domination of the crime" is one useful description of it.[296]

An elaborate theoretical explanation—which clearly and openly relies on Lampe's fundamental categorisation—of this approach can be found in Kai Ambos' writings. He underlines that the theory of domination in indirect perpetration through an organisation must rest on a twofold understanding of domination of the crime.

The first aspect of indirect perpetration through an organisation is naturalistic and concerns the actor's factual control or domination over the organisation ("*Steuerungsherrschaft*" in Ambos' words).[297] As previously mentioned, this type

---

[289] Lampe describes this as "relational wrongdoing" ("*Beziehungsunrecht*"), see ibid., p 702.

[290] Ibid., pp 702–3.

[291] Lampe's essay recognizes other systems of wrongdoing besides criminal states, such as the spontaneous "system" that develops in traditional situations of co-perpetration. For the purpose of this work, however, only the categorisation of states and organisations as systems of wrongdoing is relevant.

[292] Lampe 1996, p 703.

[293] Ibid., p 703.

[294] Ibid., pp 716, 745. This thought can also be found in Bloy 1996, p 441, who underlines that an indirect perpetrator would be responsible for an "organisational wrong" (translation by the author) and Heine 2000, p 926. Ambos acknowledges the same in Ambos 2011, p 847 (connecting the mode of liability of perpetration through an organisation to the substantive crimes of forming criminal or terrorist organisations pursuant to sections 129, 129a GCC); see also Weisser 2019, p 249.

[295] Lampe 1996, p 743.

[296] Heine 2000, pp 923, 925, 926.

[297] Ambos 2018, § 7 mn. 27.

of domination is considered to be vague by supporters of this approach. It is criticized as abstract and not constituting factual domination over the current events of a specific crime.[298]

Because of this alleged lack of factual domination of the crime through an organisation, the theory is therefore augmented by a normative element: The architect or decision maker in the organisation must be considered an indirect perpetrator because of their overall role within the organisation.[299]

The theory of indirect perpetration through an organisation thus becomes a normative model of imputation.[300] It is argued that perpetration through an organisation is thereby cast into a more convincing shape because it normatively mirrors the increasing responsibility of architects and decision makers of crimes in the higher echelons of an organisation, whilst not having to rely on vague and questionable notions of factual domination.[301]

2.4.1 *Elements of Indirect Perpetration Through an Organisation Pursuant to the Systemic Approach*

With its twofold, naturalistic and normative approach this doctrine differs from the original approach which relies solely on the notion of domination. As has been examined, the original concept of domination in indirect perpetration through an organisation is naturalistic, rather than normative.[302] By contrast, the systemic approach recognizes the naturalistic element to be limited (see at Sect. 2.4.1.1) and therefore adds another, normative element (see at Sect. 2.4.1.2).

2.4.1.1 The Naturalistic Element: Domination Over the Organisation

Supporters of this theory acknowledge that the domination exerted by a decision maker in the upper ranks of an organisation does not extend to the factual commission of crimes on the ground. Heine described domination in perpetration through an organisation as "very abstract" and proposed the wording of "functional domination over the system" ("*funktionale Systemherrschaft*") to describe the form of influence that a high-level member of an organisation has.[303]

---

[298] This line of criticism will be explored in detail in Chap. 3, see Sect. 3.3.3.

[299] Ambos 2018, § 7 mn. 27.

[300] Ibid., § 7 mn. 28.

[301] Heine, in his analysis speaks of the joint responsibility of individuals for systemic wrongdoing, see Heine 2000, p 924. Thus, the theory relies more directly on the well-known determination by the District Court of Jerusalem that responsibility for mass atrocities in fact often grows with growing distance between the actor and the specific crime.

[302] See above Sect. 2.2.4.

[303] Heine 2000, pp 924, 925. Heine's observations rest mostly on the *Mauerschützen* cases which were tried before the BGH. He states that one would have to accept a "very abstract" notion of

Other authors speak of domination or control "over the organisation" to underline the difference between such a—more general—domination of an apparatus as opposed to the narrow notion of dominating the respective physical perpetrator or the specific crime.[304]

The form of domination of the crime which follows from controlling the organisation can be described as "abstract, not always possible to prove and therefore significantly diminished".[305]

The conduct which may qualify as dominating an organisation can be characterized as follows: The persons at the apex of an organisation create a functional system for the overall criminal action ("*Gesamttatsystem*"[306]), a system of order and obedience in which the higher criminal goal of the system is obvious and therefore the commission of crimes (i.e., the violation of legally protected rights) is produced automatically. The programming of this apparatus does not need to be updated for specific situations. Instead, the general goal towards which the apparatus works, will put itself into effect through the commission of specific crimes.[307] The procedures surrounding the mass murders which took place at Nazi concentration camps are discussed as an example in this regard. Once a train filled with deported Jews arrived in an extermination camp, the persons within it would be killed based on automatic proceedings.[308] While this example seems to describe a rather narrow concept, given the static situation of a concentration camp, its reasoning may be equally applied to other situations. If a person establishes and leads an armed group within an internal conflict, they may delegate the planning and execution of operations in which crimes are committed to subordinate commanders. However, if the person makes it clear from the outset that the armed group is to commit war crimes and crimes against humanity and the group's structure and organisation reflect this orientation, the person will—under this approach—qualify as dominating the organisation.

To counterbalance this rather abstract, indirect and diminished form of influence over the specific perpetrator, supporters of this theory hint at the structural, systemic consequences of the leader's domination of the organisation. The organisation, for

---

domination of the crime, if such domination exists where "any member of the border troops shot any random fugitive based on a plethora of more or less standardized procedures" (at 925), translation by the author.

[304] See already Ambos 2018, § 7 mn. 26–7 (who uses the terms of "*Steuerungsautomatik*" (roughly "controlling automatism") and "*Steuerungsherrschaft*" in German which is translated into the simple, but catchy term of "control" (over the organisation) in his English writings); Ambos 2013, p 159 ("this lack of control is compensated by the control of the criminal organization"); Ambos 2016, Art. 25, Art. 25 mn. 15; Ambos 2011, pp 840 (speaking of a form of "indirect" domination through the organisation); Bloy 1996, p 441; Schlösser 2007, p 162; in the same vein, Heine and Weisser 2019b, § 25 mn. 27; Weisser 2019, p 249.

[305] Ambos 2018, § 7 mn. 27. Ambos also acknowledges that fungibility in the relevant situations must be described as "abstract" or "post-factual" at mn. 27.

[306] For the concept of overall criminal action ("*Gesamttat*") see below at Sect. 2.4.2.4, and Chap. 8, Sects. 8.2.5 and 8.3.

[307] Weisser 2019, p 249.

[308] Ibid., p 249.

the purpose of most crimes,[309] leads to a diminished institutional autonomy of the physical perpetrator (compared to a perpetrator outside of an organisation). This diminished autonomy makes the physical perpetrator mostly irrelevant.[310]

In summary, this approach in its first step shifts the focus of domination from the specific perpetrator and crime to the influence over the organisation.

2.4.1.2 Normative Element: Responsibility for the Organisational Wrong

The second step of this approach constitutes the true novelty in comparison to the more traditional theory (besides acknowledging the limited domination of the crime). According to the supporters of this theory, the domination over the organisation is precisely what leads to the categorisation of the decision maker as an indirect perpetrator. However, this cannot be based on a factual notion of domination alone. Therefore, the systemic approach is based on a second, normative pillar. In this doctrine, responsibility arises because of the decision maker's role and influence within and over the organisation—a normative responsibility based on the importance of the organisation for the overall criminal action.

Ambos describes this second step as a "normative adjustment" to the factual notion of domination. This adjustment or addition is necessary due to the decreased actual influence over the specific actor and crime.[311] Such a view is justified because the organisation, which the actor controls is the engine of the system of wrongdoing and its centre. Responsibility, in Ambos' view, is therefore gathered or accumulated through the organisation.[312] This coincides with Lampe's description of responsibility for systemic wrongs as amassed through a system of wrongdoing (see above). A similar view has been expressed by Bloy, who distinguishes between the front man's responsibility for "individual wrong" and the architect's responsibility for "organisational wrong".[313]

This can be said to be the manifestation of a "normative imputation model", which considers the fact that mass atrocities are always organised, channelled through, or at least tolerated by organisations.[314] The aspect of organisational wrong also explains what the Jerusalem District Court already held and underlined in 1961 and what is readily accepted by virtually everybody in international criminal law: With growing

[309] For Ambos the situation at the inner German border poses an atypical case with a lot of rather untypical autonomy on the part of the physical executioners. In his view, usually, specific fungibility would be given, see Ambos 2018, § 7 mn. 26 with. fn. 132.

[310] Ibid., § 7 mn. 26–7; Ambos 2013, p 159.

[311] Ambos 2018, § 7 mn. 28; Weisser, in a similar vein, speaks of "normative imputation" (*normative Zuschreibung*), see Weisser 2019, p 249.

[312] Ambos 2011, pp 846–7.

[313] Bloy 1996, p 441.

[314] See Ambos 2018, § 7 mn. 12, 28; this is also endorsed by Kress 2018, VStGB § 6, § 6 VStGB mn. 100.

distance through the ranks of an organisation, responsibility for the crimes committed by its members usually rises.[315]

2.4.2 *Consequences in Comparison to the Traditional Concept*

As the third German approach to the topic of indirect perpetration through an organisation, this doctrine entails certain changes in concepts and features in comparison to the traditional approach as devised by Roxin and others.

2.4.2.1 Notion of Domination

As a consequence of this approach, domination of the crime necessarily differs from the way it is understood in the more traditional theory.

Ambos describes this as an organisational-theoretical understanding of perpetration through an organisation. In his view, domination of the crime is the certainty of success achieved by "*dominating an organisation*". The "tool" in the hands of the decision maker is the organisation, not one of its members.[316] Thus, domination over the organisation leads to an indirect domination of its members.[317]

In contrast to the traditional approach, this doctrine therefore builds less on a direct link because it does not hinge solely on a factual notion of domination of the crime.[318] The link between the actor's behaviour and the misconduct that establishes criminal responsibility lies in the actor's role in the overall organisation. Expressed more in line with Lampe's theoretical groundwork, the notion of domination of the crime becomes a normative one, as a reflex of the normative consideration of the organisational wrong. A decision that somehow affects future crimes is made by a decision maker or architect on a higher level of the hierarchical organisation. This decision does not have to concern the "whether and how" of the crimes in their entirety but is limited to the person's authority over and role in the organisation. The person does not have to be able to influence the further development of the action. Their "domination" is rather based on their influence over the organisation as a whole, especially where it extends to such functionally vital and decisive acts as its establishment and maintenance. Through this, the theory avoids relying on the kind of "abstract" domination of a specific crime which can be seen in the traditional

---

[315] *Judgment Against Adolf Eichmann*, No. 197.

[316] Ambos 2011, pp 840, translations by the author; Heine and Weisser 2019b, § 25 mn. 27. See also van Sliedregt and Weisser 2022, p 634 with a view to the Rome Statute.

[317] Ambos 2011, pp 841.

[318] See for the description of direct and indirect linkage principles in models of imputation for mass atrocities van Sliedregt 2012, pp 181–2.

concept and in the initial jurisprudence of the BGH. Consequently, the notion of domination of the crime loses some importance within this doctrine.[319]

To deviate from Roxin's concept of (factual) domination of the crime and supplement the theory with normative groundwork does not necessarily entail a change in requirements or the classification of perpetration through an organisation as a mode of liability. Given its different basis, it is not surprising however, that certain changes in details are advanced by supporters of this theory as well.

2.4.2.2 Further Defining the Organisation and Its Mechanism

One demand raised especially by Ambos, concerns a more thoroughly defined concept of "organisation".[320] With a view to more recent judgments from both the international and national sphere, Ambos identifies factors which have been regarded as enabling indirect perpetration through an organisation and which differ from Roxin's strict "fungibility" requirement.

These aspects can be grouped into "hard factors" (hierarchical organisation and fungibility) and "soft factors" (ethnic allegiance, indoctrination, training regimens etc.).[321] Ambos asserts that soft factors may complement and partly replace the hard factors within an organisation and would still lead to indirect perpetration by the organisation's leader. This does not mean that a hierarchy would no longer be necessary, but e.g., fungibility could be replaced through one of the softer factors. The consequence would be a form of "personal" authority of the decision maker. However, such authority cannot be purely personal or based exclusively on personal ties as this would—in Ambos' view—inhibit the leader's capability of dominating the members of the organisation. The repressive pressure to act within the organisation must still exist.[322]

Weisser chooses another focus when describing the "industrial" killing machinery of Nazi extermination camps as an example where the systemic view on indirect perpetration through an organisation makes sense. Her description focuses on how such a system is shaped primarily by the "automatism" which is created ("programmed") and established by the higher levels within the organised power structure. In her view, the consequence of such an automatism is that specific instructions to commit a crime become unnecessary. Once a certain operation, such as the deportation of Jews into an extermination camp like Auschwitz is instructed, no specific order to commit crimes, i.e., to murder people, is necessary. Instead, the pursuant murders are said to happen automatically.[323]

This example is comparable to Roxin's focus on the *Eichmann* case, however, the reason for attributing responsibility, and thus the notion of domination of the crime,

[319] Ambos 2013, p 178.

[320] Ambos 2011, pp 848–9; Ambos 2018, § 7 mn. 28.

[321] Ambos 2011, pp 848–9.

[322] Ibid., p 849.

[323] Weisser 2019, p 249.

is different. Domination is based on creating or programming the automatism. This interpretation is not applied to other mass atrocities by Weisser. One could therefore suspect that such an automatism requires certain stable or static surroundings, tantamount to those of the highly organised Nazi killing machinery. The consequence would be that armed groups or branches of the military in civil war scenarios would perhaps not qualify under such an approach to indirect perpetration.

However, the automatism as described by Weisser can also be interpreted in a broader sense. One could consider the commission of specific crimes as a natural, automatic consequence of the action of certain organisations and thereby find that an automatism may yet be affirmed in other types of cases.[324] It should not be overlooked that even the Holocaust, as described in the *Eichmann* case, did not progress completely automatically. Heinrich Himmler—most certainly in consultation with Hitler—still made decisions regarding the regions and times of deportations and instructed both the organisers and executioners, either through the chains of command or directly. For organisers like Adolf Eichmann, the description of the organisation, i.e., the system of wrongdoing, as one of automatisms which are merely triggered without the necessity of issuing further orders, makes perfect sense. As we have seen, Eichmann could not command any of the physical perpetrators, and he did not have to. His conduct fuelled a murderous automatism.

2.4.2.3 Restriction at the Leadership Level

Based on the normative finding that domination over the organisation itself is the reason for indirect perpetration, Ambos asserts that only persons in the highest echelons of an organisation should be indirect perpetrators. This is because only they can exert "undisturbed" power over the organisation as a whole.[325] Mid-level actors could always be interfered with from above, their orders for example, could be revoked on a higher level.[326] They may instead be classified as co-perpetrators pursuant to Ambos' view.[327] Something else may be true, where a system as a whole consists of several (criminal) organisations which act more or less independently from each other and through which a "mid-level" actor can act undisturbed.[328]

[324] Picture, e.g., a part of a government's armed forces that is created to suppress the widespread protest of the population of a certain part of the country. If that branch is formed with a specific aim to crack down on the population, and the commission of crimes is included as part of the strategy from the beginning, one could validly say that a wide range of conduct, such as the mere deployment of troops into a certain area or providing information regarding the presence of opposition members in certain places will automatically lead to the commission of crimes. A person who undertakes such conduct (provision of information, stationing troops somewhere etc.) could then be said to trigger such an automatism and therefore be responsible for the systemic wrongdoing.

[325] Ambos 2011, pp 850; Ambos 2013, pp 159–60; Ambos 2018, p § 7 mn. 29.

[326] Ambos 2011, pp 850–1.

[327] Ibid., pp 850–1; Ambos 2013, p 160; Ambos 2018, § 7 mn. 29.

[328] Ambos 2011, pp 850–1. Ambos affirms the possibility of such an exception for top and mid-level bureaucrats of the Nazi regime, see Ambos 2013, p 160 with fn. 501.

2.4.2.4 Making Responsibility for Perpetration Through an Organisation an Independent Mode of Liability and Reworking Attribution of Responsibility in General

The systemic approach is mostly normative and attributes responsibility based on functional control over the system through which a crime is committed. This also means, however, that the mediated conduct *through* another person is no longer the focus of the mode of liability. Instead, the organisation is the centre of attention. As such, scholars invoke that perpetration through an organisation should be made an independent mode of liability.[329] In this vein, Heine questioned whether Section 25 GCC would still be the correct *locus legis* to accommodate perpetration through an organisation. In his view, the attribution of organisational, systemic wrongdoing is shaped by conduct that establishes or maintains an apparatus of power, which in turn systemically creates certain risks for legally protected rights. He states that therefore this kind of attribution of responsibility should be domesticated and, above all, limited by the future development of criminal law.[330] Ambos and Weisser both point out that the ongoing debate on the issue has produced numerous proposals which would enable an emancipation of a normative "perpetration through an organisation" from the traditional modes of liability. Both limit this call to the area of international criminal law based on the typical collective nature of mass atrocities.[331]

This call for an emancipation of indirect perpetration through an organisation is sometimes connected to the notion of an overall criminal situation ("*Gesamttat*").[332] Brought to the ambit of international criminal law, the concept centres on the organization or entity carrying out mass atrocities and on the whole context of the atrocity, rather than on specific crimes.[333]

According to this model, participation in a crime of a mass atrocity can be established in various steps, which take the typical collective circumstances into account. For the context of mass atrocities, the concept requires: (1) An act of the accused, (2) an overall criminal context and (3) the specific criminal outcome of the charged crime. These three requirements are connected because through their conduct, the accused contributes to the overall criminal context and, out of this context the crime is committed by another person. [334] This model therefore shifts the question of causality from the connection between the act and the outcome to the connection between the overall criminal context and the outcome.[335]

---

[329] Ambos 2011, pp 851–2; Ambos 2018, § 7 mn. 28; Eidam 2015, p 172–4; Heine 2000, p 926. Weisser 2011, p 295; Weisser 2019, p 250.

[330] Heine 2000, p 926.

[331] Ambos 2018, § 7 mn. 28; Weisser 2011, p 295; Weisser 2019, p 250.

[332] See Ambos 2013, p 177–9 with fn. 666; Ambos 2018, § 7 mn. 29; the concept of "Gesamttat" was first constructed by Dencker in Dencker 1996, p 125 et seq.; 152 et seq., 229 and for a perspective on mass atrocities by Marxen 1998, p 231–2.

[333] On the concept of *Gesamttat* itself in international criminal law see Vest 2002, pp 244–50; the specific connection to Lampe's "system of wrongdoing" is mentioned at 245.

[334] Marxen 1998, pp 231–2; Vest 2011, p 400.

[335] Marxen 1998, p 233; Vest 2011, p 400.

This model represents a rethinking of the attribution of criminal responsibility which is also known to general criminal law theory in Germany.[336]

Weisser, for example, has developed a normative approach to the concept of perpetration of individual crimes based on a European comparison.[337] It works in a two-step approach. In the first step, all contributions that are connected to a crime are put together for a comprehensive picture of the overall crime (*Gesamttat*). In a second step, the individual contribution of a person serves as the basis to determine their role in the overall crime. If the contribution was formative for the crime, the person can be a perpetrator.[338] The weight of the contribution, measured in its formative influence on the crime, can lead to persons in the background being perpetrators.[339] Based on this model—which was not developed specifically for mass atrocities—a person who shapes an individual crime by having an influential role will be a perpetrator, precisely because of this influential role.[340] The model therefore produces a similar outcome based on similar considerations as the concept of *Gesamttat* in international criminal law, but applied to individual crimes in everyday criminality.

A consequence of relying on such models can be that the notion of domination of the crime loses importance because these models focus more on the collective nature and the underlying importance of the overall crime or criminal action.[341]

2.4.2.5 Comparison and Summary

This section described certain alterations to the traditional concept and the BGH's approach which result from shifting the focus of the doctrine. From responsibility for specific crimes based on specific contributions, the systemic approach shifts the view to the system. Specific contributions are made to the functioning of the system which in turn justifies attributing the system's wrongdoing to the actor. Based on this link responsibility for committing specific crimes is attributed to the actor who contributed to the functioning of the system.

In comparison to the traditional concept by Roxin and to the approach in the *Mauerschützen* cases, the concept of domination is less factual and more systemic

[336] See already Ambos 2013, p 177 with fn. 666 who points to Weisser 2011, pp 490–511 and Robles, "Die Zwei Stufen der Beteiligungslehre—am Beispiel der Beteiligung durch Unterlassen", GA 2012, 276–290.

[337] Weisser 2011, p 490 et seq.

[338] Ibid., pp 549–50.

[339] A consequence of Weisser's model is that the distinction between individual, indirect and joint perpetration in German criminal law would become moot (see ibid., p 551), which is one of the reasons why she describes it as irreconcilable with the current German legislation, which clearly embodies these different concepts of perpetration (ibid., p 548).

[340] See Weisser 2019, p 255 with fn. 48, pointing to Weisser 2011, p 504 et seq.

[341] Ambos 2013, p 178; Vest also criticises the notion of domination of the crime for mass atrocities, although mostly based on the common concept of joint perpetration, pursuant to which a co-perpetrator dominates the crime by being able to frustrate it through the withdrawal of his or her contribution, see Vest 2011, pp 327–8, 340, 369, 382.

and normative in this approach. It acknowledges that factual domination is hardly a convincing concept when the decision maker played their role in the crime at another time and in another place. Instead of viewing domination as the actual, immediate decision regarding the "whether" and "how" of the crime, the theory states that the factual domination is exerted only over the organisation. It consequently concerns organisational structures and procedures and, as far as crimes are committed based on such structures and procedures, the decision maker or architect dominates the crime.[342]

The systemic approach to indirect perpetration is thus based on an indirect linkage principle because the contribution to the system does not establish a direct connection between the perpetrator's conduct and the crime. Responsibility is not attributed because someone, allegedly, dominated a specific crime through instruction. Instead, the perpetrator contributed to the overall system (the organisation) that is responsible for the system of wrongdoing. The link in this theory is therefore an indirect one, provided by the overall systemic wrong, to which the perpetrator contributed, and which enabled and led to the commission of specific crimes.[343]

In contrast to the traditional doctrine and the BGH's approach, this doctrine explicitly combines the ascription of responsibility with the collective dimension of the crimes. This cannot be explicitly found within Roxin's concept or the theory applied by the BGH. Both of the latter recognize the collective nature of mass atrocities and large-scale organised crime, but nowhere does this collective nature serve to justify the ascription of guilt.[344] The call to make indirect perpetration through an organisation an independent mode of liability is mirrored neither by Roxin, nor the BGH, in fact, Roxin explicitly rejects it.[345] The German jurisprudence may in practice already be applying something comparable to this in the form of the "organisation offence".

---

[342] Ambos 2018, § 7 mn. 27.

[343] In German literature such terminology is used by Marxen as an effect of the above-mentioned concept of *Gesamttat* (overall crime). He outlines "A link between the acting individual and the criminal consequence must still exist, but it does not have to be a direct link" (Marxen 1998, p 233, translation by the author). For the English terminology in general, see van Sliedregt 2012, p 181–2.

[344] Roxin in his initial textbook analysis of indirect perpetration through an organisation underlines how forms of liability would not fit the collective nature of mass atrocities (Roxin 2019, p 280). Roxin has also recognized that the actual tool in his version of indirect perpetration through an organisation would not be the respective actor but the organisation (Roxin 2007, p 9). However, none of the systemic arguments described above made it into Roxin's theory and he also rejects the necessity of construing an individual form of liability (see Roxin 2019, Chapter 12 mn. 406–10). Heine, as previously quoted, describes the BGH approach as systemic functional based on the relatively weak or abstract link between the accused's conduct and the specific crimes (killings of fugitives at the border). However, the collective or systemic dynamics were never used by the BGH to justify its approach at all. As seen above, its ever-broader notion of indirect perpetration may represent a practical approach which is fuelled by the observation of responsibility for systems of wrongdoing, but this is done unconsciously and not connected to any (possible) consequent restrictions, such as to a certain type of organisation or a certain level of hierarchy.

[345] Roxin 2019, Chapter 12 mn. 406-10.

However, it does not recognize the doctrine in theory or draw any consequences from it.[346]

Despite these differences, the systemic approach does not necessarily entail requirements which are much different from those of the traditional approach; an organised apparatus must exist and have certain features to establish a system of wrongdoing. The indirect perpetrator must—logically—have a certain position in this apparatus to justify the ascription of responsibility to them. The mechanism that leads to the functioning of the apparatus is something which may be redefined in the systemic-functional approach depending on the focus. One may favour a focus on automatisms or acknowledge a variety of factors instead of the single fungibility or readiness criteria as familiar from the traditional doctrine. Furthermore, with this approach, one can acknowledge the organisational, planning role of a person as sufficient to establish perpetrator liability. Such a person contributes to the functioning of the system, i.e., to the systemic wrong.

In contrast to the BGH's version of the doctrine, the systemic approach does not usually seem to lead to an expansion of indirect perpetration. Certainly, some types of conduct which may be more organisational than directly linked to the commission of the crimes are recognized under both approaches but based on different premises. The BGH, by ultimately relying on the subjective element—garnishing it with certain phrases about organisations and the accused's position in it—broadens the scope of potential perpetrators. In the systemic approach, the focus shifts, but—depending on the view of different scholars—also leads to the narrowing of certain requirements (restriction to the leadership level, restriction to certain types of organisations or automatisms). Therefore, the systemic approach is doctrinally better founded and more restrictive than the BGH's approach.

Naturally, all three approaches share the view on the relation between principal perpetration and secondary participation in German criminal law.

2.5 Views on a Hierarchy of Blameworthiness

As stated in the introduction, the issue of distinguishing between perpetration and participation is connected to the question of whether the underlying system of modes of liability contains a gradation of seriousness. Discussing whether someone is a perpetrator or participant only has added value when simultaneously examining the necessity of and reasons for such a distinction. Whether a system of perpetration and participation establishes a hierarchy between all or some of the modes of liability is therefore logically part of the inquiry.

Roxin's vision of perpetration and participation in German criminal law implies a hierarchy of blameworthiness between commission, instigation and aiding and abetting.[347]

---

346 See above at Sect. 2.3.2.2.

347 See above Sect. 2.2.5.

The systemic approach equally builds upon such a notion. After all, it strives to deliver a solid, more credible foundation that allows the ascription of perpetration responsibility to decision makers, architects, and organizers of crimes who operate in the background. In the absence of a hierarchy of blameworthiness, such a theoretical-dogmatic venture would be partly ill-founded; instigation and aiding and abetting would be equally befitting for those who design and implement systems of wrongdoing.

All things considered, it can be deduced that practically every opinion that endorses the doctrine of indirect perpetration through an organisation implies a gradation of blameworthiness between commission, instigation and aiding and abetting.[348]

It is noteworthy that the relevant opinions rely on an intuitional impression of the necessity to "properly express the wrongdoing" of leaders of criminal organisations when the hierarchy of blameworthiness is discussed. Roxin provides a striking example of this reasoning, stating that common linguistics dictate the preference of (indirect) perpetration over instigation because one would speak of a "desk perpetrator" not "desk instigator".[349]

This perceived necessity is usually expressed through an implied downgrading of instigation, which is illustrated through wording, but is often unaccompanied by specific arguments for such an implication of hierarchy.

For example, authors speak of "mere" instigation or ask whether a commander or high-ranking politician could be considered "only an instigator".[350]

Additionally, the assertion that the actor—a military or political leader—has a "central position" or that the "objective weight" of their contribution can only be expressed through a form of perpetration is common.[351]

This reflex can be found in jurisprudence as well,[352] and was certainly a reason for the establishment of the doctrine. Although, as discussed, the opportunity to establish perpetrator liability for business managers was also attempted via this vehicle. Interestingly, in its first practical application, this approach did not lead to harsher sentencing.[353]

---

348 See in this regard Weisser 2011, p 458, who states that certain untypical cases in which indirect perpetration through an organisation was applied by the BGH would illustrate the "special blameworthiness" (*besonderes Unwerturteil*) intrinsic to perpetration in German law.

349 Roxin 2010, p 456.

350 Roxin 2011, p 196 (mere accessory), 198 (only instigators), 203 (merely instigators) (for more examples on Roxin's view, see above Sect. 2.2.5); Schünemann 2007, § 25 mn. 65; see also the description by Weigend 2011a, p 96.

351 Ambos 1998, p 232; Jung 1995, p 174; Murmann 1996, p 272; regarding Roxin in this matter, see above Sect. 2.2.5; on the BGH's recurrence on such thoughts see Sect. 2.3.2.3.

352 German Federal Court of Justice, Judgment, 26.7.1994, above n 196, p 2706: "Not to treat the person in the background as a perpetrator in such cases would not do justice to the objective weight of his contribution" (translation by the author); see also the description of jurisprudence in this regard by Fletcher 1998, p 199; see above Sect. 2.3.2.3.

353 German Federal Court of Justice, Judgment, 26.7.1994, above n 196, p 2707; the court asserts that, given the identical margin of sentencing for instigation (which was the form of liability used

In summary, a relevant part of German academic literature and jurisprudence imply a hierarchy of blameworthiness between perpetration and participation in German criminal law. This is especially underlined by their desire to convict criminal leaders as perpetrators.[354]

2.6 Summary

The findings of this chapter open certain perspectives which will be considered in the following chapters of this work when analysing the doctrine and cases in international criminal law.

2.6.1 Summary and Comparison

The traditional version of the theory was first described by Roxin and later received suggested alterations or amendments by other scholars. It implies a hierarchy of blameworthiness between the forms of commission and instigation in German criminal law. The BGH "adopted" the doctrine, but—in practice—remodelled it up to a point where it bears little resemblance with its academic precursor. The courts' "normative combination theory" leads to a nearly unlimited discretion of judges when distinguishing perpetration from participation.[355] Based on this very broad approach, a person in the background with a certain influence over the crime can be an indirect perpetrator (depending on the size and structures of his or her gang or organisation) or an instigator.[356] Logically, at times it may be very difficult to determine which mode of liability will be applied. Furthermore, this broad interpretation of forms of perpetration by courts and literature diminishes the role of accessorial modes of liability.[357] As a consequence, some describe the German jurisprudence on perpetration and participation as being far from certain or transparent.[358]

The systemic approach underlines the indirect perpetrator's responsibility for the establishment and maintenance of the system and its mechanisms or automatisms.

by the district court), the court of the trial stage would not have sentenced the accused harsher had it convicted under the head of perpetration right away.

[354] See also Weisser 2011, p 458.

[355] See already Zieschang 1995, p 370.

[356] Puppe 2013, p 514.

[357] See Fletcher 1998, p 199, who states regarding the application of indirect perpetration through an organisation by the BGH that: "The pressure to make this symbolic point constitutes one of the factors that have driven the doctrine of complicity into retreat". See also Zazcyk 1996, p 415, who postulated the danger of a profound confounding of modes of liability.

[358] Zieschang 1995, p 370; in a similar vein regarding co-perpetration, see Heine and Weisser 2019b, § 25 mn. 67, stating that in jurisprudence any random and marginal act may constitute a sufficient objective contribution.

Consequently, the notion of domination of the crime is different to the one that applies in Roxin's approach. In the systemic theory, the concept of domination is more normative and less factual.[359]

In other words, it is not only the requirements that vary between the three versions of indirect perpetration through an organisation, but also the underlying concepts. The traditional doctrine relies on a rather factual view on domination of the crime. In a way, the same kind of influence is postulated in earlier BGH jurisprudence on the *Mauerschützen* cases where the court affirmed a high degree of influence of the indirect perpetrators over the specific crimes. It is worth noting, however, that the BGH does not only rely on this concept but maintains the option of reverting to purely subjective criteria, or, at times, an overall evaluative view. The BGH's approach to indirect perpetration through an organisation has never been truly or narrowly based on the doctrine of domination of the crime and is nowadays removed very far from it. In the systemic approach, domination is only recognized as far as the architect's contribution goes. This can be limited to organisational roles.

This comparison demonstrates that, despite the *Eichmann* case serving as its intellectual catalyst, the traditional approach to indirect perpetration through an organisation is still a model of imputation based on a direct link. Domination is established as a factual evaluation of the (perceived) influence that a leader exerts over specific crimes by "hitting a button". This is different under the systemic approach where the concept of domination becomes a normative label given to a person whose contribution to the overall system of wrongdoing is considered to deserve the classification as an indirect perpetrator. The BGH's approach is difficult to categorize in these terms, partly because it relies on subjective criteria.

All three versions of the theory rely on a hierarchy of blameworthiness between modes of liability in German criminal law. Commission is deemed more blameworthy than instigation, which in turn is believed to be more blameworthy than aiding and abetting. Aiding and abetting receives a mandatory mitigation of the sentence according to Section 27 para. 2 GCC, whilst instigation is punished just as harshly as perpetration according to Section 26 GCC. Therefore, the hierarchy of blameworthiness is usually backed with the idea that instigation would not be the "appropriate form" or "sound right" to describe the grave responsibility of persons with a central role in a crime, including architects and decision makers of mass atrocities.

As observed thus far, German literature and jurisprudence have produced differing approaches to the issue of leadership criminality. These approaches correspond only in two points: (1) high-ranking individuals behind mass atrocities are considered indirect perpetrators and (2) this is the correct outcome because of an assumed hierarchy of blameworthiness. The doctrinal concepts underlying these outcomes, however, vary greatly and are irreconcilable with each other. This demonstrates that one should be cautious in speaking of "one" German approach to the issue, or to overestimate the productiveness of the relation between German academia and jurisprudence in this topic.[360]

---

[359] See above Sects. 2.4.1 and 2.4.2.1.

[360] But see for such an appraisal Ohlin 2015, p 537.

2.6.2 *Concluding Remarks: The* Eichmann *Case and Its Implications for International Criminal Law*

The different approaches to domination of the crime also emphasise a particularity of the *Eichmann* case and the description of persons like him in this chapter. The "desk perpetrator" has mostly been described herein as a decision maker and/or architect of the crime. As examined in the beginning, a person like Adolf Eichmann made decisions which would contribute to the murder of millions of European Jews. However, Eichmann did not decide over the commission of the crime *per se*.[361] The decision to deport and murder Jewish people from a certain area was made by Himmler. This decision was then either passed down through another branch of the apparatus, the *WVHA* which ran the extermination camps, or the commanders of these camps were instructed directly by Himmler. If an order for a mass murder passed through the *WVHA* or the security police, the subordinate officials in this branch can be described as making their own decisions by further refining and specifying Himmler's orders before they would ultimately reach the physical perpetrators of the crimes. With Eichmann's decisions, that was not the case. However, his decisions and other organisational contributions were crucial to the deportation and consequent murders. Based on this and regarding the specific crimes, one might say, that Eichmann was an architect, i.e., an organizer and planner, rather than a decision maker.

Following this observation, it does not seem convincing to state that Adolf Eichmann dominated the crimes by deciding "whether" and "how" they would be committed in the traditional sense of domination by will. From this perspective it seems questionable whether he would have qualified as an indirect perpetrator under Roxin's doctrine. Despite his inability to influence their eventual commission, Eichmann did, however, decide over important and causal parts of the preparation of the crimes. Eichmann has therefore been described as a "mid-ranking bureaucrat … who enables a part of the plan to run smoothly".[362] Under the systemic view on indirect perpetration through an organisation, it could be concluded that Eichmann dominated the crime within the margins of his organisational capacity and by controlling and maintaining vital parts of the criminal system through which the crimes were committed.

This role, fulfilled by Eichmann and many others in the system of Nazi Germany can be described as that of an architect, rather than a decision maker as far as the commission of crimes is concerned. As has been submitted, the traditional view on domination of the crime seems too narrow to justify the attribution of perpetrator liability in such cases, but the systemic view aptly grasps this role. By contrast, it seems that both approaches in German academia always encompass the role of clearly identified decision makers, i.e., those who would otherwise qualify as instigators.

---

[361] But see Roxin's interpretation of the case in Roxin 2003, § 25 mn. 106, speaking of Hitler, Himmler or Eichmann giving orders to kill.

[362] Guilfoyle 2011, p 257-8.

This analysis pre-shapes the following research into the doctrine in international criminal law because it touches on two intertwined issues: a factual and a legal one.

From a factual perspective, it is important to recognize similarities and differences between the *Eichmann* case and cases before the ICC. Observing the roles of high and mid-level actors in their respective organisations is important to distinguish between different forms of influence on the crime. This comparison is also important when answering the question of whether many actors like Eichmann are brought before the ICC today, i.e., architects of crimes who participate in mass atrocities through logistical, sometimes abstract, contributions.

From a legal perspective, it is not only important to analyse and compare the requirements of indirect perpetration as laid out by the ICC in comparison to those devised in German theory and practice. Rather, we will also have to consider the notion of domination (control in the ICC's language) and its implications. Does the ICC understand domination/control as factual and specific as the traditional German view does? Or is it more of a normative concept in this regard, attributing responsibility based on thoughts of domination over the organisation and its structures rather than directly over the crime?

These two factors are decisive in analysing criticism of the doctrine in international criminal law, as well as in comparing the doctrine with potential alternatives.

References

Ambos K (1998) Tatherrschaft durch Willensherrschaft kraft organisatorischer Machtapparate. Goltdammer's Archiv 226–245

Ambos K (2009) Command Responsibility and Organisationsherrschaft: Ways of attributing international crimes to the 'most responsible'. In: Nollkaemper A, van der Wilt H (eds) System Criminality in International law. Cambridge University Press, Cambridge, 127–157

Ambos K (2011) Zur "Organisation" bei der Organisationsherrschaft. In: Heinrich M, Jäger C, Schünemann (eds) Strafrecht als Scientia Universalis Festschrift für Claus Roxin zum 80 Geburtstag am 15 Mai 2011. De Gruyter, Berlin, 837–852

Ambos K (2013) Treatise on International Criminal Law—Volume I: Foundations and General Part. Oxford University Press, Oxford

Ambos K (2016) Art. 25. In: The Rome Statute of the International Criminal Court—A Commentary. C.H. Beck/Hart/Nomos, Munich

Ambos K (2018) Internationales Strafrecht. C. H. Beck, Munich

Arendt H (2018) Eichmann in Jerusalem—Ein Bericht über die Banalität des Bösen. Piper, Munich

Bloy R (1996) Grenzen der Täterschaft bei fremdhändiger Tatausführung. Goltdammer's Archiv 424–442

Cesarani D (2004) Adolf Eichmann—Bürokrat und Massenmörder. William Heinemann, London

Dencker F (1996) Kausalität und Gesamttat. Duncker & Humblot, Berlin

Díaz y García Conlledo M (2017) Das Handeln im Rahmen eines organisatorischen Machtapparates: Täterschaft oder Teilnahme? Goltdammer's Archiv 711–720

Eidam L (2015) Der Organisationsgedanke im Strafrecht. Mohr Siebeck, Tübingen

Erdmann K-D (1983) Rassenpolitik und Judenvernichtung. In: Bracher KD, Funke M, Jacobsen H-A (eds) Nationalsozialistische Diktatur 1933–1945. Bundeszentrale für politische Bildung, Bonn

Fletcher GP (1998) Basic Concepts of Criminal Law. Oxford University Press, Oxford

Fletcher GP (2000) Rethinking Criminal Law. Oxford University Press, Oxford
Gropp W (1996) Die Mitglieder des Nationalen Verteidigungsrates als "Mittelbare Mit-Täter hinter den Tätern"?—BGHSt 40, 218. Juristische Schulung 13–18
Guilfoyle D (2011) Responsibility for Collective Atrocities: Fair Labelling and Approaches to Commission in International Criminal Law. Current Legal Problems 64:255–286
Heine G (2000) Täterschaft und Teilnahme in staatlichen Machtapparaten—NS- und DDR-Unrecht im Vergleich der Rechtsprechung. Juristenzeitung 920–926
Heine G, Weisser B (2019a) Vor §§ 25ff. In: Schönke/Schröder-StGB. C.H. Beck, Munich
Heine G, Weisser B (2019b) § 25. In: Schönke/Schröder-StGB. C.H. Beck, Munich
Heinrich M (2002) Rechtsgutszugriff und Entscheidungsträgerschaft. C.H. Beck, Munich
Heinrich M (2010) Zur Frage der mittelbaren Täterschaft kraft Ausnutzung hierarchischer Organisationsstrukturen bei Wirtschaftsunternehmen. In: Amelung K, Günther H-L, Kühne HH (eds) Festschrift für Volker Krey zum 70 Geburtstag am 9 Juli 2010. Kohlhammer, Stuttgart, 147–167
Herzberg RD (2000) Mittelbare Täterschaft und Anstiftung in formalen Organisationen. In: Amelung K (ed) Individuelle Verantwortung und Beteiligungsverhältnisse bei Straftaten in bürokratischen Organisationen des Staates, der Wirtschaft und der Gesellschaft. Pro Universitate, Sinzheim, 33–53
Herzberg RD (2009) Das Fujimori-Urteil: Zur Beteiligung des Befehlsgebers an den Verbrechen seines Machtapparates. Zeitschrift für internationale Strafrechtsdogmatik 11:576–580
Hoyer A (2008) Kombination von Täterschaft und Teilnahme beim Hintermann. In: Putzke H, Hardtung B, Hörnle T (eds) Strafrecht zwischen System und Telos: Festschrift für Rolf Dietrich Herzberg zum siebzigsten Geburtstag am 14 Februar 2008. Mohr Siebeck, Tübingen, 379–394
Hoyer A (2017) § 25. In: Systematischer Kommentar zum Strafgesetzbuch, Band I §§ 1–37 StGB. Carl Heymanns Verlag, Cologne
Hruschka J (1998) Regreßverbot, Anstiftungsbegriff und die Konsequenzen. Zeistschrift für die gesamte Strafrechtswissenschaft 110:581–639
Jain N (2014) Perpetrators and Accessories in International Criminal Law—Individual Modes of Responsibility for Collective Crimes. Hart Publishing, Oxford
Joecks W (2017) § 25. In: Münchner Kommentar zum Strafgesetzbuch: StGB, Band I §§ 1–37. C.H. Beck, Munich
Jung H (1995) Besprechung von BGH Urteil vom 26.07.1995. Juristische Schulung 173–174
Keiler J (2019) Chapter X. Forms of Participation. In: Keiler J, Roef D (eds) Comparative Concepts of Criminal Law. Intersentia, Cambridge, 285–332
Kress C (2018) VStGB § 6. In: Münchener Kommentar Strafgesetzbuch—Nebenstrafrecht III Völkerstrafgesetzbuch. C.H. Beck, Munich
Krey V, Nuys M (2009) Der Täter hinter dem Täter—oder die Liebe der Strafrechtler zum Glasperlenspiel. In: Böse M, Sternberg-Lieben D (eds) Grundlagen des Straf- und Strafverfahrensrechts: Festschrift für Knut Amelung zum 70 Geburtstag. Duncker & Humblot, Berlin, 203–223
Küpper G (1998) Zur Abgrenzung der Täterschaftsformen. Goltdammer's Archiv 519–529
Lampe E-J (1996) Systemunrecht und Unrechtssysteme. Zeitschrift für die gesamte Strafrechtswissenschaft 106:683–745
Marxen K (1998) Beteiligung an schwerem systematischen Unrecht—Bemerkungen zu einer Völkerstrafrechtlichen Straftatlehre. In: Lüderssen K (ed) Aufgeklärte Kriminalpolitik oder Kampf gegen das Böse?—Band III: Makrodelinquenz. Nomos, Baden-Baden, 220–236
Maurach R, Gössel KH, Zipf H, Dölling D, Laue C, Renzikowski J (2014) Strafrecht Allgemeiner Teil—Teilband 2—Erscheinungsformen des Verbrechens und Rechtsfolgen der Tat. C.F. Müller, Heidelberg
Morozinis I (2010) Dogmatik der Organisationsdelikte. Duncker & Humblot, Berlin
Murmann U (1996) Tatherrschaft durch Weisungsmacht. Goltdammer's Archiv 269–281
Nack A (2006) Mittelbare Täterschaft durch Ausnutzung regelhafter Abläufe. Goltdammer's Archiv 342–345
Noltenius B (2003) Kriterien der Abgrenzung von Anstiftung und mittelbarer Täterschaft. Europäischer Verlag der Wissenschaften, Frankfurt am Main

Ohlin JD (2015) Co-Perpetration: German Dogmatik or German Invasion? In: Stahn C (ed) The Law and Practice of the International Criminal Court. Oxford University Press, Oxford, 517–537
Orozco López HD (2021) Roxins mittelbare Täterschaft kraft organisatorischer Machtapparate—Eine kritische Analyse. Zeitschrift für internationale Strafrechtsdogmatik 233–248
Orozco López HD, Silva Santaularia N (2022) Reflections on Indirect (Co-)Perpetration through an Organization. Journal of International Criminal Justice 20:657–676
Orth K (1999) Das System der Nationalsozialistischen Konzentrationslager—eine politische Organisationsgeschichte. Hamburger Edition, Hamburg
Otto H (2001) Täterschaft kraft organisatorischen Machtapparates. Juristische Ausbildung 753–759
Puppe I (2013) Die Architektur der Beteiligungsformen. Goltdammer's Archiv 514–536
Reichenbach P (2016) Uneigentliche Organisationsdelikte. Juristische Ausbildung 139–149
Rengier R (2019) Strafrecht Allgemeiner Teil. C.H. Beck, Munich
Renzikowski J (1997) Restriktiver Täterbegriff und fahrlässige Beteiligung. Mohr Siebeck, Tübingen
Richter I (2020) Nazi Crimes Before West German Courts: Fritz Bauer as a Visionary of International Criminal Justice? Journal of International Criminal Justice 18:167–183
Rotsch T (1998) Die Rechtsfigur des Täters hinter dem Täter bei der Begehung von Straftaten im Rahmen organisatorischer Machtapparate und ihre Übertragbarkeit auf wirtschaftliche Organisationsstrukturen. Neue Zeitschrift für Strafrecht 491–495
Rotsch T (2000) Tatherrschaft kraft Organisationsherrschaft? Zeitschrift für die gesamte Strafrechtswissenschaft 112:518–562
Rotsch T (2005) Neues zur Organisationsherrschaft. Neue Zeitschrift für Strafrecht 13–18
Rotsch T (2009) Einheitstäterschaft statt Tatherrschaft. Mohr Siebeck, Tübingen
Roxin C (1963) Straftaten im Rahmen organisatorischer Machtapparate. Goltdammer's Archiv 193–207
Roxin C (1995) Anmerkung zum Urteil des BGH vom 26.7.1994—5 StR 98/9. Juristenzeitung 49–52
Roxin C (2003) Strafrecht Allgemeiner Teil Band II Besondere Erscheinungsformen der Straftat. C. H. Beck, Munich
Roxin C (2006) Organisationsherrschaft und Tatentschlossenheit. In: Hoyer A, Müller HE, Pawlik M, Wolter J (eds) Festschrift für Friedrich-Christian Schroeder zum 70 Geburtstag. C.F. Müller Verlag, Heidelberg, 387–400
Roxin C (2007) Organisationsherrschaft als eigenständige Form mittelbarer Täterschaft. Schweizerische Zeitschrift für Strafrecht 125:1–23
Roxin C (2010) Organisationssteuerung als Erscheinungsform mittelbarer Täterschaft. In: Amelung K, Günther H-L, Kühne HH (eds) Festschrift für Volker Krey zum 70 Geburtstag am 9 Juli 2010. Kohlhammer, Stuttgart, 449–464
Roxin C (2011) Crimes as Part of Organized Power Structures. Journal of International Criminal Justice 9:191–205
Roxin C (2012) Zur neuesten Diskussion über die Organisationsherrschaft. Goltdammer's Archiv 395–415
Roxin C (2019) Täterschaft und Tatherrschaft. De Gruyter, Berlin
Schild W (2017) § 25. In: Nomos Kommentar Strafgesetzbuch. Nomos, Baden-Baden
Schlösser J (2004) Soziale Tatherrschaft—Ein Beitrag zur Frage der Täterschaft in organisatorischen Machtapparaten. Duncker & Humblot, Berlin
Schlösser J (2007) Organisationsherrschaft durch Tun und Unterlassen—Zugleich Besprechung von BGH, Beschluss vom 26.08.2003 und Urteil vom 13.05.2004. Goltdammer's Archiv 161–174
Schmidhäuser E (1982) Strafrecht Allgemeiner Teil. J. C. B. Mohr (Paul Siebeck), Tübingen
Schroeder F-C (1965) Der Täter hinter dem Täter: Ein Beitrag zur Lehre von der mittelbaren Täterschaft. Duncker & Humblot, Berlin
Schroeder F-C (1995) Der Sprung des Täters hinter dem Täter aus der Theorie in die Praxis. Juristische Rundschau 177–180

Schroeder F-C (2009) Tatbereitschaft gegen Fungibilität. Zeitschrift für internationale Strafrechtsdogmatik 569–571
Schroeder K, Staadt J (eds) (2018) Die Todesopfer des DDR-Grenzregimes an der innerdeutschen Grenze 1949–1989. Peter Lang, Berlin
Schünemann B (2006) Die Rechtsfigur des "Täters hinter dem Täter" und das Prinzip der Tatherrschaftsstufen. In: Hoyer A, Müller HE, Pawlik M, Wolter J (eds) Festschrift für Friedrich-Christian Schroeder zum 70 Geburtstag. C.F. Müller, Heidelberg, 401–413
Schünemann B (2007) § 25. In: Leipziger Kommentar Strafgesetzbuch: StGB, Band 1: Einleitung; §§ 1–31. De Gruyter, Berlin
Simester AP, Spencer JR, Stark F, Sullivan GR, Virgo GJ (2019) Simester and Sullivan's Criminal Law—Theory and Doctrine. Hart Publishing, Oxford
Sternberg-Lieben D, Bosch N (2019) Vor §§ 52 ff. In: Schönke/Schröder-StGB. C.H. Beck, Munich
Stewart JG (2012) The End of "Modes of Liability" for International Crimes. Leiden Journal of International Law 25:165–219
Urban C (2004) Mittelbare Täterschaft kraft Organisationsherrschaft—Eine Studie zur Konzeption und Anwendbarkeit, insbesondere im Hinblick auf Wirtschaftsunternehmen. Vandenhoeck & Ruprecht Verlage, Osnabrück
van Sliedregt E (2012) Individual Criminal Responsibility in International Criminal Law. Oxford University Press, Oxford
van Sliedregt E, Weisser B (2022) The Ntaganda Case and Individual Criminal Liability at the ICC—Foreword. Journal of International Criminal Justice 20:627–635
Vest H (2002) Genozid durch organisatorische Machtapparate. Nomos, Baden-Baden
Vest H (2011) Völkerrechtsverbrecher verfolgen—Ein abgestuftes Mehrebenensystem systemischer Tatherrschaft. Stämpfli Verlag AG, Bern
von Lang J (1982) Das Eichmann-Protokoll—Tonbandaufzeichnungen der israelischen Verhöre. Severin und Siedler, Berlin
Weigend T (2011a) Perpetration through an Organization—The Unexpected Career of a German Legal Concept. Journal of International Criminal Justice 9:91–111
Weigend T (2011b) Germany. In: Heller J, Dubber MD (eds) The Handbook of Comparative Criminal Law. Stanford University Press, Stanford, 252–287
Weigend T (2014) Problems of Attribution in International Criminal Law. Journal of International Criminal Justice 12:253–266
Weisser B (2011) Täterschaft in Europa. Mohr Siebeck, Tübingen
Weisser B (2012) Die mittelbare Täterschaft kraft Organisationsherrschaft—Über den Werdegang einer Rechtsfigur vom Ausnahmeinstrument zur Allzweckwaffe. Ad Legendum 244–250
Weisser B (2019) Organisationsherrschaft und organisationsbezogene Beihilfe. Goltdammer's Archiv 244–256
Werle G, Burghardt B (2010) Die mittelbare Mittäterschaft—Fortentwicklung deutscher Strafrechtsdogmatik im Völkerstrafrecht? In: Bloy R (ed) Gerechte Strafe und legitimes Strafrecht—Festschrift für Manfred Maiwald zum 75 Geburtstag Duncker & Humblot, Berlin, 849–864
Werle G, Burghardt B (2011) Anthology—Claus Roxin on Crimes as Part of Organized Power Structures, Introductory Note. Journal of International Criminal Justice 9:191–191
Wessels J, Beulke W, Satzger H (2019) Strafrecht Allgemeiner Teil. C.F. Müller, Heidelberg
Zazcyk R (1996) Die "Tatherrschaft Kraft organisatorischer Machtapparate" und der BGH. Goltdammer's Archiv 411–415
Zieschang F (1995) Mittäterschaft bei bloßer Mitwirkung im Vorbereitungsstadium. Zeitschrift für die gesamte Strafrechtswissenschaft 107:361–381

Other Documents

District Court of Jerusalem, *Judgment Against Karl Adolf Eichmann—Unofficial Translation*, 40/61

German Federal Court of Justice, Judgment, 15.09.1988, in: Neue Juristische Wochenschrift, 1989, 912

German Federal Court of Justice, Judgment, 03.11.1992, in: Neue Juristische Wochenschrift, 1993, 141

German Federal Court of Justice, Judgment, 25.03.1993, in: Neue Juristische Wochenschrift, 1993, 1932

German Federal Court of Justice, Judgment, 18.01.1994, in: Neue Juristische Wochenschrift, 1994, 2237

German Federal Court of Justice, Judgment, 19.04.1994, in: Neue Juristische Wochenschrift, 1994, 2240

German Federal Court of Justice, Judgment, 20.10.1993, in: Neue Juristische Wochenschrift, 1994, 267

German Federal Court of Justice, Judgment, 26.7.1994, in: Neue Juristische Wochenschrift, 1994, 2703

German Federal Court of Justice, Judgment, 26.07.1994, in: Neue Juristische Wochenschrift, 1994, 2708

German Federal Court of Justice, Judgment, 03.11.1994, in: Neue Juristische Wochenschrift, 1995, 1564

German Federal Court of Justice, Judgment, 04.03.1996, in: Neue Juristische Wochenschrift, 1996, 2042

German Federal Court of Justice, Judgment, 06.06.1997, in: Neue Zeitschrift für Strafrecht, 1997, 544

German Federal Court of Justice, Judgment, 23.10.1996, in: Neue Juristische Wochenschrift, 1997, 951

German Federal Court of Justice, Judgment, 11.12.1997, in: Neue Juristische Wochenschrift, 1998, 767

German Federal Court of Justice, Judgment, 08.11.1999, in: Neue Juristische Wochenschrift, 2000, 443

German Federal Court of Justice, Decision, 07.07.2001, in: Neue Juristische Wochenschrift, 2001, 3060

German Federal Court of Justice, Judgment, 08.03.2001, in: Neue Juristische Wochenschrift, 2001, 2409

German Federal Court of Justice, Judgment, 06.11.2002, in: Neue Juristische Wochenschrift, 2003, 522

German Federal Court of Justice, Decision, 26.08.2003, in: Neue Juristische Wochenschrift, 2004, 375

German Federal Court of Justice, Decision, 02.11.2007, in: Neue Zeitschrift für Strafrecht, 2008, 89

German Federal Court of Justice, Decision, 29.07.2009, in: Neue Zeitschrift für Strafrecht, 2010, 103

German Federal Court of Justice, Judgment, 22.04.2014, in: Neue Zeitschrift für Strafrecht, 2014, 459

German Federal Court of Justice, Decision, 20.09.2016, in: Neue Juristische Wochenschrift, 2017, 498

Trials of War Criminals Before the Nuernberg Military Tribunals Under Control Council Law No. 10, Vol. V, U.S. Government Printing Service 1950

Chapter 3
Indirect Perpetration Through an Organisation Under the Rome Statute

Contents

Abstract This chapter analyses the jurisprudence of the International Criminal Court (ICC) on its theory of indirect perpetration through an organisation and its control theory. The doctrine with its legal requirements and implications is outlined in depth, making use of the elaborations of ICC jurisprudence and academic literature. It is argued that the requirements of indirect perpetration through an organisation at the ICC are well-described in theory. In practice however, it seems unclear which facts will suffice for the court to affirm the theory's requirements and which ones will not. The comparison of the ICC's theory with the German approaches as outlined in Chap. 2 shows that the former is an own theoretical construct that does not

J. Block, *Reconciling Responsibility with Reality*, International Criminal Justice Series 33, https://doi.org/10.1007/978-94-6265-607-9_3

completely resemble any of the German doctrines, despite being closest to the traditional German approach. This chapter criticises the ICC's theories of control over the crime and indirect perpetration through an organisation, applying arguments from both the international as well as the German academic debate. Other valid points of criticism aside, the theories are found to be based on an unconvincing concept of control over the crime that cannot credibly explain why a decision maker in a leadership position should qualify as someone committing the crime in the sense of Art. 25(3)(a) Rome Statute.

Keywords International Criminal Court · Indirect perpetration through an organisation · Control over an organisation · Apparatus of power · Almost automatic compliance · Control over the crime · Hierarchy of blameworthiness · Fungibility · Detachment from law · Autonomy principle

3.1 Indirect Perpetration Through an Organisation in the Rome Statute's System of Perpetration and Participation

The ICC adopted a notion of indirect perpetration through an organisation very early in its existence. This chapter analyses the doctrine as adopted by the ICC and the underlying theory of "control over the crime".

Chambers of the ICC have stressed that, unlike the Rome Statute, no national legal system is particularly designed to deal with international mass atrocity crimes.[1] The appeals chamber also underlined that the interpretation of the Rome Statute should be derived from the text, rather than from national legal systems.[2] In addition, the trial chamber in *Lubanga* stated that the need to properly address and express the responsibility of the accused is paramount in interpreting Art. 25 (3) Rome Statute.[3]

This chapter aims to answer the question whether the doctrine of indirect perpetration through an organisation stays true to these assertions. Is it a doctrine derived from the text of the Rome Statute that is particularly well-suited to describe and adjudicate the participants of international crimes?

To answer this question, this section outlines the contents and limits of indirect perpetration through an organisation and of the notion of control under ICC jurisprudence (Sect. 3.1). The findings of this analysis are compared to the approaches of indirect perpetration through an organisation from the German legal system as outlined in Chap. 2 in the following section (Sect. 3.2). In the third section of this chapter, the doctrines of the ICC are analysed critically (Sect. 3.3).

---

[1] ICC, *The Prosecutor v. Thomas Lubanga Dyilo*, Trial Judgment, 14 March 2012, ICC-01/04-01/06, para 976.

[2] ICC, *The Prosecutor v. Thomas Lubanga Dyilo*, Appeals Judgment, 1 December 2014, ICC-01/04-01/06 A 5, para 470.

[3] *Lubanga*, 14 March 2012, para 976.

3.1.1 Forms of Responsibility—The Structure of Art. 25 (3) Rome Statute

Art. 25 (3) Rome Statute embodies forms of individual criminal responsibility in its *litterae* (a) to (d).[4]

Art. 25 (3) (a) covers the "commission" of crimes and emphasises that a crime can be committed "as an individual, jointly with another or through another person". The rule furthermore states that a crime can be committed through another "regardless of whether that other person is criminally responsible". Art. 25 (3) (b) refers to ordering, inducing or soliciting a crime, (c) to aiding and abetting a crime and (d) to contributing to a crime which is committed or attempted by a group of persons with a common plan.

Art. 25 (3) Rome Statute is interpreted by the court as establishing a differential system of perpetration and participation, in which commission (perpetration) in *littera* (a) constitutes principal liability, while the modes in *litterae* (b) to (d) constitute secondary liability.[5]

---

[4] **Article 25—Individual criminal responsibility**

1. The Court shall have jurisdiction over natural persons pursuant to this Statute.
2. A person who commits a crime within the jurisdiction of the Court shall be individually responsible and liable for punishment in accordance with this Statute.
3. In accordance with this Statute, a person shall be criminally responsible and liable for punishment for a crime within the jurisdiction of the Court if that person:

(a) Commits such a crime, whether as an individual, jointly with another or through another person, regardless of whether that other person is criminally responsible;
(b) Orders, solicits or induces the commission of such a crime which in fact occurs or is attempted;
(c) For the purpose of facilitating the commission of such a crime, aids, abets or otherwise assists in its commission or its attempted commission, including providing the means for its commission;
(d) In any other way contributes to the commission or attempted commission of such a crime by a group of persons acting with a common purpose. Such contribution shall be intentional and shall either:

(i) Be made with the aim of furthering the criminal activity or criminal purpose of the group, where such activity or purpose involves the commission of a crime within the jurisdiction of the Court; or
(ii) Be made in the knowledge of the intention of the group to commit the crime; ...

[5] ICC, *The Prosecutor v. Thomas Lubanga*, Confirmation of Charges, 29 January 2007, ICC-01/04-01/06, para 320; ICC, *The Prosecutor v. Germain Katanga and Mathieu Ngudjolo Chui*, Confirmation of Charges, 30 September 2008, ICC-01/04-01/07, paras 466–7; ICC, *The Prosecutor v. Omar Hassan Ahmad Al Bashir*, Issuance of a Warrant of Arrest, 4 March 2009, ICC-02/05-01/09, para 210; ICC, *The Prosecutor v. Jean-Pierre Bemba Gombo*, Confirmation of Charges, 15 June 2009, ICC-01/05-01/08, para 479 (although discussing another topic at that point); *Lubanga*, 14 March 2012, e.g. paras 997–8; ICC, *The Prosecutor v. Germain Katanga*, Trial Judgment, 7 March 2014, ICC-01/04-01/07, para 1383–4; ICC, *The Prosecutor v. Jean-Pierre Bemba et al.*, Confirmation of Charges, 11 November 2014, ICC-01/05-01/13, para 31; *Lubanga*, 1 December 2014, para 462; ICC, *The Prosecutor v. Charles Blé Goudé*, Confirmation of Charges, 11 December 2014,

Art. 28 Rome Statute stipulates that a person can be liable as a superior in what is called superior responsibility.[6] This is considered a mode of responsibility rather than a crime (of omission), although this interpretation is questioned by some authors.[7] Superior responsibility rests on the omission to prevent, supress or investigate crimes that are committed by persons under the effective command or authority and control of a military, quasi-military or civilian superior.[8]

As has been outlined earlier, Art. 28 Rome Statute is excluded from the comparative analysis of this work as it concerns omission liability.[9]

This chapter focuses on the form of responsibility for active conduct, which forms the core of the ICC's approach to persons in leadership positions: indirect perpetration through an organisation. This doctrine builds upon another, underlying theory, the

---

ICC-02/011-02/11, para 135; ICC, *The Prosecutor v. Ahmad Al Faqi Al Mahdi*, Trial Judgment, 27 September 2016, ICC-01/12-01/15, para 58; ICC, *The Prosecutor v. Jean-Pierre Bemba Gombo et al.*, Trial Judgment, 19 October 2016, ICC-01/05-01/13, para 55; ICC, *The Prosecutor v. Al Hassan Ag Abdoul Aziz Ag Mohamed Ag Mahmoud*, Issuance of a Warrant of Arrest, 22 May 2018, ICC-01/12-01/18, para 168 with fn. 237; ICC, *The Prosecutor v. Bosco Ntaganda*, Trial Judgment, 8 July 2019, ICC-01/04-02/06, para 1200.

[6] **Article 28—Responsibility of commanders and other superiors**

(a) A military commander or person effectively acting as a military commander shall be criminally responsible for crimes within the jurisdiction of the Court committed by forces under his or her effective command and control, or effective authority and control as the case may be, as a result of his or her failure to exercise control properly over such forces, where:

(i) That military commander or person either knew or, owing to the circumstances at the time, should have known that the forces were committing or about to commit such crimes; and
(ii) That military commander or person failed to take all necessary and reasonable measures within his or her power to prevent or repress their commission or to submit the matter to the competent authorities for investigation and prosecution.

(b) With respect to superior and subordinate relationships not described in paragraph (a), a superior shall be criminally responsible for crimes within the jurisdiction of the Court committed by subordinates under his or her effective authority and control, as a result of his or her failure to exercise control properly over such subordinates, where:

(i) The superior either knew, or consciously disregarded information which clearly indicated, that the subordinates were committing or about to commit such crimes;
(ii) The crimes concerned activities that were within the effective responsibility and control of the superior; and
(iii) The superior failed to take all necessary and reasonable measures within his or her power to prevent or repress their commission or to submit the matter to the competent authorities for investigation and prosecution.

[7] See the summary by Werle and Jessberger 2020b, mn. 657; see van Sliedregt 2009 who identifies both concepts in the jurisprudence of the *ad hoc* tribunals (at 427).

[8] Note that Art. 28 (a) requires command and control for military commanders and persons who effectively act as such, while *littera* (b) requires authority instead of command for superiors who do not fall into the category of (a).

[9] See above, Introduction, II. Methodology and Limitations.

"control theory". Not unlike in Germany, these two doctrines are connected in the sense that the latter serves as the theoretical groundwork of the former.

3.1.2 Analysis of Indirect Perpetration Through an Organisation in the ICC's Jurisprudence

Beginning with the decision on the confirmation of charges in *Lubanga,* the ICC conceived its theory on how to distinguish between principal commission in Art. 25 (3) (a) and accessorial modes of liability in Art. 25 (3) (b) to (d) Rome Statute.

The chamber lays out three different approaches to distinguish between modes of liability: An objective approach, a subjective approach and what it calls the control over the crime approach.[10]

The control over the crime approach is described by the chamber as follows:

> This approach involves an objective element, consisting of the appropriate factual circumstances for exercising control over the crime, and a subjective element, consisting of the awareness of such circumstances.[11]

The chamber then goes on to outline the three forms of control which it finds embodied within the approach:

- Control through physically carrying out the offence (direct perpetration)
- Control over the will of those who carry out the crime (indirect perpetration)
- Control over the offence, along with others, by reason of the essential tasks assigned to the actor (co-perpetration).[12]

The other two approaches—the objective and subjective approach—are briefly discussed and then dismissed by the chamber.

The objective approach, which is defined here as one in which a perpetrator is only who physically commits a crime, is ruled out because of the existence of indirect perpetration "through another" in *lit.* (a). If a crime can be committed through another, the ruling criterion for commission cannot be the physical, hands-on commission at the same time.[13]

The subjective approach is—interestingly—equated by the chamber with the doctrine of Joint Criminal Enterprise (JCE). The chamber explains how in JCE, the focus is shifted from objective contributions to the state of mind in which the contribution is made.[14] This approach is then discarded by stating that the form of

---

[10] *Lubanga*, 29 January 2007, paras 327–30.

[11] Ibid., para 331.

[12] Ibid., para 332.

[13] Ibid., paras 328, 333; the pre-trial chamber in *Katanga and Chui* later picked this up and added that "modern doctrine generally rejected the objective criterion approach"; see *Katanga and Chui*, 30 September 2008, para 482.

[14] *Lubanga*, 29 January 2007, para 329.

responsibility in the Rome Statute, which is similar to JCE, can be found in Art. 25 (3) (d)—the contribution to a crime committed by a group of persons—not in *littera* (a).[15] Additionally, the chamber observes the wording of Art. 25 (3) (d) ("in any other way contributes to the commission…"), which is interpreted as establishing a residual form of accessorial liability. According to the chamber, this form is meant to criminalize actions which are committed in the necessary state of mind but where the objective contributions do not reach the threshold of the other forms.[16]

Subsequently, the *Lubanga* pre-trial chamber identifies the existing rule on indirect perpetration (commission through another) as the central reason to rely on the control over the crime approach.[17] Since then, the court has established the control over the crime theory in numerous decisions.[18]

As concerns indirect perpetration, the Rome Statute, for the first time, explicitly embodies a regulation on this mode of liability in the legal framework of an international criminal tribunal. There is no direct precedence for indirect perpetration in international criminal law history,[19] but it is said to be known and recognized in most legal systems of the world.[20]

---

[15] Ibid., para 334; this again is later reiterated by the pre-trial chamber in *Katanga and Chui* and amended by the statement that "modern legal doctrine rejects this approach for distinguishing between principals and accessories". See *Katanga and Chui*, 30 September 2008, para 483.

[16] *Lubanga*, 29 January 2007, para 336–7.

[17] Ibid., para 339. See in detail below at Sect. 3.1.2.

[18] See on the control over the crime approach: *Katanga and Chui*, 30 September 2008, paras 480, 485; *Al Bashir*, 4 March 2009, para 210; *Bemba*, 15 June 2009, para 348; ICC, *The Prosecutor v. Bahar Idriss Abu Garda*, Confirmation of Charges, 8 February 2010, ICC-02/05-02/09, para 152; ICC, *The Prosecutor v. Abdallah Banda Abakaer Nourain and Saleh Mohammed Jerbo Jamus*, 7 March 2011, ICC-02/05-03/09, para 126; ICC, *The Prosecutor v. Laurent Koudou Gbagbo*, Warrant of Arrest, 23 November 2011, ICC-02/11, para 10 ("joint control over the crimes"); ICC, *The Prosecutor v. Callixte Mbarushimana*, Decision on the confirmation of charges, 16 December 2011, ICC-01/04-01/10, para 279; ICC, *The Prosecutor v. Francis Kirimi Muthaura, Uhuru Muigai Kenyatta and Mohammed Hussein Ali*, Confirmation of Charges, 23 January 2012, ICC-01/09-02/11, para 296; ICC, *The Prosecutor v. William Samoei Ruto, Henry Kiprono Kosgey and Joshua Arap Sang*, Confirmation of Charges, 23 January 2012, ICC-01/09-01/11, para 291; ICC, *The Prosecutor v. Abdel Raheem Muhammad Huseein*, Arrest Warrant Decision, 1 March 2012, ICC-02/05-01/12, para 37 ("joint control over the commission of the crimes"); ICC, *The Prosecutor v. Simone Gbagbo*, Arrest Warrant Decision, 2 March 2012, ICC-02/11-01/12, para 25 ("joint control over the crime"); *Lubanga*, 14 March 2012, para 1005; *Katanga*, 7 March 2014, para 1393–4; ICC, *The Prosecutor v. Bosco Ntaganda*, Confirmation of Charges, 9 June 2014, ICC-01/04-02/06, paras 121, 135 ("control over the commission of a crime"); ICC, *The Prosecutor v. Laurent Gbagbo*, Confirmation of Charges, 12 June 2014, ICC-02/11-01/11, para 230 ("joint control over the commission of the crime"); *Lubanga*, 1 December 2014, para 462; *Blé Goudé*, 11 December 2014, para 135; ICC, *The Prosecutor v. Dominic Ongwen*, Confirmation of charges, 23 March 2016, ICC-02/04-01/15, para 38; *Al Hassan*, 22 May 2018, para 168; *Ntaganda*, 8 July 2019, para 774, 779–80; ICC, *The Prosecutor v. Patrice-Edouard Ngaïssona and Alfred Yekatom*, Document Containing the Charges, 18 September 2019, ICC-01/14-01/18, para 123.

[19] Werle and Jessberger 2020b, mn. 644.

[20] See *Katanga and Chui*, 30 September 2008, para 495; Fletcher 2000, p 639; Werle 2007, p 963; Werle and Jessberger 2020b, mn. 644. Ambos speaks of a "general recognition". See Ambos 2018, § 7 mn. 23.

Art. 25 (3) (a) Rome Statute speaks of the commission "through another, regardless of whether that other person is criminally responsible". This clarifies that the criminal responsibility of the "human tool" through whom the crime was committed, is irrelevant.[21]

The typical form of indirect perpetration is based on the assumption that an innocent agent or a "human tool" is used by the indirect perpetrator (also "perpetrator by means") to commit the material elements of the crime.[22] The agent often acts without the necessary *mens rea* (due to mistake) or has a defence for his actions (in some legal systems divided into justifications and excuses), e.g., duress or lack of capacity for blameworthiness.[23]

This traditional concept of indirect perpetration has gained very little importance in international criminal law. The *Erdemović* case before the ICTY famously dealt with a physical perpetrator who credibly pleaded to have acted under threat of life.[24] Dražen Erdemović was convicted, nonetheless. The higher-level commanders responsible for the Srebrenica massacre in which he participated were neither indicted nor tried as indirect perpetrators, but rather under the doctrine of Joint Criminal Enterprise (JCE).[25]

Additionally, the nature of mass atrocities and its procedural implications render the traditional concept of indirect perpetration somewhat marginal: The physical perpetrators are often unknown, and in many cases, it will not be determinable whether they acted criminally responsible. Contrary to statements frequently made by participants in mass atrocities, duress and other defences are often unavailable to executioners who participated more willingly than they would care to admit afterwards.[26]

In theory there is a range of cases in international criminal law in which the idea of innocent agents is conceivable. One example is the targeting of civilians or protected objects through physical actors (bomber and drone pilots, artillery crews) who are mistaken about the true nature of their target, whilst the commanding superior is aware of the relevant facts. However, such cases have not gained importance. A fact which might be explained either due to the anonymity of the physical actors or the use of other modes of liability for the respective actors in the background.

A common point of discussion regarding indirect perpetration is whether it can extend to responsibly acting tools or whether the autonomy of the physical perpetrator bars indirect perpetration. The narrow view—the "autonomy principle"—rules out indirect perpetration in such cases. It relies on the assumption that to act "through

---

[21] Ambos 2018, § 7 mn. 25; Cryer et al. 2019, p 353; Weigend 2015, pp 542–3.

[22] See *Katanga and Chui*, 30 September 2008, para 495; Ambos 2016, Art. 25, Art. 25 mn. 12; Cryer et al. 2019, p 352; Weigend 2015, pp 538–9.

[23] *Katanga and Chui*, 30 September 2008, para 495; *Katanga*, 7 March 2014, para 1402; Cryer et al. 2019, p 352; Weigend 2015, pp 538–9.

[24] Ambos 2018, § 7 mn. 24; Olásolo 2009, pp 114–5.

[25] See on JCE and leadership-participation in the *Srebrenica* massacre Chap. 5, Sect. 5.2.

[26] Roxin 2011, p 197; for a criminological perspective on the issue, see Anderson 2018, p 131.

another" (*"durch einen anderen", "por conducto de otro"*) is *only* possible where that other is not criminally responsible.[27]

This autonomy principle is explicitly rejected by the Rome Statute as can be seen in its wording. The indirect perpetrator acts through another "regardless of whether that other is criminally responsible".[28]

Following this, the Rome Statute must be regarded as open to the concept of the "perpetrator behind the perpetrator". The pre-trial chamber in *Katanga and Chui* listed a few cases of this legal figure, which are all explicitly taken from German criminal law.[29] However, it is not surprising that the single most relevant manifestation of this mode of liability became indirect perpetration through an organisation.[30]

In the ICC's first pertinent decision[31] Germain Katanga and Matthieu Ngudjolo Chui were accused as indirect perpetrators acting through their respective non-state armed groups which had allegedly consisted of several hundred fighters. Given that the accused were not believed to have participated personally in the attacks, this case provided the ICC with the opportunity to elaborate on its version of indirect perpetration through an organisation.[32]

It is noteworthy that, since then, only the *Katanga* trial chamber and the pre-trial chamber in *Gaddafi et al.* considered indirect perpetration through an organisation in its "pure" form, i.e., where the accused allegedly held control over the organisation alone.[33] All other proceedings rely on a combination of forms of responsibility: indirect co-perpetration.[34] Indirect co-perpetration is a form of co-perpetration but

[27] See already Chap. 2, Sect. 2.2.3.

[28] *Lubanga*, 29 January 2007, para 339, quoting Eser 2002, p. 795; *Katanga and Chui*, 30 September 2008, para 501; Jessberger and Geneuss 2008, pp 857–8; Cryer et al. 2019, p 353; Weigend 2015, pp 542–3; Werle 2007, p 964; see also Ambos 2018, § 7 mn. 25 with fn. 115 for further sources.

[29] See *Katanga and Chui*, 30 September 2008, para 498 with fn. 658, hinting at different German textbooks. The cases listed by the chamber are: Misleading the direct perpetrator about the seriousness of the offence or the qualifying circumstances or the identity of the victim. See on this also Goy 2012, p 46. Also compare this with the list in Chap. 2, Sect. 2.2.3.

[30] See already the pre-trial chamber's statements in *Katanga and Chui*, 30 September 2008, paras 496–8, 501. See also Werle and Jessberger 2020b, mn. 646 ("of particular relevance").

[31] Several earlier decisions paved the path to this. The pre-trial chamber pointed to its understanding of commission and its applicability to leaders in the arrest warrant decisions against Katanga and Chui (ICC, *The Prosecutor v. Germain Katanga*, Arrest Warrant Decision, 6 July 2007, ICC-01/04-01/07, paras 54, 60; ICC, *The Prosecutor v. Matthieu Ngudjolo Chui*, Arrest Warrant Decision, 6 July 2007, ICC-01/04-02/07, paras 55, 61). The Bemba Arrest Warrant Decision went into the same direction (ICC, *The Prosecutor v. Jean-Pierra Bemba Gombo*, Arrest Warrant Decision, 10 June 2008, ICC-01/05-01/08, para 78).

[32] Note that the prosecution had charged Katanga and Chui with ordering the crimes in question. The pre-trial chamber, however, changed this into indirect co-perpetration, see Steer 2017, p.

[33] And in these cases, only partially. All convictions concerning this doctrine examine indirect co-perpetration, see also van Sliedregt and Yanev 2019, mn. 53.

[34] See ICC, *The Prosecutor v. Muammar Mohammed Abu Minyar Gaddafi, Saif Al-Islam Gaddafi and Abdullah Al-Senussi*, Arrest Warrant Decision, 27 June 2011, ICC-01/11, paras 66, 71. The prosecutor originally regarded Muammar Al Gaddafi as an indirect perpetrator, but the pre-trial chamber recharacterized the mode of liability into indirect co-perpetration. The criminal responsibility of Abdullah Al-Senussi was characterized by the pre-trial chamber as that of an indirect

relies on a set of requirements from both indirect and co-perpetration.[35] The relevant observation for this book is that one half of that doctrine relies on the established requirements of indirect perpetration through an organisation. The test for an indirect co-perpetrator usually ascertains whether they performed an "essential contribution" to the crime (co-perpetration). However, the doctrine always rests on the assumption that the indirect co-perpetrators, by ways of their essential contributions, exercised control over the crime through their respective subordinates (indirect perpetration through an organisation).[36] The respective decisions based on indirect co-perpetration are therefore included here, as far as their findings on the "indirect perpetration" part of the doctrine are concerned.

In the doctrine of the ICC, indirect perpetration through an organisation requires that:

- The accused has control over an organisation (Sect. 3.1.2.1);
- This organisation is an organised and hierarchical apparatus of power (Sect. 3.1.2.2);
- The execution of the crimes is secured by almost automatic compliance with orders issued by the accused (Sect. 3.1.2.3); and
- The accused fulfils the relevant mental element, including the awareness of their control over the crime through the organisation (Sect. 3.1.2.4).

3.1.2.1 Control Over an Organisation

The indirect perpetrator must have control over an organisation.[37]

According to the trial chamber in *Katanga*, persons who control the apparatus are "those in the organisation who conceived the crime, oversaw its preparation at different hierarchical levels, and controlled its performance and execution".[38] According to the chamber, only a person who wields authority over an apparatus as such could be viewed as an indirect perpetrator. This person must control at least a part of the apparatus "effectively and undisturbed". Consequently, those who only

perpetrator. Al Senussi was Gaddafi's former chief of the entire security apparatus. His case was, however, declared inadmissible before the ICC later.

[35] Cf. for in-depth explanations: van Sliedregt and Yanev 2019, mn. 53 et seq.; see Weigend 2014, p 260 explaining how the doctrine of indirect co-perpetration from the viewpoint of the German doctrine naturally qualifies as a sub-category of co-perpetration.

[36] For an instructive explanation of indirect co-perpetration, see Osten 2022, pp 679–83.

[37] *Katanga and Chui*, 30 September 2008, paras 514, 518; *Muthaura et al.*, 23 January 2012, para 407; *Ruto et al.*, 23 January 2012, para 313; *Katanga*, 7 March 2014, para 1405; *Ntaganda*, 9 June 2014, paras 104, 118, 120; see also *Al Bashir*, 4 March 2009, para 222; ICC, *The Prosecutor v. Omar Hassan Ahmad Al Bashir*, Arrest Warrant Decision 12 July 2010, ICC-02/05-01/09, paras 42–3; *Abu Garda*, 8 February 2010, para 23; *Abdel Raheem*, 1 March 2012, para 30–33; *Gbagbo*, 12 June 2014, para 230; *Blé Goudé*, 11 December 2014, para 149; *Ntaganda*, 8 July 2019, paras 769, 778; *Gaddafi et al.*, 27 June 2011, para 69.

[38] *Katanga*, 7 March 2014, para 1412.

"control" a part of the organisation also qualify under this criterion.[39] At another point, the chamber describes "control" over the organisation as

> ...requiring that the indirect perpetrator use at least part of the apparatus of power subordinate to him or her, so as to steer it intentionally towards the commission of a crime, without leaving one of the subordinates at liberty to decide whether the crime is to be executed.[40]

In the *Katanga* trial judgment, the chamber also explained that control could lie with different persons within an organisation. It elaborated that control could be exercised by those who "conceived the crime, oversaw its preparation at different hierarchical levels and controlled its performance and execution".[41]

Aside from these interpretations, little has been done by chambers to elaborate *in abstracto* on this criterion. However, many decisions shed light on the factual basis which is perceived to provide evidence for it.

In the confirmation of charges in *Katanga and Chui*, the pre-trial chamber stated that both of the accused were "*de jure* supreme commanders" of their respective forces and had "*de facto* ultimate control" over the commanders of these forces. The lower-ranking commanders therefore allegedly sought orders from Germain Katanga and Matthieu Ngudjolo Chui to obtain weapons and generally reported to them.[42] The trial chamber in *Chui* asked for factors such as the role, position, function of the accused and the authority he exercised over the group.[43] It considered whether he had given orders and whether he had taken disciplinary or other measures to enforce such orders.[44] Since the chamber could not determine the latter, it could not find Ngudjolo Chui to have been the leader of the relevant organisation.[45]

In *Katanga,* the chamber determined that the accused had held a high office ("presidency") in the relevant militia and was therefore at the apex of the organisation. However, it could not be determined whether this position's powers went further than providing weapons and ammunition to several groups of the militia. Furthermore, whether a "centralised command" existed could not be determined. Therefore, the element of control over the organisation by the accused was not fulfilled.[46]

In the arrest warrant decision in *Al Gaddafi*, the pre-trial chamber also elaborated at length on the positions and resulting competence and powers of the three wanted persons.[47]

A similar reliance on the accused's role in the government and an alleged parallel hierarchical structure can be found in the reasoning on control over an organisation

---

[39] Ibid., para 1412.

[40] Ibid., para 1411. See also *Ntaganda*, 8 July 2019, para 778.

[41] *Katanga*, 7 March 2014, para 1412; see also Kiss 2019, mn. 22.

[42] *Katanga and Chui*, 30 September 2008, paras 540–1.

[43] Ibid., paras 342, 345, 405 et seq., 496, 499.

[44] Ibid., para 502.

[45] Ibid., para 503.

[46] *Katanga*, 7 March 2014, paras 1419–20. Note that the existence of a hierarchical and organised apparatus of power was also denied, based on the same finding.

[47] *Gaddafi et al.*, 27 June 2011, 72, 84–6.

in *Gbagbo* and *Blé Goudé*.[48] In *Ntaganda,* the pre-trial chamber also underlined the accused's position as deputy chief of staff,[49] as did the chamber in *Ruto et al.*, stressing one of the accused's "position on top of the network" (which was allegedly used to carry out crimes).[50] The same is true for the pre-trial and trial chamber's findings on Dominic Ongwen as the commander of one of the four brigades of the Lord's Resistance Army (LRA).[51] Finally, in *Muthaura et al.* one of the findings was that one of the accused gained control over the Kenyan *Mungiki* sect by an agreement with the organisation's actual leader, which would place the organisation under their control. In other words: they gained a type of leadership position by agreement with the former or original leadership.[52] The pre-trial chamber in *Ruto et al.* also stressed the accused's "leadership over a community".[53] In the arrest warrant decision in *Gaddafi et al.*, the pre-trial chamber emphasized, that it would not matter whether a person held an official or *de jure* position of power within a state apparatus, as long as a *de facto* position was indeed occupied.[54]

Finally, the findings of the *Katanga* trial chamber on the necessary *mens rea* also shed light on this part of the requirement. The knowledge of the actor must generally include all circumstances that lead to the fulfilment of the objective requirements.[55] The trial chamber found that the accused must be aware of their position within the organisation, thus clearly implying that this position would play a role as an objective requirement.[56]

Part of the chambers' primary approach when determining whether control over the said apparatus existed, includes a consideration of the accused's position within their organisation. In this context, "authority" and "effective command" are mentioned as relevant factors.[57] The pre-trial chamber in *Abdel Raheem* also points out the alleged *de jure* and *de facto* power and authority of the wanted person over certain branches of the Sudanese apparatus of power. Both of these factors—authority

---

[48] *Gbagbo*, 12 June 2014, para 233; *Blé Goudé*, 11 December 2014, para 150. Note that in Blé Goudé's case the strong tie with Gbagbo, the former president, may have played a definitive role in asserting his position. Nominally, he was a minister of youth at that point, see ibid., para 60.

[49] *Ntaganda*, 9 June 2014, para 120.

[50] *Ruto et al.*, 23 January 2012, para 316.

[51] *Ongwen*, 23 March 2016, para 12; ICC, *The Prosecutor v. Dominic Ongwen*, Trial Judgment, 4 February 2021, ICC-02/04-01/15, para 2860.

[52] *Muthaura et al.*, 23 January 2012, para 408.

[53] *Ruto et al.*, 23 January 2012, paras 329–332; see also Kiss 2019, mn. 51.

[54] *Gaddafi et al.*, 27 June 2011, para 72; Goy 2012, p 47.

[55] See below at Sect. 3.1.2.4.

[56] *Katanga*, 7 March 2014, para 1415. See in the same vein: *Ntaganda*, 9 June 2014, para 135.

[57] *Katanga and Chui*, 30. September 2008, para 513 ("authority and control"); *Abu Garda*, 8 February 2010, para 23 ("effective command and control"); *Abdel Raheem*, 1 March 2012, paras 30-1 ("authority and control"); *Gbagbo*, 12 June 2014, para 234 ("exert authority over the FDS", i.e. the Ivorian armed forces); *Ongwen*, 23 March 2016, para 13 ("effective command and control or authority and control", note that this paragraph primarily seems to refer to the requirements of superior responsibility, however, it is under the headline of "...facts regarding common elements of modes of liability"); *Ntaganda*, 8 July 2019, para 814 (describing the accused and two others as the highest authorities in the organisation).

and power—are based on the accused's position as a Minister and special representative of then-president Al Bashir.[58] A similar reliance on the accused's high-ranking position, first in the government and later within a parallel hierarchical structure, can be identified as part of the reasoning on control over an organisation in *Gbagbo* and *Blé Goudé*.[59] In *Ntaganda,* the pre-trial chamber also underlined the accused's position as deputy chief of staff,[60] as did the chamber in *Ruto et al.*, stressing one of the accused's "position on top of the network" (which was allegedly used to carry out crimes).[61] The same is true for the pre-trial and trial chamber's findings on Dominic Ongwen as the commander of one of the four brigades of the LRA.[62] Finally, in *Muthaura et al.* it was found that one of the accused gained control over the Kenyan *Mungiki* sect through an agreement with the organisation's actual leader, which placed the organisation under their control.[63] The pre-trial chamber in *Ruto et al.* also stressed the accused's "leadership over a community".[64] In the arrest warrant decision in *Gaddafi et al.*, the pre-trial chamber made clear, that it would not matter whether a person held an official or *de jure* position of power within a state apparatus, as long as a *de facto* position was indeed occupied.[65]

Considering the foregoing, it is evident that holding a leadership position within the organisation seems to be an essential point when determining "control" over it. In this context, "authority" and "effective command" are mentioned as relevant factors.[66] Sometimes the *de jure* and *de facto* power and authority based on the actor's position in the organisation are mentioned as well.[67]

However, these findings reveal little about the actual implications of such a position, especially given that, in theory, it should encompass something distinct from the separate requirement of almost automatic execution of orders.

Control can presumably be exercised through various functions,[68] i.e., through different forms of conduct. Decisions of the ICC discuss these ways of exercising control in differing terms.

---

[58] *Abdel Raheem*, 1 March 2012, para 31.

[59] *Gbagbo*, 12 June 2014, para 233; *Blé Goudé*, 11 December 2014, para 150. Note that in Blé Goudé's case the strong tie with Gbagbo, the former president, may have played quite a role in asserting his position. Nominally, he was a minister of youth at that point, see ibid, para 60.

[60] *Ntaganda*, 9 June 2014, para 120.

[61] *Ruto et al.*, 23 January 2012, para 316.

[62] *Ongwen*, 23 March 2016, para 12; *The Prosecutor v. Dominic Ongwen*, 4 February 2021, para 2860.

[63] *Muthaura et al.*, 23 January 2012, para 408.

[64] *Ruto et al.*, 23 January 2012, paras 329–332; see also Kiss 2019, mn. 51.

[65] *Gaddafi et al.*, 27 June 2011, para 72; Goy 2012, para 47.

[66] *Katanga and Chui*, 30 September 2008, para 513; *Abu Garda*, 8 February 2010, para 23; *Abdel Raheem*, 1 March 2012, paras 30–1; *Gbagbo*, 12 June 2014, para 234; *Ongwen*, 23 March 2016, para 13; *Ntaganda*, 8 July 2019, para 814.

[67] *Abdel Raheem*, 1 March 2012, para 31.

[68] Cf. Kiss 2019, mn. 22; *Katanga*, 7 March 2014, para 1412.

In *Gaddafi et al.*, the relevant conduct of the wanted Al Senussi was described as using his power over military forces, commanding them and directly instructing troops to fire into crowds of people.[69] The power to "control and instruct" certain youth militias was also mentioned in the arrest warrant decision against Simone Gbagbo.[70] Similarly, the reliance on troops to which "instructions could be issued" was outlined in a pre-trial chamber decision in the *Blé Goudé* case.[71]

In addition to this direct exercise of control through instruction, many other functions fulfilled by the accused were also considered.

In the cases of *Gbagbo* and *Blé Goudé*, the support of armed groups through financing and the provision of weapons was deemed (one of several) crucial factors in establishing control over militias and mercenaries.[72]

In this regard, it is striking that Germain Katanga was acquitted *inter alia* because his position as President, in which he handed out weapons and ammunition, was deemed insufficient to assert that he wielded control over the relevant armed group.[73]

This contradiction can only be reconciled if "control over an organisation" is tested by examining different indicators, a sufficient number of which must be fulfilled.

Decisions of ICC chambers provide some examples of what such indicators could be.

The capability of the accused to ensure compliance with orders within the organisation is often assessed. However—due to the sometimes-imprecise evaluation of requirements—it often remains unclear whether this examination concerns the criterion of "control" or the "almost automatic execution".[74]

In this regard, the chamber in *Katanga and Chui* stated that the means to exercise control may include the "capacity to hire, train, impose discipline, and provide resources" to subordinates.[75] In addition to these factors directly concerning the members of the organisation, the *Ntaganda* pre-trial chamber also elaborated on the strategic military responsibilities of the accused, who was found to have been the military expert of the group, developing and implementing strategies as well as securing weapons.[76]

---

[69] *Gaddafi et al.*, 27 June 2011, para 87.

[70] *Simone Gbagbo*, 2 March 2012, para 32.

[71] *Blé Goudé*, 11 December 2014, para 153.

[72] *Gbagbo*, 12 June 2014, para 233; *Blé Goudé*, 11 December 2014, para 152.

[73] *Katanga*, 7 March 2014, para 1420. Note that the chamber denied the second requirement, the hierarchical and organized apparatus of power, with respect to the militia as well.

[74] See e.g. *Katanga and Chui*, 30 September 2008, para 512; *Ntaganda*, 9 June 2014, para 120 ("insisted on compliance with orders", "ensured respect for discipline"); *Ntaganda*, 8 July 2019, paras 815 (on an effective communication system), 816 (on ensuring discipline and the ability to rely on organisation to implement plans).

[75] *Katanga and Chui*, 30 September 2008, para 513.

[76] *Ntaganda*, 9 June 2014, para 120.

Representative leadership functions such as the signing of official documents and agreements have also been considered at times.[77] The competence to appoint and assign commanders was mentioned by the chamber in *Ruto et al.* as an indicator of control over an organisation.[78] The same chamber also stressed the accused's "leadership over a community".[79]

In the situation in Côte d'Ivoire, a pre-trial chamber found that there was a well-functioning chain of communication between the accused and the members of the organisation.[80] However, it is again unclear in how far these findings differ from the necessary determination of the second requirement, i.e., the "organised and hierarchical apparatus".[81] Additionally, the chamber in the situation in Côte d'Ivoire also considers the "personal ties" to relevant militia leaders as a relevant aspect.[82]

From an evidentiary perspective, the fact that crimes were committed pursuant to issued orders was considered as proof of control exercised by the accused over an organisation.[83]

The confirmations of charges in *Gbagbo* and *Blé Goudé* contain some striking assessments on control over an organisation. In post-election violence in Côte d'Ivoire, violent youth militias allegedly committed crimes against the perceived supporters of the political opponent of the accused. The accused had allegedly exercised control over these youth groups "in the context of the campaign activities and their related mobilisation to use violence, as well as later calls for their enrolment" in the national armed forces.[84] Despite not being organised in a hierarchical style, the youth groups had "a clearly defined leadership" in the person of Charles Blé Goudé, who supported them financially and controlled them "primarily through the manipulation at mass rallies", or so the pre-trial chamber held.[85]

These findings deviate from the remainder, as they do not rely on the accused's formal or factual position at the top of an organisation through which instructions were channelled and executed. Instead, control over this "organisation" was seemingly believed to have been established by Charles Blé Goudé becoming a known figurehead who would then control the youth group—presumably through speeches—at rallies.

Another interesting observation can be made in the confirmation of charges against William Samoei Ruto in the situation in Kenya. The defence in this case pointed out how the accused had disseminated peace messages during the Kenyan post-election violence, which had not had any effect on the ongoing commission of crimes. Given

[77] *Katanga and Chui*, 30 September 2008, para 542.

[78] *Ruto et al.*, 23 January 2012, para 328.

[79] Ibid., paras 329–332; see also Kiss 2019, mn. 51.

[80] *Blé Goudé*, 11 December 2014, para 153.

[81] In line with the judgment, Kiss interprets the provision of weapons and financial support as a factor establishing control over an organisation, see Kiss 2019, mn. 53.

[82] *Gbagbo*, 12 June 2014, para 233; *Blé Goudé*, 11 December 2014, para 152.

[83] *Muthaura et al.*, 23 January 2012, para 408.

[84] *Gbagbo*, 12 June 2014, para 233; *Blé Goudé*, 11 December 2014, para 151.

[85] *Blé Goudé*, 11 December 2014, para 151.

that the perpetrators of these crimes had been members of the organisation in question, the defence argued that Ruto—obviously—did not have control over said organisation, because his calls for the end of violence had not been heeded.[86] One may of course object to such reasoning, as public calls for the end of violence are not internal instructions and may be declared to hide one's own malign intentions or as part of general propaganda. However, this is not the reasoning applied by the chamber. Instead, the chamber argues that "[t]he fact that Mr. Ruto may have disseminated peace messages does not obliterate the evidence supporting the Prosecutor's allegation that Mr. Ruto planned, coordinated and supervised the implementation of the plan to commit the acts of violence". Furthermore: "Based on the evidence available, the Chamber is convinced to the degree of substantial grounds to believe that Mr. Ruto played a major role in the development, coordination and implementation of the plan to attack PNU supporters, and thus, the Defence's argument is without merit".[87]

In other words: Given that the perpetrators did not adhere to the accused's calls to end violence, the chamber decided that control over the organisation on his part would have presented itself differently and simply relied on other factors, such as his role in planning, coordination, and implementation of the violence.[88]

Considering the foregoing, doubts arise as to the scope of the requirement that the indirect perpetrator must have "control over an organisation". Some ICC decisions seem to require a certain *de facto* and *de jure* position of the accused, while others do not. However, if such a position is the essence of the requirement, this begs the question whether it adds anything to the other two requirements, pursuant to which a hierarchical organised apparatus must exist and in which the suspect's orders must be complied with almost automatically.

Given this uncertainty, one could suspect that "control over the organisation" is less its own requirement, and more a description of what the theory of indirect perpetration through an organisation conveys. This would mean: Instead of adding anything substantial to the other requirements, control would follow where an actor

---

[86] *Ruto et al.*, 23 January 2012, para 318.

[87] Ibid., para 319. PNU—Party of National Unity, see ibid., para 32.

[88] It must be remarked here that William Ruto was charged as an indirect co-perpetrator. The control over the organisation would therefore—in the extremely vague terms of that doctrine—be joint control over the crime. This could probably be established by Mr. Ruto making an essential contribution by planning and organizing the ethnic violence. The other accused co-perpetrator, Mr. Kosgey, is already acquitted at this point in the judgment, see para 293, but the charges speak of other, unknown, co-perpetrators. However, if other co-perpetrators and their acts are unknown, the chamber would face difficulties in attributing any such other acts (which would have to amount to control over the organisation) to William Ruto. This may be the reason, why the chamber—three paragraphs earlier—decidedly speaks of William Ruto's "control over the organisation". It only changes its vocabulary regarding his conduct, when casting aside the defence's argument. In other words, given the lack of co-perpetrators at this point of the findings, it is the accused William Ruto who is believed to have exercised the direct control over the organisation. In essence, it is therefore necessary to conclude that the chamber applied the standard that planning, coordinating, and implementing a plan could amount to control over an organisation, despite the fact that the actor's calls for peace were not heeded by his supposed subordinates. For a different reading of the judgment see Kiss 2019, mn. 52, stating that the defence's argument was rejected due to lack of evidence.

is part of a hierarchical organisation in which his orders lead to the commission of crimes almost automatically. Consequently, control over the organisation would be roughly equivalent to the notion of control over the crime. The earlier decision on the confirmation of charges against *Katanga and Chui* points towards such an interpretation.[89] However, chambers have subsequently repeatedly inquired into the existence of not two, but three objective requirements of the doctrine.[90]

Therefore, this criterion is part of an established jurisprudence.

As outlined in this section, this criterion is often, albeit not always associated with a high-ranking position of the accused which is formalized in some way. This position is often associated with authority or power over the subsequent levels of the organisation. In fact, most of the relevant suspects and accused individuals held very high positions in their respective organisations.[91] However, given that the control does not have to extend over an entire organisation but can be limited to certain parts or branches of it,[92] it would be contradictory to assume that the accused must be one of the highest-ranking or most influential members.

Apart from this, the findings are rather inconsistent. The pertinent jurisprudence seems to provide a catalogue of potential factors to establish control over the organisation, but the requirements' actual limitations were not identified.

Due to these ambiguous findings, it remains questionable, whether the criterion adds its own substantial function, despite being accepted as a requirement. It does not help that, at times, chambers "address the elements [of indirect perpetration through an organisation] collectively".[93]

Aside from this ambiguity, the same question concerning control arises as previously discussed under the German traditional approach: Is the division of the organisation over which control is exerted irrelevant? Or must the indirect perpetrator have

---

[89] See *Katanga and Chui*, 30 September 2008, para 500, where the chamber elaborates that "[f]or the purposes of this Decision, the control over the crime approach is predicated on a notion of a principal's 'control over an organisation'". This decision lists "b. organised and hierarchical apparatus of power" (paras 511 et seq.) and "c. Execution of the crimes by almost automatic compliance with orders" (paras 515 et seq.) as requirements, while "a. Control over an organisation" (paras 500 et seq.) does not outline any requirement but instead explains the notion of the theory in general and its national law precedents, see paras 500–10. But somewhat differently already *Katanga*, 7 March 2014, paras 1407–12: para 1407 speaks of "two legal criteria". Para 1408 clearly identifies the almost automatic execution as one of them. Para 1411, however, identifies the "exertion of control and genuine authority over the organisation" as the second criterion (effectively leaving the nowadays recognized "hierarchical organisation" aside).

[90] See e.g. the listing of three requirements in *Muthaura et al.*, 23 January 2012, para 407 (including headline); *Ruto et al.*, 23 January 2012, para 313 (including headline); *Ntaganda*, 9 June 2014, para 104. This categorization is also mirrored by scholarly literature, see Kiss 2019, mn. 51 (with headline).

[91] This is true for the suspects/accused Katanga and Chui, Al Bashir, Gbagbo, for the Gaddafis and Al Senussi, for Ntaganda, for Banda and Jerbo, Muthaura and Ruto. The positions of other suspects/accused were somewhat lower and/or less formalized, as can be seen with Blé Goudé and Abdel Raheem.

[92] Gaddafi *et al.*, 27 June 2011, para 73; *Abdel Raheem*, 1 March 2012, para 35; Kiss 2019, mn. 22.

[93] *Muthaura et al.*, 23 January 2012, para 407; *Ruto et al.*, 23 January 2012, para 313; square brackets added by the author.

control over the executioners, the physical perpetrators of the crime? In practice, this has not become relevant yet. In all the cases before the ICC, the organisations, or relevant branches thereof consisted of potential physical perpetrators (i.e., not purely logistical or administrative support units). Whether a person is exercising control over an administrative or logistically relevant branch of a state or military apparatus, or a non-state actor could qualify as having "control over the organisation", must therefore be deduced from the overall assessment of the doctrine's requirements.

3.1.2.2 Organised and Hierarchical Apparatus of Power

The second criterion requires that the organisation through which the perpetrator acts be an organised and hierarchical apparatus of power.[94]

The *Katanga* trial chamber laid out certain cornerstones of this criterion *in abstracto*.

According to the chamber, the organised and hierarchical apparatus of power must be shaped by hierarchical relations between its members, i.e., between superiors and subordinates.[95] It must also possess a sufficiently high number of such members, more precisely of low-level members.[96] The latter is in close relation to the requirement that instructions within the organisation will be carried out automatically, which will be discussed below. Furthermore, the apparatus has been described as acting autonomously in that its existence is independent of its members and their relations to each other.[97] The trial chamber in *Katanga* asserted that its application should not only be restricted to bureaucratic regimes. In this context, the chamber also acknowledged the difficulty of determining the dynamics and natures of criminal organisations.[98]

In concreto, chambers have taken different aspects into account when determining the existence of an organised and hierarchical apparatus of power.

A centralised command structure can be found as a cornerstone of organisations in many decisions. This usually implies that an unequivocal hierarchy exists within which all relevant actors and branches have a certain place and are under the command of superiors.[99]

In *Katanga*, the trial chamber found that the relevant militia was organised as a single group and had a central system for the allocation of weapons and ammunition.

---

[94] *Katanga and Chui*, 30 September 2008, headline with para 511; *Abu Garda*, 8 February 2010, para 23; *Gaddafi et al.*, 27 June 2011, para 69; *Muthaura et al.*, 23 January 2012, para 407; *Ruto et al.*, 23 January 2012, para 313; *Abdel Raheem*, 1 March 2012, para 35; *Katanga*, 7 March 2014, para 1410; *Ntaganda*, 9 June 2014, para 119; see also *Gbagbo*, 12 June 2014, para 234 ("organised and hierarchical nature of pro-Gbagbo forces").

[95] *Katanga and Chui*, 30 September 2008, para 512.

[96] Ibid., para 512.

[97] *Katanga*, 7 March 2014, para 1409.

[98] Ibid., para 1410.

[99] See e.g. *Gaddafi et al.*, 27 June 2011, para 73; *Ntaganda*, 9 June 2014, paras 14, 119; *Ongwen*, 23 March 2016, p. 72 para 10; *Ongwen*, 4 February 2021, para 2856.

However, whether its president—the accused Germain Katanga—had held the power of a centralised command, remained unclear. The militia was therefore not found to have been an organised apparatus of power.[100]

In the situation in Darfur, pre-trial chambers repeatedly based their findings on the structure of the groups suspected to have been involved in the violent campaign against the civilian population. They found that so-called "security committees" brought organisations involved in the campaign together.[101] Through intermediaries, these committees were ultimately controlled by the minister of the interior—Abdel Raheem Hussein—and his superior, the President, Al Bashir.[102] The effective integration of the *Janjaweed* militias into the command structures of the state of Sudan was outlined in this context.[103] Similarly, the pre-trial chamber in *Gbagbo* and *Blé Goudé* found that the pro-Gbagbo forces—national military, militias and mercenaries—had a centralised command structure into which the irregular forces had been integrated.[104] Likewise, the pre-trial chamber in *Gaddafi* found that all branches of the Libyan state were ultimately subject to Muammar Gaddafi's orders and control.[105]

Findings of the existence of military-like structures within an organisation are closely related to this aspect.[106] The same is true for elaborations concerning the organisation's (military-like) division into units and staff, as well as the existence of a headquarter and communication channels.[107] Other factors resembling common armed forces are also frequently mentioned, such as the training of members and the expanded weaponry at their disposal.[108] Discipline among the members and the existence of disciplinary regimes are also examined by the chambers.[109]

The findings on the youth militias allegedly involved in the violence in Cote d'Ivoire, however, draw a somewhat different picture of an "organised and hierarchical" apparatus of power. With regards to these groups, the pre-trial chamber in *Gbagbo* and *Blé Goudé* found that despite not being organised in a formal hierarchy, these groups had "a clearly defined leadership in the Person of Charles Blé

[100] *Katanga*, 7 March 2014, paras 1417–9.

[101] These committees included the national armed forces and police and intelligence organs of Sudan, the *Janjaweed* militias and government representatives, see e.g. *Abdel Raheem*, 1 March 2012, para 20.

[102] *Al Bashir*, 4 March 2009, paras 217–20; *Abdel Raheem*, 1 March 2012, paras 20, 32.

[103] *Abdel Raheem*, 1 March 2012, para 33.

[104] *Gbagbo*, 12 June 2014, paras 233–4; see also *Ntaganda*, 8 July 2019, para 18.

[105] *Gaddafi et al.*, 27 June 2011, para 73.

[106] See especially *Ntaganda*, 9 June 2014, paras 118–9, 14; *Ongwen*, 23 March 2016, p. 72 para 10; *Ntaganda*, 8 July 2019, para 814.

[107] *Ntaganda*, 9 June 2014, para 15 (division into sectors, brigades, battalions etc., existence of staff, strategic meetings, subordinate commanders of units), 16 (effective system of communication); *Blé Goudé*, 11 December 2014, para 153; *Ntaganda*, 8 July 2019, para 814 (division into units), 815 (communication and reconnaissance system); *Ongwen*, 23 March 2016, p. 72 para 10 (Headquarters, division into units, chain of communication and command).

[108] *Katanga*, 7 March 2014, para 1418; *Ntaganda*, 9 June 2014, paras 17, 119; *Ntaganda*, 8 July 2019, para 814.

[109] *Katanga*, 7 March 2014, para 1418; *Ntaganda*, 9 June 2014, para 15.

Goudé, received financial support, and were controlled primarily through manipulation at mass rallies".[110] Financial support is identified as a factor which establishes a hierarchical apparatus in other decisions as well.[111]

However, apart from this, these pre-trial chamber decisions do not seem to fit into the broader picture. They rely on a considerably broader version of the requirement by expressly stating that an organisation—or rather a group of people—can fulfil the criterion despite lacking a hierarchy and only having a leadership figure. The divergence is immediately apparent, as a violent youth group with a vast number of members is far from resembling a conventional army. Such a resemblance, however, has been invoked in other decisions and may sum up many of the other findings above.[112]

Finally, the number of members may be of relevance in ascertaining the organised and hierarchical nature of an organisation.[113]

The organizations which chambers of the ICC considered to (potentially) fulfil the criterion vary greatly in their outward appearance: The state of Sudan with its branches of military, police and intelligence forces and integrated militias has been considered an organised and hierarchical apparatus of power,[114] as has the Libyan state under Muammar Al Gaddafi.[115] The same holds true for the *Union Patriotique du Congo* and its military wing the *Front Patriotique pour la Liberación du Congo* (UPC/FPLC) which was headed by Thomas Lubanga and Bosco Ntaganda.[116] Somewhat comparable to this, the Lord's Resistance Army under Joseph Kony (and Dominic Ongwen) in Uganda qualified as an organised, hierarchical apparatus.[117] The *Munigki* sect and a "criminal network" of perpetrators, allegedly relied upon the accused in the cases against *Muthaura et al.* and *Ruto et al.* respectively, broaden the scope of organised apparatuses. They could be described as vast Mafia- or sect-type organisations, operating primarily in the Kenyan urban areas.[118] The pro-Gbagbo youth groups in Abidjan, Côte d'Ivoire are situated at the other end of the spectrum of (not quite organised and hierarchical) apparatuses of power.[119]

[110] *Gbagbo*, 12 June 2014, para 234; see also *Blé Goudé*, 11 December 2014, para 151.

[111] See e.g. *Ruto et al.*, 23 January 2012, para 317, where a system of payment and punishment was believed to have led to the almost automatic compliance with orders (see below Sect. 3.1.2.3). In *Ntaganda*, 9 June 2014, paras 17, 118–9, the pre-trial chamber among other factors relied on the secured funding of the armed group of Thomas Lubanga, Bosco Ntaganda and Floribert Kisembo to conclude that it was an operational force with considerable military capacities.

[112] *Ntaganda*, 8 July 2019, para 814.

[113] Ibid., paras 814, 817. See also *Katanga and Chui*, 30 September 2008, para 512. Note however, that this may be a by-product of the "almost automatic compliance" criterion, which will be discussed below.

[114] *Al Bashir*, 4 March 2009, para 216.

[115] *Gaddafi et al.*, 27 June 2011, para 73.

[116] *Ntaganda*, 8 July 2019, paras 813–7.

[117] *Ongwen*, 23 March 2016, p. 72, para 10.

[118] *Muthaura et al.*, 23 January 2012, para 408, note however that the *Mungiki* were also believed to have "quasi-military capabilities", see para 214; *Ruto et al.*, 23 January 2012, paras 197, 315.

[119] *Gbagbo*, 12 June 2014, para 234; *Blé Goudé*, 11 December 2014, para 151.

In summary, the factors which serve to establish the organised and hierarchical apparatus of power can be outlined quite specifically in most decisions: They concern organisational structures in a narrower sense, including a division into units, communication channels and disciplinary methods. Classifying groups under this criterion is usually readily comprehensible: states and non-state armed groups that resemble state military structures qualify as organisations. As do criminal sects and networks with the necessary multi-layered structures, the respective chambers taking care to outline how these organisations would function. The affirmation of this requirement for pro-Gbagbo youth groups in Abidjan, Côte d'Ivoire is surprising in this context. The pre-trial chamber basically admits that no hierarchy was in place and instead bases its affirmative findings on financial support through the accused and his general recognition as a leadership figure.

Despite and apart from the latter reasoning, the jurisprudence on this requirement can be described as mostly coherent.

3.1.2.3 Execution of Crimes Must Be Secured by Almost Automatic Compliance with Orders Issued by the Suspect

As established in the confirmation of charges in *Katanga and Chui*, indirect perpetration through an organisation requires that the execution of crimes, which are instructed by the accused, is secured by almost automatic compliance with their orders.[120] The chamber summed this criterion up as follows:

> In essence, the leader's control over the apparatus allows him to utilise his subordinates as 'a mere gear in a giant machine' in order to produce the criminal result 'automatically'.[121]

The requirement of almost automatic compliance with orders was seemingly deduced by the pre-trial chamber from the fungibility criterion. After portraying how fungibility supposedly works, the chamber went on to describe how a sufficient number of subordinates was only one way to assure the specific functioning of the apparatus.[122] Another mechanism to ensure such automatic compliance would be through intensive, strict and violent training regimens.[123]

This criterion in the ICC's doctrine was seen as central to justify the ascription of principal liability from the beginning.[124] Its necessity has since been reiterated in many instances.[125]

---

[120] *Katanga and Chui*, 30 September 2008, paras 515, 517.

[121] Ibid., para 515.

[122] Ibid., paras 517–8.

[123] Ibid., para 518.

[124] Ibid., para 517 ("An authority who issues an order within such an organisation therefore assumes a different kind of responsibility than in ordinary cases of criminal ordering"); para 518 ("The highest authority does not merely order the commission of the crime, but through his control over the organisation, essentially decides whether and how the crime would be committed").

[125] *Abu Garda*, 8 February 2010, para 23; *Gaddafi et al.*, 27 June 2011, para 69; *Muthaura et al.*, 23 January 2012, para 407; *Ruto et al.*, 23 January 2012, para 313; *Simone Gbagbo*, 2 March 2012,

As evident from the formulation, the criterion implies that the organisation, through whatever kind of mechanism, ensures that the orders of the perpetrator will be carried out automatically. Therefore, the indirect perpetrator can be certain that the crimes will be committed.[126] This perceived certainty has been identified as a difference to ordering a crime, where, in the view of the deciding chamber, such certainty would not exist.[127] This connection between almost automatic compliance and certainty is therefore the most direct link to the actor having "control over the crime".[128]

Automatic compliance with orders is seen as the relevant circumstance leading to such certainty and several factors are considered by chambers of the ICC to determine whether it exists.

The fungibility of the physical perpetrators has been invoked in a number of cases when discussing this criterion. The confirmation decisions in *Gaddafi et al., Muthaura et al.*, *Ntaganda* and *Ongwen*, as well as the *Ntaganda* and *Ongwen* trial judgments mention the existence of a sufficient number of fungible individuals capable of being replaced by others.[129] In all four decisions, however, this aspect is combined with the finding that the respective organisations upheld strict and violent disciplinary regimens.[130] The same is true for the *Ongwen* trial judgment.[131] Circumstances evidencing fungibility included the vast number of low-level members of organisations, but also single incidents concerning the replacement of

para 34; *Katanga*, 7 March 2014, paras 1408–9; *Ntaganda*, 9 June 2014, para 104; *Gbagbo*, 12 June 2014, para 234; *Ongwen*, 23 March 2016, p. 72, No. 11; see for a slightly different take *Ntaganda*, 8 July 2019, paras 818–9, which do not explicitly rely on this criterion. However, the judgment takes similar criteria to the other decisions into account when elaborating on Ntaganda's control and influence over the physical perpetrators.

[126] Cf. especially *Katanga and Chui*, 30 September 2008, para 515 ("...particular characteristics of the organised and hierarchical apparatus enable the leader to actually secure the commission of crimes.").

[127] Ibid., para 517.

[128] As is correctly suspected by Kiss 2019, at mn. 42 in fn. 107.

[129] *Gaddafi et al.*, 27 June 2011, paras 75, 86; *Muthaura et al.*, 23 January 2012, para 409; *Ntaganda*, 9 June 2014, para 119; *Ongwen*, 23 March 2016, para 56 and p. 72, No. 11; see also without using the term of fungibility: *Ntaganda*, 8 July 2019, para 819 ("taking also into account the number of persons within the UPC/FPLC military structure at the relevant time..."); *Ongwen*, 4 February 2021, para 2784. Note that for Judge del Carmen Ibáñez Carranza fungibility, or replaceability, seemingly constitutes the most central of the potential mechanisms to ensure automatic compliance with orders, see ICC, *The Prosecutor v. Bosco Ntaganda*, Appeals Judgment, 30 March 2021, ICC-01/04-02/06-A A2, Separate Opinion of Judge Luz del Carmen Ibáñez Carranza, para 234.

[130] See *Gaddafi et al.*, 27 June 2011, para 75 (where the chamber combines this with the finding that each member of the organisation would fear the other); *Muthaura et al.*, 23 January 2012, paras 408 with 208-13; *Ntaganda*, 9 June 2014, para 120; *Ongwen*, 23 March 2016, p. 72, No. 11; *Ntaganda*, 8 July 2019, paras 817–9; *Ongwen*, 4 February 2021, see para 2784 elaborating on the requirements to exercise control and paras 2856–8 on the factual circumstances establishing it.

[131] *Ongwen*, 4 February 2021, see para 2784 elaborating on the requirements to exercise control and paras 2856-8 on the factual circumstances establishing it.

defected fighters through other individuals before an attack.[132] Somewhat contrary to the aforementioned, in her concurring opinion on the *Ntaganda* appeals judgment Judge Del Carmen Ibáñez Carranza seemingly implies that interchangeability of the physical perpetrators would be the dominant aspect in establishing almost automatic compliance with orders.[133]

Regardless, many ICC decisions also base their findings on the matter on factors such as menacingly strict disciplinary regimens or the threat of violence as a response to disobedience.[134]

In all these cases, the disciplinary measures that are believed to have been in place involved physical punishment including the death penalty.[135] The *Ongwen* trial chamber also elaborated on recruitment through abduction, violent initiating ceremonies and extremely harsh living conditions as relevant factors for the obedience of the LRA's fighters.[136] In a similar vein, the appeals chamber in *Ntaganda* found that the defendant's control had stretched over groups of civilians who—under the threat of the fighters of the organisation—participated in crimes. These civilians were found to have acted "in the context of the general coercive circumstances" and the chamber seemingly considered this as a factor granting control within indirect perpetration through an organisation.[137] Such findings raise the question, to what extent the physical perpetrators in the relevant cases were responsibly acting tools, given that the circumstances described amounted to some level of coercion.[138] The trial chambers in *Katanga* and in *Ongwen* addressed this issue, emphasizing that not all physical perpetrators carrying out crimes under the notion of indirect perpetration through an organization must necessarily be responsible actors.[139]

A certain differentiation can be seen within the aspect of "violent and strict" regimens. In contrast to *Katanga and Chui*, some later decisions do not rely so heavily on training regimens within which people (children) learn to commit crimes from a young age and thus undergo what could be referred to as a "socialisation

[132] See *Muthaura et al.*, 23 January 2012, para 409 on the replacement of some defected members of the organisation before the beginning of the crimes; see the list by Kiss 2019, mn. 56.

[133] Cf. *Ntaganda*, 30 March 2021, Separate opinion of Judge Luz del Carmen Ibáñez Carranza on Mr. Ntaganda's appeal, paras 233, 237, 257, 267. Other aspects that could lead to almost automatic compliance are seemingly not recognized by Judge del Carmen Ibáñez Carranza in the same way.

[134] *Muthaura et al.*, 23 January 2012, paras 208–213, 408; *Ruto et al.*, 23 January 2012, paras 324–5; see also the description in *Ongwen*, 4 February 2021, para 2856.

[135] *Muthaura et al.*, 23 January 2012, paras 208, 210–1, 213; *Ruto et al.*, 23 January 2012, paras 324–5; *Ntaganda*, 9 June 2014, para 120; *Ongwen*, 23 March 2016, para 56; *Ntaganda*, 8 July 2019, para 817; *Ongwen*, 4 February 2021, para 2856.

[136] *Ongwen*, 4 February 2021, para 2856.

[137] *Ntaganda*, 30 March 2021, para 957.

[138] See Article 31 (1) (d) Rome Statute for duress as a ground to exclude criminal responsibility under the imminent threat of death or serious bodily harm.

[139] *Katanga*, 7 March 2014, para 1404; *Ongwen*, 4 February 2021, para 2783.

of violence".[140] Instead, the conditioning that violent punishment would follow disobedience is the more present aspect.[141]

In the *Ongwen* trial judgment, violent and strict training regimens seem to be connected to fungibility in a sense that the former aspect would provide the organisation with a certain number of fungible executioners.[142]

Somewhat obtrusively, a mixture of the threat of violence and a payment mechanism led the pre-trial chamber in *Ruto et al.* to conclude that the accused's orders would be carried out almost automatically by members of his "Network".[143] The reward system allegedly established by the accused was thought to have involved payments on a regular basis ("stipend or salary") as well as rewards for the killing of the members of the political opponent's party.[144]

Additionally, the pre-trial chamber in *Ruto et al.* found that the "dominant role" of the accused during the preparation and execution of the violence had added to securing the almost automatic compliance with orders.[145]

In summary, this means that chambers have so far outlined four specific mechanisms to secure automatic compliance:[146]

- Fungibility of physical perpetrators based on their numbers,
- violent and strict training regimens in a sense of a conditioning to violence, especially when child soldiers are concerned,
- violent and threatening disciplinary or punishment regimens and
- payment mechanisms.[147]

Judge del Carmen Ibáñez Carranza outlined in her separate opinion in the *Ntaganda* appeals judgment, that in her view the "willingness" of the physical perpetrators would also play a role in ensuring almost automatic compliance. In her statement, this is closely connected to the replaceability (fungibility) of the hands-on perpetrators.[148] This could be read as a necessary connection of at least two of the

140 This seems to be one aspect considered in *Katanga and Chui*, 30 September 2008, paras 518 and 547 besides the threat of violence through the organisation.

141 See especially *Ongwen*, 23 March 2016, p. 72 No. 11; *Ntaganda*, 8 July 2019, para 817.

142 *Ongwen*, 4 February 2021, paras 2858, 2914, 2964, 3011, 3091.

143 *Ruto et al.*, 23 January 2012, para 317.

144 Ibid., para 320.

145 Ibid., para 327.

146 See also Ambos 2018, § 7 mn. 25; van Sliedregt and Yanev 2019, mn. 76. But see for a different categorization Kiss 2019, mn. 26, 57, taking the opinion that all factors can be grouped in two: Fungibility or the physical perpetrator's willingness to execute any kind of order.

147 Note that this latter aspect has been relied on only in the case against *Ruto et al.* to explain the almost automatic compliance by members of a network of an ethnic group affiliated with one of Kenya's political parties. Whether a payment mechanism alone would suffice in other cases in the view of ICC chambers seems doubtful. In the end, many organisations, especially any kind of organisation within a state hierarchy, usually offer payment. Contra see Steer 2017, p 304 who takes the position that there would in theory be little reason not to affirm control exercised through positive incentives.

148 *Ntaganda*, 30 March 2021, Separate Opinion of Judge Luz del Carmen Ibáñez Carranza, paras 234, 280, 307, 315.

abovementioned factors: Fungibility and one of the other mechanisms to establish "willingness". However, such a narrow two-fold requirement has not been explicitly required by the chambers. Furthermore, the above-mentioned mechanisms have not been phrased in the generally broad term of willingness thus far.

It is also noteworthy that in some cases, no explanation has been given as to the specific factor that would secure almost automatic compliance whilst in others, the respective chambers simply used the same findings to establish automatic compliance and other requirements.

The former was the case in the instances related to the situation in Darfur, Sudan.[149]

The latter is illustrated in the confirmation of charges in *Ruto et al.,* in which the chamber referenced all the factors which it had already listed as proof of "control over an organisation" to also determine "automatic compliance with orders".[150]

The decisions regarding the situation in Côte d'Ivoire also remain silent regarding a specific mechanism to ensure automatic compliance. In fact, the confirmation of charges decision in *Blé Goudé* does not mention automatic compliance as a requirement at all.[151]

The *Gbagbo* confirmation of charges states that the accused and his companions had joint control over the organisation, which "was possible due to the organised and hierarchical nature of the pro-Gbagbo forces, which ensured an almost automatic compliance" with orders. The relevant paragraph furthermore contains a long list of findings to support this evaluation.[152] Despite the plethora of evidence produced, the decision fails to mention which of these factors would lead to the almost automatic compliance with orders. Furthermore, the beginning of the quoted paragraph seems to establish that automatic compliance was ensured *because of* the organised and hierarchical nature of the forces in use. This is also mirrored by the fact that the same paragraph apparently serves to establish the evidence for both requirements.[153]

Such an equalisation of the two requirements has not been reiterated as can be seen in the newer decisions quoted above. However, it may serve as a reminder of how challenging a meaningful delineation between the requirements of indirect perpetration through an organisation can be. Despite these demarcating difficulties,

---

[149] In *Al Bashir*, 4 March 2009, para 211 the necessity of compliance with orders within the mode of perpetration through an organisation is mentioned. Apart from that, no explanation is given. The same is true for the second Arrest Warrant against Al Bashir and the Arrest Warrant decision against Abdel Raheem Hussein.

[150] *Ruto et al.*, 23 January 2012, para 328.

[151] See especially the part on "The co-perpetrators' joint control over the pro-Gbagbo forces" in *Blé Goudé*, 11 December 2014, paras 149–53.

[152] *Gbagbo*, 12 June 2014, para 234. In a similar vein see *Blé Goudé*, 11 December 2014, para 149–53.

[153] The paragraph before (233) concerns the "control" requirement which is treated as the first objective criterion, the one following (235) concerns the mental element; cf. *Gbagbo*, 12 June 2014, paras 233–235.

the necessary distinction between the criteria must not be ignored to avoid that they amount to the same requirement in practice.[154]

Additionally of note is the interplay of indirect and co-perpetration as applied in many decisions. This may be connected to the last point, the absence of the almost automatic compliance criterion. In decisions such as the *Ntaganda* trial judgment and the *Blé Goudé* confirmation of charges, chambers connected acting through an organisation with the capacity of the accused to—jointly with others—"rely on the organisation to implement their common plan".[155] This wording effectively mixes both requirements on a terminological level. It makes it difficult to distinguish between the implementation of the common plan on the one hand and the capacity to have the criminal elements of this plan carried out almost automatically through members of the organisation on the other.

The jurisprudence can be summarized as follows: the requirement has so far mostly been established through a specific set of factors. However, drawing a distinction between this and the "hierarchical and organised apparatus" criterion can prove difficult.

It seems that this requirement establishes a narrow standard concerning the position and conduct of potential indirect perpetrators. The commission of crimes must be secured through almost automatic compliance *with orders issued by the accused.*[156] This emphasises that the accused must directly address or control the physical perpetrators and their involvement in committing crimes. A person in a purely planning or organisational function cannot fulfil this requirement. Their instructions and influence do not extend to the physical perpetrators and the commission of crimes is not secured through their orders, even if their actions are vital for the overall criminal circumstances. This corresponds with the fact that jurisprudence emphasises how the almost automatic compliance would lead to a perceived certainty that crimes will be committed.

---

[154] Note in *Ruto et al.*, 23 January 2012, para 328 the pre-trial chamber also used the same evidence which it had referred to for the control requirement, again as additional evidence for almost automatic compliance.

[155] *Ntaganda*, 8 July 2019, para 816. See in a similar vein *Blé Goudé*, 11 December 2014, para 153, which speaks of the co-perpetrator's joint control over the pro-Gbagbo forces "in the sense of their capacity to rely on them for the pursuance of the shared common plan".

[156] *Gaddafi et al.*, 27 June 2011, para 69; *Muthaura et al.*, 23 January 2012, para 297; *Ruto et al.*, 23 January 2012, para 292; *Ntaganda*, 9 June 2014, para 104. See also *Katanga and Chui*, 30 September 2008, para 515 with headline and *Ntaganda*, 9 June 2014, para 118 with headline and 120, speaking of "almost automatic compliance with *the* orders" (italics added), but referring only to the relevant accused and their orders within the respective text.

3.1.2.4 Mental Element

The common rule for *mens rea* in the Rome Statute is Art. 30 and as such applies to all forms of perpetration and participation.[157]

Pursuant to Art. 30 (2) (a) Rome Statute, the actor must mean to engage in the relevant conduct, i.e., mean to perform the acts that fulfil the objective requirements of the relevant mode of liability.[158]

Furthermore, in order to establish intent regarding a consequence, they must mean to cause said consequence or be aware that it will occur in the ordinary course of events according to Art. 30 (2) (b).[159] This means, as the statute clarifies itself, that the acting person must at least be aware that the crime will be committed due to their conduct in the ordinary course of events.[160]

The necessary degree of probability or certainty for the "ordinary course of events" has been somewhat obscure in earlier ICC jurisprudence. In the decision on the confirmation of charges against Thomas Lubanga Dyilo, the Pre-Trial Chamber stated that a risk of the consequence occurring could be sufficient if the accused had reconciled himself with this risk. This standard would amount to *dolus eventualis*.[161] However, in the *Lubanga* trial judgment, the chamber stated that a low risk is not enough to satisfy the requirement.[162] This was upheld by the appeals chamber, thus rejecting *dolus eventualis*.[163] Instead the formulation that the actor must be aware that the consequence will occur with "virtual certainty", now seems to be the established standard of Art. 30 (2) (b). This standard implies that "the consequence will follow, barring an unforeseen or unexpected intervention that prevent this occurrence".[164]

---

[157] Ambos 2013, p 266; Pigaroff and Robinson 2016, Art. 30 mn. 6; see also *Ongwen*, 4 February 2021, para 2785.

[158] Pigaroff and Robinson 2016, Art. 30 mn. 21.

[159] Ibid., mn. 21–2.

[160] See the description at ibid., mn. 22.

[161] *Lubanga*, 29 January 2007, para 352; Pigaroff and Robinson 2016, Art. 30 mn. 26. *Dolus eventualis* or conditional intent is known in the German and Dutch legal systems. Pursuant to this standard, the mental element is given where a person is aware of the possible effects of their actions and nevertheless decides to act, thereby accepting the effects as the consequence of their conduct. Therefore, the key aspect of *dolus eventualis* is the actor's awareness of a risk and the question whether they accepted it. As can be seen, the concept operates with two elements of *mens rea*; a volitional element and a cognitive element. In *dolus eventualis*, both elements are given only in weak forms: The person neither wants the effect as the goal of their conduct, nor do they know for certain that it will occur. However, the actor knows of the potential effect (cognitive element) and reconciles him- or herself with it, acting despite the awareness of this risk (volitional element). See in detail Blomsma and Roef 2019, pp 182–9. But see Pigaroff and Robinson 2016, Art. 30 mn. 26–7 who warn of focussing too heavily on the term, as it embodies different degrees of probability in different legal systems and therefore runs the risk of complicating matters.

[162] *Lubanga*, 14 March 2012, para 1012, Pigaroff and Robinson 2016, Art. 30 mn. 26; in the same vein already: *Bemba*, 15 June 2009, para 363, stating that a mere possibility does not suffice.

[163] *Lubanga*, 1 December 2014, paras 448–50; Cryer et al. 2019, p 367.

[164] *Bemba et al.*, 19 October 2016, para 29; see for the unanimous jurisprudence after and contrary to the *Lubanga* confirmation of charges decision: Werle and Jessberger 2020b, mn. 574–5.

The trial chamber in the acquittal of *Gbagbo and Blé Goudé* seemingly set another standard for *mens rea* and foreseeability in indirect perpetration through an organisation. The chamber determined that the instructions by persons who ordered security forces to prevent a demonstration would not prove that such persons "wanted their subordinates to engage in unprovoked violent acts, much less that they controlled it".[165] The chamber goes on:

> The idea that control over a crime can be established on the basis of foreseeability of risk of criminal behaviour is antithetical to the notion of control over an organisation. Organisations are controlled by way of orders and directives, not by telepathy or risk calculus.[166]

It is submitted here that this interpretation does not fit the general approach to *mens rea* by the ICC. If a person instructs their organisation to block and supress a demonstration, this person exercises control over the organisation. The general standard for *mens rea* as outlined by chambers would in this case require, that the person issuing these instructions, was aware that their implementation would lead to the commission of crimes with virtual certainty. The trial chamber in *Gbagbo and Blé Goudé* apparently denied this and instead connected the exercise of control—through "orders and directives"—more tightly with the mental element of the indirect perpetrator. According to the trial chambers, a person would only be deemed to act with the necessary mental element if the criminal consequence (Art. 30 (2) (b)) was intended and not merely foreseen with virtual certainty. This would constitute a strict *mens rea* standard, stricter in fact than Art. 30 (2) (b) requires. It is questionable whether this narrower standard is helpful. It is of course correct, that organisations are steered through orders and directives. Additionally, the objective requirements seem to be more tailored towards blatantly criminal instructions that are channelled through organisations than towards legal instructions that could be implemented in illegal ways. However, this does not necessarily warrant a narrower *mens rea* standard. A commander or military leader may issue a directive to the subordinate branches of an organisation that will lead to the commission of crimes if implemented. This does not mean, however, that they necessarily *want* this result. The direct intent of the person in the background can still be aimed at something else (a political goal like keeping him- or herself in power), whilst they know for certain, that the implementation of the directive will lead to crimes. Therefore, the trial chamber's approach—as far as it concerns the mental element for criminal consequences—should not be followed.

According to Art. 30 (3) Rome Statute, the actor must furthermore have knowledge regarding the circumstances of the crime. This also applies to the circumstances of the form of responsibility, i.e., the facts which lead to the actor's conduct being qualified as perpetration. For indirect perpetration this means the circumstances establishing

---

[165] ICC, *The Prosecutor v. Laurent Gbagbo and Charles Blé Goudé*, Reasons for oral decision of 15 January 2019 on the Requête de la Défense de Laurent Gbagbo afin qu'un jugement d'acquittement portant sur toutes les charges soit prononcé en faveur de Laurent Gbagbo et que sa mise en liberté immédiate soit ordonnée, and on the Blé Goudé Defence no case to answer motion, 16 July 2019, ICC-02/11-01/15, Annex B, para 1930.

[166] Ibid., Annex B, para 1930.

control over the crime through another and joint control through another for indirect co-perpetration.[167]

The necessity that the actor voluntarily engages in their conduct means that they must mean to engage in the acts constituting the relevant behaviour within the framework of indirect perpetration. Examples of statements regarding this part of *mens rea* can be found in *Gbagbo, Blé Goudé* and *Ntaganda*, in which the respective chambers explicitly focused on the intent to engage in own actions, relevant for the mode of liability.[168]

Chambers also frequently determine that the actor was aware that the relevant crimes would be committed as a consequence of their conduct.[169]

Due to the focus of chambers on indirect co-perpetration, all findings on the *mens rea* regarding the perpetrators' conduct, thus far, refer to their contributions to the common plan. No chamber had to determine whether an accused meant to engage in a conduct which led to the commission of crimes, by virtue of their control over an organisation based on hierarchical structures and automatic compliance with orders. It equally did not have to be determined, whether they were aware of the criminal consequences which would occur with virtual certainty following the utilisation of the organisation. However, given the straightforward formulation of the requirement and sufficient examples from indirect co-perpetration—which necessarily involves an organisation and considerations on the likelihood of crimes being committed—this part of *mens rea* seems unlikely to cause specific issues for the mode of indirect perpetration.

Chambers of the ICC emphasised in detail the necessity of the accused's awareness of several factors which align with the objective elements above.

In *Katanga and Chui*, the pre-trial chamber determined that the accused would have to be aware of their authority, the character of their organisation and the circumstances enabling the near automatic compliance with orders.[170] In line with the control over the organisation criterion, jurisprudence has repeatedly required that the accused be aware of their "role", "position", "status" or "authority" in the

---

[167] *Katanga and Chui*, 30 September 2008, para 534; *Gaddafi et al.*, 27 June 2011, para 69; *Muthaura et al.*, 23 January 2012, para 410; *Ruto et al.*, 23 January 2012, paras 292, 333; *Abdel Raheem*, 1 March 2012, para 37; *Katanga*, 7 March 2014, para 1414; *Ntaganda*, 9 June 2014, para 121; *Gbagbo*, 12 June 2014, para 230; *Ongwen*, 4 February 2021, para 2869. See also Cryer et al. 2019, p 353.

[168] In *Ntaganda*, 8 July 2019, para 1174–5, the chamber clarifies that the object of the accused's intent must be their own conduct under the respective mode of liability—in this case the essential contribution in indirect co-perpetration. It continues to establish that the accused engaged in this conduct deliberately. In *Gbagbo*, 12 June 2014, para 236 and *Blé Goudé*, 11 December 2014, para 154, the pre-trial chamber determines that the accused meant to engage in their activities in the Ivorian post-election crisis and that they deliberately issued orders and instructions, which allegedly led to the commission of crimes.

[169] *Katanga and Chui*, 30 September 2008, para 533 (referring to the necessary awareness of the indirect co-perpetrators in general), paras 564 et seq.; *Muthaura et al.*, 23 January 2012, para 410; *Ruto et al.*, 23 January 2012, para 333; *Ntaganda*, 9 June 2014, para 135; *Gbagbo*, 12 June 2014, para 236; *Blé Goudé*, 11 December 2014, para 154.

[170] *Katanga and Chui*, 30 September 2008, para 534.

organisation.[171] The accused's awareness of their own control, exercised through the apparatus, has also been mentioned by chambers.[172]

A range of decisions also mention the accused's awareness of the organised and hierarchical apparatus of power.[173] Finally, some chambers have explicitly elaborated on the accused being aware of the circumstances which led to almost automatic compliance with their orders.[174]

As evidence of such awareness, the pre-trial chamber in *Katanga and Chui* found that the accused were aware of the large number of low level "interchangeable" soldiers, the brutal training regime for recruits of all ages and the ethnic allegiance of the soldiers.[175] Some assessments of the accused's *mens rea* refer more generally to their knowledge or awareness of the circumstances enabling control over the crime through an organisation.[176] Charles Blé Goudé, for example, was believed to have been aware of his "capacity to direct the conduct of the pro-Gbagbo youth by way of publicly issuing instructions to them".[177]

Further, where the charged crimes require a specific or special intent (*dolus specialis*) on behalf of the perpetrator, the indirect perpetrator must fulfil this intent him- or herself.[178]

---

171 Ibid., para 562; *Gaddafi et al.*, 27 June 2011, paras 81, 88; *Ruto et al.*, 23 January 2012, para 348; *Katanga*, 7 March 2014, para 1415; *Ntaganda*, 9 June 2014, para 135; *Gbagbo*, 12 June 2014, para 240 ("authority by claim of being president").

172 *Gbagbo*, 12 June 2014, para 240; see also *Gaddafi et al.*, 27 June 2011, paras 81, 88, speaking of full control over subordinates; *Blé Goudé*, 11 December 2014, para 157, about the knowledge that he had the capacity to direct youth groups. The latter two findings may also refer to the requirement of almost automatic compliance, or to both requirements.

173 *Katanga and Chui*, 30 September 2008, para 562; *Katanga*, 7 March 2014, para 1415. See also the implicit reference to this in *Gaddafi et al.*, 27 June 2011, paras 81, 88 where the accused's awareness of their role within the state apparatus of Libya and its armed forces is mentioned.

174 *Katanga and Chui*, 30 September 2008, para 562; *Katanga*, 7 March 2014, para 1415; seemingly also *Gaddafi et al.*, 27 June 2011, paras 81, 88.

175 *Katanga and Chui*, 30 September 2008, para 562; see also Kiss 2019, mn. 58.

176 *Ntaganda*, 9 June 2014, paras 121, 135.

177 *Blé Goudé*, 11 December 2014, para 157.

178 This requirement uniformly applies to all forms of perpetration, see on this general requirement for different forms of perpetration: Most importantly, see *Al Bashir*, 12 July 2010, paras 1–6 and 41–3 concluding that, Al Bashir's arrest shall also be sought over charges of genocide, due to his then established genocidal intent. See also *Ruto et al.*, 23 January 2012, para 333 (referring to indirect co-perpetration); *Katanga*, 7 March 2014, para 772; *Ntaganda*, 9 June 2014, para 121; cf. also the specific findings on the discriminatory intent of the accused under indirect (co-)perpetration in *Gbagbo*, 12 June 2014, para 236; *Blé Goudé*, 11 December 2014, para 154.

3.1.2.5 Analysis and Open Questions

The foregoing sections show that indirect perpetration through an organisation is featured with clearly denominated requirements in the jurisprudence of the ICC.[179]

In detail, however, many aspects seem unclear.

The Scope and Role of the Requirements

Control over an organisation is mostly associated with a position of power or authority within an organisation. At times, this is complemented with other considerations on the ability of the actor to steer the apparatus' actions. The latter was offered by the *Katanga* trial chamber seemingly as a definition of control over the organisation.[180] However, if this is indeed the definition of control over the organisation, the scope of this requirement still remains unclear. As seen in *Ruto et al.*, chambers do not necessarily deny control where parts of, or groups within the organisation ignore orders. If this observation is considered together with the one from *Katanga,* control means that the accused can give instructions which will generally move (steer) things within the organisation. This holds true even if the commands are not always carried out precisely as ordered or not every unit or group within the organisation adheres to them. Consequently, one may question whether control over the organisation embodies the possibility of stopping the apparatus from acting, or whether it is sufficient to only be able to set it in motion. A similar issue was identified by Judge Morrison in the *Ntaganda* trial. Therein control over civilians who participated in attacks on the civilian population was affirmed, although credible evidence existed that these individuals did not stop killing and looting, even after the leadership of the group had issued orders to do so.[181]

Other doubts concern the requirement of automatic compliance with orders. As illustrated above, ICC jurisprudence accepts fungibility, but also other mechanisms to establish this criterion. However, a vast number of low-level members in an organisation has been one factor in determining whether an organised apparatus exists. Given that a replaceability of physical perpetrators is not mandatory, one must question whether the number of members is to play a role at all in future decisions. Will a certain (high) number of low-level actors be necessary, or can the organisation consist of a few—say a dozen—members, provided they are violently trained and subjected to the threat of violence within their group?

In addition to these doubts, the precise features of the requirement of a hierarchical and organised apparatus seem unclear. In particular, the necessary internal structures of organisations through which an actor may exercise control over the crime through another seem unclear. As shown above, the chamber in *Blé Goudé*

[179] Cf. also the descriptions in Ambos 2018, § 7 mn. 25; Cryer et al. 2019, p 353; Werle and Jessberger 2020b, mn. 648–51.

[180] *Katanga*, 7 March 2014, para 1411.

[181] See *Ntaganda*, 30 March 2021, Separate opinion of Judge Howard Morrison on Mr. Ntaganda's appeal, para 19 with reference to *Ntaganda*, 8 July 2019, para 512. On the implications of this finding for the notion of control see van Sliedregt and Weisser 2022, p 634.

deemed it sufficient that a youth organisation which had been provided with finances and, more importantly, adhered to Charles Blé Goudé as their "leader" would qualify as a hierarchical and organised apparatus. The chamber explicitly pointed out that the group lacked a hierarchical structure. However, due to Blé Goudé's alleged recognition as leader and financier, the accused was believed to have had the ability to control the youth groups through manipulation at mass rallies.[182] These findings, albeit singular and not confirmed by a trial chamber, cast doubts on the necessary structures of the organisation and—consequently—on the features required to exercise control over it and ensure automatic compliance. It seems that in the *Blé Goudé* decision on the confirmation of charges, the threshold for all three requirements was lowered significantly following the acknowledgement of the youth groups as a hierarchical and organised apparatus of power. The hierarchy was reduced to two tiers with the accused being the "clearly defined leadership" and the youth group being the rank and file. The only factor of control over this "organisation" in line with other jurisprudence is the provision of finances. The accused allegedly controlled the group through campaign activities and manipulations at mass rallies. To describe these findings more sceptically: The accused was allegedly very popular among the youth, providing them with money and publicly calling upon them to engage in violence. One could therefore conclude that the margin of the hierarchical organisation is reduced to a group which has a common leadership figure, who is also known to provide some support. By contrast, the *Katanga* trial chamber denied the existence of an organised apparatus and control over an organisation despite the fact that Germain Katanga was the president and figurehead of the militia and responsible for the central provision of weapons and ammunition.[183]

The trial chamber in the joint *Gbagbo and Blé Goudé* case partly rejected control over the alleged organisations. This was *inter alia* due to missing evidence regarding the characteristics of the organisation(s). Thereby, the chamber made clear that such evidence must be provided.[184] In light of the pre-trial chamber's exaggerated interpretation of the requirement, this ruling is to be welcomed. Additionally, the case demonstrates that evidence for organisational structures will be difficult to obtain in many situations.

The foregoing observations also lead to the issue of delineating the three objective elements from one another. Certain facts may prove more than one requirement. While this is not a problem in general, it becomes one, where requirements do not differ from each other, or their delineation is blurred and therefore the doctrine leads to uncertainty. This observation could lead to the conclusion that the ICC does not require any organisational features apart from internal dynamics that will also prove near automatic compliance.[185]

Such a verdict seems justified considering the broad decisions in *Blé Goudé* and *Ruto et al.* However, some circumstances, such as a prominent position within a

---

[182] See above at Sect. 3.1.2.2.

[183] *Katanga*, 7 March 2014, paras 1419–20.

[184] *Gbagbo and Blé Goudé*, 16 July 2019, para 1942.

[185] See Kiss 2019, mn. 42.

hierarchy and certain organisation structures, have often played a role in determining the necessary shape of and control over the organisation. Given that the broadest decisions on the objective requirements were made by pre-trial chambers which did not lead to convictions, it may still be too early to disregard the requirements of "control" over a "hierarchical and organised apparatus" as hollow criteria. Should the court be willing to restrict the doctrine to organised groups of perpetrators instead of violent masses, the careful elaborations of many chambers on the internal structures of an organisation (referring to chains of communication, the division into units etc.) could provide a guideline to defining the criterion.

The Necessity of a Conduct Element and the Causal Nexus

The foregoing sections display the requirements of indirect perpetration through an organisation in the way in which it is usually referred to and tested by the court and in academic literature. This leads to an important issue: the difference between possessing and exercising power over an organisation.

This concerns the necessary conduct which eventually triggers responsibility for indirect perpetration through an organisation. We have seen above that a position of authority and power is often associated with having control over an organisation. Such a position can be proven by demonstrating certain types of conduct such as the recruitment of soldiers, the provision of weapons and more. A specific conduct element, as can be identified in hands-on commission, has not yet been pinpointed and is usually not mentioned by the ICC. However, this creates a theoretic blind spot in the analysis of the accused's wrongdoing. Indirect perpetration through an organisation constitutes liability for active behaviour. Therefore, a chamber must identify the conduct through which the accused "controlled the commission of the crime".[186] This behaviour is not tantamount to the conduct that constitutes control over the organisation.[187] Control over the organisation is a separate requirement, but one does not become an indirect perpetrator simply because one controls an organisation. This is evident given that such a form of liability would be more akin to superior responsibility pursuant to Art. 28 Rome Statute. This is applicable where a person with command or authority and effective control over subordinates (members of the organisation) fails to act.[188] Instead, it is submitted that the form of responsibility implicitly demands a special type of conduct that will actively lead to the commission of the crimes which shall then be attributed to the indirect perpetrator. Such a conduct element is quickly identified and implicitly considered by practitioners and scholars: It is the active triggering of the organisation's automatism, which usually

---

[186] Ambos has outlined the issue of mixing a role or position in a group or hierarchy with personal conduct when elaborating on problems of the doctrine of JCE, see Ambos 2007, p 173.

[187] It must also be distinguished from the necessary contribution made by an indirect co-perpetrator. The conduct element of this combined mode of liability is supposedly much broader and only comparable to that of indirect perpetration through an organisation where the contributor exercises control over the organisation him- or herself and thereby contributes to the common plan.

[188] On the requirements of effective command/authority and control of a commander in Art. 28 Rome Statute see, Triffterer 2016, Art. 28, 26 et seq.

happens through an instruction or order.[189] This cannot only be determined through the wording of multiple decisions but also through the criterion of almost automatic execution of orders. As seen above, this principle requires the indirect perpetrator to be certain that compliance with their orders is ensured. In this way, the automatic compliance criterion is inherently connected to the conduct of the indirect perpetrator which must consist of "pressing a button" in the sense of instructing the commission of crimes.[190] Identifying and underlining this "secret" conduct element of indirect perpetration through an organisation is important for analytical reasons. There is a difference between "possessing" power over an organisation and "exercising" it, both of which are necessary to trigger perpetration liability under the doctrine.

As a logical consequence, it can also be determined that a causal nexus—in the *conditio sine qua non* sense—is necessary between the accused's conduct and the criminal consequences. For indirect perpetration through an organisation this is difficult to determine directly, however must be a necessary prerequisite, given that such a causal connection is repeatedly required in cases of indirect co-perpetration.[191]

The Responsibility of Architects of Crimes without Decision-making Powers

Subsequently to the analysis in Chap. 2,[192] the issue of organisational and planning (architecting) roles within an organisation arises again. It has been outlined

---

[189] See e.g. *Gaddafi et al.*, 27 June 2011, para 87 (describing the relevant conduct as commanding them and directly instructing troops to fire into crowds of people); *Muthaura et al.*, 23 January 2012, paras 402 (stating that the essential contribution in indirect co-perpetration can "*consist of activating the mechanisms* which lead to the automatic compliance" with orders, this activation of mechanisms is then seen in the instructions issued to the perpetrators, emphasis added); *Blé Goudé*, 11 December 2014, para 153 (outlining that instructions could be issued to troops); *Gbagbo and Blé Goudé*, 16 July 2019, Annex B, para 1930 ("Having control over an organisation means that the one(s) in control decide if and when crimes are committed by the organisation. Accordingly, if a member of the organisation commits a crime, he or she must be acting pursuant to an instruction from authority within the organisation"), 1932 ("in the absence of direct evidence of orders or instructions that overtly or implicitly called for the commission of crimes, it falls upon the Prosecutor to show that the existence of such orders instructions is the only reasonable explanation of the conduct of the relevant members of the organisation… No reasonable trial chamber could thus infer that when Mr. Gbagbo decided to prohibit the RTI march, this implied an order to the FDS to kill, injure or rape the marchers"; *Ongwen*, 4 February 2021, para 2862 ("…led a group of attackers…, before directing them to attack the trading centre. …personally ordered LRA attackers to loot…"), see in the same manner paras 2913, 2963, 3010, 3110.

[190] The *Gbagbo and Blé Goudé* acquittal decision raises one pertinent question concerning this conduct element. Namely, whether the conduct must aim at the commission of crimes or whether the instruction can concern legitimate conduct which only bears the risk of leading to crimes. The trial chamber seemingly denies the latter, requiring that the indirect perpetrator's conduct aims at the commission of crimes, see *Gbagbo and Blé Goudé*, 16 July 2019, Annex B, para 1930.

[191] See *Katanga and Chui*, 30 September 2008, para 560 ("…without their agreement on the common plan and their participation in its implementation, the crimes would not have been committed as planned"); *Gbagbo*, 12 June 2014, paras 230, 232 ("the crimes would not have been committed or would have been committed in a significantly different way"); *Blé Goudé*, 11 December 2014, paras 143, 145, 148. But see for criticism on a strict causality requirement: Cupido 2022, p 644.

[192] See Chap. 2, Sects. 2.2.3.7 and 2.2.6.

earlier, that the traditional German approach aims at attributing responsibility to decision makers and architects of crimes alike. However, given the interplay of certain criteria and the notion of domination of the crime in the traditional German approach, doubts pertaining to the second category of actors have been voiced.[193] The foregoing account of the doctrine's requirements at the ICC raise the same doubts. In general, control over an organisation—as under the German theory—can be exercised by steering only a part of the apparatus. However, the chambers also quite unanimously require the execution of the crimes to be secured through almost automatic compliance with the *accused's* orders. This criterion emphasises the need of direct instructions issued by the accused and their consequent influence over the physical perpetrators. It is highly unlikely that a chamber would find that the commission of crimes was secured through almost automatic compliance with orders, issued by someone with considerable internal power, but that this internal power only stretched over matters such as provisions and materiel, transport and logistics, training, or external relations.[194] Orders issued by persons, whose competence is restricted to such "supportive" areas, do not ultimately secure the commission of a crime. Not even if these orders are complied with automatically. This issue is closely related to the notion of control that follows from the perceived certainty of the commission of the crime.

3.1.3 The Notion of Control Over the Crime Under the ICC's Jurisprudence

The pre-trial chamber in *Lubanga* first applied the notion of control over the crime to distinguish between forms of responsibility, delineating this approach from an objective and a subjective approach.[195]

The chamber explained:

> The notion underpinning this third approach is that principals to a crime are not limited to those who physically carry out the objective elements of the offence, but also include those who, in spite being removed from the scene of the crime, control or mastermind its commission because they decide whether and how the offence will be committed.[196]

The notion of control has since been established as the court's approach to the topic and has been affirmed by the appeals chamber.[197] The central formula that a person is a perpetrator if they decide whether and how the offence will be committed,

---

[193] See Chap. 2, Sects. 2.2.3.3, 2.2.3.7 and 2.2.6.

[194] It can be presumed that this is one of the reasons for the extensive reliance on indirect co-perpetration, a mode in which such organisational and planning conduct can be considered as a relevant contribution to the common plan.

[195] *Lubanga*, 29 January 2007, paras 327–32.

[196] Ibid., para 330.

[197] *Lubanga*, 1 December 2014, para 462; Ambos 2016, Art. 25 mn. 14 et seq.; see also above at Sect. 3.1.2.

has been reiterated in numerous decisions.[198] For indirect perpetration, this has been formulated as "the one(s) in control decide if and when crimes are committed".[199] These descriptions form the core of the concept and can be regarded as the court's definition of control over the crime.[200]

But how does the court determine whether an actor enjoys such control over the crime?

Control over a crime has repeatedly been associated with the person's role in the implementation of an underlying plan. This stands to reason in cases in which indirect co-perpetration is the pertinent form of liability, as it relies on mutual attribution of responsibility based on a common plan.[201] However, this leads no further when exploring the notion of control in indirect perpetration.

As underlined in a few decisions, control over the crime requires a normative evaluation of the accused's actions.[202] According to the Appeals Chamber, this means that the assessment cannot be made "by reference to how close the accused was to the actual crime and whether he or she directly carried out the incriminated conduct".[203]

The pre-trial chamber in *Al Hassan* refers to the same concept when emphasising how a co-perpetrator would not have to carry out a crime directly or be present at the crime scene. Instead, their role would have to be determined in "a normative assessment" of their role in the specific circumstances and considering the division of tasks.[204]

The aforementioned instances, by reference to the necessary requirements of co-perpetration rule it out to restrict the application of co-perpetration to persons who physically act during the commission and are present at the scene of the crime.[205] Furthermore, describing the approach as normative serves to distinguish

---

[198] *Katanga and Chui*, 30 September 2008, paras 485, 518; *Abu Garda*, 8 February 2010, para 152; *Gaddafi et al.*, 27 June 2011, para 89; *Muthaura et al.*, 23 January 2012, para 409; *Lubanga*, 14 March 2012, para 1003; *Katanga*, 7 March 2014, para 1396, 1401, 1405; *Lubanga*, 1 December 2014, para 456; *Gbagbo and Blé Goudé*, 16 July 2019, Annex B, para 1930 ("Having control over an organisation means that the one(s) in control decide if and when crimes are committed by the organisation"); implicitly also *Ntaganda*, 8 July 2019, para 778; *Ntaganda*, 30 March 2021, Separate Opinion of Judge Luz del Carmen Ibáñez Carranza, para 232. See also Weigend 2015, p 548: "Under that theory, a perpetrator is a person who 'controls' (that is, determines) whether the acts constituting an offence are carried out".

[199] *Gbagbo and Blé Goudé*, 16 July 2019, Annex B, para 1930.

[200] In its first decision on the doctrine in *Lubanga,* the Appeals Chamber did not expressly use this wording. However, given the chamber's full endorsement of the control over the crime approach, it seems unlikely that this definition should not be seen as part of it. See e.g. the appeals chamber's description of co-perpetration, emphasising that the co-perpetrator would have the power to frustrate the crime's commission, at *Lubanga,* 1 December 2014, paras 469, 473.

[201] Cf. on the predominant application of the combined mode of indirect co-perpetration van Sliedregt and Yanev 2019, mn. 53.

[202] *Lubanga,* 1 December 2014, para 473; *Al Hassan,* 22 May 2018, para 170; *Ntaganda,* 8 July 2019, paras 779, 780.

[203] *Lubanga,* 1 December 2014, para 473.

[204] *Al Hassan,* 22 May 2018, para 170.

[205] Ambos 2018, § 7 mn. 22; Werle and Jessberger 2020b, mn. 639.

it from the other two approaches—namely the objective and the subjective one.[206] However, beyond this it remains unclear whether and how the "normativity" of the control requirement influences the application of the modes of commission. Indeed, it seems that the description as "normative" is a reflection of the existence of indirect perpetration, because there is no "naturalistic" way to act "through another".[207]

According to the pre-trial chamber in *Katanga and Chui,* control over the crime requires taking objective and subjective criteria into account.[208] This chamber, and others following its example, thus allows an insight into how control over the crime should be tested in a specific case.

With specific reference to the mode of indirect perpetration through an organisation, ICC decisions outline this type of control in the following ways.

The *Katanga* trial chamber described control over an organisation by stating that:

> [p]ersons wielding control over the apparatus of power, therefore are unquestionably those in the organisation who conceived the crime, oversaw its preparation at different hierarchical levels, and controlled its performance and execution.[209]

This rather broad enumeration of conduct could apply to persons in different functions within an apparatus of power. However, the final connection between the different ways to exercise control, reads "…and controls its performance and execution". In light of the earlier findings on the requirements of the ICC doctrine, this final part of the description seems to be the most important.

Furthermore, the type of control exercised in indirect perpetration is commonly described as control over the will of those who physically carry out the crimes.[210] Some chambers describe this type of control more vividly as "subjugating the will" of the direct perpetrator,[211] or as controlling the action of another person.[212] On a different tone, some chambers asserted that control means that the will of the physical perpetrators becomes "irrelevant".[213] Despite their apparent similarity, the latter could describe something different from the former. To subjugate the will of a physical perpetrator is one thing, to simply bypass and thus render it irrelevant is another. The *Ongwen* and the *Ntaganda* confirmation decisions, which employ this phrase, count among those that rely on interchangeability and violent disciplinary

[206] *Lubanga,* 1 December 2014, para 473.

[207] *Lubanga,* 29 January 2007, para 332; *Lubanga,* 1 December 2014, para 465.

[208] *Katanga,* 7 March 2014, para 1393.

[209] Ibid., para 1412.

[210] *Lubanga,* 29 January 2007, para 332; *Katanga and Chui,* 30 September 2008, para 488; *Abu Garda,* 8 February 2010, para 153; *Gbagbo,* 12 June 2014, para 230; *Blé Goudé,* 11 December 2014, para 136; *Katanga,* 7 March 2014, paras 1402 (referring to "normal" cases of indirect perpetration), 1410 (referring to control over persons within the organisation); *Ongwen,* 23 March 2016, para 39 ("controlling the action of another person").

[211] *Blé Goudé,* 11 December 2014, paras 136, 137; *Ntaganda,* 8 July 2019, paras 774, 778; *Ongwen,* 4 February 2021, para 2783.

[212] *Ntaganda,* 8 July 2019, para 777.

[213] *Ongwen,* 23 March 2016, para 39; *Ntaganda,* 8 July 2019, para 819; *Ntaganda,* 30 March 2021, para 954; *Ongwen,* 4 February 2021, paras 2858, 2914, 2964, 3011, 3091.

and training regimens to justify indirect perpetration.[214] On this basis, the different descriptions of control could be read as pertaining to the respective forms of ensuring automatic compliance. This means control over the crime through automatic compliance within an organisation can either be built on interchangeability, which makes the will of the physical perpetrator irrelevant (because it can simply be bypassed), or on conditioning or the threat of violence, which subjugates the will of the individual perpetrator.

It is noteworthy that control over another person can be intermitted through persons who are, themselves, under the control of an indirect perpetrator. This has been affirmed by the trial chamber in *Ntaganda*, where fighters of the relevant militia forced civilians of their ethnic group to join the killing and plundering.[215]

Some scholars describe the notion of control over the crime as a graded concept in which control decreases from commission under Art. 25 (3) (a)—encapsulating the strongest form of control—down to *littera* (d), which embodies the weakest form.[216] This view is not mirrored in the chambers' general approach.[217] Instead, control over the crime in the ICC's jurisprudence is a two-sided concept. It serves to distinguish forms of (principal) perpetration pursuant to Art. 25 (3) (a) from all other modes of liability in Art. 25 (3) (b) to (d). None of these latter forms is considered to establish any form of control over the crime, as it is precisely this that only forms of commission are understood to do.[218] Either a person controls the commission of a crime, or they do not. Whether different forms of participation in Art. 25 (3) encapsulate different levels of wrongdoing is another question to be discussed in another section.

Certain other decisions, however, seem to rely on a much broader concept of control. As highlighted above, the *Gbagbo* and *Blé Goudé* confirmation decisions stand out as the broadest regarding the different requirements of indirect perpetration. It should be remarked that the notion of control logically widens as well if indirect perpetration through an organisation is affirmed in a situation like the one presumed by the pre-trial chamber in the situation of Côte d'Ivoire.

214 *Ongwen*, 23 March 2016, p. 72, No. 11; *Ntaganda*, 8 July 2019, para 819.

215 *Ntaganda*, 8 July 2019, para 822–4.

216 Olásolo and Carnero Rojo 2015, p 556. The only decision sharing this view is the pre-trial chamber decision in *Mbarushimana*, 16 December 2011, para 279.

217 This must be distinguished from the question of a hierarchy of blameworthiness between different forms of accessorial liability. Such a hierarchy has indeed been implied by chambers and scholars (see *Bemba et al.*, 19 October 2016, paras 85–6; Werle and Jessberger 2020b, mn. 616–17 and will be discussed in Chap. 7.

218 See only *Lubanga*, 29 January 2007, paras 327–32 (especially para 330 "the concept of control over the crime constitutes a third approach for distinguishing between principals and accessories..." and para 332 "According to this approach, only those who have control over the commission of the offence... may be principals..."); Furthermore, regard the approach on delineating perpetration through another from ordering in *Katanga and Chui*, 30 September 2008, para 517. See also *Ntaganda*, 30 March 2021, Separate Opinion of Judge Luz del Carmen Ibáñez Carranza, para 223 and van Sliedregt 2015, p 507 ("Control is the defining line between principals and accessories"), 511–2. For an analysis of control as a multidimensional concept see Cupido 2022, pp 639, 651, 654.

Another point concerns the scope or intensity of control, which must be exercised. Control over an organisation was affirmed in a case in which the alleged leader failed to stop the physical perpetrators from committing crimes.[219] In such a case, control would thus require the capacity to set the apparatus in motion, but not to stop it, once the commission of crimes is under way. Such a notion of control over an organisation, would widen the concept of control over the crime considerably, because it would mean that both, the "whether" and "how" of the commission of the crime would be highly questionable beyond a certain point, i.e., as soon as the relevant instruction is given, or the commission is under way.

In light of these two findings, one might consider rephrasing the concept of control, or rather, of the influence described through the term of control. This could read: Control over the crime lies with the person who decides that crimes (of a certain type) will be committed by members of the organisation with virtual certainty when following his or her instructions and barring the occurrence of an unforeseen event.

The findings of this section also confirm the earlier doubts concerning control exercised by architects of crimes. We have seen that control over the crime must be exercised through subjugating or bypassing the will of the physical perpetrators. However, this is not what an organiser or planner does, when ordering their subordinate staff—which is equally concerned with organizing and planning—to engage in certain conduct. Such a person does not subjugate or bypass the will of the physical perpetrators. Thus, the concept of control only describes the direct consequence of a person acting with control over a hierarchical apparatus in which the commission of crimes is secured because their orders lead to it almost automatically. Indirect perpetration through an organisation is therefore restricted to decision makers who instruct the physical perpetrators to commit crimes. This can of course happen through various layers of a hierarchy, but it is restricted to such direct instructions. This may be the reason why the ICC has expanded its notion of indirect co-perpetration over the years. This construct—in contrast to indirect perpetration alone—allows the contributions of architects of crimes to be captured, if they contribute to a common plan through planning or organising.[220]

Finally, the foregoing allows the conclusion that the notion of control under the ICC's doctrine is only "normative" in a limited fashion. As stated at the beginning of the section, it is normative because there is no natural commission of a crime "through another", but apart from that, it relies on factual considerations. It contains an assessment through the acting chamber. The judges can assess under which factual circumstances the will of the members of the organisation could be bypassed or subjugated and assign perpetrator liability if they believe such circumstances are given. This notion of control is therefore only normative in its choice of requirements. However, these requirements essentially establish a factual view of the circumstances

---

[219] See above on the indictment of William Ruto, Sect. 3.1.2.1.

[220] On indirect co-perpetration's broad possibility to encompass the conduct of persons who are involved in planning on a higher level see Cryer et al. 2019, pp 354–5. Note that the decision of the pre-trial chamber in *Ruto et al.* could be read as establishing a broader notion of control in indirect perpetration through an organisation, see above Sect. 3.1.2.1 and Sect. 3.1.3, immediately above.

under which a person can supposedly decide over the "whether" and "how" of the crimes.

3.1.4 A Hierarchy of Forms of Responsibility Under the Control Theory

The notion of control over a crime serves as a distinction criterion between forms of perpetration and participation in Art. 25 (3) Rome Statute. The approach therefore necessarily leads to a differential system. Whether this system establishes a hierarchy of blameworthiness between forms of participation is contentious.

There are unequivocal statements by chambers of the ICC that interpret the differentiation model under the Rome Statute as a normative one, where commission is the most serious form of contribution to the crime.[221]

In the *Lubanga* case, both the trial and the appeals chamber expressed that perpetration conveys a higher level of responsibility than forms of accessorial liability. In the trial judgment, the majority first stated that the contribution to a crime by a co-perpetrator was "necessarily of greater significance" and that commission "objectively" required a greater contribution than accessorial liability.[222] The majority of the chamber listed two arguments in favour of this view: First, the fact that the attempted commission of a crime was punishable but not the attempted contribution pursuant to lit. b) to d), and second the dependence of accessorial liability on the act of a perpetrator. They thus concluded that these points confirmed the "predominance of principal over secondary liability".[223] When elaborating on the objective threshold necessary for perpetration, the majority of the trial chamber stated that "lowering that threshold would deprive the notion of principal liability of its capacity to express the blameworthiness of those persons who are most responsible for the most serious crimes of international concern".[224]

The appeals chamber followed this approach, stating that the distinction between principal and accessory liability was not "mere[ly] terminological", but important because "generally speaking and all other things being equal" a perpetrator of a crime bears a higher blameworthiness than an accessory.[225] The trial chamber in *Al Mahdi*, explicitly followed the approach of the appeals chamber.[226]

---

[221] For an earlier analysis of jurisprudence in this regard, see Aksenova 2016, pp 164–7.

[222] *Lubanga*, 14 March 2012, paras 996–7; see also already the PTC decision on the confirmation of charges at *Lubanga*, 29 January 2007, para 321.

[223] *Lubanga*, 14 March 2012, para 998.

[224] Ibid., para 999.

[225] *Lubanga*, 1 December 2014, para 462.

[226] *Al Mahdi*, 27 September 2016, para 58.

The pre-trial chamber in *Katanga and Chui* seems to have taken the same stance by stating that finding the accused responsible as principals would render questions of accessorial liability moot.[227]

A similar approach can be found in the *Bemba et al.* trial judgment. The trial chamber found that due to the difference in control required by Art. 25 (3) (a) and (c), the latter implies a lesser degree of blameworthiness. It also describes a gradation in blameworthiness between Art. 25 (3) (b) and (c), with the former bearing a higher degree of blameworthiness. This is substantiated with the claim that the instigator, as the intellectual author of the crime, directly prompts its commission.[228] Unlike the aforementioned, this judgment explicitly determines a graded hierarchy of seriousness, where perpetration is considered more serious than aiding and abetting. It also differentiates between the other *litterae,* with ordering and instigating being more blameworthy than aiding and abetting. The relationship between *litterae* a) and b) is not explicitly touched upon, but it can be assumed that a gradation in seriousness between these two *litterae* is also implied.

The *Katanga* trial chamber on the other hand explicitly rejected the notion of different degrees of blameworthiness being *per se* attached to different forms of responsibility. After explaining the difference between perpetration and participation, the chamber asserted that Art. 25 (3) Rome Statute does not concern guilt, but individual responsibility and that therefore, an accessory may incur a sentence "akin or even identical" to the one of a perpetrator. The chamber went on to state that "the distinction between a perpetrator of and an accessory to a crime does not under any circumstances constitute a 'hierarchy of blameworthiness'. In addition, the trial chamber asserted that it could mitigate the sentence of an accessory but was not obliged to do so in light of the statute. Interestingly, it then concluded that "a perpetrator of a crime is not *always* viewed as more reprehensible than an accessory".[229] In the following paragraph, the chamber again pondered the issue, ascertaining that the distinction between perpetrators and accessories does not entail a hierarchy, neither in respect of guilt nor of penalty. Instead, the different characteristics of modes of liability simply reflect different forms of involvement in the crime, without leading to the accused being found more or less culpable or incurring a lesser penalty.[230]

The appeals chamber in *Bemba et al.* also seemingly aimed to restrict earlier decisions that implied a hierarchy of blameworthiness. In particular, it pointed out that it would not generally recognize an instigator of being less culpable than a perpetrator and a perpetrator of deserving a higher sentence than an accessory. In the chamber's view, the Rome Statute does not indicate an automatic correlation between forms of responsibility and the sentence.[231]

---

[227] *Katanga and Chui*, 30 September 2008, para 471.

[228] *Bemba et al.*, 19 October 2016, paras 85–6.

[229] *Katanga*, 7 March 2014, para 1386; emphasis in original.

[230] Ibid., para 1387.

[231] ICC, *The Prosecutor v. Jean-Pierre Bemba Gombo et al.* , Judgment on Sentencing Appeal, 08 March 2018, ICC-01/05-01/13 A6 A7 A8 A9, paras 59–60. See also *Ntaganda*, 30 March 2021, Partly concurring opinion of Judge Chile Eboe-Osuji, para 98.

Early arrest warrant decisions do not rely on a hierarchy of blameworthiness when determining the modes of liability under which the respective individuals were sought. This was the case with Joseph Kony,[232] and all the high-level leaders of the LRA, which were sought under the head of ordering.[233] The same holds true for the initial arrest warrant applications in the cases of *Katanga* and *Chui*, which also charged both suspects with ordering the crimes, without stating that their responsibility was reduced.[234] Given the well-known discussion about models of perpetration and participation in international criminal law, these early decisions imply the rejection of a hierarchy of blameworthiness by the competent pre-trial chambers.

Some chambers have stated that the behaviour of a person may be able to fulfil several modes of responsibility at once.[235] However, this should not be understood as rejecting a hierarchy of blameworthiness. In fact, it is inherent to a *normative* distinction between modes of responsibility that behaviour satisfying the narrowest requirements is also encompassed by broader (and "less blameworthy") forms of liability.[236]

Several judges appended separate opinions to decisions in other cases, rejecting a hierarchy of blameworthiness.

In line with his rejection of a differentiated model of perpetration and participation, Judge Fulford criticises the idea that Art. 25 (3) Rome Statute adopts a hierarchy of seriousness. His criticism is based on the conviction that several of the concepts in Art. 25 (3) overlap and therefore a categorization of these modes into different degrees of seriousness finds no basis in the statute. His opinion implies that the majority in *Lubanga* interprets Art. 25 (3) as a graded hierarchy with a different level of blameworthiness ascribed by each of the four *litterae*. Consequently, he also states that a differentiation between lit. (c) and (d) is unconvincing, as coordinated group action was inherent to many of "history's most serious crimes".[237] His arguments against such a hierarchy include the fact that there is no connection between the mode of liability and the sentencing range in the Rome Statute, as opposed to the German legal system where the control over the crime theory originated.[238]

---

[232] ICC, *The Prosecutor v. Joseph Kony*, Issuance of a Warrant of Arrest, 27 September 2005, 02/04-01/05, para 42 see counts 1, 4–33.

[233] ICC, *The Prosecutor v. Raska Lukwiya*, Issuance of a Warrant of Arrest, 8 July 2005, ICC-02/04, para 30, counts 6–8 (being all counts); ICC, *The Prosecutor v. Okot Odhiambo*, Issuance of a Warrant of Arrest, 8 July 2005, ICC-02/04, para 32, counts 10–19 (being all counts); ICC, *The Prosecutor v. Dominic Ongwen*, Issuance of a Warrant of Arrest, 8 July 2005, ICC-02/04, para 30, counts 27–33 (being all counts); ICC, *The Prosecutor v. Vincent Otti*, Issuance of a Warrant of Arrest, 8 July 2005, ICC-02/04, para 42, counts 1, 4–33 (count 3 as the only other ground for the decision to rest on, refers to inducing the commission of war crimes).

[234] *Katanga*, 6 July 2007, para 54; *Chui*, 6 July 2007, para 55; Steer 2017, p 307.

[235] See e.g. ICC, *The Prosecutor v. Jean-Pierre Bemba Gombo*, Trial Judgment, 21 March 2016, ICC-01/05-01/08, para 174; *Ntaganda*, 8 July 2019, para 1200.

[236] See accordingly *Ntaganda*, 8 July 2019, para 1200.

[237] *Lubanga*, 14 March 2012, Separate Opinion of Judge Adrian Fulford, para 8.

[238] Ibid., Separate Opinion of Judge Adrian Fulford, paras 9-10. As seen in Chap. 2, this is entirely correct for the relation between commission and aiding and abetting in German law. It is furthermore

Judge Christine Van den Wyngaert's criticism is based on the perception that no permitted way of interpreting the Rome Statute can lead to the adoption of the latter theory.[239] She further explains that, in her view, there are no reasons that a distinction between principals and accessories must lead to a hierarchy of blameworthiness. She points to the manifold ways of participating in international crimes, which, in her opinion, will not all fall under commission liability, yet embody highly blameworthy contributions to crimes.[240] She also contests that Rule 145 (1) (c) of the Rules of Procedure and Evidence (RPE) establishes a mandatory reduction of sentence for accessorial modes of liability.[241] Finally, she expresses her support for the necessity of fair labelling in ICC judgments, but asserts that this cannot be adequately achieved through modes of participation, as many architects of crimes would often not fall under Art. 25 (3) (a) of the statute.[242]

In his partly concurring opinion on the *Ntaganda* Appeals Judgment, Judge Chile Eboe-Osuji also criticises the adoption of a differentiated system,[243] as well as the adoption of a hierarchy of blameworthiness.[244] From his perspective, an import of the German doctrine of control over the crime is unnecessary, due to the particularities of the German legal system and its differences to the Rome Statute.[245] His criticism is *inter alia* based on the observation that no mitigated punishment for participants under *litterae* (b) to (d) in Art. 25 (3) is previsioned in the Rome Statute.[246] He also illustrates how every participant is punished for the crime under the Rome Statute (his example references actors soliciting genocide being convicted "*plainly* for genocide"). The purpose of Art. 25 (3) Rome Statute would therefore be a dragnet, aiming to encompass the conduct of starkly different forms of contribution.[247] In his view, there is consequently no difference in blameworthiness between forms of participation in Art. 25 (3) Rome Statute, rendering all modes of participation under *litterae* (b), (c) and (d) equally blameworthy to forms of commission.[248]

In his separate opinion on the *Ntaganda* Appeals Judgment, Judge Howard Morrison joined the three aforementioned judges in expressing his criticism of the court's adoption of a hierarchy of blameworthiness,[249] as well as its reliance on a

---

asserted as an unwritten rule of facultative mitigation for instigators by commentators, including by Roxin, see Chap. 2, Sect. 2.2.5 In a similar vein, see Ohlin 2022, p 249.

[239] ICC, *The Prosecutor v. Mathieu Ndgudjolo Chui*, Trial Judgment, 18 December 2012, ICC-01/04-02/12, Concurring Opinion of Judge Christine Van den Wyngaert, paras 9–21.

[240] Ibid., Concurring Opinion of Judge Christine van den Wyngaert, paras 22–5.

[241] Ibid., Concurring Opinion of Judge Christine van den Wyngaert, para 27.

[242] Ibid., Concurring Opinion of Judge Christine van den Wyngaert, paras 28–9.

[243] *Ntaganda*, 30 March 2021, Partly concurring opinion of Judge Chile Eboe-Osuji, para 33.

[244] Ibid., Partly concurring opinion of Judge Chile Eboe-Osuji, para 43, see also para 49 in favour of a unitary/monistic system.

[245] Ibid., Partly concurring opinion of Judge Chile Eboe-Osuji, paras 34 et seq.

[246] Ibid., Partly concurring opinion of Judge Chile Eboe-Osuji, para 42.

[247] Ibid., Partly concurring opinion of Judge Chile Eboe-Osuji, paras 47–8.

[248] Ibid., Partly concurring opinion of Judge Chile Eboe-Osuji, paras 64, 72, 102.

[249] Ibid., Separate opinion of Judge Howard Morrison on Mr. Ntaganda's appeal, paras 3, 8, 11.

differentiated system of perpetration and participation.[250] His criticism aligns with that of Judge Van den Wyngaert in that contributions falling under modes like aiding and abetting can consist of highly blameworthy conduct in mass atrocity crimes.[251] Judge Morrison also expressed caution regarding attempts to clearly distinguish all modes of responsibility in Art. 25 (3) from each other, stating that such an endeavour would be a "doomed enterprise".[252]

The ICC's jurisprudence on the choice of forms of responsibility and their relation to one another has been interpreted differently. Kress theorised that the matter had for now been settled, with the jurisprudence, in his view, clearly relying on a normative differentiated model.[253] Weigend regards this as an open question,[254] while Aksenova even asserts that certain convictions under Art. 25 (3) (d) show a tendency to move away from the "prioritising of commission".[255]

Notwithstanding these different views, most chambers of the ICC currently read Art. 25 (3) Rome Statute as establishing a normative hierarchy of blameworthiness, despite the vehement opposition brought forward by some judges.

Indirect perpetration through an organisation is thus considered to give rise to principal liability, which is mostly deemed more blameworthy than the liability attached to any other form of responsibility under *litterae* (b) to (d) of Art. 25 (3) Rome Statute.

3.1.5 Summary

Indirect perpetration through an organisation has gained certain contours through the ICC's jurisprudence, but many aspects yet remain unclear.

The details of the requirements of "control over an organisation" and "organised and hierarchical apparatus of power" remain largely undefined. Automatic compliance with orders has so far been established in decisions based on a limited set of factors. It remains to be seen whether these factors are definite. A more problematic issue in this regard is the equation of this requirement with the criterion of an organised and hierarchical apparatus. Lastly, the *Gbagbo* acquittal decision casts

---

250 Ibid., Separate opinion of Judge Howard Morrison on Mr. Ntaganda's appeal, para 10.

251 Ibid., Separate opinion of Judge Howard Morrison on Mr. Ntaganda's appeal, para 8.

252 Ibid., Separate opinion of Judge Howard Morrison on Mr. Ntaganda's appeal, para 9.

253 Kress 2016, p 269.

254 Weigend 2015, pp 540–1.

255 Aksenova 2016, p 149 ("clear rift in the jurisprudence"), 166, 177. She backs this view with the emerging practice of charging modes of liability "in the alternative" (see page 166). However, it could be remarked that this practice does not mirror any view by the OTP on a hierarchy of modes of participation, but instead simply aims to secure a conviction under any form of participation—irrespective of the blameworthiness of the charged individual's conduct. The same would then be true for the resulting judgments. If interpreted in this way, judgments convicting under Art. 25 (3) (d) do not demonstrate another tendency if they do not explicitly decide to convict under Art. 25 (3) (d) *instead of* (a) where both are fulfilled. This has not yet happened.

doubts on the applicable *mens rea* standard in cases of indirect perpetration through an organisation. The decision calls into question whether an instruction to engage in legal conduct that is given knowing with virtual certainty that it will lead to crimes, suffices to establish the mental element.

The analysis shows that a specific conduct is necessary to qualify as an indirect perpetrator by controlling an organisation. This conduct involves direct instructions that specifically aim at or entail the commission of crimes.

Control over the crime through another is thought to be control over the physical perpetrator and thereby over the specific crime. It is based on factual considerations of circumstances under which chambers believe a decision maker can decide whether and how a specific crime will be committed.

Most relevant decisions affirm or imply a hierarchy of blameworthiness between forms of commission and forms of participation. The conduct of someone who has control over the crime is more blameworthy. Consequently, they are less blameworthy if the conduct does not amount to control over the crime.

3.2 Comparison

Having explored the scope of indirect perpetration through an organisation as applied by the chambers of the ICC, this approach can be compared to the relevant theories as developed in German scholarly writings and jurisprudence.

It is noteworthy that, from the beginning, the ICC and scholars supporting the implementation of the doctrine have spoken of "the" theory of indirect perpetration through an organisation.[256] However, as explored in Chap. 2, such a uniform understanding of this doctrine does not exist in German legal practice or theory.[257]

This section outlines similarities and differences between the ICC's version of the doctrine and the three above-mentioned versions from Germany. Based on this, the notions of control and domination of the crime are also compared, as far as indirect perpetration is concerned.

Some chambers, including the appeals chamber, have outlined how the control over the crime theory and the doctrine of perpetration through an organisation are not derived from a specific source of national law, but are based on an in-depth analysis of Art. 25 (3) Rome Statute.[258] However, the appeals chamber in the *Lubanga* judgment also explained that it would seek guidance from approaches developed in national legal systems.[259]

---

[256] See e.g.: *Katanga and Chui*, 30 September 2008, para 505: "...German jurisprudence was in fact applied to this notion in the East German Border Trials"; Jessberger and Geneuss 2008, p 862.

[257] See Chap. 2, Sect. 2.6.1.

[258] See already *Katanga*, 7 March 2014, para 1395; *Lubanga*, 1 December 2014, para 470.

[259] *Lubanga*, 1 December 2014, para 470.

The concept—compatible with Art. 25 (3) (a) as it may be—must therefore be seen as imported from Germany and some Spanish speaking jurisdictions.[260] Given the origin of the theory and the influence of the German doctrine on the restructuring of legal systems in Spanish speaking countries, it has been asserted that the ICC essentially only considered the German legal system when developing the doctrine.[261]

Based on this observation, the following comparison prepares a part of the critical assessment of the theory as applied by the ICC. Where elements from German doctrine were imported by the court, it is likely, that its inherent weaknesses were also assumed. On the other hand, other shortcomings may not apply, because the ICC avoids certain features known in German doctrine.

3.2.1 The Theoretical Foundation of Indirect Perpetration Through an Organisation

Chambers of the ICC have elaborated on their theoretical approach to perpetration and participation in some detail. For the purposes of the subsequent comparison, it must be briefly examined, whether and to what extent the provisions of the different legal systems and the underlying interpretational concepts are parallel to one another.

3.2.1.1 The Different Provisions on Commission Liability

The doctrine of indirect perpetration through an organisation is based on an interpretation of the respective provisions of commission liability in the Rome Statute and the GCC.

The relevant provisions read:

---

[260] See only the conception as described in the earlier decisions in *Katanga and Chui*, 30 September 2008, para 485 with fn. 647 (quoting Roxin's standard book "Täterschaft und Tatherrschaft", as well as a list of literature on the German legal system and certain Spanish speaking systems), para 496 ("This doctrine is based on the early works of Claus Roxin and is identified by the term 'perpetrator behind the perpetrator' (*Täter hinter dem Täter*).") with fn. 657 hinting at Roxin's initial article on perpetration through an organisation, see again para 498 with fn. 659; *Katanga*, 7 March 2014, paras 1396 with fn. 3195, 1404 with fn. 3200, 1405 with fn. 3201, 1409 with fn. 3207, 1411 with fn. 3208, 1412 with fn. 3209. See also van Sliedregt 2015, pp 499, 507; Weigend 2008, p 479; Weigend 2015, p 547 ("most heavily influenced by German legal theory"); Ambos 2018, § 7 mn. 17; Steer 2017, pp 301, 304–5.

[261] Manacorda and Meloni 2011, p 170; van Sliedregt 2015, p 507; Zahar and Sluiter 2008, p 249; but see Ambos 2018, § 7 mn. 17 with fn. 74 emphasising the transnational acknowledgment of the doctrine of domination of the crime.

"Article 25 Rome Statute—Individual Criminal Responsibility

(3) In accordance with this Statute, a person shall be criminally responsible and liable for punishment for a crime within the jurisdiction of the Court if that person:

(a) Commits such a crime, whether as an individual, jointly with another or through another person, regardless of whether that other person is criminally responsible..."

and

"Section 25 German Criminal Code—Commission of Offence

(1) Whoever commits an offence themselves or through another incurs a penalty as an offender.

(2) If several persons commit an offence jointly, each person incurs a penalty as an offender (joint offenders)."

As can be seen, both provisions are worded in a similar fashion. The most relevant stipulation for this book is the provision that a person can commit an offence "through another".[262] The major difference lies in the rule of the Rome Statute declaring that, where a crime is committed through another, the criminal responsibility of that other person is irrelevant. The German provision does not contain this addition.

Both rules refer to "another" as the necessary tool for committing the crime. This seems to indicate the necessity of another, natural person. Overall, the resemblance of both provisions is quite striking.[263]

3.2.1.2 Theory of Domination/Control Over the Crime

Chambers of the ICC have explicitly identified several theories for the imputation of responsibility and compared the control over the crime theory to them.[264] As outlined in Chap. 2, according to the absolute majority opinion, the notion of domination of the crime is the correct approach to distinguishing perpetrators from accessories in German criminal law.[265] However, German jurisprudence has never taken up this theoretical groundwork. As previously discussed, especially when dealing with indirect perpetration, German courts rely on an approach which has been described in different terms, none of which are akin to control or domination of the crime. The most striking realisation is that in order for a German court to classify somebody as a perpetrator, it can revert to the requirement of a perpetrator having to "want

---

[262] The relevant part of Art. 25 (3) (a) Rome Statute in other languages reads: *"durch einen anderen"* (German), *"por conducto de otro"* (Spanish), *"par l'intermédiaire d'une autre personne"* (French), *"por intermédio de outrem"* (Portuguese).

[263] See e.g. Satzger 2020, § 15 mn. 53, 59.

[264] *Lubanga*, 29 January 2007, paras 322–41; *Katanga and Chui*, 30 September 2008, paras 480–6; *Katanga*, 7 March 2014, paras 1390–4.

[265] See Chap. 2, Sects. 2.2.2 and 2.2.6.

a crime as his or her own".[266] Although this does not rule out the approach of the German jurisprudence for further comparison, it must be kept in mind when comparing the weight which is given to different requirements and evidence by the different approaches.[267]

With regard to the ICC's approach as well as both the traditional and the systemic view[268] on indirect perpetration through an organisation in Germany, the respective "definitions" of domination/control are quite similar: Domination/control over the crime requires the actor deciding whether and how the crime will be committed.[269] One should add, however, that Roxin's original conception of domination as an "open concept" focusses more on the perpetrator being a "central figure" to the commission of the crime. This description may be regarded more open and abstract than the aforementioned definition. The ICC does not use this description of a central figure as part of its "control theory".[270]

3.2.1.3 The Autonomy Principle

The autonomy principle has been described as a precise way to delineate indirect perpetration from instigation in German law. However, the majority of German scholars reject the principle as being too narrow, precisely because it rules out the perpetrator behind the perpetrator.[271] Although occasionally elaborating on the issue and rejecting the autonomy principle, German jurisprudence has never been bound to the concept as it did not subscribe itself to a strict notion of domination of the crime.[272]

However, the Rome Statute clearly chooses another path by declaring that indirect perpetration is possible through innocent and guilty agents alike.[273] As a structuring

---

266 See Chap. 2, Sect. 2.3.2.3. See also for an explanation in connection with the ICC's adoption of the control theory: Weigend 2008, p 479.

267 This important doctrinal and practical difference is seldom given attention in the discussion on international criminal law, see, e.g., *Ntaganda*, 30 March 2021, Separate Opinion of Judge Luz del Carmen Ibáñez Carranza, para 239.

268 No special deviation from the definition of the notion of domination of the crime is usually proposed along with the systemic concept of indirect perpetration in German scholarly writing, which has been outlined above in Chap. 2, Sect. 2.4. Whether domination of the crime still plays a major role, if the concept is applied, is another question, which is discussed below at Sect. 3.2.3.

269 See above, for Germany at Chap. 2, Sect. 2.2.2 and for the ICC at Sect. 3.1.3. For the ICC see also Kiss 2019, mn. 4; van Sliedregt 2015, p 507.

270 However, as shown above at Sect. 3.1.2 the determination of the accused's role within the apparatus plays a role for the mode of indirect perpetration through an organisation.

271 See Chap. 2, Sect. 2.2.3.

272 See Chap. 2, Sect. 2.3.2.3. Within the subjective approach, the autonomy principle does not play a role, because the focal point to determine perpetration is only the will of the perpetrator, not their control/domination over another.

273 See above, Sect. 3.1.2; Kiss 2019, mn. 1. Kiss takes this wider notion of indirect perpetration as a suggestion that the control theory and the figure of perpetrator behind the perpetrator were meant to be recognized by the statute.

guideline to the limits of indirect perpetration, the autonomy principle is therefore unfit for modes of liability under the Rome Statute.

3.2.2 *The Legal Requirements*

The requirements of indirect perpetration through an organised apparatus of power have been described and applied distinctly in different theories.

This section compares the different requirements in groups, as far as they exist in multiple approaches to the doctrine. Such is the case with the "organised apparatus of power" (Sect. 3.2.2.1) and the actor's position within it (Sect. 3.2.2.2), it is not the case, with the detachment from law requirement (Sect. 3.2.2.3). The different mechanisms deemed relevant within the organisation are additionally compared with a view to their respective focus (Sect. 3.2.2.4). The certainty of success (Sect. 3.2.2.5) is a criterion that can be found in most approaches. Lastly, a comparison of these different criteria enables an accurate picture of resemblances and differences between the ICC and German approaches to the doctrine (Sect. 3.2.2.6).

3.2.2.1 Organised Apparatus of Power

It is relatively self-evident that within the theory an indirect perpetrator must have some organisational apparatus at their disposal. However, whether and in how far this organisation must be further defined is unclear in all versions of the theory.

In the traditional version, the requirement is described as necessitating an organisation which works independently using certain automatisms and stable structures and thereby "develops a life of its own".[274] The ICC's term of an "organised and hierarchical apparatus of power" could theoretically imply something similar. The trial chamber in *Katanga* picks up Roxin's thoughts when it states:

> The apparatus somehow operates autonomously and both its existence and survival must not depend on any personal relationships between its members.

The chamber also quotes Roxin's initial essay on the issue, in which he outlines that "half a dozen anti-social elements" joining forces to commit crimes would not constitute an apparatus of power.[275]

Furthermore, neither the traditional German concept, nor the ICC's approach limit themselves to bureaucratic, state-like institutions. From the outset, Roxin and others have recognized secret and mafia organisations as possible apparatuses, later mentioning that armed non-state actors in internal armed conflicts and ethnic violence

---

[274] See Chap. 2, Sect. 2.2.3.1; Roxin 2011, p 198.

[275] *Katanga*, 7 March 2014, para 1409 with fn. 3207 hinting at Roxin 2011, p 204.

could also be organisations under the theory.[276] The same holds true for the ICC in both theory[277] and practice.[278]

The BGH does not require any specific features of the organisation within its version of the theory. As outlined, the possibility of triggering standardized procedures in any kind of organisation suffices under German jurisprudence. Comparatively small economic "organisations" have been regarded as sufficient to fulfil this requirement.[279]

However, it should be recalled, that the state apparatus of the German Democratic Republic was the first organisation German jurisprudence referred to. The respective judgments outline its relevant features in detail.[280]

These early judgments with their detailed descriptions of hierarchies, command structures and organizational units within the apparatus bear resemblance to the ICC's elaborations on such factors. However, whilst the BGH now places significantly less emphasis on organisational features, the ICC (usually) inquiries into the structures and functioning of the relevant organisations in detail. The only ICC decision which stands in contrast to this practice is the ruling on the pro-Gbagbo youth in the situation in Côte d'Ivoire. There the pre-trial chamber's inquiries led to the realization that the youth groups did not qualify as typical hierarchical organisations, however, it decided to classify them as such anyway.

The ICC's practice regarding the details based on which an organisation is usually affirmed, stands out because, in some cases, it actively inquires whether organisations resemble conventional armies. However, this "military focus" is not actually determinative for organisations in the ICC's view. This can be seen in its findings on other organisations, such as the *Mungiki* sect and the "network of perpetrators" in the situation in Kenya.[281] The latter two embody what Roxin originally called states within a state, pertaining to his category of secret and underground organisations.[282]

The systemic approach to perpetration through an organisation does not include any specific requirement as to the organisation. However, the underlying rationale of a system of wrongdoing logically requires certain organisational structures which allow it to aggregate the individual crimes and set them in relation to an overarching systemic wrong.

Finally, a feature of the apparatus of power in the traditional German theory, as well as in the ICC's approach is closely connected to the overall concept of perpetration

---

276 See Chap. 2, Sect. 2.2.3.1.

277 See *Katanga*, 7 March 2014, para 1410, underlining that the concept should not be restricted to "bureaucracies akin to those of Third Reich Germany".

278 See the organisations which have been recognized as hierarchical apparatuses at some point by the ICC above at Sect. 3.1.2.2.

279 See Chap. 2, Sect. 2.3.2.2.

280 See Chap. 2, Sect. 2.3.2.1.

281 See above, Sect. 3.1.2.2.

282 The *Mungiki* sect especially was described as a secret organisation with a strict hierarchical regime, having its own mechanisms of justice and vast influence on the poorer population of Nairobi. It would thus probably qualify as a "mafia organisation" in the sense of Roxin's theory; see on the *Mungiki Muthaura et al.*, 23 January 2012, paras 207–13.

through an organisation: an additional requirement pertaining to the organisation. Roxin's model demands the organisation be detached from law and the physical perpetrators be fungible. The ICC demands an almost automatic compliance with the accused's orders (within the apparatus). In a similar vein, the BGH has settled on the notion of "standardized procedures" within the organisation. Thus, these three approaches share the suspicion that they do not require any tangible features from an organisation, if the mechanism leading to control/domination of the crime (which is described through another requirement) can be affirmed.[283]

This suspicion notwithstanding, the ICC's approach seems to mostly align with what Roxin, and other supporters of the traditional version devised as potential apparatuses of power. These two versions of perpetration through an organisation are therefore much narrower than the concept of "organisations" which the BGH recognizes nowadays. Supporters of a systemic view have not elaborated in unison or detail on the apparatus. However, given the theory's focus on the responsibility of leaders for establishing, organising and maintaining the system itself, one would expect the organization requirement regarding structures and automatised proceedings, to be at the higher end of what the ICC recognizes as hierarchical and organised apparatuses of power.

3.2.2.2 Position to Issue Orders in or Control Over an Organisation

Advocates of the traditional concept of indirect perpetration through an organised apparatus of power require the perpetrator to have the power to issue instructions within this apparatus.[284] The comparable requirement under the ICC's doctrine is called "control over the organisation".[285]

Originally, the power to issue instructions within an organisation referred to the actor's capability to steer the apparatus into a certain direction or action. The requirement therefore necessitates a power of command or a position of direct influence within the apparatus.[286] The same holds true in ICC jurisprudence, where the accused's *de jure* and *de facto* position of power and command plays a vital role when determining control over the organisation.[287] In its current application of its version of the theory, the BGH does not demand a special position. In fact, it does not even expect the indirect perpetrator to be part of the organisation.[288]

---

[283] Regarding the German approaches, see Herzberg 2000, p 33 et seq.; regarding the broad standardized procedures requirement, see Weisser 2012, pp 247–9, 250. Concerning the ICC, see Sect. 3.1.2.5.

[284] See Chap. 2, Sect. 2.2.3.3.

[285] See above at Sect. 3.1.2.1.

[286] See Chap. 2, Sect. 2.2.3.3.

[287] See above at Sect. 3.1.2.1.

[288] See Chap. 2, Sect. 2.3.2.2 on the case in which a civilian who was not part of the GDR apparatus reported the plans of another to flee the GDR who was consequently taken in custody. The BGH convicted the denunciator as an indirect perpetrator through an organisation, regardless of him being an *extraneus* to the GDR apparatus. See on this also Ambos 2009, pp 152.

As a supporter of a systemic view, Ambos outspokenly advocates to restrict its application to the highest echelons of an organisation's hierarchy. He bases this idea on the observation that only persons at the apex of the organisation could steer it "undisturbedly". According to his view, an exception exists where the whole system consists of several organisations (one may speak of agencies or branches) which autonomously work towards the criminal goal.[289] By contrast, the traditional theory and the ICC's approach explicitly recognize a position to issue instructions or to control the organisation where this relates only to a part of the organisation.[290] The difference between these views concerns mid-level decision makers who receive and convey orders, but whose part of the organisation does not qualify as sufficiently autonomous in Ambos' view. In such situations, the ICC clearly concurs with the wider view of the traditional theory. In practice this can be seen in cases like that of Dominic Ongwen. The accused in this case worked his way up through the ranks of Joseph Kony's LRA. Although he eventually belonged to the so-called "control altar" and therefore to the highest committee of the organisation, decisions were ultimately made by Kony. Ongwen's power of command stretched "only" over the fighters of his brigade. This was nevertheless sufficient for the pre-trial chamber to confirm the charges against him, on the basis of indirect (co-)perpetration within which his control over "parts of the organisation" was affirmed.[291]

Concerning the evidentiary basis on which these requirements are affirmed in practice, the ICC notably focusses on the actor's position in the organisation and their relation to subordinates by inquiring into chains of command and the expected level of compliance with orders.[292] This procedure supports the initial evaluation that the ICC follows the approach devised by Roxin. However, certain findings considered by the ICC could broaden the requirement's scope well beyond that of the traditional concept. In this regard, some factors such as the provision of weapons and finances as a means of ensuring control and the manipulation of youth groups as mass rallies stand out.[293]

It is questionable, whether supportive, organisational tasks suffice to establish a position to issue instructions from the perspective the traditional theory. It also seems unrealistic to affirm such a position under the original theory for a person who publicly addresses unorganised groups with calls for violence, as done by the *Blé Goudé* pre-trial chamber.

It seems plausible that sufficiently important influence over supportive conduct, such as the provision of finances and weaponry, could qualify as the necessary organisational wrong leading to the classification as an indirect perpetrator under the systemic approach. This applies regardless of whether the influence is restricted

---

[289] See Chap. 2, Sect. 2.4.2.3; see in this vein also ibid., pp 152–3.

[290] Cf. Chap. 2, Sect. 2.2.3.3 and Sect. 3.1.2.1.

[291] *Ongwen*, 23 March 2016, paras 56-8, p. 72, paras 10–2.

[292] See Sect. 3.1.2.1.

[293] See Sect. 3.1.2.1 these findings are mostly found in the decisions in *Gbagbo* and *Blé Goudé*. However, financing also plays a role in establishing control over the alleged organisations in the decisions in *Muthaura et al.* and *Ruto et al.*

to the highest level of leadership. In this latter regard, a subtle parallel between the ICC's and BGH's early assessment of evidence exists and it is this aspect which led Heine to describe the BGH's approach as "systemic-functional". In Heine's view, in the trials against the members of the national defence council and the political bureau, the relevant conduct of the accused was not their voting behaviour, but their contributions to the maintenance of the GDR's overall border regime.[294] The same can be said in ICC cases about the more "supportive" kind of conduct.[295] However, one must consider that there is a difference between possessing and exercising control. From the perspective of the ICC at least, only the former of these two aspects can be affirmed for an actor playing a supportive role in the organisation without direct decision-making powers over the physical perpetrators.

One may summarize the findings on the requirements of a position to give instructions (traditional and systemic approach) or control over the organisation (ICC) as follows:

In theoretic terms, the ICC is seemingly very close to the considerations of the traditional model. No restriction of the mode of liability to the highest echelons is deemed necessary, contrary to what some authors within the systemic approach demand.

However, when considered in detail, the ICC may have occasionally taken a path already explored by the BGH in the 1990s. Where the defendant holds a more general role within an organisation, indirect perpetration is affirmed, but not necessarily backed with specific findings of the defendant's possibilities of steering the apparatus into a certain action. In this regard, both the BGH and the ICC have sometimes moved towards a more collective, systemic view on organisational responsibility, without doing so explicitly.

3.2.2.3 Detachment from Law

Roxin devised indirect perpetration through an organisation based on several observations, one of which being that the organisation must operate "detached from the law".[296] This requirement has been criticised in the ambit of German and international criminal law.[297] The BGH did not adopt it and Ambos, as a prominent advocate

[294] See Chap. 2, Sects. 2.3.2.1 and 2.4.

[295] This observation is somewhat less surprising if one considers the ICC's trend of adjudicating virtually anyone as an indirect co-perpetrator. Just as with the members of the GDR committees before the BGH, the perspective of the ICC is usually broadened by the notion of indirect co-perpetration. The mutual attribution of conduct leads to an implicit lowering of the requirements of indirect perpetration through an organisation because control over the apparatus can be exerted "together". While this theory cannot be explored here in detail, it must be remarked that such a construction—valid or not as it may be—should not lead to a lowering of the control over the organisation requirement, where a person is believed to have exercised control over this part of the organisation alone.

[296] See Chap. 2, Sect. 2.2.3.4.

[297] For a comprehensive overview, see Ambos 2004, pp 606–11; Ambos 2011b, p 154. In German scholarly literature, see e.g. Herzberg 2000, p 37, criticising the notion as unprecise and questioning

for a systemic fundament of the theory, rejects it as well.[298] The ICC also does not recognize the detachment from law as a requirement for its theory.[299]

However, it is worth mentioning that so far, all organisations which were accepted by the ICC under its theory would most likely have fulfilled this requirement. Whilst some qualified as mafia-type organizations, others were armed non-state actors and yet others were made up of the state apparatus. Nevertheless, at some point the commission of crimes was one of their common and usual means of action.[300] With every probability, persons participating in the crimes as low and mid-level actors knew this and generally did not expect to face consequences for their actions. Regardless, it seems realistic to assume that the notion of an organisation operating outside the legal order will not be incorporated into the notion of perpetration through an organisation at the ICC. However, the issue could become relevant in the future should the court ever deal with more contentious situations in which the relevant organisations as a whole—e.g., the Israeli or United States Armed Forces—would not qualify as being detached from the law.

3.2.2.4 The Organisation's Mechanism: Fungibility, Readiness to Commit the Crime, Automatic Compliance with Orders and Standardized Procedures

The discussed approaches to the theory of indirect perpetration through an organisation share a common feature which can only be categorized *in abstracto*: A certain kind of mechanism must exist within the organisation that supposedly leads to the commission of crimes if it is activated. Of course, other requirements also play a role, such as the detachment from law for Roxin, but the mechanism is often at the centre of the debate and shaped differently in the different approaches.

whether one could validly say that the GDR state apparatus as a whole had detached itself from the law based on the murders of fugitives at the border. He states that these incidents only represent a small part of the state apparatus' actions.

298 See Chap. 2, Sects. 2.3.2.3 and 2.4; see also Werle and Jessberger 2020b, mn. 650.

299 Ambos 2013, pp 156–7; Gil Gil and Maculan 2015, p 355.

300 In the situation in Kenya, the *Munigki* sect and the "network" allegedly used by William Ruto were both criminal organisations from the beginning (*Muthaura et al.*, 23 January 2012, paras 103, 204–14 establishing that the *Munigki* were involved in crimes against humanity as an organisation; *Ruto et al.*, 23 January 2012, paras 180, 186, 192, concerning the "networks'" implementation for and role in crimes against humanity). The same was true for the youth groups as allegedly incorporated into the pro-Gbagbo forces in Côte d'Ivoire (*Gbagbo*, 12 June 2014, paras 105–6, 165 (concerning the alleged use of youth groups for violence). The situations in the D.R. Congo, the Central African Republic and Uganda were shaped by the actions of armed non-state actors which did not adhere to rules of international humanitarian law from the outset. In the situation in Darfur, Sudan, the military and state apparatus are believed not to have adhered to legal boundaries either, as the widespread attack on the civilian population allegedly was part of the plan from the beginning of the campaign.

For Roxin, fungibility of the direct perpetrator is the focal point in enabling domination of the crime through an organisation.[301] Within the traditional view on the theory, however, other proposals to describe this mechanism have gained importance as well. Schroeder's readiness or disposition to act (*"Tatbereitschaft"*) is the best known of these alternatives.[302]

From the beginning, the BGH opted for another description of the relevant mechanism and emphasised the indirect perpetrator's capability to set "standardized proceduresin motion, which would almost automatically lead to the commission of the crime.[303]

For the systemic approach to indirect perpetration through an organisation, different aspects of the mechanism have been discussed: Weisser emphasised the machine-like automatism of industrial murder mechanisms, such as the one devised by the Nazis for the Holocaust. Looking at earlier ICC jurisprudence, Ambos explored a broader view on the mechanism, which is not confined to fungibility.[304]

The ICC applies the criterion of "almost automatic compliance with orders". Within this requirement, different mechanisms or aspects have been recognized by chambers that would lead to such an automatism. Fungibility of the physical perpetrators is one, violent and strict training and disciplinary regimens another. Payment and reward systems have also been mentioned in this regard.[305]

Different opinions have been voiced as to the resemblance of the ICC's approach with German precedents. For some, the ICC's "almost automatic compliance with orders" resembles the "standardized procedures" criterion known in German jurisprudence.[306] Ambos categorizes the different factors recognized by the ICC into two different groups: Where fungibility plays a role, the organisation's mechanism is based on "hard factors", as he expresses it. Other factors, such as ethnic relations, indoctrination, strict training regimens etc., are so-called "soft factors".[307] According to Kiss, the two notions ("hard" and "soft" or "weak" factors) are already being used at the ICC. He believes that the court applies the two traditional German criteria of Roxin's "fungibility" and Schroeder's "readiness to act". In his view, the readiness to act arises out of factors such as indoctrination and training regimens. Consequently, he relies on Ambos' category of "soft factors", however believes that this is practically synonymous with willingness or readiness to commit the crime.[308] This view is somewhat mirrored by the separate opinion of Judge del Carmen Ibáñez Carranza in the *Ntaganda* appeals judgment, where much emphasis is placed on the "replaceable

[301] See Chap. 2, Sect. 2.2.3.2.

[302] See Chap. 2, Sect. 2.2.3.5.

[303] See Chap. 2, Sect. 2.3.2.3.

[304] See Chap. 2, Sect. 2.4.2.2.

[305] See above Sect. 3.1.2.3.

[306] See Werle and Jessberger 2020b, mn. 649.

[307] Ambos 2011a, pp 845–6, 848–9. Ambos is in favour of adopting such a set of 'hard' and 'weak' factors to adapt the theory to situations unlike those of highly organized state crimes; see ibid., p 846. See also on the role of "soft" or "weak" factors: Lanza 2021, p 247.

[308] See Kiss 2019, mn. 26, 43.

nature of direct perpetrators who are willing to implement" the organisation's instructions.[309] This equation of "soft factors" with the willingness to commit the crime criterion is not endorsed by Ambos, who regards the latter as one of the requirements from the German debate, which has not been adopted.[310] Roxin is of the opinion that the ICC has essentially adapted his, i.e., the traditional theory of indirect perpetration through an organisation.[311]

That reality is not as simple as the latter suggests, could already be seen in the decision regarding the confirmation of charges in *Katanga and Chui*. In this decision, the pre-trial chamber departed from the fungibility criterion, instead acknowledging that "[a]n *alternative* means by which a leader secures automatic compliance via his control of the apparatus may be through intensive, strict and violent training regimens".[312]

Regarding the different factors considered as potentially establishing the "automatic compliance" requirement, one can indeed see a parallel to the BGH's jurisprudence. After all, "almost automatic compliance with orders" is usually based on standardized procedures and the BGH sometimes even uses the formulation of "automatic commission of crimes".[313] To simply equate the two, however, does a disservice to the somewhat defined jurisprudence of the ICC. As laid out above, only a limited set of factors has been recognized thus far as being capable of establishing almost automatic compliance.[314] Given the very broad and unprecise German jurisprudence on standardized procedures, one should exercise caution in equating the two.

One should also be careful when equating payment mechanisms, as well as violent and strict training and disciplinary regimens ("soft" factors in Ambos' words) with Schroeder's criterion of willingness to commit the crime. The reasoning is the same: As long as the ICC applies a set of factors which can establish automatic compliance, it is not helpful to equate this with another concept, devised in another legal system with other implications. Despite this *caveat*, it is correct that Schroeder elaborated *inter alia* on the pressure exerted over members of an organisation, which is also be present in violent and strict training regimens.[315] Only time will tell whether the ICC's approach is broad enough to resemble the "readiness to commit the crime" criterion. Should the mere existence of payment mechanisms become sufficient to establish automatic control in the future, one could refer to this component of automatic

309 *Ntaganda*, 30 March 2021, Separate Opinion of Judge Luz del Carmen Ibáñez Carranza, paras 234, 280, 307, 315.

310 Ambos 2013, pp 156–7. The inclusion of readiness or willingness to act into the ICC's jurisprudence is also denied by Gil Gil and Maculan 2015, p 355 and Werle and Jessberger 2020b, p 650.

311 Roxin 2019, Chpter 12 mn. 366.

312 *Katanga and Chui*, 30 September 2008, para 518, emphasis added. The chamber's rather explicit departure from the fungibility criterion can be followed through the elaboration on the matter in paragraphs 516–8.

313 See Chap. 2, Sect. 2.3.2.1.

314 Fungibility, strict training and/or disciplinary regimens, payment mechanisms (although it remains questionable whether the existence of only the latter would suffice), see Sect. 3.1.2.3.

315 See Chap. 2, Sect. 2.2.3.5.

compliance as willingness to commit the crime. However, as long as the ICC's focus remains on the coercive, violent element of such organisations, Schroeder's criterion seems too broad to aptly describe this.[316]

Additionally, it could be said that Schünemann's requirement of "systems of violence" is mirrored by the ICC's view on violent and strict training regimens. Schlösser's psychological factors which lead to social domination in his view, can also be identified within the ICC's approach.[317] However, both would fail to describe the situation should a chamber of the ICC decide to treat payment mechanisms alone as a factor in almost automatic compliance.

As far as it is discussed by the ICC, the fungibility aspect closely resembles Roxin's original concept, as seen in the *Muthaura et al.* decision on the confirmation of charges. The chamber in this decision explains how, allegedly, the accused ensured the execution of a certain number of crimes, despite the defection of a range of perpetrators on their way to the crime scene. Fungibility was affirmed in this decision because the accused had immediately taken measures to replace them, i.e., called a coordinator to organise replacements. Consequently, the chamber affirmed the fungibility of the physical perpetrators within this organisation.[318]

It is worth highlighting that in many cases, chambers of the ICC elaborated on evidence establishing both a sufficient number of executioners (fungibility) and the strict disciplinary and training regimens of the organisations in question. In such instances, the "automatic compliance" criterion may seem narrower than German precedents due to the combination of several requirements. However, as other cases have treated this requirement much too leniently (even mostly ignoring it in *Blé Goudé*), it would be wrong to believe that it requires the cumulative fulfilment of several of the above-mentioned criteria.

All things considered, the ICC's jurisprudence is not unanimous and definitive enough to precisely compare the requirement of almost automatic compliance with orders with the precedents from German theory and practice. The ICC's criterion obviously supersedes Roxin's original proposal of fungibility alone, but it may resemble a future model in which fungibility and readiness to commit the crime present alternative mechanisms. However, this depends on the case law's further developments. As the ICC's "almost automatic compliance", is narrower than the limitless "standardized procedures" as applied by the BGH, the requirements of the two courts should not be equated in this regard.

---

[316] The current character of the "soft" factors taken into account by the ICC may more aptly be described with what Schünemann calls an "implicit threat of violence" in the German debate, see Schünemann 2006, p 412; Schünemann 2007, § 25 mn. 129.

[317] See Chap. 2, Sect. 2.2.3.7.

[318] *Muthaura et al.*, 23 January 2012, para 409.

3.2.2.5 Certainty of Success of the Envisaged Crime

As clarified in Chap. 2, the notion of certainty of success plays a crucial role for the theoretic groundwork of the traditional theory of indirect perpetration through an organisation. Supporters of the theory argue that a decision maker in an organisation can be "certain" that the instructed crimes will be committed, and that this certainty distinguishes forms of commission from accessory liability. Particularly the distinction between indirect perpetration and instigation is often explained through certainty: whilst an instigator cannot be certain that the instigated person will commit the crime, an indirect perpetrator can, especially when they have an organisation at hand.[319] Some supporters of a more systemic view also refer to the notion of certainty. However, in such an approach responsibility is attributed based on contributions to a system of wrongdoing instead of individual crimes. Therefore, certainty of success is much less important,[320] because the indirect link between the contribution and the crime is readily accepted.

In the jurisprudence of the BGH, the certainty of success does not play an important role as an underlying *ratio* of the doctrine.

The ICC's doctrine also implies that a notion of certainty of success is a relevant part of its theoretical foundation: Chambers require that the "commission of the crimes must be secured by almost automatic compliance with orders of the accused".[321]

The well-known argument from the German theory has occasionally been reiterated in literature discussing the Rome Statute. Kiss states that the certainty that the instructed crime will be committed is what distinguishes an indirect perpetrator from someone who orders a crime.[322]

If one compares Roxin's (and others') vehement insistence on this notion with the ICC's mention of a similar concept, the conclusion that certainty that the crime will be committed represents a cornerstone of the concept of control is inevitable.

Within the concept of the German traditional view, certainty of success can be identified as both a requirement and a consequence of the "official" requirements of the mode of liability. In this regard, the ICC's approach is very similar. Both theories imply that if their respective requirements are fulfilled, an order by the indirect perpetrator will almost certainly lead to the commission of crimes. In both approaches, this certainty centres around the intra-organisational automatism.

However, a difference between the two approaches can be observed concerning the terminological references.

The ICC places more emphasis on the factors that would lead the members of an organisation to comply with orders almost automatically. The traditional theory in

---

319 See Chap. 2, Sect. 2.2.3.6.

320 Ambos 2013, p 178; see already in Chap. 2, Sect. 2.4.2.1.

321 See above Sect. 3.1.2.3; see e.g. *Gaddafi et al.*, 27 June 2011, para 69; *Muthaura et al.*, 23 January 2012, para 297; *Ruto et al.*, 23 January 2012, para 292; *Ntaganda*, 9 June 2014, para 104.

322 Kiss 2019, mn. 11.

scholarly debate focusses heavily on the (intermediate) outcome, the—supposed—certainty of success. Simultaneously, such academic literature is less concerned with the details of fungibility or readiness to commit the crime. This difference in focus is a consequence of the different perspectives of theory and practice. As part of the theory, Roxin and others elaborate on the certainty of success to develop and justify the concept.[323] For the ICC in practice, the outcome—the secured commission of the crime—is less relevant than establishing and proving the factors that lead to it, i.e., the factors establishing automatic compliance with orders. This is the case, because it is the latter that constitutes the official requirements of the doctrine. These different viewpoints, however, do not imply a different opinion on the matter, which is that an indirect perpetrator can be certain that the crimes they instruct will be committed.

3.2.2.6 Summary and Preliminary Conclusion

This section has demonstrated that indirect perpetration through an organisation as applied by the ICC mirrors certain features and tendencies as known from the different versions of its German role model.

The analysis shows a certain concordance of what has been referred to as the "secret" conduct element earlier in this chapter. As analysed, the ICC's doctrine demands conduct in the form of the exercise of control over the organisation through orders. This is also inherent to Roxin's conception of the doctrine, which he visualizes as a person who "at the nerve center of the organizational structure presses the button and issues an order to kill".[324] Such a strict conduct element is logically not inherent to the systemic approach, where the actor's role in the overall system is of more relevance than their direct link to the specific crime. The triggering of standardized procedures as required by the BGH could be seen as similar to this necessary conduct element at the ICC.

Overall, indirect perpetration through an organisation is relatively close to Roxin's theory, and certainly closer than the BGH is to its scholarly role model origin. Significant differences can be found in the rejection of detachment from law and in relying on a broader set of mechanisms that supposedly lead to certainty of the crime.[325]

The ICC's version is consequently narrower than that of the BGH, both in theory and in practice. In theory, it has stricter requirements as to the organisation and the accused's power over or in it. In practice, despite decisions with a broader tendency and the prevalent role of indirect co-perpetration, the figure is also narrower as certain features concerning the mechanism to secure the commission of crimes and

[323] Note that Roxin has emphasised that certainty within the traditional theory must be seen as "inner-organisational" in the sense that potential factors from outside—resistance by third parties or the victim—do not change the domination exercised by the indirect perpetrator. This shows that, for supporters of the traditional German theory, certainty of success is strongly connected to inner-organisational procedures; see Chap. 2, Sect. 2.2.6.

[324] Roxin 2011, p 198.

[325] Also see Orozco López and Silva Santaularia 2022, p 658 for whom the ICC's approach "constitutes an autonomous thesis" and is "not particularly close" (at 667).

the individual's position in the apparatus are necessary. The systemic approach in German literature is somewhat undefined in terms of specific requirements, which makes a comparison difficult. However, some proposals from this approach can be found in the ICC's practice: Some conduct which qualifies as establishing or maintaining an organisation, but not steering its actions has been deemed sufficient by the court to establish control over an organisation.[326] On such occasions, the ICC covertly moves towards a systemic view when emphasising the importance of the accused's conduct for the overall functioning of the organisation instead of their direct influence on specific crimes.

3.2.3 The Notion of Domination/Control Over the Crime

As mentioned above, domination and control over the crime in the traditional and systemic approach, as well as under the ICC's are defined similarly to the capacity to determine whether and how a crime will be committed.[327]

The ICC defines all forms of control for the various modes of perpetration. Pursuant to jurisprudence, the indirect perpetrator

> ...controls the will of those who carry out the objective elements of the offence (commission of the crime through another person, or indirect perpetration).[328]

In the jurisprudence of the ICC, this means that the will of the physical perpetrators is subjugated or bypassed by the indirect perpetrator.[329]

This definition differs from Roxin's original description of domination in indirect perpetration. As shown in Chap. 2, Roxin's concept is not primarily about controlling the will of the immediate perpetrator. Instead, "domination by will" means that the indirect perpetrator has a way to have their will the dominant one in the context of the crime. This does not mean that the direct perpetrator's will is necessarily overridden, although this may be the case where indirect perpetration is based on coercion (i.e., the physical perpetrator is acting under duress). In theory, the ICC's notion of control is thus narrower when it expects the indirect perpetrator to exert some form of control over *the will of the immediate perpetrator*.

Occasionally, however, this difference becomes less apparent; certain decisions determine control over the will of the immediate perpetrator by stating that it would become "irrelevant" for the commission of the crime.[330] This is hardly different from the traditional German concept in which the fungibility of the immediate perpetrator

---

[326] See again the elaborations of the pre-trial chamber in *Ruto et al.*, 23 January 2012, para 318–9. The chamber states that the accused "planned, coordinated and supervised" a plan and "played a major role in the development, coordination and implementation" of it.

[327] See above Sect. 3.2.1.2.

[328] *Lubanga*, 29 January 2007, para 332; *Katanga and Chui*, 30 September 2008, para 488; *Abu Garda*, 8 February 2010, para 153.

[329] See above at Sect. 3.1.3.

[330] See above at Sect. 3.1.3.

is supposed to provide exactly that: the decision maker's independence from the will of the executioner. Considering the factors which establish almost automatic compliance at the ICC, it is conceivable that both notions of control over the will of the immediate perpetrator have their place. The executioner's will may become irrelevant because they can be replaced (fungibility), but it may also be overridden or subjugated (violent and strict indoctrination and or disciplinary regimens).

As explained in Chap. 2, the systemic approach to indirect perpetration through an organisation shifts the focus from domination over the indirect perpetrator to dominating the apparatus of power. This theory therefore recognizes a potential lack of actual, continuous dominance or control over the executioner of a crime during its commission. The notion of control over the crime in indirect perpetration as applied by the ICC does not conform to such a view.

Many decisions by ICC chambers refer explicitly to controlling the will of the direct perpetrator, be it in plain wording, or by reference to subjugating it.[331] Another aspect that is considered is the by-passing of the executioner's will. The *Ntaganda* decision describes the effect of this control by stating that the direct perpetrators functioned as tools in the hands of the decision makers.[332] This understanding has consequently found its way into scholarly literature.[333]

In apparent contrast to this, the pre-trial chamber in *Muthaura et al.* underlined how it would not be the individual perpetrators who would be controlled by the accused, but rather the organisation.[334] However, such assertions are rare and do not support a finding that the ICC's approach is, in theory, similar to the one underlying the systemic view from German literature. Likewise, the occasional reliance on an accused's organisational conduct, which does not appear to directly steer the action of the apparatus, is not sufficient proof of an increasingly systemic approach. Instead, the occasional consideration of non-directing conduct by the accused is based on two factors: the ICC's reliance on indirect co-perpetration (which lays emphasis on the contribution of co-perpetrators to a common plan) and a lack of evidence concerning a more direct involvement. It could therefore be said that, in practice, the ICC has taken certain, unconscious, or at least under-explained steps towards a notion of control in the normative sense which underlies the systemic approach.

Nevertheless, this does not represent an active, theoretically founded change of doctrine and should instead be considered the by-product of the above-mentioned practical difficulties. As such, it may be comparable to the BGH's jurisprudence regarding the members of the National Defence Council and the Political Bureau of the GDR, should one wish to follow Heine's assessment of these judgments as being

[331] See e.g. *Gbagbo*, 12 June 2014, para 230 (control over the will); *Blé Goudé*, 11 December 2014, paras 136 (will becomes irrelevant), 137 (subjugation); *Ntaganda*, 8 July 2019, paras 774, 777 (subjugation), 778 (not leaving the perpetrator at liberty to decide whether the crime is to be executed); see in detail above at Sect. 3.1.3.

[332] *Ntaganda*, 8 July 2019, para 819.

[333] Goy 2012, p 46; Gil Gil and Maculan 2015, pp 352–3; Kiss 2019, mn. 14; van Sliedregt 2015, p 507; Ventura 2019, mn. 42. See also Weigend 2015, p 555.

[334] *Muthaura et al.*, 23 January 2012, para 409.

based on systemic considerations. However, given the lack of normative considerations, control over the crime in indirect perpetration through an organisation is a factual concept at the ICC.[335] This is also in line with the traditional German concept. This can be seen in the close and necessary connection between the doctrine's requirements and the necessary domination of the physical perpetrator's will. As discussed, the ICC relies on factual requirements. Where these requirements are established, chambers deem this sufficient to establish that the indirect perpetrator could be certain of the commission of the crime, and the will of the executioners would be rendered irrelevant.

The notion of control in indirect perpetration through an organisation has occasionally been described with the term "effective control".[336] Effective control is known as the standard for superior responsibility pursuant to Article 28 Rome Statute. It is often defined as the material ability to prevent or repress the commission of crimes together with the general possibility of issuing orders to subordinates.[337] The analysis of ICC jurisprudence has shown that such a description is unfit for the model of indirect perpetration through an organisation and does not grasp the practical scope of it. This holds true even though parallels will exist in certain cases. In theory, determining "whether and how" a crime will be committed and the capability to give orders, as well as prevent and repress the commission of crimes sound like proximate abilities. However, this overlap is only partial because "effective control" does not imply the superior's "positive" capacity to instruct the commission of specific crimes. Conversely, there is a substantial difference between being able to instruct the commission of specific crimes and being capable of stopping them once they are under way. It is therefore unconvincing to equate "effective control" with the notion of control in indirect perpetration pursuant to Art. 25 (3) (a) Rome Statute. Such a conclusion is supported by neither the theory, nor practice of the ICC.[338]

It has been proposed above that control in indirect perpetration through an organisation at the ICC could be rephrased to describe the type of influence resulting from the ICC's requirements. Control over the crime would thereby lie with the person who decides whether crimes (of a certain type) will be committed by members of the organisation when following their instructions, barring the occurrence of unforeseen events.[339] Although different from the "whether and how" formula, this formulation would not signify a departure from the traditional German concept of domination of the crime as far as the obvious, far-reaching similarities between the two concepts are concerned. Instead, this alternative wording would equally describe the kind of

---

335 See also Weigend 2011, p 100.

336 Ventura 2019, mn. 42; see also the elaborations by the *Ongwen* pre-trial chamber on the requirements of responsibility for indirect perpetration, ordering and superior responsibility in *Ongwen*, 23 March 2016, p. 72–3 with paras 11–13.

337 Schabas 2016, p 614; Triffterer 2016, Art. 28, Art. 28 mn. 28.

338 Note, however, that such tight control over subordinates has indeed been demanded in academic literature, see Eser 2002, p 795.

339 See above Sect. 3.1.3.

influence postulated by Roxin's theory, as both theories are relatively close to each other.

This resemblance of the concepts of control over and domination of the crime is affirmed by another finding made above and in Chap. 2: the notion of control and domination concern the commission of specific crimes through specific perpetrators. In conjunction with the likewise similar requirements of indirect perpetration through an organisation, both doctrines fail to grasp the conduct of architects of crimes who do not take decisions which will directly lead to the commission of crimes. This is because control/domination must be exercised over the specific crime through the use of physical perpetrators who can be replaced or pressured into the commission of the crime. However, this form of control/domination only lies with persons who can influence the physical perpetrators through a direct line of instructions, not with actors who are concerned with logistical or supportive tasks. The latter cannot replace the physical perpetrators or pressure them into committing the crime. More importantly, the above analysis of cases concerning indirect perpetration through an organisation has shown that conduct which would not amount to the court's concept of direct, factual control over the crime seems to be rare. Although nominally relying on indirect co-perpetration, many cases single out charges based on direct instructions to commit crimes. Naturally, these charges cannot always be proven in the trials. However, where this is the case, the allegations usually additionally collapse at several other points, including the perpetrator's identity and the organisational structures as such.[340] On the other hand, where the accused were convicted or the charges against them were confirmed under the head of indirect (co-)perpetration, the court believed that they had issued direct instructions to commit crimes.[341]

In other words, it seems that only a few of the people who have appeared before the ICC played a highly important role but acted as high-level facilitators and organisers of crimes without also giving direct instructions to commit such crimes. The Eichmann-type of architect of crime with extremely important, facilitating roles,

---

[340] See *Gbagbo and Blé Goudé*, 16 July 2019, paras 1925–8 (lack of command structures for the alleged control over a hierarchical organisation), 1935 (lack of evidence for the physical perpetrators belonging to the alleged organisation); *Katanga*, 7 March 2014, 1419–21 (lack of organised and hierarchical apparatus of power).

[341] See the conviction of Bosco Ntaganda: *Ntaganda*, 8 July 2019, paras 840 ("Mr Ntaganda gave the final order for the troops to advance to Mongbwalu; it was Mr Ntaganda's order which set off the assault by the UPC/FPLC soldiers"; footnotes omitted), 842 ("Mr Ntaganda was the overall commander of the assault on Mongbwalu: he gave orders to the UPC/FPLC troops who participated in this operation and these troops reported directly to him", footnotes omitted), see further paras 843, 845, 846 ("exercised oversight over the unfolding" operation), paras 847 with headline "Mr. Ntaganda gave orders to commit crimes and personally engaged in violent conduct towards enemies". See also the confirmation of charges against Dominic Ongwen: *Ongwen*, 23 March 2016, paras 67 ("Dominic Ongwen led the group of LRA fighters…"), 68, 73 ("Dominic Ongwen briefed and instructed the troops before the attack."), 78 ("To execute the attack, Dominic Ongwen issued orders to the LRA units under his command at the time … His instructions to the fighters were to attack and kill indiscriminately everyone…"), 83 ("While he did not directly participate in the attack on the ground, Dominic Ongwen had overall command of the attack, and ensured that his orders were transmitted and obeyed by appointing a leader on the ground.").

seem to be less common in mass atrocities that are committed through less industrialized mechanisms than the Holocaust. Additionally, the ICC has devised the doctrine of indirect co-perpetration that potentially addresses such contributions which do not directly steer the physical perpetrators into action.

3.2.4 A Hierarchy of Blameworthiness as the Consequence of Control Over the Crime

All four approaches to indirect perpetration are described as "normative".[342] This refers to two separate, albeit connected, aspects.

The first concerns the distinction between forms of perpetration and participation. Given the existence of indirect perpetration, it is often alleged that the underlying system must be normative as opposed to naturalistic or empirical. As there is no "natural" way to act through another person, no "natural" pulling of strings or directing another, an objective or natural distinction between, for example, indirect perpetration and instigation is often deemed impossible. The distinction must therefore be made by evaluating the facts based on certain principles, rather than naturalistic relations of cause and consequence.[343]

The second aspect of this differentiation is closely connected to the first and is found with equal frequency in theory and jurisprudence: the normative distinction criterion. Whether its domination, control or the vague "overall assessment" as applied by the BGH; this criterion carries a consequence in terms of blameworthiness. This means that if perpetration is affirmed based on a form of domination or control over the crime, or on the BGH's "overall assessment", the criminal responsibility of the perpetrator is automatically higher than that of an accessory.[344] An exception can only be found in a few decisions of the ICC and certain separate opinions.[345]

However, the four approaches stem from two legal regimes in which forms of liability either have no, or only a limited influence on sentencing. German criminal law knows no mitigation of sentencing for the instigator (if the instigation itself is successful) and the Rome Statute does not envisage a connection between modes of liability and sentencing at all.[346]

German academic literature and jurisprudence heavily rely on a vague notion of "suitability" or "appropriateness" to justify the normative view of perpetration and

---

342 See above Sect. 3.1.3. for control over the crime at the ICC, see Chap. 2, Sects. 2.2.4 and 2.4.2.1.

343 Van Sliedregt 2015, p 508; see Chap. 2, Sect. 2.2.2.

344 See for the German theories Chap. 2, Sect. 2.5. See concerning the ICC ibid., p 508.

345 See above at Sect. 3.1.4.

346 See on the equal punishment of instigators in German law, Chap. 2, Sect. 2.2.5. For the Rome Statute, it is contentious whether Rule 145 RPE establishes a connection between the form of responsibility and the sentencing length. It is submitted here that no such connection exists. See in the same vein: Gil Gil and Maculan 2015, p 362; van Sliedregt 2012, p 85. The topic of a hierarchy in the Rome Statute and the relation between liability and sentencing is treated in more length in Chap. 7, Sects. 7.2.2. and 7.2.3.

participation inherent to the doctrine of domination of the crime.[347] On an international scale, jurisprudence and academia seem to have subsumed this vague feeling under the principle of fair labelling. To label the persons most responsible for international crimes as "perpetrators" is deemed to have expressive value because it underlines their heightened responsibility.[348] Thus, whilst the call for this expressive, labelling function exits but is rarely explicitly put into words in the German debate, it is not only present but also denominated in clear vocabulary in the international sphere.

3.2.5 Conclusion

In contrast to the German legal system, the Rome Statute clearly rejects the autonomy principle as a possible rule to distinguish between indirect perpetration and instigation by expressly recognizing the perpetrator behind the perpetrator.

The underlying notion of control over the crime which is embodied in ICC jurisprudence is also similar to the traditional concept.

The BGH's vast and shapeless approach to the issue is not mirrored by the ICC's version of the theory so far.[349]

From a comparative viewpoint, the ICC's model bears the most resemblance to the traditional German model as described by Roxin and Schroeder.[350] The court does not rely on considerations of systemic responsibility for organisational wrong in its theoretic foundation. In its concept of control over the crime, it clearly utilises the opposite view;[351] factual control over the specific crime through the organisation's automatism, potentially exercised on all levels of the organisation.[352]

However, considerable differences between the ICC's and the traditional German approaches have also been identified. Therefore, the ICC's approach does not

[347] See Chap. 2, Sect. 2.5.

[348] Van Sliedregt 2012, p 81; van Sliedregt 2015, pp 510–1; Weigend 2015, p 552; Werle and Jessberger 2020b, p 616; in this vein also Jessberger and Geneuss 2008, p 866; Ohlin et al. 2013, p 745.

[349] One could argue that the ICC's common reliance on the mode of indirect co-perpetration leads to an ever-broader notion of perpetration. This is backed by the latter figure's resemblance to the *ad hoc* tribunals' JCE doctrine (as recognized by van Sliedregt and Yanev 2019, mn. 59–61). For criticism on the doctrine of JCE, see Chap. 5, Sect. 5.2.4.

[350] See contra Werle and Jessberger 2020b, mn. 649.

[351] In the same vein: Werle and Jessberger 2020a, mn. 623 (note that this statement is omitted in the English version of the textbook).

[352] This is despite Ambos' correct analysis that by adopting certain new requirements, such as the broader "automatic compliance", the ICC adapts the theory to the less bureaucratic organisations of asymmetrical armed conflicts (see Ambos 2011a, pp 846) and that such organisations would equally qualify as systems of wrongdoing within a systemic approach (see ibid., p 847).

resemble the traditional German concept closely. Instead, it broadens and modifies it, and claims of a direct "import" of "the" theory into international criminal law should be read with caution.[353]

3.3 Critical Analysis

International and German literature have produced numerous points of criticism on the doctrine, some of which will be discussed here in detail. The proximity of the ICC's concept to the traditional German model enables the import of certain arguments against this doctrine. Other points from the German debate are without relevance in the ambit of international criminal law and have no place in this book.[354] This section combines certain points of criticism from both the international and German national debate on the issue without aiming to reproduce the debate in all aspects.

3.3.1 The Conception of the Doctrine

The conception of the theories of control over the crime and indirect perpetration through an organisation are subject to ongoing criticism. This criticism concerns the textual interpretation and underlying wording of Art. 25 (3) Rome Statute (Sect. 3.3.1.1), the recognition of the doctrine in national legal systems (Sect. 3.3.1.2) and the teleological argument, which seemingly serves as the ICC's main motivator for relying on the theory (Sect. 3.3.1.3).[355]

3.3.1.1 The Wording of Art. 25 (3) (a) Rome Statute

The wording of Art. 25 (3) (a) is perhaps the most obvious point of attack. The article establishes that a person shall be criminally liable for a crime under the court's

---

[353] See ibid., p 838.

[354] See above on the rejection of the autonomy principle through Art. 25 (3) (a) Rome Statute at Sect. 3.1.2.

[355] The *travaux préparatoires* of the article do not yield any preference of the preparatory commission for the control over the crime approach (Yanev 2018, pp 477–83). Saland does not mention the question of the system of perpetration and participation as a crucial point of debate during the preparatory sessions, although he recalls that delegations showed little understanding of the concepts of legal systems other than their own, see Saland 1999, p 198–200. Given that no consensus of the delegates on how to interpret Art. 25 (3) Rome Statute can be produced and in light of the obvious competition between systems and ideas during the preparatory stages, the drafting history must be considered futile for its interpretation and will not be followed any further.

jurisdiction if he or she "[c]ommits such a crime, whether as an individual, jointly with another or through another person..."

It can therefore be criticised that the ICC's doctrine equates "acting through another" with "acting through an organisation".[356] In this regard, Weigend stresses that acting through a responsible tool must not necessarily include acting through an organisation.[357] Judge Christine Van den Wyngaert even takes the stance that acting through an organisation is incompatible with the term of acting through another. She points out that, despite organisations being made up of people, the interaction among people is fundamentally different to the exercise of authority over a branch of an organisation.[358] Judges Eboe-Osuji and Morrison share this concern. Eboe-Osuji states that the Rome Statute simply does not contain a word or phrase that reads "indirect co-perpetration". The doctrine would consequently be an analogy contrary to the legality principle.[359] Judge Morrison adds that such an understanding of Art. 25 (3) (a) Rome Statute is not possible through principles of statutory interpretation in accordance with Art. 21 of the Statute.[360]

Somewhat contrary to Judge Van den Wyngaert's view, Steer has pointed out that the statute already quite explicitly recognises the perpetrator behind the perpetrator. In her opinion, it is therefore "not unthinkable" to go a step further and include the commission through an organisation.[361]

It has also been submitted that one could accept that an indirect perpetrator in such cases acts through "other persons", i.e., through the members of the apparatus.[362]

Chambers of the ICC have stressed that the perpetrator acts through the organisation, although it is seemingly difficult to read this interpretation into Art. 25 (3) (a) Rome Statute.[363] However, the analysis above illustrates that the notion of control over the crime in indirect perpetration through an organisation relies on a concept of control over the individual perpetrator through the organisation's mechanisms.[364] When considered from this perspective, it seems less problematic to read the figure

[356] *Chui*, 18 December 2012, Concurring Opinion of Judge Christine Van den Wyngaert, paras 52, 57; van Sliedregt and Yanev 2019, mn. 66.

[357] Weigend 2015, p 550. In a similar vein see van Sliedregt and Weisser 2022, p 634.

[358] *Chui*, 18 December 2012, Concurring Opinion of Judge Christine Van den Wyngaert, para 52–4. Note that Judge Van den Wyngaert places a lot of emphasis on the necessity of the indirect perpetrator subjugating the will of the direct perpetrator in this mode of liability. She admits that organisational features could serve as evidence in establishing whether a person would "dominate the will of certain individuals" within the organisation (at para 55). In partial agreement, see Steer 2017, p 305.

[359] *Ntaganda*, 30 March 2021, Partly concurring opinion of Judge Chile Eboe-Osuji, paras 16, 66.

[360] See ibid., Separate opinion of Judge Howard Morrison on Mr. Ntaganda's appeal, para 12–3.

[361] Steer 2017, p 303.

[362] Ohlin et al. 2013, pp 737–8; van Sliedregt 2015, p 514; see also with reference to the German debate Weisser 2019, p 250. But see *Chui*, 18 December 2012, Concurring Opinion of Christine Van den Wyngaert, para 53, taking the view that there is a difference between personal influence exercised over persons and the exercise of abstract authority within an organisational entity.

[363] *Muthaura et al.*, 23 January 2012, para 409.

[364] See above at Sect. 3.1.3.

into the term "commission through another". In the view of the ICC, this is still what happens, albeit facilitated through the organisation.[365]

It has been suggested that interpreting Art. 25 (3) (a) as being based on the "control theory" would expand the scope of commission liability and through this violate the principle of legality.[366] However, it must be kept in mind that Art. 25 (3) (a) Rome Statute only speaks of committing a crime "through another". This wording neither contains an express statement on how the physical perpetrator can or must be influenced by the indirect perpetrator nor the reason why no direct contact between the participants is required. Therefore, the interpretation does not violate the legality principle.[367]

Chambers of the ICC have justified their choice of the control theory by ruling out other possible theories for the interpretation of Art. 25 (3) Rome Statute. These were referred to as the objective and the subjective approach.[368] Beginning with the wording of *lit.* (a), which allows perpetration "through another", chambers ruled out the objective approach.[369] The subjective one was dismissed with the reasoning that it was tantamount to the use of JCE and contributions to a group crime were clearly only provided for in *lit.* (d), but not at the beginning of Art. 25 (3). From this, the chambers inferred that no subjective approach will prevail in the interpretation of Art. 25 (3).[370] This approach to eliminating other theories of perpetration and participation has been criticised as a very selective choice of arguments. In the view of Noto, the existence of the wording "commission through another" does not rule out a material objective approach. He questions why the chamber only hints at the drawbacks of the subjective and objective approaches, whilst not mentioning the deficiencies of the control theory.[371] Yanev criticises that the wording of the statute (concerning co-perpetration and the assumption of the underlying control theory) was interpreted without sufficient regard to the solutions proposed in international jurisprudence. Instead, such precedents were discarded in favour of recurring to a feeble basis of national and international jurisprudence.[372] This leads to the issue of international recognition of indirect perpetration through an organisation and the control theory.

---

365 When viewed in this way, it could be argued that the ICC does what was proposed by van Sliedregt and Yanev, i.e. that the ICC should rely on organisations as evidence to prove the acting through another person (see van Sliedregt and Yanev 2019, mn. 66). However, as outlined above, it is also true that at times chambers of the ICC refer to the organisation as the actual tool. As long as this incongruity between the reasoning in indirect perpetration through an organisation and the underlying notion of control exist, this question cannot be answered satisfactorily.

366 Gil Gil and Maculan 2015, pp 357, 369; see with reference to the combined mode of indirect co-perpetration: *Chui*, 18 December 2012, Concurring Opinion of Judge Christine Van den Wyngaert, para 64.

367 Weigend 2015, p 551.

368 *Lubanga*, 29 January 2007, paras 327–30.

369 Ibid., paras 328, 333; *Katanga and Chui*, 30 September 2008, para 482.

370 *Lubanga*, 29 January 2007, para 334; *Katanga and Chui*, 30 September 2008, para 483.

371 Noto 2013, pp 165–6.

372 Yanev 2018, pp 483–96.

3.3.1.2 Recognition in Other Legal Systems and Reliance on Such Systems for the Interpretation of the Rome Statute

The recognition of "the" doctrine of indirect perpetration through an organisation in different national legal systems, as well as what implications this has for its application by the ICC are heavily disputed.[373]

Some chambers, judges and scholars affirm a wide-spread acknowledgment of the doctrine in national legal systems.[374] Judge del Carmen Ibáñez Carranza elaborated on the use of the doctrine in several Latin-American legal systems.[375] Kiss has pointed out, that the doctrine is the only one recognised among multiple legal systems.[376]

The latter assertion may or may not be true.[377] Regardless, it does not change the fact that the number of national legal systems, which recognize *a* model of indirect perpetration through an organisation, is limited. The ICC's chambers was able to cite five jurisdictions in which the doctrine had been applied. This included Argentina, in which the relevant decision had later been overturned by a higher court.[378] Additionally, it has been alleged that some of the Spanish judgments quoted in the confirmation decision in *Katanga and Chui* did not rely entirely on the doctrine.[379] The former *ad hoc* tribunals judge Wolfgang Schomburg declared that the doctrine of "control over the act" would be "predominantly accepted on a global level".[380] In the accompanying footnote, Schomburg refers to a study of the German *Max-Planck-Institut* for

---

[373] The *Lubanga* pre-trial chamber did not explicitly hint at national jurisdictions or customary international law as sources of law in their decisions establishing the control theory. Instead, it explicitly pointed to its interpretation of the Text of Art. 25 (3) Rome Statute, see in this regard ibid., p 461. However, the explanations of the chamber in *Katanga and Chui* reads very differently, when it states that the two reasons to establish the doctrine besides the supposed textual interpretation were that the doctrine "has been increasingly used in national jurisdictions" and "has been addressed in the jurisprudence of the international tribunals" (*Katanga and Chui*, 30 September 2008, para 500).

[374] For jurisprudence see *Katanga and Chui*, 30 September 2008, para 485 (control theory), but see also 495-9, where the concept of indirect perpetration through an organisation is credited solely to Roxin; see also *Katanga*, 7 March 2014, para 1395 (rejecting the relevance of the wide spread recognition for ICC law); *Lubanga*, 1 December 2014, para 470; Ambos 2018, § 7 mn. 25; Kiss 2019, mn. 48. For a detailed analysis of the use of national legal doctrine as interpretational guidance for Art. 25 (3) Rome Statute see: Weisser 2022, pp 393–6.

[375] *Ntaganda*, 30 March 2021, Separate Opinion of Judge Luz del Carmen Ibáñez Carranza, paras 240-3, 257–60.

[376] Kiss 2019, mn. 49.

[377] Note, for example, that many European legal systems do not recognize the doctrine, due to their different systems of perpetration and participation in which no need for such a doctrine arises. See Weisser 2011, pp 296-299. See also van Sliedregt and Weisser 2022, p 630. Additionally, Osten points out that the doctrine is not recognized in Japan: Osten 2022, p 685.

[378] Weigend 2015, pp 550-1; see also Gil Gil and Maculan 2015, p 354; Ohlin 2015, p 523 (calling the alleged wide recognition a "vast exaggeration"); van Sliedregt 2015, p 507.

[379] Gil Gil and Maculan 2015, p 355 with fn. 28.

[380] See ICTY, *Prosecutor v. Fatmir Limaj, Haradin Bala, Isak Musliu*, Appeals Judgment, 27 September 2007, IT-03-66-A, Partially Dissenting and Separate Opinion and Declaration of Judge Schomburg, para 11, see also fn. 13.

foreign and international criminal law. The study, which was commissioned by the ICTY, ascertains the criminal liability of leaders of criminal groups and networks. It confirms that leaders of criminal groups and networks are usually considered the "primarily responsible offender". Concerning the legal technicalities behind this finding, it states that "structurally differing concepts of the doctrine of complicity yield results that are, to a large extent, functionally equivalent". The summary of the findings determines that:

> [v]arying concepts of complicity may indeed lead to different solutions at the offense level; however, they are consistent in the relative weighting of characteristic contributions to the offense.[381]

Therefore, the study revealed that national legal systems agree that a leader of a criminal group usually bears the most responsibility for the crimes. However, they do not agree on how this result is achieved in terms of legal requirements and concepts on the attribution level. In other words, national legal systems seemingly differ in their solution of the problem just as much as approaches in international criminal law differ. An international preference or universal recognition of the concept of control over the crime was not confirmed by the study.

Following doubts over the actual application in certain legal systems, it has been criticised that the doctrine merely represents a one-sided import of German criminal law doctrine.[382] It has been pointed out that the legal systems of Spanish speaking countries that apply the theory largely rely on the German doctrine. This calls the doctrine's suitability to inform international criminal law into question.[383] Consequently, it could be argued that only one country's doctrine lies at the heart of the theory as devised by the ICC: the German doctrine.[384]

This criticism can be supplemented with earlier observations. As discussed in Chap. 2, the German legal system does not recognize the doctrine unanimously. Three approaches have been identified, with other theories on how to deal with desk perpetrators existing in scholarly literature.[385] Thus, it would not be correct to refer

---

[381] See the summary of the studies at https://csl.mpg.de/en/research/projects/general-legal-principles-of-international-criminal-law-on-the-criminal-liability-of-leaders-of-criminal-groups-and-netwo/ (last accessed on 25 May 2021).

[382] Rastan 2009, p 267; van Sliedregt and Weisser 2022, p 630; *Lubanga*, 14 March 2012, Separate Opinion of Judge Adrian Fulford, para 10.

[383] van Sliedregt 2015, p 507; van Sliedregt and Yanev 2019, mn. 69. See also the criticism in *Chui*, 18 December 2012, Concurring Opinion of Judge Van den Wyngaert, paras 5, 17. Also see Steer 2017, p 304. But see Weisser 2022, p 395, who advocates looking for solutions in customary international criminal law nevertheless.

[384] Ohlin 2015, p 517; van Sliedregt 2015, p 507. This was the impression of Judge Adrian Fulford (see *Lubanga*, 14 March 2012, Separate Opinion of Judge Adrian Fulford, para 10) and Judge Christine Van den Wyngaert (see *Chui*, 18 December 2012, Concurring Opinion of Judge Christine Van den Wyngaert, paras 5, 17, 50) as well. The latter criticised the reliance on German doctrine especially with a view to the "universalist mission" of the ICC.

[385] These approaches encompass joint-perpetration or instigation as the modes of choice for leaders behind large scale crimes. In favour of joint perpetration, see mainly Frister 2018, § 27 mn. 40; Jakobs 1983, Section 21 mn. 60, 103; Jakobs 1995, pp 26–7; Jescheck and Weigend 1996, p 670. In

to "the" doctrine in the German legal system. This holds true, especially in light of the differences examined in Chap. 2, as well as the fact that the general approach (indirect perpetration through an organisation) is not unanimously recognized in Germany.[386] When developing the theories of control over the crime and the modes of liability connected to them, the practice of individual chambers of the ICC is therefore selective and partial and does not ascertain whether these sources are representative for their respective legal system.[387] It must also be kept in mind that any import of the doctrine, which simultaneously relies on scholarly literature and German jurisprudence inevitably considers two different, partially incompatible theories.[388]

Finally, it is questionable whether adopting national doctrines is a wise approach at all, irrespective of their general acceptance. It could be unreasonable to consider national legal approaches when exploring responsibility for universally recognized crimes.[389]

Moreover, even if one should adopt the view that a considerable number of legal systems recognize one doctrine of indirect perpetration through an organisation, this still raises the question of why these legal systems should guide the interpretation of the Rome Statute.

The application of national criminal law doctrine to the interpretation of the statute is based on Article 21 (1) (c) (general principles of law derived from national laws). Considering the above, it is however highly dubious whether the rules applied by the ICC in this regard could qualify as such general principles.[390]

---

favour of applying instigation Herzberg 2000, p 48 et seq.; Herzberg 2009, p 579; Hruschka 1998, p 606; Noltenius 2003, p 322; Renzikowski 1997, p 91; Rotsch 2000, pp 561–2; Zazcyk 1996, p 414.

[386] See only Roxin and his confrontation with criticism in Roxin 2019, Chpter 12 mn. 378 et seq.; cf. the list of criticisms in Heine and Weisser 2019, § 25 mn. 28. See also Gil Gil and Maculan 2015, p 354, criticising the selective choice of sources by chambers of the ICC which, in their view, leads to a misinterpretation of the degree of acceptance of the imported theories; but see *Ntaganda*, 30 March 2021, Separate Opinion of Judge Luz del Carmen Ibáñez Carranza, paras 240 et seq. reproducing such a selective choice of sources.

[387] Gil Gil and Maculan 2015, p 356; Weigend 2011, p 105.

[388] See Chap. 2, Sect. 2.5. German academic literature relies on the domination of the crime approach, whilst the jurisprudence has always recognized a subjective approach and nowadays oscillates between subjective and vague "overall evaluative" criteria. This fact is not always recognized in international criminal law literature, see e.g. Ohlin 2015, p 521 stating that "Roxin's theory moved from academic theory to doctrinal reality" (footnote omitted).

[389] See Stewart 2014, p 320 et seq., especially 330–1; 334–5. Contrary to this see *Ntaganda*, 30 March 2021, Separate Opinion of Judge Luz del Carmen Ibáñez Carranza, paras 240–3, 257 relying explicitly on the treatment of the doctrine in a few Latin-American systems to refine the theory in use at the ICC.

[390] *Chui*, 18 December 2012, Concurring Opinion of Judge Christine Van den Wyngaert, para 17 (with a view of the control theory as a general principle of law); Gil Gil and Maculan 2015, p 355, also raise this doubt concerning the court affirming co-perpetration for contributions in the preparatory stage. But see on methodology applied by the ICC: Weisser 2022, pp 394–5.

Instead, Article 21 (1) (b), which refers to international practice and custom could serve as a basis to adopt a theory, which would have to be derived from customary international law.[391]

However, as of now, there is no general theory on perpetration and participation in customary international criminal law that could qualify under Article 21 (1) (b) of the Rome Statute.[392] The pre-trial chamber in *Katanga and Chui* hinted at examples of the control theory and indirect perpetration through an organisation in ICTY jurisprudence.[393] These instances, however, are limited to a separate opinion and a trial chamber judgment, which were both authored by German ICTY Judge Wolfgang Schomburg.[394] The appeals chamber later reversed the findings of the trial chamber in *Stakić* and applied the doctrine of JCE instead of indirect perpetration through an organisation.[395]

In connection with such observations regarding the majority and minority opinions in international judgments, the suspicion has been raised that the higher number of civil law jurisdiction judges in certain ICC decisions favoured the adoption of the control theory because it is derived from a civil law tradition.[396]

It has also been asserted that the doctrine was applied by the district court of Jerusalem in the *Eichmann* trial.[397] However, the judgment against Adolf Eichmann does not rely on the requirements or concepts of either the doctrine of indirect perpetration through an organisation or the control theory. It is correct that, in convicting Eichmann as a perpetrator of the crimes, the court was driven by his crucial role and the magnitude of the crimes that he facilitated.[398] However, the judgment does not discuss or even identify requirements that resemble the later doctrines of indirect

[391] deGuzman 2016, Art. 21, Art. 21 mn. 23–4; Schabas 2016, pp 519–23.

[392] See only Kiss 2019, mn. 45; Ohlin 2015, p 524; van Sliedregt and Yanev 2019, mn. 69; Yanev 2018, p 485 (with further sources in fn. 96 and 97), 492, who all deny the status of customary international law to the control theory or indirect perpetration through an organisation.

[393] See *Katanga and Chui*, 30 September 2008, para 506 with fn. 672.

[394] ICTY, *Prosecutor v. Milomir Stakić*, 31 July 2003, IT-97-24-T, paras 439 et seq.; ICTR, *Sylvestre Gacumbitsi v. The Prosecutor*, 7 July 2006, ICTR-2001-64-A, Separate Opinion of Judge Schomburg on the criminal responsibility of the appellant for committing genocide, paras 14–22; van Sliedregt and Yanev 2019, mn. 9. As Yanev points out, Judge Schomburg later authored several further separate opinions in the same vein in the appeals judgments of *Limaj et al, Martić* and *Simić*, see Yanev 2018, p 486.

[395] ICTY, *Prosecutor v. Milomir Stakić*, 22 March 2006, IT-97-24-A, paras 58–63; note that neither prosecution nor defence had appealed the trial judgment based on the notion of commission that was used in it, but the appeals chamber saw it necessary to "remedy this error" (para 63) anyways. See also already the criticism by Judge Adrian Fulford in *Lubanga*, 14 March 2012, Separate Opinion of Judge Adrian Fulford, para 10. See also Steer 2017, p 304. Ohlin points out that judgments of international tribunals do not establish customary international law because they do not constitute state practice, see Ohlin 2015, pp 524–5.

[396] Steer 2017, pp 304–5; see also Christensen and Orina 2022, p 714.

[397] Ambos 2018, § 7 mn. 25.

[398] See the court's statement on its application of a label of "perpetration" on Eichmann in District Court of Jerusalem, *Judgment Against Karl Adolf Eichmann—Unofficial Translation*, 40/61, at No. 197.

perpetration through an organisation. Therefore, it does not represent an early application of the doctrine of indirect perpetration through an organisation. Instead, it "only" embodies one early, top-down approach to properly displaying the responsibility of an architect of a crime.[399]

In Ambos' view, the *Justice* case, in which lawyers working for Nazi Germany were tried for their involvement in the regime's juridical terror, mirrors the doctrine of perpetration through an organisation to some degree.[400] In a similar vein, Clark asserts that the control theory can be found in the *RuSHA* judgment because the tribunal tested whether the accused had "decisive" or "integral" roles in the Nazi state branches in which they worked.[401] This, however, cannot be sustained. The convictions of former Nazi judges, prosecutors, and officials in the *RuSHA* case were based on a broad notion of participation in an overall endeavour, but the judgments neither rely on a legal concept of control, nor on the requirements discussed in any of the theories of perpetration through an organisation. Instead, they describe the factual behaviour of the accused without construing a legal doctrine around it.[402] Identifying an application of indirect perpetration through an organisation or of the control theory in these judgments would therefore be an over-interpretation.[403]

The doctrine has now been applied consistently by the ICC.[404] However, this cannot serve as an argument in its favour. Consistency in the court's own jurisprudence does not—logically—indicate any prior international custom or practice from which the theory could be derived.[405] The appeals chamber elaborated on the doctrine of control over the crime in the *Lubanga* appeal and underlined that the interpretation would not be primarily guided by international or national legal precedents, but rather by an interpretation of the text of the Rome Statute.[406] Its findings on the text

[399] The application of the doctrine by the Jerusalem district court is also rejected by Kress 2006, p 306. Kress defines the approach of the district court as being shaped by joint perpetration of the overall criminal situation (*Gesamttat*).

[400] Ambos 2018, § 7 mn. 25. The *Justice* case saw charges and convictions of former Nazi judges, prosecutors and officials of the ministry of justice of Nazi Germany, see Trials of War Criminals Before the Nuernberg Military Tribunals Under Control Council Law No. 10, Vol. III, U.S. Government Printing Service 1950.

[401] Clark 2015, p 466. The *RuSHA* case concerned the charges against former officials of the Nazi's SS Race and Settlement Main Office (*Rasse- und Siedlungshauptamt, RuSHA*), see Trials of War Criminals Before the Nuernberg Military Tribunals Under Control Council Law No. 10, Vol. IV, U.S. Government Printing Service 1950.

[402] Yanev 2018, pp 487–9 who also hints at the fact that the tribunals described the accused's contributions as "active" and "energetic" as well.

[403] In this vein also Kress 2006, p 306 with fn. 18; Yanev 2018, pp 487–9. See also Chap. 4, Sects. 4.3.2. and 4.3.3.

[404] To avoid misunderstandings: This means the doctrine in its specific form at the ICC as analysed and discussed in the first section of Sect. 3.1.2 above.

[405] In the same vein: Steer 2017, p 306, criticising that the judicial and scholarly repetition renders the question of any customary law status redundant. But see apparently in a different vein Kiss 2019, mn. 5, 59, who emphasises the repeated affirmation of the theory by the court itself.

[406] *Lubanga*, 1 December 2014, para 470.

of Art. 25 (3) (a) Rome Statute have been discussed above.[407] There is nothing to be said against ruling out certain interpretations of the statute by explaining their incompatibility with it. However, the adoption of the notion of control over the crime and indirect perpetration through an organisation is neither the only, nor a compulsory conclusion of ruling out the two other approaches. The decision pertaining to the control over the crime theory must therefore actively be drawn from one (or a few) legal tradition(s),[408] and from one in which the doctrine does not stand unchallenged.

The process through which the control theory and indirect perpetration through an organisation found their way into ICC jurisprudence has been evaluated differently.[409] It has been suggested that the court should only rely on the theory if it was to construct a *Dogmatik* best mirroring the wording of Art. 25 (3) (a) Rome Statute.[410] In the words of Judge Adrian Fulford, "…a chamber should undertake a careful assessment as to whether the policy considerations underlying domestic legal doctrine are applicable at this Court, and it should investigate the doctrine's compatibility with the Rome Statute framework."[411] Whether this has been done by the ICC so far is questionable.

3.3.1.3 Circular Teleological Argument

The pre-trial chamber in *Katanga and Chui* justified its decision to read indirect perpetration and the control theory into the statute, hinting at the court's mission and the typical nature of the crimes. This appears to be the or one of the reasons why the court interprets Art. 25 (3) (a) the way it does:

> The most important reason for this Chamber's deciding for this mode of liability is that it has been incorporated into the framework of the Statute. The crimes falling within the jurisdiction of this Court—those of "the most serious [...] concern to the international community as a whole", and which "threaten the peace, security, and well-being of the world"—will almost inevitably concern collective or mass criminality. The chamber finds that by specifically regulating the commission of the crime through another responsible person, the Statute targets the category of cases which involves a perpetrator's control over the organisation.[412]

This statement is valid as far as it implies that the mode of indirect perpetration can be perceived as being incorporated into the statute to tackle leadership criminality. The wording has been discussed above, but the underlying possible interpretation of the wording of Art. 25 (3) (a) does not appear to be the driving force behind this paragraph.

---

[407] See above Sect. 3.1.2.

[408] See also Steer 2017, p 305.

[409] Ibid., p 303 speaks of a patchworking process; see also Aksenova 2016, p 149 who suspects that a thorough analysis of arguments against the doctrine would have led the court to reject it.

[410] Gil Gil and Maculan 2015, p 356.

[411] *Lubanga*, 14 March 2012, Separate Opinion of Judge Adrian Fulford, para 10.

[412] *Katanga and Chui*, 30 September 2008, para 501, footnotes omitted.

Instead, the Rome Statute's purpose and target of high-level participants in international crimes can validly be construed as the actual reason behind the doctrine's application.

Considering this and notwithstanding other potential (doctrinal) reasons for the theory's conception, the driving motive behind its adaptation could be rephrased as: this interpretation of the Rome Statute is due to the fact that an effective adjudication of persons involved in high-level leadership criminality is presumably enabled as a consequence. This has been aptly described as a policy choice considering that other statutory interpretations may be possible as well.[413] Despite the mass atrocities at hand, the application of the control theory with its hierarchy of blameworthiness, as well as indirect perpetration through an organisation, is not a logical consequence. Another system of perpetration and participation could also provide for the adjudication of the most responsible participants in international crimes and simply apply other forms of liability to do so.[414]

The reasoning on which the chamber relies can thus be described as "putting the cart before the horse".[415] Interestingly, the same allegation has been raised against the implementation of the Joint Criminal Enterprise (JCE) doctrine by the ICTY. When implementing this latter doctrine, the ICTY appeals chamber equally used the purpose of the tribunal to adjudicate all those who were involved in the mass atrocities in the former Yugoslavia as an argument.[416] In both cases, the same criticism thus applies: the purpose and statute of a criminal tribunal do not predefine the way in which people can be found responsible for crimes under it.

This finding regarding one of the apparent motives behind its implementation must be kept in mind when assessing the ICC's doctrine. A policy choice, driven by the goals of the court, is no compelling starting point for such a doctrine.

3.3.2 *On Indirect Perpetration Through an Organisation*

The doctrine of indirect perpetration through an organisation can be criticised from different angles, as has been done in the international and German national debate.

---

413 Steer 2017, p 307. See also the analysis of the role of professional ICC staff by Christensen and Orina 2022, p 707, 715. Whether any feature of Art. 25 (3) Rome Statute compels an interpretation in the way which is proposed by the ICC is discussed in Chap. 7, Sects. 7.2.2. and 7.2.3.

414 Steer 2017, p 307; van Sliedregt and Yanev 2019, mn. 66; Weigend 2011, p 106.

415 van Sliedregt and Yanev 2019, mn. 66.

416 ICTY, *Prosecutor v. Duško Tadić*, 15 July 1999, IT-94-1-A, paras 189–90; the reasoning applied there is criticized by Ohlin 2007, p 72. For details on JCE see Chap. 5, Sect. 5.2.

3.3.2.1 The Organised Apparatus of Power

The organised apparatus of power, or organised structure of power[417] is the centrepiece of the doctrine. Regardless of the differences between the three German approaches and the one developed at the ICC an organisation must exist for an indirect perpetrator to act "through" it.

However, the very necessity of this requirement has been criticised both in the international and the German national debate.

Broadness of the Terminology

The broadness of the terminology applied to characterize the basis of the doctrine—organisation, organised apparatus or power structure—can and has been criticised.

Ascertaining whether an organised power structure exists, may prove more difficult than one would expect. Based on the original theory, judges would have to rely on facts such as an organisation's number of members, period of existence and size and scope.[418] However, the threshold established by the traditional German version of the theory is completely obscure in this regard. It is obvious that the machinery of Nazi Germany was the stereotype example behind the concept. However, Roxin asserted early on that different kinds of organisations, including criminal gangs, the Mafia and (recently) terrorist organisations would also be encompassed by it.[419] In practice, the state apparatus of the former German Democratic Republic has been regarded as such an organisation by the BGH.[420] The same holds true for the *Grupo Colina*: a 30-members death squad, instructed by former Peruvian president Alberto Fujimori, which was responsible for 23 murders.[421] Notwithstanding the horrible crimes committed by its members, it can be suggested that *Grupo Colina* was negligibly small in comparison to Nazi Germany.[422]

The same applies before the ICC: strictly necessary numbers, levels of hierarchy, organisational structures and procedures have never been identified despite the vast amount of case material from which one could draw such conclusions. In the pre-trial stage of the case against *Abdallah Banda and Jerbo*, one of the defendants was accused as an indirect co-perpetrator (suggesting his contribution to the common plan through his own organisation). According to the findings of the pre-trial chamber, his organisation comprised 4-12 vehicles, manned with the necessary fighters and supplied with the necessary ammunition.[423] Considering the different possible factors

---

[417] See for this terminology: Olásolo 2009, p 116; van Sliedregt and Yanev 2019, mn. 56.

[418] Herzberg 2009, p 577.

[419] See Chap. 2, Sect. 2.2.3.1.

[420] See Chap. 2, Sect. 2.3.2.1.

[421] Herzberg 2009, p 577. The case of Alberto Fujimori was tried before Peruvian courts but, according to scholarly literature, the applied doctrine oscillates somewhere between Roxin's and Schroeder's proposals (see e.g. Schroeder 2009, p 569 et seq.; critical in general: Herzberg 2009, p 576 et seq).

[422] Herzberg 2009, p 577.

[423] *Abdallah Banda*, 7 March 2011, para 141. The second accused, Saleh Jerbo, was believed to have commanded a much bigger group, consisting of 24–26 vehicles, see para 142. Note that the

establishing "almost automatic compliance" with orders in the organisation, its size seemingly matters less to the ICC than it would under the traditional theory in German law. In the latter, the necessity of fungibility logically implies a higher number of potential low-level perpetrators. At the ICC, this is not necessarily the case if automatic compliance is ensured in other ways. This leads to the question whether "half a dozen antisocial elements"[424] can be considered an organisation if their leader personally chose and indoctrinated them to act according to their orders. It should be kept in mind that the organisation was initially described as existing independently of its individual members. This implicitly excludes very small "organisations" under this doctrine.[425]

As stated earlier, individual chambers outlined certain necessary features of the organisation. These included a high number of low-ranking members, a hierarchy between superiors and subordinates and the independence of the apparatus' existence from its individual members. Chambers of the ICC in individual cases have largely adhered to a broad set of findings displaying certain tendencies. For example, military-like structures and/or chains of command etc. have frequently served as evidence.[426] Despite allowing the identification of certain relevant factors, these elaborations have thus far hardly served to establish any boundaries of the doctrine.[427]

These insecurities raise another issue, namely, the alleged similarity in structure and functioning of groups, which are treated as possible organisations by Roxin and the ICC. Additional "stereotypes" listed by Roxin are terrorist organisations, civil war parties and groups involved in "tribal wars".[428] The ICC's concept of an organisation proves equally broad, with its choice of "organisations" to date leading to little certainty. Abdallah Banda's group seemingly represented the smallest "organisation", while the Sudan's or Côte d'Ivoire's state apparatus may have been the largest organisation found in cases before the court. Armed non-state military actors (in the situations in the D.R. Congo, Uganda and the Central African Republic) and certain violent underground movements (situation in Kenya) range somewhere between these extremes in terms of membership numbers, but differ in their goals, means of achieving them and fields of action and operations.

If all these organisations are to fall under the basic requirement of the theory, where must the line be drawn? It has been observed that it may be misguiding to only consider the sheer size of an organisation, as control is often much tighter in

---

charges against both accused were confirmed in the form of (direct) co-perpetration due to their physical presence and participation in the attack which is the object of the trial. The notion of organisation within indirect perpetration therefore played no further role in the case.

424 Roxin 2011, p 204.

425 See above Sect. 3.1.2.2.

426 See above Sect. 3.1.2.2.

427 The acquittal of Germain Katanga sheds some light on the issue: The existence of an organisation can be denied where no hierarchical relations can be determined between certain branches or levels of the organisation. Such was the case between the position of presidency and the different local commanders in Germain Katanga's militia, see *Katanga*, 7 March 2014, paras 1419–20.

428 Roxin 2019, Chpter 12 mn. 370.

smaller organisations, whereas the left hand may not know what the right hand is doing in bigger ones.[429]

Additionally, one must question whether other factors the ICC regards as relevant for the establishment of a *hierarchical and organised* apparatus of power are well-defined and can be proven or rejected at trial. The trial chamber in *Katanga* shed some light on this issue by not being able to determine any power of command for the office of president of the *Ngiti* militia, which Katanga was believed to have led. Whilst the chamber found that the militia acted as a single group, it denied its hierarchical apparatus of power due to the lack of an effective command structure from the group's apex downwards.[430]

Apart from this, neither supporters of the traditional theory nor the ICC have specified the required aspects of an apparatus of power.

Proponents of the German scholarly view often invoke additional descriptors of members being "cogs in the machine" of the apparatus. Such metaphors, however, are not very helpful in this regard.[431]

Occasionally, chambers of the ICC will elaborate on essential features, yet ultimately treat them very differently. Whilst certain hierarchical relationships are required by one chamber, another explicitly rejects their necessity, as long as the accused can be seen as a "leadership figure".[432] Many of the ICC's other factual findings provide insight into the respective chamber's reasoning as to why *in concreto* a certain group of people can be considered an organisation.[433] However, *in abstracto* the jurisprudence has clarified very little—the *Katanga* judgment standing out as a helpful example—and it remains unclear under which circumstances a plurality of persons would be deemed a hierarchical and organised apparatus of power through which an indirect perpetrator could act.

Thus, the theory so far provides few tangible features of the organisation requirement.[434] Given that the ICC—in different but comparable terms to Roxin—expects the indirect perpetrator to have "control" over the apparatus, some kind of factual hierarchy must exist.[435] Further, *some* members of the organisation must exist because the concept of indirect perpetration would otherwise be led to absurdity. Beyond that there is nothing.

---

[429] Herzberg 2000, p 36; the same question on the delineation between a non-hierarchical gang and an organisation is posed by Krey and Nuys 2009, p 214.

[430] *Katanga*, 7 March 2014, paras 1417–20.

[431] Herzberg 2009, p 577.

[432] See *Katanga and Chui*, 30 September 2008, para 512 reading "…the organisation must be based on hierarchical relations between superiors and subordinates" and in contrast to that *Blé Goudé*, 11 December 2014, para 151 "… the pro-Gbagbo youth, which despite not being organised in a formal hierarchy, had a clearly defined leadership in his person…"

[433] See for example the emphasis on hierarchies, communication lines, unit-structures and supplies which lead to a group resembling an army in *Ntaganda*, 8 July 2019, para 814; and similarly in *Ongwen*, 23 March 2016, p. 72, para 10. For details see above Sect. 3.1.2.2.

[434] In the same vein already Weigend 2015, pp 552-3 and Morrison, see *Ntaganda*, 30 March 2021, Separate opinion of Judge Howard Morrison on Mr. Ntaganda's appeal, para 17.

[435] See above, Sects. 3.1.2.1 and 3.2.2.2.

In the German debate, the same unsatisfying situation has led to the allegation that a judgment based on the theory can neither be verified nor rebutted, at least not by proving that certain organisational structures did not exist.[436]

Under the ICC's theory, as long as some kind of organisation with a hierarchy exists and a crime was committed by a member due to a direct instruction or within a generally existing structure of command, it seems plausible that the requirement of an organised power structure could always be affirmed. If a crime was in fact committed, who would doubt that the group's structure was tight enough to lead to its commission?[437] In practice, this seems dangerously close to reversing the burden of proof. If all that is required for a conviction is a crime, a (potentially anonymous) physical perpetrator affiliated with a group and a defendant in a position of power who gave an instruction—what relevance remains for the organised apparatus of power criterion? As suspected earlier, it should therefore be questioned whether the requirement fulfils a purpose at all.[438]

Unsuitability of the Criterion for Actors in Asymmetrical Conflicts and Other Modern-day Situations of Mass Atrocities

Since the first import of the doctrine, a difference between the *Katanga and Chui* case and the examples which first inspired the doctrine has been debated.[439]

The pre-trial chamber consciously altered the requirements of the original doctrine to adapt it to certain organisations.[440] This alteration also broadened the requirement of automatic compliance with orders, which will be discussed below.[441] However, due to the heavy reliance on the "organisation" component, many authors doubt that the theory of indirect perpetration through an organisation is suitable to describe the dynamics and relevant factors of modern mass atrocities.

This is often established through a comparison to the case which inspired Roxin. If indirect perpetration through an organisation was created to deal with bureaucratically organised mass atrocities in Nazi Germany, how can it suitably address the violence committed by disorganised militias?[442]

---

[436] See already Herzberg 2009, p 577, referring to Roxin's original approach.

[437] Again: The *Katanga* trial judgment, by ways of rejecting certain requirements of that mode of liability, helps to clarify the matter, but that alone does not enable a clear picture of the necessary features of the apparatus.

[438] In the same vein Herzberg 2009, p 577.

[439] The doctrine was first and foremost conceived by Roxin based on the *Eichmann* case (see Chap. 2, Sects. 2.1 and 2.2.1). It was first applied in practice by a court in Argentina on the country's former military Junta, but revoked by a higher instance in this case (see Ambos 2018, § 7 mn. 25; Maculan 2013, p 82 with fn. 45; 84) and later by the German BGH on high-level politicians from the former GDR (see Chap. 2, Sect. 2.3.2.1).

[440] *Katanga and Chui*, 30 September 2008, paras 515–8.

[441] See above Sect. 3.1.2.3 for elaborations on this requirement.

[442] Cupido 2022, p 649; Guilfoyle 2011, p 265; Manacorda and Meloni 2011, p 171; Osiel 2005, pp 1834–5; Weigend 2011, p 107; Weigend 2015, p 553; Yanev 2018, p 469. But see Kiss 2019, mn. 43, advocating for applying this doctrine, *inter alia* based on the broadened set of requirements (i.e., automatic compliance in comparison to fungibility, see comparison above at Sect. 3.2.2.4). See

Some perceive this as a practical, evidentiary disadvantage. The argument being that if the theory requires strict hierarchical and organisational structures, however, these cannot be proven in the relevant cases, it must be unfit for international criminal law.[443]

The implications of such criticism are twofold: as the most prominent actors in cases before the ICC, non-state armed groups are generally badly organised and, despite this lack of organisation, their decision makers and architects should be treated as indirect perpetrators.

The Myth of Disorganised Non-state Actors and the Correct Comparative Angle

It is correct that in terms of the number of people involved at different levels of different branches, authorities, or entities, the murder machinery of Nazi Germany in the Holocaust remains a sad particularity. However, whether this means that "African militias" are usually disorganised is questionable.

Indeed, the ICC's decisions are often packed with elaborations on many organisational features, such as: chains of command, disciplinary regimens, training and equipping of fighters, chains of communications and communication logs, supply of ammunition and provisions, even occasional training in international humanitarian law.[444] Judging by some of the suspects' backgrounds, it is to be suspected that some enjoyed military officer training in western countries of the northern hemisphere.[445] Additionally, the sheer number of alleged physical perpetrators cast doubts on the

---

also Eldar 2013, p 341, criticising the reliance on "bureaucratic organizational structures", which would prove unfit for "other types of collective frameworks".

443 See van Sliedregt 2015, p 514; Weigend 2015, p 553 with fn. 92, referring to the lack of evidence that led to the dismissal of the charge of indirect perpetration through an organisation in *Katanga*, 7 March 2014, paras 1417–21. See also *Chui*, 18 December 2012, Concurring Opinion of Judge Christine Van den Wyngaert, para 29, underlining that this lack of evidence of specific positions is problematic in a hierarchical system of modes of liability and could be circumvented by not relying on a hierarchy of blameworthiness.

444 See e.g. *Ongwen*, 23 March 2016, paras 56-7 (division into operational units, system of hierarchy); *Ntaganda*, 8 July 2019, paras 309–332 (organisational structures), 334–340 (available weaponry), 341–6 (communications); 813–5 (summary); see also the findings in *Katanga*, 7 March 2014, paras 1417–8, concerning the Ngiti militia with "thousands of combatants" who received military training, the trial chamber could not find proof of centralised command and therefore rejected the existence of an organisation in the sense of the doctrine. However, many other findings supported the picture of an organisation, albeit perhaps not one which was headed by the accused in his function as president. The pre-trial chamber in *Bemba* found that the fighters of Jean-Pierre Bemba's *Mouvement de Libération du Congo* had been trained in and informed about the importance of international humanitarian law, see *Bemba*, 15 June 2009, para 491.

445 This was the case with several Rwandan military officers who participated in the genocide, see ICTR, *Prosecutor v. Bagosora et al.*, 18 December 2008, ICTR-98-41-T, para 44 (concerning Théoneste Bagosora, speaking of advanced military training in Europe), 66 (concerning Anatole Nsengiyumva, who received military training in France). According to a Rwandan Newspaper, Sylvestre Mudacumura, who was wanted by the ICC before notice of his death in 2019, received military officers training at the leadership academy of the German armed forces before the genocide in Rwanda, see https://www.newtimes.co.rw/section/read/13673. Accessed 6 April 2023.

picture of a wide-spread lack of organisation.[446] To have even a relatively small group train, move and commit crimes at the same pace, time and place requires hierarchies, procedures, weaponry and provisions. The bigger the crowd, the higher the organisational necessities to enable its functioning as a group.[447] Naturally, the degree of organisation varies in such cases. With regards to certain constellations, such as the pro-Gbagbo youth groups in Côte d'Ivoire, the existence of any degree of organisation seems questionable. On the other side of the spectrum, armed militias such as the UPC/FPLC of Thomas Lubanga and Bosco Ntaganda, as well as Jean-Pierre Bemba's *Mouvement de Liberación du Congo/Armée de Liberación du Congo* (MLC/ALC) clearly show high degrees of organisation and certain standards as to their forces' training and equipment.[448] Additionally, it would be ill-advised not to consider the Rwandan Genocide when discussing this issue. Even though it has not been dealt with before the ICC, that does not change the fact that it was organised over years in advance through the involvement of different state authorities and party organisations. Especially considering the simplicity of the means with which it was carried out, its horrific unfolding can only be explained by a very effective organisation.[449] Finally, two aspects of the Nazi state as the "stereotype" comparison case of indirect perpetration through an organisation must be kept in mind.

First, some contemporary historians argue that the Nazi murder machinery did not actually work as one unified whole but was constantly hung up on internal struggles over competences and influence.[450] If true, this assertion shows how, despite such struggles, the state apparatus managed to murder millions of people. This would mean that even though the machinery did not function as smoothly as imagined, it was able to plan, organize and perpetrate the Holocaust and countless other crimes, nonetheless.

Second, to compare non-state armed groups on the African (or really any) continent with the Nazi state does not make sense in terms of the relevant "theatres of crime", i.e., the object of comparison. Especially for the purpose of the doctrine of indirect perpetration through an organisation, a comparison should be made between the situations in which the relevant crimes were committed, such as unlawful attacks on villages that resulted in mass atrocities.

---

[446] See e.g. *Katanga*, 7 March 2014, para 1418 ("thousands of combatants"); *Ntaganda*, 8 July 2019, para 314 speaking of 1800–2000 recruits at a time. Note also that Jean-Pierre Bemba's armed group was found to have numbered up to 20,000 fighters (*Bemba*, 21 March 2016, para 390) and Alfred Yekatom's *Anti Balaka* militia, allegedly numbered up to 3,000 fighters (ICC, *The Prosecutor v. Alfred Yekatom and Patrice-Edouard Ngaïssona*, 5 May 2020, ICC-01/14-01/18, para 65). The latter two persons were not charged under the head of indirect perpetration through an organisation but were nevertheless believed to have headed vast groups of organized fighters.

[447] For a criminological perspective on the role of organisations for genocide see Anderson 2018, in general pp 60–61 (on the "genocidal state as an organizational culture"), pp 150–4 (on mobilizing the physical perpetrators of genocide through different levels of organisational structures).

[448] *Ntaganda*, 8 July 2019, para 813–5; *Bemba*, 21 March 2016, paras 696–705 (summary of the structure of the *MLC/ALC* (*Mouvement de Libération du Congo/Armée de Libération du Congo*).

[449] Cf. Anderson 2018, on the fact that genocide does not require elaborate technological skill at p 55.

[450] Cesarani 2004, pp 181, 183.

The doctrine, in the way Roxin devised it, focused on the *Eichmann* case and its link to Nazi extermination camps, however the murderous campaign of the Nazi state was not restricted to this. *SS Einsatzgruppen* (operation units, effectively death brigades) incited terror among people—Jews, Poles, "Communists"—behind the German lines during the war in eastern Europe. Villages were raided and civilians murdered *en masse*.[451] Similar events unfolded in certain occupied countries through *Wehrmacht* forces in "response" to partisan attacks.[452]

These are the incidents and organisational units to which "disorganised" African militias should be compared.[453] It is doubtful that the degree of organisation in general would vary greatly between an infantry brigade of the *Wehrmacht* or *SS* and the military divisions of groups like the Lord's Resistance Army (LRA), *the Forces Démocratiques de Libération du Rwanda* (*FDLR*) or the *UPC/FPLC*. Such organisations may be part of a bigger apparatus (the Nazi state) or not (like in the armed conflict in the eastern provinces of the Congo) but examined individually they share many common features in terms of ranks, levels of hierarchy, chains of command and communication, necessities in supplies and more. Individual training may vary greatly, but one might be surprised by the level of "proficiency" that members of such non-state armed groups may develop over years in harsh conflict situations in which they participate as combatants. Even where this is not the case, such individual differences are mostly irrelevant where the victims are unprepared and undefended inhabitants of a village or town.

These observations demonstrate that speaking of largely "disorganised" militias runs the risk of establishing a dangerous narrative of the reality of the situation. If the findings of many ICC decisions are considered and the comparison with the Nazi state's crimes is based on a more careful case selection, the differences between "organisations" may turn out to be much less significant than what is argued by commentators. In other words, under closer inspection, "African militias" will often turn out to not be all that disorganised if compared with the correct counterpart—military units of a comparable size and acting in a comparable area of operation.[454]

---

451 See on the organisation and scale of crimes committed through the *Einsatzgruppen*: Trials of War Criminals Before the Nuernberg Military Tribunals Under Control Council Law No. 10, Vol. IV 1950, 414–6, 427–33.

452 Trials of War Criminals Before the Nuernberg Military Tribunals Under Control Council Law No. 10, Vol. XI, U.S. Government Printing Service 1950, 765–9.

453 For a similar comparison of *Einsatzgruppen* with the *Interahamwe* of the Rwandan genocide from a criminological viewpoint see Anderson 2018, pp 54–5. Pursuant to the traditional theory, it is submitted that a commander of a *Wehrmacht* unit would qualify as an indirect perpetrator in such cases. He steers this part of the (much bigger) apparatus through his orders, hierarchies are in place, the *Wehrmacht* (in massacres of civilians) acted detached from the law and the soldiers were fungible. Within his version of the systemic view, Ambos' theory would reject this because a brigade commander steers a small part of the apparatus, but he does not carry responsibility for the systemic wrong as such. He could thus probably be a co-perpetrator according to Ambos (see Chap. 2, Sect. 2.4.2.3).

454 To a certain extent, the organisations that were part of the allegations in *Muthaura et al.* and *Ruto et al.* may be less comparable to the "military-style" non-state actors that are discussed here. These apparatuses more closely resemble mafia-like or sect-type organisations. However, one should not

Furthermore, despite the myriad of differences which could be pointed out, a comparison of Rwanda and Nazi Germany shows that mass atrocities can very well be organised on other continents by decision makers and architects in other states. In these cases, a significant level of preparation and organisation will be necessary to initiate the murders.[455]

In sum, the allegation that organisations before the ICC are too disorganised should be seen critically.

What remains is an evidentiary problem. If organisational structures cannot be proven, as was the case with the powers and competences of Germain Katanga as president of the *Ngiti* militia, people cannot be convicted, despite their organisation potentially—materially—fulfilling the necessary requirements.[456]

An evidentiary problem leaves at least two possible solutions:

1. Increasing the capacities and mechanisms to acquire reliable evidence. However, this is a fight that the Office of the Prosecutor (OTP) regularly fights, which has been discussed elsewhere and is not the topic of this book.[457]
2. If the theory does not match the facts, change the theory.[458] This is an obvious and promising approach. However, it must be tackled cautiously as the requirements of indirect perpetration through an organisation are designed to reflect the belief that certain factors are responsible for the special role and blameworthiness of the indirect perpetrator. If one was to rely on the theory, any change of it must be examined with care.

Towards Abolishing the Organisation Requirement?

If one wishes to change the theory on indirect perpetration through an organisation, one inevitably discovers proposals of scholars to get rid of the organisation requirement.

Such a point is made by Jain, who stresses that indirect perpetration through an organisation would unnaturally "simplif[y] … the conditions under which mass

forget, that such organisations are the second group of apparatuses in the traditional German theory. Additionally, what is true for military-style actors applies to these groups as well: the bigger the organisation, the more sophisticated its structures must be to enable concerted action through it.

455 This is not to say that the technical automatization of the killing would be the same. The *modus operandi* of the massacres of the Nazis and the Hutu-Power Government in Rwanda varied significantly. However, whether it would truly make a difference to the necessary organisation whether people are gassed upon their arrival at an extermination camp or cornered in a soccer stadium and slaughtered is questionable. Cf. on this Anderson 2018, pp 54–5 on the role of organisations in the perpetration of genocide and at 55 on the low-key technical skill needed for mass murder.

456 See also van Sliedregt 2015, p 514. As far as bureaucratic documentation as evidence is concerned the shape of the doctrine might be problematic, despite the high degree of organisation. If the requirements can be better proven through evidence typically produced after the fall of bureaucratic regimes than after the collapse of a non-state armed group, the "organisation" requirement—despite its factual correctness—may stand in the doctrine's way to procedural effectiveness.

457 See e.g. de Vos 2013, p; SáCouto and Thompson 2015, p 329 et seq.

458 The saying is credited to Albert Einstein.

atrocity occurs: a vertical, tautly structured hierarchical organisation that gives rise to an automatic implementation of commands..."[459]

This reaction to the perhaps disenchanting practical results of the doctrine is understandable.

Albeit not concerning the requirement of a hierarchical and organised apparatus, changes to the doctrine have already been made by the ICC. As illustrated in the comparison, the ICC has altered the theory regarding certain components, e.g., the mechanism which is supposedly at work within the organisation. The court recognizes different ways to determine almost automatic compliance and thereby applies a broad and flexible approach to the organisation's mechanism. In the view of certain authors, this approach was necessary to adapt the theory to the environment of asymmetrical conflict.[460]

Furthermore, the above-mentioned criticism should be recalled: Thus far, a functioning chain of command connecting higher and lower organs or units of an organisation is the only, relatively reliable aspect upon which the chambers of the ICC have based positive and negative findings.[461] A further consequence of this is that it remains unclear whether the organisation requirement actually plays much of a role under the current jurisprudence.

If the doctrine were to remain intact, it therefore seems questionable whether abolishing any of its requirements would do any good.

Moreover, concerns about abolishing the criterion are even farther reaching. It should be remembered that opting to prosecute decisions makers and architects of crimes as indirect perpetrators is a normative choice. Based on the factual notions of domination/control over the crime, it is the normative evaluative decision that under certain factual circumstances the perpetrator behind the perpetrator can control the crime and is therefore considered a principal of the crime. Indirect perpetration through an organisation rests on the assumption that it is precisely the form of organisational procedures, which are described by the requirements (a hierarchical, organised apparatus of power, fungibility, almost automatic compliance etc.) that allows such an attribution of perpetrator liability.

It is possible to contradict this normative evaluation of factual dynamics and decide that other factors should decide over the question of how a person becomes an indirect perpetrator under Art. 25 (3) (a) Rome Statute. However, any such approach would have to be critically tested for its underlying conviction of why a person should be regarded a perpetrator under its alternative requirements.

Weigend proposes to utilise the more general definition of control in such cases. Pursuant to his proposal, an indirect perpetrator should be determined through the "control over the will" test.[462] This means that only where a chamber considers it proven that the person in the background actually—and irrespectively of organisational features—controlled the actions of the physical perpetrator, they can be an

459 Jain 2014, p 139.

460 Ambos 2011a, pp 851–2; Kiss 2019, mn. 43.

461 See above Sect. 3.3.2.1.

462 Weigend 2015, p 555.

indirect perpetrator. According to Weigend, mere leadership over an organisation does not in itself establish such control. Instead, indirect perpetration must involve the exercise of intense psychological or physical pressure or the creation of a misconception about relevant facts.[463] Under this approach, organisational features could still play a role as evidentiary factors, a point which has also been favoured by others.[464] If the exercise of pressure must amount to a situation in which the physical perpetrator acts under duress, then this approach would effectively not fall into the category of the perpetrator behind the perpetrator anymore.[465]

It is unclear whether such an approach would change any of the evidentiary problems, although it may release the court from the necessity of inquiring into organisational dynamics to the same extent it does now. Regardless, circumventing evidentiary standards is not the function of modes of liability.[466] However, this approach would have the effect that the court would no longer be able to prosecute decision makers and architects of crimes as perpetrators in all circumstances. Evidentiary problems aside, it seems more likely that most actors presented to the court had relatively stable organisations at their disposition than that they deceived or coerced their subordinates.[467]

Weigend's approach would therefore lead to a narrower notion of indirect perpetration which does not amount to the ideas of other scholars criticising the organisation requirement. However, this illustrates how any notion of indirect perpetration is carried by an assessment of criteria that justify the attribution of perpetrator liability. If one were to depart from the organisation requirement in the (debatable) belief that it fails to grasp certain characteristics of the groups through which mass atrocities are committed, alternative requirements must be produced. As demonstrated by Weigend's proposal, this then leads to the dilemma that such requirements tend to be even narrower than what is currently applied by the ICC.

Considering this and the foregoing section, it would be wise for the organisation requirement to remain as long as the doctrine of indirect perpetration through an organisation is regarded as the correct approach to the issue by the majority opinion.

An Unclear Requirement, Not Unfit for International Criminal Law

The requirement of an organised and hierarchical apparatus of power is underdefined, but not out of place in the ambit of international crimes which have been presented before the ICC to date. Many of the organisations found in ICC jurisprudence demonstrate a certain degree of structures and internal procedures. The problem with this

---

[463] Ibid., p 539 (on control over the will in the ambit of international criminal law), 555-6.

[464] See *Chui*, 18 December 2012, Concurring Opinion of Judge Van den Wyngaert, para 55; van Sliedregt and Yanev 2019, mn. 66.

[465] Art. 25 (3) (a) Rome Statute implies the existence of the perpetrator behind the perpetrator, as previously mentioned. However, this does not mean that the category of perpetration through an organisation must be the relevant constellation for the perpetrator behind the perpetrator.

[466] Weigend 2011, p 109.

[467] Although, in light of the wide-spread use of child-soldiers and menacingly strict regimens, there would probably be more cases of "classic" indirect perpetration through coercion and deception than there were in Nazi organisations, in this vein see also ibid., pp 109–10.

criterion is therefore mostly an evidentiary one. Abolishing or broadening the organisation criterion must therefore be critically analysed. As the mode of liability is based on normative decisions concerning the factual dynamics, a replacement or abolishment is conceivable. However, it is precisely this kind of normative evaluation which forces us to consider: If indirect perpetration through fully responsible actors is removed from the boundaries of an organisation, what is the reason behind attributing perpetrator liability to the actor? Is someone who does not control an organisation with certain minimum requirements as blameworthy as someone who does? This seems doubtful considering the underlying theory of control over the crime and would be highly questionable under the German domination of the crime theory. If ICC jurisprudence were to adopt such an approach by discarding the organisation requirement either explicitly or implicitly by not actually requiring any organisational features, accessory liability would become even more redundant in practice. The underlying hierarchy of blameworthiness would equally become redundant in the ICC's practice, as most accused would more readily be considered principals.

This leads to a second approach to the issue with organisations. The use of a narrower focus on indirect perpetration has been proposed, in which coercion and deception are the factors which determine the control of the decision maker.[468] Organisational features can serve as evidence but are not requirements in and of themselves.[469] This is a possibility. However, due to the fact that instructing responsibly acting persons to commit crimes would consequently not fall under indirect perpetration, this would only be satisfying if suitable alternatives for decision makers and architects of crimes exist.

The question therefore presents itself: How convincing are the other requirements of the doctrine and does the notion of control over the crime, as applied by the ICC, serve to appropriately describe the wrongdoing of high-level actors? If this is not the case, but an alternative mode of liability can serve the same purpose, this would speak in favour of taking a narrower approach to indirect perpetration. Consequently, the hierarchy of blameworthiness stipulated by the ICC would become questionable.

3.3.2.2 Almost Automatic Compliance with Orders

As discussed, almost automatic compliance with orders can be broken down into the factors of fungibility, indoctrination (violent and strict training regimens), menacingly strict disciplinary regimens and payment mechanisms.[470] The first of these corresponds to the requirement singled out by Roxin and his supporters in the traditional German theory. Some believe that the other factors correspond to Schroeder's criterion of readiness to commit the crime.[471]

[468] See Weigend 2015, pp 555–6.

[469] *Chui*, 18 December 2012, Concurring Opinion of Judge Christine Van den Wyngaert, para 55; van Sliedregt and Yanev 2019, mn. 66; Weigend 2015, pp 555–6.

[470] For the latter, it seems doubtful whether this alone would suffice, see above Sect. 3.1.2.3.

[471] See the comparison above at Sect. 3.2.2.4.

The two differing cornerstones in the German traditional theory—fungibility and readiness to commit the crime—have seen vigorous criticism over the years, which must be considered when evaluating the doctrine.

Fungibility of the Physical Perpetrators

The fungibility criterion has first and foremost been criticised as incapable of grasping important constellations of cases. It has been pointed out that whenever a highly trained specialist is needed to commit a crime, the criterion fails. This seems persuasive if one considers the time and effort necessary for specialized training.[472]

Roxin agrees with this criticism but asserts that most cases for which indirect perpetration through an organisation is devised would not deal with specialists but with "replaceable" low-level perpetrators without special knowledge.[473]

When looking at cases before the ICC, this assertion is partly correct; mass atrocities in these cases were often carried out with simple means at the disposition of large numbers of perpetrators.[474] In other cases the equipment was more elaborate, yet the organisation through which the crimes were initiated might have had additional personnel to operate the equipment at their disposition.[475]

Finally, one must examine the function of this criterion in Roxin's traditional theory. Fungibility is one of the fundamental criteria enabling domination of the crime. Where fungibility is denied, so should domination of the crime. Without this requirement it is not justified to determine a background actor as truly dominating the crime. Requiring fungibility thus constitutes a normative decision on a factual requirement through which Roxin justifies the attribution of perpetrator liability. It is therefore not necessarily valid to state that certain cases will not be grasped by this criterion.

At the same time, however, if the requirement ultimately fails to reflect the realities on the ground, it is worth considering whether the criterion aptly describes reasons relevant for the attribution of perpetrator liability to the decision maker in the organisation.

It has been suggested that the requirements as laid out by Roxin are rather accidental and closely connected to his first object of study: The *Eichmann* case and the industrial murder machinery of Nazi extermination camps.[476]

From this perspective, the further aspects which the ICC's chambers consider can be regarded as a positive addition.

---

[472] Schroeder 2009, p 570; in the same vein Ambos 2009, pp 145–6.

[473] Roxin 2003, mn. 119.

[474] Cf. e.g. the pre-trial chamber's findings in *Katanga*, 6 July 2007, that the members of the militias that carried out the crimes were trained with and used firearms, spears and machetes at paras 255, 282, 300.

[475] See on the use of heavy weapons e.g. in *Gbagbo*, 12 June 2014, paras 176, 232; *Ntaganda*, 8 July 2019, para 323. The violent campaign object of the ICC's Sudan situation was allegedly carried out with the support of bombings by Sudan's state air force, cf. *Al Bashir*, 4 March 2009, para 85.

[476] Weigend 2015, pp 552–3; Weisser 2019, p 247 (calling the procedures in the extermination camp of Auschwitz the "prototype" of indirect perpetration through an organisation). See also van Sliedregt 2015, p 509.

Readiness to Commit the Crime in the Form of Violent and Strict Training and Disciplinary Regimens

Whether Schroeder's readiness to commit the crime criterion actually modelled for these additions remains unclear. However, as stated earlier, the effect of violent and strict training (indoctrination) and disciplinary regimens can be described as resulting in a readiness to commit the crime in the minds of the low-level members of an organisation.

As far as the ICC would rely on it, this requirement must also be examined critically.

In German scholarly debate, it has been pointed out that a pre-existing readiness to commit a crime has nothing to do with organisational structures.[477] Furthermore, it is a feature which could equally be affirmed in instigation.[478] Consequently, basing domination of the crime on the exploitation of the pre-existing readiness of another, would significantly and unjustifiably broaden the scope of this mode of responsibility. In any case of instigation, it would have to be explored whether the instigator had known of and relied on the pre-existing readiness to commit a crime.[479] Additionally, it has been criticised that the criterion focusses on the situation preceding the crime when the desk perpetrator would exploit the pre-existing readiness. However, domination must be given during the crime and a pre-existing willingness can subsequently change.[480]

Concerning the lacking relation between organisational structures and readiness to commit the crime, the criticism above seems to be generally accurate. A perpetrator may be ready to commit a crime in the ambit of mass atrocities for manyfold reasons, hatred, fear and hope for material gains being among them. However, as far as the factors that are considered by the ICC are concerned, this criticism is only partly valid. Psychological or physical pressure can be exerted over someone else outside of organisations. However, it is evident that this becomes easier and more manageable where a system to implement such pressure is in place—such as an organised apparatus based on obedience and strict disciplinary rules. It has been underlined that the Nazi machinery seldom exerted such brute pressure on its members, but this seems to be different in several cases with which international criminal law is concerned today.[481]

Based on this, however, the criticism that instigation can equally be given by turning to a person already prepared to commit the crime remains valid. The forms of ordering, encouraging and soliciting under Art. 25 (3) (b) of the Rome Statute

---

[477] Rotsch 1998, p 493.

[478] Ambos 1998, p 230; Rotsch 1998, p 493; Rotsch 2000, p 525; see also Roxin 1995, p 51, who focusses more on Section 30 para 2 GCC which punishes the "declaring of willingness" towards another to commit a crime.

[479] Herzberg 2009, pp 578–9, who also speaks of a "domination through compliance" (*Willfährigkeitsherrschaft*).

[480] Jain 2014, pp 127–8; Rotsch, ZStW 2000, 525.

[481] On the lack of brute psychological pressure in the Nazi apparatus see Anderson 2018, p 131; Jain 2014, pp 125–6; Roxin 2011, p 197.

can also be affirmed where a background actor approaches someone who is ready to commit a crime when told to do so. This is most evident with "ordering" a crime. The authority necessary to order a crime under Art. 25 (3) (b) Rome Statute could be based on the physical actor's general readiness to commit a crime. This in turn could stem from violent and strict training and disciplinary measures (or payment mechanisms).[482] It can therefore be remarked that the criteria chosen by the ICC in this regard do not explain where the difference between indirect perpetration and a form of responsibility like ordering, soliciting or encouraging would be very well. The "temporal criticism" generally applies before the ICC as well. The physical perpetrator's readiness to commit the crime is exploited by the person in the background when instructing the former to act. However, this does not necessarily mean that the physical perpetrator will remain equally ready to act on site; they could still change their minds. This also holds true for a member of a non-state armed group. However, it must be acknowledged that the range of factors considered by the ICC is narrower than the broad "readiness to commit the crime" factor. Where psychological pressure comes into play, the generally correct assertion that the perpetrator may simply change their mind becomes questionable. It remains true that even where insubordination carries the threat of violence, a militia member can decide (more or less) freely not to perform certain actions. However, they might be less inclined to do so than a recruit who joined a group due to the prospect of material gain, who is under no similar pressure.

Finally, Roxin's view that readiness to commit a crime is merely the consequence of fungibility cannot stand as far as the ICC's criteria are concerned. If readiness to commit a crime arises out of specific psychological or physical pressure or from indoctrination, this is not a by-product of fungibility. It is something else which can or cannot be instilled through an organisation. Whether an organisation is comprised of a large number of low-ranking members has nothing to do with it.

In conclusion, only parts of the criticism of Schroeder's readiness criterion can be translated into valid criticism of the ICC's approach. The most relevant point concerns the ICC's choice of factors explaining the particularity of indirect perpetration through an organisation in comparison to other modes of liability. If violent and strict training regimens lead to almost automatic compliance with instructions by a decision maker, how does this differ from forms of responsibility under Art. 25 (3) (b) Rome Statute, especially regarding the mode of ordering?

Necessity of Strict Interpretation of Almost Automatic Compliance

This inconsistency notwithstanding, the amendment of fungibility with further factors has been welcomed by scholars as a suitable transcription of this part of the doctrine into international criminal law. Given the different characteristics of armed groups and organisations behind international crimes, the consideration of different factors, which can be fulfilled to varying degrees and can jointly lead to

[482] Authority is defined as the ordering-person's capability to issue instructions under which the recipient feels compelled to act. See on the requirements of ordering under Art. 25 (3) (b) Rome Statute Chap. 6, Sect. 6.2.2.

an "almost automatic compliance with orders" is seen as a major advantage of the ICC's approach.[483]

Despite this general approval, commentators have repeatedly stressed that only a certain level of control will suffice for indirect perpetration, meaning that not any kind of factor should be allowed to fulfil the almost automatic compliance criterion.[484] For instance, Ambos demands that, despite the welcome alteration, leadership authority cannot be allowed to dwindle too much. He concludes that authority cannot solely be based on personal relationships.[485]

Cases like those in the situation in Côte d'Ivoire show the danger of not heeding these calls for a restrictive handling of the requirements. As outlined earlier, in the decisions on the confirmation of charges in *Gbagbo* and *Blé Goudé*, little (*Gbagbo*) to nothing (*Blé Goudé*) was elaborated regarding the facts necessary to establish this criterion.[486] Consequently, the simple observation that Charles Blé Goudé had—allegedly—served as a leadership figure to the pro-Gbagbo youth, was enough for the pre-trial chamber to believe that Gbagbo had controlled them. He had supposedly done so through "manipulation at mass rallies".[487] This incident vividly illustrates how chambers of the ICC can deem factors as satisfactory, which are the exact opposite of what scholars have expressed as necessary. The pre-trial chamber ignored the necessity of proving specific ways of ensuring almost automatic compliance and thereby took a step towards undermining the figure's theoretic foundation. By ignoring the requirement of almost automatic compliance in the case of Charles Blé Goudé, the chamber not only cut out a central consideration of the doctrine of indirect perpetration through an organisation, but further blurred the lines between indirect perpetration and soliciting, encouragement and incitement. Although the latter is only criminalized in the case of genocide,[488] the case nevertheless demonstrates what may happen with the doctrine if chambers start ignoring its central requirements. Perpetration liability will be attributed to prominent persons who publicly called for violence without any specification of their influence over the audience. In this regard, and as far as these specific findings are concerned, it is a good sign that the trial chamber overturned the allegations against Laurent Gbagbo and Charles

---

[483] See Ambos 2011a, pp 846; Ambos 2013, pp 156–7, explaining that such a set of factors also better explains the institutional autonomy deficit of the actor, i.e. their inability to actively decide over the final commission of the crime; Ambos 2016, Art. 25 mn. 14; in the same vein Kiss 2019, mn. 59.

[484] Ambos 2011a, pp 849; Jessberger and Geneuss 2008, p 867; Kiss 2019, mn. 44. In a somewhat similar vein, Gil Gil and Maculan endorse the view taken by the *Katanga* trial chamber on the matter which they identify as a rather narrow approach, see Gil Gil and Maculan 2015, pp 367, 370.

[485] Ambos 2011a, pp 849; see also Kiss 2019, mn. 44.

[486] See above Sect. 3.1.2.3, it has been observed that whilst the *Gbagbo* decision does not elaborate separately on the matter, the *Blé Goudé* decision does not even treat almost automatic compliance as a separate criterion.

[487] *Blé Goudé*, 11 December 2014, para 151.

[488] Cf. Art. 25 (3) (e) Rome Statute; Ambos 2016, Art. 25 mn. 43.

Blé Goudé, elaborating *inter alia* on the incomplete picture of Blé Goudé's alleged involvement with the youth groups.[489]

Conclusion

Moving forward, it would be preferable if chambers of the ICC would strive to develop features that qualify as ensuring almost automatic compliance instead of casually avoiding the criterion. Otherwise, it may meet a similar fate to the German jurisprudence: becoming a shapeless, ever-broader doctrine with the primary aim of convicting anyone as a perpetrator.[490]

Apart from this, the problem of delineating indirect perpetration through an organisation from other modes of liability also remains. The question of how to distinguish indirect perpetration from ordering a crime self-evidently presents itself where a person uses their authority over others to instruct them to commit crimes. A common answer to the delineation question, presented in debates surrounding both national legal systems and the Rome Statute is the following: if the decision maker can be certain that the crime will be committed, they have control over the crime and are therefore a perpetrator and not a "mere" accessory.[491]

3.3.2.3 Irrelevance of Certainty of Success

It has been asserted that the theory of indirect perpetration through an organisation in Germany is built around a notion of "certainty of success". This is not its own criterion, but rather an implied intermediate step, which is nevertheless vital.[492] This consideration is also part of the figure in the practice of the ICC. The ICC equally defines and justifies perpetrator liability through considerations on the actor's capability to secure the automatic compliance with orders and consequently the commission of the crime.[493]

Certainty of success,[494] i.e., certainty of the crime eventually being committed, is also central to the reasoning of many authors. However, its relevance to determining the boundaries of a mode of responsibility is highly questionable.

First and foremost, distinguishing between indirect perpetration and ordering, soliciting, and inducing (instigation[495]) seems impossible if certainty of success is the criterion used to do so. Supporters of the theory in German national and international

---

489 Cf. *Gbagbo and Blé Goudé*, 16 July 2019, paras 1935–6.

490 Cf. the analysis of German jurisprudence in Chap. 2, Sect. 2.3.2.2.

491 Kiss 2019, mn. 11; on the same argument in German doctrine see Chap. 2, Sects. 2.2.4.6 and 2.2.4.

492 See Chap. 2, Sect. 2.2.3.6.

493 See above at Sect. 3.1.2.3.

494 To rely on a uniform terminology, the term "certainty of success" will be used hereinafter.

495 "Instigation" is the category referred to in the German debate, as no ordering exists in the provisions of the GCC. However, one could subsume soliciting and inducing in Art. 25 (3) (b) Rome Statute under the term of instigation as well (see Chap. 6, Sect. 6.1). Instigation will therefore be used as a synonym for soliciting and inducing under the Rome Statute from this point forward.

criminal law frequently allege that the certainty of success would distinguish the desk perpetrator from the person who orders or instigates, as only the former can rely on whatever criterion is deemed relevant (be it fungibility, readiness to commit a crime or almost automatic compliance).[496] This means that a person without an organised power structure who utilises an autonomously acting physical perpetrator can only be liable for ordering or instigating. However, is the commission of a crime in this situation less certain? This is hardly convincing. Depending on the circumstances, an instigator could be as certain of the success of the crime as a decision maker with an organisation at their disposal.[497]

Following this logic, the instigation of a skilled and reliable assassin, who is motivated by an extremely high bounty is equally reliable to using members of an organisation.[498] Alternatively, one can consider a scenario involving members of a branch of the Ku Klux Klan, or a fanatic organisation of religious extremists.[499] If within such an organisation, a leader privately and under the oath of secrecy asks a befriended, lower ranking member to commit a specific (racist/religiously motivated) crime, this would be considered instigation. If the same leader invokes his superior knowledge, morals and position in the private conversation vis-à-vis his subordinate (but does not issue an instruction through the group's chain of command), this may be considered ordering.[500] Meanwhile, a more general instruction within the same group would be indirect perpetration if it led to the commission of the crime. The success of the crime would be equally, or perhaps more probable in the first case. If a person instigates another with whom they share a common ideological goal and are bound to by friendship, loyalty or an agreement, the crime may be committed just as certainly as in cases in which organisational procedures and protocols are set into motion.[501] The same is true where a person relies on their authority to give a compelling instruction to their subordinates, which would amount to ordering. Indeed, as exemplified, the boundaries between these situations can be blurry.

---

[496] Kiss 2019, mn. 11 ("...those who issue an order without being indirect perpetrators face a higher degree of uncertainty as to whether or not the crime will be committed"); Olásolo 2009, p 141 (following *Katanga and Chui*, 30 September 2008, paras 517–8); Ventura may imply the same when he explains the difference between indirect perpetration and ordering based on "control", see Ventura 2019, mn. 10, 42; For the German debate see only Roxin 2007, pp 10–11 ("This certainty of success is the reason for domination of the crime"); Schroeder 2009, p 570 (*Fehlen der Erfolgsunsicherheit*—Missing of the uncertainty of success); translations by the author.

[497] Herzberg 2009, p 578; Murmann 1996, p 274; Noltenius 2003, p 321; Renzikowski 1997, p 89; Rotsch 2000, p 525.

[498] In this vein Renzikowski 1997, p 89.

[499] The Ku Klux Klan is one of Roxin's examples for his theory, see Chap. 2, Sect. 2.2.3.1.

[500] The mode of ordering under the Rome Statute is explored below (see Chap. 6). A privately made call to commit a crime such as this, in which the group's structures are deliberately not used, but the "superiority" of the inducing person is still invoked, may qualify as a case of ordering under Art. 25 (3) (b) Rome Statute, but not necessarily of indirect perpetration.

[501] See also Rotsch 2009, p 392: "The instigation of a loyal and reliable friend ... can lead to the commission of the crime with the same certainty as the use of a blindly acting, human tool" (translation by the author).

The same doubts arise when considering the certainty argument from another angle. As Herzberg points out in the German debate, there are many "traditional" cases of perpetration in which the success of the crime is all but certain. If a terrorist (acting alone) plants a bomb with a time fuse in a car or a father tells his son to steal money from the child's grandmother, the success of the respective crime is far from certain. However, if the victim gets into the car in time or the child actually steals the money, both, terrorist and father will be perpetrators,[502] despite the lack of certainty.[503]

Given the central position of these unconvincing explanations, a German commentator concludes that, "indirect perpetration through an organisation is domination reduced to certainty of the criminal result".[504] Although this sounds convincing, criticism of the notion of certainty should not end there. Instead, and as the foregoing analyses demonstrate, certainty is no viable criterion to distinguish between perpetrators and participants.[505]

Furthermore, it is necessary to go a step further and ask: Is the eventual commission of the crime even certain in the way described above? Or are typical situations of indirect perpetration through an organisation dependent on too many different decisions made by different actors to speak of certainty, despite the existence of a power structure?

3.3.3 The Theory of Control Over the Crime/Domination of the Crime as an Unconvincing Concept

It has been outlined how control over the crime can be interpreted differently in indirect perpetration through an organisation. The traditional German concept of domination of the crime uses the term in a narrow sense. Whoever decides over the "whether" and "how" of the specific crime dominates it, a definition which would also be true for indirect perpetrators. The systemic approach to indirect perpetration uses a more normative, abstract concept of domination of the crime in which it is recognized that the organisation's decision maker has relatively little influence and thus only an abstract say in the "whether" and "how" of the specific crime.[506] As discussed, the ICC's approach more closely resembles the traditional German concept and may even be narrower in detail. It focusses on the indirect perpetrator's

[502] The terrorist uses the victim as a "human tool" against him- or herself (they do not know about the bomb and of course, would not be liable for harming him- or herself); the father uses the child as an innocent agent given that the child is unable to grasp the implications of the action and is exempt from criminal liability. This evaluation is based on German criminal law.

[503] Herzberg 2009, p 578.

[504] Rotsch 1998, p 493; Rotsch 2009, p 329.

[505] The same has been asserted by various commentators in the German debate, see Haas 2008, p 57; Murmann 1996, p 274; Noltenius 2003, p 321; Herzberg 2009, p 578; Orozco López 2021, p 247; Renzikowski 1997, p 89; Rotsch 2009, p 329.

[506] See Chap. 2, Sects. 2.2.4 and 2.4.2.1.

perceived capability to subjugate or bypass the direct perpetrator's will and identifies factual criteria under which this is deemed plausible by the court. It thereby rests on a strict and factual notion of control over the specific crime, which is much closer to the traditional German concept than the systemic one.[507]

Criticism of the theory of control over the crime in international criminal law arose soon after its adoption and draws from international and national debate.

In his separate opinion for the *Lubanga* trial judgment, judge Adrian Fulford criticised the control theory for its implementation of a strict distinction between modes of liability. In his view, a strict dividing line between modes of liability in Art. 25 (3) Rome Statute can and should not be drawn. According to him, the forms of responsibility in this article are not meant to be mutually exclusive and will self-evidently overlap.[508]

For the sake of clarity, it must be remarked that the doctrine of domination or control over the crime as developed in German law and the ICC's practice until now, does not establish "mutual" exclusivity between modes of liability. Instead, one must determine whether specific behaviour satisfies a form of perpetration besides a form of participation, the latter of which will then be overruled in concurrences. Materially they are not mutually exclusive, although this will not affect the judgment. This is the exact point which Judge Fulford refers to when arguing that modes of liability are not exclusive in this sense in ICTY and ICTR jurisprudence.[509]

Distinguishing between modes of liability based on the criteria which are thought to convey control over the crime in indirect perpetration through an organisation may prove extremely difficult. Commentators have taken to reiterating the well-known line from national legal systems, according to which a perpetrator is simply the person "who had control over the crime", whilst someone ordering, instigating or aiding and abetting would "not control the crime".[510] But what is control over the crime? The notion of certainty that the crime will be committed has already been dismissed as being a meaningless term when distinguishing between modes of perpetration and participation. It can therefore hardly lie at the core of the "control" concept.

Due to this uncertainty about the actual meaning of control, it is no surprise the adoption of the control theory and its application in the practice of the ICC has been criticised from various angles over the years.[511]

Weigend criticised the development of the theory at the ICC, which started with the amendment of the traditionally known requirements, arguing that it does not contain any theoretical limits. In his view, any kind of influence exerted through or in the

---

[507] See Sects. 3.1.3 and 3.2.3.

[508] *Lubanga*, 14 March 2012, Separate Opinion of Judge Adrian Fulford, paras 6–7.

[509] Ibid., Separate Opinion of Judge Adrian Fulford, para 7 with fn. 13. The jurisprudence of the *ad hoc* tribunals is divided and partially contradictory on this issue, see Chap. 5, Sect. 5.3.4.

[510] Jessberger and Geneuss 2008, p 865; Kiss 2019, mn. 11, who also quotes Roxin on the certainty argument; Ventura 2019, mn. 10. All of this was established by the pre-trial chamber in *Katanga and Chui*, 30 September 2008, para 517.

[511] It remains controversial, as put in Ohlin et al. 2013, p 726.

organisation could qualify as establishing control in the future.[512] The yet unclarified role of "payment mechanisms" within the automatic compliance requirement comes to mind.[513] Should it ever be developed into an individual factor of automatic compliance by the court, this would render the requirement boundless, thus proving Weigend's prediction.

In general, the theory has been condemned as vague, broad and under-justified; therefore, granting no doctrinal guidance.[514] This criticism seems warranted given the earlier observations on the ambiguous and underdefined requirements of indirect perpetration through an organisation. If the requirements are not thoroughly defined, the notion of control will consequently appear shapeless as well.

Perhaps in light of this opinion, Steer warns that the notion of control must be interpreted strictly and rigorously proven. Clear evidence that the accused could indeed ensure almost automatic compliance with orders must be produced, as the court would otherwise be applying a strict liability standard.[515] In a similar vein, Eboe-Osuji warned that the control theory might ultimately broaden, not restrict criminal responsibility.[516]

The theory's potential to designate decision makers in organisations as perpetrators is considered by commentators and judges as having a positive effect on fair labelling.[517] This point has played a vital role in the German debate for years, with the caveat that the principle of fair labelling is less known and referred to in German academia.[518]

In contrast to this, the figure of indirect perpetration through an organisation has also been criticised as being unable to explain the complex individual relations at play in the organisation and execution of collective violence.[519] As far as architects who do not make decisions that reign directly over the physical perpetrators are concerned, this is correct. Such persons cannot validly be subsumed under this doctrine. This

---

[512] Weigend 2015, pp 548–9.

[513] See above at Sect. 3.1.2.3.

[514] Dubber 2007, p 1001; Gil Gil and Maculan 2015, p 352.

[515] Steer 2017, p 308.

[516] *Ntaganda*, 30 March 2021, Partly concurring opinion of Judge Chile Eboe-Osuji, para 92.

[517] Cupido 2022, p 640; Ohlin et al. 2013, p 725; van Sliedregt 2012, pp 80–1; van Sliedregt 2015, pp 510–1; Weigend 2015, p 539; *Ntaganda*, 30 March 2021, Separate opinion of Judge Luz del Carmen Ibáñez Carranza, para 224. See also Guilfoyle 2011, p 255 et seq. analysing the apparent need of fair labelling in international justice. This topic will gain importance below in the comparison of indirect perpetration through an organisation and ordering crimes, see Chap. 7, Sects. 7.2.2. and 7.2.3.

[518] Instead, it is said that one would justifiably feel "uncomfortable" if high-level decision makers and architects of crimes would be convicted as "mere" instigators, see e.g. Roxin 2011, pp 196 (mere accessory), 198 (only instigators), 203 (merely instigators); Schünemann 2007, § 25 mn. 65. See also the description by Weigend 2011, p 96. Additionally, German authors argue with the "objective weight" of the decision maker's contribution, inferring that modes of accessory liability would be unfit to describe it; see in this regard Ambos 1998, p 232; Jung 1995, p 174; Murmann 1996, p 272.

[519] In this vein Jain 2014, p 139.

conclusion *inter alia* hinges on the factual concept of control over the crime at the ICC.

Additionally, it is this control that makes the direct perpetrators look like soulless automatons in the hands of the decision makers, or so it is remarked by Jain.[520] This interpretation is certainly plausible, especially if one is not familiar with the intricacies of the underlying concept of the perpetrator behind the perpetrator.

These points aside, criticism on the concept of control over the crime must go deeper. Is it convincing to say that the decision maker exercises an influence which grants them "control" over the crime and renders the decision of the individual direct perpetrators meaningless? This leads to an issue which lies at the theoretic foundation of the control or domination of the crime theory: the necessarily hypothetical dimension of control in cases of perpetration through an organisation.[521]

According to the traditional German approach, a person who dominates a crime holds the "criminal action" in their hands and decides over the "whether" and "how" of the crime. They are therefore the central figure of its realisation.[522] For indirect perpetration through an organisation this means that the background actor's direct influence over the specific crime is affirmed. The same is true for the ICC's doctrine of control over the crime, in which the decision maker of an organisation is thought to control (subjugate or bypass) the direct perpetrators' will and therefore decides whether and how the specific crime will be committed.[523] The systemic notion of domination of the crime plays no visible role in the ICC's jurisprudence. Despite its obvious "normative" dimension due to its reference to commission "through another", control over the crime is determined in a predominantly factual way at the ICC. The doctrine examines the actual influence of the decision maker over the crime.

However, it is questionable whether this logic provides a convincing explanation as to why the actor in the background controls the crime and acts through another.

3.3.3.1 The Traditional Approach to Domination/Control: The Organisation's Mechanisms Lead to Certainty which Leads to Domination/Control

Domination of the crime in the traditional German doctrine, as well as control over the crime pursuant to the ICC's construct, are first and foremost based on the "automatic mechanisms" of the organisation: Fungibility, readiness to commit the crime or the almost automatic compliance with orders.

Under Roxin's approach, fungibility of the perpetrator plays the central role in allowing the person on a higher level of the organisation to dominate the crime. In

520 Ibid., p 139. See in a similar vein: Guilfoyle 2011, pp 265–6, 275, 276.

521 See already *Lubanga*, 14 March 2012, Separate Opinion of Judge Adrian Fulford, para 17 on the necessary hypothesis on how the crime would have evolved without the accused's involvement.

522 See Chap. 2, Sect. 2.2.6.

523 See above Sect. 3.1.3.

Roxin's view, being able to randomly replace a person previously chosen to commit a crime, is one of three possibilities to have a crime "committed through another".[524] This is where his metaphor of a working apparatus, in which physical perpetrators are nothing but randomly replaceable cogs in a machine originates. Fungibility is thought to convey domination of the crime, because the free choice of the "human tool" to not carry out an order would not inhibit the commission of the crime. Instead, the leader of the organisation could "immediately" and "randomly" replace the refusing actor and have the crime committed by the new actor. This leads Roxin to the astonishing assertion that, if the leader of an organisation orders an assassination which fails three times, but succeeds on the fourth try, they would have had domination over the last crime. In other words, the high number of potential executioners leads to an equally high number of possible attempts—a plethora of opportunities to commit the crime. Based on this, Roxin believes that any crime committed through fungible physical perpetrators, will be dominated by the respective person in the background. This is closely connected to his inference of a perceived "certainty" that the crime will be committed.[525] As discussed, Roxin would ascribe responsibility for indirect perpetration through an organisation to leaders and officials of the Nazi murder machinery (including the mid-level bureaucrat Eichmann), leaders in secret service organisations, terrorist and extremist underground groups, civil war parties, as well as in the Mafia and other criminal gang structures.[526]

Schroeder's readiness to commit the crime represents another theoretical focus. For Schroeder, it is the exploitation of this readiness that creates virtual certainty of the commission of the crime for the person in the background and thus makes them an indirect perpetrator.[527] Other proposals require that the organisation be "embedded in a system of violence", or place emphasis on the social construct of the organisation. Both approaches would lead to (different) forms of psychological pressure on the physical actor.[528]

The ICC's approach resembles and combines these requirements as factors of its almost automatic compliance criterion. This requirement is narrower than Schroeder's readiness to commit the crime, however, the ICC considers fungibility and psychological pressure as factors in almost automatic compliance. The resulting notion of control is comparable to that of the traditional German theory: fungibility or psychological pressure presumably lead to an almost automatic compliance with orders, which in turn secures the indirect perpetrator's capacity to have the crime committed, i.e. certainty of success of the crime. They therefore have control over the crime.[529]

---

524 The other two supposedly are coercion and mistake. See Chap. 2, Sect. 2.2.3.2.

525 As stated above, this is not a relevant objective criterion to evaluate forms of responsibility, see Sect. 3.3.2.3.

526 See Chap. 2, Sect. 2.2.3.1.

527 See Chap. 2, Sect. 2.2.3.5.

528 See Chap. 2, Sect. 2.2.3.7.

529 See above Sects. 3.1.2.3, 3.1.3 and 3.2.3.

Thereby, the concepts of domination/control are factual rather than normative and imply that the indirect perpetrator can factually control the crime, i.e., decide whether and how the specific crime is committed.[530]

However, this view seems rather theoretical and an analysis of cases—especially ones which are typical for mass atrocities—unveils serious doubts as to this reasoning. Do fungibility of the physical perpetrator and psychological pressure through violent, strict training and disciplinary regimens truly grant the person in the background a final decision over whether and how a specific crime will be committed?

3.3.3.2 Stereotypical Cases and the Decisive Influence on the Specific Crime by Mid-level Actors and Executioners

The development of indirect perpetration through an organisation was triggered first and foremost by reflections on former Nazi officials, such as Adolf Eichmann and the apparatus which stood ready at their disposal.[531]

Given that "architects" of crimes usually fulfil neither Roxin's nor the ICC's requirements of the doctrine, this section focusses on actors whose conduct qualifies them as decision makers of international crimes and their supposed control over such crimes under the ICC's doctrine of indirect perpetration through an organisation.[532]

If it is to be ascribed to an individual, criminal responsibility must be attributed to a specific crime. Therefore, a crime committed in a concentration camp or by members of death brigades must be attributed specifically to leaders and organisers of the Holocaust. Likewise, each crime committed during attacks on towns and villages or during outbreaks of post-election violence must be specifically attributed to leaders of non-state organisations or governments.[533]

It is this connection between individual criminal responsibility and a specific criminal act which must be kept in mind when assessing the theory of domination of the crime through an organisation. The question must thus be: Can a decision maker of a criminal organisation have control over the crime if the specific crime is committed by members of this organisation at another time and place?

This question has been debated in Germany with regard to leaders within Nazi Germany and the crimes committed in extermination camps. In the ambit of international criminal law, it concerns the leaders and decision makers of any relevant group of people, such as governments with state forces and potential affiliated militias, non-state armed groups and vast criminal networks. The issue also concerns any

---

[530] See also Weigend 2011, p 100.

[531] See Chap.2, Sects. 2.1, 2.2.2 and 2.2.3.1.

[532] See on the earlier findings in this regard: Chap.2, Sects. 2.2.6 and 2.6.2 as well as Sect. 3.2.3. Note again that the conduct of such organisers may be grasped through the combined mode of indirect co-perpetration.

[533] See already with reference to the German debate: Herzberg 2000, p 38, reaffirming that every instance of perpetration and participation must have a link to a specific crime and a specific victim ("*tatkonkret und tatopferkonkret*").

potential situation and *modus operandi*: concentration or prison camps, military-like field operations and any other outbreaks of violence.

To approach the issue, one should consider two things.

First, criminal states as well as smaller non-state organisations are shaped by hierarchies, division of labour and often bureaucracy. The enterprises of organisations are determined from above, but initial orders do not tend to be specific. The execution of crimes is thus highly dependent on the subsequent organisational steps and specifying orders. This dynamic logically seems to grow with the size and structural complexity of an organisation. This means that it will be more prevalent in cases where crimes are conceived in the highest echelons of a state, as alleged in the situations in Sudan (Darfur), Libya and Côte d'Ivoire. However, the dynamic that instructions "take on flesh and blood" with every involved lower level of a hierarchy, exists in much smaller organisations as well.[534]

This leads to the second point: to have the crimes carried out, an organisation necessarily relies on the decisions of mid-level actors—planners, organisers and commanders responsible for certain areas—and on low-level officers and the rank and file.[535]

These observations are not novel and are widely known, but are they mirrored by the concept of domination of/control over the crime? In other words, is domination/control over the crime a convincing description of the kind of influence exercised by decision makers on higher levels of the organisations over the specific crimes?

Exemplary Cases from the Genesis of the Doctrine

Two real life cases served as examples to Roxin for the conception of the doctrine: (1) the mass murders in Nazi extermination camps during the Holocaust and (2) the assassinations of exiled politicians through a KGB agent.[536] Additionally, the so called *Mauerschützen* cases before the German BGH became a jurisprudential example of the application of a version of the doctrine.[537]

It has been pointed out that the commission of a specific crime in Nazi extermination camps depended on the decisions and actions of many of the involved personnel. Officials on different organisational levels, including the commanders of concentration camps, decided to spare groups or individuals and thus prevented their killing.[538]

---

[534] This formulation has been used to describe organisational dynamics in the *Judgment Against Adolf Eichmann*, at No. 232. See also Anderson 2018, p 61 on the delegation of authority to lower levels in order to effectively pursue the (genocidal) objectives set on higher levels of the Nazi state apparatus and how this is typical for large-scale crimes such as genocide.

[535] Similarly see Herzberg 2009, p 580.

[536] See Chap. 2, Sect. 2.2.3.

[537] See Chap. 2, Sect. 2.3.2.

[538] Herzberg points out how Rudolf Höß, commander of the concentration camp Auschwitz, could have prevented a high number of murders, had he wanted to do so, see Herzberg 2009, p 580. Of course, it is probably correct to assume that a commander of a concentration camp could not have spared the majority or all inmates. However, regarding actual survivors, their potential murder under another commander remains hypothetical.

Officials tasked with the identification of Jewish people in their respective communities omitted to list, warned, and thus enabled the escape of some families. This certainly happened in a few and could have happened in many more instances.[539] In other words, mid and low-level officials made decisions that impeded the commission of certain crimes.

On the level of organisers, planners, and commanders, this was possible due to their significant influence over the way in which instructions were ultimately carried out. Contrary to the belief of some, for the most part directives and instructions from a political leadership involved in mass atrocities do not specify the victims, times, and dates of the crimes. Instead, decision makers on various levels are given considerable discretion regarding how and against whom to act.[540] This discretion can be used to manipulate or sabotage plans from higher echelons of an organisation. Whilst such "internal resistance" was not a frequent occurrence within the Nazi regime, it is known to have occurred and succeeded in some cases.[541]

Equivalent scenarios are conceivable during the "cleansing operations" of death brigades in occupied territories.[542] A low-ranking officer could attempt to enable the escape of persons apprehended by his squad, or a soldier could decide not to point out the places that he identified as hideouts of wanted Jewish people or members of another persecuted group.

The devastating truth that such acts of humanity were scarce reminds us of the overall murderous functionality of the Nazi machinery. "In general" it worked all too well and, naturally, no one person within the apparatus could have stopped it as a whole.[543] However, this does not alter the veracity of the previous statement:

---

[539] See Herzberg 2000, pp 38–9; Herzberg 2009, p 579.

[540] "[A]s is customary in any hierarchical regime, an order becomes more and more detailed and takes on flesh and blood as it is passed down from one level to the next", see *Judgment Against Adolf Eichmann*, No. 232. See in more detail Herzberg 2009, p 580, who describes how the Nazi officers upon the arrival of Jews in concentration camps would decide who would be murdered right away and who would not. During *Tschistka* (the great terror by Stalin's Soviet Russia on (perceived) opponents), Stalin would usually not specify the deportation and murder victims, but rather give out general instructions to the agencies loyal to him. Herzberg also quotes Hitler's so-called "euthanasia order", which led to the mass killing of people with disabilities. This order by Hitler simply tasked two officials with the "naming of physicians" who would consequently be authorised to "allow" the killing of people with disabilities. None of the victims or respective perpetrators were specified by Hitler beforehand, nor was the order phrased in a way which would oblige the decision makers on other levels to include or exclude specific next level decision makers in the process. A similar relationship between the highest echelons of power and the lower officers has been described for the apparatus of the Argentinian Junta. Osiel describes how the latter enjoyed considerable discretion concerning the question of how to proceed with the victims of their abductions, ranging from the possibility of simply setting them free to murdering them; see Osiel 2005, p 1836.

[541] See Arendt 2018, pp 275-8 who elaborates on authorities within the German occupying forces in Denmark which were apparently involved in warning and evacuating Jews before they could be deported.

[542] These have not been addressed in the conception of the theory by Roxin. As seen above, however, (at Sect. 3.3.2.1) such situations make for a better point of reference for crimes committed in current cases before the ICC.

[543] Herzberg 2009, p 579.

the commission of specific crimes depends on the decisions of different people at different times, places and positions. Officers and the executioners themselves had the power to decide whether specific crimes would happen or not.[544]

The other original example for domination of the crime is the assassination of a person through the member of a secret service organization.[545] With regards to such a situation, Roxin asserts that an assassination attempt may fail a few times, but if it is eventually committed, the person in the background would have domination over this crime.

This evaluation can also cast doubt on the notion of control. The repeated defection or failure of agents calls the domination of the background actor into question. Should the agent tasked with the assassination choose to warn their target, this would seriously inhibit the commission of the crime. Furthermore, the victim may have other chances of self-defence or of going undercover after a failed attempt on their life. Finally, even if the crime is eventually committed, this could take weeks or months longer than originally intended.[546]

This example is therefore unconvincing with regard to domination/control of the crime. Admittedly, unlike in mass atrocities, a victim is already specified in this case. However, the time and date are not, and neither is the perpetrator because—as the example itself illustrates—they can still refuse. The idea that the person in the background decides over the "whether" and "how" in such a situation is extremely far-fetched.[547] It would be more accurate to state that the person in the background "instructs and hopes that everything goes as planned".

As far as state organised crime is concerned, the German BGH addressed the issue with regards to the shooting of persons trying to flee East Germany.[548] This is another example of soldiers committing specific crimes, based on very general orders issued by the highest echelons of power. Based on its own version of the theory,[549] the BGH decided that a person in the background, relying on the apparatus and with

---

[544] In the same vein: Herzberg 2000, pp 38–9; Herzberg 2009, pp 579–80; based on this Schlehofer calls the domination, which is invoked by Roxin's theory "potential domination" because the persons in the background would only dominate the potential crime which would replace the first attempt should the executioner decide not to carry it out; see Schlehofer 2008, p 361.

[545] See above Sect. 3.2.2.3.

[546] Herzberg 2000, p 38. Note that Roxin has argued that factors from outside of the organised power structure could not serve to impede domination of the crime. This is important as any kind of perpetrator must expect a victim to defend him- or herself, try to escape or impede the commission of the crime. Potential factors originating in the victim's sphere or out of coincidence should therefore indeed not play a role in assessing a theory of perpetration and participation. Instead of "outside factors", Roxin asserts it would be important that the members of the organisation not "act on their own and in contradiction to the organisation's goal, but as organs of the leadership whose authority they recognize" (translation by the author), see Roxin 2019, p 278. The foregoing examples and argumentation, however, demonstrate that not even Roxin's model organisation of Nazi Germany worked the way he imagined.

[547] See also Ambos 2004, pp 596–8; Herzberg 2000, p 38.

[548] See Chap. 2, Sect. 2.3.2.

[549] For differences between the BGH's approach and the traditional version of the doctrine, see Chap. 2, Sect. 2.3.2.3; see also the comparison above under Sect. 3.2.2.

the necessary mental element, would have domination of the crime and thus be an indirect perpetrator.[550] Domination was affirmed for the members of the political bureau and the national defence council. As stated *obiter dictum*, it would have also been affirmed for regiment commanders, but was denied (together with instigation) for lower-level officers responsible for the briefing of the border guards before their regular shifts.

Two of the seven killings at the GDR border in the trial against the members of the national defence council were committed by guards who shot the victims while they were crossing the border fortifications. The other victims were killed by spring-guns which had been installed by personnel of the border troops.[551] In the two instances in which border guards personally shot the victims, it is obvious that the members of the national defence council did not have actual influence over the specific crime.[552] Contrary to the traditional German theory, these guards were not fungible in a way that would have ensured the commission of the specific crimes, i.e. the killing of the two victims. If the respective soldiers had decided not to shoot, or to deliberately miss their target, the men trying to flee the GDR could have possibly been successful. The guards could not have been replaced like "cogs in a machine" with sufficient time for the crime—the shooting of the victims—to still be committed.[553]

The BGH decided not to use the fungibility criterion, instead stressing how the crimes would be committed "almost automatically" due to the "standardized procedures" (the passing down of orders) and the "unconditional willingness of the perpetrators to commit the crime". Due to this, the leadership level could be certain that the crime would be committed. The decision of the physical perpetrator would be "predetermined by the framework conditions".[554]

This is equally unconvincing. At the time of the judgment, the former border guard and shooter of one of the victims had already been convicted for murder (*Totschlag*).[555] His actions were not excused due to duress or a similar defence.[556] The question arises why the decision of a person acting completely autonomously be

---

[550] Although not prominently featured as the only necessary precondition for being a perpetrator, the judgments of the BGH clearly and explicitly mention domination of the crimes, see German Federal Court of Justice, Judgment, 26.7.1994, in: Neue Juristische Wochenschrift (NJW), 1994, p 2706; German Federal Court of Justice, Decision, 02.11.2007, in: Neue Zeitschrift für Strafrecht, 2008, p 90. As displayed in Chap. 2, this somewhat less central notion of domination of the crime nowadays plays little to no role in the BGH's jurisprudence (see Chap. 2, Sects. 2.3.2.2, 2.3.2.2).

[551] German Federal Court of Justice, Judgment, 26.7.1994, above n 541, p 2704.

[552] In the same vein: Herzberg 2000, pp 37–8; Weisser 2019, p 248.

[553] Herzberg 2000, pp 37–8; Murmann 1996, p 280; Noltenius 2003, pp 321–2; Rotsch 1998, p 493; Rotsch 2000, pp 528–9; The District Court of Berlin rejected indirect perpetration through an organisation precisely because of these considerations, see German Federal Court of Justice, Judgment, 26.7.1994, above n 541, p 2705.

[554] German Federal Court of Justice, Judgment, 26.7.1994, above n 541, p 2706.

[555] See ibid., p 2704, No. 7 in list of incidents; the Judgment referred to is: German Federal Court of Justice, Judgment, 25.03.1993, in: NJW, 1993, p 1932.

[556] However, the BGH determined that, based on the position of the soldier at the end of the hierarchy, a low sentence would be passed because the GDR's system would make him a victim of the border regime as well, see German Federal Court of Justice, Judgment, 25.03.1993, above n 546, p 1937.

"predetermined" in such a case? One could argue that a (very) high possibility existed that border guards would opt to execute their orders, but this is far from certain. Any of the soldiers could decide not to shoot.[557] The case is less clear concerning the killings through pre-installed spring guns which were activated by the victims trying to climb the fences. However, in these cases, one should still be mindful of what was outlined earlier: the vast number of officers of different ranks tasked with ordering and organising the set-up of such traps speaks against domination or control by GDR leadership.[558] Interestingly, the District Court of the first instance judgment in *Nationaler Verteidigungsrat* denied indirect perpetration and affirmed instigation (for two of the three defendants) applying this exact reasoning, i.e. that no control could have been exercised by the members of the national defence council.[559] It is additionally noteworthy that, after replacing the convictions by establishing indirect perpetration, the BGH did not alter the respective sentences. Its reasoning being that, had it convicted "correctly", the District Court would have handed down the same sentences for perpetration as it had for instigation and aiding and abetting.[560]

These cases have been analysed by scholars and the courts with a view to the respective requirements of their approaches. As outlined above, whilst these requirements differ, the ICC's requirement of almost automatic compliance matches the various proposals in German theory to a certain extent. Furthermore, the certainty of the commission of the crime is a central point for both the traditional German theory and the ICC. It is this certainty which cannot be convincingly established in the cases above. Neither the fungibility of, nor the psychological pressure on the physical perpetrators led or could have led to any certainty that they would eventually commit the crime.

These three cases lie at the heart of the theory's conception and raise serious doubts about the ability of the doctrines of control over the crime and indirect perpetration through an organisation to provide a justification as to why persons in the background, far removed in time and space, should be indirect perpetrators.

It is submitted that this dynamic—the influence of various people's decisions on the commission of a specific crime—shapes any mass atrocity in which people on different levels act autonomously in the instruction, organisation, planning, and execution of these crimes.

---

557 Herzberg 2000, p 38.

558 See also Noltenius 2003, p 321 who stresses how the many different levels of hierarchy, all occupied by persons with autonomous decisions, denies the politicians domination over the commission of specific crimes.

559 See the description in German Federal Court of Justice, Judgment, 26.7.1994, above n 541, p 2705.

560 Ibid., p 2707. Consequently, the BGH believed that even the difference between aiding and abetting (already vested with a mandatory mitigation of punishment at the time of the crimes) and perpetration would not have altered the sentencing.

Exemplary Cases from the ICC's Practice

As the foregoing reasoning could apply to any situation involving mass atrocities, one must examine cases which have come before the ICC as well. In certain cases, examples of groups of defecting perpetrators were examined by the chambers.

In the confirmation of charges in the *Banda and Jerbo* case, the pre-trial chamber examined the unlawful attack on an African Union military compound through a coalition of militias. The chamber found that when troops on the way to the attack learned the identity of their target—African Union soldiers instead of Government soldiers as they had been previously told—some of the troops left the convoy and withdrew.[561]

In *Muthaura* et al., the defence called one of the accused's control over the *Mungiki* sect into question, because on the way to an attack, a number of persons left the group before arriving at their destination.[562] However, the chamber rejected considering such a defection as an argument against control, as the accused was able to promptly organize replacement for the defecting members of the group.[563] He did so by contacting an individual, to whom he promised money and who then recruited replacements for the missing attackers.[564]

Especially the latter case could be regarded as a textbook example of the theory of indirect perpetration through an organisation based on automatic compliance through fungibility. However, this is only due to the specific situation: the original attackers could only be replaced because they decided against the attack before it happened. The same was true for the fighters in *Banda and Jerbo*, where the crews of the respective vehicles withdrew before the attack. Aside from this limitation to the specific situation, these examples additionally illustrate how low-ranking subordinates may decide to exercise their free will to abandon their superiors' plans. It is conceivable that this free decision to disengage from unfolding crimes could also be made where a replacement was impossible due to the action already being underway and/or superiors not having sufficient oversight to gain awareness of the perpetrators' disengagement and consequently replace them. In the latter incident, the defecting persons were members of the *Mungiki* sect, known for brutal punishment of disobedience. This demonstrates that violent and strict disciplinary regimens do not necessarily lead to the type of control associated with them either. Apparently, the threat of violent punishment, including the death sentence, did not stop these persons from disengaging.[565]

Another case illustrates the significant influence of mid-ranking actors on mass atrocities. The trial judgment against Bosco Ntaganda elaborates on the refusal of a commander known as "Americain" to participate in an attack on the town of Kobu

561 *Abdallah Banda*, 7 March 2011, para 134 b). Note again that the chamber ultimately confirmed charges of co-perpetration and did not elaborate on the alternative charge of indirect co-perpetration (at para 162).

562 *Muthaura et al.*, 23 January 2012, para 409.

563 Ibid., paras 395–6, 409.

564 Ibid., paras 395–6.

565 On the disciplinary and punishment system of the *Mungiki* sect, see ibid., paras 208–13, 408.

in the eastern D.R. Congo. Americain was the commander of one of the battalions which were intended to carry out the attack.[566] It is not entirely clear in the judgment, but it seems that as a consequence of Americain's refusal, only two instead of three battalions attacked the town.[567] In order to show his control over the lower tiers of officers, the chamber refers to Ntaganda's subsequent messages via radio, in which he stated that insubordination is intolerable and that his orders must be obeyed.[568] However, this incident may equally prove how Ntaganda had no ultimate say over whether and how certain crimes would be committed, given that mid-level commanders were apparently able to definitively refuse to participate in an attack. From the little information presented in the judgment, it seems that Americain was not replaced as a commander, nor was his battalion replaced through another. This shows that the menacingly strict disciplinary regime of the *UPC/FPLC* obviously did not persuade Americain to order his men to participate in the attack.

The confirmation of charges against *Ruto et al.* elaborates on the important role of mid-level actors as well. Here, the chamber found that a range of mid-level actors were responsible for punishment and payment, the two aspects that led the chamber to affirm the almost automatic compliance criterion for the "network" of perpetrators in the case.[569]

Finally, a third critical aspect emerged in ICC jurisprudence that raises doubts about the type of "control" that decision makers in organisations exercise. In the case against *Ruto et al.*, the defence noted that the accused had disseminated peace messages, but the crimes had not stopped. As portrayed above, the chamber's reaction to this seemingly indicates that these calls for an end to violence were genuine and not countered by the accused through internal orders to the contrary.[570] The pre-trial chamber affirmed control over the organisation, nonetheless. Considering the aforementioned, however, it cannot still be affirmed that the accused could decide whether the crimes would be committed when "his" organisation was loose and no longer abiding by his orders.[571]

These points may serve as an illustrative example of different situations that arose in "modern" international criminal law. They show that the concept of control over the crime as applied by the ICC is just as questionable in these cases as it would be in the historic cases that led to the conception of the doctrine. Furthermore, it should be noted that these examples are not hypothetical but based on actual failures within presumably tight organisational procedures that led to the commission of crimes.

---

566 *Ntaganda*, 8 July 2019, para 565.

567 See ibid., para 572 with fn. 1757 speaking of two battalions led by other commanders.

568 Ibid., paras 565 with fn. 1723 especially.

569 *Ruto et al.*, 23 January 2012, paras 322 (coordinators deciding over and handing out payment), 325 (competence of local coordinators to decide over punishment), 328 (coordinators being told to "take charge" of the attacks).

570 See the evaluation above at Sect. 3.1.2.1.

571 See *Ruto et al.*, 23 January 2012, paras 318–9. If it is true that the accused's calls for peace were genuine, this case would serve as an example of dynamics which have not been discussed yet. It would show how the capacity to instruct the commission of crimes does not necessarily entail the capacity to order their halt as well.

The theoretical potential of mid- and low-level actors in ICC decisions to impede or obstruct crimes could be explained at length and with the aid of many examples.[572]

For example, in *Katanga and Chui,* the crimes in question were mostly committed during an attack on the village of Bogoro in Ituri Province, D.R. Congo. The fighters of the two militias attacked from two sides, making escape difficult. However, this does not mean that situations in which individual fighters or low-level officers could have altered the course of events are inconceivable. Just as their cruelty could aggravate the harm brought over the population of Bogoro, their decisions to not kill, rape, loot or burn in certain instances could change the course of events with regards to specific crimes. These decisions could be made at any moment during the attack, as an individual decision in a specific moment could ultimately mean that a certain victim or person's property would be left unscathed.

The Case of Irreplaceable Specialists

Another frequently mentioned point from the German debate concerns the use of highly trained specialists. It is questionable whether there can be control over the crime if a specialist is ordered to act.[573] Concerning such cases, some German scholars maintain that fungibility is not suitable to describe how an actor in the background could dominate the crime. A specialist cannot be replaced at will, instead an organisation is highly dependent on their decision to co-operate. Should they decline, no one can take their place.[574] Roxin takes the view that in such cases, instigation would be the correct form of responsibility,[575] and the Rome Statute would additionally provide the mode of ordering in such situations.

Given that the ICC recognises other factors enabling control, it would have to assess whether in the specific case, it was fungibility or rather strict and violent training that enabled such control. The argument of irreplaceability is not relevant to those acting under menacingly strict training regimens.

Regardless, the irreplaceability argument can only be persuasive if one generally accepts that a background actor can dominate a specific crime through their will by using persons who ultimately make their own decisions. As discussed in the previous subsections, such a notion of domination or control should be rejected. The specialist argument adds little to the criticism as any physical perpetrator is not fungible when committing a certain crime. Whether they are specialists makes no difference because both can decide not to act, thus potentially impeding the crime's commission. Additionally, a specialist's heightened, pre-existing readiness to commit the crime does not alter the evaluation of the presumed "control" of the

---

572 Note in this vein also *Ntaganda*, 30 March 2021, Partly concurring opinion of Judge Chile Eboe-Osuji, para 45, explaining how Osama Bin Laden would not have had control over the 9/11 attacks in the sense of the doctrine, given that the suicide pilots of the hijacked planes themselves could have decided not to carry out the attacks.

573 Schroeder 1995, p 178; Schroeder 2009, p 569.

574 Schroeder 1995, p 178; Schroeder 2009, p 569. This is one of Schroeder's main arguments in favour of his theory in which domination is the consequence of the "pre-existing readiness to commit the crime", see Chap. 2,Sect. 2.2.3.5.

575 Roxin 2003, § 25 mn. 118.

indirect perpetrator. As already discussed, a person previously determined to commit a crime, can abandon this intent at any given moment, thus negating the "control" which the person in the background exercised when instructing the commission of the crime.

Preliminary Conclusion Regarding Control in Stereotypical Cases

The commission of specific crimes, which are ordered by a leader or authority within an organisation, often depends on the willingness to cooperate and further planning by mid- and low-level actors. Mid-level planners, organisers, and executioners make decisions which influence the way in which crimes are committed.

Some scholars argue that domination of and control over the crime, in such cases, would only (but sufficiently) be domination/control of the result. I.e., a person in a leadership position would dominate/control the organisation and consequently have domination/control over the consequence of the crime.[576]

However, this assertion is also incorrect. As discussed, there are many instances throughout the commission of mass atrocities during which a member on the execution level of an organisation can decide not to commit an individual crime. Depending on the specific situation, they will not be replaceable and consequently, a specific crime will not be committed.[577] A planner or organiser can decide to warn and even enable the escape of potential victims. But, under the ICC's factual notion of control, criminal responsibility arises for the commission of a specific crime against a specific victim and its specific legally protected right. A decision maker who instructs the commission of mass atrocities has therefore no control, no ultimate decision concerning the question whether a specific crime and its criminal consequence will occur.[578]

The planners, organisers and executioners in an organised power structure may be replaceable "cogs in the machine" as far as its general functioning is concerned. Their malfunction may not stop the entire apparatus from working, but it stops the commission of a specific crime or, depending on their position and influence, of several crimes. In this regard, the apparatus does not work independently from its members' will and its leaders have no control over the commission of a specific crime.[579]

---

[576] Roxin 2006a, p 299; see the description by Ambos 2004, p 598 and Rotsch 2009, p 328; Schünemann turns this into his central criterion of domination of the crime, see Schünemann 2006, p 411.

[577] See in the same vein in English literature: Ambos 2009, pp 145-6; Guilfoyle 2011, p 275; Orozco López and Silva Santaularia 2022, p 663.

[578] See already with reference to the German traditional approach: Herzberg 2000, pp 37–8; Weisser 2019, p 249; in a similar vein Eidam 2015, p 169. See also the explanation in English by Guilfoyle 2011, p 275. In the same vein: Zazcyk 1996, p 414 who states that the "automatism" and responsibility of the executioner are mutually exclusive concepts. By this, he is of course relying on the autonomy principle, but nevertheless correctly describes the factual dependence of the person in the background on the executioners and others.

[579] See already Herzberg 2000, pp 37–8; Herzberg 2009, p 579; see also Ambos 2009, pp 145–6; Eidam 2015, p 169; Guilfoyle 2011, p 275; Hoyer 2017, § 25 mn. 90; Murmann 1996, pp 269, 272–4 ("*Tatherrschaft* is only the functioning of organisational relations" (at 273), "The system does not

3.3.3.3 An Unconvincing Counterargument

German supporters of the theories try to counter this assertion with the argument discussed below. Given the resemblance between the traditional German model and the ICC's approach, this line of reasoning is valid for the theory in international criminal law as well.

The counter argument can be summed up as follows: The *actual* or *current* domination/control exercised by the person in the background is proven by the functioning of the apparatus in the specific situation.[580] In other words, the fact that the crime was committed demonstrates the functioning of the apparatus and is therefore proof of the leader's domination of the crime.[581] Thoughts on the *potential* possibility to impede the crime's commission through decisions made by the executing actor (or others) are labelled as hypothetical and therefore invalid.[582]

In this vein, Schünemann states that domination of the crime does not have to be complete or seamless, and that hinting at hypothetical realities of non-compliance would be a distraction from the current domination (*aktuelle Tatherrschaft*). He further adds that where the crime is committed, there is obviously no non-compliance.[583] Similarly, Roxin contests the validity of the criticism, stating that the murders committed through the myrmidons of the Nazi or GDR regime show that the "automatism of the apparatus" worked.[584] Roxin relies on the notion that the functioning of the organised apparatus grants the person in the background what he calls "domination of surrogate causes" or "substitute measures" (*Ersatzursachenherrschaft*). This would lead to the effect that the physical actor would not get to decide whether the crime is eventually committed.[585] In this context, it is sometimes stressed that domination of the crime is not based on a factual observation but on a guiding principle. Roxin explains that this principle takes the facts as presented by reality into account, as normative principles must be inspired by reality.[586]

This line of thought of the supporters of the control theory relies on two interconnected ideas:

- Reality shows that the organisation works and thus proves the validity of the concept of indirect perpetration through an organisation.

become a soul-less thing through the number of members. All the members still have a free will and this creates uncertainty" (at 274), translations by the author)); Noltenius 2003, pp 320–1; Osiel 2005, p 1836; Rotsch 1998, p 493; Rotsch 2009, p 333; Weisser 2019, p 248. Also note *Ntaganda*, 30 March 2021, Partly concurring opinion of Judge Chile Eboe-Osuji, paras 77 et seq.

580 Schünemann 2007, § 25 mn. 127.

581 Roxin 2003, § 25 mn. 114–117; Roxin 2006b, pp 391-2; Roxin 2019, Chpter 12 mn. 388.

582 Schünemann 2007, § 25 mn. 127.

583 Ibid., § 25 mn. 127, translation by the author; note also how this reference to the executioner's knowledge of their replaceability indeed seems closer to Schroeder's concept of pre-existing readiness to commit the crime.

584 Roxin 2003, § 25 mn. 114–5.

585 Ibid., § 25 mn. 117.

586 Roxin 2006b, p 392; Roxin 2019, Chpter 12 mn. 380–81.

– To rely on other hypothetical realities, in which the crime is not committed, is therefore invalid.

Given what has already been discussed about the stereotypical cases of mass atrocities, these counter arguments must be evaluated critically.

3.3.3.4 Domination/Control Through an Organisation as a Hypothetical Basic Assumption that Ignores Rather than Considers Reality

Section 3.3.3.2) above has given rise to doubts on the notion of control over the crime through an organisation based on the factual dynamics, i.e., the many decisions made by all people involved in large scale crimes. The question is whether the counterarguments, as listed in Section. 3.3.3.3), remove these doubts?

Does reality demonstrate how the organisation works and thus prove the validity of the theory of indirect perpetration through an organisation? Does reality prove how, through a general order, a political leader has control over the commission of a specific crime against a victim they do not single out?

The answer must be in the negative. The factual, eventual commission of the crime only proves that some dynamic is at work in situations in which mass atrocities are committed. It does not prove that this dynamic is the result of factors such as fungibility or violent and strict training regimens. Neither does it show that "domination of" or "control over the crime" are the correct descriptions for this dynamic, and that a decision maker in an organisation can and should be described as holding such control. Instead, the fact that the crime was committed only shows that some factors—probably a combination of various ones—lead to the regular and frequent commission of crimes by members of an organisation if instructed from above.[587] However, this only means that supporters of the theories correctly describe the core issue of the debate. It is not a convincing argument for their legal description of this real-life phenomenon. This evaluation is not altered by speaking of "current domination when a crime is committed (Schünemann) or by pointing out that "the automatism works as Nazi crimes show" (Roxin). Likewise, suggesting that the indirect perpetrator acts "through the organisation" not through an individual does not make a difference.[588] The traditional German approach and the ICC interpret domination/control as factual, crime-specific concepts. As previously discussed, it is precisely the decision of individuals that will decide over the commission of the crime. Whilst the argument of the theory's supporters may be true that the organisation as a whole functions along predetermined paths, the commission of specific crimes does not.[589]

[587] In a similar vein see Weisser 2019, p 247 and Morrison in *Ntaganda*, 30 March 2021, Separate opinion of Judge Howard Morrison on Mr. Ntaganda's appeal, para 32.

[588] This wording has been used occasionally by the ICC (see *Muthaura et al.*, 23 January 2012, para 409) and by Roxin (Roxin 2007, p 9).

[589] See also Herzberg, ZIS 2009, 578; Weisser 2019, p 249.

Roxin's term of "domination of surrogate causes" does not alter any of the findings above. The conclusion that the time and dynamics of a situation often do not allow for a replacement of a failing executioner, still holds true if the presumed "fungibilityis replaced by the term "substitute measures" or "surrogate causes". Equally true is that through their power to shape instructions, mid-level actors decisively influence subsequent crimes. As has further been illustrated with exemplary cases above, the implementation of violent and strict training regimens does not affect this assessment. These examples show how the threat of punishment does not function as a reliable deterrent to decisions of mid and low-ranking members of organisations that may influence and effectively impede the commission of specific crimes.

Roxin is correct when stating that a form of criminal responsibility must consider real-life circumstances. However, the arguments supporters advance in this regard provide no additional reasoning as to why indirect perpetration through an organisation would grasp real life circumstances especially well.

In fact, the cases above clearly show the opposite, i.e., that the commission of the crime is not under the "control" of persons in the background. This is first and foremost because of the free choice of the planners, organisers, and executioners who, despite existing pressure, can decide not to have a certain crime committed, yet will not be replaced.[590] Even if their defection is ultimately discovered and the crime ultimately committed, it must be questioned why in this situation (with another, replaced executioner) control would be the correct description of the leader's influence over the crime.

Based on the foregoing, one must conclude that supporters of the theory of indirect perpetration through an organisation in academia advance the factual circumstances of mass atrocities in the belief that the commission of crimes proves that their theory is correct. The ICC regards the theory in a similar way and affirms control based on the same considerations.[591]

However, the cases and their analysis show that this perception is wrong. It seems that it is based on a very narrow view on systemic crimes, which simplifies matters to make reality fit the concept. Roxin states that, "in most cases of indirect perpetration through organised power structures—consider murders in concentration camps, ethnical 'cleansings' and the liquidation of opponents of the regime through special units—the power to prevent the commission of the crime is simply not given".[592] When solely considering the execution level, this view may be partially persuasive

[590] In the German debate, scholars have therefore advanced the autonomy principle as the distinction criterion of choice, rejecting indirect perpetration through an organisation as "erroneously factual", see Herzberg 2000, pp 46–7. This option is no longer available when interpreting the Rome Statute; it was made by those commenting on the German regulations and is exclusively available within the ambit of the GCC, where the perpetrator behind the perpetrator is not explicitly recognized. In a similar vein see Orozco López and Silva Santaularia 2022, p 661 et seq.

[591] Although the elaborations are shorter and fewer because they are usually only employed when made necessary through defence arguments.

[592] Roxin 2019, Chpter 12 mn. 389. The same can be seen in other instances, e.g. Roxin 2006b, p 391: "The action to be carried out can be modified by the executioner at best, but it cannot be changed"; and Roxin 2003, § 25 mn. 119: "Perpetration through an organisation is not tailored for crimes by specialists, but rather for crimes in repeating patterns such as the concentration camp

where crimes are committed in static situations, e.g. in concentration camps or against inmates of prisons. However, the other examples expose the blindness to reality, the type-cast view on mass atrocities,[593] which has been criticised above. Who, if not the soldiers or members of paramilitary units or special forces, can decide over the commission of a specific crime? Who, if not them, can decide not to expose the (already identified) hideout of a wanted person, or decide to let a potential victim escape and randomly fire into the air to feign a successful flight?

The assertion that an indirect perpetrator in an organisation could "replace unwilling perpetrators beforehand"[594] is not helpful. Control over the crime means control during, not before its commission, and in the situations described above, the replacement of the actors is not possible.[595] Further, the threat of violent disciplinary measures and punishment does not impact this either and the designated executioners of crimes retain their free will.

In summary, during the commission of specific crimes, the executioners are (very often) not replaceable because if one executioner decides not to act—be it out of mercy, laziness or due to bribery[596]—the opportunity to have a specific crime committed, will not repeat itself.[597] The same is true for the influence exerted through violent and strict training and disciplinary regimens; despite the pressure put on them, mid- and low-level actors still make active choices about their conduct and thus, influence whether and how specific crimes are committed.[598]

Apart from this, the narrow view on the characteristics of atrocity crimes completely disregards the decision power of mid-level actors. The counter arguments and descriptions exclusively focus on the (incorrect) assumption that the actors at the execution level cannot influence the crime, i.e., prevent it. The same underlying reasoning can be found in ICC decisions.[599] However, if a high political leader or general is to have control over the crime, then all subordinate levels of command would have to equally lack the power to influence the specific crime. In reality, this is not the case.

---

murders and shooting at the berlin wall" (translation by the author). The latter is especially prone to raise doubts on that view as the static situation in a concentration camp is very different from a situation of a fugitive's flight to safety over a fortified border.

593 This view can also be seen in descriptions of what is perceived as relevant in and characterising for such situations, see e.g. the belief that the desk perpetrator would have "*Gestaltungsmacht*" ("Power to design [the crime]", Roxin 2006b, p 391) and the reference to "repeating patterns" (see Roxin 2003, § 25 mn. 119). Critical also Rotsch 2000, p 528.

594 This has been stated by Roxin 2003, § 25 mn. 115; the ICC has relied on exactly this reasoning in *Muthaura et al.*, 23 January 2012, para 409.

595 Rotsch 2000, p 528; in the same vein Timpe 2016, p 239.

596 Herzberg 2009, p 578.

597 In the same vein see Rotsch 2000, pp 528–9.

598 In the German debate, the line is drawn between autonomously acting direct perpetrators and those which can defend themselves on grounds of mistake or coercion, especially duress. The line between such cases and violent and strict training regimens (in the sense of indoctrination), which do not yet amount to a ground of defence, can be difficult to find.

599 Cf. Sects. 3.1.2.3 and 3.1.3.

Consequently, it is simply not true that the unsuccessful executioner of a specific crime would be replaced "immediately". Roxin's metaphor of the apparatus which keeps functioning irrespective of the malfunction of certain cogs in the machine, is unsustainable.[600] Thus, the assertion of the structural difference between an instigator and a desk perpetrator is also unsustainable. The same is true for the pre-trial chamber's finding in *Katanga and Chui*, that an indirect perpetrator could ensure automatic compliance with orders in contrast to an ordering person under Art. 25 (3) (b).[601] The foregoing part has demonstrated how, in the stereotypical cases, the executioners are often just as independent, and the leader in the background just as dependent on the direct perpetrator as would be the case in "classic" scenarios of instigation.[602]

The same holds true for the other aspect of almost automatic compliance with orders in ICC jurisprudence: Violent and strict training and disciplinary regimens do not lead to an unconditional, unchangeable willingness of the direct perpetrator to commit a crime. The individual can change their mind and decide not to engage in the criminal conduct.[603]

For both types of mechanisms, fungibility and violent and strict training regimens, the perception of "certainty" that a crime will be committed through the structures of the organisation is equally untrue.[604]

Consequently, fungibility and violent and strict disciplinary regimens do not create "control" over the crime for a decision maker of an organisation. In fact, concerning leaders in higher ranks and mass atrocities, no factual control over specific crimes seems to exist. This is not meant to question the influence and power of decision makers over international crimes, nor does it doubt the reprehensibility of their actions. However, in the way it is used in the traditional German theory and by the ICC, domination/control is an incorrect and misleading description of the role and influence of such persons in these crimes.[605]

---

600 See also Herzberg 2009, p 578; but see Roxin's assertion of exactly that consequence of his theory in Roxin 2003, § 25 mn. 107 and Roxin 2011, p 200. Ambos reaches a similar conclusion on the factual interchangeability, but sticks to the concept which he wishes to reinforce through normative value-based considerations; see Ambos 2009, pp 144–51. See also Orozco López 2021, p 237.

601 *Katanga and Chui*, 30 September 2008, para 517.

602 Herzberg has criticised the unconvincing distinction between indirect perpetration (through an organisation) and instigation in Roxin's theory in a similar manner, although from the opposite starting point. He explains that in the theory, a desk perpetrator uses the organisation just as an instigator uses the physical perpetrator. He points out that if the use of an apparatus of power leads to indirect perpetration, it is unconvincing why the use of a reliable physical perpetrator in other circumstances would not lead to indirect perpetration but to instigation; see Herzberg 2000, p 48.

603 Rotsch 2000, p 525; Rotsch 1998, p 493.

604 Herzberg 2009, p 578; Noltenius 2003, p 321; Rotsch 2000, pp 528–9.

605 This may be different with the normatively defined notion of domination of the crime in the German systemic approach, which recognizes the lack of factual domination/control and therefore recurs to the decision maker's or architect's responsibility for creating and maintaining the apparatus of power, the system of wrongdoing, see above Sect. 3.2.4. However, this approach cannot be found in the ICC's view on indirect perpetration through an organisation, see above Sect. 3.3.3.3.

In the German debate, supporters of the theory have criticised the reasoning of this section as "hypothetical" because it questions domination of the crime where the crimes have been committed.[606] This "counter argument" misses the point. If the crime was committed, considerations on possible defections, refusals and interventions by mid- and low-level participants are hypothetical because they are made after the fact. However, this is not the hypothesis under discussion. As can be seen in the cases above, the concept of control itself is purely hypothetical.[607] The "arguments" proving "control"—such as the fact that members of an organisation commit a crime based on the instructions of their superiors—are nothing but the cornerstones of the entire debate: the recognition of the fatal potential of groups of people in mass atrocities.[608]

3.3.3.5 The Dissociation from the Specific Crime Through the Theory

The hypothetical concept of domination in cases of indirect perpetration through an organisation leads to a dissociation of perpetrator responsibility from the specific crime. Based on the theory, a decision maker is someone who triggers certain procedures in an organisation, but does not control the crimes committed by its members.[609] The theory therefore blames the perpetrator for the functioning of the apparatus but it does not ascribe guilt based on the control over a specific crime.[610] Perpetration is therefore defined abstractly without requiring a tangible link between the actor and the crime.[611] The danger that the doctrine could lead to a "strict liability standard" is therefore real as far as the lack of a tangible link between the conduct and the crime is concerned.[612]

---

[606] See e.g. Schünemann 2007, § 25 mn. 127.

[607] This has already been described for the—somewhat comparable—"essential contribution" test in joint perpetration under the control over the crime doctrine, see *Lubanga*, 14 March 2012, Separate Opinion of Judge Adrian Fulford, para 17; in the same vein *Chui*, 18 December 2012, Concurring Opinion of Judge Van den Wyngaert, para 42; Ohlin et al. 2013, p 727. See in this vein from German academic writings: Eidam 2015, p 169; Noltenius 2003, pp 319–20; Orozco López 2021, p 244; Renzikowski 1997, p 89; Schlehofer 2008, p 361 speaks of "potential" domination.

[608] Or as Renzikowski puts it, "If the foundation of the theory of domination of the crime is not to be blasted, one should not replace the actual domination of the crime in an individual case through the background actor's possibility to eventually reach his goals" (translation by the author), see Renzikowski 1997, p 89.

[609] Herzberg 2009, p 578; Noltenius 2003, p 319; Rotsch 2000, pp 527, 561.

[610] Noltenius 2003, p 319. Note that the doctrine's reliance on abstractly controlling an apparatus instead of the specific crime has even triggered the criticism that it would be incompatible with the rest of Roxin's original theory of domination of the crime, see Orozco López 2021, p 233 et seq.

[611] In the same vein Noltenius 2003, pp 319–20 and see Rotsch 2009, p 329: "the conduct of the person in the background is completely decoupled from the bringing about of the elements of the crime", translation by the author. See also Zazcyk 1996, p 414.

[612] See Steer's warning in Steer 2017, p 308.

The dissociation of responsibility from specific crimes can be seen in the wording of Roxin's work. Roxin himself underlines the importance for indirect perpetration to attribute responsibility for specific crimes.[613] Despite this statement, when considering indirect perpetration for mass atrocities, his works occasionally seem to abandon this perspective, succumbing instead to the temptation of attributing guilt based on contributions to the overall mass atrocity. This seems to be the case when the theory and its requirements are explained with consideration to the "overall plan" instead of the specific crime.[614] Such wording raises the suspicion that for Roxin the pledge to focus on the specific crime is sometimes overshadowed by the manyfold aspects of systemic crimes.[615] By relying on the specific groundwork of Roxin's traditional concept of indirect perpetration through an organisation, the ICC imports this theoretical flaw.

The tendencies and expressions in Roxin's writings resemble the underlying rationale of systemic or indirect linkage models.[616] Given Roxin's and the ICC's goal to develop a theory on the imputation of responsibility for mass atrocities, this is not surprising, as the contributions to an overall criminal plan are often easier to identify than those to specific crimes.

However, neither the traditional German nor the ICC's approach mirror such a systemic or indirect linkage theory in their notions of domination/control. Instead, domination and control are defined on a crime-specific basis. It is this definition that is not suitable for indirect perpetrators in an organisation. The ICC fails to explain the link between the decision maker's actions and the commission of the specific crime. It must therefore be concluded that the theory of indirect perpetration, as applied by the ICC, dissociates criminal responsibility from the specific crime, instead ascribing it to the accused for being in a central position within an organisation. It does so without considering any of the necessary foundations of a systemic approach to the doctrine, instead clinging to a misguided notion of realities in mass atrocities.

---

[613] See Roxin 2019, p 243.

[614] "No one would hesitate to ascribe to those giving the orders here a central position in the overall course of events", "without affecting the accomplishment of the overall plan" see Roxin 2011, p 198; the same can be found in German in Roxin 2019, p 272 ("*Schlüsselstellung innerhalb des Gesamtgeschehens*", "Key position in the overall course of events"); this view is mirrored by Roxin's idea of mid-level and executing actors, whose influence on the commission of crimes is frequently denied by him, see e.g. Roxin 2006b, p 391, where he speaks of "designing power" of the person in the background while asserting that the executing actors could "modify but not impede the course of events".

[615] As established at the end of Chap. 2, one might say that Roxin misses the point about Adolf Eichmann's specific involvement by devising a theory that would—if at all—fit direct decision makers and not the planners and organisers, the architects of the crimes (see Sect. 2.6.2).

[616] See van Sliedregt 2012, pp 181–2 who outlines that broad notions of commission such as indirect perpetration through an organisation and Joint Criminal Enterprise (Cf. Sect. 5.2) constitute models of indirect linkage.

3.3.3.6 Conclusion: Control Over the Crime as an Illusory, Hypothetical Concept in Indirect Perpetration Through an Organisation

This section has demonstrated that the guiding metaphor in the traditional German and the ICC's approach, pursuant to which an organisation would be a machine which keeps working unconcerned with the malfunctioning of certain cogs, is unsustainable.[617] Eventually, it must be recognized that even if only a single cog in a large machine breaks, this incident does not leave the machine unharmed. It will probably fail to work, at least as far as its output in the specific "production line" is concerned. The broken small part must be identified, a spare must be supplied and the faulty part must be replaced. In the interim, the machine—or at least an operational part of it—stands still. Its surroundings, however, do not.

To believe that a decision maker of an organisation controls the specific crime—or even only its outcome—is misguided, irrespective of the denomination of its requirements, be they fungibility or violent and strict disciplinary and training regimens.

Control over the crime as an indirect perpetrator acting through an organisation, is therefore an illusory, hypothetical concept that fails to credibly explain the influence of decision makers in different positions on systemic crime.

3.3.3.7 Summary

Criticism of the control theory hints at the danger of over-broadening the doctrine by accepting too many factors for establishing control. Furthermore, the question of how the control theory would properly serve to delineate modes of perpetration from participation remains unanswered. This leads to the more profound question of whether control in indirect perpetration through an organisation is defined meaningfully at all.

As we have seen, it is not. Instead, the concept of control over the crime as applied in indirect perpetration through an organisation by the ICC is not only vague, but also based on hypothetical considerations. Decision makers in organisations usually do not actually decide whether and how specific crimes are committed.

This theoretical flaw is a homemade problem, following the import of German criminal law doctrine. In consequence, it leads to doctrinal issues which are already known in the national legal system of origin, and which equally apply or even intensify under the Rome Statute. The reaction by supporters of the theory is an import of unconvincing arguments on what control would be and how this would help in delineating perpetration from participation.[618]

---

617 The ICC relied on this metaphor as well when introducing the doctrine, see *Katanga and Chui*, 30 September 2008, para 515 ("In essence, the leader's control over the apparatus allows him to utilise his subordinates as "a mere gear in a giant machine" in order to produce the result automatically".).

618 See above under Sects. 3.3.2.3 and 3.3.3.

Consequently, the theory as applied by the ICC does not provide for a convincing description of the wrongdoing of decision makers in criminal organisations,[619] and it is true that the court is "losing sight of the facts on the ground" due to its unrealistic view on the factual dynamics of mass atrocities.[620]

Other characterisations of the influence that decision makers behind mass atrocities enjoy are conceivable.[621] Descriptions which can better serve in the further comparison with responsibility for ordering. The factual influence of the "indirect perpetrator" could be described as "taking the decision that crimes of certain types shall be committed by members of the organisation if this is not impeded by the occurrence of an unforeseen event". This description is not a novel definition of control because, as we have seen, control is a misguided description of the influence of decision makers. Instead, this phrase should be considered as the essence of the actual decision-making power of a leader in an organisation.

3.3.4 *Uncertainties in Dealing with the Doctrine in Theory and in Practice*

Judge Adrian Fulford remarked that the doctrine of control over the crime had originated in post-war Germany to deal with particularities of this system.[622] The development of the doctrine in Germany has been discussed in Chap. 2 and the underlying regulations have been compared above, highlighting certain differences.[623] In addition, German criminal law is aimed at any kind of crime, whilst the Rome Statute applies exclusively to mass atrocities. Judge Fulford's observation is therefore well-founded and leads to certain delicate speculations.

It is submitted that the import of a complex doctrine that widens the scope of forms of perpetration, whose origin is in one national legal system necessarily creates uncertainties about its practical scope and possible application.

The former of these points has been criticised in the debate surrounding perpetration and participation in Germany as well, with suggestions being made that the

619 This would be different, if the ICC had adopted a more systemic approach on indirect perpetration through an organisation. As outlined in Chap. 2 (Sect. 2.4), the notion of control would consequently be less important, and emphasis would be placed on the decision maker's role in the functioning of the apparatus. Armed non-state actors and vast criminal organisations in the typical ICC cases can qualify as systems of wrongdoing (see Ambos 2011a, pp 847).

620 van Sliedregt 2015, p 515.

621 See above Sect. 3.3.1.3. The proposed reformulation reads "Control over the crime has who decides that crimes (of a certain type) will be committed by members of the organisation with virtual certainty when following his or her instructions and barring the occurrence of an unforeseen event".

622 *Lubanga*, 14 March 2012, Separate Opinion of Judge Adrian Fulford, para 10.

623 See Sect. 3.2.1.1.

broad and flexible use of forms of perpetration and participation potentially blurs the delineation and thus leads to uncertainty.[624]

This uncertainty regarding the doctrine of control over the crime and its application are visible in judicial practice and scholarly writing pertaining to the ICC's doctrine as well.[625] In practice, the distinction between indirect perpetration and the combined mode of indirect co-perpetration is apparently unclear. There is a clear tendency at the ICC to charge under the latter, combined mode of liability.[626] However, in several cases, it remains unclear why this is the mode of liability best suited to capture the accused's responsibility.

The *Al Bashir* case contains alternative charges against Omar Al Bashir, the former president of Sudan. He is sought by the court as an indirect perpetrator or indirect co-perpetrator.[627] The arrest warrant against *Gaddafi et al.* contains charges for former Libyan leader Muammar Al Gaddafi and his son Saif Al-Islam Gaddafi, as well as former chief of security police Abdullah Al-Senussi. Charges against Muammar Al Gaddafi originally rested on indirect perpetration.[628] However, the pre-trial chamber reclassified Al Gaddafi's liability as indirect co-perpetration. Saif Al-Islam Gaddafi was equally indicted as an indirect co-perpetrator, whilst Al-Senussi faces charges as an indirect perpetrator.[629]

Without prejudice to the pre-trial chamber's knowledge of the cases,[630] the classification of the indicted as indirect perpetrators or indirect co-perpetrators seems somewhat confusing. Both Al Bashir and Al Gaddafi are believed to have held a position of superior and unrivalled power in their respective state apparatus. These positions are implied by the chamber whilst elaborating on the respective persons as indirect co-perpetrators.[631] However, this categorization is confusing, given the role of and picture drawn by the co-perpetration part of the doctrine.[632] If Gaddafi

[624] Puppe 2013, p 514 et seq; Zieschang 1995, p 370.

[625] Note that such uncertainty is even conceded by outspoken supporters of the theory, such as Judge Luz del Carmen Ibáñez Carranza. Cf. her impression that "there is still much misunderstanding and misinterpretation" which, for her, became clear through the submissions in the different stages of the *Ntaganda* case, see *Ntaganda*, 30 March 2021, Separate Opinion of Judge Luz del Carmen Ibáñez Carranza, para 206.

[626] As van Sliedregt and Yanev point out, so far only the combined mode of indirect co-perpetration has played a greater role in decisions of the ICC (van Sliedregt and Yanev 2019, mn. 53). In the decisions regarding Germain Katanga and Ngudjolo Chui (after the separation of the proceedings against them), indirect perpetration was treated in its stand-alone form, but both accused were acquitted under this head of responsibility.

[627] *Al Bashir*, 4 March 2009, paras 214–21 (indirect co-perpetration); para 222 (indirect perpetration); *Al Bashir*, 12 July 2010, para 43 (reaffirming the alternative indictment).

[628] *Gaddafi et al.*, 27 June 2011, para 66.

[629] Ibid., para 71.

[630] All three arrest warrants were issued by pre-trial chamber I. However, its composition changed after the first decision in *Al Bashir* (in 2009).

[631] See *Al Bashir*, 4 March 2009, para 221; *Gaddafi et al.*, 27 June 2011, para 72.

[632] It was first established in *Katanga and Chui* and generally aims at situations in which an accused cannot be said to have acted through another, because their contributions would not constitute the exercise of control. In the first decisions this was either based on the fact that the accused only

had "absolute, ultimate and unquestioned control over the Libyan State apparatus of power, including the Security Forces",[633] then why would he be an indirect *co*-perpetrator? Where would he lack the necessary control over the apparatus that would lead to the necessity to attribute to him the acts of other co-perpetrators?

In the case of Al Bashir, the same question arises. His role is described as being the *de jure* and *de facto* president of the state of Sudan. He allegedly had "full control over all branches of the 'apparatus' of the State of Sudan",[634] a description which raises doubts about his dependency on other decision makers for the realisation of his criminal plans.[635]

Moreover, the arrest warrant decision in *Mudacumura* is shaped by a similarly confusing approach. Sylvestre Mudacumura was sought over charges as an indirect co-perpetrator and for ordering the same crimes.[636] The pre-trial chamber affirmed the ordering charges but denied charges under indirect co-perpetration. The reasoning behind the latter being that the chamber was unable to determine a common plan between Mudacumura and other members of the leadership circle of his armed group, the *FDLR*.[637] On the other hand, ordering was affirmed based on the findings that the accused had been the "top military commander" of the armed group, which was a "well organised organisation" with a "clear hierarchical structure". According to the pre-trial chamber's findings, Mudacumura had "control over his forces and authority over recruiting, promoting, removing and disciplining them". "Mr. Mudacumura's dominance and control over FDLR troops" allegedly included his capability to impede their demobilisation and authorise marriages.[638] In other words, Sylvestre Mudacumura is the stereotype indirect perpetrator (through an organisation) under the doctrine of the ICC. Given the elaborations of the pre-trial chamber, this is evident. However, for unknown reasons, the charges against him relied on the combined mode of indirect co-perpetration.

These cases demonstrate how a uniform approach to the doctrine of indirect perpetration and its delineation from indirect co-perpetration does not exist and leads to contradictory results in practice. It can be assumed that this relates to the above-mentioned uncertainty about the scope of the doctrine.

---

controlled one of several organisations involved in the commission of the crimes (*Katanga and Chui*, 30 September 2008, para 492–3) or because the accused could only control one organisation together with others (*Al Bashir*, 4 March 2009, paras 213–21). From then on, the notion developed into something broader. It now captures the contributions of persons who do not exercise any kind of control over the organisation themselves as long as they contribute to a common plan with others and one of the other persons exercises control over the physical perpetrators (see *Gbagbo and Blé Goudé*, 16 July 2019, Annex B, para 1922).

[633] *Gaddafi et al.*, 27 June 2011, para 72.

[634] *Al Bashir*, 4 March 2009, paras 221–2.

[635] See already Ambos 2016, Art. 25 mn. 17 with fn. 128.

[636] ICC, *The Prosecutor v. Sylvestre Mudacumura*, Issuance of a Warrant of Arrest, 13 July 2012, ICC-01/04-01/12, para 59.

[637] Ibid., para 62.

[638] Ibid., para 64.

In academic writing, certain interpretations and comments also demonstrate how scholars are unsure of the theoretic groundwork of the doctrine.

Guilfoyle notes that the doctrine runs the risk of displaying only the indirect perpetrator as a blameworthy participant of the crime whilst marginalising the guilt of the direct perpetrators.[639] From a German scholar's view, this could be countered by stating that Roxin never implied such a downgrading of the direct perpetrator's responsibility or guilt.[640] However, this is only half the reality of the "German" perspective, as certain authors in German language literature have voiced their support for a necessary mitigation of sentence for direct perpetrators who act under an organisation's pressure in mass atrocities.[641] Additionally, Guilfoyle's point is coherent if seen as referring to a broader audience. Irrespective of the interpretation of the German and some Spanish speaking jurisdictions, lawyers from other jurisdictions and lay persons may find that blaming a decision maker as the perpetrator of a crime seems to ignore the physical perpetrator.

Another issue seemingly arises when examining the notion of control. Olásolo and Carnero Rojo interpret the control criterion as a graded concept: a perpetrator under Art. 25 (3) (a) Rome Statute would be allocated the highest degree of control, with control "decreasing" down through the modes of *litterae* (b) to (d).[642]

This could be a valid, new approach to interpreting the control concept, but currently it seems to be a misconception of the doctrine as applied by the ICC.[643] This is due to the fact that control over the crime is an all-or-nothing-approach both in German criminal law theory[644] and at the ICC. This is illustrated in numerous assertions by the court.[645]

The examples in this section may be situational and as far as jurisprudence is regarded, other factors invisible to the reader of the decisions, may have played a role in the classification of the accused's conduct as well. Nevertheless, they speak to a certain confusion or uncertainty concerning the theoretic groundwork and scope of indirect perpetration through an organisation and the control theory at the ICC.

---

639 Guilfoyle 2011, pp 265–6, 275, 276.

640 Elbers 2018, p 128.

641 See Vest 2011, pp 171–2. See also Orozco López 2021, pp 238–9 emphasising that the attribution of an equal level of responsibility to the phyiscal perpetrator and the indirect perpetrator still fails to adequately describe the outstanding role of the decision maker.

642 Olásolo and Carnero Rojo 2015, p 557.

643 The authors do not indicate any new interpretation or approach in this regard but simply refer to the existing case law of the ICC, see ibid., pp 557–8.

644 At this point the lack of regard for other legal systems that apply the control theory may become obvious. From this point of view, it is not unthinkable that the legal systems of Spain or certain Latin American countries employ such a graded concept of control. It is submitted that, in such a system, distinguishing between perpetration and participation would be even more difficult.

645 See only *Lubanga*, 29 January 2007, paras 327–32 (especially para 330 "the concept of control over the crime constitutes a third approach for distinguishing between principals and accessories…" and para 332 "According to this approach, only those who have control over the commission of the offence… may be principals…"); see also the distinction between indirect perpetration and ordering made by the pre-trial chamber in *Katanga and Chui*, 30 September 2008, para 517.

3.3.5 *Summary and Conclusion*

This section has shown different aspects of criticism of indirect perpetration through an organisation and the underlying control theory.

The first point raised is the dubious groundwork based on which the theories have made their way from the national legal systems of Germany, Spain and some Latin American countries into the practice of the ICC.

The second point concerns the requirements of the doctrine. Although they do not seem off point in their tendency, they remain vague and therefore very broad. As can be seen in comparison to the development in Germany, an unrestricted broadening of the doctrine is possible.

It can even be suspected that the implied hierarchy of blameworthiness under the control theory leads the jurisprudence to spiral under its application. If only control conveys the highest level of seriousness and chambers are confronted with a case of (morally) highly blameworthy conduct, the pressure to subsume it under the doctrine of indirect perpetration (or indirect co-perpetration) is high.

This in turn can lead to the recognition of other factors and a broadening of requirements. The result could soon be similar to the application of JCE in *ad hoc* jurisprudence: perpetrator liability for everyone who somehow got involved in a common plan or somehow played a role within an organisation.[646] A loss of relevance of modes of participation under the Rome Statute can be the consequence.[647]

The third point concerns the underlying doctrine of control over the crime, as far as control in indirect perpetration through an organisation is concerned. It has been shown that this concept of control can at best be called hypothetical but may simply be illusory in many cases.

3.4 Concluding Remarks

We have seen in this chapter, that the ICC's jurisprudence reveals an identifiable, yet rough and undefined set of criteria and factors for the doctrine of indirect perpetration through an organisation. With its doctrine, it is relatively close to the traditional German concept, as far as the underlying notion of control/domination is concerned. The specific requirements laid out by the ICC differ in several ways from Roxin's original concept and, to a certain extent, resemble a synthesis of several ideas that have been voiced in academic literature.

Three observations from this chapter stand out as crucial for the further exploration of the topic.

---

[646] See already Ohlin et al. 2013, pp 745–6.

[647] Fletcher has already described this regarding the application of the German theory to the *Mauerschützen* cases, see Fletcher 1998, p 199; see also regarding this threat in German jurisprudence Puppe 2013, pp 514–5.

Firstly, the notion of control as applied in the doctrine of indirect perpetration through an organisation by the ICC, is focussed on decision makers, rather than architects of crimes. This is connected to the naturalistic view on factors that enable control over the crime. The doctrine shares this focus with the traditional German theory. This restriction of the doctrine must be considered in the further course of this book.

Secondly, as far as the respective chambers determined their involvement in crimes, this restriction to decision makers behind crimes does not rule out the responsibility of many persons brought before the ICC. Usually, relatively direct involvement in the form of direct orders was identified. Mass atrocities do not require a high degree of technological understanding. However, it seems that the limited temporal and spatial frames of the cases before the ICC imply the existence of less actors who take on purely architecting, facilitating roles. Instead, most of those tried before the ICC until now took part in direct decisions that triggered the commission of crimes.

Thirdly, criticism not only of the doctrine's criteria, but primarily of its underlying notion of control has been voiced. The notion of control as applied by the ICC is hypothetical and therefore unconvincing because it builds on a misconception of factual dynamics and circumstances. Given this extensive criticism, it must be questioned, why the control theory and indirect perpetration through an organisation were adopted and are held on to by the court when adjudicating decision makers of international crimes.[648]

Given the possibility presented by the doctrine to designate decision makers as perpetrators, the consideration of fair labelling is apparently very important. The fact that, aside from this, a lot speaks against the doctrine, has rightly led to the assertion that the ICC has made a "policy choice" in this regard.[649] The same has been asserted in the German debate: arguments against the traditional German approach are legion and have nevertheless been cast aside by judges and scholars alike, because they apparently wish the theory to prevail.[650]

This tendency may well be objectionable. However, the "wish to give evil a name" through appropriately describing a participant's role in the crime, is an important aspect of international criminal justice.[651] At some point, the question must therefore

---

648 As discussed earlier, the doctrine in its use at the ICC rules out blaming a person who takes on the role of an architect without own decision-making powers over the commission of the crime, see above at Sects. 3.1.3 and 3.2.3.

649 See Steer 2017, p 307; see also Aksenova 2016, p 149 (criticising a lack of in-depth consideration on behalf of the ICC concerning the adoption of the theory).

650 For this conclusion see Herzberg 2009, p 579 (asserting that only the wish to stick to indirect perpetration keeps supporters of the theory from realizing its doctrinal flaws); Hruschka 1998, p 608; Krey and Nuys 2009, p 212 (calling this a "legitimate concern"); Noltenius 2003, p 319 ("considerations of legal policies"); Renzikowski 1997, p 90 (saying that what remains is the thought that "the big must be punished harder than the small ones"); Weigend 2011, p 102 (conceding that it is intuitive to hold Nazi leaders as perpetrators); translation of all quotes by the author.

651 On the relevance of properly expressing the wrongdoing of leaders behind international crimes see only: *Ntaganda*, 30 March 2021, Judge Luz del Carmen Ibáñez Carranza, para 224; van Sliedregt 2015, p 511; van Sliedregt 2012, p 81; Weigend 2015, p 552. This topic is discussed in detail under the terms of fair labelling and expressive justice in Chap. 7, Sect. 7.2.3.5.

be, whether the doctrine actually provides for an accurate expression of a decision maker's role and influence. However, this must be done in comparison to possible alternatives.

Considering all this, it must be scrutinized whether the adherence to the doctrine is understandable or misplaced with a view to the system of Art. 25 (3) Rome Statute in which indirect commission is settled. This question will be answered through a comparison to the other form of responsibility for active conduct of persons in leadership positions which the Rome Statute provides for: responsibility for ordering a crime.

References

Aksenova M (2016) Complicity in International Criminal Law. Hart Publishing, Oxford

Ambos K (1998) Tatherrschaft durch Willensherrschaft kraft organisatorischer Machtapparate. Goltdammer's Archiv 226–245

Ambos K (2004) Der Allgemeine Teil des Völkerstrafrechts. Duncker & Humblot, Berlin

Ambos K (2007) Joint Criminal Enterprise and Command Responsibility. Journal of International Criminal Justice 5:159–183

Ambos K (2009) Command Responsibility and Organisationsherrschaft: Ways of attributing international crimes to the 'most responsible'. In: Nollkaemper A, van der Wilt H (eds) System Criminality in International law. Cambridge University Press, Cambridge, 127–157

Ambos K (2011a) Zur "Organisation" bei der Organisationsherrschaft. In: Heinrich M, Jäger C, Schünemann B, al. e (eds) Strafrecht als Scientia Universalis Festschrift für Claus Roxin zum 80 Geburtstag am 15 Mai 2011a. De Gruyter, Berlin, 837–852

Ambos K (2011b) The Fujimori Judgment—A President's Responsibility for Crimes Against Humanity as Indirect Perpetrator by Virtue of an Organized Power Apparatus. Journal of International Criminal Justice 9:137–158

Ambos K (2013) Treatise on International Criminal Law—Volume I: Foundations and General Part. Oxford University Press, Oxford

Ambos K (2016) Art. 25. In: The Rome Statute of the International Criminal Court—A Commentary. C.H.Beck/Hart/Nomos, Munich

Ambos K (2018) Internationales Strafrecht. C. H. Beck, Munich

Anderson K (2018) Perpetrating Genocide—A Criminological Account. Routledge, Abingdon

Arendt H (2018) Eichmann in Jerusalem—Ein Bericht über die Banalität des Bösen. Piper, Munich

Blomsma J, Roef D (2019) Chapter VII. Forms and Aspects of Mens Rea. In: Keiler J, Roef D (eds) Comparative Concepts of Criminal Law. Intersentia, Cambridge, 177–206

Cesarani D (2004) Adolf Eichmann—Bürokrat und Massenmörder. William Heinemann, London

Christensen MJ, Orina NM (2022) The International Criminal Court as a Law Laboratory—Professional Battles of Control and the 'Control of the Crime' Theory. Journal of International Criminal Justice 20:699–716

Clark RC (2015) Together Again? Customary Law and Control over the Crime. Criminal Law Forum 26:457–495

Cryer R, Robinson D, Vasiliev S (2019) An Introduction to International Criminal Law and Procedure. Cambridge University Press, Cambridge

Cupido M (2022) The Control Theory as a Multidimensional Concept—Reflections on the Ntaganda Appeal Judgment. Journal of International Criminal Justice 20:637–656

de Vos C (2013) Investigating from Afar: The ICC's Evidence Problem Leiden Journal of International Law 26:1009–1024 deGuzman MM (2016) Art. 21. In: The Rome Statute of the International Criminal Court—A Commentary. C.H. Beck Munich

Dubber MD (2007) Criminalizing Complicity—A Comparative Analysis. Journal of International Criminal Justice 5:977–1001

Eidam L (2015) Der Organisationsgedanke im Strafrecht. Mohr Siebeck, Tübingen

Elbers S (2018) Die mittelbare Mittäterschaft im Völkerstrafrecht. Dissertation deposited at the library of University of Münster

Eldar S (2013) Exploring International Criminal Law's Reluctance to Resort Modalities of Group Responsibility. Journal of International Criminal Justice 11:331–349

Eser A (2002) Individual Criminal Responsibility. In: Cassese A, Gaeta P, Jones JRWD (eds) The Rome Statute of the International Criminal Court—A Commentary. Oxford University Press, Oxford, 767–822

Fletcher GP (1998) Basic Concepts of Criminal Law. Oxford University Press, Oxford

Fletcher GP (2000) Rethinking Criminal Law. Oxford University Press, Oxford

Frister H (2018) Strafrecht AT. C.H. Beck, Munich

Gil Gil AG, Maculan E (2015) Current Trends in the Definition of 'Perpetrator' by the International Criminal Court: From the Decison on the Confirmation of Charges in the *Lubanga* case to the *Katanga* judgment. Leiden Journal of International Law 28:349–371

Goy B (2012) Individual Criminal Responsibility before the International Criminal Court—A Comparison with the Ad Hoc Tribunals. International Criminal Law Review 12:1–70

Guilfoyle D (2011) Responsibility for Collective Atrocities: Fair Labelling and Approaches to Commission in International Criminal Law. Current Legal Problems 64:255–286

Haas V (2008) Die Theorie der Tatherrschaft und ihre Grundlagen—Zur Notwendigkeit einer Revision der Beteiligungslehre. Duncker & Humblot, Berlin

Heine G, Weisser B (2019) § 25. In: Schönke/Schröder-StGB. C.H. Beck Munich

Herzberg RD (2000) Mittelbare Täterschaft und Anstiftung in formalen Organisationen. In: Amelung K (ed) Individuelle Verantwortung und Beteiligungsverhältnisse bei Straftaten in bürokratischen Organisationen des Staates, der Wirtschaft und der Gesellschaft. Pro Universitate, Sinzheim, 33–53

Herzberg RD (2009) Das Fujimori-Urteil: Zur Beteiligung des Befehlsgebers an den Verbrechen seines Machtapparates. Zeitschrift für internationale Strafrechtsdogmatik 11:576–580

Hoyer A (2017) § 25. In: Systematischer Kommentar zum Strafgesetzbuch, Band I §§ 1–37 StGB. Carl Heymanns Verlag Cologne

Hruschka J (1998) Regreßverbot, Anstiftungsbegriff und die Konsequenzen. Zeistschrift für die gesamte Strafrechtswissenschaft 110:581–639

Jain N (2014) Perpetrators and Accessories in International Criminal Law—Individual Modes of Responsibility for Collective Crimes. Hart Publishing, Oxford

Jakobs G (1983) Strafrecht Allgemeiner Teil—Die Grundlagen und die Zurechnungslehre. Walter de Gruyter, Berlin

Jakobs G (1995) Mittelbare Täterschaft der Mitglieder des Nationalen Verteidigungsrates. Neue Zeitschrift für Strafrecht 26–27

Jescheck H-H, Weigend T (1996) Lehrbuch des Strafrechts—Allgemeiner Teil. Duncker & Humblot, Berlin

Jessberger F, Geneuss J (2008) On the Application of a Theory of Indirect Perpetration in *Al Bashir*. Journal of International Criminal Justice 6:853–869

Jung H (1995) Besprechung von BGH Urteil vom 26.07.1995. Juristische Schulung 173–174

Kiss A (2019) Indirect Commission. In: de Hemptinne J, Roth R, van Sliedregt E (eds) Modes of Liability in International Criminal Law. Cambridge University Press, Cambridge, 30–57

Kress C (2006) Claus Roxin's Lehre von der Organisationsherrschaft und das Völkerstrafrecht. Goltdammer's Archiv 304–310

Kress C (2016) *Joachim Vogels* Regelungsmodelle der Beteiligung und das Völkerstrafrecht. In: Tiedemann K et al. (eds) Die Verfassung moderner Strafrechtspflege—Erinnerung an Joachim Vogel. Nomos Baden-Baden 259–273

Krey V, Nuys M (2009) Der Täter hinter dem Täter–oder die Liebe der Strafrechtler zum Glasperlenspiel. In: Böse M, Sternberg-Lieben D (eds) Grundlagen des Straf- und Strafverfahrensrechts: Festschrift für Knut Amelung zum 70 Geburtstag. Duncker & Humblot, Berlin, 203–223

Lanza G (2021) Indirect Perpetration and Organisationsherrschaftslehre. Duncker & Humblot, Berlin

Maculan E (2013) La fertilización cruzada jurisprudencial y los modelos de responsabilidad—Acordes y desacuerdos en la jurisprudencia latinoamericana. In: Gil Gil A, Maculan E (eds) Intervención Delictiva y Derecho Penal Internacional—Reglas de atribución de la responsabilidad en crímenes internacionales. Dykinson, Madrid, 207–232

Manacorda S, Meloni C (2011) Indirect Perpetration versus Joint Criminal Enterprise. Journal of International Criminal Justice 9:159–178

Murmann U (1996) Tatherrschaft durch Weisungsmacht. Goltdammer's Archiv 269–281

Noltenius B (2003) Kriterien der Abgrenzung von Anstiftung und mittelbarer Täterschaft Europäischer Verlag der Wissenschaften Frankfurt am Main

Noto F (2013) Secondary Liability in International Criminal Law. Dike, Zurich

Ohlin JD (2007) Three Conceptual Problems with the Doctrine of Joint Criminal Enterprise. Journal of International Criminal Justice 5:69–90

Ohlin JD (2015) Co-Perpetration: German Dogmatik or German Invasion? In: Stahn C (ed) The Law and Practice of the International Criminal Court. Oxford University Press, Oxford, 517–537

Ohlin JD (2022) The Hierarchy of Blameworthiness. In: Jessberger F, Vormbaum M, Burghardt B (eds) Strafrecht und Systemunrecht. Mohr Siebeck, Tübingen, 247–256

Ohlin JD, van Sliedregt E, Weigend T (2013) Assessing the Control-Theory. Leiden Journal of International Law 26:725–746

Olásolo H (2009) The Criminal Responsibility of Senior Political and Military Leaders as Principals to International Crimes. Hart Publishing, Portland

Olásolo H, Carnero Rojo E (2015) Forms of Accessorial Liability under Article 25(3)(b) and (c). In: Stahn C (ed) The Law and Practice of the International Criminal Court. Oxford University Press, Oxford, 557–591

Orozco López HD (2021) Roxins mittelbare Täterschaft kraft organisatorischer Machtapparate - Eine kritische Analyse. Zeitschrift für internationale Strafrechtsdogmatik 233–248

Orozco López HD, Silva Santaularia N (2022) Reflections on Indirect (Co-)Perpetration through an Organization. Journal of International Criminal Justice 20:657–676

Osiel M (2005) The Banality of Good: Aligning Incentives against Mass Atrocity. Columbia Law Review 105:1751–1862

Osten P (2022) Indirect (Co-)Perpetration and the Control Theory—A Japanese Perspective. Journal of International Criminal Justice 20:677–697

Pigaroff DK, Robinson D (2016) Art. 30. In: The Rome Statute of the International Criminal Court—A Commentary. C.H.Beck—Hart—Nomos Munich

Puppe I (2013) Die Architektur der Beteiligungsformen. Goltdammer's Archiv 514–536

Rastan R (2009) Review of ICC Jurisprudence 2008. Northwestern Journal of International Human Rights 7:261–298

Renzikowski J (1997) Restriktiver Täterbegriff und fahrlässige Beteiligung. Mohr Siebeck, Tübingen

Rotsch T (1998) Die Rechtsfigur des Täters hinter dem Täter bei der Begehung von Straftaten im Rahmen organisatorischer Machtapparate und ihre Übertragbarkeit auf wirtschaftliche Organisationsstrukturen. Neue Zeitschrift für Strafrecht 491–495

Rotsch T (2000) Tatherrschaft kraft Organisationsherrschaft? Zeitschrift für die gesamte Strafrechtswissenschaft 112:518–562

Rotsch T (2009) Einheitstäterschaft statt Tatherrschaft. Mohr Siebeck, Tübingen

Roxin C (1995) Anmerkung zum Urteil des BGH vom 26.7.1994—5 StR 98/9. Juristenzeitung 49–52

Roxin C (2003) Strafrecht Allgemeiner Teil Band II Besondere Erscheinungsformen der Straftat. C. H. Beck, Munich

Roxin C (2006a) Organisationsherrschaft und Tatentschlossenheit. Zeitschrift für internationale Strafrechtsdogmatik 293–300
Roxin C (2006b) Organisationsherrschaft und Tatentschlossenheit. In: Hoyer A, Müller HE, Pawlik M, Wolter J (eds) Festschrift für Friedrich-Christian Schroeder zum 70 Geburtstag. C.F. Müller Verlag, Heidelberg, 387–400
Roxin C (2007) Organisationsherrschaft als eigenständige Form mittelbarer Täterschaft. Schweizerische Zeitschrift für Strafrecht 125:1–23
Roxin C (2011) Crimes as Part of Organized Power Structures. Journal of International Criminal Justice 9:191–205
Roxin C (2019) Täterschaft und Tatherrschaft. De Gruyter, Berlin
SáCouto S, Thompson KC (2015) Investigative Management, Strategies, and Techniques of the ICC's OTP. In: Stahn C (ed) The Law and Practice of the International Criminal Court. Oxford University Press, Oxford, 328–349
Saland P (1999) International Criminal Law Principles. In: Lee RS (ed) The International Criminal Court—The Making of the Rome Statute. Kluwer Law International, The Hague, 189–216
Satzger H (2020) Internationales und Europäisches Strafrecht. Nomos, Baden Baden
Schabas (2016) The International Criminal Court—A Commentary on the Rome Statute. Oxford University Press, Oxford
Schlehofer H (2008) Täterschaftliche Fahrlässigkeit. In: Putzke H, Hardtung B, Hörnle T (eds) Strafrecht zwischen System und Telos: Festschrift für Rolf Dietrich Herzberg zum siebzigsten Geburtstag am 14 Februar 2008. 355–375
Schroeder F-C (1995) Der Sprung des Täters hinter dem Täter aus der Theorie in die Praxis. Juristische Rundschau 177–180
Schroeder F-C (2009) Tatbereitschaft gegen Fungibilität. Zeitschrift für internationale Strafrechtsdogmatik 569–571
Schünemann B (2006) Die Rechtsfigur des "Täters hinter dem Täter" und das Prinzip der Tatherrschaftsstufen. In: Hoyer A, Müller HE, Pawlik M, Wolter J (eds) Festschrift für Friedrich-Christian Schroeder zum 70 Geburtstag. C.F. Müller, Heidelberg, 401–413
Schünemann B (2007) § 25. In: Leipziger Kommentar Strafgesetzbuch: StGB, Band 1: Einleitung; §§ 1–31. De Gruyter Berlin
Steer C (2017) Translating Guilt—Identifying Leadership Liability for Mass Atrocity Crimes. Asser Press, The Hague
Stewart JG (2014) Ten Reasons for Adopting a Universal Concept of Participation. In: van Sliedregt E, Vasiliev S (eds) Pluralism in International Criminal Law. Oxford University Press, Oxford, 320–341
Timpe G (2016) Die strafrechtliche Geschäftsherrenhaftung. Strafverteidiger Forum 237–245
Triffterer O (2016) Art. 28. In: The Rome Statute of the International Criminal Court—A Commentary. C.H.Beck Munich
van Sliedregt E (2009) Article 28 of the ICC Statute: Mode of Liability and/or Separate Offense? New Criminal Law Review 12:420–432
van Sliedregt E (2012) Individual Criminal Responsibility in International Criminal Law. Oxford University Press, Oxford
van Sliedregt E (2015) Perpetration and Participation in Article 25(3). In: Stahn C (ed) The Law and Practice of the International Criminal Court. Oxford University Press, Oxford, 499–516
van Sliedregt E, Weisser B (2022) The Ntaganda Case and Individual Criminal Liability at the ICC—Foreword. Journal of International Criminal Justice 20:627–635
van Sliedregt E, Yanev L (2019) Co-Perpetration Based on Joint Control over the Crime. In: de Hemptinne J, Roth R, van Sliedregt E (eds) Modes of Liability in International Criminal Law. Cambridge University Press, Cambridge, 85–120
Ventura MJ (2019) Ordering. In: de Hemptinne J, Roth R, van Sliedregt E (eds) Modes of Liability in International Criminal Law. Cambridge University Press, Cambridge, 284–306
Vest H (2011) Völkerrechtsverbrecher verfolgen—Ein abgestuftes Mehrebenensystem systemischer Tatherrschaft. Stämpfli Verlag AG, Bern

Weigend T (2008) Intent, Mistake of Law and Co-Perpetration in the *Lubanga* Decision on the Confirmation of Charges. Journal of International Criminal Justice 6:471–487

Weigend T (2011) Perpetration through an Organization—The Unexpected Career of a German Legal Concept. Journal of International Criminal Justice 9:91–111

Weigend T (2014) Problems of Attribution in International Criminal Law. Journal of International Criminal Justice 12:253–266

Weigend T (2015) Indirect Perpetration. In: Stahn C (ed) The Law and Practice of the International Criminal Court. Oxford University Press, Oxford, 538–556

Weisser B (2011) Täterschaft in Europa. Mohr Siebeck, Tübingen

Weisser B (2012) Die mittelbare Täterschaft kraft Organisationsherrschaft—Über den Werdegang einer Rechtsfigur vom Ausnahmeinstrument zur Allzweckwaffe. Ad Legendum 244–250

Weisser B (2019) Organisationsherrschaft und organisationsbezogene Beihilfe. Goltdammer's Archiv 244–256

Weisser B (2022) Pluralismus und Rechtsvergleichung im Völkerstrafrecht. In: Jessberger F, Vormbaum M, Burghardt B (eds) Strafrecht und Systemunrecht. Mohr Siebeck, Tübingen, 385–398

Werle G (2007) Individual Criminal Responsibility in Art. 25 ICC Statute. Journal of International Criminal Justice 5:953–975

Werle G, Jessberger F (2020a) Völkerstrafrecht. Mohr Siebeck, Tübingen

Werle G, Jessberger F (2020b) Principles of International Criminal Law. Oxford University Press, Oxford

Yanev L (2018) Theories of Co-Perpetration in International Criminal law. Brill Nijhoff, Leiden

Zahar A, Sluiter G (2008) International Criminal Law—A Critical Introduction. Oxford University Press, Oxford

Zazcyk R (1996) Die "Tatherrschaft Kraft organisatorischer Machtapparate" und der BGH. Goltdammer's Archiv 411–415

Zieschang F (1995) Mittäterschaft bei bloßer Mitwirkung im Vorbereitungsstadium. Zeitschrift für die gesamte Strafrechtswissenschaft 107:361–381

Other Documents

District Court of Jerusalem, *Judgment Against Karl Adolf Eichmann—Unofficial Translation*, 40/61

German Federal Court of Justice, Judgment, 25.03.1993, in: Neue Juristische Wochenschrift, 1993, 1932

German Federal Court of Justice, Judgment, 26.7.1994, in: Neue Juristische Wochenschrift, 1994, 2703

German Federal Court of Justice, Decision, 02.11.2007, in: Neue Zeitschrift für Strafrecht, 2008, 89

Trials of War Criminals Before the Nuernberg Military Tribunals Under Control Council Law No. 10, Vol. III, U.S. Government Printing Service 1950

Trials of War Criminals Before the Nuernberg Military Tribunals Under Control Council Law No. 10, Vol. IV, U.S. Government Printing Service 1950

Trials of War Criminals Before the Nuernberg Military Tribunals Under Control Council Law No. 10, Vol. XI, U.S. Government Printing Service 1950

Part II
Responsibility for Ordering a Crime

Responsibility for ordering a crime can be found in Art. 25 (3) (b) Rome Statute. The regulation looks back on a long history of similar precedents. Whilst the statutes of the Nuremberg and Tokyo tribunals after World War II did not contain a specific provision regarding modes of liability and did not elaborate on questions thereof, certain judgments referred to defendants who had "ordered" the commission of crimes.[1] However, responsibility for ordering appeared in Control Council Law No. 10 which was established by the allied control council in Germany.[2]

The Geneva Conventions of 1949 contain a provision for states parties to criminalise and punish the commission and ordering the commission of violations of international humanitarian law.[3]

The Report of the International Law Commission (ILC) on the work of its 43rd session in 1991 contained a provision that criminalised the commission and the ordering of the commission of genocide.[4]

---

[1] Finnin S (2012) Elements of Accessorial Modes of Liability—Article 25 (3) (b) and (c) of the Rome Statute of the International Criminal Court. Martinus Nijhoff Publishers, Leiden, pp 14–15; see also Heller's statement, that the IMT produced "almost nothing" on modes of participation: Heller KJ (2011) The Nuremberg Military Trials and the Origins of International Criminal Law. Oxford University Press, Oxford, p 3.

[2] On the history and establishment of Control Council Law No. 10, see Heller (fn. 1), pp 12–17.

[3] Cf. Geneva Convention I, Art. 49; Geneva Convention II, Art. 50; Geneva Convention III, Art. 129; Geneva Convention IV, Art. 146. Bantekas I (2002) Principles of direct and superior responsibility in International Humanitarian Law. Manchester University Press, Manchester, p 51.

[4] Cf. A/46/10, Report of the International Law Commission on the work of its forty-third session, 29 April–19 July, Official Records of the General Assembly, Forty-sixth session, Supplement No. 10, at 101 (Article 19 of the Draft Code of Crimes against the Peace and Security of Mankind). See on this Vest H (2002) Genozid durch organisatorische Machtapparate. Nomos, Baden-Baden, pp 243–4; Vest H (2011) Völkerrechtsverbrecher verfolgen—Ein abgestuftes Mehrebenensystem systemischer Tatherrschaft. Stämpfli Verlag AG, Bern, p 365.

The Draft Code of Crimes against the Peace and Security of Mankind that was adopted by the ILC in 1996 listed "ordering" in Article 2 (3) (b) as a form of individual responsibility for international crimes.[5]

Both the statutes of the tribunals for the former Yugoslavia and for Rwanda recognise responsibility for ordering crimes,[6] the same is true for the regulations of the Special Court for Sierra Leone.[7]

The provisions on certain crimes in the ILC draft code and in the statutes of the ICTY, ICTR and SCSL additionally use the wording "committing and ordering" as the description of the relevant conduct to fulfil the crimes' *actus reus*.[8]

The German legal system in contrast does not recognise "ordering a crime" as a form of responsibility.[9]

In the first part of this book, the development of indirect perpetration through an organisation was illustrated. This second part will explore the responsibility for ordering as a potential alternative form of responsibility to indirect perpetration through an organisation.

Given that the mode of ordering is old and deeply entrenched in the history of international criminal law, it is possible that it emerged to target cases of high and mid-level actors, i.e. to target decision-makers and architects of international crimes.

If this is correct, ordering would be the original international mode of liability utilised to address the types of case which currently fall under indirect perpetration through an organisation according to the jurisprudence of the ICC, Germany and other countries applying this doctrine.

This theory will be explored by shedding light on the requirements, the legal classification and the cases addressed under ordering in its different developmental stages within international criminal law. Additionally, the theory will be scrutinised when analysing whether ordering could have served as an alternative in certain situations, where courts applied other solutions.

If ordering was indeed developed as a means to grasp and adjudicate the wrongdoing of high and mid-level decision-makers, it would stand in sharp contrast to the application of indirect perpetration through an organisation to such cases by

---

[5] Cp. The Art. 2 (3) (b) of the Draft Code of Crimes Against the Peace and Security of Mankind of 1996; see also Finnin (fn. 1), p 18.

[6] Cp. Art. 7 (1) ICTY Statute; Art. 6 (1) ICTR Statute. On their genesis see Finnin (fn. 1), pp 19–20.

[7] Cp. Art. 6 (1) of the Statute of the Special Court for Sierra Leone.

[8] See Art. 16 of the Draft Code of Crimes Against the Peace and Security of Mankind ("An individual who, as leader or organser, actively participates in or orders the planning, preparation…" referring to the crime of aggression); Art. 2 ICTY Statute ("…prosecute persons committing or ordering to be committed grave breaches…"); Art. 4 ICTR Statute ("…prosecute persons committing or ordering to be committed…"); Art. 3 SCSL Statute ("… prosecute persons who committed or ordered the commission…").

[9] In the German version of the Rome Statute, ordering is translated to "*Anordnen*". Consequently, the noun would be "*Anordnung*". In this context, *Anordnung* can be translated to mean an "order", "command", "instruction" or "ruling". Another possible translation into German would have been the term of *"befehlen"/"Befehl"*, which means ordering or commanding in a more narrow, mostly military, sense.

the ICC. An overlap of these modes of liability would have to be solved meaningfully. If this turns out to be impossible, the better arguments may speak for applying ordering instead of indirect perpetration through an organisation in cases of leadership criminality.

The genesis of the mode of ordering and its relation to other modes of Art. 25 (3) Rome Statute will also enable conclusions as to the underlying relation between forms of responsibility. If ordering was developed to describe and adjudicate the same wrongdoing as indirect perpetration through an organisation, the existence of a hierarchy of blameworthiness between forms of commission and ordering would be highly questionable.

Responsibility for ordering will be explored in a chronological order, starting with post-World War II trials (see Chap. 4), followed by the jurisprudence on ordering at the *ad hoc* tribunals for the Former Yugoslavia and for Rwanda (Chap. 5) and finally the interpretation of ordering under the Rome Statute of the International Criminal Court (Chap. 6).

Chapter 4
Historic Precedents: Ordering in Post-World War II Trials

Contents

Abstract Ordering the commission of crimes as a form of individual criminal responsibility in international criminal law dates back to the trials against former German politicians, military officers and administrative personnel after World War II. Most prominently, the provision on criminal liability in Control Council Law No. 10 encompassed ordering liability. Many former *SS* and *Wehrmacht* officers were convicted by the U.S. Military Courts in Nuremberg *inter alia* based on the allegation of having ordered the commission of crimes. This chapter analyses the pertinent judgments of the Nuremberg subsequent trials, as well as certain other cases of the time, to shed light on the requirements and implications of the first instances of the use of ordering liability in international criminal law. The chapter concludes that both decision makers and architects of crimes could be described as having ordered the commission of crimes as it sufficed to exercise authority or authorship with regards to a criminal order. The chapter rejects the idea that a form of indirect perpetration liability was recognized by the U.S. Military Tribunals. It acknowledges that besides ordering liability, other, broader and more indirect, concepts of attribution of responsibility were also practiced by the courts.

J. Block, *Reconciling Responsibility with Reality*, International Criminal Justice Series 33, https://doi.org/10.1007/978-94-6265-607-9_4

Keywords Ordering · U.S. Military Courts · Nuremberg subsequent trials · Control Council Law No. 10 · Authority · Authorship

4.1 The Structure of Art. 2 Para. 2 CCL 10

Whilst the trials at the International Military Tribunal (IMT) and International Military Tribunal for the Far East (IMTFE) did not elaborate on modes of participation, other criminal proceedings, following World War II, became an important basis for the development of international criminal law. The most significant of these trials against former Nazi officials took place before U.S. Military Courts in Nuremberg.[1] In addition to that, British courts conducted several hundred trials within the British zone in Germany and other European countries.[2] Other trials took place under Soviet and French authority or in formerly occupied countries.[3]

The so-called Nuremberg subsequent trials were conducted under Control Council Law No. 10 (CCL 10).[4] The Allied Control Council had issued this regulation on 20 December 1945 to provide for a common legal basis for the prosecution of officials of the Nazi regime in occupied Germany.[5]

The trials before British military courts were not conducted under CCL 10. Instead, the Royal Warrant of 14 June 1945 was the regulation under which these courts acted.[6] Despite this difference, some of the cases which were tried by British and, in one case, Canadian military courts provide valuable insights into the development of the mode of ordering despite being based on legal frameworks other than CCL 10.

British military courts elaborated on ordering in two cases which subsequently became known in international criminal law: The *Buck* case, tried in Wuppertal, Germany and the trial against Nickolaus von Falkenhorst, tried in Brunswick (Braunschweig), Germany.[7] Additionally, a Canadian military court, acting under the Canadian War Crimes Regulation, tried the former *SS* commander Kurt Meyer in what is known as the *Abbaye Ardenne* case in Aurich, Germany.[8] These cases will be

---

[1] Cryer 2005, p 41.

[2] Ibid., p 41; Form 2007, p 57.

[3] Cryer 2005, p 41.

[4] CCL 10 is considered part of the "Nuremberg Law" together with the Nuremberg Principles and the Statute of the IMT and the jurisprudence of IMT and the subsequent trials, see Ambos 2018, § 6 mn. 2; also acknowledging its prevailing importance for international criminal law: Werle and Jessberger 2020, mn. 38–41.

[5] Lippmann 1992, p 9 et seq.; Werle and Jessberger 2020, mn. 38.

[6] Form 2007, p 57; Rogers 1990, pp 780, 786. For an analysis of the trials conducted under the Royal Warrant see Cheah and Vormbaum 2018. Regarding the relation of CCL 10 and the Royal Warrant see at 673.

[7] Law Reports of Trials of War Criminals Vol. V, 1948, p 39; Law Reports of Trials of War Criminals Vol. XI, 1948, p 18.

[8] Law Reports of Trials of War Criminals Vol. IV, 1948, p 97 et seq.

considered in addition to the more comprehensive jurisprudence of the Nuremberg subsequent trials for a broader insight into ordering in post-World War II trials.

As the most relevant regulation on participation in post-World War II trials, Art. 2 para. 2 CCL 10 deserves a closer look before attempting to analyse the requirements of ordering.

CCL 10 contained provisions for crimes against peace, war crimes and crimes against humanity. In contrast to the Nuremberg Charter, it did not link the latter with the former two, thus treating crimes against humanity as a separate crime.[9] Unlike the Nuremberg Charter, it also explicitly contained a list of modes of, or ways to incur individual criminal responsibility: Art. 2 para. 2 established that persons could be responsible if they were a principal (a), an accessory to the commission of the crime or ordered or abetted the same (b), took a consenting part therein (c) or were connected with plans or enterprises involving its commission (d). It also provided for criminal responsibility for being a member of organizations which committed the crimes (e).[10]

While this was by far more developed than the rules in the Nuremberg Charter, Art. 2 para. 2 CCL 10 seems to lack a coherent system of perpetration and participation.[11] Its structure does not seem to be overly consistent: It distinguishes between principals and accessories, but primarily by using abstract terms. Only within the various modes of lit. (b) to (d) does it differentiate between ordering and abetting, taking a consenting part in or being connected with criminal plans or enterprises. Judging by the order of the letters, it seems conceivable that all modes following lit. (b) should be considered accessorial whilst only (a) provides for (abstract) principal perpetration. When interpreted literally, ordering and abetting must mean something different, or at least more specific than the general "being an accessory" as they are connected to the latter by the conjunction "or".[12]

It has been contended that the tribunals hardly cared to elaborate on the specific modes of responsibility on which their judgments rested due to the broad formulation

---

[9] Werle and Jessberger 2020, mn. 39.

[10] The provision reads:

> 2. Any person without regard to nationality or the capacity in which he acted, is deemed to have committed a crime as defined in paragraph 1 of this Article, if he was (a) a principal or (b) was an accessory to the commission of any such crime or ordered or abetted the same or (c) took a consenting part therein or (d) was connected with plans or enterprises involving its commission or (e) was a member of any organization or group connected with the commission of any such crime or (f) with reference to paragraph 1 (a), if he held a high political, civil or military (including General Staff) position in Germany or in one of its Allies, co-belligerents or satellites or held high position in the financial, industrial or economic life of any such country.

[11] Von Knieriem 1953, p 223. Besides the fact that von Knieriem had himself been accused (but acquitted) in the *Flick* trial, his remarks on difficulties in interpreting the letters of Art. 2 Para 2 CCL 10, still seem comprehensible.

[12] An analysis of the potentially underlying system of perpetration and participation follows below in Sect. 4.5.

of Art. 2 para. 2 CCL 10.[13] It has been alleged that in many cases the tribunals only ascertained the crime and were content with stating that a defendant had participated in it.[14] Heller has highlighted that to participate knowingly was the base concept of imputation of responsibility under CCL 10, whose more specific requirements subsequently depended on the particular mode of participation.[15] The alleged opaqueness of the judgments under CCL 10 must be taken into account. Nevertheless, these trials have greatly influenced the development of international criminal law.[16] The following analysis *inter alia* explores whether the judgments of the twelve U.S. Military Tribunals in Nuremberg provide a valuable basis of research on the mode of ordering in international criminal law.

4.2 Legal Requirements

In the follow up trials against former Nazis, allied military courts have often referenced orders that were issued by the defendants. The legal requirements laid down in these cases vary in detail yet enable conclusions as to the situations and actions deemed sufficient for the imputation of responsibility under ordering.

For this section, the twelve Nuremberg subsequent trials based on CCL 10 remain the main object of research, whilst the few other cases from British and Canadian military courts serve as additional, alternative insight where appropriate.

4.2.1 Actus Reus—*The Conduct Element of Ordering*

To incur responsibility for ordering, the actor, naturally, must have given an order. But what kind of conduct would be deemed sufficient and necessary by the Nuremberg tribunals and other courts to qualify as ordering?

Orders in the context of a state and its military were regarded as extremely important by the Nuremberg tribunals. In the *High Command* case, the tribunal stressed the importance of orders in a military context, saying that they were "the basis on which an army operates". In the view of the tribunals, an army cannot work effectively without such orders and its discipline is built on them.[17] Civilians within the state apparatus of Nazi Germany and even some officials of business enterprises were also convicted under the terminology of ordering crimes.[18]

---

[13] Von Knieriem 1953, pp 228, 229.

[14] Ibid., p p229.

[15] Heller 2011, p 252.

[16] Cryer 2005, p 41; Heller 2011, p 2 et seq.

[17] Trials of War Criminals Before the Nuernberg Military Tribunals Under Control Council Law No. 10, Vol. XI, U.S. Government Printing Service 1950, p 510.

[18] Cf. also Heller 2011, p 257 et seq.

The language employed to describe the relevant conduct of persons who were found to have ordered a crime, varied significantly.

The Nuremberg military tribunals often referred to the "passing down", "transmission", "distribution" or "dissemination" of orders.[19] At other points, the judgments speak of "issuing" an order or instruction, or simply of "ordering".[20] Additionally, the phrases "application" or "implementation" of the order were used.[21] A Tribunal stated that "the transmittal through the chain of command constitutes an implementation of an order".[22] In other instances, a tribunal spoke of "executing" or "carrying into effect" certain orders.[23]

The *High Command* tribunal has also described behaviour which led to a conviction for ordering as responsibility for "criminal connection with participation in and formulation of" and for "contribution to the formulation of" an illegal order.[24]

The tribunal in the *Hostages* case described the conduct which the courts saw as relevant for ordering under CCL 10 as follows: "One who distributes, issues or carries out a criminal order becomes a criminal…".[25] *Heller* summarizes the range of acts that fall under ordering, slightly differently, as "issuing, drafting, or transmitting" an order.[26] The latter description seems to adequately capture the differently shaped acts that could in general lead to a conviction for ordering a crime.[27]

Based on this, the different types of conduct that were considered to constitute the *actus reus* of ordering can be described as follows.

"Issuing" and "ordering" may be regarded as descriptions of an act of handing out an instruction to subordinates by one's own initiative and authorship and under one's

---

[19] Trials of War Criminals Before the Nuernberg Military Tribunals Under Control Council Law No. 10, Vol. XI 1950, see e.g., pp 563 (von Leeb); 567, 573, 577 (von Kuechler); 581, 584 (Hoth); 597, 600 (Reinhardt); 615–617, 620 (von Salmuth); 645, 647 (von Roques); 1265 (List); 1274 et seq. (Kuntze); 1294 (Rendulic); 1306 et seq. (Felmy).

[20] Ibid., p p584, 588 (Hoth); 619 (von Salmuth); 645 (von Roques); 651, 653, 654, 657 (Reinecke); 1263 et seq. (List); 1274 et seq. (Kuntze); Trials of War Criminals Before the Nuernberg Military Tribunals Under Control Council Law No. 10, Vol. IV, U.S. Government Printing Service 1950, pp 539, 545, 547; Trials of War Criminals Before the Nuernberg Military Tribunals Under Control Council Law No. 10, Vol. V, U.S. Government Printing Service 1950, pp 106, 115, 118, 130, 131, 147, 149.

[21] Trials of War Criminals Before the Nuernberg Military Tribunals Under Control Council Law No. 10, Vol. XI 1950, pp 560, 563 (von Leeb); 614 (Reinhardt); 647 (von Roques).

[22] Ibid., p 510.

[23] Trials of War Criminals Before the Nuernberg Military Tribunals Under Control Council Law No. 10, Vol. IV 1950, pp 511, 517, 533; Trials of War Criminals Before the Nuernberg Military Tribunals Under Control Council Law No. 10, Vol. XI 1950, p 1274 et seq.

[24] Trials of War Criminals Before the Nuernberg Military Tribunals Under Control Council Law No. 10, Vol. XI 1950, pp 693 and 674.

[25] Ibid., p 1271.

[26] Heller 2011, p 255.

[27] In contrast to the tribunal's summary, Heller's description includes the drafting of an order. The "execution" of an order is not mentioned by Heller. This seems plausible because the implementation or putting into effect of orders as considered by the tribunals usually happened through other orders and did not mean the hands-on physical implementation of an order by the respective person.

own authority. In *High Command*, both the defendants Hoth and von Roques were found guilty of directly instructing their subordinates to execute commissars and to conduct mass shootings.[28] In *Hostages*, defendant Kuntze was found guilty because he issued orders to shoot or hang insurgents on the spot and burn down villages with communist administrations.[29]

"Transmission" and its synonyms (dissemination, distribution, passing down) meant the transferring of an order issued by higher ranking officers to lower subordinates.[30] To incur liability for ordering in these instances it was necessary that a commander added his[31] authoritative weight to the order, i.e. that his headquarters were not merely used by a higher authority to convey instructions to lower subordinates, thus bypassing him.[32] This was apparently seen likewise by the British military court in the *Buck* case. The defendant Wunsch had transmitted an order to the chief of the secret police in his camp, whilst the defendant Nussberger issued an order to shoot prisoners of war.[33] Wunsch was the camp commander but was not in charge of the police in it. The court sentenced him to four years imprisonment, whilst sentencing Buck, who had issued the original order, and Nussberger to death.[34] It has been submitted that, by finding Wunsch guilty, the court extended liability for ordering to mere transmissions,[35] implying that the addition of authoritative weight is unnecessary. However, the judgment can also be interpreted differently. Given the massive discrepancy in punishment, it is possible to infer that the defendant Wunsch was convicted for another form of participation.[36] This interpretation would mean an alignment of the jurisprudence of this particular British military court with the above-mentioned necessity of authoritative weight in the transmission of orders under the Nuremberg tribunals.

The third type of conduct recognized as a potential *actus reus* by the Nuremberg subsequent tribunals is the drafting of an order. This deserves special attention with

---

[28] Trials of War Criminals Before the Nuernberg Military Tribunals Under Control Council Law No. 10, Vol. XI 1950, pp 584, 645; Heller 2011, p 255 et seq.

[29] Trials of War Criminals Before the Nuernberg Military Tribunals Under Control Council Law No. 10, Vol. XI 1950, p 1277 et seq.

[30] Ibid., p 510; cf. also the description in Heller 2011, p 257.

[31] Given that the trials against war criminals under CCL 10 and the other cases considered in this chapter only involved male defendants and the body of law is historical and no longer applied, this chapter will refer to the relevant actors, including in their abstract form, as male.

[32] Trials of War Criminals Before the Nuernberg Military Tribunals Under Control Council Law No. 10, Vol. XI 1950, p 510; Heller 2011, p 257.

[33] Law Reports of Trials of War Criminals Vol. V 1948, p 39.

[34] Ibid., p 41.

[35] Finnin 2012, p 48 et seq.

[36] This is merely an alternative interpretation of the judgment, which admittedly implies that said Military Court would have awarded different sentences to different forms of participation, which is unclear.

a view to the earlier and subsequent chapters of this book.[37] In *High Command*, the court stated that "(i)deas and general directives must be translated into properly prepared orders if they are to become effective in a military organization".[38] It further determined that staff officers who moulded a basic criminal idea (of their superiors) into properly prepared orders or who took action to ensure that such orders were properly distributed, committed a criminal act under international criminal law.[39] With regards to the defendant Walter Warlimont, such acts lead to him being guilty "of a participating part in the formulation of [a] criminal order". Warlimont had drafted the notorious Commissar Order, pursuant to which captured political commissars of the Soviet Red Army should be executed.[40] Similarly, the defendant Lehmann, who served as chief legal advisor to the *Oberkommando Wehrmacht* (*OKW*, High Command of the Wehrmacht), "became the main factor in determining the final form in which the criminal ideas of Hitler were put".[41] This was described as "the making of a substantial contribution to the drafting of an order".[42]

Whether an order was mandatory or directory did not make any difference in the court's view, as long as it authorized the crime.[43] In one instance, a defendant in the *Justice* case was found to have authorized the transferal of prisoners, who had been sentenced to death, to the *Gestapo* for execution.[44] This raises the question of whether authorizing criminal conduct upon request by subordinates satisfies the requirements for giving an order.[45] Due to the lack of clear wording when ascertaining the responsibility of the defendant, the *Justice* tribunal left an option open that suggests that using one's authority to permit a crime, thought of by someone else, could qualify as giving an order to commit it. In the *I.G. Farben* case, the tribunal used ordering and authorizing as different descriptions of criminal responsibility ("conduct… which constitutes ordering, approving, authorizing or…").[46]

---

[37] The drafting of an order may in certain instances correspond to the "architect" mode of participation in mass atrocities, if the drafter does not exercise any influence over whether the order is ultimately issued in the form chosen by them.

[38] Trials of War Criminals Before the Nuernberg Military Tribunals Under Control Council Law No. 10, Vol. XI 1950, p 513.

[39] Ibid., p 513.

[40] Ibid., p 665.

[41] Ibid., p 693.

[42] Law Reports of Trials of War Criminals Vol. XV, 1948, p 78.

[43] Trials of War Criminals Before the Nuernberg Military Tribunals Under Control Council Law No. 10, Vol. XI 1950, p 1269, the same wording of "authorization" can also be found with the defendant Steimle in Trials of War Criminals Before the Nuernberg Military Tribunals Under Control Council Law No. 10, Vol. IV 1950, p 541, as well as with Pohl in Trials of War Criminals Before the Nuernberg Military Tribunals Under Control Council Law No. 10, Vol. V 1950, p 983.

[44] Trials of War Criminals Before the Nuernberg Military Tribunals Under Control Council Law No. 10, Vol. III, U.S. Government Printing Service 1950, p 1141.

[45] Ibid., p 1141 et seq.

[46] Trials of War Criminals Before the Nuernberg Military Tribunals Under Control Council Law No. 10, Vol. VIII, U.S. Government Printing Service 1950, pp 1157, also at 1162.

It is striking that the charge of ordering a crime is not discussed in much detail in the *Ministries* case, despite the fact that many of the defendants played vital roles in formulating or drafting laws and decrees.[47] Apparently, the tribunal did not find the actions sufficient to categorise them as ordering.

As to the necessary specifications, the *Hostages* tribunal described the orders for which the defendants were to blame as "orders, directives and instructions" which they had sent or received by virtue of their position.[48] This statement, especially in the given context, seems to refer primarily to formal, written instructions.

It becomes evident in many instances in the Nuremberg judgments, that orders did not have to concern the commission of a "specific" crime. The instruction to generally act in a way that qualified as a crime sufficed. Based on this, the defendant List in the *Hostages* case was found guilty, even though, by virtue of his higher rank, he did not order the commission of specific crimes, but rather passed on and issued general orders.[49]

In the cases before the Nuremberg Tribunals, many of the judgments rested on written orders as evidence. However, oral orders were considered equally relevant, as can be seen e.g., in the testimony of one defendant who, in a face-to-face discussion with his subordinate commander, ordered unwarranted court martial proceedings against officers of capitulated Italian troops. The officers were consequently shot.[50]

Furthermore, the *Hostages* tribunal was confronted with the defences of some of the defendants claiming that they had, alongside the written criminal orders, issued oral orders not to execute the written ones.[51] The judges did not find any credible evidence for these oral counter orders, but examined the statements as potential defences. This speaks for an equal relevance of oral orders in the opinion of the tribunals.[52]

Applying an even broader interpretation, a judge advocate before a Canadian Military Court in the *Abbaye Ardenne* case stated that *SS* commander Kurt Meyer could be held responsible for orders for which no evidence in written or oral form could be found. Instead, in the judge advocate's opinion, the existence of such an order could be inferred from the circumstantial evidence.[53] This not only confirms the possibility of oral orders, but also clarifies that the order itself did not have to be recorded in writing or testimony but could, in the view of certain military tribunals, be inferred from the circumstances.

---

[47] Trials of War Criminals Before the Nuernberg Military Tribunals Under Control Council Law No. 10, Vol. XIV, U.S. Government Printing Service 1950, p for formulation as a contribution to the policies and crimes see e.g., pp 400 et seq., 698 et seq., 702, 809, for drafting see e.g., pp 400 et seq., 416, 484, 597.

[48] Trials of War Criminals Before the Nuernberg Military Tribunals Under Control Council Law No. 10, Vol. XI 1950, p 1258.

[49] Ibid., p 1269 concerning the reissuing of the so called "Keitel Order", which established that for each killed German soldier, 100 hostages should be killed.

[50] Ibid., p 1311 et seq., for the testimony of defendant Lanz see 1106 et seq., 1108.

[51] Ibid., p 597 (Reinhardt), 615 (von Salmuth).

[52] Ibid., p 597, 615.

[53] Law Reports of Trials of War Criminals Vol. IV 1948, p 108.

An ambiguously worded order could qualify as ordering, if it bore the possibility of being carried out illegally, i.e., if it could lead to criminal behaviour.[54]

An order had to be considered binding by the sender and the recipient, i.e., the latter had to be "compelled to comply".[55]

In summary, the analysis shows that three types of conduct could fulfil the *actus reus* of ordering under Art. 2 para. 2 CCL 10: The drafting or preparing of orders, the issuance of them and the transmission of orders from higher levels which had to be passed down. In the latter case, the actor needed to add his authoritative weight to the order, i.e., it would not suffice if an order was only transmitted via his office as a communication point without involving his authority. This was seemingly handled in the same way by the British court in the *Buck* case. By contrast, the first category of conduct, the drafting of orders, required no additional authority. The relevant conduct could seemingly lie solely in the intellectual effort put into the formulation of an order.

4.2.2 Unlawfulness of the Order

The order either had to be criminal in itself, or bear the possibility of being applied in a criminal way.[56] The tribunal in *High Command* found that both the Commissar and the Commando Order were "criminal upon [their] face",[57] the latter even constituting an order "to commit murder".[58] The Barbarossa Jurisdiction Order contained both aspects: It conferred upon junior officers the authority to shoot individuals upon suspicion of being involved in illegal acts and was, in this regard, a criminal order. Furthermore, it contained no provisions to prevent its illegal application—leaving it up to the field commanders whether they would restrain the actions of their subordinates by disciplinary measures.[59] This made it possible to apply it in

[54] Trials of War Criminals Before the Nuernberg Military Tribunals Under Control Council Law No. 10, Vol. XI 1950, p 560 et seq., 685 et seq.; Heller 2011, p 255.

[55] Trials of War Criminals Before the Nuernberg Military Tribunals Under Control Council Law No. 10, Vol. XI 1950, p 651; Heller 2011, p 255.

[56] Trials of War Criminals Before the Nuernberg Military Tribunals Under Control Council Law No. 10, Vol. XI 1950, p 512; 560 et seq.; Heller 2011, p 255.

[57] Trials of War Criminals Before the Nuernberg Military Tribunals Under Control Council Law No. 10, Vol. XI 1950, p 567.

[58] Ibid., p 581; Heller 2011, p 255.

[59] Trials of War Criminals Before the Nuernberg Military Tribunals Under Control Council Law No. 10, Vol. XI 1950, p 524 et seq.; Heller 2011, p 255.

a criminal manner.[60] Criminal liability for orders that could be applied in a criminal fashion could be averted by formulating safeguards eliminating the margin for criminal application.[61]

4.2.3 *Position of Authority*

Issuing or passing on an order logically presupposes that the actor exercises some form of power or authority over certain subordinates. However, as discussed above, the mere drafting of an order sometimes sufficed for ordering. This raises the question of whether a position of authority was deemed necessary by the tribunals at all.

Authority or the power to give orders was discussed by some of the U.S. military tribunals in Nuremberg. In the *Pohl* case, the court hinted at the superior authority to issue certain orders which defendant Pohl enjoyed.[62] In *High Command*, the tribunal emphasised that a defendant had given orders that were considered binding by the recipients as well as the senders.[63] Many defendants in the more famous post-World War II trials held higher positions within the military, state apparatus or economic enterprises.[64] However, the question of whether the tribunals always required the actor to exercise some form of authority when giving an order must be evaluated closely.

A differentiation between "rank" and "position" is helpful in the analysis of these cases. Especially in military or para-military hierarchies, the rank someone possessed not always corresponded with his influence and opportunity to shape a criminal endeavour; this depended on his position within the organization and in its chain of command.

4.2.3.1 Positions of the Accused in the Nazi State Apparatus

In the *High Command* case, all defendants were part of the military hierarchy of Nazi Germany. Most of them had served as commanding officers at the front, whilst a few, namely Reinecke, Warlimont and Lehman, held positions within different

---

[60] Trials of War Criminals Before the Nuernberg Military Tribunals Under Control Council Law No. 10, Vol. XI 1950, p 560 et seq.; Heller 2011, p 255.

[61] Trials of War Criminals Before the Nuernberg Military Tribunals Under Control Council Law No. 10, Vol. XI 1950, p 525.

[62] Trials of War Criminals Before the Nuernberg Military Tribunals Under Control Council Law No. 10, Vol. V 1950, p 983; Heller 2011, p 255.

[63] Trials of War Criminals Before the Nuernberg Military Tribunals Under Control Council Law No. 10, Vol. XI 1950, p 651; Heller 2011, p 255.

[64] According to Heller, the position of most of the defendants in the U.S. Military Trials in Nuremberg to demand obedience from their subordinates might have been precisely the reason why the tribunals did not elaborate on such a requirement at length (cf. Heller 2011, p 255).

offices of the *OKW* in Germany.[65] The same held true in the *Hostages* case where all defendants were commanding officers or chiefs of staff in foreign countries occupied by the *Wehrmacht*.[66]

Thus, those who were ultimately convicted for ordering had a *de jure* position of authority. Without any evidence to the contrary, it seems conceivable that their instructions would usually be obeyed, leading to them having *de facto* authority as well. In the case of defendant Reinecke in the *OKW*, the tribunal also found that he issued certain directives signed "by order" ("*im Auftrag*"). This indicated that it was him acting instead of his superior.[67] In these instances, the court found that a defendant could not evade responsibility merely because he issued instructions "by order".[68] Whether the *de jure* authority emanated from the individual's own position within the hierarchy or was derived from the consent of a superior therefore did not make a difference.

In practice, there were hardly any differences between the authority of these defendants anyway. Most of the men in the *High Command* and *Hostages* cases, who were convicted on grounds of ordering were military commanders in the field or in occupied territories. The size of the military formations they commanded varied from "Panzer Groups"[69] and "Corps"[70] to an "Army Group".[71] Thus, the number of soldiers under their command varied, as did the range of officer ranks which were subordinate to them. Ultimately, however, they all had a strict chain of command below them.

The same held true for Reinecke: The orders he issued directly, "by order" or in his own name, primarily concerned prisoners of war camps and were transferred down the chain of command to the authorities responsible for their execution.[72]

In the *Einsatzgruppen* case, the defendants had all been part of the hierarchy of the *SS Einsatzgruppen*, the death squads charged with the execution of Hitler's and Himmler's monstrous plans of extermination for the civilian populations of eastern Europe.[73] Those who were proven to have ordered crimes also held positions of authority.[74] In one instance, the tribunal in *Einsatzgruppen* pointed out that the

[65] Trials of War Criminals Before the Nuernberg Military Tribunals Under Control Council Law No. 10, Vol. XI 1950, p 648 (Reinecke); 661 et seq. (Warlimont); 690 (Lehmann).

[66] Ibid., p 1230 et seq.

[67] Ibid., p 652.

[68] Ibid., p 653.

[69] Ibid., pp 581 (Hoth); 597 (Reinhardt).

[70] Ibid., pp 1300, 1309 et seq.

[71] Ibid., p 553 (von Leeb).

[72] Ibid., p 650 et seq.

[73] Trials of War Criminals Before the Nuernberg Military Tribunals Under Control Council Law No. 10, Vol. IV 1950, p 414 et seq.

[74] The positions varied from chief of an *Einsatzgruppe* (comparable to an infantry battalion, comprised of 800 to 1200 men (Ibid, 414)), to commanders of *Sonderkommandos* (comparable to an infantry company (Ibid, 414)); cf. e.g., for commanders of *Einsatzgruppen* defendants Ohlendorf, 511 et seq., Nauman, 517; for commanders of *Einsatzkommandos* or *Sonderkommandos* defendants Sandberger 532 et seq., Steimle, 539 et seq., Biberstein, 542 et seq.

defendant Steimle had commanded a firing squad himself.[75] This implies his presence at the crime scene of the specific shooting as well as his direct communication with the men acting as physical perpetrators. The case of Steimle is thus an example of an order that was given directly to the physical perpetrators of the crime, which is scarcely found in the Nuremberg military trials. It also implies that commanding only a relatively small group of perpetrators would suffice to earn the mark of "ordering a crime".

The *Medical* case saw the trying of many physicians, of whom nearly all had held officer ranks in the *Wehrmacht* or *SS* and occupied positions of varying importance. The defendants Mrugowsky and Rose were convicted of ordering crimes.[76]

In the *Pohl* case, members of the *SS* economic and administrative office (*WVHA*) were convicted *inter alia* for ordering the commission of war crimes and crimes against humanity.[77] Among the convicted were the former *WVHA*'s chief Oswald Pohl, who had been directly subordinated to Himmler,[78] and the chief of an "*Amt*",[79] which was a subordinated organizational unit.[80]

The *RuSHA* case dealt with the so called "germanization programme". The defendants, who were convicted for having ordered certain measures or acts,[81] or having issued directives related to the programme, had held high positions within the Race and Settlement Main Office (*Rasse- und Siedlungshauptamt—RuSHA*) or in the Staff Main Office of Himmler as Reich Commissioner for the Strengthening of Germanism (*Reichskommissar für die Festigung des deutschen Volkstums—RKFDV*).[82]

---

[75] Trials of War Criminals Before the Nuernberg Military Tribunals Under Control Council Law No. 10, Vol. IV 1950, p 540.

[76] Trials of War Criminals Before the Nuernberg Military Tribunals Under Control Council Law No. 10, Vol. II, U.S. Government Printing Service 1950, p 247, 271. Mrugowsky, as Chief of the Hygiene Institute of the Waffen SS was a military superior and commander with the power to issue orders (ibid., p 242). In this position, the tribunal was convinced, he had given orders to his subordinate, Dr. Ding, to conduct typhus experiments on inmates of the Buchenwald concentration camp (see ibid., p 245).

[77] Trials of War Criminals Before the Nuernberg Military Tribunals Under Control Council Law No. 10, Vol. V 1950, p 983, 1031, 1039 et seq.

[78] Ibid., p 980.

[79] Ibid., p 1024.

[80] Another person found responsible for ordering crimes was the chief dental officer, who had held authority over dental matters within the jurisdiction of the *WVHA* and who was therefore responsible for these matters in concentration camps (ibid., p 1035).

[81] The structure of the *RuSHA* judgment makes it difficult to determine whether the tribunal greatly distinguished between the description of modes of participation in the sense of Art. 2 Para 2 CCL 10. This is due to the fact that the crimes and criminal endeavours of the involved entities are described generally and reference is made to the defendants where determined appropriate instead of addressing the accused's contributions all at once.

[82] Regarding the organizations in the centre of the case against members of the former *Rasse- und Siedlungshauptamt* (*RuSHA*, "Race and Settlement Main Office") see: Trials of War Criminals Before the Nuernberg Military Tribunals Under Control Council Law No. 10, Vol. IV 1950, p 599. The defendants Greifelt and Creutz had served as chief of the staff main office and his deputy respectively (see Trials of War Criminals Before the Nuernberg Military Tribunals Under Control

As several of the Nuremberg trials illustrate, the position of authority does not, however, need to emanate from a military or para-military hierarchy.

In dealing with the judicial administration of Nazi Germany (*Justice* case), Tribunal III found that the defendants Schlegelberger, Klemm and Joel had ordered the commission of certain crimes.[83] Schlegelberger had acted in his position as provisional Reich Minister of Justice.[84] Klemm had been State Secretary in the Reich Ministry of Justice.[85] Joel had been a prosecutor and liaison officer to the *SS* and *Gestapo*, and in this function ordered or authorized the transferral of polish prisoners to the *Gestapo* for execution.[86]

Although none of the defendants were held responsible for ordering, the so-called industrialist cases show that a position of authority within a distinctly civilian context could have sufficed to be held responsible for ordering a crime.[87]

4.2.3.2 Analysis of Positions of the Defendants

We have seen that ordering was invoked frequently in many of the Nuremberg subsequent trials. The findings of the tribunals concerning the positions of the defendants enable a range of observations.

Positions Within the Hierarchy and Presence During the Crime

When comparing the ranks of the defendants in the cases before the U.S. Military Tribunals, it seems that ordering in the sense of CCL 10 did not imply any specific amount of subordinates, number of following ranks or other restriction on the organizational authority of the actor. Someone as high up the state hierarchy as the defendants Pohl, Reinecke or Lammers,[88] who obtained their instructions from the

---

Council Law No. 10, Vol. V 1950, p 154 et seq.). The defendants Hofmann and Hildebrandt had both been Chiefs of the *RuSHA* (see ibid., p 160 et seq.).

[83] Trials of War Criminals Before the Nuernberg Military Tribunals Under Control Council Law No. 10, Vol. III 1950, pp 1085, 1105, 1141.

[84] Ibid., p 1082.

[85] Ibid., p 1087.

[86] Ibid., pp 1135 et seq., 1141 et seq.

[87] Regarding the *Farben* case, the involvement of certain defendants in terms of ordering and other forms of participation is rejected by the Tribunal, see Trials of War Criminals Before the Nuernberg Military Tribunals Under Control Council Law No. 10, Vol. VIII 1950, pp 1157, 1162, 1165. In the *Krupp* case, defendant Max Ihn directed defendant Werner Lehmann to execute a decision of the directorate of the Krupp works in Essen providing that Hungarian Jews, working as forced labourers, should be sent back to Buchenwald, where they would be killed (see Trials of War Criminals Before the Nuernberg Military Tribunals Under Control Council Law No. 10, Vol. IX, U.S. Government Printing Service 1950, p 1428). However, it remains unclear whether this would be regarded as ordering in a narrower sense because the tribunal does not refer to this again.

[88] The position and role of Pohl as Chief of the *WVHA* have been outlined briefly in Chap. 2, Sect. 2.1, see also Trials of War Criminals Before the Nuernberg Military Tribunals Under Control Council Law No. 10, Vol. V 1950, p 980 et seq.; Reinecke headed the General Wehrmacht Office in the High Command of the *Wehrmacht* and was thus responsible *inter alia* for all matters of

first row of state officials after Himmler or even Hitler himself, could incur liability in connection with a criminal order as much as a person like Steimle who personally commanded a firing squad.[89]

It is logical that the tribunals consequently did not deem it important whether a person who ordered a crime had been present at the crime scene or not.

As for the defendants of the *High Command* and *Hostages* cases, it is obvious that they had usually not been present at the site of the crimes. Sometimes they were not even aware that specific criminal acts were being committed and even in the *Einsatzgruppen* trial, the tribunal often did not elaborate on the (possible) presence of the defendants at the scene.

It can therefore be summarized that holding a position of authority on basically any level of the state apparatus sufficed to establish liability for ordering when placed in front of the Nuremberg Military tribunals.

De Jure or de Facto Authority

Notwithstanding the aforementioned cases, the position of authority did not have to be strictly *de jure* or be originally embedded in the position which the actor held. In *High Command,* the tribunal explained that from its findings, chiefs of staff, who did not hold official authority over subordinate troops, but worked directly under and for the commander in chief, held a variety of *de facto* executive powers. These depended largely on the personality of the commander and other factors.[90] In the situations described by the tribunal in *High Command*, one could speak of a form of derived authority, as chiefs of staff would enjoy a certain freedom to sign orders, which they had prepared on their own, "by order" of their superior.[91] The tribunal held that in practice, a chief of staff could sign orders for, and by order of, the commanding officer notwithstanding that the commander might not have seen the order.[92] Accordingly, the lack of *de jure* authority over subordinate officers and ranks and file would not relieve a chief of staff from responsibility for the participation in criminal orders.[93] Based on this, the defendant Woehler, who had been a chief of staff, was held responsible for orders involving the shooting of civilians suspected of sabotage and espionage, which he signed in this capacity.[94] The tribunal was satisfied that he had either issued the order without submitting it to the commander

prisoners of wars, see Trials of War Criminals Before the Nuernberg Military Tribunals Under Control Council Law No. 10, Vol. XI 1950, pp 648, 650; Lammers had been the *Reich Minister* of the Reich Chancellery, see Trials of War Criminals Before the Nuernberg Military Tribunals Under Control Council Law No. 10, Vol. XIV 1950, p 589.

[89] Steimle was chief of a *Sonderkommando*, see Trials of War Criminals Before the Nuernberg Military Tribunals Under Control Council Law No. 10, Vol. IV 1950, p 539.

[90] Trials of War Criminals Before the Nuernberg Military Tribunals Under Control Council Law No. 10, Vol. XI 1950, p 512 et seq.

[91] Ibid., p 512 et seq.

[92] Ibid., p 514.

[93] Ibid., p 514, where the court describes that (command) responsibility, however, did not attach to a chief of staff in absence of his participation in criminal orders or their execution.

[94] Ibid., p 685.

in chief beforehand, or, having done so, had been responsible for the formulation of the order.[95] He was thus found to be criminally responsible for the order.[96] In the same case, defendant Reinecke was convicted for crimes against prisoners of war, because he had—as head of the office responsible for these matters—issued many consequential decrees regarding the ill treatment of prisoners.[97] Reinecke had issued such decrees "by order" of his superior Wilhelm Keitel, the chief of the *OKW*, and yet the tribunal asserted here that Reinecke "was not a mere stenographer". His task included the drafting and preparation of orders, however the tribunal found that many orders did not bear Keitel's initials or signature, implying that Keitel had not seen or specifically approved them.[98] This suggests a certain acceptance by the tribunal of a purely *de facto* position of authority, at least as long as the system in which a person functioned would lead to his orders being recognized by subsequent levels of the hierarchy.[99]

Authority as a Strict Requirement of Ordering?

A tribunal in Nuremberg stated that the position of authority must enable the actor to add his authoritative weight to a decision when passing it down the hierarchy.[100] A mere transmittal through the office of a commander would not be sufficient.[101] This means, that even where an individual generally held authority, he would not be liable where an order simply passed through his office due to communicational procedures, without touching upon his competences.

However, whether this means that an ordering person must always act from a position of authority needs clarification.

As we have seen, even the preparation of orders could amount to ordering. The question is whether this would also allow for a finding of liability for ordering where persons did not exercise any authority in the preparation. If so, authority would only play a role in certain constellations of ordering before the Nuremberg tribunals.

In accordance with the authority requirement, the tribunal in the *Hostages* case made it clear that the actor will not be criminally responsible if he signs or "initials" an instruction, e.g., to approve a certain form of a written order, but does not have the power to issue orders on his own behalf or amend or rescind the order.[102] Accordingly the tribunal did not find the defendants Foertsch and von Geitner responsible for ordering crimes. Foertsch had been a chief of staff and was said not to have given any orders nor to have had the power to do so. His mere distribution of the orders, in his

---

95 Ibid., p 685.

96 Ibid., p 686.

97 Ibid., pp 649 et seq., 657 et seq.

98 Ibid., p 652 et seq.

99 See for such an interpretation Finnin 2012, p 57.

100 Trials of War Criminals Before the Nuernberg Military Tribunals Under Control Council Law No. 10, Vol. XI 1950, p 510.

101 Ibid., pp 510, 556 et seq.

102 Ibid., pp 1284 et seq., 1287 et seq.

function as chief of staff, was not sufficient to qualify his behaviour as ordering.[103] The same was held for von Geitner: As chief of staff he had performed a range of tasks which included the signing or initialling of orders by the commander in chief, General Bader. These included orders for the shooting of hostages and reprisal prisoners. General Bader, however, had reserved the authority to order such reprisals or the taking of hostages for himself. Additionally, the orders of such acts were not prepared by von Geitner either, but by another, special legal officer, who reported to General Bader directly. The tribunal therefore found that the evidence did not show any criminal responsibility for ordering in the case of von Geitner.[104]

The *Hostages* case could therefore be read as stating that only if someone acted with authority in the preparation of orders, would that person be liable for ordering a crime.

The *High Command* case, however, draws another picture of authority and the drafting of orders. As mentioned before, in this case the defendants Warlimont and Lehmann, who had both held high offices in the *OKW*, were found guilty due to specific orders.[105]

Lehmann, as chief of the legal department of the *OKW*, had played a vital role in the formulation of the Barbarossa Jurisdiction Order. In particular, by determining that the collective executions of civilians be left up to the decision of lower ranking field commanders.[106] However, the final order was not introduced into the chain of command by Lehmann, who probably did not have the authority to do so. Instead, the court blamed him for casting "the whole into an effective military order".[107] The order in its final form was issued by Keitel, the chief of the *OKW*.[108] Consequently, the tribunal described Lehmann's responsibility as that of "criminal connection with, participation in, and formulation of this illegal order".[109] The wording of the judgment leaves little room to interpret it as anything different than criminal responsibility for ordering.[110] However, this finding does not contain any reliance on authority, as long as authority means the addition of authoritative weight. A department chief, such as Lehmann, who prepares a draft for an order or general directive, does not add such authoritative weight.[111] He may have authority over his own subordinate officers and clerks, but his draft goes up the hierarchy to his superior, who then

[103] Ibid., p 1284.

[104] Ibid., p 1287 et seq.

[105] See above in Sect. 4.2.1; Heller 2011, p 256.

[106] Trials of War Criminals Before the Nuernberg Military Tribunals Under Control Council Law No. 10, Vol. XI 1950, p 692 et seq.

[107] Ibid., p 693, see p 691 et seq. for a description of the drafting process of the Barbarossa Jurisdiction Order.

[108] Ibid., p 692.

[109] Ibid., p 693.

[110] Heller 2011, p 256.

[111] Cf. Finnin 2012, p 50 et seq., who describes the issue, but regards it under the *actus reus* of preparing orders.

decides whether to amend, sign or discard the draft. This raises the suspicion that ordering does not always require a position of authority.

Walter Warlimont was deputy chief of the Wehrmacht Operation Office (*Wehrmachtführungsstab*) and chief of the office's department of National Defence. As such, he reported directly to Jodl (Chief of the Operation Office) and Keitel (Chief of the *OKW* as a whole) and thus to the first tier of state military officials under Hitler.[112] In this role he was one of the leading influences behind the formulation of the notorious Commissar Order.[113] The tribunal found that, notwithstanding the fact that the murder of political commissars was not Warlimont's idea, "he contributed his part to moulding it into its final form".[114]

The Commissar Order was issued by Warlimont with the addition "by order".[115] It seems unlikely that he issued this far-reaching order to commit a war crime—the killing of prisoners of war—signing "by order" of his superiors yet was still exercising his own discretion. Instead, one must assume that when he signed the Commissar Order he was doing so under direct instruction of his superiors (Jodl, Keitel or even Hitler).

Warlimont was also involved in the preparation of the so-called Commando Order according to which the members of allied "commandos" operating behind the Nazi lines should be killed if they fell into the hands of the *Wehrmacht*. Warlimont's conduct concerning this order was described *inter alia* as a contribution to its formulation.[116] The tribunal did not bother differentiating between the official authority that came with his position and the authority he could exercise at his own discretion but in the name of his superiors.

One must conclude that the tribunal did not blame Warlimont for exercising his own authority, but for participating in the formulation of the orders. The tribunal's verdict regarding Warlimont is thus comparable to the one regarding Lehmann: The accused were not found guilty of ordering because they exercised their own *de jure* or *de facto* authority over others. Instead, their contribution to, or authorship of the order was at the centre of their conviction.

It can thus not be sustained that ordering under the rulings based on CCL 10 required the actual exercise of authority in every circumstance. Alternatively, individual "authorship", i.e., a central role in the formulation (or drafting) of an order, could suffice to qualify as ordering a crime. The range of defendants in the analysed cases before the Nuremberg Military Trials does not allow for an assessment of whether a certain rank or position was even necessary to qualify as this specific variety of ordering. The defendants,—Lehmann and Warlimont—whose participation was labelled ordering, but was based on authorship, held higher positions in the state apparatus. This makes it impossible to ascertain whether a low-ranking officer

[112] Trials of War Criminals Before the Nuernberg Military Tribunals Under Control Council Law No. 10, Vol. XI 1950, p 661 et seq.

[113] Ibid., p 663 et seq.

[114] Ibid., p 665.

[115] Ibid., p 665.

[116] Ibid., p 674.

who contributed to the formulation of an order would have similarly been convicted under the term of ordering.

Heller sees a contrast between the rulings in *Hostages* and *High Command*, due to the different outcomes for the defendants, von Geitner in one case and Lehmann and Warlimont in the other case, concerning their contribution to the drafting of specific orders.[117] In light of the aforementioned, however, such a contradiction cannot be sustained. The tribunal found that von Geitner did not have any opportunity to influence the formulation of the order because his commanding General kept him out of such matters and appointed a special legal officer to deal with them. By contrast, Lehmann and Warlimont decisively influenced the formulations and thus the content of orders.

The judgment against defendant Otto Woehler in the *High Command* case may support this finding. Just as von Geitner, Woehler had served as a chief of staff, with the difference that von Geitner was only tasked with formally checking and signing the orders formulated by another and given to him by his direct superior. Woehler, on the other hand, had the freedom to issue orders on his own initiative. A prerogative which the tribunal believed he took advantage of, consequently finding that Woehler had ordered certain crimes. In conjunction with the conviction of Lehmann and Warlimont, this observation demonstrates the different possibilities of incurring responsibility for ordering in the tribunal's view. Whilst Woehler had a range of possibilities allowing him to exercise his authority on his own initiative, Lehmann and Warlimont influenced orders through their authorship, making the exercise of authority unnecessary. Von Geitner had neither: He did not have the authority to issue instructions to commit crimes, nor was he involved in the material drafting of the respective orders to commit such crimes.[118]

Consequently, it must be found that the necessity of authority seemingly depended on the way in which a person was involved in the order. When issuing or transmitting an order, the actor had to add his authoritative weight; when drafting it, it was unnecessary to hold a position of authority.

4.2.4 *The* Mens Rea *of Ordering a Crime*

The tribunal in the *High Command* case held that, to be responsible for ordering, the commanders had to know that the orders they were passing on were unlawful or, where the order was "criminal upon its face", should have known of its unlawfulness. In other words: A commander had to know about the illegality of an order (if it was ambiguous) or the order had to be criminal upon its face (in which case the commander should have known about its illegality).[119]

[117] Heller 2011, p 256.

[118] Cf. Trials of War Criminals Before the Nuernberg Military Tribunals Under Control Council Law No. 10, Vol. XI 1950, p 1287 et seq.

[119] Ibid., p 511; cf. also Heller 2011, p 258.

This requirement would apply to all of the different acts—issuing, drafting and transmitting—that could constitute ordering.[120] Likewise, the tribunal in the *Hostages* case asserted that a person distributing, issuing or carrying out a criminal order had to know or should have known of its criminal character.[121]

These assertions can be read as establishing the following: Where an order is criminal upon its face it leads to criminal responsibility if the actor should have known of this. Where it isn't, i.e., because the illegality is less obvious or the order is in itself not illegal, but can be applied illegally, the actor must have had positive knowledge of its unlawfulness or its capacity of being applied so.[122] With regards to the latter case, the judgment in *High Command* enables such a conclusion. The judgment states that the accused von Leeb had expressed his disapproval of an order that could be applied illegally by subordinate officers as it allowed them to shoot persons, suspected of being involved in certain activities, on the spot. Subsequently the defendant had transmitted the order, without clarifying the ambiguity. In light of the broad competence granted to low-ranking officers to perform on-the-spot executions, the tribunal assumed that von Leeb was aware of the order's capacity of being applied illegally.[123]

The specific crimes committed as a result of a commander's directive or policy did not have to come to his attention. I.e., he did not need to have knowledge of single incidents if they were within the scope of these directives or policies.[124]

4.2.5 Commission of the Crime, Ordering as a Substantive Crime and Attempt

The jurisprudence of the Nuremberg Military Trials is divided over the issue of whether the crime must have actually been committed, i.e., if liability for ordering could be incurred, if the orders were not executed.[125]

In the *High Command* case, the tribunal only found a defendant guilty for giving orders if a crime was actually committed because of the order.[126] It has been submitted by Heller that the tribunal in *High Command* also viewed ordering as a substantive

[120] Cf. Trials of War Criminals Before the Nuernberg Military Tribunals Under Control Council Law No. 10, Vol. XI 1950, p 512, where the tribunal confirms that "any participation" in implementing such orders were criminal acts; Heller 2011, p 258.

[121] Trials of War Criminals Before the Nuernberg Military Tribunals Under Control Council Law No. 10, Vol. XI 1950, p 1271.

[122] Heller 2011, p 258.

[123] Trials of War Criminals Before the Nuernberg Military Tribunals Under Control Council Law No. 10, Vol. XI 1950, p 560.

[124] Ibid., p 1271.

[125] Heller 2011, p 258.

[126] Cf. for instances where the respective charge was not sustained Trials of War Criminals Before the Nuernberg Military Tribunals Under Control Council Law No. 10, Vol. XI 1950, pp 615, 647.

crime, based on the conviction of defendant Reinhardt.[127] Concerning his involvement in the deportation of the civilian population into concentration camps and their exploitation as forced labour, the tribunal stated that Reinhardt was "criminally responsible for issuing the orders and for the acts done in implementation of them".[128] The connecting word "and" in this statement is interpreted by Heller as establishing ordering as a substantive crime. The tribunal explained that "[T]he orders to do those things were criminal orders and they were fully implemented by him".[129] But the judgment can also be interpreted differently: the tribunals often stated that someone had issued or transmitted orders and had overseen their implementation, which in turn led to the commission of the crime.[130] The reasoning concerning defendant Reinhardt in the *High Command* case is no different. He could be convicted for ordering the commission of crimes precisely because he also undertook other acts, which eventually led to the commission of the crime. This, however, does not mean that he would have been guilty of ordering (as a substantive crime) had the orders not been implemented. The tribunal describes the defendant's acts as ordering and other contributions. One of these contributions being the order, which does not establish independent liability but is seen as one of the acts leading to the (necessary commission of the) eventual crimes.[131] It can therefore be said that the *High Command* tribunal did not believe in a substantive liability for ordering, irrespectively of the commission of the crimes.

In *Einsatzgruppen*, the tribunal explained that contrary to what it considered to be the law of CCL 10, Article 47 of the German Military Penal Code provided for punishment for illegal orders whether they were executed or not.[132] It thereby emphasized that it saw no room for ordering where the crimes were not committed.

Defendant Brueckner in the *RuSHA* case was also acquitted of the charge of forcibly conscripting foreigners into the *Wehrmacht* because the draft order he had formulated had never been put into action.[133]

The tribunal in *Hostages* took a different stance on this issue. With respect to the notorious "commissar order", which established that political commissars of the

---

[127] Heller 2011, p 259.

[128] Trials of War Criminals Before the Nuernberg Military Tribunals Under Control Council Law No. 10, Vol. XI 1950, p 614.

[129] Ibid., p 614.

[130] Cf. for examples of illegal orders leading to the commission of crimes in *High Command*, ibid., pp 560 et seq., 584, 599, 647.

[131] Cf. Ibid., p 647. The description of defendant von Roques' acts and responsibility makes it clear that he is considered responsible because his orders led to his subordinates committing the crimes and, with other agencies, because he acquiesced in their actions.

[132] Trials of War Criminals Before the Nuernberg Military Tribunals Under Control Council Law No. 10, Vol. IV 1950, p 486; Heller 2011, p 258 et seq.

[133] Trials of War Criminals Before the Nuernberg Military Tribunals Under Control Council Law No. 10, Vol. V 1950, p 147; Heller 2011, p 259.

Russian army should be shot and not treated as prisoners of war, it was deemed sufficient that the order was given, even if no one was consequently shot.[134] In this regard, one must keep in mind that the declaration that no quarter will be given was already incorporated as contrary to the laws and customs of war in the Hague Convention from 1907.[135] The issuance of the commissar order could therefore perhaps constitute a separate crime under said convention. The tribunal in *Hostages*, however, chose to describe defendant Rendulic's guilt as "the crime of [...] passing on a criminal order", clearly indicating criminal responsibility for the ordering of a crime that had not been committed.[136]

The judgment in the *von Falkenhorst* case, delivered by a British military court, is comparable to the *Hostages* ruling: Nickolaus von Falkenhorst had been charged with and convicted for passing on an order, according to which Jewish prisoners of war should be deprived of their status and handed over to the *SD* (*Sicherheitsdienst*—Security Service of the SS), which would have meant their certain death.[137] The tribunal found the defendant guilty of ordering this illegal treatment, even though the order had not been carried out.[138]

Heller has interpreted the *Hostages* case as establishing the issuance of an order that was not carried out as a substantive crime in contrast to the mode of liability of ordering in cases where orders were carried out.[139] From a civil law perspective, the two latter incidents would be more aptly described as the attempt to order a crime. To view it as a substantive crime in civil law terminology would run counter to the regulation of Art. 2 para. 2 CCL 10, in which ordering is clearly (only) a mode of liability.

In summary, post-World War II jurisprudence is divided over the matter. While most tribunals of the Nuremberg subsequent trials denied a possible attempt or substantive crime of ordering, at least one tribunal (in the *Hostages* case) and a British military court affirmed this possibility.

4.2.6 Summary and Conclusion

As discussed in this section, there are three types of conduct that could fulfil the *actus reus* of ordering under Art. 2 para. 2 CCL 10: Drafting, issuing, and transmitting an order. To trigger criminal liability, an order had to be unlawful or be capable of being applied unlawfully. For actors who issued or transmitted orders, the tribunals held

[134] Trials of War Criminals Before the Nuernberg Military Tribunals Under Control Council Law No. 10, Vol. XI 1950, p 1294; Cf. also Heller 2011, p 258 et seq.

[135] Cf. Art. 23 (d) of the Hague Convention from 1907.

[136] Trials of War Criminals Before the Nuernberg Military Tribunals Under Control Council Law No. 10, Vol. XI 1950, p 1294.

[137] Law Reports of Trials of War Criminals Vol. XI 1948, pp 20, 22.

[138] Ibid., p 24; Cryer et al. 2019, p 360.

[139] Heller 2011, p 258–9.

that they had to add their authoritative weight to the order, i.e., they had to hold a position of authority *vis-à-vis* the recipients of the order. For the drafting of an order, however, no such authority was necessary. A person who ordered a crime had to know that the order could lead to the commission of crimes if the order was not evidently unlawful. If it was "criminal upon its face", the *mens rea* standard was lower, i.e., a should-have-known standard applied.

The jurisprudence is divided over whether an order that was never put into effect could trigger responsibility for ordering.

This section shows that under the mode of ordering different types of conduct, relevant orders and mental element standards could play a role. The picture emerging from this analysis is one of a mode of ordering that fulfilled several descriptive functions at once, describing decision makers in high, middle, and low-ranking positions of authority. However, it could also apply to persons involved in the preparation and drafting of orders, who would not make the final decision of whether an order would be carried out. These individuals had to significantly influence the content or shape of the order. Following the distinction made in earlier chapters, one can say that this last group represented a type of architects of crimes.

Furthermore, it is worth underlining that certain tribunals resorted to ordering as a mode of liability more than others. Ordering was seemingly employed more where defendants acted in military-like situations (*High Command, Hostages, Einsatzgruppen*), than in administrative or civilian surroundings (*Pohl, Ministries, RuSHA, Justice*, the industrialist cases). Much less instances from the latter judgments could be quoted in this section because the respective tribunals seemingly preferred other descriptions of the accused's involvement.

4.3 Observations on Ordering and Authority in Post-World War II Trials

Based on the analysis of the requirements of ordering in post-World War II trials, some observations can be made, which can be helpful in the further description of the development of the mode of ordering.

4.3.1 Authority or Authorship as a Determining Factor

The different types of conduct and the limited authority requirement connected to them enable an analysis of what the tribunals deemed relevant aspects in the preparation and issuance of orders.

One can observe a difference in the types of order considered by post-World War II tribunals and courts. This concerns the actor's positions of authority and responsibility within their branches of the Nazi state, in these cases specifically within the Wehrmacht. In many instances the defendants were found responsible for ordering, because they passed on certain orders. As explained above, this must go hand in hand with the authoritative weight of the person passing on the order. A simple "technical" transmission of the order does not constitute responsibility for ordering.[140]

In other instances, however, the defendants were charged for "issuing" certain orders or "ordering" that something had to be done by their subordinate units. At first, the difference in wording seems to be only of a stylistic nature, but it actually turns out to describe two different types of orders or conduct. The first type has been described above and can be characterised as the passing on of instructions to subordinate units or entities with the weight of one's own authority.

The second type describes the issuing of orders that, in their specific form, do not originate from a higher authority.[141] Instead, these types of orders are given to implement other, more general, orders, directives or policies. These may sometimes not have been detailed enough to be passed on without further "operational" clarifications and instructions.[142] It can be assumed that any order issued on the independent initiative of a commander would additionally fall under this category.

A third type of behaviour that qualified as ordering can be found in the acts of certain defendants that were described as a "formulation of"[143] or "contribution to the formulation of"[144] orders. As outlined above, the respective defendants did not exert their own authority in these instances. Instead, the determining factor of their criminal responsibility was the intellectual contribution to the drafting process of the criminal order.[145]

One difference between the three lies in the measure of individual initiative and "creativity" of the actor. A second difference concerns the reliance on authority and hierarchy. In the first type of case, the actor adds his authoritative weight to the order and assumes responsibility for his subordinates obeying it. However, he does not, personally or through his staff, develop ideas on what must be done. This kind of initiative only occurs in the second type of case: Here the commander issues an own order within his scope of competence. The ideas and details contained therein are either a product of his own mind, or a mental appropriation of an order prepared by his staff. The orders in this second type of case may specify or reiterate the content of

140 Trials of War Criminals Before the Nuernberg Military Tribunals Under Control Council Law No. 10, Vol. XI 1950, pp 510, 556 et seq.

141 Ibid., p 588 (defendant Hoth issued an order resembling Hitler's language and goals); 619 (von Salmuth issued an order pursuant to which soldiers would not be punished for crimes committed against the civilian population under orders); 645 (von Roques issued an order specifically commanding the shooting of civilians found in the possession of arms).

142 Cf. Ibid., p 645, where von Roques issued the order to execute civilians found in possession of weapons to implement the more generally phrased Barbarossa Jurisdiction order.

143 Ibid., p 693.

144 Ibid., p 674.

145 Cf. again the description of Warlimont's role in the drafting of the Commissar order and Lehmann's involvement in the Barbarossa Jurisdiction and Commando orders (ibid., pp 665, 693, 694).

broader directives,[146] or serve the implementation of such directives by instructing the use of certain measures.[147] Of course, this second category may also concern completely different affairs, unattached to higher orders, but capable of leading to criminal acts, nevertheless.

In the third type of case, the actor does not exert authority or hierarchical weight to issue the order because he is reliant on the decision of a superior to do so. However, he significantly shapes the order by introducing ideas which he, by himself or through his personnel, developed. Alternatively, he cast the order into the necessary shape and form to turn it into a ready-to-issue product.

The judgment against von Leeb in the *High Command* case contains an example of the first type of conduct: von Leeb was found responsible for transmitting the Barbarossa Jurisdiction order to which he added his authoritative weight.[148] He was not involved in the order's drafting, nor did he exercise initiative in its issuing; he "merely" transmitted it. However, the authoritative position from which he did so, made it relevant for the massive conglomeration of troops under his command.

The cases of defendants Woehler and Reinecke serve to illustrate the second type of conduct, i.e., the issuing of instructions, based on independent initiative. Defendant Woehler, as chief of staff, issued orders to shoot civilians suspected of sabotage. Despite his competence to do so (derived from his superior, who had left such matters to him), he was not transmitting an instruction received from a higher level but reacting to specific circumstances in his area of competence.[149] In the case of defendant Reinecke, the tribunal pondered his contribution to orders concerning the mistreatment of prisoners of war. Given that Reinecke apparently gave the orders himself and no specific superior instructions existed in this regard, he also falls into this second category of conduct, i.e., the issuance of orders with authority and out of an individual's own initiative.[150]

The cases of the defendants Warlimont and Lehmann serve as examples for the last category: Both were found to have crucially contributed to the formulation, the drafting of orders. Given their positions in the military apparatus, they could not issue the orders themselves, and instead had to pass them to their superiors who then issued them.[151]

These observations on three different types of case show two different requirements, each of which, by itself, would suffice for a conviction for ordering: Authority and Authorship. The first category of conduct only requires authority. The last category only requires authorship without authority. Naturally, a meeting of both requirements leads to ordering liability as well.

---

[146] Cf. e.g. Ibid., p 588.

[147] Cf. e.g. Ibid., p 645.

[148] See for a description above in Sect. 4.2.4.

[149] See again Trials of War Criminals Before the Nuernberg Military Tribunals Under Control Council Law No. 10, Vol. XI 1950, p 685. Note that the tribunal was convinced that Woehler had alternatively drafted the orders, by grace of which he would fall into the third category of conduct.

[150] Ibid., p 651 et seq.

[151] See above Sect. 4.2.3.2.

These two requirements, to a certain extent, resemble the categorisation of decision makers and architects of crimes that has been discussed in earlier chapters. If a member of a department or general staff would draft criminal orders but could not issue them due to a lack of authority, he could be described as an architect of the crime. A commander on the other hand, who merely decided to transmit a criminal order to their subordinates and did so in ways commensurate with their authority, would be a decision maker.[152] Finally, a person could be both an architect and decision maker, where he drafted and issued an order himself. Given the necessary authority, however, he would primarily remain a decision maker who did or did not draft his own decisions to have crimes committed.

4.3.2 Exercising Authority or Power Without Being Charged Under Ordering

Notwithstanding the above, it remains unclear whether ordering was really employed to grasp the conduct of a broader category of architects of crimes. More precisely, it seems questionable whether people in roles like the one Adolf Eichmann had occupied would be found responsible for ordering crimes. This is not due to the scope of the head of ordering, which would be broad enough as we have just seen. However, the analysis of Nuremberg subsequent trials questions whether decision-making authority or the drafting of directives would always be primarily treated as ordering.

This issue can be seen in the *Pohl, Ministries, Justice, RuSHA* and the industrialist cases, where the idea of ordering is mentioned far less than in the other examined cases. The difference between these and the other cases mostly lies in the area of application, the proximity to the crimes and the specific tasks of the defendants. In the *RuSHA* case, the defendants were primarily employed in one of the main offices of the SS. The defendants in *Pohl* had been employed by the *WVHA*, the economic main office of the SS. They thus held ranks within a para-military hierarchy, but quite a few of them were not directly concerned with the planning, organisation, or execution of crimes.[153]

[152] Despite the commander's duties as part of a chain of command, he made decisions over the commission of crimes by not issuing parallel directives to circumvent or differently implement the criminal orders.

[153] It has been outlined in the second chapter, how a branch of the *WVHA* was responsible for running the extermination camps. Instructions issued in this branch would have concerned the murder of prisoners in these camps very directly; see Chap. 2, Sect. 2.1. However, the U.S. military tribunal in the *Pohl* case did not share this view and instead stated that, "Neither Pohl, nor any other member of the WVHA had authority to order the execution of concentration camp prisoners" (Trials of War Criminals Before the Nuernberg Military Tribunals Under Control Council Law No. 10, Vol. V 1950, p 981). Consequently, the charges against Oswald Pohl do not reflect the statements made in Chap. 2. The emphasis laid by the tribunal was a different one and focused on several separate "actions" or enterprises in which the *WVHA* and Pohl were involved. The tribunal deemed

The tasks of many of the defendants differed from those of the defendants in other cases insofar as they did not concern the immediate perpetration of the crimes (in this case primarily slave labour and extermination via forced labour and cruel circumstances). None of them were charged directly with organizing and instructing the guards. Some are nevertheless directly responsible for the deaths of uncountable inmates of concentration camps. If someone assigns at least 11 working hours per day, knowing that the food rations of the forced workers are minimal, this person directly sets a condition for their deaths by exhaustion. Another person who audits the economic functioning of a camp and concludes that it does not yield the desired output, can come to this conclusion and expect that others will raise the working hours in the camp as a consequence. However, his own conduct does not directly determine anyone's fate.[154]

Although most of the defendants in *Ministries* and *Justice* were eventually convicted, few were charged with the specific ordering of crimes. In this instance as well, they were not part of a military hierarchy. Instead, they had served as ministers, secretaries of state, judges, and prosecutors or in other positions within ministries, the judicial branch or other authorities and financial institutions of Nazi Germany. Many of them thus held a position in which they had exercised authority over a range of subordinates, if not a whole organization or executive branch of the Nazi regime. Yet again, many of their tasks and areas of action seem to have been detached from the crimes to which they eventually led. A striking example is the role of Lammers, Reich Minister of the Reich Chancellery. Lammers signed or co-signed many decrees and laws, often putting his signature next to Hitler's.[155] Many of them concerned the position and allocation of posts to prominent figures, such as Karl Hermann Frank in Bohemia and Moravia or Himmler in the occupied Poland.[156] These acts were vital to enable the subsequent ordering or commission of crimes, but they did not, in themselves, violate norms of international criminal law or contain the instructions to do so. Lammers also co-signed decrees or laws, which directly deprived certain parts of the population (mostly people that fell under the Nazi label of Jews or "Poles") of certain rights and which were thus considered criminal by the tribunal.[157] In these cases, no subsequent acts were necessary as the violation of the norm lay in the signing of the decree itself. "Ordering" did not play a role and Lammers was finally found guilty without the tribunal using the terminology of Art. 2 para. 2 CCL 10.

A similar description is found in the case of Schlegelberger, the highest-ranking defendant in the *Justice* case. By instituting and partly drafting consequential Nazi legislation in both Germany and occupied territories, Schlegelberger employed the

---

Pohl's involvement as highly blameworthy nonetheless, and he was finally convicted for his "direct participation" in these actions (see ibid., pp 984, 988, 989) and sentenced to death (ibid., p 1062).

[154] Ibid., p 983. This refers to Pohl's own conduct as an administrator of the concentration camps. Note the contradiction to newer descriptions of his direct involvement as described in Chap. 2, Sect. 2.1.

[155] Trials of War Criminals Before the Nuernberg Military Tribunals Under Control Council Law No. 10, Vol. XIV 1950, p 590 et seq.

[156] Ibid., p 590 et seq.

[157] Ibid., p 600 et seq.

ministry of Justice as a means to further and support the aims of the Nazi regime and his responsibility was described with reference to his role in the regime.[158]

The industrialists in the *Farben, Flick* and *Krupp* cases staffed high positions in economic enterprises. They joined the common cause of the Nazis and supported them through the total subjection of their enterprises' economic output under the aggressive war efforts. Slave labour was employed in their plants, and they relied on plundered materials and machinery.[159] But scarcely did they engage in the formulation of criminal plans, nor did they receive any instructions from others which they could then put into motion by themselves. In many cases they depended on the decisions of the *SS* and its vast bureaucratic organization and would often not decide over the allocation or treatment of forced labourers by themselves.[160] Thus, they were less probable to order the commission of crimes.

These cases demonstrate how different roles or positions of persons and the difference between the acts which are necessary to commit certain international crimes influenced the description of responsibility in post-World War II trials.

Quite a range of defendants provided invaluable support for the execution of the Nazis' murderous plans, some by drafting these plans themselves, adding more detailed criminal ideas; others by working out meticulous manuals for the completion of such plans. Yet some supported the execution of these plans by wilfully functioning within their sphere of competence in the state apparatus. However, among all these participants, only those who gave a definite instruction that a crime be committed—whether it be a specific offence or the command to generally engage in criminal behaviour in certain situations—were convicted for ordering the commission of crimes.[161] The others were scarcely found guilty of ordering. Instead, they were blamed for having participated in the crimes or the formulation of the plans or policies that led to them. This leads to the conclusion that ordering a crime was not consistently applied as a mode of liability for decision makers and architects of Nazi crimes. Instead, it seems that such persons usually fell under ordering if they were involved in a military context, where orders rapidly and directly led to crimes. Although some situations in which persons issued instructions that led to crimes

---

158 Trials of War Criminals Before the Nuernberg Military Tribunals Under Control Council Law No. 10, Vol. III 1950, e.g., at pp 1086–7.

159 Cf. for plunder and spoliation by I. G. Farben: Trials of War Criminals Before the Nuernberg Military Tribunals Under Control Council Law No. 10, Vol. VIII 1950, p 1141 et seq.; cf. also the findings in *Krupp*, Trials of War Criminals Before the Nuernberg Military Tribunals Under Control Council Law No. 10, Vol. IX 1950, p 1338 et seq. and in *Flick*, especially count one on deportation and slave labour, Trials of War Criminals Before the Nuernberg Military Tribunals Under Control Council Law No. 10, Vol. VI, U.S. Government Printing Service 1950, p 1194 et seq.

160 In *Flick*, the tribunal found that the industry did not have actual control over the slave labour programme, but depended on state authorities which "vigorously" supervised the programme, Trials of War Criminals Before the Nuernberg Military Tribunals Under Control Council Law No. 10, Vol. VI 1950, p 1196 et seq.

161 Arguably, even this was not done consistently in the cases discussed in this section. Whether Pohl's decisions concerning working hours in concentration camps, which obviously lead to more people dying of exhaustion, could not also have been qualified as an order is questionable.

were described as ordering, in the proceedings against members of primarily administrative branches of Nazi Germany, other descriptions of responsibility were often additionally chosen. In Heller's view, in such cases, a form of enterprise liability was used by the tribunals.[162] He principally refers to situations in which ordering could seldom be found, as was the case in the *RuSHA, Ministries, Justice* and *Pohl* decisions. According to Heller's analysis, "participation" in the enterprise was the description used by the courts. Such participation was possible as creator or executor of instructions and often involved the actors enjoying "authority and discretion".[163]

By combining Heller's observations with the abovementioned findings, one can conclude that ordering a crime played a role mostly in military contexts and where direct links between the relevant instructions and crimes could be established. In cases where defendants primarily contributed to the overall system and worked outside of military-operational contexts, a broad notion of participation in an enterprise was used.[164]

4.3.3 Control Over Parts of the Nazi Apparatus and "Direct Participation"

Earlier chapters of this book elaborated on indirect perpetration through an organisation. This mode of responsibility, regardless of its form under a specific legal system, relies on the idea that the actor controls an organisation and therefore becomes an indirect perpetrator of the crimes, which are committed by members of that organisation.

As seen above, ordering was not applied to many defendants outside of the strictly military and fighting *SS* division of the Nazi state apparatus. Given that the term control is frequently used by some tribunals and a notion of "participation" often played a role in judgments where ordering was not relied on, this section will explore whether and to what extent a notion of control played a role in such cases. Could this be an indicator for another mode of liability close to perpetration through an organisation?

The tribunal in *High Command* described the position of the defendant Reinecke as having the "general control and responsibility" and "over-all control and supervision" over matters of prisoners of war in the *OKW*.[165] Reinecke was held responsible for orders he gave (partly in form of directives), but was also considered by the tribunal as guilty of "participation in the criminal segregation of prisoners of war".[166] In his

---

[162] Heller 2011, pp 281–90.

[163] Ibid., p 284 et seq.

[164] Heller describes the notion of participation in such enterprises as "extremely broad", see ibid., p 284.

[165] Trials of War Criminals Before the Nuernberg Military Tribunals Under Control Council Law No. 10, Vol. XI 1950, pp 650, 653.

[166] Ibid., p 657.

case, both ordering and a more general notion of controlling and participating in crimes fell together.

Similarly, the tribunal in *Pohl* described Oswald Pohl's position as one where he had "absolute control" over the *WVHA* as an organization.[167] His position was believed to be one where he could "exercise substantial supervision and control".[168] Pohl, however, was not convicted under the head of ordering, but was found guilty of direct participation in war crimes and crimes against humanity.[169] The wordings of both judgments resemble basic thoughts on perpetration through an organization in an abstract way: By being the chiefs of an agency/office with far reaching competences, Pohl and Reinecke were believed to have had control over matters of prisoners of war and concentration camps respectively.

The tribunal in the *Hostages* case also referred to questions of control, albeit in a somewhat different fashion. It asserted that many of the higher-ranking defendants did not have direct control over units. Instead, it was said that, due to their high ranks, their control was of an indirect nature.[170] Their generally valid orders would thus be sufficient to establish responsibility.[171]

The term control can also be found in the *Einsatzgruppen* case where a defendant was said to have had "control and jurisdiction" over the Estonian "Home Guard".[172] Regarding another defendant, the tribunal stated that a "high ranking officer who plans an operation or participates in the planning and has control over officers taking part in the movement certainly cannot escape responsibility for the action by absenting himself the day of execution of the plan".[173]

The same tribunal followed a line of reasoning which appears somewhat familiar in the light of the control theory when it determined the responsibility of a defendant named Schubert. Schubert had supervised the execution of several hundred people. He had done so by orders of his superior and had inspected every step from the deportation of the victims to the actual killing. He had chosen the location for the crime and ensured that the orders of his superior would be neatly followed. He stated that he would have intervened if anything would not have gone according to these orders.[174] The trial therefore found that the defendant's "criminal involvement in the

---

167 Trials of War Criminals Before the Nuernberg Military Tribunals Under Control Council Law No. 10, Vol. V 1950, p 980 et seq.

168 Trials of War Criminals Before the Nuernberg Military Tribunals Under Control Council Law No. 10, Vol. XI 1950, p 981 et seq.

169 Trials of War Criminals Before the Nuernberg Military Tribunals Under Control Council Law No. 10, Vol. V 1950, p 984. As mentioned previously, the description does not mention any direct involvement of Pohl in the conveyance of execution orders, although modern historians believe this happened as well (see Chap. 2, Sect. 2.1).

170 Trials of War Criminals Before the Nuernberg Military Tribunals Under Control Council Law No. 10, Vol. XI 1950, p 1259.

171 Ibid., p 1259.

172 Trials of War Criminals Before the Nuernberg Military Tribunals Under Control Council Law No. 10, Vol. IV 1950, p 533.

173 Ibid., p 549.

174 Ibid., p 581 et seq.

Christmas massacre of Simferopol is complete…".[175] In this specific instance, one can observe how the organisational supervision of a range of crimes led the tribunal to affirm a high degree of responsibility for an officer.

There is another instance in which the *Pohl* tribunal verbalized thoughts which can later be identified in the theory of perpetration through an organization. With regards to the defendants Kiefer and Eirenschmalz, the tribunal described their roles as "integral" and "material" "cogs in the machine".[176] Neither were said to have been either executioner or "trigger man".[177] Yet their indispensable role for the functioning of the machinery was recognized. With regards to Kiefer, his responsibility was not named in technical terms, but the tribunal focused especially on the evaluation that the planning and erection of concentration camps would not have been possible without him.[178] In the case of Eirenschmalz, the tribunal concluded that he had played the role of a principal in and accessory to the crime.[179] Certain considerations as to the role within and the control over the machinery can be identified in this case as well.[180]

These statements by the tribunals contain assessments of what was believed to be crucial in determining a person's responsibility. In so far, they all contain some resemblance to the doctrine of indirect perpetration through an organisation and the theories of domination/control. This resemblance lies in the position of the accused within the Nazi state agencies and the accused's consequent influence over a certain subject area or part of an organization.

The tribunals thus identified two factors they deemed relevant when assessing a person's role within a criminal organization. Responsibility is either attributed to the actor (1) by virtue of his control over a certain area of the organization, i.e., by his ability to set the apparatus in motion in a specific direction; or (2) by asserting his own possibilities of directing and interfering with the specific crime whose execution he supervises. The latter involves a certain spatial and temporal proximity to the crime.

However, these findings do not enable conclusions on a legal concept of control over an organisation because they are limited to descriptions of influence without outlining legal requirements. The tribunals did not identify necessary thresholds or requirements to establish responsibility based on a notion of "organisational control". Furthermore, their terms of control are descriptions of facts and refer to organisational matters, subsequently serving as a basis for the evaluation of the defendants' involvement in crimes. Undoubtedly, these descriptions mirror systemic approaches

175 Ibid., p 584.

176 Trials of War Criminals Before the Nuernberg Military Tribunals Under Control Council Law No. 10, Vol. V 1950, pp 1023, 1031.

177 Ibid.

178 Ibid., p 1023.

179 Ibid., p 1031.

180 The metaphor of cogs in the machine is usually used to describe the physical perpetrators which are treated as fungible (replaceable) in the doctrine of indirect perpetration through an organisation, see Chap. 2, Sect. 2.2.3.2). That is obviously not meant here. Instead, the defendants Kiefer and Eirenschmalz were mid-level bureaucrats, for which the traditional theory would generally affirm the possibility of indirect perpetration.

to leadership liability in some way. This makes sense given the roles of the defendants in a vast apparatus with a highly differentiated division of labour. However, it does not mean that the tribunals settled on a doctrine of control (especially not of control over crimes) or perpetration through an organisation.

This reasoning equally applies in the *Justice* case, in which Ambos identifies an early form of indirect perpetration through an organisation. Ambos bases this finding on the formulation that the defendants are charged with "conscious participation in a nation wide(sic) government-organised system of cruelty and injustice ... perpetrated in the name of law by the authority of the Ministry of Justice, and through the instrumentality of the courts".[181] As stated above, this evaluation cannot be endorsed,[182] although it is conceded that the underlying considerations of this judgment are akin to those relied on by supporters of the systemic theory of indirect perpetration through an organisation. As with other cases previously discussed, the wording of the judgment first and foremost resembles thoughts on the dynamics and roles of actors in organisations. There is no underlying doctrine comparable to that of domination or control over the crime, nor are specific requirements examined. A certain linguistic resemblance between the description of responsibility in the *Justice* case and the doctrine of indirect perpetration through an organisation can be identified, however, it remains just that: a description of factual circumstances and not a legal doctrine.[183]

Another aspect which must be mentioned is the diverging denominations used in the above-mentioned instances. Whilst the tribunals sometimes labelled the criminal behaviour as direct participation, as was the case with Pohl, similar behaviour was considered ordering in other cases, as was the case with Reinecke in *High Command*, whose issuing of directives is explicitly stated in the context of his position and control.

Therefore, control exercised within an organization did not lead to one specific mode of participation.[184] It cannot be established that the tribunals saw a material difference between such control leading to liability as a "principal" (direct participant) or to "ordering" a crime under Art 2 para. 2 CCL 10. In a similar manner, the notion of indirect perpetration through an organization is not implied.[185] However, the judgments show that it is an obvious point of interest, regarding how far a participant

[181] Trials of War Criminals Before the Nuernberg Military Tribunals Under Control Council Law No. 10, Vol. III 1950, p 985; Ambos 2007, p 182 with fn. 152.

[182] See Chap. 3, Sect. 3.3.1.2.

[183] See also Kress 2006, p 306; Yanev 2018, pp 487–9.

[184] Note possible overlaps of the parts of judgments examined in this section and Heller's observation on a broad notion of participation in crimes/enterprises as discussed above under Sect. 4.3.2.

[185] Heller asserts a similarity between indirect perpetration through an organisation and the case of defendant Berger in the *Ministries* case, see Heller 2011, p 272. He bases this on the descriptions of how Berger had organized a notorious unit, selected the man who trained it and kept the unit under his protection. Furthermore, he had been informed of the unit's savage conduct and had tried to justify it. Finally, the tribunal underlined how the unit had been formed to commit crimes, see Trials of War Criminals Before the Nuernberg Military Tribunals Under Control Council Law No. 10, Vol. XIV 1950, pp 545–6. It is submitted that this description may satisfy the requirements of the systemic approach, although certain inquiries into the role of the defendant would still have

in a mass atrocity exercised influence ("control") over their branch of an apparatus or direct subordinates. Apart from this, it remains obscure whether notions of control played a role in determining the description under a certain mode of liability. The role of defendant Schubert in the *Einsatzgruppen* trial, who had apparently supervised and assured the "orderly" execution of a massacre, was not described as "ordering", despite the military-like context. In the *High Command* and the *Hostages* cases, i.e., in cases against members of the Wehrmacht, control was sometimes associated with orders and the mode of ordering. In cases less shaped by military or *SS* death squad actions, ordering was less frequently used whilst some notion of control within the state organisation was considered. It can therefore be suspected that considerations on control were broadly used to explain a defendant's influence over certain procedures and crimes but were not connected to certain modes of liability.

4.4 Sentencing Practice and Possible Implications on Ordering and the Over-All System of Forms of Liability

To determine the role that ordering played for the imputation of responsibility and guilt in post-World War II trials, an analysis of sentences may prove helpful. Many judgments suffered from a certain neglect of clear labelling of modes of responsibility. Additionally, defendants were often convicted on multiple counts for participation in numerous cases of various crimes. The role of the mode of ordering in post-World War II jurisprudence can therefore not be determined by simply examining convictions and sentencing lengths. This section will focus on different factors that were considered in sentencing and could also be related to modes of liability.

The most obvious of these factors is the position the convicted held within the hierarchy of Nazi Germany's agencies and organisations. This again refers to an individual's position within the respective branches of the Nazi state, not to their military or *SS* rank.

In the *High Command* case, sentences between three years and lifelong imprisonment were imposed.[186] Due to the innumerable incidents attributed to the actors, establishing a clear link to their respective modes of responsibility is impossible. A connection to the military rank of the defendants did not exist.[187] The two lifelong imprisonments were imposed on the defendants Reinecke and Warlimont. They

---

to be made. Under the narrower views of the traditional German approach and the ICC, it seems questionable whether the defendant Berger could have been said to have domination/control over the actions of the unit.

[186] Trials of War Criminals Before the Nuernberg Military Tribunals Under Control Council Law No. 10, Vol. XI 1950, p 695 et seq.

[187] Heller 2011, p 321 et seq.

were not the highest-ranking defendants by far.[188] However, regarding their position to make or influence decisions, Reinecke and Warlimont held very high and relevant positions in the overall state apparatus. In fact, by being responsible for or involved in the drafting of orders and the management of a certain area of affairs respectively,[189] the impact of their actions on state policy and consequentially committed crimes could be regarded as even more decisive than the influence of commanders in the field. Reinecke and Warlimont were both convicted *inter alia* for ordering crimes by drafting certain orders or directives.

In the *Hostages* case, the sentences tend to become harsher, i.e. longer, the higher the position of the defendant.[190] Both life imprisonments were imposed on two of the highest ranking commanders[191] and decreased from there.[192]

This pattern does not, however, repeat itself in the *Einsatzgruppen* case. There, the highest positions were the commanders of the *Einsatzgruppen*, followed by the commanders of *Einsatzkommandos* or *Sonderkommandos*. Irrespective of their ranks, many of them received the death penalty.[193] Others were sentenced to life imprisonment or fixed-term sentences.[194]

The same holds true for the *Medical* case. Whilst convictions for ordering were handed down, a link between the description of responsibility and the severity of the sentence cannot be established. The same holds true for the connection between the position in the state apparatus and the severity of punishment: Many of the convicted were given the death penalty.[195] Others had held positions as chiefs of various medical

---

[188] Von Leeb and von Kuechler as field marshals had held much higher ranks within the Wehrmacht, see Trials of War Criminals Before the Nuernberg Military Tribunals Under Control Council Law No. 10, Vol. XI 1950, pp 553, 565.

[189] For Reinecke see ibid., p 648 et seq.; for Warlimont see ibid., p 661 et seq.

[190] Cf. also the assessment in Heller 2011, p 317 et seq.

[191] For the sentencing cf. Trials of War Criminals Before the Nuernberg Military Tribunals Under Control Council Law No. 10, Vol. XI 1950, p 1318 et seq. Defendant List had been the Armed Forces Commander Southeast, and thus the highest Wehrmacht representative in occupied southeast Europe (see ibid., p 1262 et seq.). Kuntze had been List's deputy and as such exercised the same functions in many instances (ibid., p 1274 et seq.).

[192] The defendant Rendulic received a 20-year sentence and had first served as a Tank Army Commander in Croatia, later as Armed Forces Commander North in Finland and Norway (ibid., pp 1288, 1318). Heller explains the shorter sentence of Rendulic in comparison to von List and Kuntze by his comparatively smaller area of occupied territory and subordinate soldiers in Heller 2011, p 318. The same sentence was given to Speidel who had been the military commander in southern Greece (Trials of War Criminals Before the Nuernberg Military Tribunals Under Control Council Law No. 10, Vol. XI 1950, pp 1313, 1319). Defendant Felmy, who had been the commander of Army Group Southern Greece, received a 15 year term (ibid., pp 1305, 1319). From this sentence, the terms decrease in accordance with the positions and executive powers of the defendants.

[193] Out of the 21 convicted in the *Einsatzgruppen* case, 14 were given the death penalty, Trials of War Criminals Before the Nuernberg Military Tribunals Under Control Council Law No. 10, Vol. IV 1950, p 587 et seq.

[194] Ibid., p 587 et seq.

[195] Among them Mrugowsky, Chief of the Hygiene Institute of the Waffen SS, Hoven, Chief Camp Physician of Buchenwald, but also Brack, who had worked in the Staff Main Office SS, apparently without holding a higher position, see Trials of War Criminals Before the Nuernberg Military

offices of the *Wehrmacht*, the *Luftwaffe* or the *SS* and were sentenced to lifelong imprisonment.[196]

The sentencing in *Pohl* saw various death sentences, as well as prison sentences between 10 years and life imprisonment.[197] Pohl, chief of the *WVHA* of the SS, as well as the defendants Loerner and Eirenschmalz were sentenced to death. The latter two had mostly acted as chiefs of an *Amtsgruppe* and an *Amt* respectively and had thus been responsible for organisational units one and two ranks below that of defendant Pohl. Loerner also became Pohl's deputy of the *WVHA* at some point.[198] None of them had been explicitly connected to illegal orders,[199] but the central role of certain branches of the *WVHA* for the operation of the extermination camps must have played a role in sentencing. This can be seen with defendant Frank, Chief of another *Amtsgruppe* and deputy to Pohl, who was sentenced to life imprisonment, although he held the same hierarchical positions as defendant Loerner.[200] However, Loerner and Eirenschmalz were determined as being essential for certain parts of the slave labour programme and for the concentration camps, whilst Frank only assisted *ex post facto* by administering the distribution of valuables obtained from murdered inmates.[201]

In the *RuSHA* case, all the convicted received terms between life imprisonment and 10 years.[202] Some had been found guilty of ordering the commission of crimes,[203] but no correlation between certain modes of responsibility and sentencing can be established. The amount of criminal plans or endeavours in which the defendants had engaged may have influenced the sentencing in this case.[204] The position of the defendants apparently played a role in the determination of sentences in the *RuSHA* case: Greifelt as chief of the *RKFDV* was given life imprisonment and Hofmann and Hildebrandt, both having been chiefs of the *RuSHA*, received a sentence of 25 years each.[205]

In the *Ministries* case, sentences between 3 and 25 years were imposed.[206] The term of ordering was hardly used in the judgment. The highest sentences were imposed on defendants Berger, Veesemeyer and Lammers with the former receiving

---

Tribunals Under Control Council Law No. 10, Vol. II 1950, pp 242, 299 (Mrugowsky), 287, 300 (Hoven), 277, 300 (Brack).

[196] Such as Handloser (ibid., pp 199, 298), Schroeder (210, 298), Genzken (217, 298).

[197] Trials of War Criminals Before the Nuernberg Military Tribunals Under Control Council Law No. 10, Vol. V 1950, p 1062 et seq.

[198] Ibid., p 1005.

[199] Ibid., pp 1004 et seq., 1023 et seq.

[200] Ibid., p 992.

[201] Cf. Ibid., pp 997, 1008 et seq., 1030 et seq.

[202] Ibid., p 165 et seq.

[203] Namely: Greifelt, Creutz, Hofmann and Hildebrandt (ibid., pp 106, 115, 147, 149).

[204] Heller 2011, p 320.

[205] Trials of War Criminals Before the Nuernberg Military Tribunals Under Control Council Law No. 10, Vol. V 1950, pp 154 et seq., 160 et seq.; Heller 2011, p 320.

[206] Trials of War Criminals Before the Nuernberg Military Tribunals Under Control Council Law No. 10, Vol. XIV 1950, p 866 et seq.

25 and the latter two 20 years of imprisonment.[207] However, other individuals who had held a very high office in the Nazi state received considerably lower sentences.[208]

The sentences in the *Justice* case ranged from 5 years to life imprisonment.[209] All the defendants held varying ranks in the judiciary system and or the justice administration of Nazi Germany, but no correlation between their positions and the length of sentence can be identified.[210]

In the so-called industrialist cases against officials of the enterprises *Flick*, *Krupp* and *I.G. Farben*, the sentences ranged from 1½ to 12 years of imprisonment.[211] A connection to the respective positions of the accused is not possible.[212]

In the *Buck* and *von Falkenhorst* cases, the defendants who were convicted on the grounds of ordering were given the death sentence.[213] However, the same held true for Kurt Meyer in the *Abbaye Ardenne* case, whose charge of ordering had

---

207 Berger had been chief of the Main Office SS (*SS-Hauptamt*), and as such *inter alia* responsible for the recruitment of the Waffen-SS (ibid., pp 528, 538, 540). Veesenmeyer had been Minister and Plenipotentiary to Hungary, which resulted in him being the *de facto* ruler of Hungary. In his position he selected the responsible officials for the mass deportation of the Jewish population in Hungary and oversaw and reported on their activities (ibid., pp 646, 653, 654 et seq.). Lammers had been *Reich Minister* and Chief of the Reich Chancellery, a position which the tribunal found Hitler conferred upon him to relieve himself of many details in the drafting of his plans (ibid., pp 590 et seq., 701).

208 Cf. for sentences ibid., p 866 et seq.

209 Trials of War Criminals Before the Nuernberg Military Tribunals Under Control Council Law No. 10, Vol. III 1950, p 1199 et seq.

210 Schlegelberger as provisional *Reich Minister* of Justice had probably held the highest position among the defendants, but among his co-convicted for lifelong imprisonment were Rothaug, who had been a director of a district court and a public prosecutor at the people's court, Oeschey, a notorious judge of a special court and Klemm, who rose up to the position of state secretary (see ibid., pp 1082, 1087, 1143, 1159). Yet many of the other defendants had held comparatively high positions, such as Lautz, a chief public prosecutor at the people's court, who received ten years of imprisonment (see ibid., pp 1118 et seq., 1200).

211 Trials of War Criminals Before the Nuernberg Military Tribunals Under Control Council Law No. 10, Vol. VI 1950, p 1128; Trials of War Criminals Before the Nuernberg Military Tribunals Under Control Council Law No. 10, Vol. VIII 1950, p 1206 et seq.; Trials of War Criminals Before the Nuernberg Military Tribunals Under Control Council Law No. 10, Vol. IX 1950, p 1449 et seq.

212 In the *Krupp* case, the highest sentences were imposed on Alfried Krupp (12 Years), who was the sole owner of the Krupp enterprises since 1943 (Trials of War Criminals Before the Nuernberg Military Tribunals Under Control Council Law No. 10, Vol. IX 1950, pp 226, 1449 et seq.) and Erich Mueller, who had been only one of several deputy directors of the executive board (ibid., pp 226, 1450). Another deputy director, defendant Korschan, was given only six years (ibid., pp 226, 1451), the same punishment was imposed on Lehmann, who had been a lower ranking official (ibid., pp 395, 1451). In *Farben*, the highest and lowest sentences respectively were given to lower ranking officials of the firm who had not been members of the executive board: Duerrfeld and Kugler (see Trials of War Criminals Before the Nuernberg Military Tribunals Under Control Council Law No. 10, Vol. VIII 1950, pp 1166, 1208). In *Flick*, all of the three convicted had held very high offices in the Flick enterprise (Law Reports of Trials of War Criminals Vol. V 1948, p 41; Law Reports of Trials of War Criminals Vol. XI 1948, p 23).

213 Law Reports of Trials of War Criminals Vol. V 1948, p 41; Law Reports of Trials of War Criminals Vol. XI 1948, p 23.

been dismissed.[214] The sentences of the higher ranking von Falkenhorst and Kurt Meyer were later commuted to life imprisonment. Defendant Buck, who had been a *Hauptsturmführer* and in charge of two prisoner camps in Alsace, had held a relatively low rank and position. The same is true for defendant Nussberger, who only commanded the police in one of the camps.[215]

The position of the actor in the hierarchy of the German *Wehrmacht*, *SS* and state apparatus of Nazi Germany or one of the affiliated business enterprises alone does thus not allow for a conclusion regarding the severity of responsibility and guilt in the opinion of the tribunals. However, in some trials it did play a role, amongst other factors, in sentencing.[216]

Different modes of responsibility did not in and of themselves influence the severity of punishment as long as a direct connection between active behaviour and the crimes existed.

Some cases create the impression that the tribunals determined the responsibility and guilt of an individual to be higher the greater the temporal and spatial proximity of their involvement to the specific crime. This would explain many of the death sentences for actors of various ranks in the *Einsatzgruppen* and *Medical* cases, who were directly connected to the victims of their brutal plans. However, this interpretation stands in contrast to the hierarchy of sentencing in the *High Command* and *Hostages* cases, where responsibility was apparently deemed to be greater the higher up a defendant had been in the hierarchy and thus the farther removed he was from the scene in terms of time and space. This is also confirmed by the sentencing in other cases where a higher position within the Nazis state apparatus was associated with the opportunities and responsibility for participating in the criminal endeavours of the state.

Such direct influence would often either be termed responsibility for ordering or described as active or direct participation in criminal plans.

Therefore, it can be concluded that high sentences resulted from either personal involvement in mass atrocities on the ground as a leadership figure or organiser or the exertion of direct influence over crimes by persons in higher positions. Naturally, this remains a merely rough outline of factors that could determine responsibility and guilt in the view of the Nuremberg military tribunals.

Heller has observed something similar. He underlines that the mere acquiescing or knowing and approving of crimes would seldom lead to grave punishment.[217]

Additionally, all death sentences in the *Einsatzgruppen*, *Pohl*, and *Medical* cases were imposed on individuals who had contributed to crimes while in active service at the SS. One could thus conclude that a membership or working position within the

---

[214] Law Reports of Trials of War Criminals Vol. IV 1948, p 109.

[215] Cf. for a description of the defendants' position: Law Reports of Trials of War Criminals Vol. V 1948, p 39.

[216] Cf. Heller 2011, Chapter 14, who concludes in the findings on the *Justice* case (316), the *Einsatzgruppen* case (319), the *RuSHA* case (320) and the *Krupp* case (321).

[217] Heller found a certain connection to the crime, by directly or actively participating in it, to be vital for sentencing in the *Einsatzgruppen*, *Medical*, *Pohl* and *RuSHA* case, see ibid., pp 315, 316 et seq., 319, 320.

SS heavily influenced the severity of the sentence. However, it must be observed that due to their active positions in the *SS*, most of the accused had a direct connection to the committed crimes by planning, organizing or executing the respective plans, programmes or at least parts thereof.[218] This finding fits well into the perception that a direct connection to the planning or execution of crimes was deemed especially blameworthy.

Finally, the fact that the tribunals often did not identify the modes of responsibility, which they saw fulfilled in specific instances, impedes the establishment of a more precise link between these modes and the sentences.[219]

Other factors such as the sheer number of incidents and victims must have also played a role, as the findings above, alone, do not explain certain differences in the judgments. The actions of *SS* members (e.g., in *Einsatzgruppen*) were apparently perceived as more blameworthy than the acts of individuals committed within the *Wehrmacht* (e.g., in *High Command* or *Hostages*). This is astonishing as the tribunals themselves ascertained the large-scale involvement of the latter in horrendous crimes. These did not differ from those committed by the *SS Einsatzgruppen* in their nature, but perhaps in the number of specific crimes.

This section has illustrated, that in some cases, certain correlations between the high position of an actor and his sentence can be established. The more important finding, however, concerns the type of influence an actor had and the commission of crimes. Where tribunals could establish an individual's direct influence over the commission of crimes, sentences were higher. Such was the case with *Wehrmacht* officers who drafted general orders and directives that led to the commission of crimes; with officers in *SS Einsatzgruppen* who orchestrated the massive killing operations in occupied regions of eastern Europe; and with officials who controlled the branches of the Nazi state which were most intimately involved with organised mass murder, i.e. Oswald Pohl and some of his subordinates from the *WVHA*.[220] Heller found that less direct forms of participation like acquiescing or knowing and approving of crimes, led to lighter sentences. These two findings read in conjunction may suggest that forms of participation described as being a principal or participating in a plan or ordering of a crime would establish the more direct link between actors and crimes, leading to higher sentences.

---

[218] Cf. also the analysis in ibid., pp 315, 316 et seq., 319, 322.

[219] Ibid., pp 328.

[220] Such direct influence is not to be confounded with a "direct link". If one would like to recur to the terminology used earlier, sentencing in the Nuremberg subsequent trials apparently valued the direct linkage established in "ordering" crimes highly blameworthy. However, it also regarded the indirect linkage provided by the more systemic functional conduct ("participation") of persons like Oswald Pohl as extremely serious.

4.5 The Relation Between Ordering and Other Modes of Responsibility

Art. 2 para. 2 CCL 10 neither explicitly states anything as to the relation of its modes of responsibility, nor regarding the gravity or guilt associated with them.

An early German commentator asserted that the mode of liability would have had to be of much importance both in formulating the judgment and in assessing the sentence. In his view, a focus should have been laid on whether someone conducted an act themselves, instigated its commission, only approved of it or was involved in a plan connected with its commission.[221] Heller called analysing the Nuremberg judgments with regard to the factors influencing sentencing an exercise in frustration.[222]

Such frustration indeed arises when looking upon the apparent discrepancies between the structure of Art. 2 para. 2 CCL 10, and its application in the practice of the military tribunals. With its distinction between "principals" and "accessories and others", the text of Art. 2 para. 2 CCL 10 seemingly implies a differential model of perpetration and participation.[223] However, the common view is that the military tribunals interpreted the law as a unitary system. Given the disregard of the tribunals as to the delineation of modes of liability, this is the most convincing conclusion.[224] Heller suspects that this is due to the fact that any participant under Art. 2 para. 2 CCL 10 was "deemed to have committed" the crime.[225] Heine believes that the categories of perpetration and participation in Art. 2 para. 2 CCL 10 were "especially tailored" for mass atrocities committed in an inhumane regime. His analysis implies that, irrespectively of questions of accessorial liability, the regulation was deliberately formulated broadly to encapsulate the behaviour of everyone who had in any way been associated with the Nazi crimes.[226]

Notwithstanding the analysis above, these statements, as well as the work of others, seem to indicate that a certain differentiation was made between forms of participation and their respective blameworthiness. This distinction was apparently made between "direct" connections to the crime and less active forms of contribution such as the acquiescence into or the knowing approval of crimes.[227]

In the supplemental judgement to the *Pohl* case, the tribunal elaborated on its view on a hierarchy between the modes incorporated in Art. II para. 2 CCL 10. Referring to the provision, the tribunal stated that "[i]t enumerates, in a descending scale of

[221] Von Knieriem 1953, p 229.

[222] Heller 2011, p 330.

[223] In this vein see Finnin 2012, p 16; Heller 2011, p 254; Olásolo 2009, p 21.

[224] Finnin 2012, p 17; Heller 2011, p 254; Olásolo 2009, p 21; Werle and Jessberger 2020, p 611. Heine hints to the fact that questions of accessorial liability, concerning the relation between the responsibility of the physical perpetrator and the higher levels were never elaborated on, due to "pragmatical reasons", see Heine 2000, p 922.

[225] Heller 2011, p 254. For the according text of Art. 2 Para 2 CCL 10, see above fn. 1057.

[226] Heine 2000, p 922.

[227] In the same vein, Heller with regards to the sentencing in *Einsatzgruppen* in Heller 2011, p 319.

culpability, the persons who are deemed to have committed crimes". The judgment then lists the forms of participating in a crime starting with "(1) Principals".[228]

The tribunal in the *RuSHA* case, took the opposite stand and underlined its perception of the culpability of a person who had ordered the commission of a crime as follows: "While in such a case the defendant might not have actually carried out the physical evacuation in the sense that he did not personally evacuate the population, he nevertheless is responsible for the action, and his participation by instigating the action is more pronounced than that of those who actually performed the deed."[229]

Hence the relation between the different modes of culpability on Art. II para. 2 CCL 10 is not obscure, but there is an outright contradiction as to its interpretation within the judgments from the Nuremberg subsequent trials.

The judgment in the *Pohl* case seems to be the only one in which a tribunal asserted such a hierarchy of seriousness. This could lead to the conclusion that in general no hierarchy between the forms of liability existed.[230]

On the other hand, as explored in the section above, certain active and direct contributions to plans aimed at the commission of crimes, or to the organization and execution of such plans were deemed more culpable than the mere acquiescing into, taking a consenting part in or knowing and approving of such enterprises.[231] The same has been said about command responsibility which was referred to extensively in some cases, but which was apparently regarded as a less culpable manner of incurring responsibility.[232]

Within these more active ways of participation—ordering and participating in criminal plans or endeavours—a hierarchy or relation between them cannot be established by ways of interpreting the Nuremberg judgments under CCL 10. This means that in regard to a hierarchy of seriousness under CCL 10, ordering has been perceived as being more severe than less active involvements. However, a hierarchical relation between ordering and the other more active forms, which the tribunals often identified as "direct participation", cannot be established. Consequently, ways of "direct participation", which have been described using differing terminology, and ordering are to be seen as the more blameworthy, active forms of participation in the Nuremberg subsequent trials.

---

[228] Trials of War Criminals Before the Nuernberg Military Tribunals Under Control Council Law No. 10, Vol. V 1950, p 1180, Heller 2011, p 314.

[229] Trials of War Criminals Before the Nuernberg Military Tribunals Under Control Council Law No. 10, Vol. V 1950, p 153; Heller 2011, p 314.

[230] See Van Sliedregt 2015, p 502–3, outlining how accomplices were treated "as perpetrators" in post-World War II jurisprudence.

[231] Heller reaches the same conclusion regarding some cases in Heller 2011, pp 315, 316 et seq., 319, 320.

[232] Ibid., p 328.

4.6 Conclusion

The observations of this chapter lead to the conclusion that ordering was among the forms of responsibility under CCL 10 that served for the adjudication of high and mid-level decision makers and architects of crimes, although it did so mostly within the limited contexts of military and *SS* death brigade operations.

The Nuremberg subsequent trials were followed by a long term of relative lethargy in international criminal law until the international tribunals emerged during the brutal conflicts in the former Yugoslavia and in Rwanda. For an accurate picture of the historic development of this form of responsibility, it must be analysed whether ordering was maintained as a form of liability for leaders behind mass atrocities under the jurisprudence of these tribunals.

References

Ambos K (2007) Joint Criminal Enterprise and Command Responsibility. Journal of International Criminal Justice 5:159–183

Ambos K (2018) Internationales Strafrecht. C. H. Beck, Munich

Cheah W, Vormbaum M (2018) British War Crimes Trials in Europe and Asia, 1945–1949: A Comparative Study. Leiden Journal of International Law 669–692

Cryer R (2005) Prosecuting International Crimes. Cambridge University Press, Cambridge

Cryer R, Robinson D, Vasiliev S (2019) An Introduction to International Criminal Law and Procedure. Cambridge University Press, Cambridge

Finnin S (2012) Elements of Accessorial Modes of Liability—Article 25 (3) (b) and (c) of the Rome Statute of the International Criminal Court. Martinus Nijhoff Publishers, Leiden

Form W (2007) Justizpolitische Aspekte west-allierter Kriegsverbrecherprozesse 1942–1950. In: Eiber L, Sigel R (eds) NS-Verbrechen vor amerikanischen Militärgerichten in Dachau 1945–1948. Wallstein Verlag, Göttingen, 41–66

Heine G (2000) Täterschaft und Teilnahme in staatlichen Machtapparaten—NS- und DDR-Unrecht im Vergleich der Rechtsprechung. Juristenzeitung 920–926

Heller KJ (2011) The Nuremberg Military Trials and the Origins of International Criminal Law. Oxford University Press, Oxford

Kress C (2006) Claus Roxin's Lehre von der Organisationsherrschaft und das Völkerstrafrecht. Goltdammer's Archiv 304–310

Lippmann M (1992) The Other Nuremberg: American Prosecutions of Nazi War Criminals in Occupied Germany. Indiana International and Comparative Law Review 2:1–100

Olásolo H (2009) The Criminal Responsibility of Senior Political and Military Leaders as Principals to International Crimes. Hart Publishing, Portland

Rogers APV (1990) War Crimes Trials under the Royal Warrant: British Practice 1945–1949. The International and Comparative Law Quarterly 39:780–800

Van Sliedregt E (2015) Perpetration and Participation in Article 25(3). In: Stahn C (ed) The Law and Practice of the International Criminal Court. Oxford University Press, Oxford, 499–516

Von Knieriem A (1953) Nürnberg - Rechtliche und menschliche Probleme. Ernst Klett Verlag, Stuttgart

Werle G, Jessberger F (2020) Principles of International Criminal Law. Oxford University Press, Oxford

Yanev L (2018) Theories of Co-Perpetration in International Criminal law. Brill Nijhoff, Leiden

Other Documents

Law Reports of Trials of War Criminals Vol. IV, 1948
Law Reports of Trials of War Criminals Vol. V, 1948
Law Reports of Trials of War Criminals Vol. XI, 1948
Law Reports of Trials of War Criminals Vol. XV, 1948
Trials of War Criminals Before the Nuernberg Military Tribunals Under Control Council Law No. 10, Vol. II, U.S. Government Printing Service 1950
Trials of War Criminals Before the Nuernberg Military Tribunals Under Control Council Law No. 10, Vol. III, U.S. Government Printing Service 1950
Trials of War Criminals Before the Nuernberg Military Tribunals Under Control Council Law No. 10, Vol. IV, U.S. Government Printing Service 1950
Trials of War Criminals Before the Nuernberg Military Tribunals Under Control Council Law No. 10, Vol. V, U.S. Government Printing Service 1950
Trials of War Criminals Before the Nuernberg Military Tribunals Under Control Council Law No. 10, Vol. VI, U.S. Government Printing Service 1950
Trials of War Criminals Before the Nuernberg Military Tribunals Under Control Council Law No. 10, Vol. VIII, U.S. Government Printing Service 1950
Trials of War Criminals Before the Nuernberg Military Tribunals Under Control Council Law No. 10, Vol. IX, U.S. Government Printing Service 1950
Trials of War Criminals Before the Nuernberg Military Tribunals Under Control Council Law No. 10, Vol. XI, U.S. Government Printing Service 1950
Trials of War Criminals Before the Nuernberg Military Tribunals Under Control Council Law No. 10, Vol. XIV, U.S. Government Printing Service 1950

Chapter 5
Responsibility for Ordering a Crime Under the Jurisprudence of the *Ad Hoc* Tribunals for the Former Yugoslavia and Rwanda

Contents

Abstract Both the statutes of the International Criminal Tribunals for the former Yugoslavia and for Rwanda contain a provision on ordering liability. This chapter explores the pertinent jurisprudence and elaborates on the legal requirements and implications of ordering responsibility under these statutes. It is shown that ordering liability under these statutes was shaped by the *ad hoc* tribunals' jurisprudence, leaving few questions as to the legal requirements of this mode of liability. Its categorisation within the overarching system of perpetration and/or participation in the statutes is less clear though. This chapter argues to interpret ordering responsibility

J. Block, *Reconciling Responsibility with Reality*, International Criminal Justice Series 33, https://doi.org/10.1007/978-94-6265-607-9_5

under the *ad hoc* tribunals' statutes as a highly blameworthy form of accessorial liability. This is based *inter alia* on a comparison with the doctrine of Joint Criminal Enterprise (JCE) which leads to the conclusion that JCE is not better suited than ordering liability to depict the highly blameworthy conduct of decision makers behind international crimes. The conclusion is further backed by a textual interpretation of jurisprudence, as well as an analysis the implications of modes of liability on sentencing.

Keywords International Criminal Tribunal for the former Yugoslavia · International Criminal Tribunal for Rwanda · Ordering · Joint criminal enterprise · Hierarchy of blameworthiness · Authority · Common plan · Accessory liability · Customary international criminal law · Special intent · Attempt to order

5.1 Legal Requirements and Categorization of Ordering in the Law of the *Ad Hoc* Tribunals

The jurisprudence of the International Criminal Tribunals for the former Yugoslavia and for Rwanda has played a crucial role in the development of the system of international criminal law.[1]

Regarding forms of responsibility, the statutes of the International Criminal Tribunals for the former Yugoslavia and for Rwanda stipulate in their respective Articles 7 (1) and 6 (1) that:

> A person who planned, instigated, ordered, committed or otherwise aided and abetted in the planning, preparation or execution of a crime [...] of the present Statute, shall be individually responsible for the crime.[2]

The following jurisprudence interpreted these provisions on many occasions, creating a canon of rules for the different forms of responsibility. As opposed to post-World War II jurisprudence, the *ad hoc* tribunals treat modes of criminal responsibility with care, differentiating and delineating between them.[3]

Specifically, the statutes differentiate between planning, instigating, ordering, committing, and aiding and abetting a crime. Their respective Articles 7 (3) and 6 (3) furthermore contain a provision on superior responsibility.[4] Additionally, Articles 4 (3) of the ICTY Statute and 2 (3) of the ICTR Statute contain a provision

---

[1] Boas et al. 2007, p. 425.

[2] Article 7 (1) Statute of the International Criminal Tribunal for the former Yugoslavia (ICTY Statute); Article 6 (1) Statute of the International Criminal Tribunal for Rwanda (ICTR Statute). Parts omitted for uniform citation.

[3] Werle and Jessberger 2020, at mn. 612 believe that the jurisprudence of the *ad hoc* tribunals has provided a breakthrough in the use of a differentiated system of perpetration and participation in international criminal law. See also Finnin 2012, p. 20.

[4] Articles 7 (3) and 6 (3) read: "The fact that any of the acts referred to in articles [...] of the present Statute was committed by a subordinate does not relieve his [...] superior of criminal responsibility if he [...] knew or had reason to know that the subordinate was about to commit such acts or had

on "complicity in genocide", which has been interpreted as a form of responsibility as well.[5] As exemplified in their application of the term "committing" a crime to participation in a Joint Criminal Enterprise (JCE), both tribunals, but primarily the ICTY, often interpret the term extensively.[6] By contrast, other forms of responsibility, including ordering, planning and instigating have received comparatively little attention by the jurisprudence.[7] The following chapter will focus on the form of ordering, and—where possible and necessary—planning and instigating, to shed light on these presumably underestimated modes of liability. It will pursue the question whether ordering could have adequately described and adjudicated the criminal conduct of high and mid-level actors, of decision makers and architects behind international crimes in cases where it was not used.

Where necessary or useful, the jurisprudence of the Special Court for Sierra Leone will be considered in this chapter as well.[8]

This chapter first analyses the legal requirements of ordering[9] and outlines the common views on the relation of ordering to other forms of responsibility (Sect. 5.1). It then portrays the *ad hoc* tribunals' jurisprudence on participation in a JCE, compares this with responsibility for ordering and assesses the extent to which ordering would have provided for the adjudication of some characteristic cases before the *ad hoc* tribunals (Sect. 5.2). The third part (Sect. 5.3) explores the relation between ordering and other modes of liability in the jurisprudence of the *ad hoc* tribunals and develops an original categorization of liability for ordering in a system of perpetration and participation under the statutes of the ICTY and ICTR.

The criminalization of ordering the commission of a crime was embedded as a form of responsibility in Article 7 (1) ICTY Statute and Article 6 (1) ICTR Statute.

It is noteworthy that ordering is also mentioned in both statutes in their respective provisions concerning the jurisdiction over violations of the Geneva Conventions.[10] In this regard, the provisions are similar to the one concerning genocide in the ILC's Draft Code proposal of 1991, and the SCSL Statute apparently followed this example

---

done so and the superior failed to take the necessary and reasonable measures to prevent such acts or to punish the perpetrators thereof". Minor parts omitted for uniform citation.

[5] Boas et al. 2007, p. 282–4.

[6] Werle and Jessberger 2020, mn. 612; see *infra* Sect. 5.2.

[7] See already Boas et al. 2007, p. 379.

[8] The SCSL's provision on individual criminal responsibility in Article 6 (1) SCSL Statute reads: "A person who planned, instigated, ordered, committed or otherwise aided and abetted in the planning, preparation or execution of a crime referred to in Articles 2–4 of the present Statute shall be individually responsible for the crime", and thus closely mirrors the provision of the ICTY and ICTR.

[9] Where helpful and possible, this analysis will point to parallels to the requirements of planning and instigating.

[10] Article 2 of the ICTY Statute reads: "The International Tribunal shall have the power to prosecute persons committing or ordering to be committed grave breaches of the Geneva Conventions of 12 August 1949 …". Article 4 of the ICTR Statute reads: "The International Tribunal for Rwanda shall have the power to prosecute persons committing or ordering to be committed serious violations of Article 3 common to the Geneva Conventions of 12 August 1949…".

as well.[11] The presence of ordering in the articles regarding breaches of the Geneva Conventions has, however, not been interpreted as establishing any other requirements for its application. Hence, the special emphasis on ordering violations of the Geneva Conventions has apparently been perceived as merely declaratory.[12] The similar sounding provisions in all four Geneva Conventions, which oblige the States Parties to criminalize the commission or ordering of the commission of crimes may explain the inclusion of ordering into the wording of these provisions of the statutes.[13] The vocabulary of these rules will consequently not play a role in the following interpretation.

5.1.1 Legal Requirements

The jurisprudence of the *ad hoc* tribunals elaborates extensively on the requirements necessary to incur responsibility for ordering.[14]

5.1.1.1 Criminal Conduct: The Giving of an Order

The requirements of the criminal act of ordering have been explicitly treated by the chambers and been reiterated in many instances.

As a general description, many chambers of the ICTY and ICTR state that ordering involves, "a person in a position of authority using that position to convince another to commit an offence".[15]

---

[11] See above, Introduction to Part II.

[12] The *Tadić* appeals chamber has mentioned the term "ordering" in Article 4 ICTY Statute to underline its perception that the scope of the statute should not be limited to those physically fulfilling a crime, but also to "other offenders", see ICTY, *Prosecutor v. Duško Tadić*, 15 July 1999, IT-94-1-A, para 189.

[13] Cf. Article 49 Geneva Convention for the Amelioration of the condition of the wounded and sick in armed forces in the field of 12 August 1949; Art. 50 Geneva Convention for the Amelioration of the condition of the wounded, sick and shipwrecked members of the armed forces at sea of 12 August 1949; Article 129 Geneva Convention relative to the treatment of prisoners of war of 12 August 1949; Article 146 Geneva Convention relative to the protection of civilian persons in time of war of 12 August 1949; Bantekas 2002, p. 50; van Sliedregt 2012, p. 62.

[14] It does so, despite the ignorance of the tribunals regarding ordering, and other modes of liability apart from "commission (JCE)" when it comes to convicting and sentencing.

[15] ICTR, *Prosectuor v. Jean-Paul Akayesu*, 2 September 1998, ICTR-96-4-T, para 483; ICTR, *Prosecutor v. Georges Anderson Nderubumwe Rutaganda*, 6 December 1999, ICTR-96-3-T, para 39; ICTY, *Prosecutor v. Tihomir Blaskić*, 3 March 2000, IT-95-14-T, para 281; ICTR, *Prosecutor v. Ignace Bagilishema*, 7 June 2001, ICTR-95-1A-T, para 31; ICTY, *Prosecutor v. Radislav Krstić*, 2 August 2001, IT-98-33-T, para 601; ICTR, *Prosecutor v. Laurent Semanza*, 15 May 2003, ICTR-97-20-T, para 382; ICTY, *Prosecutor v. Milomir Stakić*, 31 July 2003, IT-97-24-T, para 445; ICTR, *Prosecutor v. Juvénal Kajelijeli*, 1 December 2003, ICTR-98-44A-T, para 763; a similar wording can be found in: ICTY, *Prosecutor v. Dario Kordić and Mario Čerkez*, 17 December 2004, IT-95-14/2-A, para 28; SCSL, *Prosecutor against Brima, Kamara, Kanu*, 20 June 2007, SCSL-04-16-T,

An order does not have to be given in writing or any other particular form.[16] Regarding the wording of the order, the tribunals hold that it can be explicit or implicit.[17] The trial chamber in *Dragomir Milošević* stated that the order need not be explicit "in relation to the consequences it will have".[18] Additionally, ICTR case law shows that the derogatory language typical for genocidal criminal patterns—such as the request to "get to work", which meant to start killing—does not raise any doubts as to the nature of certain orders.[19]

Whether the order must be illegal is treated relatively indirectly by the tribunals. Concerning the *actus reus*, the *Blaskić* trial chamber stated that it is irrelevant whether the order's illegality is "apparent on its face".[20] While this could imply that the order must itself contain the request for illegal conduct, later judgments seemingly contradict this. The chambers in *Mladić* and *Gotovina* stated that an order to engage in conduct that results in the commission of crimes is enough to trigger criminal responsibility for ordering.[21] However, the most striking argument against a necessity

---

para 772; ICTY, *Prosecutor v. Ljube Boškoski and Johan Tarčulovski*, 10 July 2008, IT-04-82-T, para 400; ICTR, *Prosecutor v. Bagosora et al.*, 18 December 2008, ICTR-98-41-T, para 2008; ICTY, *Prosecutor v. Dragomir Milošević*, 12 November 2009, IT-98-29/1-A, para 290; ICTY, *Prosecutor v. Ljube Boškoski and Johan Tarčulovski*, 19 May 2010, IT-04-82-A, para 160; ICTR, *Prosecutor v. Yussuf Munyakazi*, 5 July 2010, ICTR-97-36A-T, para 432; ICTR, *The Prosecutor vs. Dominique Ntawukulilyayo*, 3 August 2010, ICTR-05-82-T, para 416; ICTR, *Prosecutor v. Gaspard Kanyarukiga*, 1 November 2010, ICTR-2002-78-T, para 620; ICTY, *Prosecutor v. Vlastimir Đorđević*, 23 February 2011, IT-05-87/1-T, para 1871; ICTR, *Théoneste Bagosora et al. v. The Prosecutor*, 14 December 2011, ICTR-98-41-A, para 277; ICTR, *The Prosecutor v. Grégoire Ndahimana*, 30 December 2011, ICTR-01-68-T, para 719; ICTR, *Prosecutor v. Édouard Karemera et al.*, 2 February 2012, ICTR-98-44-T, para 1428; ICTY, *Prosecutor v. Ramush Haradinaj et al.*, 29 November 2012, IT-04-84bis-T, para 624; ICTR, *The Prosecutor v. Augustin Ngirabatware*, 20 December 2012, ICTR-99-54-T, para 1292; *Prosecutor v. Mićo Stanišić and Stojan Župljanin*, 27 March 2013, IT-08-91-T, para 97; ICTY, *Prosecutor v. Radovan Karadžić*, 24 March 2016, IT-95-5/18-T, para 573; see already Finnin 2012, para 53; Mettraux 2005, p. 282.

[16] *Blaskić*, 3 March 2000, para 281; ICTY, *Prosecutor v. Dario Kordić and Mario Čerkez*, 26 February 2001, IT-95-14/2-T, para 388; ICTY, *Prosecutor v. Mladen Naletilić and Vinko Martinović*, 31 March 2003, IT-98-34-T, para 61; ICTY, *Prosecutor v. Stanislav Galić*, 5 December 2003, IT-98-29-T, para 168; ICTY, *Prosecutor v. Radoslav Brđanin*, 1 September 2004, IT-99-36-T, para 270; ICTY, *Prosecutor v. Pavle Strugar*, 31 January 2005, IT-01-42-T, para 331; ICTR, *The Prosecutor v. Jean de Dieu Kamuhanda*, 19 September 2005, ICTR-99-54A-A, para 76; *Boškoski et Tarčulovski*, 10 July 2008, para 400; ICTY, *Prosecutor v. Milan Milutinović et al.*, 26 February 2009, IT-05-87-T, para 87; *Boškoski and Tarčulovski*, 19 May 2010, para 160; *Đorđević*, 23 February 2011, para 1871; *Haradinaj et al.*, 29 November 2012, para 624; *Stanišić and Župljanin*, 27 March 2013, para 98; *Karadžić*, 24 March 2016, para 573. The SCSL has followed this approach in *Brima et al.*, 20 June 2007, para 772; SCSL, *Prosecutor v. Charles Ghankay Taylor*, 18 May 2012, SCSL-03-01-T, para 476. Boas et al. 2007, p. 366; Mettraux 2005, p. 282.

[17] *Blaskić*, 3 March 2000, para 281; *Naletilić*, 31 March 2003, para 61; Boas et al. 2007, p. 366.

[18] *D. Milošević*, 12 November 2009, para 267.

[19] *Akayesu*, 2 September 1998, paras 275, 308; ICTR, *The Prosecutor v. Jean de Dieu Kamuhanda*, 22 January 2004, ICTR-95-54A-T, para 502; *Kamuhanda*, 19 September 2005, paras 71, 74.

[20] *Blaskić*, 3 March 2000, para 282.

[21] ICTY, *Prosecutor v. Ante Gotovina et al.*, 15 April 2011, IT-06-90-T, para 1959; ICTY, *Prosecutor v. Ratko Mladić*, 22 November 2017, IT-09-92-T, para 3566.

of the unlawfulness of the order results from the *mens rea* requirements, which are examined below.[22]

The relevant acts are described as "instructing", "ordering" or "directing" the commission of crimes.[23]

Whether an order can be given together with other persons is a subject that has not been discussed explicitly. This concerns situations in which the instruction must be issued through a collective, e.g., a committee or council. The *Brđanin* trial chamber decision, for example, suggests this possibility. In this case, the accused was found guilty of ordering crimes because of decisions which he made as a member of the regional crisis staff of a Bosnian-Serb regional entity.[24]

In the situations in the former Yugoslavia, Rwanda and Sierra Leone, many of the orders that constituted criminal behaviour involved specific instructions to carry out a certain crime.[25] Naturally, instructions in the context of military operations within a small or medium sized area within a proximate time frame, qualify as ordering.[26] However, more general instructions also fall under the head of ordering. For example, Tharcisse Renzaho, who had been prefect of Kigali at the time, was convicted for ordering crimes, which were committed at roadblocks throughout the city.[27] During several meetings he ordered several *conseillers* and *responsables des cellules*, government officials responsible for small scale administration units, to supervise the erection of roadblocks. *Interahamwe*, the notorious, violent and racist militia of the Hutu Power Government, and other armed militia conducted identity screenings at these roadblocks, and it was well-known that Tutsis and members of the Hutu opposition would be killed there.[28] In a similar manner, Jean Kambanda, prime minister of Rwanda during the genocide of 1994, plead guilty to ordering the erection of roadblocks where militia would kill Tutsis and moderate Hutu.[29] Hence, an order for a specific behaviour, carried out by different actors, at different locations and at no specific time or date, can qualify as ordering. The conduct of Radoslav Brđanin poses as an example for an administrative or legislative type of action that can lead to responsibility for ordering. The trial chamber found, that as a member of a regional crisis staff, he had been the key figure and driving force behind the

---

[22] See at Sect. 5.1.1.4.

[23] ICTR, *Sylvestre Gacumbitsi v. The Prosecutor*, 7 July 2006, ICTR-2001-64-A, para 184; for instructing see also ICTY, *Prosecutor v. Stanislav Galić*, 30 November 2006, IT-98-29-A, para 176; *D. Milošević*, 12 November 2009, para 267.

[24] *Brđanin*, 1 September 2004, paras 1063–7.

[25] Cf. e.g. *Akayesu*, 2 September 1998, paras 648, 656–7, 664–5; see also *Bagosora et al.*, 18 December 2008, paras 1067, 1167, 1204, 1253; see also the summary of the accused Kordić's role in *Kordić and Čerkez*, 26 February 2001, paras 829, 834.

[26] Cf. *Karemera*, 2 February 2012, paras 1229–1234.

[27] ICTR, *Prosecutor v. Tharcisse Renzaho*, 14 July 2009, ICTR-97-31-T, paras 179–181, 766.

[28] Ibid., paras 157, 180, 763–6; note that the appeals chamber quashed Renzaho's conviction for ordering the killings at roadblocks, cf. ICTR, *Tharcisse Renzaho v. The Prosecutor*, 1 April 2011, ICTR-97-31-A, para 321.

[29] ICTR, *The Prosecutor vs. Jean Kambanda*, 4 September 1998, ICTR-97-23-S, para 39 (xi); Kambanda's appeal against the guilty-plea-based trial judgment was overturned in October 2000.

staff's decisions.[30] Hence, he was held responsible for the *en-masse* dismissal of non-Serbs from "all areas of employment", which had been decided by the crisis staff on a regional level and passed down to municipal crisis staffs for execution. This amounted to ordering persecution as a crime against humanity.[31]

It must be remarked that the *ad* hoc tribunals usually convicted officials in the highest echelons of governments and administration for their participation in a Joint Criminal Enterprise, even if they had enabled and encouraged the commission of crimes through their orders.[32] Whether such broad and general orders that possibly entailed the commission of countless (different) crimes can in fact qualify as ordering under the *ad hoc* tribunals' statutes, is part of the assessment further below.[33]

Responsibility for ordering can be incurred by a person who passes an order down the chain of command.[34] This means that a person who initially issues an order, which then passes through intermediaries before reaching the physical perpetrators can incur liability for ordering.[35] The same is true for any intermediate superior who transmits and therefore reissues an order.[36] Consequently, the members of an entire chain of command, be it military or civilian, can incur responsibility for ordering a crime, provided that the other requirements are fulfilled.

The order need not address a specific perpetrator, but the perpetrators must be sufficiently identified to establish the authority requirement.[37] The chambers were usually content with naming the respective groups to which the physical perpetrators belonged.[38] The *Gacumbitsi* appeals chamber referred to "*conseillers*", the "communal police", "*Interahamwe*", or "soldiers" when describing the physical perpetrators who acted pursuant to orders of the accused.[39] In *Semanza*, the chambers

---

[30] *Brđanin*, 1 September 2004, para 319.

[31] Ibid., paras 1063–7. The underlying international crime committed with the necessary discriminatory intent was the denial of fundamental rights as a crime against humanity (Article 5 ICTY Statute).

[32] Cf. e.g., the findings about the roles of Đorđević, Nyiramasuhuko and Karadžić below at Sect. 5.2.2.3.

[33] See *infra* Sect. 5.2.3.

[34] ICTY, *Prosecutor v. Kupreškić et al.*, 14 January 2000, IT-95-16-T, paras 827, 862; *Brima et al.*, 20 June 2007, para 774; *Milutinović et al.*, 26 February 2009, para 87; *Đorđević*, 23 February 2011, para 1871; *Taylor*, 18 May 2012, para 476; *Haradinaj et al.*, 29 November 2012, para 624.

[35] *Blaskić*, 3 March 2000, para 282; *Kordić and Čerkez*, 26 February 2001, para 388; *Naletilić*, 31 March 2003, para 61; *Brđanin*, 1 September 2004, para 270; *Strugar*, 31 January 2005, para 331; *Brima et al.*, 20 June 2007, para 772; *Milutinović et al.*, 26 February 2009, para 87; *Đorđević*, 23 February 2011, para 1871; *Taylor*, 18 May 2012, para 476; *Haradinaj et al.*, 29 November 2012, para 624; *Karadžić*, 24 March 2016, para 573; Boas et al. 2007, p. 365.

[36] *Kupreškić et al.*, 14 January 2000, para 827, 862; *Brima et al.*, 20 June 2007, para 774; *Boškoski and Tarčulovski*, 19 May 2010, para 167.

[37] *Boškoski and Tarčulovski*, 19 May 2010, para 75.

[38] Ibid., para 75 with Footnote 216.

[39] *Gacumbitsi*, 7 July 2006, paras 184–7.

found that the accused had directed attacks by groups "including soldiers and *Interahamwe*",[40] and "*gendarmes*".[41] The *Blaskić* appeals chamber spoke of "HVO troops" (troops of the Croatian Defence Council) that Blaskić had ordered to commit war crimes.[42]

Thus, it does not matter whether an individual, a spontaneously gathered group or a (para-)military unit is addressed by the order. Whether obedience can be expected, and whether the crime will thus be committed, is therefore not a question of the *actus reus*, but examined within the authority requirement.[43]

Some chambers also elaborated on the question of presence at the crime scene and asserted that such presence was not necessary.[44]

The tribunals frequently expressed the view that the existence of orders can be proven by circumstantial evidence.[45] However, this presupposes that the inference of the existence of orders is the only reasonable one, and it was underlined that great caution must be taken when making such inferences.[46] The *Galić* trial chamber laid out a range of factors that can serve as circumstantial evidence for ordering.[47] These comprise factors regarding the illegal acts themselves (the number of illegal acts, their widespread occurrence, and the *modus operandi* of similar acts), the organization and actors (number, identity and type of troops, logistics involved, tactical tempo of operations, officers and staff involved) and features of the respective superior (effective command and control over the actors, location of the superior at the time of commission and that officer's knowledge of criminal acts committed under his command).[48] In *Bagosora et al.*, the trial chamber relied on the "centralized and hierarchical nature of the army", as well as parallel criminal incidents to attribute a

---

[40] *Semanza*, 15 May 2003, paras 178, 196; ICTR, *Prosecutor v. Laurent Semanza*, 20 May 2005, ICTR-97-20-A, para 363.

[41] *Semanza*, 15 May 2003, para 196.

[42] ICTY, *Prosecutor v. Tihomir Blaskić*, 29 July 2004, IT-95-14-A, paras 588, 597.

[43] See below Sect. 5.1.1.2.

[44] *D. Milošević*, 12 November 2009, para 290; *Boškoski and Tarčulovski*, 19 May 2010, para 125. The *Tadić* trial chamber stated more generally that "not only does one not have to be present but the connection between the act contributing to the commission and the act of commission itself can be geographically and temporally distanced", ICTY, *Prosecutor v. Duško Tadić*, 7 May 1997, IT-94-1-T, para 687.

[45] ICTY, *Prosecutor v. Ivica Rajić*, Rule 61 Decision, 13 September 1996, IT-95-12-R61, paras 59 *et seq.*; *Blaskić*, 3 March 2000, para 282; *Kordić and Čerkez*, 26 February 2001, para 388; *Naletilić*, 31 March 2003, para 61; *Strugar*, 31 January 2005, para 331; *Kamuhanda*, 19 September 2005, para 76; *Gacumbitsi*, 7 July 2006, para 115; *Brima et al.*, 20 June 2007, para 772; *Boškoski et Tarčulovski*, 10 July 2008, para 400; *D. Milošević*, 12 November 2009, para 265; *Boškoski and Tarčulovski*, 19 May 2010, paras 160; *Munyakazi*, 5 July 2010, para 432; ICTR, *Prosecutor v. Callixte Kalimanzira*, 20 October 2010, ICTR-05-88-A, para 213; *Đorđević*, 23 February 2011, para 1871; *Haradinaj et al.*, 29 November 2012, para 624.

[46] *D. Milošević*, 12 November 2009, para 265; *Kalimanzira*, 20 October 2010, para 213; *Haradinaj et al.*, 29 November 2012, para 624.

[47] *Galić*, 5 December 2003, para 171; see already the quotes in Boas et al. 2007, p. 366 and Finnin 2012, p. 46.

[48] *Galić*, 5 December 2003, para 171; the *Galić* trial chamber itself quotes the *Čelebići* trial judgment which identifies the same factors as possible circumstantial evidence for the mental element of

number of crimes to Théoneste Bagosora, who had held a high military post and had been far removed from the site of the attributed crimes.[49]

ICTY and ICTR jurisprudence quite clearly reject the idea that an order can be given by omission and instead require positive action.[50] However, the chambers in *Galić* evaluated certain omissions as circumstantial evidence for a given order.[51]

5.1.1.2 Position of Authority

Without doubt, the person giving an order must exert some form of influence to incur responsibility for ordering under the jurisprudence of the ad hoc tribunals. The ICTR especially has elaborated in several instances, and in detail on the relationship between the emitter and the recipient of the order.[52]

Authority or a Superior-Subordinate Relationship: The Not So Divided Jurisprudence on the Legal Requirement

The literature on the jurisprudence of the *ad hoc* tribunals is divided over the precise contours of the requirement concerning the ordering person's relation to the recipient of the order.[53]

In some early cases, the *ad hoc* tribunals invoked a superior-subordinate relationship as a requirement of ordering.[54]

In the majority of cases, however, the tribunals convicted on grounds of ordering if the actor had (only) exercised authority over the perpetrators. The trial chamber in *Kordić and Čerkez*, ruled that a formal superior-subordinate relationship was not necessary, and underlined its disagreement with the chambers in *Akayesu* and *Blaskić*.[55] The appeals chamber of the ICTR did the same in *Semanza* and

superior responsibility (Article 7 (3) ICTY Statute), see ICTY, *Prosecutor v. Zejnil Delalić et al.*, 16 November 1998, IT-96-21-T, para 386 (note: the proceedings against Zejnil Delalić and Hazim Delić are usually referred to as the *Čelebići* case, named after the prison camp, where they committed their crimes).

[49] *Bagosora et al.*, 18 December 2008, paras 1067, 1167, 1204, 1253.

[50] *Galić*, 30 November 2006, para 177; *D. Milošević*, 12 November 2009, para 267; *Đorđević*, 23 February 2011, para 1817; *Bagosora et al.*, 14 December 2011, para 277; *Taylor*, 18 May 2012, para 476; *Haradinaj et al.*, 29 November 2012, para 624; Cryer et al. 2019, p. 360; Werle and Jessberger 2020, mn. 665.

[51] *Galić*, 5 December 2003, para 749; *Galić*, 30 November 2006, para 177.

[52] A reason for the ICTY to concern itself less with the specific requirement of authority or a superior-subordinate relationship might be its heavy reliance on the figure of Joint Criminal Enterprise, see *infra* Sect. 5.2.1.

[53] Boas et al. 2007, p. 367; Schabas describes the jurisprudence as divided over the matter in Schabas 2016, para 574.

[54] *Akayesu*, 2 September 1998, para 483; ICTR, *The Prosecutor v. Alfred Musema*, Trial Decision, 27 January 2000, ICTR-96-13-A, para 121; *Blaskić*, 3 March 2000, para 281.

[55] *Kordić and Čerkez*, 26 February 2001, 388.

Gacumbitsi.[56] This view seemingly prevailed, as the later jurisprudence of the *ad hoc* tribunals shows.[57]

The rejection of a formal superior-subordinate relationship means, that the person must have authority over the recipient of the order instead. This authority can be of an informal and purely temporary nature.[58] It can, as the trial chamber in *Gotovina et al.* described it, be "formal or informal".[59]

The trial chamber in *Gacumbitsi* held that "the authority of an influential person can derive from his social, economic, political, or administrative standing, or from his abiding moral principles. Such authority may also be *de jure* or *de facto*".[60] The tribunals reiterated this statement with some frequency.[61]

The controversy over the requirement of authority or a superior-subordinate relationship has been frequently referred to by the tribunals' chambers themselves and by commentators.[62]

However, an analysis of the judgments in the centre of this debate shows that the controversy is superfluous. The differences between the chambers' views concerning

---

[56] *Semanza*, 20 May 2005, para 361; *Gacumbitsi*, 7 July 2006, para 181–2.

[57] See judgments of the appeals chambers in: *Kordić and Čerkez*, 17 December 2004, para 28; *Kamuhanda*, 19 September 2005, para 75; *Boškoski and Tarčulovski*, 19 May 2010, para 164; as well as of the trial chambers in *Naletilić*, 31 March 2003, para 61; *Kajelijeli*, 1 December 2003, para 763; *Brđanin*, 1 September 2004, para 270; *Strugar*, 31 January 2005, para 331; *Bagosora et al.*, 18 December 2008, para 2008; *Renzaho*, 14 July 2009, para 738; *Munyakazi*, 5 July 2010, para 432; *Ntawukulilyayo*, 3 August 2010, para 416; *Kanyarukiga*, 1 November 2010, para 620; *Gotovina et al.*, 15 April 2011, para 1959; ICTR, *The Prosecutor v. Pauline Nyiramasuhuko et al.*, 24 June 2011, ICTR-98-42-T, para 5593; *Ndahimana*, 30 December 2011, para 719; *Karemera*, 2 February 2012, para 1428; *Haradinaj et al.*, 29 November 2012, para 624; *Ngirabatware*, 20 December 2012, para 1292; *Stanišić and Župljanin*, 27 March 2013, para 98; ICTY, *Prosecutor v. Jovica Stanišić and Franko Simatović*, 30 May 2013, IT-03-69-T, para 1263; *Karadžić*, 24 March 2016, para 573; *Mladić*, 22 November 2017, para 3566; Cf. also Boas et al. 2007, p. 368; Goy 2012, pp. 50–1; Olásolo and Carnero Rojo 2015, p. 562. This standard has also been applied by the SCSL, see *Brima et al.*, 20 June 2007, para 772; *Taylor*, 18 May 2012, para 475.

[58] *Semanza*, 20 May 2005, para 363; *Bagosora et al.*, 18 December 2008, para 2008; *Milutinović et al.*, 26 February 2009, para 86; *Munyakazi*, 5 July 2010, para 432; *Ntawukulilyayo*, 3 August 2010, para 416; *Kanyarukiga*, 1 November 2010, para 620; *Ndahimana*, 30 December 2011, para 719; *Karemera*, 2 February 2012, para 1428; *Taylor*, 18 May 2012, para 475; ICTY, *Prosecutor v. Zdravko Tolimir*, 12 December 2012, IT-05-88/2-T, para 905; *Ngirabatware*, 20 December 2012, para 1292; *Karadžić*, 24 March 2016, para 573. See also Mettraux 2005, p. 282.

[59] *Gotovina et al.*, 15 April 2011, para 1959; the same can be found in *Stanišić and Simatović*, 30 May 2013, para 1263.

[60] ICTR, *Prosecutor v. Sylvestre Gacumbitsi*, 17 June 2004, ICTR-2001-64-T, para 288.

[61] *Đorđević*, 23 February 2011, para 1871; *Haradinaj et al.*, 29 November 2012, para 624; *Tolimir*, 12 December 2012, para 905; for earlier judgments see the extensive list in Finnin 2012, p. 54 with Footnote 60.

[62] *Kordić and Čerkez*, 26 February 2001, para 388 with fn. 533; the chamber in *Semanza* referred to the aforementioned as "clarifying" the requirement, see *Semanza*, 20 May 2005, para 361; Mettraux 2005, p. 282 with Footnote 19; Olásolo and Carnero Rojo 2015, p. 562 with Footnote 25; Schabas 2016, p. 574.

this requirement are marginal and suggest that the terms of authority and superior-subordinate relationship were used to express the same and not a different relation between the persons involved.

The trial judgment against *Jean-Paul Akayesu* may serve as an example. *Akayesu* had been a *bourgmestre* of a Rwandan commune called Taba. As such, the chamber found, he had held official, *de jure* authority over the communal police. Additionally, his *de facto* powers were believed to have been greater. His word would often be obeyed, even if instructing illegal actions, and the local population regarded him as a "parent".[63] It was also conceded that the extent to which a *bourgmestre*'s commands would be obeyed depended on his personal popularity within the local population.[64] The position of *bourgmestre* was summarized by the chamber as being "the most powerful man in the commune". It also stated that "his *de facto* authority in the area [was] significantly greater than that which [was] conferred upon him *de jure*".[65] The chamber was silent with regards to *Akayesu*'s relation to the notorious *Interahamwe* militia. *Akayesu* was found guilty of ordering several murders. Members of the local police, whose superior he was by law, committed the first of these murders in his presence and under his orders.[66] The second and third murders were committed by *Interahamwe* militia, and "the local population".[67] The tribunal found Akayesu guilty of ordering them to commit those crimes. Hence, it found the requirement of a superior-subordinate relationship fulfilled.[68]

This shows that, even the *Akayesu* chamber only expected a relatively informal, and not a *de jure* relationship of superiority and subordination, as most of the perpetrators he had ordered to act were not under his *de jure* command.

The chambers in *Gacumbitsi* required no formal superior-subordinate relationship, instead demanding that the person who gave the orders have acted out of a position of authority.[69] *Sylvestre Gacumbitsi* had been a *bourgmestre* as well, and the trial chamber elaborated on his position, drawing from the expert witness' statements in *Akayesu.*[70]

The chamber found that *Gacumbitsi* had been an influential figure in his *commune*. He had held legal authority over the communal workers and police but no "superior authority" over the *gendarmerie*, soldiers or the *conseillers de secteurs* (the chief administrative workers on the next lower level).[71] The trial chamber thus denied his authority to give orders and convicted him only for ordering the communal police to commit crimes.[72]

---

[63] *Akayesu*, 2 September 1998, para 56–77.

[64] Ibid., para 76.

[65] Ibid., para 77.

[66] Ibid., paras 218, 648.

[67] Ibid., paras 269, 658, 668.

[68] Cf. the conviction in ibid., paras 737–9.

[69] *Gacumbitsi*, 17 June 2004, para 281 and *Gacumbitsi*, 7 July 2006, para 181.

[70] *Gacumbitsi*, 17 June 2004, paras 229–36.

[71] Ibid., paras 242–243.

[72] Ibid., paras 283–284.

The trial chamber elaborated on its perception of the necessary authority with the following considerations:

> The authority of an influential person can derive from his social, economic, political or administrative standing, or from his abiding moral principles. Such authority may also be de jure or de facto. When people are confronted with an emergency or danger, they can naturally turn to such influential person, expecting him to provide a solution, assistance or take measures to deal with the crisis. When he speaks, everyone listens to him with keen interest; his advice commands overriding respect over all others and the people could easily see his actions as an encouragement. [...] In certain circumstances, the authority of an influential person is enhanced by a lawful or unlawful element of coercion, such as declaring a state of emergency, the de facto exercise of an administrative function, or even the use of threat or unlawful force. The presence of a coercive element is such that it can determine the way the words of the influential person are perceived. Thus, mere words of exhortation or encouragement would be perceived as orders within the meaning of Article 6 (1) referred to above. Such a situation does not ipso facto lead to the conclusion that a formal superior-subordinate relationship exists between the person giving the order and the person executing it. [...] [I]nstructions given outside a purely informal context by a superior to his subordinate within a formal administrative hierarchy, be it de jure or de facto, would also be considered as an "order" within the meaning of Article 6 (1) of the Statute.[73]

With a view to these thoughts, the appeals chamber evaluated the facts differently than the trial chamber had. It stated that under the specific circumstances, the people and the members of the *Interahamwe* militia considered *Gacumbitsi*'s words as orders, which led to him having authority over them, despite not being their *de jure* superior.[74]

The situations in the *Akayesu* and *Gacumbitsi* cases are therefore similar: Both men had been *bourgmestres* and both were found to have ordered the commission of crimes. They did so by virtue of their *de facto*, non-formalized, superior social standing, which led to their words being perceived as orders.

Some other ICTR judgments, also elaborated on the relation between the terms, "authority" and "superior-subordinate relationship".

The *Semanza* trial chamber pointed out that ordering required a position of authority and concluded that responsibility for ordering implied the existence of a superior-subordinate relationship.[75] The trial chamber in *Ntagerura* referred to this, yet only explicitly spoke of the necessity of a "superior-subordinate relationship".[76] The appeals chamber in *Semanza*, found that the implied superior-subordinate relationship was no contradiction to the fact that no "formal" relationship had to be proven.[77] The trial chamber in *Bagosora et al.* picked up this notion, stating that no formal superior-subordinate relationship was necessary. Instead, a position of authority would suffice for "creating the kind of relationship envisaged under Article 6 (1) of the Statute for ordering..."[78]

---

[73] Ibid., para 282.

[74] *Gacumbitsi*, 7 July 2006, para 184–185.

[75] *Semanza*, 15 May 2003, para 382.

[76] ICTR, *Prosecutor v. André Ntagerura et al.*, 25 February 2004, ICTR-99-46-T, para 624.

[77] *Semanza*, 20 May 2005, para 361.

[78] *Bagosora et al.*, 18 December 2008, para 2008.

Later judgments also required a position of authority on behalf of the accused that would compel another person to commit a crime when following their order.[79]

In summary, while the chambers in the later jurisprudence all rejected the necessity of a "formal" superior-subordinate relationship, the earlier judgments that still demanded a superior-subordinate relationship never described it as a formal one. The comparison between the *Akayesu* and the *Gacumbitsi* cases illustrates that there was no requirement of a formalized superior-subordinate relationship in the jurisprudence of the *ad hoc* tribunals. The only chambers to explicitly refer to such a relationship were those rejecting it.[80] As far as it's based on jurisprudence, the discussion can thus be described as an illusory debate.

The comparison of cases above shows that the (supposedly) broader authority requirement mirrors the reality of international criminal law more adequately. The factors leading to the accused's instructions being followed are sometimes of a formal hierarchical nature where an actor is integrated into a professionalized civil or military hierarchy.[81] However, many times they are not. Due to their bearing, behaviour, and commitment, political leaders may rise to a *de-facto* position of authority over military commanders and troops, which they could not command legally.[82] Others may exercise authority, based on traditions, social status and their perceived moral superiority, although this authority may also depend on their personal popularity.[83] Regardless, others will carry out their instructions once they are given.

When expressed in this way, the conclusion of the chambers in *Semanza*, that a certain superior-subordinate relationship is "implied" or "created" by the authority that one person has over the other, is only logical.[84] Consequently, in some cases, the relation between the actor who gives an order, and the recipient who carries it out can be described as a *de-facto* superior-subordinate relationship.[85] Hence, such a

---

[79] Ibid., para 2008; *Munyakazi*, 5 July 2010, para 432; *Ntawukulilyayo*, 3 August 2010, para 416; *Kanyarukiga*, 1 November 2010, para 620; *Nyiramasuhuko*, 24 June 2011, para 5593; *Ndahimana*, 30 December 2011, para 719; *Karemera*, 2 February 2012, para 1428; *Taylor*, 18 May 2012, para 475; *Ngirabatware*, 20 December 2012, para 1292; *Karadžić*, 24 March 2016, para 573. See also Boas et al. 2007, p. 265.

[80] In the view of Boas et al., the *Kordić* chamber had interpreted the *Akayesu* judgment as requiring a formal superior-subordinate relationship in Boas et al. 2007, p. 367.

[81] Cf. e.g. the observations on the accused's position towards and control of various military formations in *Blaskić*, 3 March 2000, paras 442–66; see also on the *de jure* command of *bourgmestre's* over the communal police in Rwanda in *Akayesu*, 2 September 1998, paras 63–6.

[82] Cf. the trial chamber's findings on the role and position of *Kordić* in *Kordić and Čerkez*, 26 February 2001, paras 545–56; 763–72.

[83] Cf. e.g. the description of the role of *bourgmestres* in Rwanda and of the accused by the trial chamber in *Akayesu*, 2 September 1998, paras 72–7; 180. See also the reflections on the perception of authority in *Gacumbitsi*, 17 June 2004, para 282; van Sliedregt describes this as being "of an informal nature" in van Sliedregt 2012, p. 106.

[84] *Semanza*, 15 May 2003, para 382; *Semanza*, 20 May 2005, paras 361, 363.

[85] The trial chamber in *Gacumbitsi* stated that the necessary authority requirement could be "*de jure* or *de facto*" in *Gacumbitsi*, 17 June 2004, para 282; see also: *Boškoski and Tarčulovski*, 19 May 2010, para 163. Such a definition is mentioned for ordering under Articles 25 (3) (b) of the Rome

relationship can follow from the authority, but is not a requirement in and of itself.[86] Alternatively, the necessary authority could be described as creating a situational superior-subordinate relationship between the persons involved, at least as far as each specific order is concerned.

For some chambers, the existence of a superior-subordinate relationship also served as circumstantial evidence to prove authority over others.[87]

The Shaping of the Authority Requirement

The necessary contours of the authority requirement have been described in different ways.

The *Akayesu* trial chamber used the description of "convincing" someone to commit a crime.[88] However, the *Milutinović* trial chamber stated the opposite and explicitly underlined that the ordering person did not have to "convince" the physical perpetrator.[89] Other judgments chose to describe the necessary influencing *vis-à-vis* another as one that enables the ordering person to "persuade" or to "impel" the other.[90]

These examples notwithstanding, the most common definition of ordering, which is widely used in the *ad hoc* tribunals' jurisprudence provides that the ordering person, by use of their authority, "compelled" the recipient of the order to commit the crime.[91]

The Oxford Dictionary defines "to compel" as "force or oblige (someone) to do something". In line with this, the trial chamber in *Gacumbitsi* elaborated on the necessity of an element of coercion within the authority requirement.[92] The chamber stated that the words and actions of influential people could be qualified as incitement or aiding and abetting, if they led to crimes. However, wherever they were accompanied by a lawful or unlawful element of coercion, they could be perceived

Statute by Ambos 2016, Article 25 mn. 22. See also Finnin 2012, pp. 56–7 (in favour of a rather narrow notion of superior-subordinate relationship but one which should be evaluated *de facto*).

[86] See also Finnin 2012, p. 55, who sums this up by saying that a superior-subordinate relationship is not required but might be sufficient to prove the necessary authority.

[87] ICTR, *Prosecutor v. Tharcisse Muvunyi*, 12 September 2006, ICTR-2000-55A-T, para 467.

[88] *Akayesu*, 2 September 1998, para 483.

[89] *Milutinović et al.*, 26 February 2009, para 87; the same was ruled by the chamber in *Taylor*, 18 May 2012, para 476.

[90] *Rutaganda*, 6 December 1999, para 39 (to persuade); *Musema*, 27 January 2000, para 121 (to persuade); *Kajelijeli*, 1 December 2003, para 763 (to impel); *Kamuhanda*, 22 January 2004, para 594 (to impel); Boas et al. 2007, p. 365.

[91] Cf. *inter alia Bagilishema*, 7 June 2001, para 30; *Semanza*, 15 May 2003, para 483; *Gacumbitsi*, 17 June 2004, para 281; *Muvunyi*, 12 September 2006, para 467; *Bagosora et al.*, 18 December 2008, para 2008; *Renzaho*, 14 July 2009, para 738; *Munyakazi*, 5 July 2010, para 432; *Ntawukulilyayo*, 3 August 2010, para 416; *Kanyarukiga*, 1 November 2010, para 620; *Nyiramasuhuko*, 24 June 2011, para 5593; *Ndahimana*, 30 December 2011, para 719; *Karemera*, 2 February 2012, para 1428; *Taylor*, 18 May 2012, para 475; *Tolimir*, 12 December 2012, para 905; *Ngirabatware*, 20 December 2012, para 1292; *Stanišić and Župljanin*, 27 March 2013, para 97; *Karadžić*, 24 March 2016, para 573. See also Boas et al. 2007, p. 365. *Tolimir*, 12 December 2012, para 905.

[92] *Gacumbitsi*, 17 June 2004, para 282; see already the quote of this paragraph above in Sect. 5.1.1.2.

as orders in the sense of Article 6 (1) ICTR Statute.[93] In the view of the chamber, whether such an element of coercion existed would depend on the perception of the recipient.[94] Accordingly, the *Gacumbitsi* appeals chamber described the authority to order as "a more subjective criterion that depends on the circumstances and the perceptions of the listener".[95] Such a "coercive" element as a prerequisite of authority implies that some kind of psychological pressure on the listener exists. However, one must be careful not to confound this with coercion leading to a state of duress for the recipient of the order. The latter interpretation would clearly go too far if the abovementioned descriptions of the *Gacumbitsi* chambers is considered.

As for the person exercising the authority, it is evident that both military and civilian personnel can incur liability for ordering.[96]

Under ICTY and ICTR jurisprudence, persons in very different ranks and positions were found to have exercised authority. Amongst them were ministers and highest military authorities, but also regional and local government representatives.[97]

The *Gacumbitsi* trial chamber asserted that instructions given within a *de jure* or *de facto* administrative hierarchy would also be considered "ordering".[98] The *Brđanin* trial judgment serves as an example of ordering in such an administrative hierarchy.[99]

The trial chamber in *Strugar* believed that the ability to issue "binding" orders was necessary to constitute the authority to compel someone to act.[100] In light of the clear rejection of a formal superior-subordinate relationship, this description used by the chamber is surprising. The chamber in *Muvunyi* chose a different wording and asserted that an actor would have authority if they could issue a binding order or

---

93 Ibid., para 282.

94 Ibid., para 282; *Gacumbitsi*, 7 July 2006, para 182.

95 *Gacumbitsi*, 7 July 2006, para 182.

96 *Kordić and Čerkez*, 26 February 2001, para 367; Del Ponte 2006, p. 548.

97 Pauline Nyiramasuhuko served as Minister of Family and Women's Development, see *Nyiramasuhuko*, 24 June 2011, para 8; Théoneste Bagosora served as *directeur de cabinet* in the Rwandan Ministry of Defence and therefore as the highest military authority after the minister, see *Bagosora et al.*, 18 December 2008, paras 25, 50, 1067, 1167; Tharcisse Renzaho was prefect of Kigali-Ville prefecture and as such the representative of the national government, vested with the authority of the state, see *Renzaho*, 14 July 2009, paras 1, 80, 750; Radoslav Brđanin headed the influential crisis staff of the autonomous region of Krajina which comprised many municipalities in western Bosnia and Herzegovina, see *Brđanin*, 1 September 2004, paras 1–9, 163 *et seq.*; Jean-Paul Akayesu and Sylvestre Gacumbitsi were *Bourgmestres* and as such served as the administrative and traditional heads of the Rwandan municipal units of *communes,* see *Akayesu*, 2 September 1998, paras 56–77, *Gacumbitsi*, 17 June 2004, paras 5–6. Jean Kambanda, prime minister of Rwanda during the genocide was *inter alia* convicted for ordering the killing of Tutsis and Hutu opposition members throughout the country, see *Kambanda*, 4 September 1998, para 39 (xi), note, however, that this conviction has been entered under a guilty plea.

98 *Gacumbitsi*, 17 June 2004, para 282.

99 Radoslav Brđanin was convicted for ordering persecution (by ways of the discriminatory mass lay-off of non-Serbian workers as a denial of the right to employment), see *Brđanin*, 1 September 2004, paras 319, 1063–7.

100 *Strugar*, 31 January 2005, para 331; endorsing this view: Finnin 2012, p. 56.

"otherwise compel another to commit a crime".[101] On the other hand, the *Milutinović* trial chamber explicitly rejected that the authority had to encompass the ability to issue binding orders, which was later reiterated by the SCSL in the *Taylor* trial judgment.[102]

Olásolo and Carnero Rojo describe the relation as one where the ordering person must "exercis[e] significant influence" over the recipient.[103] Such a broad interpretation of ordering would mean that the authority, i.e. the *de-facto* superior-subordinate relationship which contains an element of coercion and compels the recipient to act, could be affirmed where it only extends to the circumstances of the specific order.[104] A person might utter words of encouragement or endorsement which are perceived as orders, and in the next moment, their opinion can become less important to the physical actors.[105] When expressed in these terms, the authority requirement may seem broad at first. However, in this form it still has the effect that a *de facto* powerless actor, who only held a ceremonial or representative function is excluded from the criminal responsibility for ordering. Furthermore, if ordering requires the actor having the authority to compel another to commit a crime, it provides a clear distinguishing criterion *vis-à-vis* instigation. Simultaneously, the requirement grasps different cases in which an individual, by exercising their strong influence, can decisively influence the commission of crimes by either instructing others or refraining from doing so.[106]

The authority requirement is therefore comparable to the one employed by the U.S. military tribunals in Nuremberg, which required the addition of authoritative weight to orders for some alternatives of ordering. A comparison with post-WWII jurisprudence also illustrates different viewpoints on ordering. Whilst the "addition of authoritative weight" as applied by the military tribunals seems influenced by typical military situations, "compelling" another person seems tailored to various circumstances, including situations of military command and obedience, as well as more informal, social relationships of power. Both terms seemingly refer to the same or a comparable influence of the ordering person over others.

Regardless, the "authorship" of a criminal order is not included under the *ad hoc* jurisprudence on ordering in the way in which the law under CCL 10 encompassed it.[107] If a person under the jurisdiction of the *ad hoc* tribunals contributes to the

---

[101] *Muvunyi*, 12 September 2006, para 467.

[102] *Milutinović et al.*, 26 February 2009, para 86; *Taylor*, 18 May 2012, para 475.

[103] Olásolo and Carnero Rojo 2015, p. 562.

[104] Cf. Mettraux 2005, p. 282 who states that the "authority [...] may only last as long as it takes for the order to be given and obeyed".

[105] Cf. in this regard, the Trial Chamber in *Gacumbitsi* which held that the authority relationship may depend on the way that the words of another person are perceived in *Gacumbitsi*, 17 June 2004, para 282; van Sliedregt 2012, p. 106.

[106] In the same vein as regards the delineation of ordering from instigation, see already Cryer 2004, pp. 245–6.

[107] See Chap. 4, Sect. 4.2 on the legal requirements and application of ordering in post-World War II.

formulation of an order that leads to the commission of crimes, but does not exercise independent authority—perhaps because the draft or plan must go up the chain of command for approval and issuance—this cannot qualify as ordering a crime. However, it is conceivable that in such cases responsibility for planning a crime under Articles 7 (1) and 6 (1) of the *ad hoc* tribunals' statutes arises.[108]

The Recipient of the Order

Considering the complex structures of command and responsibility in many cases, it is important to determine exactly over whom the authority must extend to give rise to liability for ordering.

The authority must enable the ordering person to compel "another to commit" a crime,[109] which seemingly only refers to the physical perpetrator. Some commentators describe the necessary authority of the ordering person as exercising authority over the "perpetrator" or "principal perpetrator".[110] However, it was rather common in the cases before the *ad hoc* tribunals that the ordering actor would not communicate with or even know the identity of the physical perpetrator of the crime. Instead, an actor would issue an order and pass it down the chain of command. It is therefore unclear whether authority existed where the ordering actor exercised authority over an intermediary in the chain of command, but not over the physical perpetrator or vice versa.

Does a commander who exerts authority over a loyal subordinate officer also have authority over this officer's unit, even if this unit is an unruly group of paramilitaries who only obey their own commander? Alternatively; Does a commander who has the obedience of a group, but not that of the intermediary officer still enjoy authority over these men and women? Both cases are conceivable, especially in more loosely structured organizations, e.g., non-state actors or paramilitary units.

In the first case the *ad hoc* tribunals would most likely affirm the authority of the commander. The tribunals have frequently convicted persons for ordering crimes based on the conception that an order could be passed down a chain of command.[111] Additionally, if they were charged before the tribunals, the orders had usually been carried out. As stated above, this could be regarded as circumstantial evidence for authority. However, even where evidence supports the view that a group of physical perpetrators only obeyed their direct superior, authority could probably still be affirmed for the higher-ranking individual, if they had authority over the direct superior of the group. If someone can compel another person to act pursuant to their

---

[108] Planning, in general terms, requires that a person designed a criminal conduct with the intent that the crime will be committed, or designed an act or omission being aware of the substantial likelihood that a crime will be committed in relation to that respective conduct, see e.g. *Kordić and Čerkez*, 17 December 2004, paras 26, 31; Boas et al. 2007, p. 354.

[109] ICTR, *The Prosecutor v. Ferdinand Nahimana et al.*, 3 December 2003, ICTR-99-52-T, para 719; *Bagosora et al.*, 14 December 2011, para 277; *Semanza*, 20 May 2005, para 361; *Haradinaj et al.*, 29 November 2012, para 624, *Ngirabatware*, 20 December 2012, para 1292; *Stanišić and Župljanin*, 27 March 2013, para 97; *Karadžić*, 24 March 2016, para 573.

[110] *Strugar*, 31 January 2005, para 331; Olásolo and Carnero Rojo 2015, p. 562.

[111] This suffices as the giving of an order, see *supra* Sect. 5.1.1.1.

instruction, and this other person can do the same with their subordinates, a "chain of authority" is set into motion. Although, the higher-ranking commander might only be able to compel their direct subordinate, this lower ranking paramilitary commander will compel their unit to act in the way which the higher-ranking commander expects and intends. This form of "chain authority" would thus nevertheless lead to affirming authority over the physical perpetrators under the law of the *ad hoc* tribunals.

In the second case, a person is unable to compel another, say lower ranking officer, to act the way they want. The question is whether this person still enjoys authority over the group that physically commits the crime. This would be a question of fact and depend heavily on the way in which the order is given. If the higher-ranking commander communicates directly with the obedient unit, this will naturally constitute an exercise of authority. If the commander instead instructs the intermediary officer, who is not subject to their authority, authority of the commander would have to be denied. In the latter scenario no "chain-authority" exists due to the lack of compelling authority of the higher commander over the lower-ranking one. Instead, the intermediary commander can relay the order based on their uncompelled decision, which presumably makes the difference between ordering and instigating. If the order is transmitted, only the intermediary officer exercises authority over the unit. The higher-ranking commander would not be liable for ordering but might be liable for instigating.

These examples illustrate that, irrespective of the chain of command or the number of intermediaries, the authority of the ordering person must effectively extend to and compel the physical perpetrators of the crime.

However, a second point must also be underlined. As shown, authority must enable the ordering person to compel another to *commit* the crime. This must be read as referring to commission in the narrower sense of the word, i.e., in the sense of hands-on, commission or indirect commission. An order directed at someone who will aid and abet a crime by providing the necessary means in advance will not suffice. In other words, only where (chain) authority is exercised over the physical perpetrator of a crime can the authority criterion be affirmed.

The Difference Between Authority and Effective Control in Virtue of Article 7 (3)/6 (3) of the *Ad Hoc* Tribunals' Statutes

According to the *Seromba* trial chamber, to prove the superior-subordinate relationship implied by the authority requirement, it would be necessary for the ordering actor to have exercised effective control over the direct perpetrators.[112]

However, the earlier *Kamuhanda* appeals judgment had already ruled that authority over another, enabling this other person to be compelled to commit a crime, was not tantamount to the effective control requirement of superior responsibility.[113] The chamber in the *Seromba* appeal consequently quashed the trial chamber's ruling

[112] ICTR, *The Prosecutor vs. Athanase Seromba*, 13 December 2006, ICTR-2001-66-1, para 305.

[113] *Kamuhanda*, 19 September 2005, para 75; Cf. Boas et al. 2007, pp. 369–70; Mettraux 2001, p. 274. In the *Kamuhanda* trial, the same had already been held by the trial chamber, see *Kamuhanda*, 22 January 2004, para 612.

and affirmed that no effective control over the direct perpetrators would be necessary to establish the authority criterion.[114] In the same vein, the trial chamber in *Kordić and Čerkez* found earlier that Kordić had exercised authority over soldiers and ordered them to commit crimes, yet it denied Kordić's superior responsibility for the acts of these soldiers.[115] The latter requires effective control over the subordinates who committed the crime.[116] Such control would lie in the ability to prevent subordinate troops or persons from perpetrating the crime.[117] However, Kordić's "substantial influence" would not amount to such effective control.[118]

The authority criterion is thus understood as broader and less rigorous than the effective control criterion under Article 6 (3) ICTR and Article 7 (3) ICTY Statutes. Of course, these elements can still coincide if a person exerts authority that suffices not only to make another commit a crime, but also to prevent them from committing said crimes.[119]

Superior responsibility at the *ad-hoc* tribunals also requires a *de facto* or *de jure* superior-subordinate relationship.[120] However, this is understood more narrowly than authority to order,[121] and refers to factual or legal commanders and other superiors. Individuals in such a position are expected to have a more generalized command over the perpetrators whose crimes they are expected to prevent, suppress, or punish.[122]

Evidence to Prove Authority

Authority of the ordering person can also be proven through the circumstances.[123]

---

[114] ICTR, *The Prosecutor v. Athanase Seromba*, 12 March 2008, ICTR-2001-66-A, para 202.

[115] *Kordić and Čerkez*, 26 February 2001, para 388 and 840; Mettraux 2001, p. 274.

[116] *Kordić and Čerkez*, 26 February 2001, paras 401, 840; Mettraux 2001, p. 274.

[117] *Kordić and Čerkez*, 26 February 2001, 405, 840; Mettraux 2001, p. 274.

[118] *Kordić and Čerkez*, 26 February 2001, para 840–1.

[119] For such an example, see the elaboration by Mettraux on a potential superior responsibility for the breach of duty precisely by giving an order to act in Mettraux 2001, pp. 275–6.

[120] The jurisprudence has been shaped by the ruling in *Delalić et al.*, 16 November 1998, paras 354, 370; see also ICTR, *The Prosecutor vs. Ignace Bagilishema*, 3 July 2002, ICTR-95-1A-A, paras 50, 61; ICTR, *Juvénal Kajelijeli vs. The Prosecutor*, 23 May 2005, ICTR-98-44A-A, para 85; ICTR, *Ferdinand Nahimana et al. v. The Prosecutor*, 28 November 2007, ICTR-99-52-A, para 483; *Karadžić*, 24 March 2016, para 580; Boas et al. 2007, p. 182–3.

[121] Cf. the above-mentioned example of Dario Kordić.

[122] See *Delalić et al.*, 16 November 1998, para 370 reading "... the existence of such a position cannot be determined by reference to formal status alone. Instead, the factor that determines liability for this type of criminal responsibility is the actual possession, or non-possession, of powers of control over the actions of the subordinates". More recently see *Karadžić*, 24 March 2016, para 580 ("A superior is someone who possesses 'the power or authority in either a *de jure* or a *de facto* form to prevent a subordinate's crime or to punish the perpetrators of the crime").

[123] *Brđanin*, 1 September 2004, 270; ICTY, *Prosecutor vs. Fatmir Limaj et al.*, 30 November 2005, IT-03-66-T, para 515; ICTY, *Prosecutor v. Mile Mrkšić et al.*, 27 September 2007, IT-95-13/1-T, para 550; *Boškoski et Tarčulovski*, 10 July 2008, 400; *Đorđević*, 23 February 2011, para 1871; Finnin 2012, p. 56.

According to the trial chamber in *Kamuhanda* the existence of authority can be inferred from the fact that the recipients obeyed (i.e., carried out) the order.[124] This can potentially be difficult where the order itself has already been inferred from the circumstances.[125]

In *Kordić and Čerkez* the trial chamber based its findings of Dario Kordić's authority *inter alia* on the presence of security guards around him, the central position of his seating in the meeting room and the deferential behaviour of officers towards him.[126] As previously mentioned, the existence of a (formalized or visible) superior-subordinate relationship can serve as evidence for the authority of the superior over the subordinates.[127]

Summary: Authority as a Broad and Flexible Criterion

As shown, authority can be formal or informal, and may only be temporary. In the specific situation and for the specific order, it suffices that the relationship between the ordering person and the recipients is shaped in such a way that the order is obeyed because the recipients feel compelled to do so. Authority must be exercised over the perpetrators of the crime in a narrow sense, not over persons who e.g., aid and abet the crime.

Authority is not tantamount to effective control in the sense of superior responsibility. The latter refers to a narrower concept, where a superior essentially restrain their subordinates.

Authority for ordering has thus developed under ICTY and ICTR jurisprudence into a broad and flexible criterion.[128]

However, authority must eventually compel the physical perpetrators to act, and no alternative "authorship" is recognized as was done in post-World War II jurisprudence under CCL 10. In this regard, the authority requirement is rather narrow because it only allows for a conviction under ordering, where instructions compel the executioners of a crime to act, i.e., where instructions lead directly to the commission of crimes.

5.1.1.3 The Necessary Nexus Between the Order and the Commission of the Crime

The *ad hoc* tribunals' jurisprudence establishes that a certain nexus must exist between the order and the commission of the crime. In a range of judgments, chambers determined that the prosecution does not need to prove that the act would not

---

[124] *Kamuhanda*, 22 January 2004, para 594; Boas et al. 2007, p. 366.

[125] See above under Sect. 5.1.1.1 for the possibility to infer the existence of an order from the circumstances.

[126] Cf. *Kordić and Čerkez*, 26 February 2001, paras 556, 764.

[127] *Muvunyi*, 12 September 2006, para 467.

[128] Finnin has criticised the broad notion of authority as laid out *inter alia* by the *Gacumbitsi* appeals judgment, see Finnin 2012, p. 56.

have occurred but-for the order of the accused, but that the order must have had a 'direct and substantial effect' on the commission of the illegal act.[129]

A similar criterion is required for acts falling under "planning" and "instigating" pursuant to Articles 7 (1) and 6 (1) of the respective statutes.[130]

The trial chamber in *Galić* chose more careful wording in which it stated that the ordering person's behaviour must have had a "positive effect" in bringing about the commission of crimes.[131]

The *Renzaho* case may serve as an example for the different causality standards accepted by the *ad hoc* tribunals for ordering. Tharcisse Renzaho, who had been prefect of Kigali in Rwanda in 1994, was convicted by a trial chamber for ordering the killings of Tutsi civilians at roadblocks. According to the trial chamber, Renzaho had ordered his administrative subordinates to oversee the erection of roadblocks, intending the killing of civilians at these checkpoints. Pursuant to this, his subordinates supervised the construction of additional roadblocks and assured the authorities' support for already existing ones.[132] Hence, the chamber determined that "Renzaho's instructions reinforced the message that the local authorities' (sic) supported roadblocks, and substantially contributed to the targeted killings at them".[133] This case demonstrates how the substantial contribution requirement encompasses both cases in which the order is *conditio sine qua non*, and such in which it merely furthers the commission of a crime. Pursuant to the trial chamber's findings, Renzaho's orders led to the setup of new roadblocks. Without his orders the crimes committed at these specific roadblocks would not have taken place.[134] Additionally, his orders to encourage the armed militias at already existing checkpoints were found to have substantially contributed to the commission of crimes at these locations. For the latter, it was apparent that such crimes occurred prior to Renzaho's order and would have continued without them as well. His orders in this regard only had a contributory effect.

The direct and substantial effect formula has thus implemented a moderate causal nexus requirement. It grasps more than only *sine qua non* orders (without excluding them), however orders which are only minor contributions to the crime will not suffice.

---

[129] *Tadić*, 7 May 1997, para 674; *Strugar*, 31 January 2005, para 332; *Milutinović et al.*, 26 February 2009, para 88; *Boškoski and Tarčulovski*, 19 May 2010, para 160; *Munyakazi*, 5 July 2010, para 432; *Nyiramasuhuko*, 24 June 2011, para 5593; *Karemera*, 2 February 2012, para 1428; *Taylor*, 18 May 2012, para 477; *Haradinaj et al.*, 29 November 2012, para 624; *Ngirabatware*, 20 December 2012, para 1292; *Stanišić and Župljanin*, 27 March 2013, para 98; ICTR, *The Prosecutor v. Pauline Nyiramasuhuko et al.*, 14 December 2015, ICTR-98-42-A, para 976; *Karadžić*, 24 March 2016, para 573. See also Boas et al. 2007, p. 370.

[130] *Strugar*, 31 January 2005, para 332; Boas et al. 2007, pp. 357–8, 362–3, Mettraux 2005, p. 281.

[131] *Galić*, 5 December 2003, para 169; this seemingly broader formulation has, however, been quite unique in the jurisprudence.

[132] *Renzaho*, 14 July 2009, paras 179–81.

[133] Ibid., para 181.

[134] Note that this order was *conditio sine qua non* but not necessarily in the sense that it triggered the physical perpetrators' decisions to act.

5.1.1.4 Mens Rea

The statutes of the ICTY and ICTR do not provide specific rules for *mens rea*. Therefore, the tribunals had to identify and clarify the boundaries of the mental element.[135]

Besides the *mens rea* that is generally necessary to incur liability for ordering, the requirement of a special intent for ordering crimes, such as genocide or persecution is of enormous importance.

General Rules From ICTY, ICTR and SCSL Case Law

The ordering person must intend for the offence to be committed[136] or to "have awareness of the substantial likelihood that a crime will be committed in the execution of the order".[137] In the view of the ICTY appeals chamber, an order given with such awareness must be regarded as accepting the crime.[138] The appeals chamber regarded this form of mental element, which is lower than direct intent, to be sufficient. It thus disregarded the broader formula of the *Blaskić* trial chamber. The latter had held that the *mens rea* for ordering would be fulfilled if the actor had intentionally or knowingly taken the risk that the crime would occur.[139]

The *Orić* judgment established that *mens rea* in instigation required a volitional and a cognitive element. For the former, it would suffice if the instigator knew that his instigation would "more likely than not" lead to the commission of the crime. This would then equate to accepting that the crime would be committed.[140] It has been suggested that this corresponds to the notion of *dolus eventualis*.[141] From the wording chosen by the appeals chamber in *Blaskić*, it could be deduced that this *dolus*

---

[135] van Sliedregt 2012, p. 50.

[136] *Gotovina et al.*, 15 April 2011, para 1959; *Haradinaj et al.*, 29 November 2012, para 624; *Karadžić*, 24 March 2016, para 573; *Mladić*, 22 November 2017, para 3566; Boas et al. 2007, pp. 364–5.

[137] *Blaskić*, 29 July 2004, para 42; *Brđanin*, 1 September 2004, para 270; *Kordić and Čerkez*, 17 December 2004, para 30; *Galić*, 30 November 2006, para 152; *Nahimana et al.*, 28 November 2007, para 481; ICTY, *Prosecutor v. Milan Martić*, 8 October 2008, IT-95-11-A, paras 220-2; *Munyakazi*, 5 July 2010, para 432; *Gotovina et al.*, 15 April 2011, para 1959; *Nyiramasuhuko*, 24 June 2011, para 5593; *Karemera*, 2 February 2012, para 1428; *Haradinaj et al.*, 29 November 2012, para 624; *Stanišić and Župljanin*, 27 March 2013, para 97; *Stanišić and Simatović*, 30 May 2013, para 1263; *Nyiramasuhuko et al.*, 14 December 2015, para 976; *Karadžić*, 24 March 2016, para 573; *Mladić*, 22 November 2017, para 3566. See also *Stakić*, 31 July 2003, para 445 according to which the person who ordered has "the required *mens rea* of the crime" and is aware of the substantial likelihood that the crime will be committed. See also for SCSL jurisprudence *Brima et al.*, 20 June 2007, para 773; *Taylor*, 18 May 2012, para 474.

[138] *Blaskić*, 29 July 2004, para 42; *Kordić and Čerkez*, 17 December 2004, para 30; *Nyiramasuhuko et al.*, 14 December 2015, para 976. See also Mettraux 2005, pp. 282–3.

[139] *Blaskić*, 3 March 2000, paras 592, 738.

[140] ICTY, *Prosecutor v. Naser Orić*, 30 June 2006, IT-03-68-T, para 279; van Sliedregt 2012, pp. 104–5.

[141] van Sliedregt 2012, p. 104. On the notion of *dolus eventualis* see Chap. 3, Sect. 3.1.2.4.

eventualis standard would be necessary for ordering.[142] In fact, the appeals chamber explicitly mentioned the necessity of a volitional element as part of the *mens rea*.[143] As mentioned, the characteristic wording of accepting the crime explicitly found its way into some appeals judgments.[144] However, the notion of "accepting the crime" does not play a crucial role in the definition of the mental element proposed in many other judgments.[145]

Hence, the jurisprudence of the *ad hoc* tribunals requires a cognitive element, described as the awareness of the substantial likelihood that the crime would occur. However, the role of a separate volitional element of accepting the crime remains somewhat obscure.[146] The volitional element—where deemed necessary—could be inferred from the cognitive element.[147] It seems improbable that a chamber would deny acceptance where awareness is given, as acceptance implies something less than aiming or wishing to bring about the crime. Therefore, despite its mention in individual judgments, one could conclude that a volitional element has not gained an autonomous meaning.[148]

With regards to the act of giving of an order, the accused must possess direct intent.[149]

The trial chamber in *Blaskić* determined that the *mens rea* of the person ordering the crime was determinative of the specific crime for which they would be responsible.[150]

Consequently, it is also irrelevant whether the order, in and of itself, was criminal "on its face".[151] In *Boškoski and Tarčulovski*, the appeals chamber held that even a

---

142 Ibid., p. 106.

143 *Blaskić*, 29 July 2004, para 41; *Martić*, 8 October 2008, para 222.

144 *Kordić and Čerkez*, 17 December 2004, para 30; *Nyiramasuhuko et al.*, 14 December 2015, para 976.

145 See instead the typical wording of "awareness of substantial likelihood" in many, also recent, trial chamber decisions: *Nahimana*, 3 December 2003, para 481; *Strugar*, 31 January 2005, para 333; *Brima et al.*, 20 June 2007, para 773; *Milutinović et al.*, 26 February 2009, para 85; *Nyiramasuhuko*, 24 June 2011, para 5593; *Taylor*, 18 May 2012, para 474; *Haradinaj et al.*, 29 November 2012, para 624; *Tolimir*, 12 December 2012, para 904; *Mladić*, 22 November 2017, para 3566.

146 In the same vein: Werle and Jessberger 2020, mn. 563.

147 Cf. the wording in *Martić*, 8 October 2008, para 223: "...person giving the order acted with awareness of the substantial likelihood that a crime would be committed in the execution of the order, *thus* accepting the crime" [emphasis added]. Werle and Jessberger 2020, mn. 563 with Footnote 82, who also point out that the *ad hoc* tribunals do not always differentiate material and procedural remarks as strictly, as is typical *inter alia* in German criminal law.

148 In the same vein: Burghardt 2008, p. 281.

149 *Kordić and Čerkez*, 17 December 2004, para 29; ICTR, *The Prosecutor v. André Ntagerura, Emmanuel Bagambiki and Samuel Imanishimwe*, 7 July 2006, ICTR-99-46-A, para 365; *Seromba*, 13 December 2006, para 306; *Stanišić and Župljanin*, 27 March 2013, para 97. The same is true for instigating and planning, see *Kordić and Čerkez*, 17 December 2004, para 29.

150 *Blaskić*, 3 March 2000, para 282; see also *Kordić and Čerkez*, 26 February 2001, para 388.

151 *Blaskić*, 3 March 2000, para 282; *Kordić and Čerkez*, 26 February 2001, para 388.

lawful order, or plan of operation could give rise to criminal responsibility, e.g., for ordering, under the above-mentioned substantial likelihood requirement.[152]

The case law does not elaborate specifically on the requisite *mens rea* regarding the circumstances of ordering a crime. Whether the ordering person needs to know of their own authority, and the substantial effect that their orders have, is not explicitly clear. Yet it is very likely that the actor's intent must include knowledge of the circumstances concerning their person and influence.[153]

If not through case law, the answer may be deduced through the following consideration. As awareness of the substantial likelihood that the crime will be committed pursuant to the order is necessary, an awareness of the causal link between the order and the crime is logically implied. The same can be deduced concerning the actor's knowledge of their authority, as these elements are linked. The substantial likelihood that the crime will occur stems from the effect that the order will have. The influence of the order on the perpetrator taking action comes from the authority exercised by the ordering person. It is thus highly questionable whether the *ad hoc* tribunals would affirm the mental element in cases where an actor does not know of their own position of authority and the resulting influence.

The *mens rea* can be inferred from the circumstances.[154] The presence at the crime scene can serve as evidence.[155] The trial chamber in *Kajelijeli* stated that the accused's prior and similar behaviour, the failure to punish and verbal encouragement were among the relevant circumstances from which one could infer the *mens rea* of a person in a position of authority.[156]

The Special Intent Requirement for Ordering

From the jurisprudence of the *ad hoc* tribunals, Olásolo finds that a person ordering the commission of a crime does not need to fulfil its specific *mens rea* requirements (such as any ulterior or special intent).[157] He states that the chambers in *Blaskić* and *Kordić and Čerkez* did not explicitly mention such a requirement for individuals accused of ordering.[158] Indeed, these chambers used the then-established formulation

---

[152] *Boškoski and Tarčulovski*, 19 May 2010, paras 172, 174; see also Werle and Jessberger 2020, mn. 666.

[153] Olásolo and Carnero Rojo seem to conclude that this was required in *Blaskić*, 29 July 2004, paras 40–2, see Olásolo and Carnero Rojo 2015, p. 567 with Footnote 58. The cited paragraphs refer to the trial chamber's findings, which elaborated on Blaskić's orders. However, neither of the chambers addresses the issue directly.

[154] *Strugar*, 31 January 2005, para 333; *Haradinaj et al.*, 29 November 2012, para 624; as a general rule on *mens rea* this had already be mentioned in *Tadić*, 7 May 1997, para 676; *Delalić et al.*, 16 November 1998, para 328.

[155] *Kajelijeli*, 1 December 2003, para 769; *Boškoski and Tarčulovski*, 19 May 2010, para 132; *Haradinaj et al.*, 29 November 2012, para 624.

[156] *Kajelijeli*, 1 December 2003, para 769.

[157] Olásolo 2009, pp. 139–40.

[158] See ibid., pp. 139–40, referring to the *Blaskić* and *Kordić* cases; *Blaskić*, 29 July 2004, para 166; *Kordić and Čerkez*, 17 December 2004, para 112.

that the actor had to be aware of the substantial likelihood that the crime would be committed, but did not elaborate further on the *mens rea* requirement of ordering.

However, this interpretation of the *ad hoc* tribunals' statutes and jurisprudence must be reconsidered. In general, it is true that ICTY and ICTR jurisprudence have frequently reiterated the mental element requirements for ordering, i.e., that an "awareness of the substantial likelihood that the crime will be committed in the execution of the order", which can be seen as "accepting the crime", is necessary.[159]

The *Blaskić* and *Kordić and Čerkez* chambers used the "substantial likelihood" description in the respective parts of their judgments concerning the crime of persecution.[160] One might therefore conclude that the requirements described in these paragraphs are meant to be the exclusive description of what is necessary to incur liability for ordering persecutions—a crime which requires a special discriminatory intent.[161]

However, further analysis of the jurisprudence leads to a more differentiated picture. The trial chamber in *Semanza* e.g., referred to all modes of liability besides commission as accomplice liability and stated that, to incur such responsibility, the actor did not need to fulfil the *mens rea* of the crime.[162] This is in line with the interpretation by Olásolo.

In other instances, the accused were convicted under "committing" and "ordering" a crime. As the commission of genocide undoubtedly requires the special intent to be given on part of the actor. Therefore, it cannot be inferred whether the chambers also deemed this relevant for ordering because they determined the accused's special intent in general, without specifying for which mode of liability this *dolus specialis* would be necessary.[163]

However, other judgments elaborate on the ordering person's special intent explicitly: in a number of cases, chambers have tested the accused's *special intent* for genocide or persecution when assessing their liability for ordering the respective crimes.[164] The *Seromba* trial chamber explicitly outlined that ordering and instigating would require the special intent of the actor.[165] In *Brđanin*, the accused was found responsible for ordering persecution because he had ordered crimes with the

159 Cf. the respective descriptions and explanations in Cryer et al. 2019, p. 360; Schabas 2016, pp. 574–5; Werle and Jessberger 2020, mn. 666. The formulation goes back to *Blaskić*, 29 July 2004, para 42. See under Sect. 5.1.1.4.

160 *Blaskić*, 29 July 2004, para 166; *Kordić and Čerkez*, 17 December 2004, para 112.

161 *Kordić and Čerkez*, 26 February 2001, paras 211–12; ICTY, *Prosecutor v. Milomir Stakić*, 22 March 2006, IT-97-24-A, para 329; Badar 2013, pp. 295–7.

162 *Semanza*, 15 May 2003, para 377, 388.

163 *Akayesu*, 2 September 1998, paras 727, 734; *Rutaganda*, 6 December 1999, paras 397, 399, 402; *Musema*, 27 January 2000, paras 891, 934, 936; *Gacumbitsi*, 17 June 2004, paras 260, 287–8.

164 *Kajelijeli*, 1 December 2003, paras 836-8; *Nahimana*, 3 December 2003, paras 968, 977A; *Kamuhanda*, 22 January 2004, paras 648–652; *Brđanin*, 1 September 2004, paras 1063–7; ICTR, *The Prosecutor v. François Karera*, 7 December 2007, ICTR-01-74-T, paras 539-40; *Renzaho*, 14 July 2009, paras 765-6; *Nyiramasuhuko*, 24 June 2011, paras 5867-5871, 587.

165 *Seromba*, 13 December 2006, para 312.

necessary discriminatory intent.[166] The appeals chamber in *Nyiramasuhuko* affirmed that the accused had possessed the specific intent of genocide and thus ordered the crime.[167]

In the latter case, the appeals chamber used the common formula of "accepting the crime by ordering it with awareness of the substantial likelihood", but did not believe that this excluded the need for a special intent.[168] In a similar manner, the trial chamber in *Kajelijeli* explained that to incur accomplice liability, one must be aware of the essential elements of the crime and of one's own support of the crime.[169] The chamber then tested the accused's special intent. The *Karera* judgment only refers to the "well established" case law and goes on to find that the accused had genocidal intent, and that he is guilty of ordering crimes that therefore amounted to genocide.[170]

Ad hoc jurisprudence thus shows a certain pattern here. Tribunals only use the common wording for the *mens rea* requirements for ordering without referring to a special intent requirement. However, when determining the facts of the accused's *mens rea* they do elaborate on their special intent. This pattern can also be found in *Nahimana*,[171] *Kamuhanda*,[172] *Renzaho*[173] and *Ntawukulilyayo*.[174]

In a similar way, the *Bagosora* trial chamber determined that the accused "was aware of the genocidal intent of the perpetrators and *shared it*".[175] The accused was also convicted of superior responsibility for genocide pursuant to Article 6 (3) ICTR Statute. Regarding this, his own intent was not mentioned, and the chamber only elaborated on the direct perpetrator's intent.[176] This difference shows how the formulation of an accused "sharing" the specific intent of the perpetrators refers to them fulfilling the (necessary) special intent requirement themselves.

Additionally, the trial chamber in *Milutinović et al.* explained that the special discriminatory intent could be fulfilled by any involved person, namely physical perpetrators, or persons who planned, ordered, or instigated the crimes. This test only serves to determine whether the crime of persecution is fulfilled in the first

[166] *Brđanin*, 1 September 2004, paras 1063–7; the same chamber found him responsible for instigating crimes as well, because he had instigated persecution with the necessary special intent, see at para 1052.

[167] *Nyiramasuhuko et al.*, 14 December 2015, paras 984–7, especially at 986.

[168] Compare the formulations in ibid., para 976 and *Kordić and Čerkez*, 17 December 2004, para 112.

[169] *Kajelijeli*, 1 December 2003, para 768.

[170] *Karera*, 7 December 2007, paras 539–40.

[171] *Nahimana*, 3 December 2003, paras 968, 977A.

[172] *Kamuhanda*, 22 January 2004, paras 648–50.

[173] *Renzaho*, 14 July 2009, paras 765–6 with Footnote 856–7.

[174] *Ntawukulilyayo*, 3 August 2010, paras 28, 456–7 with fn. 645. The findings on his special intent were appealed by Ntawukulilyayo, but his conviction for ordering genocide was quashed for another reason (insufficient notice), and the appeals chamber did thus not elaborate on the question of genocidal intent (see ICTR, *Dominique Ntawukulilyayo v. The Prosecutor*, 14 December 2011, ICTR-05-82-A, paras 180, 207).

[175] *Bagosora et al.*, 18 December 2008, para 2126 (emphasis added), see conviction at 2158.

[176] Ibid., paras 2144, 2149, 2154, 2158.

place, not to determine a participant's responsibility. However, it has been construed as implying that ordering a special intent crime also requires such special intent.[177]

An additional observation on the matter can be made with a view to jurisprudence on aiding and abetting. The *Tolimir* trial chamber summed up the ICTY case law, stating with respect to aiding and abetting that, "[i]t is not necessary for the accused to share the *mens rea* of the principal perpetrator. Regarding the specific intent crimes, such as genocide and persecution, it must be shown that the accused knew of the principal perpetrator's genocidal or discriminatory intent".[178] This renouncement of a special intent requirement for the aider and abettor was established by earlier ICTY judgments.[179]

With this in mind, it is striking how trial chambers employed very different descriptions for the necessary requirements when elaborating on the *mens rea* of aiding and abetting and ordering.[180] The explicit rejection of the special intent requirement in these judgments was only aimed at aiding and abetting and did not renounce the necessity of a special intent for ordering, planning, or instigating. Meanwhile, the jurisprudence described the necessary *mens rea* for planning and instigating by referencing the awareness criterion which became common for ordering, without elaborating on the special intent.[181] There is no obvious reason why the tribunals should have excluded the special intent requirement for all modes of responsibility, while only explicitly mentioning it when elaborating on aiding and abetting.

The relevant jurisprudence therefore illustrates the following: aside from limited statements to the contrary, the tribunals usually tested the special intent of people they convicted of ordering the relevant crimes. They did so without explicitly requiring such intent in the abstract description of the modes' requirements. However, when abstractly describing the requirements of aiding and abetting, the chambers often underlined that a special intent was not necessary.[182]

[177] Cp. Goy 2012, pp. 55–6, who identifies this interpretation in the chamber's reasoning but rejects it.

[178] *Tolimir*, 12 December 2012, para 911, footnotes omitted.

[179] ICTY, *Prosecutor v. Milorad Krnojelac*, 17 September 2003, IT-97-25-A, para 52; ICTY, *Prosecutor v. Mitar Vasiljević*, 25 February 2004, IT-98-32-A, para 142; ICTY, *Prosecutor v. Radislav Krstić*, 19 April 2004, IT-98-33-A, para 140; *Brđanin*, 1 September 2004, para 273; *Muvunyi*, 12 September 2006, para 470; ICTY, *Prosecutor v. Blagoje Simić*, 28 November 2006, IT-95-9-A, para 86; see also Burghardt 2008, pp. 302-3. But see differently ICTR, *The Prosecutor v. Callixte Kalimanzira*, 22 June 2009, ICTR-05-88-T, paras 293, 393, 474 where the chamber explicitly tested the accused's special intent before convicting him for aiding and abetting genocide; see also the criticism by Mettraux, who deems this to be contrary to customary law on genocide in Mettraux 2005, pp. 211–12.

[180] *Brđanin*, 1 September 2004, paras 270-3; *Mrkšić et al.*, 27 September 2007, paras 550, 556; *Tolimir*, 12 December 2012, paras 904, 911.

[181] *Kanyarukiga*, 1 November 2010, para 653–4; *Nyiramasuhuko*, 24 June 2011, paras 5591–2; *Karemera*, 2 February 2012, paras 1426–7; *Tolimir*, 12 December 2012, paras 899, 901; Instigating only: *Brđanin*, 1 September 2004, para 269; *Muvunyi*, 12 September 2006, para 465.

[182] See also Burghardt 2008, pp. 302–3.

These findings suggest that special intent is indeed necessary for the mode of ordering pursuant to Articles 7 (1) and 6 (1) of the ICTY and ICTR Statutes respectively.[183]

"What Matters is the Mental Element of the Ordering Person"

Another typical formulation of some ICTY judgments supports the above-mentioned interpretation of a special intent requirement for ordering. In the *Blaskić* and the *Kordić and Čerkez* cases, the trial chambers ruled that "what is important is the commander's *mens rea*, not that of the subordinate executing the order."[184]

These rulings have been said to establish that a person can incur responsibility for ordering in cases where the perpetrator is not criminally liable.[185] Badar describes the situation in which a commander orders his subordinates to open artillery fire on a non-military target where civilians are taking refuge. Where the commander knows of the civilian nature of the target, yet orders his men, who believe the target to be a military one, to attack, the commander can be liable for ordering war crimes.[186]

This is a possible conclusion from the rulings in *Blaskić* and *Kordić and Čerkez*. However, there are two alternative interpretations to these judgments.

It could be interpreted that, as far as the ordering person's *mens rea* exceeds the usual intent to commit a crime, their state of mind—not the executioner's—will determine the crime for which they are responsible. This would be of relevance where a special intent is necessary, which only the ordering person and not the physical perpetrator possesses.

Alternatively, the chambers' statement could be referring to the *mens rea* of the ordering person in a declaratory way. The two rulings would then mean that, to establish responsibility for ordering, the actor must possess the necessary intent him- or herself.

Badar's interpretation that this renders the physical perpetrator's intent unnecessary, is thus only one possible interpretation of the phrase that "what matters is the mental element of the ordering person". This interpretation could be supported by the statement in the judgment that "[T]herefore, it is irrelevant whether the illegality of the order was apparent on its face".[187] Consequently, responsibility for ordering would depend solely on the *actus reus* of the physical actor, whereas their *mens*

---

[183] This was already been suspected by Burghardt in ibid., p. 303; in the same vein see Ambos and Bock 2016, pp. 214–15, but based on the assumption that ordering would be a form of indirect perpetration. See also Boas et al. 2007, pp. 352, 429, affirming this for cases in which the ordering, planning, or instigating person intended the crimes to be committed (as opposed to cases in which the person was only aware of the substantial likelihood). This finding would consequently also apply to instigating and planning because the chambers usually only denied the special intent requirement for aiding and abetting.

[184] *Blaskić*, 3 March 2000, para 282; this was taken up by the chamber in *Kordić and Čerkez*, 26 February 2001, para 388. See also Mettraux 2005, p. 282.

[185] Badar 2013, p. 335; but see for an interpretation of the *Blaskić* and the *Kordić and Čerkez* cases to the contrary: Olásolo 2009, p. 140.

[186] Badar 2013, p. 335.

[187] *Blaskić*, 3 March 2000, para 282.

rea would be irrelevant. In other words, the (punishable) commission of a crime by another would not be a requirement for ordering, instead only the physical perpetration of the crime's *actus reus* would be necessary.[188] Such a concept is reminiscent to the use of an innocent agent and forms of indirect perpetration.

However, tribunals have repeatedly pointed out that ordering requires the crime in question be committed.[189] Should this frequent statement refer to the commission of a crime in the sense of the "punishable fulfilment of objective and subjective elements", this would not be reconcilable with Badar's view that ordering only requires the *actus reus* of a crime.

Considering this, it seems equally possible that the tribunals' statement ("what matters is the mental element of the ordering person") was merely meant to underline the necessity of the ordering actor having to fulfil the necessary *mens rea* requirements him- or herself. The ordering actor would have to be aware of the circumstances and the substantial likelihood that crimes (i.e., their *actus reus* fulfilled with the necessary *mens rea*) could be committed because of the order. The above statement would then have a declaratory function and would not reduce the necessary commission of a crime by another to the objective elements of that crime.

It is of little surprise that the chambers' elaborations on the crimes in question do not enable any conclusion on this matter. The identity of the physical perpetrators was usually unknown to the chambers, and the question of whether they had acted with the relevant intent was often not touched upon.

The precise meaning of these statements will therefore remain unclear. However, given the elaborations on the special intent requirement, it also seems possible that the chambers meant that the ordering person's special intent would matter when their liability was discussed.

Regardless, Badar's interpretation also leads to the conclusion that the ordering person must possess a special intent where this is prerequisite for a crime. However, his interpretation also implies a certain consequence for the system of accessorial liability under the *ad hoc* tribunals' statutes.

5.1.2 Ordering as Principal or Accessorial Liability in the Jurisprudence of the Ad Hoc *Tribunals*

It is still slightly contentious whether Article 7 (1) ICTY Statute and Article 6 (1) ICTR Statute establish a differentiated system of perpetration and participation or a unitary system of perpetration, although the majority view nowadays affirms a differentiated system.[190] Some authors ascertain that the tribunals apply neither of

[188] Which in turn would lead to ordering being very close to a form of indirect perpetration through another person, or as agency, as pointed out by Badar 2013, p. 335.

[189] See *supra* Sect. 5.1.1.1.

[190] For a differentiated system of (principal) perpetration and (secondary) participation: Burghardt 2008, pp. 303–4; Finnin 2012, p. 20; Jain 2014, pp. 43–44; Olásolo 2009, pp. 23, 26; Werle and

the two concepts consistently.[191] Whether such a differentiated model implies a hierarchy of blameworthiness, rendering commission the most blameworthy form of responsibility remains equally controversial.[192]

For those who recognize a differentiated system it is also contentious whether the mode of ordering was conceptualized as primary or secondary liability, i.e., whether a person ordering a crime would be a principal of, or an accessory to the crime under the *ad hoc* tribunals' law.[193]

The view that ordering constitutes secondary liability is often connected with the understanding that the statutes imply a hierarchy of blameworthiness with commission constituting the single most serious form of responsibility.[194]

Ambos and Bock endorse another interpretation, according to which ordering is a special form of indirect perpetration and thus functions as primary responsibility.[195]

Some ICTR judgments have been interpreted as establishing ordering as "a third form of responsibility" in the sense that it is an independent form of participation.[196] This description as a third form can be found in *Rutaganda, Musema* and *Kajelijeli.*[197] However, if read in conjunction with the accompanying paragraphs, these judgments show that they merely contain an enumeration of the forms of responsibility listed

---

Jessberger 2020, mn. 612. See also Schabas 2006, p. 297 being critical of a hierarchy of modes of liability, but recognizing such a distinction in the jurisprudence. Against a differentiation between perpetration and participation: Separate Opinion of Judge David Hunt on Challenge by Ojdanić to Jurisdiction Joint Criminal Enterprise, ICTY, *Prosecutor v. Milan Milutinović et al.*, Decision on Ojdanić's Motion Challenging Jurisdiction—Joint Criminal Enterprise, 21 May 2003, IT-99-37-AR72, para 31. But see Cryer 2004, p. 244 in favour of interpreting ordering under the ICTR and ICTY statutes as principal liability.

[191] van Sliedregt 2007, p. 190. See also van Sliedregt 2012, p. 154 ("There is no coherent grounding for any of the systems of responsibility"); in the same vein Eser 2002, p. 786. See also ICC, *The Prosecutor v. Bosco Ntaganda*, Appeals Judgment, 30 March 2021, ICC-01/04-02/06-A A2, Partly concurring opinion of Judge Chile Eboe-Osuji, para 30, on his view that the preoccupation of distinguishing principals from accessories is new to the ICC, i.e., played no role in former international courts.

[192] Against a hierarchy of blameworthiness: Boas et al. 2007, p. 422, criticizing that, in their view, the tribunals implied such a hierarchy; Schabas 2006, p. 297; Zorzi Giustiani 2008, pp. 798–9. In favour see especially the judgments discussed in Sect. 5.3.5. Also note that for many commentators a differentiated system of perpetration and participation seems to automatically imply a hierarchy, which was opposed earlier in this thesis (see Introduction).

[193] In the same vein Burghardt 2008, pp. 305, 308.

[194] Olásolo 2009, pp. 135 with fn. 238, 139-40.

[195] Ambos and Bock 2016, pp. 214–15; see already Ambos 2004, p. 645–6. This was seemingly endorsed by the prosecution in the *Semanza* appeal, *Semanza*, 20 May 2005, para 352; it was embraced by the trial chamber in ICTR, *The Prosecutor vs. Siméon Nchamihigo*, 12 November 2008, ICTR-01-63-T, para 388.

[196] Ambos 2018, § 7 mn. 45 with Footnote 251.

[197] *Rutaganda*, 6 December 1999, para 39; *Musema*, 27 January 2000, para 121; *Kajelijeli*, 1 December 2003, para 763.

in Article 6 (1) ICTR Statute.[198] Hence, the descriptions as "first", "second" etc. do not enable any conclusions on a system of perpetration and participation.

These different interpretations offer a noteworthy insight into possibilities of interpreting the role of ordering in the statutes. However, most of the jurisprudence interprets the relevant provisions as establishing a differentiated system of perpetration and participation.[199]

Ad hoc jurisprudence quite clearly differentiates between the commission of a crime and aiding and abetting a crime, often labelling the latter as accomplice liability.[200] The same label has been affixed to ordering, planning, and instigating in a range of judgments.[201]

This notwithstanding, the precise classification of ordering (and planning and instigating) within a differential participation system remains unclear. The jurisprudence shows that some form of differentiation exists, as many chambers distinguished between perpetrator and accomplice liability. Yet, the precise relation of responsibility forms to each other is undefined and does not seem to follow common doctrinal standards of criminal law.

In connection thereto, the precise shape of the "accessorial object" under the differentiated approach of the *ad hoc* tribunals is in question. We have seen how tribunals have stated that the necessary *mens rea* of ordering is "what matters". Badar's suggestion that a person could be liable for ordering, even where the physical perpetrator does not fulfil the mental element of the crime, comes to mind.[202] In this vein, Vogel advanced the idea that customary international criminal law recognizes

---

[198] Cf. *Rutaganda*, 6 December 1999, paras 36–40 ("firstly...planning", "second form of participation, that is, incitement", "ordering, which is a third form", "fourthly... commission"); *Musema*, 27 January 2000, paras 118–122 ("the first form of participation, planning", "The second form of participation, incitement", "the third form of participation, ordering", "the fourth form of participation in which...he actually commits"); *Kajelijeli*, 1 December 2003, paras 762–3 ("the second form of participation, 'instigating'", "the third form of participation, 'ordering'").

[199] See e.g. the following decisions that imply a differentiation between perpetration and participation: *Kordić and Čerkez*, 26 February 2001, para 373 (accomplices/accomplice liability, principal perpetrator); *Krstić*, 2 August 2001, para 643 (accomplice liability, secondary participation, direct or principal perpetrator); *Semanza*, 15 May 2003, para 436 (accomplice, principal perpetrator); *Prosecutor v. Milorad Krnojelac*, 17 September 2003, paras 72–3 (principal offender/perpetrator); *Kajelijeli*, 1 December 2003, para 963 (principal perpetrators, secondary or indirect forms of participation); *Vasiljević*, 25 February 2004, paras 102 (accessory); ICTR, *The Prosecutor v. Aloys Simba*, 13 December 2005, ICTR-01-76-T, para 389 (principal perpetrator); ICTY, *Prosecutor v. Miroslav Kvočka et al.*, 28 February 2005, IT-98-30/1-A, para 91 (principal perpetrator); ICTY, *Prosecutor v. Milan Martić*, 12 June 2007, IT-95-11-T, para 438 (principal perpetrator); *Karera*, 7 December 2007, para 583 (secondary forms of participation); *Nyiramasuhuko et al.*, 14 December 2015, para 3422 (secondary forms of responsibility), 3424 (principal perpetrators).

[200] See e.g. the *Tadić* appeals judgment which first elaborated on the delineation of Joint Criminal Enterprise and Aiding and Abetting, *Tadić*, 15 July 1999, para 229.

[201] See e.g. *Delalić et al.*, 16 November 1998, para 334; *Kordić and Čerkez*, 26 February 2001, para 373; ICTR, *The Prosecutor v. Clément Kayishema and Obed Ruzindana*, 1 June 2001, ICTR-95-1-A, para 185; see also ICTR, *The Prosecutor vs. Emmanuel Ndindabahizi*, 15 July 2004, ICTR-2001-71-I, para 457(instigating); *Semanza*, 15 May 2003, para 557 (instigating).

[202] See above, Sect. 5.1.1.4.

that only the *actus reus* must be fulfilled in what he called "very limited" accessorial liability.[203] Under this observation, it would be possible to make sense of the different statement on the necessary *mens rea* and the mode of ordering as accessorial liability: if the concept of accessorial liability in *ad hoc* jurisprudence is limited to someone else fulfilling the crime's objective elements, then what matters for the *mens rea* of accessories is their own state of mind.

However, depending on the presentation of the relevant crimes, chambers of the *ad hoc* tribunals often elaborated on the physical perpetrator's *mens rea*, implying that both objective and subjective elements played a role in determining the crime (the accessorial object) in which an accused had participated.[204]

Additionally, many ICTR chambers elaborated explicitly on the special intent of Rwandan *génocidaires* who physically committed the crimes.[205] This would be unnecessary if the accessorial object for ordering, planning, instigating, or aiding and abetting were merely the respective *actus reus*, e.g., acts of killing.

The very limited accessorial liability is therefore not an approach that has been taken by most chambers of the *ad hoc* tribunals. Instead, accessorial liability requires both *actus reus* and *mens rea* of the physical perpetrator. Without prejudice to remaining issues and reservations, this categorisation will be subsequently applied.

This does not yet answer the question of whether the tribunals interpret their statutes as embodying a hierarchy of blameworthiness between principal perpetration and accessorial participation. The latter issue will be discussed again below, considering the conclusions of the rest of this chapter, as well as terminology and the jurisprudence on legal concurrences.[206]

---

[203] Vogel 2002, pp. 425, 427, 434.

[204] See e.g. *Brđanin*, 1 September 2004, paras 465 (physical perpetrator's intent to kill or inflict serious injury), 1001, 1013, 1020 (physical perpetrator's discriminatory intent); *Bagosora et al.*, 18 December 2008, paras 2172, 2177, 2193, 2202, 2212 (awareness of the physical attackers and the accused that the attacks were part of a widespread and systematic attack); *Gotovina et al.*, 15 April 2011, paras 1722 (physical perpetrator's knowledge of the attack on the civilian population as an element of crimes against humanity), 1729 (perpetrator's intent to kill and knowledge that the victims will die), 1746 (physical perpetrator's intent to forcibly displace the people in the town which they were attacking); *Ngirabatware*, 20 December 2012, para 1376 (physical perpetrator's knowledge of widespread and systematic attack). In the same vein, Burghardt 2008, pp. 306–7.

[205] See e.g. *Bagosora et al.*, 18 December 2008, paras 2126, 2135, 2138–9, 2144, 2149, 2155, 2212 (finding that an accused knew about the genocidal intent of the perpetrators and shared it), 2119 and 2121-2 (denying the genocidal intent of the physical perpetrators); *Nyiramasuhuko*, 24 June 2011, e.g. paras 5756–7; 5771, 5783, 5825 (referring to the respective genocidal intent of the attackers); *Ntawukulilyayo*, 3 August 2010, para 456; *Ngirabatware*, 20 December 2012, para 1345.

[206] See *infra* Sect. 5.3.

5.1.3 The Attempt of Ordering a Crime

Whether the ordered crime must actually be committed to give rise to liability for ordering, remained unclear in early ICTY and ICTR jurisprudence.[207] In 2003, the trial chambers in *Kajelijeli* and *Semanza* took the view that a crime under the ICTR Statute had to be committed to give rise to criminal liability in general, or to liability for planning.[208] The *Brđanin* trial judgment stated that "to establish individual criminal responsibility for planning, instigating, ordering and otherwise aiding and abetting [...], proof is required that the crime in question has actually been committed by the principal offender(s)".[209] The chamber relied *inter alia* on the *Stakić* trial judgment, which it believed had implied this view on ordering.[210] The view of the *Brđanin* trial chamber has since been adopted on several occasions by chambers of the ICTY and ICTR.[211]

To date, none of the chambers of the ICTY or ICTR has expressed a view to the contrary. Regarding the attempt of the commission of the offence, scholarly literature recognizes a punishable attempt under international criminal law.[212] However, scholars concede that the criminalization of an attempt in customary international law seems to have been incorporated in the *ad hoc* statutes only through the inclusion of the modes of "planning" and "aiding and abetting in the planning and preparation" of the crime.[213]

In line with the latter, *ad hoc* jurisprudence rejects the criminalization of the attempted commission of a crime with the exception of attempted genocide.[214] Consequently, no punishable attempts have been subject of the tribunals' jurisprudence.

Therefore, the attempted commission of a crime is not criminalized as such under the *ad hoc* tribunals' law. Consequently, the order to commit a crime, which is then attempted but not completed, does not lead to criminal responsibility for ordering the crime. As the attempt to commit a crime is not punished as commission, ordering the attempt of a crime cannot be punished because to incur liability for ordering, "the crime has to be committed".

---

[207] Mettraux 2005, p. 283; van Sliedregt 2012, p. 106.

[208] *Semanza*, 15 May 2003, para 278; *Kajelijeli*, 1 December 2003, para 758.

[209] *Brđanin*, 1 September 2004, para 267.

[210] Ibid., para 267 with fn. 705, quoting for ordering: *Stakić*, 31 July 2003, para 445. The *Stakić* chamber in this paragraph stated *inter alia* that a conviction for ordering would not be entered where commission was also fulfilled (cf. on this topic Sect. 5.3.4. *infra* on concurrences).

[211] *Martić*, 12 June 2007, para 441; *Nahimana et al.*, 28 November 2007, para 481; *Nyiramasuhuko*, 24 June 2011, para 5593; *Stanišić and Župljanin*, 27 March 2013, para 98; *Karadžić*, 24 March 2016, para 573.

[212] Ambos 2016, Article 25 mn. 48; Cassesse 2004, pp. 266 *et seq.*; Eser 2002, pp. 807–8; Mettraux 2005, p. 283; van Sliedregt 2012, pp. 150–1; Werle and Jessberger 2020, mn. 803.

[213] Ambos 2016, Article 25 mn. 48; Eser 2002, pp. 807–8.

[214] *Akayesu*, 2 September 1998, para 473; ICTY, *Prosecutor vs. Milorad Krnojelac*, 15 March 2002, IT-97-25-T, para 432 with fn. 1292; agreeing Mettraux 2005, p. 293; Olásolo 2009, p. 30.

The same is true for an order which does not substantially contribute to the commission of a crime (irrespective whether the crime was committed). This latter case touches upon the issue of "failed ordering", which is structurally different to the former case.[215] However, both cases lead to the same result: giving an order that does not have a substantial effect on the crime (failed ordering), cannot be punished as (attempted) ordering because no such form of responsibility is recognized by the tribunals. Instead, aiding and abetting the preparation of the crime could possibly be fulfilled.

5.1.4 Summary

The requirements of responsibility for ordering under the law of the *ad hoc* tribunals have been defined through jurisprudence with few contentious issues. Most of these can be reconciled through a thorough interpretation of the pertinent judgments.

It remains unclear whether the system of perpetration and participation of the ICTY and ICTR Statutes contains a hierarchy of blameworthiness and where ordering would be classified in such a hierarchy. What is relatively clear is that ordering is considered accessorial liability by most chambers. For accessory liability to arise, the crime must be committed by the physical perpetrator with the necessary intent.

It has been illustrated in this section that ordering can encompass the conduct of persons in the highest echelons of power and attribute responsibility for widespread coordinated violence. However, the most important tool of the *ad hoc* tribunals in dealing with high- and mid-level contributors to mass atrocities is another form of responsibility: Participation in a Joint Criminal Enterprise.

5.2 The Difference Between Ordering and Contributing to a Joint Criminal Enterprise

The *ad hoc* tribunals developed the Joint Criminal Enterprise (JCE) or common purpose responsibility to charge and convict all those who had taken part in a criminal design or scheme. Consequently, this figure was used extensively and led to the conviction of many political and military leaders.

The appeals chamber in *Tadić* developed this new form to attribute responsibility, after the accused had been acquitted by the trial chamber. The latter had found that members of the armed group to which Tadić belonged had killed five civilians in

[215] The former is the question of "ordering an attempted crime", the latter that of "attempting to order a crime".

the village of Jaskići in 1992, but that Tadić had not been involved directly.[216] The chamber then developed its understanding of Article 7 (1) ICTY Statute: as its purpose was to capture all those responsible for international crimes in the former Yugoslavia, a broad understanding of the modes of liability in the statute was indicated.[217] Thus, Article 7 (1) would "not exclude those modes of participating in the commission of crimes which occur where several persons having a common purpose embark on a criminal activity, that is then carried out either jointly or by some members of this plurality of persons".[218]

Any group of people can embark on a Joint Criminal Enterprise. In some cases, such as *Tadić*, the mode of JCE serves to convict persons who were very close to the committed crimes, but did not directly, i.e., personally, participate in their commission.[219] A certain hierarchical or superior position within a JCE, conveying power to the actor is not necessary.[220] Yet, in many cases, high-level politicians, military and administrative officials were convicted under JCE for their contributions to crimes.[221]

Liability through participation in a JCE has gained enormous importance in the jurisprudence of the ICTY[222] and has found its way into ICTR[223] and SCSL[224] jurisprudence.

---

216 See the description at *Tadić*, 15 July 1999, paras 172–77; Cryer et al. 2019, p. 344. But see Boas et al. 2007, pp. 10 *et seq*.. who identify the earlier *Furundžija* trial judgment as the first source on JCE.

217 Cryer et al. 2019, pp. 344–5.

218 *Tadić*, 15 July 1999, paras 188–90.

219 When establishing the JCE doctrine, the appeals chamber found that the accused Tadić had been involved in the attack on Jaskići, rounding up and beating men, who were later shot. Tadić had also been part of the armed group of which other members later carried out the shooting, see: ibid., paras 183, 232.

220 Osiel 2005, p. 1788.

221 See e.g. the trials against: Radovan Karadžić (IT-95-5/18), Ratko Mladić (IT-09-92), Vlastimir Đorđević (IT-05-87/1), Augustin Bizimungu (ICTR-99-50), Édouard Karemera (ICTR-98-44), Charles Taylor (SCSL-03-01), as well as the indictment against Slobodan Milošević (IT-02-54); in the same vein Mettraux 2005, p. 292 with further sources.

222 Burghardt 2008, p. 314; Mettraux 2005, p. 292; Werle and Jessberger 2020, mn. 625.

223 Cf. e.g. ICTR, *The Prosecutor v. Yussuf Munyakazi*, 28 September 2011, ICTR-97-36A-A, paras 160–3; ICTR, *The Prosecutor v. Casimir Bizimungu et al.*, 30 September 2011, ICTR-99-50-T, paras 1905–13; ICTR, *Édouard Karemera et al. v. The Prosecutor*, 29 September 2014, ICTR-98-44-A, paras 145 *et seq.*; see also Werle and Jessberger 2020, mn. 625. But see on the somewhat slow incorporation of JCE into ICTR practice Boas et al. 2007, pp. 28 *et seq*..

224 SCSL, *Prosecutor against Moinina Fofana et al.*, 2 August 2007, SCSL-04-14-T, para 206–19; SCSL, *Prosecutor against Alex Tamba Brima et al.*, 22 February 2008, SCSL-2004-16-A, paras 72 *et seq.*; *Taylor*, 18 May 2012, paras 457–68.

5.2.1 *Joint Criminal Enterprise—The ICTY's and ICTR's Approach to Dealing with Various Contributions to Large-Scale Crimes*

To compare responsibility for participation in a JCE with ordering, an overview over the former doctrine's legal requirements (Sect. 5.2.1.1), the nature of ensuing responsibility (Sect. 5.2.1.2) and the perceived advantages and common critiques on it (Sect. 5.2.1.3) is necessary.

5.2.1.1 Legal Requirements for Participation in a Joint Criminal Enterprise

Pursuant to the *ad hoc* tribunals' jurisprudence, the actus reus of a JCE requires:

- A plurality of persons.
- The existence of a common plan, design, or purpose, which amounts to or involves the commission of a crime provided for in the Statute.
- Participation of or contribution by the accused in the common design involving the perpetration of one of the crimes provided for in the Statute.[225]

The plurality of persons does not have to be organised in a military, political or administrative structure.[226]

The common plan must amount to or involve the commission of crimes.[227] These crimes can thus be a means to achieving another—not in itself criminal—aim.[228] Large scale criminal schemes, such as the country-wide persecution of a group of people can also form the common purpose.[229] The common plan does not have to be arranged or formulated. It can materialize extemporaneously.[230] The tribunals can infer the existence of a common plan from the fact that several persons acted in unison to implement a criminal enterprise.[231] When determining whether a person

[225] *Tadić*, 15 July 1999, para 227.

[226] Ibid., para 227; *Tolimir*, 12 December 2012, para 889; see also Cryer et al. 2016, p. 357.

[227] *Tadić*, 15 July 1999, para 227; Werle and Jessberger 2020, mn. 626.

[228] Cf. *Đorđević*, 23 February 2011, para 2003 where the chamber notes that the demographic modification of Kosovo was not a crime and that this (non-criminal) purpose needed to amount to or involve a crime; in the same vein: van Sliedregt 2012, p. 137.

[229] ICTR, *Édouard Karemera et al. v. The Prosecutor*, Decision on Jurisdictional Appeals—Joint Criminal Enterprise, 12 April 2006, ICTR-98-44-AR72.5—ICTR-98-44-AR72.6, para 12; ICTY, *Prosecutor v. Momčilo Krajišnik*, 27 September 2006, IT-00-39-T, para 876; ICTY, *Prosecutor v. Radoslav Brđanin*, 3 April 2007, IT-99-36-A, paras 420–25; Werle and Jessberger 2020, mn. 626.

[230] *Tadić*, 15 July 1999, para 227; *Haradinaj et al.*, 29 November 2012, para 618; *Tolimir*, 12 December 2012, para 891; Cryer et al. 2019, p. 345; Werle and Jessberger 2020, mn. 626.

[231] *Tadić*, 15 July 1999, para 227; *Taylor*, 18 May 2012, para 460; *Tolimir*, 12 December 2012, para 891; Cryer et al. 2019, p. 345; Werle and Jessberger 2020, mn. 626. Cf. also ICTR, *Aloys Simba v. The Prosecutor*, 27 November 2007, ICTR-01-76-A, paras 74, 90, 250.

was a member of the JCE, a certain remoteness of this person from the crime is irrelevant.[232]

The individual contribution has not been clearly defined by the *ad hoc* jurisprudence.[233] A direct participation in the commission of the crime is not required, neither is a necessary or substantial contribution to the plan.[234] However, in its later jurisprudence, the ICTY started requiring that the accused make a "significant" contribution to the enterprise.[235]

In addition to the physical perpetration of a crime, such a contribution can lie in procuring or providing assistance to its commission.[236] The trial chamber in *Milutinović et al.*, clarified that the assistance provided as a contribution to the JCE must only be in furtherance of the common plan. In contrast to aiding and abetting, the assistance does not have to support another person committing the crime.[237] A chamber in *Haradinaj et al.* also stated that "conduct which is not criminal when considered alone may also satisfy" the contribution element.[238] Whilst group membership alone does not qualify as a contribution *per se*, membership in a certain criminal organization is also not a prerequisite for responsibility.[239] An omission can suffice as a contribution as long as a legal duty to act exists.[240] The perpetrators on the ground do not have to be involved in the JCE. If one member of the JCE utilises a direct perpetrator and thereby pursues the common plan, the crime can be imputed to them and all other members of the JCE.[241] Some argue that in this case, the physical perpetration through a third party outside of the JCE must be part of the common plan to have these crimes committed.[242] Such "tools" or third

[232] ICTY, *Prosecutor v. Momčilo Krajišnik*, 17 March 2009, IT-00-39-A, para 663.

[233] Werle and Jessberger 2020, mn. 627.

[234] *Gotovina et al.*, 15 April 2011, para 1953; Cryer et al. 2019, p. 345; Werle and Jessberger 2020, mn. 627. With regards to direct participation see *Tadić*, 15 July 1999, para 227; *Krajišnik*, 17 March 2009, para 663; *Ndahimana*, 30 December 2011, para 721; with regards to contribution see: *Kvočka et al.*, 28 February 2005, paras 97, 104, 187; *Haradinaj et al.*, 29 November 2012, para 619.

[235] *Brđanin*, 3 April 2007, para 430; *Gotovina et al.*, 15 April 2011, para 1953; *Haradinaj et al.*, 29 November 2012, para 619; Cryer et al. 2019, pp. 345–6. These seem to be in contrast to the earlier ruling in *Kvočka et al.*, 28 February 2005, paras 97, 104, 187.

[236] *Brđanin*, 1 September 2004, para 263; *Gotovina et al.*, 15 April 2011, para 1953.

[237] *Milutinović et al.*, 26 February 2009, para 103.

[238] *Haradinaj et al.*, 29 November 2012, para 619.

[239] *Milutinović*, 21 May 2003, para 25; see Boas et al. 2007, p. 46 on the delineation from membership crimes.

[240] *Galić*, 30 November 2006, para 175; *Milutinović et al.*, 26 February 2009, 103; *Haradinaj et al.*, 29 November 2012, para 619.

[241] *Brđanin*, 3 April 2007, paras 410-14, see also Judge Shahabuddeen's partly dissenting opinion paras 10–13; Cryer et al. 2019, p. 346. The *ad hoc* tribunals refer to this as "interlinked" JCEs, to describe how (at least) one co-perpetrator of a criminal enterprise on a leadership level links this JCE to the lower-level group of physical perpetrators. See on this in detail: van Sliedregt 2012, pp. 158–64.

[242] Werle and Jessberger 2020, mn. 627, quoting *inter alia Krajišnik*, 17 March 2009, paras 225, 598, 714; *Karemera*, 2 February 2012, para 1440; *Taylor*, 18 May 2012, para 464; *Haradinaj et al.*, 29 November 2012, para 618; *Tolimir*, 12 December 2012, para 890; *Stanišić and Župljanin*, 27 March

persons who carried out the crime do not need to have the relevant *mens rea* for the crime.[243]

The ICTY established three forms of JCE which differed in their *mens rea* requirements: the basic, the systemic, and the extended form.[244]

The basic form is given where a plurality of persons conceives a common plan and execute it with the same *mens rea.*[245] All members are then liable for the crimes committed under the common plan.[246] Whilst the common plan need not be criminal in its ultimate goal, the intent that certain crimes will be committed in its execution is required.[247]

The systemic form refers to the so-called concentration camp cases.[248] In these cases, the JCE is characterized by a system of ill-treatment in which the members contribute to the repressive acts within the system. The intent of the members must be directed to further this system.[249] If such intent is given the respective member of the JCE is responsible for all crimes committed within the operation of the system of ill-treatment.[250] The knowledge of this system can be inferred for people having a prominent position within the system.[251]

Crimes, which were originally not part of the common plan, can still be attributed to the other members of the JCE. The tribunals refer to this as the extended (third) form.[252] They test if the commission of the crime has been foreseeable for the other members of the JCE. If this has been the case, and the participants have willingly taken the risk that such crimes be committed, they bear responsibility for them.[253] It has been submitted that these requirements impose a recklessness or *dolus eventualis* standard for the crimes, not one of negligence.[254]

2013, para 104; *Stanišić and Simatović*, 30 May 2013, para 1258; ICTY, *Prosecutor v. Vlastimir Đorđević*, 27 January 2014, IT-05-87/1-A, para 63.

243 *Krajišnik*, 17 March 2009, para 226; Cryer et al. 2016, p. 358.

244 *Tadić*, 15 July 1999, para 228; *Vasiljević*, 25 February 2004, para 97–9; Werle and Jessberger 2020, mn. 628.

245 See for an extensive elaboration on the necessary mental element: Badar 2013, pp. 354, 357, 359.

246 *Tadić*, 15 July 1999, paras 196, 220, 228; Werle and Jessberger 2020, mn. 629.

247 *Tadić*, 15 July 1999, para 228; Badar 2013, p. 354; Cryer et al. 2019, pp. 346–7.

248 *Tadić*, 15 July 1999, paras 198, 220, 228; Werle and Jessberger 2020, mn. 630.

249 *Tadić*, 15 July 1999, para 228; Badar 2013, p. 357.

250 Werle and Jessberger 2020, mn. 630; on the historic precedents of type 2 JCE see the trial chamber in ICTY, *Prosecutor v. Miroslav Kvočka et al.*, 2 November 2001, IT-98-30/1-T, paras 268–89, especially 278, 282.

251 *Tadić*, 15 July 1999, para 203; Werle and Jessberger 2020, mn. 630.

252 *Tadić*, 15 July 1999, para 204; *Haradinaj et al.*, 29 November 2012, para 621; Werle and Jessberger 2020, mn. 631.

253 See already *Tadić*, 15 July 1999, paras 204, 220; see also the confirmation of the jurisprudence in MICT, *Prosecutor vs. Radovan Karadžić*, 20 March 2019, MICT-13-55-A, para 433; also Cryer et al. 2019, p. 347; Werle and Jessberger 2020, mn. 631.

254 Cryer et al. 2019, p. 347.

Burghardt states that these "different" requirements, in fact, do not differ. Intent in the language of the court (which is necessary for JCE types I and II) encompasses everything within the awareness of the substantial likelihood that the crimes would be committed. JCE III liability instead requires that the excess crimes are the natural and foreseeable consequence of the JCE. These formulas, although different in wording, in Burghardt's view do not formulate deviating concepts.[255]

The *ad hoc* tribunals elaborated on the necessity of the specific intent of certain crimes for members of the JCE III and asserted that they do not need to share it. Consequently, a member of a JCE could incur liability for committing genocide without fulfilling the *dolus specialis* requirement.[256] At the SCSL, the trial chamber in *Taylor* took the opposite stand and denied this possibility.[257]

5.2.1.2 Nature of Responsibility for Participation in a JCE

The ICTY has consistently stated that JCE entails responsibility for "committing" a crime, as mentioned in Article 7 (1) ICTY Statute.[258] In terms of a differentiation between primary (or principal) and secondary (or accessorial) liability, JCE thus, in the view of the tribunals, leads to being responsible as a primary perpetrator (or principal) of the crime.[259] Several judgments laid out the respective chamber's perception of how such a principal (by ways of a JCE) could be distinguished from an aider and abettor.[260] This became unavoidable because of the low threshold for the contribution to the JCE.[261] The distinction between perpetration and participation is therefore a normative one, in the sense that perpetration is not limited to a hands-on commission.[262]

However, especially the categorization of JCE III as entailing principal responsibility is unconvincing.[263] One may question the uniform labelling of essentially very

---

255 In detail see Burghardt 2008, pp. 328–331.

256 Decision on Interlocutory Appeal in *Brđanin*, 19 March 2004, para 5; *Brđanin*, 3 April 2007, para 431; *Tolimir*, 12 December 2012, para 898; *Đorđević*, 27 January 2014, paras 77–84; Werle and Jessberger 2020, mn. 631.

257 *Taylor*, 18 May 2012, para 468; Werle and Jessberger 2020, mn. 631 with Footnote 236.

258 See already *Tadić*, 15 July 1999, para 188, 191; reiterated e.g. in *Vasiljević*, 25 February 2004, para 95; *Kvočka et al.*, 28 February 2005, paras 79–80; *Krajišnik*, 17 March 2009, para 662; *Tolimir*, 12 December 2012, para 885. See also Cryer et al. 2019, p. 347; Mettraux 2005, p. 290.

259 Haan 2005, p. 196; Cf. the explanation and delineation from an aider and abettor in *Tadić*, 15 July 1999, para 192; see the reference to the term "commission" e.g. in *Krajišnik*, 17 March 2009, para 662; see also Satzger 2018, § 13 mn. 55 and Cryer et al. 2019, p. 347, who agree with the tribunal only with reference to JCE I and II.

260 *Tadić*, 15 July 1999, para 229; *Vasiljević*, 25 February 2004, para 102.

261 On the problematic implications that the use of JCE entails for a distinction between primary and secondary liability: Satzger 2018, § 13 mn. 58.

262 Ohlin et al. 2013, p. 741.

263 Ambos 2007, pp. 167–176, especially 173; Cryer et al. 2019, p. 347; Ohlin 2007, pp. 85–8. See also van Sliedregt 2015, p. 503, underlining that, strictly speaking, participants in a JCE are accessories under a theory of complicity.

different acts, some of which describe a joint perpetration situation, whereas others seem to be much closer to the concept of aiding and abetting.[264] Additionally, the renouncement of a special intent requirement for members of the JCE type III seems contradictory if JCE is to convey liability for commission.[265]

5.2.1.3 Advantages and Criticism of JCE

The doctrine of JCE supposedly holds different advantages for the prosecution of large-scale atrocities.

A perceived advantage of JCE is its better suitability to the reality of criminality.[266] JCE is described as "telling a darker story" if compared to command responsibility. In contrast to the latter, it is praised as not depicting superiors as "simply asleep at the wheel", but as "driving purposively towards disaster".[267] In the opinion of some commentators, the multifaceted relationships between certain actors involved in the planning and execution of crimes can be reflected appropriately by JCE.[268]

Where the physical perpetrator knows only a part of the criminal scheme, or lacks the special intent necessary for a crime, while the senior leaders who conceived the plan fulfil these requirements, it is deemed artificial to convict the latter as "aiders and abettors".[269]

From a procedural point of view, JCE is thought to provide the prosecution with a flexibility to "impose an appropriate degree of criminal responsibility" to individual defendants.[270] Cassesse thus described the doctrine as "particularly fit" to cover the different actions of the participants in a common criminal scheme.[271]

However, the doctrine of Joint Criminal Enterprise has also been heavily criticized.[272]

When the ICTY appeals chamber introduced JCE, it heavily relied on the "object and purpose" of the tribunal.[273] The chamber determined that the statute intended to extend the jurisdiction of the tribunal to "all those 'responsible for serious violations

264 Ambos 2007, pp. 167–176; Cryer et al. 2019, p. 347; Mettraux 2005, p. 292; Ohlin 2007, pp. 76–7; see also the defence of the concept at Cassesse 2007, pp. 114–6.

265 Haan 2005, p. 200; For criticism on this renouncement see: Badar 2006, pp. 301–2; Stewart 2012, pp. 172–8.

266 Cassesse 2007, p. 115.

267 Osiel 2005, p. 1788; see also Cryer et al. 2019, p. 348.

268 Burghardt 2008, pp. 339–40; Del Ponte 2006, p. 550; Mettraux 2005, p. 292; Osiel 2005, p. 1788; van der Wilt 2007, p. 92.

269 Del Ponte 2006, p. 550; Decision on Motion Challenging Jurisdiction, *Milutinović*, 21 May 2003, para 20.

270 Gustafson 2007, p. 139.

271 Cassesse 2007, pp. 110–11.

272 For an overview see: Cryer et al. 2019, pp. 347–8; Satzger 2018, § 13 mn. 58; Werle and Jessberger 2020, mn. 633; see also Jordash 2013, pp. 133–61.

273 *Tadić*, 15 July 1999, paras 189-90; *Krajišnik*, 17 March 2009, para 654–5.

of international humanitarian law' committed in the former Yugoslavia".[274] It also relied on a report by the Secretary-General of the United Nations, which stated that he believed all persons who had participated in the planning, preparation or execution of crimes were individually responsible for these crimes.[275]

Understandably, this reasoning has been criticized as circular: to fulfil the mandate of the court, i.e., to punish everyone associated with crimes in the former Yugoslavia, the chamber decided to read the statute in a way that would enable precisely this outcome.[276] In other words: to convict all responsible actors, all actors were made responsible.

The third form of JCE was criticized as not mirroring the state of international customary law. The tribunals used a very limited number of post-World War II proceedings to deduce it. These historic precedents are mostly British cases, which a chamber of the Extraordinary Chambers of the Courts of Cambodia (ECCC) saw as a thin basis for the deduction of a form of criminal responsibility.[277] Additionally, "Joint Criminal Enterprise" or the "common purpose" doctrine in common law countries usually leads to accessorial, not principal, liability.[278]

The "elastic nature"[279] of the JCE, i.e. the possibility to apply it to large scale criminal schemes, has sparked the allegation that it may endanger the restraining force of criminal law.[280] Danner and Martinez determine that, by establishing the JCE doctrine, the tribunals have sought to ensure punishment of serious human rights violations "despite gaps in either the definitions of substantive crimes or in the liability provisions of the statute".[281] Thus, individuals like Duško Tadić were found guilty despite the lack of evidence of their direct participation in crimes.[282]

Additionally, and in light of the absence of guidelines provided by the chambers of the tribunals, it seems that only prosecutorial discretion determines the scope of the JCEs charged and the contributions made.[283] To underline the relevance of the problem, one may quote the *Zigiranyirazo* case where the prosecutor alleged that the defendant "acting in concert with others, participated in the planning, preparation or execution of a common scheme, strategy, plan or campaign to exterminate the Tutsi and the political opposition to the Interim Government",[284] a statement which

[274] *Tadić*, 15 July 1999, para 189.

[275] Ibid., para 190, the chamber quotes the Report of the Secretary-General Pursuant to paragraph 2 of Security Council Resolution 808 (1993), U.N. Doc. S/25704, 3 May 1993.

[276] Ohlin 2007, p. 72.

[277] ECCC, *Decision on the Appeals against the Co-Investigating Judges Order on Joint Criminal Enterprise (JCE)*, 20 May 2010, 002/19-09-2007-ECCC/OCIJ, paras 75–88; Cryer et al. 2019, pp. 347–8; Olásolo 2009, pp. 55–7.

[278] Olásolo 2009, pp. 55–6.

[279] Cryer et al. 2019, p. 348.

[280] Badar 2006, p. 302; Cryer et al. 2016, p. 361; Danner and Martinez 2005, p. 132.

[281] Danner and Martinez 2005, p. 132.

[282] Ibid., p. 134.

[283] Ibid., p. 135; Cryer et al. 2019, p. 348; Osiel 2005, pp. 1802–3.

[284] ICTR, *The Prosecutor v. Protais Zigiranyirazo—Indictment*, Indictment, 20 July 2001, ICTR-01-73-T, para 23; Danner and Martinez 2005, p. 136.

effectively refers to the entire genocide against the Rwandan Tutsi. As a result of these broadly defined requirements, the preparation of a proper defence becomes increasingly difficult.[285]

The low bar of the *mens rea* requirement for members of an extended JCE (third form), can also be criticized as a circumvention of the more rigid requirements which usually shape some international crimes.[286]

However, the *ad hoc* tribunals and their subsequent International Residual Mechanism for Criminal Tribunals (MICT) remain unimpressed by the criticism and continue their work based on this approach of attributing criminal liability.[287]

5.2.2 *Comparison of JCE and Ordering*

The *ad hoc* tribunals, in particular the ICTY, used the JCE doctrine extensively. In many instances, any other mode of responsibility was cast aside as the tribunals considered JCE to be the best-suited approach to convict the persons involved in these crimes. Yet, in numerous cases some of the other modes of liability under the statutes of ICTY, ICTR and SCSL would probably have been fulfilled as well. The following section compares the requirements, legal implications, and some cases of participation in a JCE and ordering. In doing so, it will explore the applicability of ordering as an alternative tool to adjudicating the wrongdoing of high- and mid-level decision makers and architects behind international crimes.

5.2.2.1 The Legal Requirements

The JCE doctrine and ordering each grasp different aspects of the organizational structures and dynamics behind such crimes through their respective requirements.

The theory of JCE builds on the common plan or design, which must include or amount to the commission of crimes.[288] It can develop spontaneously or consist of a thoroughly planned and agreed upon policy.[289] The common plan can be small scale but can also be regional or even nationwide.[290]

---

[285] Cryer et al. 2019, p. 348.

[286] See above Sect. 5.2.1.2; Badar 2006, pp. 301–2; Stewart 2012, pp. 172–8. See the rejection of grounds of appeal based on the JCE doctrine in *Karadžić*, 20 March 2019, para 437.

[287] Cryer et al. 2019, p. 348; Werle and Jessberger 2020, mn. 633; see e.g. the endorsement by Del Ponte 2006, pp. 549–551 and Piacente 2004, p. 446–9. See also more recently *Karadžić*, 20 March 2019, paras 425 et. seq.

[288] See above at Sect. 5.2.1.1.

[289] Cf. description in *Tadić*, 15 July 1999, para 227; For a criminal enterprise that was planned in detail beforehand see e.g. the lengthy findings of the trial chamber in *Đorđević*, 23 February 2011, paras 2000–130.

[290] *Tadić*, 15 July 1999, para 204, speaking of a "town village or region"; for a description of a region-wide common plan see e.g. Ibid., para 231; for Kosovo cf. *Đorđević*, 23 February 2011,

This common plan is the central attributive or linking vehicle of JCE: responsibility for all crimes that are envisaged by or foreseeable within the JCE is ascribed to the JCE's members.[291] The application of JCE thus requires a plurality of persons, as a *common* plan cannot be conceived by a single individual.[292]

Responsibility for ordering does not require the existence of a plan, scheme, design, or anything comparable.[293] The requirement which characterizes ordering as a special form of responsibility for large scale atrocity crimes is its reliance on the authority of the actor over the perpetrators.[294] As illustrated, this authority can be of a temporary, volatile nature and does not have to be embedded within any kind of hierarchy, although it often will be.[295]

The two forms of attribution place different emphases on the nexus between the commission of the crime and the relevant risk-creating factors: the participation in a common plan or design, and the use of authority over others. Consequently, the link between the actor's conduct and the crime is also shaped differently, as can be seen when comparing the relevant *actus rei.*

Any behaviour that constitutes a significant contribution to the common plan or design can fulfil the *actus reus* of JCE liability.[296] It is noteworthy that, in describing the relevant contributions, some chambers recurred to formulations that were common for the modes of liability within the statutes of the tribunals. The accused participated in a common plan by "ordering", "planning" or "instigating" the commission of certain crimes.[297] This does not mean that the tribunals tested the respective requirements of these modes.[298] Alternatively, the chambers used terminology that did not in itself resemble the language of the statutes but could easily be associated with one of the other modes of responsibility, such as *inter alia* "directing", "facilitating" or "supporting".[299] However, many acts that qualified as a contribution

paras 2000–8; for the nation-wide JCE to commit crimes against the Tutsi population see *Karemera et al.*, 12 April 2006, para 12; *Karemera*, 2 February 2012, paras 1435, 1453–4.

291 Ambos describes the JCE doctrine as an "institutional-participatory" or "systemic" model for the attribution of responsibility, see Ambos 2007, pp. 167–8.

292 See above at Sect. 5.2.1.1.

293 For a comparison of JCE and ordering, planning and instigating from the view of the ICTY appeals chamber see *Krajišnik*, 17 March 2009, para 662.

294 See above at Sect. 5.1.1.2.

295 See above at Sect. 5.1.1.2.

296 See above at Sect. 5.2.1.1.

297 *Kordić and Čerkez*, 26 February 2001, paras 828-9 (planned, instigated, ordered); *Krajišnik*, 17 March 2009, para 226 (instigated, ordered); *Karadžić*, 24 March 2016, paras 5818–9 (orders enabling the killing of Bosnian Muslim males).

298 With reference to "planning": *Simba*, 27 November 2007, para 90.

299 *Kordić and Čerkez*, 26 February 2001, paras 828–9 (preparing campaign against Bosnian Muslim population in Central Bosnia); *Krajišnik*, 17 March 2009, para 663 (facilitating); *Tolimir*, 12 December 2012, para 1092 (directing forcible removal), 1109 (supported the criminal activities in which his subordinates were engaged); *Karadžić*, 24 March 2016, para 5819 (facilitating a killing operation).

to the JCE were described in more neutral terms. The link between these acts and the common plan, and thus to the crimes, had to be explained by the tribunals.[300]

Ordering, on the other hand, requires the issuance of an order, which does not necessitate a particular form; it can be oral or in writing and can be implicit.[301] Words of encouragement which are perceived as an order, due to the circumstances and authority of the speaker, can also constitute an order.[302]

The two *actus rei* thus overlap wherever the contribution to the common plan consists of the giving of orders concerning the commission of crimes. Overlaps with "planning", "instigating" and "aiding and abetting" are probably equally frequent.[303] However, the *actus reus* of participation in a JCE can be established by any kind of conduct that contributes to the common plan and is, therefore, much broader. For this reason, JCE has been described as an "institutional-participatory" and systemic model of responsibility. Any act that furthers or supports the design of the criminal group and thus contributes to the functioning of this group, institution or organisation, leads to responsibility for the ensuing crimes.[304] This model can be described as based on a principle of indirect linkage, as contributions to the common enterprise lead to criminal responsibility without requiring a precise connection between the contribution and the crime.[305]

On the other hand, the order is a comparatively narrow attributive vehicle: responsibility arises only where the actor engages in conduct that establishes a clear line of authority from them to the physical perpetrators of the crime. In other words, responsibility arises where a direct link can be construed through the issuance of an instruction.

Regarding the necessary causal nexus, ordering requires a "direct and substantial effect" of the order on the commission of the crime. However, the effect does not

300 *Martić*, 12 June 2007, paras 450-1 (describing the accused's "fuelling of an atmosphere of insecurity and fear", and how he "deliberately refrained from intervening against perpetrators who committed crimes against the non-Serb population"); *Karemera*, 2 February 2012, para 1453 (describing the distribution of weapons by the accused); *Karadžić*, 24 March 2016, description of contributions in para 3468; see e.g., also para 3475 ("…laying the ground work for that criminal implementation through the creation of, and support for, the structures and bodies which carried out the plan."), para 3489 ("…by ordering the VRS to carry out general mobilisation…"), para 3491 ("The accused was central in promoting the creation of a separate police structure."); *Mladić*, 22 November 2017, para 4893 (containing a list of contributions to the JCE on the siege of Sarajevo), para 5097 (containing a list of contributions to the Srebrenica JCE).

301 See above Sect. 5.1.1.1.

302 *Gacumbitsi*, 17 June 2004, para 282.

303 Responsibility for planning envisions one or more persons formulating a method of design or action, procedure, or arrangement for the accomplishment of a particular crime, see *Semanza*, 15 May 2003, para 380. For a list of judgments with reference to this wording see Mettraux 2005, p. 279 with Footnote 1. See Boas et al. 2007, pp. 355–6 for several telling examples in which persons were convicted for planning.

304 Ambos 2007, pp. 167–8; Ambos 2018, § 7 mn. 30; van Sliedregt 2015, pp. 504–6.

305 van Sliedregt 2012, pp. 181–2. Note that van Sliedregt correctly limits this to "interlinked JCEs", a concept which is at some points very close to indirect perpetration (see at 157–65). The leadership JCEs to which van Sliedregt refers are those in the focus of this chapter.

need to be the necessary condition for the crime being committed, i.e., it does not have to be *sine qua non*.[306] The contribution to the common plan of the JCE must be "significant", yet not *sine qua non* either to achieve the criminal purpose.[307] The difference between the causality requirements seems marginal at first but may prove to be decisive. While the order must have an effect on the commission of the *crime*, the contribution to the JCE only needs to further the common criminal *plan*. I.e., the contribution to the JCE need not influence the crime, but only the plan encompassing the crime. The chamber in the re-trial of *Haradinaj et al.* stated accordingly, "...conduct which is not criminal when considered alone may also satisfy this element if it involved procuring or giving assistance to the execution of the common criminal purpose."[308] Hence, in terms of the necessary causal nexus, the responsibility for participation in a JCE and for ordering a crime correspond whenever the contribution to the JCE consists of an act that falls under ordering, and has a substantial effect on the commission of a specific crime. The much narrower requirements of ordering limit the correspondence in this regard. Any other significant contribution to the criminal enterprise does not qualify as ordering. This could include, e.g., an order to perform a supportive task, not amounting to committing the crime itself.

Initially, the extent to which the *mens rea* requirements differ in their application, thus leading to different consequences in terms of conviction, seemed questionable. Burghardt asserted that, when comparing JCE types I and II with liability for ordering, there appeared to be no actual differences regarding the mental element. Both modes require intent, i.e., direct intent or the awareness of the substantial likelihood that the crime will be committed.[309] Furthermore, the actor, be it a member of the JCE or someone giving orders, needs to fulfil the specific intent requirement in person.

The appeals chamber in *Krajišnik* determined that, to incur responsibility for JCE, the person had to intend to participate in and contribute to the common purpose. Whereas, when planning, instigating, or ordering a crime, the person had to intend the commission of the crime or had to have acted with the awareness of the substantial likelihood that the crime would be committed.[310] This could imply, that no intent for the subsequent crimes is necessary when participating in a JCE and that intent to participate in the common plan would suffice. However, this interpretation seems unrealistic. After all, the common plan must include the commission of crimes. Consequently, it is more realistic that the intent must include these crimes as well.[311] Therefore, Bughardt's doubts as to a different scope of *mens rea* for participation in JCEs I and II and ordering may still be valid.

The conclusion concerning the comparison of ordering with JCE III must be different. Whilst the foreseeability of the natural consequences might amount to the

---

[306] See *supra* Sect. 5.1.1.3.

[307] *Haradinaj et al.*, 29 November 2012, para 619.

[308] Ibid., para 619.

[309] See Burghardt 2008, pp. 328–331 and above at Sect. 5.2.1.1.

[310] *Krajišnik*, 17 March 2009, para 662.

[311] See only Ambos 2018, § 7 mn. 30 and Werle and Jessberger 2020, mn. 629–30 on the subjective requirements of JCE liability.

same standard as awareness of the substantial likelihood, it is more likely that a difference exists. This is because a foreseeable consequence implies only the recognition of a possibility. By contrast, the awareness of a substantial likelihood implies a certain degree of probability. Thus, the *mens rea* requirement of ordering is narrower than the one of JCE III.

Additionally, the jurisprudence has renounced a specific intent requirement in JCE III cases. By contrast, in cases of ordering such intent is typically required,[312] rendering its requirements narrower than those of JCE III.

To a certain extent, criminal responsibility for ordering and for participation in a JCE type I or II have overlapping requirements. This means wherever the participation in a JCE type I or II consists of exercising authority towards subordinates in a manner that has a substantial effect, not only on the common plan, but on the commission of a crime, such participation also qualifies as ordering. The same applies *mutatis mutandis* where a participant of a JCE plans or instigates a crime.

Concerning the acts of architects of crimes, it is apparent that under the *ad hoc* tribunals' law ordering does not encompass such conduct. JCE, with its broad "contribution" requirement, does. However, the mode of planning will often overlap with JCE to a large extent where a person engages in the substantial development of plans and organisation of mass atrocities.

5.2.2.2 The Nature of Responsibility

In the view of the tribunals, participation in a JCE entails liability for committing a crime, i.e., as a principal perpetrator. Although criticised especially for type III liability, this has not sparked any changes to the practice at the *ad hoc* tribunals.[313] Responsibility for ordering is mostly referred to as accessorial liability.[314]

The ICTY often did not enter convictions under modes of responsibility besides JCE if the latter could be proven. The trial chamber in *Mladić* took the stance that, although the prosecution had charged the accused with other forms of liability, convicting him for "committing" the crimes for his leading role in different JCEs, would best reflect the totality of his conduct.[315] Together with other ICTY judgments, this shows that JCE is often given priority over other modes of liability.[316] However, the ICTR decision in *Renzaho*, in which JCE was cast aside in favour of a conviction for ordering and aiding and abetting goes in the opposite direction.[317]

---

[312] See on this Sect. 5.1.1.4.

[313] See above Sect. 5.2.1.2.

[314] See also the comparison by Ventura 2019, mn. 9. On the categorisation as secondary liability see above Sect. 5.1.2.

[315] *Mladić*, 22 November 2017, paras 5164–5.

[316] The same explanation can be found in *Karadžić*, 24 March 2016, paras 3525, 4940, 5994; see also *Milutinović et al.*, 26 February 2009, paras 276, 474, in the former paragraph the trial chamber rejects a conviction under JCE and "[a]s a result" turns to other forms of liability.

[317] *Renzaho*, 14 July 2009, para 766 with Footnote 857.

In sum, it can be observed that JCE is undoubtedly regarded as principal liability (commission), while the classification of ordering is somewhat obscure, albeit usually described as accessory liability. It may be for these or other reasons that the tribunals, especially the ICTY, where possible, usually convict for participation in a JCE and often only consider the other modes if JCE cannot be proven.

5.2.2.3 The Relevant Circumstances of the Atrocities Grasped by Ordering and JCE

Comparing the cases and modes of responsibility under which acts were convicted can reveal whether the tribunals follow a stringent policy when applying participation in a JCE or ordering.

It is conceivable participation in a JCE is usually only applied to cases where large scale atrocities must be attributed to a person further removed from the commission of the specific crime, by grace of their position. On the other hand, ordering could possibly only grasp smaller scale cases where the actors directly influence the commission of a single criminal incident. Such a distinction would illustrate that, despite the partly concurrent legal requirements, in the tribunals' views, both modes of liability serve to describe and adjudicate different varieties of responsibility in systemic crime. To evaluate the similarities of the exemplary cases, the following section assesses three characteristics: (1) the spatial and timely extent of criminal incidents, (2) the influence the accused exerted over single criminal incidents attributed to them and (3) the position that the actor held pursuant to his political, administrative, military, or social role.

Spatial and Timely Extent of the Acts and Operations

The allocation of responsibility for numerous crimes, committed at different places and times is of crucial importance when discussing the criminal liability of high-ranking politicians, military officers, and other leaders. If participation in a JCE is better suited to reflect the responsibility of such figureheads, one would expect cases of contributions to a JCE to be mostly large-scale incidents with numerous crimes being attributed to the accused. On the other hand, if ordering cannot appropriately describe the acts of persons who triggered numerous crimes at different times and places, one would expect its application to crimes committed within a limited time frame and area.

However, responsibility for ordering has been attached to both orders for individual incidents and to countrywide actions. On the lower end of the scale, cases such as *Akayesu* serve as examples: the accused ordered the killing of small groups of victims in his custody, who were murdered in front of his office, as well as a killing next to his victims' house.[318]

In cases such as *Gacumbitsi*, *Kamuhanda* and *Semanza*, the area and the number of people affected were larger: the accused gave orders to kill Tutsi who had taken

[318] *Akayesu*, 2 September 1998, paras 268, 308–13.

refuge in large groups at different compound parishes and churches.[319] Although still relatively limited in their spatial and temporal dimension, these cases involved the murder of a large number of people.[320]

Orders can also be carried out and affect people on a local, i.e., communal, or city-wide level. Tharcisse Renzaho was convicted for ordering the killings at roadblocks in the *prefecture* of Kigali-Ville.[321] Similarly, actions on a regional scale can fall under ordering, as the *Brđanin* trial judgment shows. Brđanin was the president of the so-called Crisis Staff of the autonomous Bosnian-Serb Region of Krajina,[322] and as such was found responsible for ordering the persecution of ethnic Bosnian Muslims and Croats.[323] He had been the driving force behind orders given to the relevant municipal bodies to dismiss Muslims and Croats "from basically all areas of employment".[324] Jean Kambanda, Prime Minister of the Interim Government of Rwanda during the genocide, pleaded guilty to, and was convicted of ordering the erection of roadblocks where Tutsi and moderate Hutu were identified and killed. It is plausible to assume that these orders were handed down from the cabinet to be implemented on a countrywide scale, however, neither the indictment nor the judgment specify the scale on which these orders led to the erection of roadblocks and subsequent killings.[325] Apart from this, there is no incident in the ICTY and ICTR jurisprudence where crimes that occurred on a countrywide scale were attributed to a person based on the mode of ordering.

Likewise, an individual's responsibility for participation in a JCE can be affirmed in a wide variety of cases; from participation in criminal schemes limited in their

---

[319] *Kamuhanda*, 22 January 2004, paras 637–51; *Gacumbitsi*, 17 June 2004, paras 152–4; 167–74; *Semanza*, 20 May 2005, para 364; *Gacumbitsi*, 7 July 2006, para 184. For a description of the massacre in the *Semanza* case, see *Semanza*, 15 May 2003, paras 163, 194–206.

[320] *Semanza*, 15 May 2003, paras 163 (the prosecution alleged that there were "several hundred"); *Kamuhanda*, 22 January 2004, para 506 (witnesses estimated the number of the victims to be between one and three thousand, paras 293, 324, 334, 349); *Gacumbitsi*, 17 June 2004, paras 108 (the prosecution charged that several thousand refugees were killed), 118, 123 (a witness's estimation ranged between 12,000 and 30,000), 174 (the chamber eventually found that many of the several thousand people at the Nyarubuye compound were killed).

[321] *Renzaho*, 14 July 2009, paras 116, 766. The appeals chamber quashed this conviction (*Renzaho*, 1 April 2011, paras 316–21), but without voicing any criticism of the application of the form of liability to the situation in general. It is submitted, that the description of Renzaho's conduct and state of mind by the trial chamber, in contrast to the appeals chamber's findings, supports a conviction for ordering genocide. While instructing his subordinates to erect and man roadblocks, Renzaho was aware of the fact that Tutsi and Hutu opposition members would be identified and killed there. Renzaho also possessed the necessary genocidal intent. For this view see ibid., Partially Dissenting Opinion of Judge Güney, paras 3–4, Partially Dissenting Opinion of Judge Pocar, paras 2–6, 8–9, 12 both with references to the trial chamber's findings.

[322] For its establishment and competences see *Brđanin*, 1 September 2004, Part VI. The Regional Level of Authority, paras 163 *et seq.*

[323] Ibid., paras 1063–7.

[324] Ibid., paras 319, 1065.

[325] ICTR, *The Prosecutor v. Jean Kambanda, Indictment* 28 October 1997, ICTR-97-23-DP, para 3.17; *Kambanda*, 4 September 1998, para 39 (xi). It seems clear though that roadblocks were used as a measure to identify and kill Tutsi and moderate Hutu everywhere in the country.

extent to those that expand over an entire country. It is important to note that the temporal and spatial scope of the JCE and that of the crimes attributed due to participation in the JCE can diverge. In *Tadić*, in which the appeals chamber of the ICTY introduced the theory of JCE, the accused was found to have contributed to a criminal plan spanning over the "Prijedor Region",[326] but was "only" attributed responsibility for the killing of five men in the village of Jaskići.[327]

Crimes committed in detention camps pose the next higher level on the scale of temporal and spatial extension of JCE cases. Omarska Camp in the Prijedor region in Bosnia existed from May to August 1992 and had several thousand inmates.[328] The camp enabled a system of ill-treatment in which numerous crimes against humanity were committed against the inmates during the four months of its existence.[329]

The ICTY also found other JCEs on a municipal level, which varied in their duration. The massacres of thousands of Muslim men and boys in Srebrenica that took place in and around the town from 13 to 26 July 1995 qualified as a single criminal enterprise.[330] The campaign of shelling and sniping conducted by Serbian forces to spread terror among the civilian population of Sarajevo constituted a single JCE. This campaign was aimed at the besieged city of Sarajevo and its inhabitants, lasting from 12 May 1992 to November 1995.[331] Both of these JCEs served to allocate responsibility for a range of crimes, which were committed within the time frame and relevant area of the respective JCE.[332]

During the *Karadžić* and *Mladić* trials, the chambers also found that the accused had participated in an "overarching" JCE that comprised the various regions under Bosnian Serb control (Eastern Bosnia, the Sarajevo Region, and the Krajina Region in the West), which aimed to remove non-Serbs from these territories.[333] This common design lasted from October 1991 to November 1995.[334]

---

[326] *Tadić*, 15 July 1999, para 230.

[327] Ibid., paras 232–3.

[328] *Kvočka et al.*, 2 November 2001, paras 17–18, 21.

[329] Ibid., paras 319–320; *Kvočka et al.*, 28 February 2005, paras 182–3.

[330] *Mladić*, 22 November 2017, paras 4970. The enterprise also encompassed the concealment of the crimes, including reburial operations which extended the temporal extension of the enterprise until 1 November 1995, ibid., paras 4922, 4970.

[331] Ibid., para 4740; *Karadžić*, 24 March 2016, paras 4636, 4676.

[332] The earliest incidents of shelling and sniping in Sarajevo which were explicitly attributed to the Bosnian Serb military, and thus to Mladić, happened on 27 May and 13 December 1992 respectively (cf. *Mladić*, 22 November 2017, paras 1922, 2173). The latest confirmed incidents took place on 6 March and 28 August 1995 (ibid., paras 1974, 2150). The killings in Srebrenica were dated between 13 July and mid-August 1995 (ibid., paras 2676, 2882).

[333] *Karadžić*, 24 March 2016, paras 2627, 3463, 3465; *Mladić*, 22 November 2017, paras 3573, 4232.

[334] *Karadžić*, 24 March 2016, para 3463; *Mladić*, 22 November 2017, para 4232; however, the crimes alleged only began in spring 1992 (for the alleged incidents cp. e.g. *Karadžić*, 24 March 2016, paras 624, 730–1, 855) and lasted until 1995, although apparently ending before November (ibid., paras 657, 661).

Vlastimir Đorđević was convicted for having participated in a common criminal design that encompassed the whole of the Kosovo and lasted from October 1998 until June 1999.[335]

At the ICTR, a trial chamber found that a JCE existed from 11 April 1994, which aimed at "the destruction of the Tutsi population in Rwanda".[336]

This account highlights a limited disparity between the scale of crimes committed pursuant to criminal ordering and those attributed pursuant to JCE. Both modes served to attribute responsibility for single incidents (e.g., the murder of a specific number of victims as was the case in *Tadić* and *Akayesu*).

For the attribution of crimes on a countrywide scale through the mode of ordering, only the *Kambanda* case can serve as an example. In *Renzaho*, responsibility was attributed to the accused for the killings at roadblocks, which had lasted for several weeks and were committed in the administrative area of the country's capital.

Responsibility for participation in a JCE served to allocate liability for acts that had been committed over the course of several years and on a countrywide scale. However, despite the common purpose usually being on a larger scale, at times JCE conveyed responsibility for a single incident. Hence, both modes could lead to liability for a single incident or even a single criminal act. The description of the JCE infers a larger margin of action than that of criminal orders. However, this understanding is not mandatory as ordering can grasp criminal conduct committed throughout a long period of time and within a vast area. Finally, it is noteworthy that JCE has been advanced by the ICTY from the beginning as the tool of choice in dealing with mass atrocities in the former Yugoslavia and was given precedence over ordering. The existence of less relevant cases considered under the mode of ordering is a logical result. The existence of judgments pertaining to ordering crimes with vast spatial and temporal margins shows that the mode is not generally unfit to describe such cases.

Influence on the Specific Crime

The influence, which the accused exercised over the specific crimes that were attributed to them, is of special interest when analysing the pertinent cases. If JCE was designed to more appropriately deal with high-level officials, increasingly indirect contributions and, thus, no direct influence on the commission of specific crimes are to be expected. Regarding ordering, it could conversely be expected that the actor usually influences a smaller number of or just a single crime but has greater influence over this crime.

If JCE is specifically suited to attribute responsibility for contributions made on higher levels, one can expect it to be primarily applied to conduct concerning the establishment and maintenance of the overall machinery behind mass atrocities, as

[335] *Đorđević*, 23 February 2011, paras 2000, 2129–30; the crimes attributed to him began in January 1999 cp. Ibid., para 1615 for the crime of deportation.

[336] *Karemera*, 2 February 2012, paras 1453–4; the judgment is not as specific with regards to the specific underlying criminal acts, but refers to crimes committed between April and June 1994, cp. e.g. ibid., paras 1649, 1666.

well as to broad directives and guidelines concerning this machinery and the general commission of criminal acts. If that were the focus of ICTY and ICTR jurisprudence, it could be deduced that JCE was devised as a systemic model for the attribution of responsibility, tailored specifically to adjudicate the wrongdoing of decision makers and architects of international crimes.

Ordering, in turn, would only grasp cases in which the systemic function of the actor is reduced to specific instructions concerning a precisely shaped scope of crimes. Instructions with a broader but less specific influence would not be adjudicated under ordering but be grasped by JCE.

The issue of influence over a crime is not to be confounded with the causality requirement in a strict sense. Some conditions may be *conditio sine qua non* for the later commission of a crime, but only influence the extent to which the crime is committed in a vague way. Other conditions may shape the specific crime in terms of means, time, or place without being *conditio sine qua non,* if it is evident from the overall situation that the physical perpetrators would have committed the crime anyways.

The ICTR's jurisprudence is particularly helpful when analysing the influence of ordering actors on the specific crimes. In *Akayesu*, the accused had told persons over whom he held authority that they should kill their respective victims, which they proceeded to do immediately.[337] A similar situation was found in the case of Pauline Nyiramasuhuko. Upon arriving at the administrative building of a Rwandan *prefecture*, where Tutsi were taking refuge, she told the accompanying militia to enter the building and kill and rape Tutsi.[338] The influence of these people on the commission of the crime was direct and comprehensive: their instructions were most likely causal in the sense of a *conditio sine qua non*. Additionally, they oversaw the crime directly, communicated with the physical perpetrators and told them explicitly how to proceed. Their influence on the specific crimes was thus comparatively strong. The crimes that ensued were then limited to a group of victims identifiable due to their identity, or their presence at a certain place. The crimes were limited as to the perpetrators and their means as well, as Nyiramasuhuko and Akayesu each directed a specific group of individuals.

In the cases of *Renzaho* and *Brđanin*, the influence was less direct, as both cases involved intermediaries, however the tracing of a causal line is nevertheless possible. In *Renzaho*, the tribunal found that the accused had ordered the erection of roadblocks, which he knew were used to stop, identify, and kill Tutsis.[339] He issued these orders to his subordinate administrative functionaries who then carried them out.[340] Militias then staffed the roadblocks and killed Tutsi. Renzaho's orders were thus causal conditions for the crimes committed at the newly erected roadblocks. However, his personal influence over the single specific acts of perpetration was limited. He

[337] *Akayesu*, 2 September 1998, paras 218, 269, 648, 658, 668.

[338] *Nyiramasuhuko*, 24 June 2011, paras 5867–70.

[339] *Renzaho*, 14 July 2009, paras 116, 766.

[340] On Renzaho's influence over the *conseillers*, who were his direct subordinates and organized the road blocks see ibid., para 754.

vaguely determined the time in which the crimes were to begin, as it was only a matter of time before the first murder would be committed. Although, he did not directly command the physical perpetrators, nor specify the time and date, Renzaho could be relatively sure of the ensuing acts, thus knowing the general shape of the subsequent crimes.

In *Brđanin*, the accused had signed a directive to exclude non-Serbs from seeking employment which qualified as a crime of persecution (a crime against humanity).[341] A causal line from the committee which decided the discriminatory measure to the municipal authorities who enacted it, is visible. However, like the *Renzaho* case, Radoslav Brđanin did not influence the specific crimes. He chose neither the victims, nor time, date or physical perpetrators (as far as they were required for the legal discrimination enacted by the accused). Yet, he could be relatively certain the crimes that would be committed.

We can thus see that both types of conduct, specific orders and broad instructions, can be regarded as ordering crimes, if they lead to the commission of the crime.

As could be expected, the ICTY's jurisprudence allows an insight on the influence of specific crimes, exercised by members of a JCE. Duško Tadić, with whom the JCE doctrine originated, contributed to the criminal enterprise in the Prijedor region *inter alia* by taking part in the attack on the village of Jaskići during which he rounded up and severely beat some of the men.[342] As he was aware of the risk that people would also be killed during this operation and took part in it nevertheless, he was convicted for participating in a JCE (type III).[343] Although little is known about Tadić's personal acts in the moment when the killing took place, the influence he exerted over the crime—if he exerted any at all—can be assessed as specific and focused on the single incident. His contribution lay in his participation in the rounding up and beating of a group of men, some of whom were later shot. Thus, his influence only extended over this incident of which he was a participant.

Moreover, Ratko Mladić contributed to the Srebrenica JCE *inter alia* by issuing orders to military and police units in Srebrenica. The orders included instructions to forcibly evacuate women, children, and elderly people from Srebrenica and to relocate Muslim men to locations where some of them would later be executed.[344] These contributions were direct in their influence over the specific crime, albeit to different degrees. When Mladić ordered the deportation of inhabitants from Srebrenica, he exercised direct influence over the commission of the crime against humanity of deportation and inhumane acts (forcible transfer).[345] His subordinates began to carry out the order within hours and the order affected a quantifiable number of victims,

---

[341] *Brđanin*, 1 September 2004, paras 9, 168, 1050.

[342] *Tadić*, 15 July 1999, paras 230–2.

[343] Ibid., para 232.

[344] *Mladić*, 22 November 2017, paras 5004, 5010 (for the killings that later took place at the elementary school see para 2917), 5052, 5065.

[345] For Mladić's conviction see ibid., para 5214.

as it only concerned Bosnian Muslim persons within the Srebrenica area.[346] On the other hand, Mladić ordered the transfer of a group of detained men from a football field to detention facilities. The men were then executed within the following days.[347] Whether his orders to relocate these detainees were causal to their death is difficult to determine. The JCE encompassing the killing of Bosnian men had already been initiated, but whether they would have been murdered elsewhere is unclear.[348] Hence, by giving the relocation order, Mladić at the very least influenced time, date, and location of the later crime, while the potential victims were already identifiable.

In other cases, contributions to a JCE could hardly be described as having a formative influence on any specific crime. However, they fulfilled the broader "significant contribution" requirement, with some also being *conditio sine qua non* for the subsequent crimes. This holds true especially for persons who contributed to the common purpose through acts on a political, administrative, or organizational level.

Vlastimir Đorđević was an assistant minister of the Serbian Ministry of the Interior and, as such, held power over special police units.[349] The trial chamber found that from October 1998, a JCE to modify the ethnic balance of Kosovo existed. It encompassed waging a campaign of terror against the Kosovo Albanian population.[350] The accused significantly contributed to this plan *inter alia* by incorporating paramilitary units into the Serbian security forces. He deployed those units to Kosovo, where they committed crimes against civilians.[351] He also arranged the hiding of bodies and prevented judicial investigations into the crimes.[352] The deployment of troops was causal for their commission of crimes. However, Đorđević's influence on single criminal incidents was limited as he was apparently not concerned with giving operational orders to these units. Thus, he had no influence over whether and where these paramilitaries would act and if they would commit crimes.[353] The orders to conceal the bodies of victims and to refrain from judicial investigations were seen as a significant contribution to the JCE. However, they did not influence the crimes, as these had already been committed.

---

[346] In the findings of the chamber, Mladić ordered the transfer from Srebrenica/Potočari to the territory held by the army of Bosnia and Herzegovina on 12 July 1995, and the transfers began that same day, see ibid., paras 2982–3.

[347] Ibid., para 5010.

[348] The transfer from the football field to the elementary school was arranged on 13 July 1995 (ibid., para 5010), the JCE with the purpose of killing the able-bodied men of Srebrenica had been initiated on or around 11 July 1995 (ibid., para 4970).

[349] Cf. e.g. *Đorđević*, 23 February 2011, paras 40, 42, 61–2.

[350] Ibid., para 2007.

[351] Ibid., paras 2021, 2155.

[352] Ibid., para 2156.

[353] The trial placed the emphasis on the accused's incorporation of the paramilitary group called the "Scorpions" into the special police forces, despite his knowledge of their criminal background. It was also alleged that the accused had missed anticipating the group's commission of crimes and had failed to investigate their acts. Cf. ibid., paras 1944, 1948 (on the activities of the paramilitary unit), 1953, 1955 (on the accused's knowledge of crimes committed earlier by the unit), 2155 (personal involvement in the implementation of paramilitary units into the police and their deployment to Kosovo).

Radovan Karadžić was convicted *inter alia* because of his participation in the overarching JCE to create an ethnically homogeneous Serb state.[354] Its common purpose entailed the commission of large numbers of crimes, including persecution, extermination, and deportation as crimes against humanity.[355]

According to the chamber, Karadžić laid "the ground-work for the criminal implementation through the creation of, and support for, the structures and bodies which carried out the plan."[356] The accused distributed and promoted instructions that were vital for the establishment of Bosnian Serb Crisis Staffs. He oversaw their implementation and decided how they would function, which the chamber evaluated as his exercise of authority.[357] Additionally, Karadžić used his power over political, governmental, and military structures to further the objective of removing the Bosnian Muslims and Croats from Serb-claimed territory.[358] He also activated instructions that were "intimately linked to the physical control of Bosnian Serb claimed territory". The ensuing takeover of power resulted in widespread crimes against Bosnian Muslims and Croats.[359] Finally, Karadžić issued orders to the military, sometimes to corps and brigade commanders directly and exercised his authority over police forces.[360] The latter shows that Karadžić indeed acted from a position with the power to directly influence specific criminal incidents. However, the manifold other activities through which he contributed to the JCE were of a more detached, abstract nature not typically involving the exertion of influence over the commission of individual crimes. Undoubtedly, his instructions leading to the physical takeover of territories by Bosnian Serb forces could mark the beginning of widespread crimes. However, he did not influence the means used, the exact acts committed, or the specific victims. Nor did he communicate with the physical perpetrators, as the municipal crisis staffs and various military and police commanders existed as intermediaries.

These cases show that ordering and participation in a JCE can describe the criminal liability attached to acts with differing degrees of influence on the specific crimes. Parallel to the spatial and temporal extent, the influence exerted over single criminal incidents changes with the broadening of the stage. This is of little surprise, considering that high-level decision makers and architects usually do "not get their hands dirty". The comparison reveals that there is little variation in the influence between the accused convicted under different forms of liability. The *Akayesu, Nyiramasuhuko* and *Tadić* cases saw convictions for ordering and participation in a JCE alike for acts that only concerned a single criminal incident. In the *Renzaho, Brđanin, Mladić* and *Karadžić* cases, ordering and participation in a JCE were used to describe acts of individuals who were not personally present when or shortly before the crimes were committed. With the exception of Brđanin, they did not act to have certain crimes or

[354] *Karadžić*, 24 March 2016, para 3463.

[355] Ibid., para 3524.

[356] Ibid., para 3475.

[357] Ibid., para 3478.

[358] Ibid., para 3480.

[359] Ibid., para 3484.

[360] Ibid., paras 3489–91.

acts committed that would fall under a predestined legal description. Instead, they made decisions, which would lead to the commission of crimes without defining what would happen specifically. The future perpetrators were defined only by their affiliation with the actors' party in the conflict or widespread attack on the civilian population. The victims were unknown and defined by the area affected and by their belonging to a group, usually an ethnic or religious one. Because the accused operated on different levels, it must be ascertained whether the cases differed greatly in terms of influence over the specific crime. The acts by Renzaho and Mladić that led to numerous crimes in Kigali and Srebrenica were carried out swiftly and involved few intermediary measures. The decisions made by Brđanin, and particularly Karadžić, were of a more general, directive nature and often required implementation by the municipal administrations, and in Karadžić's case on higher military levels. Notwithstanding these differences, it would be wrong to describe the influence that Renzaho and Mladić exerted as decisively different from that of Brđanin and Karadžić. This is because the different levels at which they operated did not make any difference in terms of their direct influence over certain crimes. The policies the four men followed and goals they sought to implement defined the scope of actions that would affect the victims and thus the scope of possible (and foreseeable) crimes.[361]

Therefore, it can be observed that no general difference in terms of personal influence on specific crimes existed between cases in which the tribunals applied ordering or participation in a JCE. The differences lay in the presence of the accused during the commission of the crimes; whether they were present on the ground, influencing specific instances of criminal behaviour or whether they were removed from the scene, influencing only the pattern of crimes, but not specific crimes.

Position of the Actor: Political, Administrative, Military, or Social Authority

Another crucial characteristic is the position of the accused within politics, the administration, the military or in civil society. If responsibility for participating in a JCE was best suited to describe the liability of high-ranking personnel, one could expect that JCE cases would predominantly concern the members of the highest political and military echelons while lower ranking decision makers would be convicted for ordering. Whether this holds true is assessed in the following, keeping in mind that, from a legal perspective, participation in a JCE does not demand a position of authority from the actor, whereas ordering does.[362]

Indeed, many of those convicted on grounds of participation in a JCE at the ICTY were officials in the upper classes of the political, administrative, and military elite. Among them were Radovan Karadžić (the president and commander-in-chief), Ratko Mladić (the commander of the highest operative body of the army of the Bosnian

[361] In *Karadžić*, this was the creation of a homogeneous Serb state in Bosnia and Herzegovina which would require the expulsion of Bosnian Muslims and Croats from the claimed territory. In *Brđanin*, the same held true for the autonomous region Krajina. In *Mladić*, the policies included the expulsion of all Muslims from Srebrenica and the killing of the Muslim men. In *Renzaho*, the policy was the widespread attack on the Tutsi civilian population.

[362] See the comparison above at Sect. 5.2.2.1.

Serb "Republika Srpska")[363] and Momčilo Krajišnik (president of the Bosnian-Serb Assembly of the Republika Srpska)[364]. An assistant minister to the Serbian Minister for the Interior was also involved.[365] The president of the Republic of Serbia (and later of the Federal Republic of Yugoslavia), Slobodan Milošević was indicted on grounds of participation in various JCEs (concerning Croatia, Bosnia and Herzegovina and Kosovo), but died before trial.[366] At the ICTR, some of those convicted of participating in a JCE, held high positions in the state apparatus as well. Among them were the Minister of the Interior of the interim government, as well as the Chairman of the most influential party behind the interim government of the *génocidaires*.[367] Many of the other convicted were not in the highest echelons of government, yet, they held governmental, administrative, or military positions in the state apparatus, which equipped them with power and the competence to make decisions.[368] However, some of those convicted for participation in a JCE held positions that did not exert any authority whatsoever. Duško Tadić played a minor role in the raid on the village Jaskići yet was convicted for participating in a JCE.[369]

On the other hand, many of those convicted for giving orders that led to crimes held positions of authority in the middle tier of government, military and/or society: they were communal mayors, such as the Rwandan *bourgmestres*, prefects of cities or municipalities, military commanders or the presidents of regional councils.[370]

---

[363] *Karadžić*, 24 March 2016, paras 2, 167; *Mladić*, 22 November 2017, paras 265, 275–6.

[364] *Krajišnik*, 27 September 2006, para 4.

[365] *Đorđević*, 23 February 2011, paras 38–40

[366] ICTY, *Prosecutor v. Slobodan Milošević, Second amended Indictment "Kosovo "*, 16 October 2001, IT-99-37-PT, paras 3, 16; ICTY, *Prosecutor v. Slobodan Milošević, Amended indictment "Bosnia and Herzegovina"*, 22 November 2002, IT-02-54-T, paras 4, 6; ICTY, *Prosecutor v. Slobodan Milošević, Second amended Indictment "Croatia"*, 28 July 2004, IT-02-54-T, paras 4, 6.

[367] See the description and conviction of: Édouard Karemera in *Karemera*, 2 February 2012, paras 4, 1457; Matthieu Ngirumpatse in ibid., paras 10, 1458.

[368] Radislav Krstić had been the General of the "Drina Corps" a military formation of the Bosnian Serb Army that was deeply involved in the massacres of Srebrenica, where Krstić had also been present, see *Krstić*, 2 August 2001, paras 3, 631. Zdravko Tolimir was an Assistant Commander and Chief of Intelligence and Security of the Main Staff of the Bosnian Serb Army, and as such involved in the Srebrenica massacre, see *Tolimir*, 12 December 2012, para 2; Ljubiša Beara and Vujadin Popović both held different ranks as security officers and were Tolimir's subordinates, and as such participated in the Srebrenica JCE (ICTY, *Prosecutor v. Vujadin Popović et al.* , 10 June 2010, IT-05-88-T, paras 1090, 1168, 1202, 1302). Aloys Simba had been an influential figure in Rwandan society, but did not hold any official position at the time when he participated in a JCE that encompassed the massacre of Tutsi refugees (*Simba*, 13 December 2005, paras 56–7, 403–6).

[369] *Tadić*, 15 July 1999, 230–3, see also the description of Tadić beating men during the raid of a village, constituting his contribution to the JCE, at *Tadić*, 7 May 1997, paras 352–3.

[370] Jean-Paul Akayesu and Sylvestre Gacumbitsi had been *bourgmestres*, and as such the administrative and traditional heads of the Rwandan municipal units of *communes* (cp. *Akayesu*, 2 September 1998, paras 56–77; *Gacumbitsi*, 17 June 2004, paras 5–6). Tharcisse Renzaho was the first prefect of Kigali-Ville prefecture, and as such the (civilian) guarantor of peace, superior of the subordinate levels of administrative functionaries and simultaneously retained his rank as a colonel of the army (see *Renzaho*, 14 July 2009, paras 80–1, 754). Radoslav Brđanin headed the influential crisis staff

However, others held higher positions, such as those of ministers.[371] Finally, Jean Kambanda, the president of the interim government of Rwanda pled guilty to the charge of ordering the commission of crimes.[372]

In summary, whilst a number of those convicted for participating in a JCE held higher political or military positions, the application of JCE was all but limited to those cases. Instead, it stretched over all tiers of decision makers down to actors who held no superior position at all. Fewer instances of actors in the highest echelons of states can be identified for cases of ordering, yet such cases existed. As ordering requires some form of authority,[373] none of those convicted under ordering completely lacked a position of such authority.

No Significant Factual Differences in Cases Grasped by JCE and Ordering

As illustrated, the two modes of responsibility are largely used to adjudicate actors in the same cases. There is no stringent policy determining which cases warrant a conviction under participation in a JCE and which under ordering. Instead, it is conceivable that other considerations and the tribunals' willingness to apply the respective modes of liability influenced the choice of these modes. These considerations could have included a potential lack of evidence to prove the explicit modes of liability under the *ad hoc* tribunals' statutes (i.e., lack of evidence for a specific order), or the wish to apply a mode of liability that undoubtedly refers to the convicted as principal perpetrators.[374] Finally, a doctrinal view on the relation between forms of perpetration and participation—i.e. a relation in which principal liability always takes precedence over accessory liability—may also lie at the heart of this preference.

5.2.2.4 Conclusion: Significant Similarities of Legal Requirements and Relevant Circumstances

The comparison of the legal and factual elements that shape the application of the modes of responsibility of ordering and participation in a JCE at the ICTY and ICTR revealed considerable similarities. However, two striking differences have been singled out.

First, through its broad "significant contribution" requirement in the *actus reus,* JCE can be applied to what has been termed architects of crimes for the purpose of this book. This is because any kind of (sufficiently significant, indirect) link to the crime can suffice to attribute liability. The contribution of a planner or organizer in

of the autonomous region of Krajina which comprised many municipalities in western Bosnia and Herzegovina (*Brđanin*, 1 September 2004, paras 1–9).

371 Pauline Nyiramasuhuko was the Minister of Family and Women's Development under the interim government during the genocide of 1994 in Rwanda (*Nyiramasuhuko*, 24 June 2011, para 8).

372 Cf. *Kambanda*, 4 September 1998, para 39 (xi); with this he adhered to the charges brought forward by the prosecution, see *Kambanda Indictment*, 28 October 1997, para 3.17.

373 See above Sect. 5.1.1.2.

374 See Sect. 5.2.1.2 on the nature of responsibility for participation in a JCE.

a crucial coordinating position can thus be grasped as participation in a JCE. This is not the case under ordering; if the actor does not instruct the direct perpetrators or does not issue instructions with authority but asks another higher-ranking individual to give the order, liability for ordering will not occur. This means that while JCE indeed gives rise to criminal responsibility for certain architects and decision makers of crimes, ordering only serves to grasp the latter. It is conceivable that responsibility for planning a crime can equally serve under the *ad hoc* tribunals' law to describe and adjudicate the conduct of architects of crimes. However, this is outside the scope of this book.

The second difference concerns the nature of liability. Principal liability only follows for participation in a JCE, whilst ordering is more commonly associated with accessory liability.

With the restriction to decision makers, the question arises whether the head of ordering would be better suited to address their responsibility in front of the *ad hoc* tribunals. The potential of this form of responsibility to describe the conduct of decision makers successfully and convincingly is therefore evaluated in the subsequent sections.

5.2.3 Ordering as an Alternative Mode of Responsibility to JCE in Leadership Cases Before the Ad Hoc *Tribunals*

The following section assesses whether the conventional mode of ordering (and occasionally of planning) could have been applied convincingly in certain cases, chosen from the jurisprudence of the tribunals.

The analysis necessarily rests on the findings of the tribunals. Difficulties may therefore arise when determining facts relevant for a mode of responsibility that was not charged or examined by the respective chamber. The analysis will also consider that a prosecutor may have different reasons to charge acts under a certain mode of liability. For example, where someone is believed to have played a crucial role, but evidence only shows their involvement in a supportive manner, a prosecutor might charge the individual with participation in a JCE or aiding and abetting because it is unlikely that other modes will clear the burden of proof. In cases with evidence for specific direct instructions to commit crimes, the prosecution and/or chamber may have other reasons to charge or adjudicate under the mode of JCE. These could include the belief that this mode best describes the criminal liability and expresses the degree of responsibility and blameworthiness of the actor. Ultimately, the findings of this section will contribute to answering whether it was reasonable to treat participation in a JCE as the preferable mode of responsibility while relying on its perceived ability to appropriately describe the accused's conduct.

5.2.3.1 Ratko Mladić's Participation in the Srebrenica Massacre

Ratko Mladić was convicted for his contributions to the Srebrenica JCE, which aimed to murder the able–bodied Muslim men of Srebrenica and forcibly deport the women, children and elderly.[375] The chamber found that his contribution to the JCE consisted *inter alia* of issuing several orders to the VRS forces, which concerned the operation in and around Srebrenica.[376] The question is whether the chamber's findings would have carried a conviction of Mladić for ordering as well.

It seems almost superfluous to state that large-scale crimes were committed in the Srebrenica area beginning on 12 July 1995, including genocide and extermination, murder, persecution, and other inhumane acts (forcible transfer).[377] The trial chamber determined that, when contributing to the JCE, Mladić acted with the necessary intent regarding the commission of the above-mentioned crimes and that he fulfilled the special intent requirements.[378]

As determined above, Ratko Mladić would have fulfilled the authority requirement had he been in a position to compel others to commit a crime by giving them orders.[379]

Mladić was the commander of the main staff of the Bosnian Serb Army.[380] The chamber described the main staff as being responsible for the planning and conduct of operations on the strategic level.[381] The commanders of the units involved were present at Srebrenica,[382] meaning that Mladić could exercise authority over them directly and thus over their troops.

Mladić took over command of all units engaged in combat in Srebrenica when he arrived on 11 July 1995.[383] During the Srebrenica massacres, he continuously issued orders to those units.[384] He retained command and control over the VRS main staff and continued giving orders, which were implemented.[385] Later he stated that the important decisions had all been made by an inner core of officials, including himself.[386] Consequently, the necessary position of authority of Ratko Mladić could have been proven.

Determining whether Mladić's personal conduct sufficed to establish the *actus reus* of ordering is more complicated. The list of contributions to the JCE, which

375 *Mladić*, 22 November 2017, para 4987, 5098.

376 Ibid., para 5097.

377 Ibid., para 5098.

378 Ibid., paras 5130–1.

379 See above Sect. 5.1.1.2.

380 *Mladić*, 22 November 2017, paras 275–6, 5047.

381 Ibid., para 265.

382 See e.g. Ibid., para 5000; for the position of Radislav Krstić, see *Krstić*, 2 August 2001, paras 3, 631.

383 *Mladić*, 22 November 2017, para 4995.

384 Ibid., paras 5049–50, 5097.

385 Ibid, para 5053.

386 *Mladić*, 22 November 2017, para 5045.

was provided in the trial judgment, does not include the direct ordering of the large-scale murders.[387] Instead, the judgment abstractly summarizes that Mladić *inter alia* "gave orders" to different recipients (VRS and law enforcement units) and provided misleading information on the whereabouts of the Muslim men and boys of Srebrenica in the aftermath of the massacres. However, the judgment contains a considerable number of circumstantial details regarding Mladić's involvement in Srebrenica.

Shortly before the killings started on 12 July 1995, Mladić held a meeting with military and civilian police commanders. He apparently attended this meeting for about 50 minutes.[388] Later on the same day, he ordered the (forcible) transfer of Bosnian Muslim women, children and elderly people from the village of Potočari to the town of Kladanj (outside of the Bosnian-Serb held area at this point).[389] On 13 July, he toured the area and visited surrounding villages.[390] At a football field, he inspected the men and boys that were detained there and later that day ordered their transfer to an elementary school. About 50 of these detainees were later shot at the school.[391] Additionally, the chamber received evidence that Mladić had ordered the execution of ten detainees on or about 23 July 1995.[392]

Of these acts, only two would qualify as ordering at first glance: The order to forcibly transfer the population of Srebrenica into the territory held by the army of Bosnia and Herzegovina, and the order to shoot ten civilians or prisoners of war on 23 July. However, the tribunals can also consider circumstantial evidence when inferring whether an accused gave an order to commit a crime.[393]

In this regard, a conversation between two officers becomes important. The chamber found that the officers met the morning of 12 July, shortly after the meeting which Mladić had held. In this conversation one officer told the other that all abled-bodied men should be killed, and they discussed potential detention and execution sites.[394] Ratko Mladić had not only participated in that meeting early on 12 July but had also been the highest-ranking commander there. The chamber seemingly determined that this meeting had some effect on the crimes encompassed by the JCE. However, it could have reasonably concluded that during this meeting, or during the preceding night, Mladić gave an order concerning the killing of Muslim men and boys in Srebrenica.[395] This holds all the truer because the chamber stressed Mladić's

[387] Ibid., para 5097–8.

[388] Ibid., paras 4970, 5000, 5067.

[389] Ibid., paras 5003–4.

[390] Ibid., para 5007.

[391] Ibid., para 5010, 5065.

[392] Ibid., para 5039.

[393] See above Sect. 5.1.1.1.

[394] This conversation between officers Popović and Nikolić transpired "prior to the third Hotel Fontana meeting", which took place at about 10 a.m. on 12 July, and thus after the early morning meeting, which has been mentioned before. *Mladić*, 22 November 2017, paras 2470, 4978.

[395] The chamber stated that the JCE initially encompassed the crimes of persecution and inhumane acts (forcible transfer), but that genocide, extermination and murder became part of the envisaged means "by the early morning of 12 July 1995", see ibid., para 5096.

control and command over the units in Srebrenica during the massacres. Together with Mladić's participation in the relevant meetings, this makes it seem more than unlikely, that the subsequent murder operation was not based on an instruction from the highest-ranking commander present.

Other pieces of evidence could have also served to prove or substantiate Mladić giving orders. Mladić was present when the women, children and elderly were forced into the busses for transfer and the men were violently separated from them. Furthermore, members of the special police who separated the families said they were acting on Mladić's orders.[396] During the day of 12 July, Mladić stated that he wanted to interrogate men between 16 and 60 years as they were potential soldiers and he wanted to screen them for war criminals.[397] Furthermore, on 13 July Mladić used a certain hand gesture which a witness understood to mean that the prisoners should be killed.[398]

It is important to delineate between liability for active behaviour and command responsibility which attaches to the failure of military commanders to act. In the case of Mladić, however, the mentioned evidence does not support an image of him as a helpless by-stander or commander without far-reaching power over his troops or knowledge of their acts. Instead, it paints a picture of Mladić acting out his position of the highest military rank; the commander-in-chief on the ground who was present (and involved) when the momentous decisions were made, and who intended the commission of the crimes.

It is furthermore conceivable that the involved forces, the executioners of the crimes, felt compelled to act when receiving instructions from their superiors. As commander-in-chief of all the troops in Srebrenica, Mladić exerted (chain-)authority over the physical executioners whenever they felt compelled to act due to their direct superiors' orders.

Hence, the trial chamber could have affirmed the objective elements for Mladić ordering the massacres at Srebrenica.

Given that Mladić's act significantly contributed to the JCE in Srebrenica, his orders should have also had at least a direct and substantial effect on the commission of the crimes.

Regarding *mens rea* for the specific mode of ordering, no problems should have arisen. There could have been little doubt that the accused was well aware of his central position, and of the fact that his acts and the orders he had given would lead to the commission of such crimes.

In summary, it is probable that the chamber could have convicted Mladić for ordering the crimes at Srebrenica and its surroundings that began on 12 July 1995.

The decision to murder the able-bodied men in the enclave of Srebrenica was apparently conceived in the night leading up to or in the early morning of 12 July 1995. Thus, one may also consider whether Mladić was responsible for planning the crimes of genocide, crimes against humanity and war crimes.

---

[396] Ibid., para 5006.

[397] Ibid., para 5005.

[398] Ibid., paras 5119–20, 5127.

Ratko Mladić's case therefore shows how circumstantial evidence can be sufficient to establish that a direct order to commit crimes must have existed. Many details which the chamber of the ICTY used to establish Mladić's contribution to the Srebrenica JCE could have served as evidence that, at some point, he must have ordered the commission of these crimes. Given his authority over the involved forces, the chamber's findings leave little doubt that it existed.

In such a case, it is questionable whether listing contributions to a JCE paints a clear picture of the convict's participation. It is true that Mladić conferred with many officers and other officials when conceiving the crimes. However, the most relevant conduct must have been the final decision and instruction to commence the killing; a decision which was his to make at this point. It is therefore probable that Mladić could have been convicted for ordering the Srebrenica massacre.

5.2.3.2 Radovan Karadžić's Participation in the Srebrenica Massacre

Radovan Karadžić was also convicted for participating in the Srebrenica JCE. However, his role was different to Mladić's. Karadžić was the political leader of the Republika Srpska, the Serbian Bosnian political and territorial entity, and he was neither on the ground nor involved in the meetings with Mladić and the other officers of the Srebrenica JCE. An examination of this case is imperative when exploring the possibilities, the tribunals might have had to convict high-level participants in crimes under the mode of ordering.

Actus Reus—Giving an Order, Authority, Causal Nexus

Karadžić held a position of authority, which was both *de jure* and *de facto* and stretched not only over the civilian administration, but also over the Bosnian Serb military, of which he was the commander in chief.[399] He also exercised such authority several times during the events in Srebrenica.[400]

The chamber described various ways in which Karadžić influenced the events. He ordered the establishment of Bosnian Serb municipal structures and promoted a man named Deronjić to be their chief.[401] Karadžić gave orders which limited the entry of humanitarian aid convoys and thus of international access to the enclave.[402] In addition, he ordered Deronjić to organize the transfer of a large group of Muslim men to a place where they were consequently killed.[403] Furthermore, he declared a state of war over Srebrenica, which enabled the military and police units to avoid lengthy administrative procedures to obtain material and personnel, which they used for the killing operation.[404] The first of these acts, the above-mentioned order to

[399] *Karadžić*, 24 March 2016, paras 2, 167.
[400] See the summary in ibid., paras 5817–9.
[401] Ibid., paras 226, 5761, 5817.
[402] Ibid., paras 5757–8, 5817.
[403] Ibid., paras 5805, 5818, 5830.
[404] Ibid., paras 5779, 5819.

move detainees, directly led to killings. In relation to this, it was found that an officer of the Bosnian Serb military had explained in a briefing that he had orders "from two presidents" to "get rid" of the detainees.[405] Additionally, the chamber found that when Deronjić discussed the movement of the detainees after talking to Karadžić, the decision to murder them had already been made.[406] The chamber asserted that the order of events showed the "malign intent" behind Karadžić's order to move the prisoners and inferred his agreement to the plan of killing the Muslim men and boys of the enclave.[407] The killings that followed this specific order resulted in the death of at least 4,204 Bosnian Muslim men and boys.[408] In light of these findings, the chamber could have also found that Karadžić had ordered the killing of these detainees. This order would be inferred from the circumstances described above and one would have to conclude that such an order was implied in Karadžić's instruction to move the detainees. It is likely that the general instruction to murder these civilians already existed when the order to move them was given by Karadžić in the evening of 13 July 1995. Even then, it could be concluded that his specific order functioned as the trigger for the killing operation.

In light of Karadžić's position it is highly likely that his instructions to his newly appointed civilian commissioner, Deronjić, compelled the latter to set the movement of the detainees in motion.[409] It is conceivable that the executioners knew that the orders to relocate the detainees came from Karadžić and thus also inferred their subsequent fate. Such an inference could be derived from the explanation given by officers that the orders to kill came from "two presidents". The executioners may therefore have felt compelled to kill the detainees once they were transferred, aware of the general plan that this should be done.

On the other hand, some acts and omissions rather portray Karadžić as a well-informed, approving spectator, acting to keep himself informed of events on the ground and supporting the actions through his instructions. Apart from the order that led to the relocation and subsequent killing of at least 4000 Muslim men, the facts do not seem to support a conviction for ordering the remaining crimes in Srebrenica. However, in the jurisprudence of the *ad hoc* tribunals, an order did not need to be *sine qua non* to trigger responsibility for ordering a crime. Thus, one must ask whether Karadžić's orders with limited effect on the commission of the crimes would have sufficed to convict him for ordering the remaining massacres and the deportation of Muslims from Srebrenica.

The establishment of the Bosnian Serb municipal administrative structure and the declaration of the state of war both facilitated the commission of the crimes.[410]

---

[405] Ibid., para 5818.

[406] Ibid., paras 5772–3, 5805, 5818, 5830.

[407] Ibid., paras 5805, 5830.

[408] Cp. the findings at ibid., paras 5307 *et seq.*, especially 5354, 5382, 5413, 5464.

[409] Ibid., para 5817.

[410] Ibid., paras 5817, 5819.

Additionally, Karadžić limited and partially prohibited the access of representatives of the international community to Srebrenica.[411]

However, even if those orders contributed to the commission of the crimes, Karadžić's authority must have compelled the physical perpetrators to commit the crimes. This cannot be affirmed for his orders to establish Bosnian Serb municipal structures, the declaration of a state of war and keeping representatives of the international community out of the area. The execution of such orders might have substantially furthered the commission of crimes, but the consequent acts (raising of administrative structures, prohibiting access etc.) did not constitute the physical commission of crimes. Whoever carried out these tasks did not commit the crimes of genocide, crimes against humanity and war crimes by doing so.

The chamber could therefore not have convicted Karadžić for ordering crimes with respect to these instructions.

Mens Rea

As to *mens rea*, the tribunal found that Karadžić possessed the necessary mental element for war crimes, crimes against humanity and genocide, as well as the special intent for the latter. Had it desired to convict him for ordering the crimes, the chamber would have had to establish that Karadžić was also aware of the substantial likelihood that genocide and the other crimes would occur because of his orders. It can be assumed that Karadžić knew of the weight and impact his orders had on the crimes in Srebrenica, and that he could be certain that he would further them by issuing the abovementioned instructions.

The chamber distinguished between Karadžić's *mens rea* before and after he learned of the commencement of killings in Srebrenica. It found that he became aware of Mladić and the other commanders' new plan to murder the Bosnian Muslim men and boys on 13 July 1995.[412] Based on this, Karadžić could not have fulfilled the *mens rea* of genocide when he established municipal structures in Srebrenica and control over humanitarian access because these had been ordered previously.[413] However, these actions have already been found not to have fulfilled the *actus reus* either and are therefore of no relevance.

The phone conversation, during which Karadžić became aware of and decided to support the massacres, took place on the evening of 13 July 1995. The evidence would have thus sufficed to find Karadžić guilty of ordering the killing of at least 4,204 Bosnian Muslim men and boys who were moved from Bratunac to Zvornik and murdered there.[414]

Conclusion on Karadžić Ordering the Srebrenica Massacres

Notwithstanding the instances of Karadžić's conduct that would not have fulfilled the *actus reus* of ordering, the chamber could have found Radovan Karadžić guilty

[411] Ibid., paras 5799, 5817.

[412] Ibid., para 5811.

[413] Ibid., paras 5761, 5757–8, 5811.

[414] Ibid., paras 5805, 5811, 5818.

of ordering war crimes, crimes against humanity and genocide with respect to the killing of at least 4,204 Bosnian Muslim men and boys. He did so by ordering the transfer of these men and boys to a place where they would be murdered. Through this act, he signalled his support and approval of the genocidal plans, which in turn would have a compelling effect on the executioners and thus have a substantial effect on the subsequent crimes.

In sum, Karadžić could have been allocated responsibility for a range of crimes committed in Srebrenica through ordering. His declaration of a state of war would have most likely qualified as aiding and abetting the other events of the massacres, as well as the deportation of the women, children, and elderly people from Srebrenica.

5.2.3.3 Radovan Karadžić's Overarching Role in the Armed Conflict in the Former Yugoslavia

Radovan Karadžić was also convicted for contributing to an "overarching JCE" that encompassed the goal to remove Bosnian Muslims and Croats from territories, which the Bosnian Serb leadership claimed as theirs.[415] Many crimes were attributed to Karadžić based on his contributions to the JCE. His actions were mostly of a political and general nature.[416] His case therefore poses an example of a political leader who, by exercising the functions of his office, facilitated and furthered large-scale crimes.

The trial chamber affirmed Karadžić's responsibility for war crimes and crimes against humanity based on the application of type I and type III JCE.[417] The crimes against humanity of deportation, inhumane acts (forcible transfer) and persecution (by forcible transfer and deportation) had been within the scope of his and the Bosnian Serb leadership's plan.[418] Murder as a war crime and a crime against humanity and extermination (a crime against humanity) were not encompassed by the JCE and were thus attributed through a JCE type III.[419]

The chamber found that numerous crimes were committed during the take-over of power in municipalities in Bosnia and Herzegovina by the Bosnian Serb military and affiliated paramilitary units.[420]

The evidence also showed that Karadžić exercised direct authority over all relevant state branches, including the government and administration, the military and police and the Bosnian Serb political party.[421]

The chamber determined that Karadžić was deeply involved in the formulation of the political goals of the Bosnian Serb "Republika Srpska", such as the expulsion of

[415] Ibid., para 3440.

[416] For the findings on Karadžić's criminal responsibility in this regard see ibid.. paras 3524–5.

[417] Ibid., para 3524.

[418] Ibid., paras 3464, 3466.

[419] Ibid., paras 3523–4; for the foreseeability criterion of JCE III liability see above Sect. 5.2.1.1.

[420] Cf. legal findings on crimes at ibid., paras 2439 *et seq.*, especially the conclusions at 2456, 2463, 2481, 2570.

[421] Ibid., paras 3478, 3480–1, 3488–9, 3491.

Muslims and Croats from the territory it claimed.[422] He pushed the implementation of alternative state structures in the newly independent Bosnia and Herzegovina that enabled the take-over of power in the territories claimed by the Bosnian Serb movement.[423] This included *inter alia* the implementation of "crisis staffs" that later became crucial in the take-over of power.[424] He also integrated so-called "territorial defence units" into the Bosnian Serb army and controlled the latter, e.g. by ordering its mobilisation.[425] In February 1992,[426] Karadžić activated the second phase of the notorious "Variant A/B Instructions", which ordered the municipal crisis staffs to gain physical control over their respective municipalities.[427] What ensued was widespread violence and the expulsion of the vast majority of Muslims and Croats from the respective municipalities.[428]

The connection between the "Varian A/B Instructions" and the crimes of deportation, inhumane acts (forcible transfer) and persecution would have easily fulfilled the requirement of giving an order. The crimes were a direct consequence of Karadžić's instruction to seize power in the municipalities, and this take-over was intimately linked to the expulsion of the non-Serb population. Given the all-encompassing authority and power of Karadžić over the government and military of the Republika Srpska, it is also conceivable that he exercised (chain) authority over the perpetrators of these crimes. Upon receiving instructions that were direct consequences of Karadžić's orders, these perpetrators felt compelled to execute them.

Additionally, Karadžić's orders had a direct and substantial effect on the commission of the crimes, as they were an immediate, and unavoidable, consequence of the implementation of the instructions.[429] A chamber could have even reached the conclusion that, without the instructions given by Karadžić in his central role, the crimes would not have been committed in the same way. Hence, this act also fulfilled the direct and substantial effect requirement.

Karadžić possessed the relevant *mens rea* for the commission of the crimes of deportation, inhumane acts, and persecution.[430] He must have been aware of his own authority over the recipients of his orders, and of the substantial likelihood that these crimes would be committed if his instructions were carried out. His orders unavoidably included the commission of such crimes, and he must have been aware thereof.

---

[422] Ibid., paras 3440, 3449, 3482–3.

[423] Ibid., paras 3435, 3477, 3488.

[424] Ibid., paras 3437, 3478.

[425] Ibid., paras 210–13, 3488–9.

[426] Ibid., para 135.

[427] Ibid., paras 3083, 3087, 3088–9, 3484; The "Variant A/B Instructions" were considered mandatory by Bosnian Serb leaders on the municipal levels who had to implement them, see ibid., para 3074-5. The implementation is described in detail at ibid., paras 132 seq.

[428] Ibid., paras 3441–4, 3446,

[429] In this regard see also the chamber's finding at ibid., para 3497.

[430] Ibid., para 3463.

Radovan Karadžić could therefore have been convicted for ordering the crimes of deportation, inhumane acts (forcible transfer) and persecution, all of which constitute crimes against humanity.

Another question concerns Karadžić's responsibility for the crimes of murder (as a war crime and a crime against humanity) and extermination (a crime against humanity). He was found guilty of these crimes under JCE III because they were not part of the common plan and he had not intended them, yet could have foreseen them.[431] Hence, the question arises whether the evidence would have sufficed to determine that his acts had a direct and substantial influence on the commission of these crimes and whether he had been aware of the substantial likelihood of them being committed.

The necessary issuance of an order could have been found in the same acts as described above. However, an issue arises in connection with the authority criterion. As authority of the ordering person must compel the perpetrator to commit the crime, it is questionable whether, based on the issuance of said instructions alone, this requirement would have been affirmed. This would have depended on circumstances, such as the formulation of the instructions and the subsequent operational orders to the military and police forces, as well as other statements made by the accused. If, from the instructions and general bearing of Karadžić, the recipients of the order would have felt compelled, not "only" to expel and deport Muslims and Croats, but also to murder them, the authority requirement could have been affirmed. However, if these crimes were a foreseeable side effect, but compelling influence of the accused could not be proven, he would not have been guilty of ordering the commission of these specific crimes.

Karadžić's responsibility would have depended on whether there is a difference between the "substantial likelihood" requirement and the "foreseeability" requirement of the JCE doctrine. As outlined earlier, this is the case. Therefore, the tribunal would have had to find that the commission of the crimes of murder and extermination had been foreseeable to Karadžić, as well as that he was aware of the substantial likelihood that the crimes would be committed.

In summary, Radovan Karadžić could have been convicted for ordering the crimes of deportation, inhumane acts (forcible transfer) and persecution, for issuing the Variant A/B instructions to the municipal crisis staffs. However, it remains unclear whether he could have been convicted for ordering murder and extermination as well.

This shows how the involvement of leaders in the highest echelons of a state can fulfil the requirements of ordering a crime. However, much depends on the wording and perception of the general directives which qualify as orders. The Variant A/B instructions could qualify as instigating the crimes of murder and persecution at the very least. Without these instructions, the physical perpetrators would not have exercised violence against parts of the civilian population, which was sanctioned by their leaders. The instructions were therefore *sine qua non* in triggering the perpetrator's decision to commit the crimes of murder, extermination etc.

[431] Ibid., paras 3466, 3523.

5.2.3.4 Vlastimir Đorđević's Acts Concerning the Serbian Campaign in Kosovo

Vlastimir Đorđević was an assistant minister of the Serbian Minister of the Interior during the campaign of persecution and deportation against the Kosovo Albanians.[432] In his role, Đorđević had *de jure* authority over the police forces in Kosovo. He regularly attended meetings of coordinating bodies within the Ministry of the Interior and had detailed knowledge about the facts on the ground, including the use of disproportionate force by police units. Đorđević also contributed to the deployment of paramilitary troops to Kosovo in 1999 and oversaw the integration of a notorious paramilitary unit into the regular security forces. When first deployed to Kosovo, this unit shot 14 civilians without any legal consequences.[433] Additionally, he played an important part in concealing the bodies of victims and in hindering investigations of different killings.[434] He did not move to punish or even investigate the crimes.[435]

These different acts were seen as a significant contribution to the Kosovo JCE.[436] The trial chamber also affirmed Đorđević's responsibility for aiding and abetting the crimes of deportation, forcible transfer, murder, and persecutions.[437]

However, it concluded that Đorđević could not be found guilty for "directly" ordering or instigating these crimes. It also rejected liability for planning. As the purpose of the common plan (within the JCE) had been to "modify the ethnic balance of Kosovo", which was not in itself a crime, the chamber found it impossible to establish that Đorđević had directly planned any of the crimes.[438] Given the findings of the chamber were based on a lack of evidence for direct ordering, and the fact that it considered the possibility of convicting the accused for such orders, one must rely on these findings.

However, the chamber's rejection of the mode of planning can be seen critically. Planning requires an act in the preparatory or execution phase of a crime, which has a substantial effect on the commission of the crime. Simultaneously, the person needs to be aware of the substantial likelihood that the plan will lead to the commission of the crime.[439] Given Đorđević's authority over police forces in Kosovo and his central position in the Ministry of the Interior, it seems conceivable that he could have been convicted for planning certain crimes. For example, he agreed with a lower ranking police commander to deploy the notorious paramilitary group "Scorpions"

---

[432] *Đorđević*, 23 February 2011, paras 38 (on Vlastimir Đorđević's position as assistant minister), 2129 (on the common plan of a campaign targeting the Kosovo Albanian population).

[433] Ibid., para 2155.

[434] Ibid., para 2154.

[435] Ibid., paras 2156–7.

[436] Ibid., para 2158.

[437] Ibid., para 2164.

[438] Ibid., paras 2166–8.

[439] See e.g. *Kordić and Čerkez*, 17 December 2004, para 26; Boas et al. 2007, pp. 354–7; van Sliedregt 2012, pp. 111–12.

to a town where they were tasked with carrying out a "mopping up operation".[440] This resulted in them shooting 19 Kosovo Albanian civilians, of which 14 died.[441] It seems conceivable that the chamber could have found that the deployment had a substantial effect on the commission of the crime and that Đorđević was aware of the risk that crimes like this would be committed.

Đorđević's role and involvement thus serve as an example of an architect or organizer of crimes. His actions facilitated the Serbian terror campaign against the Muslim population of the Kosovo. But his involvement or evidence thereof did not constitute a direct enough link to enable a conviction under ordering or planning.

5.2.3.5 Conclusion

The analysis shows that three of the legal requirements usually prove to be decisive when determining responsibility: (1) The authority, which must compel the perpetrator to commit the crime, (2) the causal nexus and (3) the *mens rea* requirement. The latter two are defined broadly by the tribunals and allow for convictions under ordering (and planning, as its requirements in this regard are the same) for an accordingly broad spectrum of conduct. The order only needs to have a direct and substantial effect on the commission of a crime. The ordering person only needs to be aware of the substantial likelihood that the crime will be committed. The cases above show that in situations of conflict and ethnic tensions, responsibility for ordering can be easily incurred. Someone who *knows* of these tensions, as well as their faction's aims and instructs others to act in a way that can directly and substantially further or causally lead to crimes, fulfils the requirements. This means that broadly worded instructions and directives can fall under ordering.

However, the ordering person must exercise authority that compels the recipient of the order to commit the crime. Ordering conduct that does not inherently involve the commission of a crime hardly suffices. Hence, ordering acts that facilitate or logistically enable the commission of a crime but do not constitute the commission of it in a legal sense, do not lead to responsibility for ordering. If the recipient of the order is not compelled to commit a crime, but only to aid and abet another person in committing a crime, this does not lead to responsibility for ordering a crime. However, it is conceivable that in these cases, the instructing person would be liable for aiding and abetting and perhaps planning, depending on their individual role.[442]

Thus, the requirements of causal nexus and *mens rea* broaden the spectrum of conduct grasped by ordering, whereas the requirement of authority narrows its scope.

[440] *Đorđević*, 23 February 2011, paras 1938, 1942.

[441] Ibid., para 1944.

[442] In German criminal law e.g., persons who instigate another to aid and abet a crime are considered aiders or abettors themselves, see Heine and Weisser 2019, § 27 mn. 25–7.

As shown, the evidence would have supported convictions for ordering crimes in two of the most notorious cases that came before the ICTY.[443]

Two ways of proving responsibility for ordering a crime can be identified in these cases. It is necessary to show the existence of an instruction that qualifies as an order with the relevant effect on the crimes, or to present an abundance of evidence that can only be reasonably interpreted as showing that, in light of their authority and position, the accused must have ordered the commission of the crimes.[444] The necessary proof of a direct link between the accused's conduct and specific crimes is narrower than the broad "contribution" that suffices under JCE. This is due to the different models of imputation; the systemic, indirect one of which (JCE) logically accepts a broader range of conduct. To a certain extent, the difference is limited through the possibility of considering some of the relevant acts as circumstantial evidence that an order must have existed.

The foregoing analysis shows that the *ad hoc* tribunals could have resorted to ordering to convict persons in higher ranks for their participation in the crimes committed in the former Yugoslavia and in Rwanda depending on the particularities of the accused's involvement.[445] Additionally, planning and instigating could have been used at other points at which the tribunals equally recurred to JCE.[446] However,

---

[443] This is hardly surprising if one considers the view that legal practitioners took concerning the evidence relevant for the JCE investigation process; see Piacente 2004, pp. 447–9, who describes how investigations to enable JCE convictions focused *inter alia* on identifying the "members of the military and political chain of command" and the "planners and instigators of the crimes committed".

[444] For the first type see especially the findings above where it was found that Karadžić's order to assume power had directly and obviously led to the crimes of deportation, inhumane acts, and persecution (crimes against humanity). For the second type see the findings, where it is submitted that, given Mladić's prominent position, his continued presence in important meetings and the description of his personal behaviour would have allowed for the conclusion that the crimes of murder, extermination, and genocide were not only committed with his permission, but were ordered by him.

[445] See Boas et al. 2007, p. 380, reaching the same conclusion.

[446] Responsibility for planning a crime could have been affirmed for all acts of the four accused where they formulated, alone or with others, a method of design or action, procedure, or arrangement for the accomplishment of a particular crime. Their contributions had to be substantial (Mettraux 2005, pp. 279, 280), but not *condition sine qua non* for the commission of the subsequent crimes (Ambos and Bock 2016, pp. 211). Such conduct could be formulating a plan or endorsing the plan of another (Mettraux 2005, p. 280, with sources from jurisprudence). According to some jurisprudence, the planning must take place "at both the preparatory and the execution phases" (see e.g. *Akayesu*, 2 September 1998, para 480; Boas et al. 2007, p. 356 with Footnote 86). Given the deep involvement of the accused in the exemplary cases of this section, there is little doubt that they could have also been convicted for planning the crimes and possibly for ordering. The description of their conduct shows their immediate participation in the preparatory stages of the respective campaigns. The plan can refer to an act or omission with the awareness of the substantial likelihood that a crime will be committed in the realisation of that act or omission, the illegality of the plan itself is not a requirement (ibid., p. 354). For Mladić and Karadžić this means that their involvement in the preparation and execution of plans in Srebrenica can amount to planning the crimes. For Karadžić the same would be true for the preparation of the "Variant A/B Instructions". In the case of Đorđević, evidence seemed to be lacking, but—given the conviction for JCE—it does not seem unlikely that his responsibility for planning, could have been inferred from circumstantial evidence.

sometimes, responsibility for aiding and abetting could have proven to be the only alternative fulfilled by the accused's conduct. The tribunals, especially the ICTY, resorted to JCE in these cases, thereby facilitating convictions for "committing" the crimes.

For organisational conduct which does not establish a sufficiently direct link to the specific crimes, it is possible that only JCE or aiding and abetting can serve under the *ad hoc* tribunals' law. However, it is equally possible that the tribunal simply lacked the necessary evidence to establish the accused's responsibility for planning, instigating, or ordering. For organisational conduct that does not fulfil the modes of planning, ordering, or instigating, one might consider whether aiding and abetting is the correct description of this conduct. It seems questionable whether commission through participation in a JCE is the more appropriate label for such indirect contributions.

Regardless, the observation that JCE is the *ad hoc* tribunals' tool of choice in dealing with decision makers in international criminal law must be questioned further. It has been shown that ordering, in conjunction with planning and instigating, would allow for a comprehensive adjudication of high-level decision makers, nevertheless JCE was and still is predominantly applied.

The possible reasons for applying JCE instead, and whether ordering should be given a more central role among the forms of liability of the ICTY's and ICTR's statute, will be discussed in the following.

5.2.4 *Critical Analysis of the JCE Doctrine and Advantages of Ordering*

We have seen that ordering a crime and participation in a JCE partially overlap, as far as their legal requirements are concerned. This shows that, strictly speaking, it is not necessary to apply JCE to adjudicate the wrongdoing of decision makers or architects of international crimes.

However, it is not only or primarily a *lacuna* in responsibility that the JCE doctrine seeks to avoid through its flexibility. It is also the perceived expressive value of the doctrine and its potential to label participants in a JCE as perpetrators that makes it interesting for practitioners and scholars.

This section analyses the JCE doctrine with a view to these points and contrasts this with ordering responsibility and its potential advantages.

5.2.4.1 Perceived Advantages of JCE

Some perceived advantages of the doctrine of JCE were outlined earlier.[447] These advantages can now be reassessed in light of the foregoing comparison between ordering and JCE.

The tribunals and some scholars are convinced that JCE is a suitable form to adjudicate the acts of high-ranking participants in international crimes and stress JCE's applicability to large-scale criminal schemes.[448] However, the analysis above shows that the application of ordering, planning, and instigating would not lead to impunity under the statutes of the *ad hoc* tribunals. Some acts of organizers of crimes may fall under aiding and abetting. Although possible, it would be very unlikely that a "significant contribution" to a JCE would not even qualify as conduct under the latter.

This means that although there is no outright danger of impunity in the absence of JCE, its application is nevertheless perceived to be important.

Flexibility and a Hierarchy of Blameworthiness

Some cases raise the suspicion that JCE serves to convict individuals for their participation where the respective chambers could otherwise not convict the accused at all or do so "only" under the head of aiding and abetting. The former was the case when the appeals chamber in *Tadić* reversed the trial judgment.[449] The latter was true in *Đorđević*. In this case, the trial chamber elaborated on other modes of liability besides JCE and discarded all apart from aiding and abetting.[450] In *Tadić*, the chamber also elaborated on the delineation between JCE and aiding and abetting, though it did not differentiate between JCE and ordering, planning and instigating.[451] This may create the impression that the doctrine of JCE was originally created to cover cases which lacked sufficient evidence to convict the accused at all,[452] or to convict them under a "more serious" head of liability than that of an aider and abettor.[453] Based on this finding, the supposed advantage of JCE is twofold: it is flexible, allowing the attribution of responsibility where other modes fail or are difficult to prove, and it provides for a conviction under commission liability where another mode would otherwise be fulfilled. The latter point touches on the issue of a hierarchy of blameworthiness in which aiding and abetting is perceived as a less serious form of liability.

---

[447] See above Sect. 5.2.1.3.

[448] *Krajišnik*, 27 September 2006, para 876; *Đorđević*, 27 January 2014, para 63; see also Burghardt 2008, pp. 339–40; Cassesse 2007, p. 115; Del Ponte 2006, pp. 549–51; Mettraux 2005, p. 292; Osiel 2005, p. 1788; van der Wilt 2007, p. 92.

[449] *Tadić*, 15 July 1999, paras 172 *et seq.*, 230–2.

[450] *Đorđević*, 23 February 2011, paras 2164, 2168.

[451] *Tadić*, 15 July 1999, para 229.

[452] In the same vein see Danner and Martinez 2005, pp. 133–4, who also criticize that this part of the approach comes at the expense of key criminal law principles, such as the culpability principle. See also Steer 2017, p. 282.

[453] For such an impression raised in literature see Del Ponte 2006, p. 550; see also *Milutinović*, 21 May 2003, para 20.

However, the first of these two points is highly problematic. A doctrine's capability to attribute liability for any contribution is not an advantage, because it blurs the lines between differently responsible actors.[454] This becomes even more problematic, if the doctrine is favoured not only because it is flexible and broad, but also carries a heightened mark of blameworthiness.

This leads to the second point: the notion that participation in a JCE is more blameworthy than aiding and abetting a crime is only sustainable if the system of perpetration and participation must be read as establishing a normative hierarchy with commission as the most blameworthy form of responsibility. However, it is highly questionable whether Articles 7 (1) and 6 (1) of the ICTY and ICTR Statute demand such an interpretation. We have seen that differentiated, hierarchical systems of perpetration and participation in this strict form are not common to international criminal law and cannot necessarily be found in national legal systems. The tribunals could have opted for any approach to dealing with perpetration and participation. Therefore, a hierarchy of blameworthiness, as far as one exists in *ad hoc* jurisprudence, has been established in conjunction with JCE as a policy choice at the tribunals without compelling reasons from the text of the statutes.[455] Consequently, a hierarchy of blameworthiness, in which a conviction under JCE would be preferable to display the accused's heightened responsibility, is not implied in the statutes and therefore cannot serve as an argument in favour of JCE.

The flexibility and hierarchy arguments in favour of a JCE are thus unconvincing. It seems that the tribunals' choices of JCE and a hierarchy of blameworthiness are based on another important aspect of international criminal justice.

Expressive Value and Fair Labelling of JCE

As described above,[456] commentators in favour of the JCE doctrine often stress its expressive value and its ability to present a "fuller and more accurate picture" of the crimes and the groups of persons who conceive a criminal plan together.[457] Some chambers of the ICTY took this view themselves when they assured that JCE "most accurately and appropriately" reflected the behaviour of accused persons in leadership positions.[458]

This holds true in theory when considering the relationships between the many people involved and to some extent in practice, as some judgments may show.[459]

[454] Cp. the criticism portrayed at Sect. 5.2.1.3.

[455] If the wording of the statutes expresses any preference for a system of perpetration it seems to be a unitary one without normative distinctions between forms of responsibility, see Steer 2017, p. 282.

[456] See Sect. 5.2.1.3.

[457] Gustafson 2007, p. 139.

[458] *Krajišnik*, 27 September 2006, para 877; *Karadžić*, 24 March 2016, paras 3525, 4940, 5994.

[459] For a description of how Mladić and other commanders apparently discussed the plan to murder thousands of Bosnian Muslims in Srebrenica, in *Mladić*, 22 November 2017, paras 5000, 5067–8; but see also the description of how Karadžić apparently discussed the plans for the Srebrenica massacres with his subordinate Deronjić on the phone, in *Karadžić*, 24 March 2016, para 5772–3. Especially this latter instance is a dialogue between Karadžić and a subordinate which does not

Additionally, the necessity of proving the existence of a common plan can lead to an accurate description of how, when and by whom the criminal scheme was developed.

Notwithstanding this advantage, the comparison with ordering liability shows that other essential factors are usually not reflected in an evaluation of the requirements of JCE. It does not require an assessment of the relation between the persons involved, nor question who made the final decision to act, nor who contributed the ideas behind the plan.[460] JCE thus runs the risk of levelling very different contributions to the crimes committed in its execution.[461]

As the highest operative commander of the Bosnian Serb army Ratko Mladić was found guilty of committing the crimes in Srebrenica based on his participation in a JCE. The JCE was believed to have been conceived by a plurality of persons including the commanders and security chiefs of different military and police units, as well as by Radovan Karadžić.[462] Given that the ICTY's chambers established in various judgments that a strict hierarchy governed the Bosnian Serb administration and military, it seems unlikely that all the members of the Srebrenica JCE contributed in similar or even comparable ways to the massacres. Yet, they could theoretically all have been guilty of committing the crimes by contributing to the common criminal purpose.[463] The outcome would have been, and partially was, a range of judgments of many perpetrators who committed genocide and other crimes without distinguishing between their—exceedingly different—contributions.[464] This highlights that the way in which political and military leaders contribute to the commission of the crimes, their central position and the decisiveness of their actions for the eventual outcome are not mirrored by this mode of responsibility. Thus, this can hardly be described as an accurate and appropriate reflection of their participation in the crimes. The doctrine therefore does not contribute to fair labelling.[465] Having committed a crime by contributing to a JCE is vague and being a perpetrator can mean anything. Thus,

involve discussion and agreement, but rather an instruction by the higher-ranking person to act in a certain way.

[460] In a similar vein van Sliedregt 2015, p. 505. Del Ponte takes the opposite stance and contests that these questions of a hierarchy or superior-subordinate-relationships play a role when determining the criminal responsibility of leadership figures, see Del Ponte 2006, p. 550. Gustafson rightly points out that, to apply JCE liability, the role of individuals within the group can be assessed (in: Gustafson 2007, p. 139). However, an assessment of a position of authority is not legally necessary for JCE liability, and the final label of responsibility also does not reflect such a position on behalf of the convicted.

[461] In the same vein Haan 2005, pp. 195–6; Ohlin 2007, p. 77; Ohlin 2015, p. 518; Ohlin 2007, p. 88. See also Steer 2017, p. 282.

[462] Cp. *Mladić*, 22 November 2017, para 4988. For the ranks and positions of some of the involved officers see *Popović et al.*, 10 June 2010, paras 1090 (Popović, Chief of Security of the Drina Corps), 1202 (Beara, Chief of Security Administration of the army's main staff), 1337 (Nikolić, Chief of Security of the Zvornik Brigade), 1434 (Borovčanin, Deputy Commander of police forces).

[463] In reality, the convictions of the involved officers were not all based on JCE as can be seen e.g. in *Popović et al.*, 10 June 2010, paras 2104 *et seq.*

[464] In the same vein Ohlin 2007, p. 88 ("Not all parts of the group agent are equal").

[465] As van Sliedregt points out, no differentiation in blameworthiness is made between different participants in a JCE, see van Sliedregt 2015, p. 505.

JCE does not single out and describe the different contributions and their importance for the crime. Instead, given the different nature of contributions to the JCE, the determination of seriousness of the participant's conduct moves to the sentencing stage and "participation in a JCE" becomes a meaningless phrase.[466]

Summary

The perceived flexibility of JCE in conjunction with its potential to mark participants as perpetrators is no valid point in favour of the doctrine. Flexibility is a dangerous asset for a form of responsibility, especially where other modes already criminalize the same conduct. As previously addressed, this is the case with ordering, planning, instigating, and aiding and abetting.[467]

As a hierarchy of blameworthiness is not dictated by the statutes, it cannot be used as a reason to support JCE. To the extent that chambers have relied on such a hierarchy, it was introduced together with the JCE doctrine. Rather than being an argument in favour, it necessitates justification itself.

JCE is not fit to properly describe the convict's wrongdoing. Its expressive value is limited as it does not reflect hierarchical and other power dynamics between the participants in the crime, thereby levelling their different contributions and roles. In other words: among the most responsible for the crime, it does not single out the true leaders, decision makers, and architects. Instead, it simply affixes the same mark on all members of the criminal enterprise. Contrary to the endorsement by tribunals and scholars, it is therefore not capable of appropriately reflecting the contributions of decision makers and architects of international crimes.

5.2.4.2 Advantages of the Legal Requirements of Ordering and Their Application to Leadership Cases

The following two sections assess responsibility for ordering, and where appropriate for planning and instigating, and explore the extent to which these modes could be applied more appropriately to the decision makers and architects of the crimes in the former Yugoslavia and in Rwanda. The legal requirements of ordering can be, and were, applied to grasp the participation of mid- and high-level actors in international crimes. Some authors have therefore described ordering, planning, and instigating as "important and suitable" mechanisms for such cases.[468] The analysis of the legal requirements and the comparison to JCE have also shown that the tribunals, especially the ICTY, could have relied more on ordering than they did.

---

466 See already in this vein Ambos 2007, p. 173, implying that JCE renders all participants equal on the level of attribution, which moves the weighing of different types of conduct into the sentencing stage.

467 See above at Sect. 5.2.3.

468 See Boas et al. 2007, p. 380.

Mens Rea as No Undue Restriction to the Scope of Ordering

The type of crimes committed and the necessary *mens rea* requirement may be of relevance in some cases. Wherever the alteration of the ethnic demographic composition of a territory or the extermination of a part of the population is part of the political agenda of the actors, attribution via ordering will usually apply. The actors' conduct in combination with their authority and personal remarks on the issue will leave no doubt that they substantially and directly furthered the crimes with the necessary intent, addressing *inter alia* the physical perpetrators of the crimes while doing so. However, difficulties arise when either the (compelling) authority is not exercised over the eventual perpetrators or when the *mens rea* or the direct and substantial effect cannot be proven.

The necessary mental element can be lacking in cases where crimes were committed that do not necessarily result out of the implementation of the political agenda. For example, the crimes of murder and extermination committed against the local populace in cases where "only" their deportation or forcible transfer was envisaged. It is unclear whether the "awareness of the substantial likelihood" requirement would be interpreted broadly enough to capture such excesses. It seems unlikely that the involved decision makers in such cases are not aware of the substantial likelihood of such crimes, however, this depends on the circumstances. However, the history of the conflicts in the former Yugoslavia shows that campaigns of deportation and forcible transfer are hardly ever unaccompanied by physical (including sexual) violence. The *mens rea* will therefore be confirmed in many cases.

The Exercise of Authority Over Others Apart from the Physical Perpetrators

The lack of the exercise of (compelling) authority over the perpetrator and the lack of instructions with a proven direct and substantial effect on the crimes, can be a restriction to the mode of ordering under ICTY and ICTR law. This is the case especially where a person exercises authority over groups of people who act as supporters and facilitators of the crime, but do not qualify as perpetrators. For example, imagine a high-ranking military officer or government official who orders the provision of weapons or the construction of prison camps. Their orders are important for the commission of the crimes without instructing the physical perpetrators to commit them.[469]

However, responsibility for planning or instigating can be affirmed in some instances where an architect of a crime is involved in the preparation of large-scale crimes.[470] In other cases, only aiding and abetting can be applied if one were to

---

[469] A parallel can be seen here to the observations on the Eichmann case and the suspicion that it falls outside of the scope of the traditional theory of indirect perpetration through an organisation (see Chap. 2, Sects. 2.2.6 and 2.6.2).

[470] Responsibility for planning can be incurred by several persons together. It must refer to a design, action, procedure, or arrangement aimed at the accomplishment of a crime or of an act or omission that will lead to a crime. It can also consist of endorsing another's plan (see Mettraux 2005, p. 280; Boas et al. 2007, pp. 354–6). Where several persons conceive such a design together, planning will

refrain from using JCE. However, given the coverage provided by ordering, planning, and instigating together, these cases are rare, as seen with the exemplary cases above.

Very few cases exist that are not covered by any of the modes of ordering, planning, instigating, or aiding and abetting. Such cases are theoretically possible where a contribution is significant enough for JCE but does not have a furthering influence on the crime. It is difficult to imagine such a case, but it must be conceded that in such an extremely rare scenario no criminal responsibility would arise under the explicit modes of responsibility of the statutes.[471]

The Lack of Authority in Groups of People with Equal Rank and Influence

It has been argued that where persons act in concert as equal partners and decide to commit a crime, ordering does not apply due to lack of authoritative relationship.[472] The analysis above has shown several points that invalidate this argument. The broad requirements of ordering and planning adequately capture criminal plans that were made as "joint decisions". The case studies have shown that in general the participants of such meetings (and consequently members of the common criminal purpose) were commanders and other persons with authority, who were portrayed to have had "agreed" on a criminal plan. Together, the modes of ordering and planning provide for the necessary means to describe and encompass these participants' contributions if they have a substantial and direct effect on the later crimes. If the highest-ranking officer (or any other person with authority over the others) exercised their authority, they can easily be convicted for ordering, even where the others in the meeting are decision makers themselves *vis-à-vis* their subordinates. It must be kept in mind that the superior does not need to actively invoke the authority.[473] Everyone in the meeting who then proceeded to instruct their subordinates to carry out crimes can still be liable for ordering crimes. Additionally, if all or some participants of a meeting combine their authority over others, this can qualify as joint ordering.[474]

If anyone (including the highest-ranking person) contributed to the criminal scheme without possessing *de facto* authority, this person can still be liable for "planning" or "instigating" the crimes. Their causal nexus and *mens rea* requirements are equally broad. The is true for persons acting as organizers on subsequent levels: if they do not directly instruct the physical perpetrators, their contributions

---

also apply to a person who contributes by affirming logistical or other organisational support to be provided through their subordinates.

[471] Whether this is a remarkable disadvantage is questionable. Many systems of violence, especially large, state-like ones, will inevitably comprise persons who support the apparatus yet remain far away from any criminal actions. If their behaviour does not even amount to aiding and abetting, whether and to what extent it can convincingly be seen as a contribution to the crimes committed through such a system must be evaluated carefully.

[472] Del Ponte 2006, p. 549.

[473] It is submitted at this point that wherever military hierarchies are involved the author deems it highly unlikely that the word of the highest-ranking person in the room would not also be attributed the most weight by the other officers.

[474] See above at Sect. 5.1.1.1.

will often amount to planning. The "authorship" of a criminal plan or order, which was described as ordering under the jurisdiction of the Nuremberg subsequent trials, can thus be adjudicated as the planning of a crime by the *ad hoc* tribunals.[475]

Summary

Liability for ordering can attach to the acts of many high- and mid-level actors. The conduct element that can relate to any kind of instruction, guideline or directive leads to a comprehensive scope. The authority requirement does not raise an insurmountable threshold either, with all relevant political, military, and social power dynamics falling under it.

However, the authority requirement is limited by the fact that the ordering actor must use their authority to compel the perpetrators of the crime. Orders for facilitating or supportive operations that do not concern or address the physical perpetrators do not qualify as ordering the commission of crimes. Ordering is understood as imputation for an instruction, and such instruction must trigger the commission of crimes through a direct line of acts, starting with the order and ending with the executioners committing the crime.

5.2.4.3 The Expressive Value of Ordering in Comparison to JCE

As previously indicated, it can be seen as established that the *ad hoc* tribunals choose and test those forms of responsibility that most accurately describe the conduct of the accused.[476] This descriptive or expressive value of a mode of responsibility is frequently mentioned, especially in the application of JCE. It is common that the chambers refrain from making findings under other modes of liability because they believe that JCE suffices to "adequately capture" the accused's responsibility.[477]

The appropriateness of a mode can *inter alia* relate to the adequate literal description of the conduct of the accused and their influence on and relation to others and the surroundings.[478]

---

[475] For planning see especially above at Sects. 5.2.2.1 and 5.2.3.5. Note that planning can also be done by several persons together (Mettraux 2005, p. 279).

[476] *Krajišnik*, 27 September 2006, para 877; *Milutinović et al.*, 26 February 2009, paras 614, 619; *Tolimir*, 12 December 2012, para 1174 ("best characterized as commission"); *Karadžić*, 24 March 2016, paras 3525, 4940, 5994; *Mladić*, 22 November 2017, para 5165.

[477] *Krajišnik*, 27 September 2006, para 877; *Karadžić*, 24 March 2016, para 5449.

[478] *Milutinović et al.*, 26 February 2009, para 619 shows that the categorization of modes as principal or secondary liability alone was not the only reference for the descriptive approach of the tribunals. The chamber abstractly describes behaviour that it found to be typically captured under the respective modes: "planning primarily applies to those who design crimes, (...) instigating primarily applies to those who prompt others to commit crimes, and (...) ordering primarily applies to those who instruct others to commit crimes; whereas aiding and abetting applies to those who provide practical assistance, encouragement or moral support to the perpetration of a crime."

As determined, the focus of liability for ordering is different to that of participation in a JCE. Ordering focusses on the authority of an actor and the relationship to subordinates, while JCE focusses on the relationship between actors without addressing hierarchical or other superior-subordinate relationships. The capacity of JCE to reflect the joint plans and decisions made by people in groups is often pointed out as an advantage of this doctrine. This perceived advantage has been called into question above.

The focus of ordering on authority and top-down relationships is different from that of JCE, but aptly describes important dynamics that lead to the commission of crimes. It focusses on the decisive position and conduct of persons in positions of authority who contribute to a crime's commission regardless of their proximity to it or their influence and oversight over specific criminal incidents. It also grasps the conduct of those who, by using their authority, encourage crimes whose commission was already underway.

Through this focus, ordering precisely describes the conduct of persons who create the risk of the commission of international crimes through their authority. More specifically, this authority is exercised either by setting a military, political or administrative chain of command into motion, or by acting as a social or moral authority to whose words people adhere.

Hence, liability for ordering pointedly portrays the conduct of persons in leadership positions. It captures how they can "cry 'havoc!' and let slip the dogs of war",[479] because people feel compelled to comply with their instructions. This central role can be played by persons giving military orders to conduct an attack, by persons in the government or administration enacting legislature or administrative guidelines, and by actors who enjoy authority based on social structures and whose words are given decisive weight.[480]

The *ad hoc* tribunals did not always share this view. In some instances, the appeals chamber of the ICTR rejected ordering as a fitting mode where the person involved had been present at the crime scene and directed the physical perpetrators. The chamber saw fit to describe the conduct as "committing" the crime, although it restricted this to liability for genocide.[481] In *Gacumbitsi*, the appeals chamber found that ordering and planning did not fully capture the responsibility of the accused, because Gacumbitsi "did not simply 'order' or 'plan' genocide from a distance and leave it to others to ensure that his orders and plans were carried out". Instead, he had been present at the scene to supervise and direct the massacre.[482] This reasoning misses a crucial characteristic of crimes committed pursuant to pre-prepared orders

[479] On the quote see Chap. 1, Sect. 1.1

[480] See also Bantekas 2002, p. 50, who outlined that legislative acts or judicial decisions could be grasped by ordering as well. See Boas et al. 2007, pp. 422–3 with doubts about JCE/commission bearing more expressive value than ordering and instigating.

[481] *Gacumbitsi*, 7 July 2006, paras 59–61; *Seromba*, 12 March 2008, para 161; in *Munyakazi*, 28 September 2011, paras 132–135, the chamber expanded this view to the commission of crimes against humanity as well; see also the trial chamber in *Munyakazi*, 5 July 2010, paras 430, 491 that picked up the reasoning of the appeals chambers.

[482] *Gacumbitsi*, 7 July 2006, para 61.

and plans. As is widely accepted and demonstrated by the analysis of cases and legal tools (in this chapter: JCE and ordering, in earlier chapters: indirect perpetration through an organisation), the conduct of decision makers and architects of large-scale atrocities does not become more dangerous when such people supervise or "control" the execution of their plans and orders themselves. Instead, it is their reliance on a working chain of command that makes their behaviour critical. In other words: they are dangerous precisely because they do not have to supervise and direct the implementation of their orders and plans. Sylvestre Gacumbitsi was present when the crimes he ordered were committed, however they were not committed because he was there and directed the attackers, but rather because he was vested with the authority to make the physical perpetrators act. The appeals chamber failed to recognise this when describing commission as the more appropriate mode of liability.

Considering the above, ordering under the *ad hoc* tribunals provides a suitable description for the responsibility attributed to leaders, who make decisions that lead directly to mass atrocities, albeit through various levels of participants.

By contrast, where a person issues orders for supportive, organisationally relevant conduct instead of the commission of the crime itself, they will not be liable for ordering under the *ad hoc* tribunals' statutes. Naturally, where a person's conduct is not encompassed by a mode of liability, this mode will not provide an adequate description of their conduct. This concerns the architect issue as identified before.[483] It has been submitted that the mode of planning would cover most such cases, while some scenarios would lead to convictions for aiding and abetting.[484] Besides offering suitable legal requirements, planning also provides for the necessary expressive value. Ultimately, planning, scheming, and plotting is exactly what architects of crimes do.

In summary, the expressive value of the mode of ordering a crime is higher than that of JCE as far as decision makers of international crimes are concerned. Architects (planners and organizers) will often be "planners", but sometimes may "only" fall under aiding and abetting. Ordering mirrors the elevated position of the decision maker in relation to subordinates and physical perpetrators. Liability for ordering therefore has a higher potential compared to JCE of appropriately describing the facts that render a person in a high political, military or other position of authority responsible for the commission of crimes. This speaks in favour of applying ordering to leadership cases under the law of the *ad hoc* tribunals.

5.2.4.4 Conclusion: The Higher Expressive Value of Ordering as a Direct Linkage Theory of Imputation

The comparison above illustrates how the indirect linkage theory behind JCE does not carry a greater expressive value than the direct imputation via ordering and planning.

Allegedly, the broader scope of JCE is an advantage as it allows adjudicating people as perpetrators who would otherwise qualify as aiders and abettors or not

[483] See already above at Sect. 5.2.4.2.

[484] See above for the potential of the mode of planning at Sects. 5.2.2.1 and 5.2.3.5.

be convicted at all.[485] This reasoning highlights the risk of applying broad indirect linkage theories instead of the statutory predetermined set of direct linkage models. Responsibility for aiding and abetting is perceived as not grave enough to mirror the liability of actors who contribute to criminal policies or their implementation. The task of the tribunals is to adjudicate everyone responsible for the crimes. Therefore, when theories of direct linkage embedded in the explicit wording of the statute seemingly proved insufficient, the tribunals apparently found themselves called upon to establish another doctrine of indirect linkage; JCE. This doctrine remains heavily contested, not least due to the assertion that the JCE's introduction was based on a circular argument. By establishing liability for commission by participation in a JCE, a model of indirect linkage is used to circumvent the perceived shortcomings of the direct linkage imputation provided for in the statutes.

Problems arise when indirect linkage theories are applied instead of those of a direct linkage. The assessment that certain behaviour must have been criminal is anticipated.[486] Equally anticipated is the assessment that aiding and abetting or other modes, which are perceived as less grave are unable to describe the accused's responsibility. The focus is shifted from the single criminal incident (the crime) to the pattern of crimes, the criminal plan, or the policy involving such crimes. Consequently, it is much easier to impute responsibility for many criminal incidents based on JCE than on the other modes of liability, including aiding and abetting. Once the indirect link (the contribution to the *plan,* not the *crime*) is established, any crime can be imputed, no matter how insignificant (or non-existent) the contribution's effect on the specific crime is.[487] This leads to an additional and misleading labelling of conduct that has already been criminalized by the explicit modes of responsibility outlined in Articles 6 (1) and 7 (1) of the statutes respectively.

Certain forms of direct linkage imputation do not run this risk. They can grasp the most reprehensible conduct whilst requiring proof of a direct link. Thus, they single out the blameworthy connection between the actor and specific crime both legally and terminologically instead of levelling essentially different contributions. Consequently, to appropriately describe and label the wrongdoing of a decision maker, ordering has a higher value than JCE. The same will usually be true to planning and instigating, as far as they overlap with contributions to a JCE.

---

[485] Del Ponte 2006, p. 550; Gustafson 2007, pp. 152–3.

[486] For an equally wide formulation see Del Ponte 2006, p. 549; she states that where someone instructs the commission of crimes as part of a broader crime, after an agreement had been reached with others that such orders would be issued, that person will *only* be found responsible for ordering the crimes which they ordered. Del Ponte's conclusion is that ordering would not fully capture the responsibility of the individual in question and JCE would allow for a better solution. The possibility of finding the person guilty for (psychologically) aiding and abetting the other crimes by agreeing to the plan is not elaborated on.

[487] This is not necessarily an advantage in terms of fair labelling because if many differently grave contributions can lead to commission liability, distinctions in seriousness are once again moved to the sentencing stage.

As previously mentioned, expressive value and fair labelling are often associated with a hierarchy of blameworthiness. Where such a hierarchy exists, it is understandably argued that the influential conduct of leaders and planners of international crimes should be categorized under the most serious mode of responsibility. The comparison above thus suggests that ordering liability should be categorized as highly blameworthy. Therefore, the question arises: does ICTY and ICTR jurisprudence support an interpretation of ordering as one of the most blameworthy forms of responsibility under their statutes?

5.3 Ordering and Its Relation to Other Modes of Liability in the *Ad Hoc* Tribunals' Jurisprudence

Responsibility for ordering a crime is considered to be accessorial liability in the majority of ICTY and ICTR decisions and by most scholars.[488] This means that a differentiated system of perpetration and participation exists. However, whether this system contains a hierarchy of blameworthiness is another question to be addressed below.

Many scholars interpret the differentiated system of the *ad hoc* tribunals as a normative one, in which commission is the single most blameworthy form of responsibility.[489] Others reject any hierarchy between the modes of liability and effectively advocate for a unitary or purely phenomenological, but differential system of perpetration and participation.[490] Some assert that a gradation of responsibility based on the forms of liability cannot lead to a realistic description of guilt, which should instead be achieved through sentencing.[491] According to some authors, the issue can be described as divided along the lines of common law and civil law approaches.[492]

However, as the development of jurisprudence was shaped by different chambers and individuals from different legal systems with different views on the appropriate way to deal with mass atrocities, a closer look at different indicators is necessary.

[488] See above Sect. 5.1.2.

[489] For such an interpretation in literature see especially: Olásolo 2009, p. 135 with Footnote 238; see also the findings and sometimes critical evaluations by Boas et al. 2007, p. 422; Burghardt 2008, p. 307; Schabas 2006, p. 297.

[490] *Krnolejac*, 15 March 2002, para 77; Separate Opinion of Judge David Hunt on Challenge by Ojdanić to Jurisdiction Joint Criminal Enterprise, *Milutinović*, 21 May 2003, para 31; Boas et al. 2007, pp. 413–4, 422–3; Zorzi Giustiani 2008, pp. 798–9.

[491] Cf. the description of possible cases in Boas et al. 2007, pp. 413–4, 422–3; see also Schabas 2006, p. 297; Zorzi Giustiani 2008, pp. 798–9, speaking of a "perverse effect of the application of a hierarchy".

[492] van Sliedregt 2012, p. 78; see also Damgaard 2008, p. 194, who refers to the then-contentious question of whether JCE would be seen as perpetration or accessory liability, which was equally draped around the question of blameworthiness, seriousness and hierarchy.

5.3.1 *The* Ad Hoc *Tribunals' Terminology for Different Modes of Perpetration and Participation*

The language used by the tribunals when referring to different modes of liability and their relation to each other is inconsistent. Considering the seriousness of crimes, the different legal cultures of the judges and the little guidance given by the statutes, it is understandable that the development of a coherent doctrine of perpetration and participation seemingly did not lie at the heart of the tribunals' work. An analysis of the language used by the tribunals can nevertheless shed light on the different concepts of perpetration and participation, which could conceivably be imbedded in the statutes.

The tribunals differentiate between "direct" and "indirect forms of responsibility", which are sometimes referred to as direct or indirect "forms of participation".[493] In addition, the tribunals also use the terms principal perpetrator and accomplice, accessory, or secondary participation.[494] Principal perpetration is used as an antonym to the others.[495]

At first it seems that the terms indirect participation or responsibility, complicity, accessory, and secondary participation all refer to the same concept and could be used synonymously. Despite chambers hardly referring to more than two of these terms simultaneously, the way in which they are generally used clearly distinguishes them from direct responsibility or principal perpetration.[496] However, there are considerable discrepancies in the jurisprudence when classifying the modes of liability within these two categories.

---

[493] *Semanza*, 15 May 2003, para 563; *Kajelijeli*, 1 December 2003, para 963; *Gacumbitsi*, 7 July 2006, para 201; *Karera*, 7 December 2007, para 583; *Renzaho*, 14 July 2009, para 766 with fn. 857; *Nyiramasuhuko et al.*, 14 December 2015, paras 3422–4.

[494] *Kordić and Čerkez*, 26 February 2001, para 373 (accomplices/accomplice liability, principal perpetrator); *Krstić*, 2 August 2001, para 643 (accomplice liability, secondary participation, direct or principal perpetrator); *Semanza*, 15 May 2003, para 436 (accomplice, principal perpetrator); *Prosecutor v. Milorad Krnojelac*, 17 September 2003, paras 72-3 (principal offender/perpetrator); *Kajelijeli*, 1 December 2003, para 963 (principal perpetrators, secondary or indirect forms of participation); *Vasiljević*, 25 February 2004, paras 102 (accessory); *Kvočka et al.*, 28 February 2005, para 91 (principal perpetrator); *Simba*, 13 December 2005, para 389 (principal perpetrator); *Martić*, 12 June 2007, para 438 (principal perpetrator); *Karera*, 7 December 2007, para 583 (secondary forms of participation); *Nyiramasuhuko et al.*, 14 December 2015, para 3422 (secondary forms of responsibility), 3424 (principal perpetrators).

[495] *Krstić*, 2 August 2001, para 643; *Kordić and Čerkez*, 26 February 2001, para 373; *Semanza*, 15 May 2003, para 436; *Kajelijeli*, 1 December 2003, para 963.

[496] See e.g.: *Delalić et al.*, 16 November 1998, para 334; *Kordić and Čerkez*, 26 February 2001, para 373; *Kayishema*, 1 June 2001, para 185; *Krstić*, 2 August 2001, para 643; *Semanza*, 15 May 2003, paras 377, 557, 563; *Kajelijeli*, 1 December 2003, para 963; *Vasiljević*, 25 February 2004, para 102; *Ndindabahizi*, 15 July 2004, para 457; *Karera*, 7 December 2007, para 583; *Nyiramasuhuko et al.*, 14 December 2015, para 3422.

Aiding and abetting qualifies as a form of indirect, secondary or accomplice responsibility or participation.[497] A range of judgments suggest that complicity in genocide also qualifies as such a form of indirect, secondary, accessorial or accomplice liability.[498] Indirect forms of responsibility, i.e., primarily aiding and abetting, tend to be associated with lower sentences than direct forms of liability.[499]

However, there is considerably more confusion with the terms of principal perpetration and direct responsibility.

In some cases, the term principal perpetrator seemingly only refers to "hands on" or "physical" perpetration.[500] Chambers in other cases applied a broader approach to the notion of principal perpetration and found participants in both a JCE and other ways of commission to be principals to the crime.[501] In *Nchamihigo*, the trial chamber seemingly described ordering and planning as principal perpetration.[502] Principal perpetration was also portrayed in contrast to aiding and abetting, without clarifying which forms of liability would be included in the former concept.[503] Only

---

[497] *Tadić*, 15 July 1999, para 229; *Kvočka et al.*, 2 November 2001, para 284; *Semanza*, 15 May 2003, para 563; *Kajelijeli*, 1 December 2003, para 963; *Ntagerura et al.*, 25 February 2004, para 813; *Đorđević*, 23 February 2011, para 1873; *Ntawukulilyayo*, 14 December 2011, para 244; *Tolimir*, 12 December 2012, para 907; *Stanišić and Župljanin*, 27 March 2013, para 107; *Nyiramasuhuko et al.*, 14 December 2015, para 3424. See also Burghardt 2008, p. 304.

[498] *Akayesu*, 2 September 1998, paras 468, 700, 734; *Krstić*, 2 August 2001, para 643; *Semanza*, 15 May 2003, para 435–6, 557; apparently also: *Nyiramasuhuko*, 24 June 2011, paras 5981–3, casting aside complicity in genocide where another form of liability for the crime of genocide was fulfilled; however, note that the *ad hoc* jurisprudence on complicity in genocide is all but consistent as described in Boas et al. 2007, pp. 282–4; van Sliedregt 2012, pp. 172–7.

[499] *Kajelijeli*, 1 December 2003, para 963; *Kanyarukiga*, 1 November 2010, para 684; SCSL, *Prosecutor v. Charles Ghankay Taylor, Sentencing Judgment*, 30 May 2012, SCSL-03-01-T, para 21; *Nyiramasuhuko et al.*, 14 December 2015, para 3422, 3424. Concerning the notion that aiding and abetting is less serious than ordering and commission (including JCE) and concerning complicity in genocide see *Semanza*, 15 May 2003, paras 557–9, see below at Sect. 5.3.3. See also van Sliedregt 2015, p. 504.

[500] *Bagosora et al.*, 18 December 2008, para 125; *Kanyarukiga*, 1 November 2010, para 625; *Gotovina et al.*, 15 April 2011, para 2602; *Taylor*, 18 May 2012, para 456, 464; *Nyiramasuhuko et al.*, 14 December 2015, para 3424. Apparently also by the chambers in *Prosecutor v. Milorad Krnojelac*, 17 September 2003, para 75, distinguishing between participants in a JCE and principal perpetrators; *Brđanin*, 3 April 2007, para 445; *Martić*, 12 June 2007, para 438; ICTY, *Prosecutor v. Dragomir Milošević*, 12 December 2007, IT-98-29/1-T, para 955; *Seromba*, 12 March 2008, para 45. See also Burghardt 2008, pp. 305–6.

[501] *Kordić and Čerkez*, 26 February 2001, para 393; *Krstić*, 2 August 2001, para 643–4 (the appeals chamber apparently followed this categorization, but reversed the judgment due to a lack of genocidal intent on behalf of Krstić, see *Krstić*, 19 April 2004, para 134); *Prosecutor v. Milorad Krnojelac*, 17 September 2003, para 73; *Vasiljević*, 25 February 2004, para 95; *Kvočka et al.*, 28 February 2005, para 91; *Simba*, 13 December 2005, para 389; *Seromba*, 12 March 2008, paras 161, 182 (with criticism in the dissenting opinion by Judge Liu, para 6); *Munyakazi*, 5 July 2010, para 430.

[502] See *Nchamihigo*, 12 November 2008, para 388: "He personally ordered, instigated and aided and abetted systematic killings of influential Tutsi and Hutu opponents. … The Chamber determined that Nchamihigo was a principal perpetrator".

[503] See e.g. the way in which the *Kalimanzira* trial chamber distinguishes between "Principal perpetration" and aiding and abetting, leaving open, which forms of responsibility would be encompassed by the former term (*Kalimanzira*, 22 June 2009, paras 744–5).

sometimes were direct and principal perpetration used synonymously.[504] In *Semanza*, the appeals chamber referred to ordering as perpetration.[505]

The only reasonable conclusion to this plethora of interpretations of the term principal perpetration, is that principal perpetration always encompasses the physical, "hands-on" commission of a crime at the least.[506] As outlined earlier, the vast majority of scholarly opinion and many judgments also suggest that liability for participation in a JCE amounts to principal liability.[507] Aiding and abetting does not qualify as principal responsibility.

The classification of responsibility into "direct" and "indirect" forms can lead to a less obscure picture of the tribunals' views on the relation between modes of liability.

There can be little doubt that criminal responsibility for committing a crime under the statutes leads to direct responsibility.[508] However, when it comes to ordering, planning, and instigating, the jurisprudence is divided over their classification.

A certain number of judgments labelled ordering, planning, and instigating as "accomplice liability", akin to aiding and abetting.[509] In line with this, other judgments imply a distinction between commission or principal liability on the one hand and ordering, planning, instigating, and aiding and abetting on the other.[510] Given the preliminary two-fold classification of forms of liability into direct (including principal perpetration and all forms of commission) and indirect (i.e., secondary, accomplice, accessorial), these judgments imply that ordering, planning and instigating qualify as indirect responsibility.

However, in other cases, chambers stated that ordering, planning, and instigating gave rise to direct responsibility.

This was the case in *Renzaho*, where the trial chamber convicted for ordering and aiding and abetting genocide instead of for JCE, despite the latter's requirements being fulfilled. The chamber took the view that ordering, which it described as a direct form of responsibility, most appropriately captured the accused's involvement. It explained that, under the circumstances, a conviction for ordering and aiding and abetting genocide would not lead to a milder sentence than a conviction under participation in a JCE.[511]

---

504 *Krstić*, 2 August 2001, para 643.

505 *Semanza*, 20 May 2005, para 388.

506 However, see the scarce but coherent jurisprudence of some trial chambers and sometimes the appeals chamber at the ICTR as displayed below at Sect. 5.3.5.

507 See above at Sect. 5.2.1.2.

508 See e.g. the delineation in *Nyiramasuhuko et al.*, 14 December 2015, paras 3422–4; the equation of ordering and participation in a JCE as direct forms of responsibility in *Renzaho*, 14 July 2009, paras 766 with fn. 857, 770 with fn. 858; see also *Simba*, 13 December 2005, para 437.

509 Quite generally referring to all mentioned modes: *Delalić et al.*, 16 November 1998, para 334; *Kordić and Čerkez*, 26 February 2001, para 373; *Kayishema*, 1 June 2001, para 185; see also *Semanza*, 15 May 2003, para 557 (instigating); *Ndindabahizi*, 15 July 2004, para 457 (instigating).

510 *Akayesu*, 2 September 1998, para 472; *Semanza*, 15 May 2003, para 377; *Kajelijeli*, 1 December 2003, para 963; *Gacumbitsi*, 7 July 2006, para 201; *Karera*, 7 December 2007, para 583; *Nyiramasuhuko et al.*, 14 December 2015, para 3422.

511 *Renzaho*, 14 July 2009, para 766 with Footnote 857.

In the same vein, after reversing the accused's conviction for ordering, the appeals chamber in *Ntawukulilyayo* stated that this had removed "the only direct form of responsibility" by which the convicted had been found to have participated in a range of killings.[512]

Besides these unequivocal referrals, other judgments, certain judges, and the prosecution also showed a certain tendency to regard ordering as a form of direct responsibility or participation.

When discussing the differences between Articles 7 (1) and (3), the trial chamber in *Kordić and Čerkez* stated:

> For instance, a superior who orders the killing of a civilian may be held responsible under Article 7 (1), as might a political leader who plans that certain civilians or groups of civilians should be executed, and passes these instructions on to a military commander. The criminal responsibility of such superiors, either military or civilian, in these circumstances *is personal or direct*, as a result of their direct link to the physical commission of the crime. The criminal responsibility of a superior for such positive acts, except where the superior orders the crime in which case he may be more appropriately referred to as primarily responsible for its commission, may be regarded as "follow(ing) from general principles of accomplice liability".[513]

This statement can be read as establishing that ordering constitutes a form of direct responsibility, despite concluding somewhat confusingly by pointing to the possibility of regarding ordering leaders as "primarily responsible" or "accessories".

In the *Semanza* appeal, the prosecution submitted that ordering resulted in responsibility as a principal perpetrator.[514] The chamber did not explicitly decide on the prosecution's claim but ruled positively on the ground of appeal. Semanza's conviction for complicity in genocide and aiding and abetting in extermination was reversed and instead a conviction for ordering genocide and extermination was entered.[515] The chamber also followed the prosecution's claim that such a conviction warranted a higher sentence in light of his level of culpability.[516] In their separate opinion, Judges Shahabuddeen and Güney stated that Semanza "having been found guilty [...] of ordering genocide, is a perpetrator of genocide".[517] Consequently, they found that a sentence of life imprisonment for genocide would have been the appropriate sentence.[518]

It was furthermore common for chambers at the ICTR to state that:

---

[512] *Ntawukulilyayo*, 14 December 2011, para 244.

[513] *Kordić and Čerkez*, 26 February 2001, para 367, emphasis added.

[514] *Semanza*, 20 May 2005, para 352.

[515] Ibid., paras 353, 364.

[516] Ibid., paras 353, 389, in sum the chamber replaced the 25 years' sentence of the trial judgment with 35 years, see IV. Disposition, page 130.

[517] Ibid., Separate Opinion of Judge Shababuddeen and Judge Güney, para 2.

[518] Ibid., Separate Opinion of Judge Shababuddeen and Judge Güney, para 3.

> Life imprisonment have (sic!) also been imposed to those at a lower level who planned or ordered the atrocities or if they participated in the crimes with particular zeal or sadism. Secondary or indirect forms of participation have usually entailed a lower sentence.[519]

This can be interpreted as contrasting planning, ordering and participation with special zeal or sadism with secondary or indirect forms of participation. The respective chambers then endorsed that planning and ordering are not indirect or secondary forms of participation. The judgment in *Nchamihigo*, in which the accused was labelled a "principal perpetrator" after being convicted of ordering, instigating, and aiding and abetting crimes, could be read in the same way. Ordering and instigating would then qualify as principal perpetration and therefore as direct responsibility.[520]

Hence, ordering, planning, and instigating have frequently been described as "direct responsibility" by chambers of the ICTY and ICTR.

These observations may be interpreted simply as two competing views on the role of ordering, planning, and instigating in a system of perpetration and participation. Whilst some chambers believed that these forms would qualify as indirect and accomplice liability, others would label them as direct, principal responsibility. However, many decisions only use one of these terms to classify ordering. Cases in which ordering is called both principal and direct responsibility in the same decision are very rare and it can be suspected that the same is true for planning and instigating.

Therefore, if indirect/direct responsibility does not refer to the same classification as principal/accomplice liability, another reading of these seemingly contradictory views is possible. Such an interpretation is conceivable if accomplice liability means "derivative" liability, in the sense that someone else needs to have committed the crime to enable such a form of accomplice liability. Principal liability would then not be tantamount to direct liability, but simply mean that no commission of the crime by another is necessary.

Pursuant to such a reading, the difference in labelling between principal/accomplice and direct/indirect liability would not be contradictory. Ordering, planning, and instigating would qualify as accomplice liability, i.e., responsibility that requires the physical commission of a crime by another (akin to aiding and abetting). Simultaneously, these forms of accomplice liability would lead to direct responsibility (in contrast to aiding and abetting). This interpretation would enable a coherent reading of many, albeit not all, judgments of the *ad hoc* tribunals.[521] Furthermore,

---

[519] *Karera*, 7 December 2007, para 583, footnotes omitted; see also ICTR, *Alfred Musema vs. The Prosecutor* 16 November 2001, ICTR-96-13-A, para 383; ICTR, *The Prosecutor v. Elizaphan and Gérard Ntakirutimana* 21 February 2003, ICTR-96-10 and ICTR-96-17-T, para 884; *Ndindabahizi*, 15 July 2004, para 500; *Gacumbitsi*, 7 July 2006, para 206, reaching this conclusion without literally reiterating the principle; *Bagosora et al.*, 18 December 2008, para 2270; *Kanyarukiga*, 1 November 2010, para 684; *Karemera*, 2 February 2012, para 1720; Holá 2012, p. 14.

[520] *Nchamihigo*, 12 November 2008, para 388. However, this must be treated with caution as "principal perpetrator" and "direct responsibility" were not used as synonyms in most judgments.

[521] Certain judgments are opposed to such a reading, treating secondary and indirect participation as synonyms, which is not compatible with the approach outlined here. See e.g. *Kanyarukiga*, 1 November 2010, para 684); *Karera*, 7 December 2007, para 583; *Kajelijeli*, 1 December 2003, para 963.

this reasoning would be in line with the—widely uncontested—view that ordering, planning, and instigating require the actual commission of the crime to trigger responsibility, as they would be treated as accomplice (but direct) liability.

Regarding blameworthiness, the classification as direct responsibility would put ordering, planning, and instigating on one level with commission (which would qualify as direct and principal liability), whilst their respective derivative, accomplice or accessorial characters would require the commission of the crime by another.

The foregoing observations can be summarized as follows:

- The term principal perpetration is not used unambiguously but comprises the physical perpetration of the crime at the least and certainly JCE liability.
- Forms of responsibility or participation are divided into direct and indirect responsibility.
- Direct responsibility encompasses "committing" a crime pursuant to Article 6 (1) ICTR Statute/7 (1) ICTY Statute, i.e., forms of principal perpetration (hands on commission, participation in a JCE).
- Indirect responsibility includes "aiding and abetting" a crime pursuant to Article 6 (1) ICTR Statute/Article 7 (1) ICTY Statute.
- The terms indirect and accomplice liability do not necessarily refer to the same concept.
  - Should they refer to the same idea, the status of ordering, planning, and instigating would be contentious.[522] Some chambers would then classify these forms as indirect/accomplice liability, whilst others would classify them as direct responsibility (potentially implying primary/principal responsibility).
  - Should they refer to different concepts, more sense could be made of the status of ordering, planning, and instigating. The forms could qualify as direct responsibility (being more serious than indirect responsibility) and simultaneously as derivative accomplice liability (i.e., requiring the commission of the crime by another).

The latter approach would ultimately mean that high- and mid-level decision makers could be convicted for ordering (planning and instigating) without conveying a lower degree of seriousness than for persons who committed the crime. To a degree, such an interpretation could be seen as the continuation of post-World War II jurisprudence. It would acknowledge that ordering is a highly reprehensible way of triggering a crime, without a notion of "principal" liability being associated with it.[523] Furthermore, this understanding would build on the common denominator of the terminology and responsibility classification, as used by the ICTY and ICTR.

Whether this interpretation is consistent with other factors that shaped the tribunals' jurisprudence, will be discussed in the following sections with regard to the requirements, sentencing length and legal concurrences of ordering.

---

[522] Although the chambers did not expressly argue about the classification of these modes.

[523] Cf. Chap. 4, Sect. 4.6.

As the term principal perpetrator was used ambiguously in the language of the tribunals, in contrast to the rest of this book, to avoid confusion the following sections will use the terms primary responsibility (for commission) and derivative liability (where the crime must be committed to give rise to criminal responsibility, i.e., aiding and abetting and, pursuant to one possible view, ordering, planning and instigating).

5.3.2 The Legal Requirements of Ordering

As described above, certain requirements of ordering imply a proximity between ordering and commission as far as seriousness is concerned. Simultaneously, certain features of ordering imply that it gives rise to derivative liability.

5.3.2.1 Compelling Authority as an Argument for Indirect Perpetration and/or the High Degree of Seriousness of Ordering a Crime

Ordering requires authority over the recipient of the order, i.e., the latter must feel "compelled to act". Hence, it has been occasionally argued that ordering is closer to cases of commission (in the form of agency or indirect perpetration).[524] The concept of indirect perpetration was recognized by few chambers of the ICTY and ICTR and was harshly criticised.[525] However, if one were to accept this concept, a certain similarity could be found between someone using their authority to compel another to act, and someone "controlling another", thereby committing the crime.

As discussed above, indirect perpetration and innocent agency require the use of a human "tool", who is usually not criminally liable him- or herself. By contrast, indirect perpetration through an organisation relies on certain mechanisms and features within the organisation. The ICC often recurs to the authority of the indirect perpetrator over the subordinates and/or organs of the organisation to determine "control over the crime".[526]

The authority to compel another is not tantamount to the use of an innocent agent. At least, no chamber of the ICTY or ICTR has invoked the necessity of such a strong coercive effect for compelling authority. This means that the authority under ordering must not be so strong as to exclude the physical perpetrator's criminal

---

[524] *Brđanin*, 3 April 2007, Partly Dissenting Opinion of Judge Shahabuddeen, para 10 with fn. 13; potentially in the same vein *Semanza*, 20 May 2005, Separate Opinion of Judge Shahabuddeen and Judge Güney, paras 2–3.

[525] *Gacumbitsi*, 7 July 2006, para 60, see also Separate Opinion by Judge Schomburg paras 18–23 (endorsing the interpretation of commission as including indirect perpetration), Partially Dissenting Opinion of Judge Güney paras 2–7 (critical); *Brđanin*, 3 April 2007, paras 412–13; *Seromba*, 12 March 2008, para 171, which clearly relies on a notion of indirect perpetration; see already van Sliedregt 2012, pp. 92–3. See also Chap. 3, Sect. 3.3.1.2 on the early, but always rejected references to the doctrine by Judge Schomburg.

[526] See Chap. 3, Sect. 3.2.2.4.

liability. Neither does authority require any formalized or organised structures. The "mere" authority over the recipient of an order suffices, regardless of how informal or temporary it may be. Therefore, it is not entirely convincing to argue that, under the ICTY and ICTR Statute and the respective jurisprudence, the authority requirement wholly resembles a form of indirect perpetration. On a more general level, however, it is correct that ordering is founded on a factor—authority—that is also deemed relevant for indirect perpetration through an organisation (in some of its versions).

In terms of seriousness and importance of the ordering person's role, it is therefore true that ordering is very close to forms of indirect perpetration as known from other systems. However, the relevant aspect is not the similarity between these forms of liability, but the recognition that the decisive factor in ordering, namely the authority over the perpetrator, renders the conduct of the ordering actor highly reprehensible. To issue an order to people over whom one holds authority creates an enormous risk and will often be the trigger for the commission of crimes. This key position makes the misuse of the authority highly blameworthy.

5.3.2.2 The Ordering Actor's *Mens Rea* as an Argument for Indirect Perpetration

The interpretation suggested by Badar that ordering would also be applicable where the ordering actor possesses the necessary *mens rea* while the recipient of the order does not,[527] would support the view of ordering as a form of commission (through another). Accordingly, a person could incur ordering liability, even if the physical perpetrators acted without the necessary mental element. This is conceivable e.g. for certain war crimes, or where the executioners lack the necessary special intent.[528] When distinguishing between primary and accessorial liability, it is a well-established rule of criminal law that the primary perpetrator must have at the least committed an unlawful principal act.[529] In many legal systems, this means that they must have fulfilled both the *actus reus* and the *mens rea* of the crime, in order to enable accessorial or accomplice liability.[530] Whether this is true for the system under the *ad hoc* tribunals is unclear.[531] By elaborating on the physical perpetrators' *mens rea* at times, the inquiries of some chambers speak toward a more comprehensive concept of accessorial liability.[532] This is in contrast to Badar's interpretation of the role of the ordering persons' *mens rea.* It has been pointed out that both understandings are possible. According to Badar, only the *mens rea* of the ordering actor would be relevant, thereby reducing the accessorial object of derivative liability to the crime's

[527] For this view see above Sects. 5.1.1.4 and 5.1.2; Badar 2013, p. 335.

[528] On the war crimes example see ibid., p. 335.

[529] Eser 2002, p. 783.

[530] See Badar 2013, pp. 70–1 (England), 75–6 (Australia), 77–8 (Canada), 157 (Germany), 167–8 (France); Eser 2002, p. 783.

[531] See above Sects. 5.1.1.4 and 5.1.2; see Vogel 2002, pp. 424–5.

[532] See above Sect. 5.1.2.

objective elements. Following this, ordering would be very close to the notion of indirect perpetration, as the criminal liability of the executioners would be irrelevant. This would undoubtedly speak in favour of a high seriousness of ordering.

Another plausible reading of the tribunals' statement on *mens rea* implies the necessity of the ordering person possessing the special intent. As will be shown below, this is also connected to a high blameworthiness in the *ad hoc* tribunals' jurisprudence.

Therefore, no matter which interpretation is followed, one arrives at the conclusion that ordering is seen as conveying a high degree of blameworthiness.

5.3.2.3 The Non-existence of Attempted Ordering

In many national criminal law systems, commission or primary perpetration is connected to the punishable attempt of a crime. Under the ICTY and ICTR Statutes, ordering, planning, and instigating require the actual commission of the crime. The attempted ordering, planning, or instigating are not punishable.[533] This could be interpreted as assigning a lower seriousness to ordering than to forms of commission, because ordering is apparently not serious enough to justify the criminalization of its attempt.

However, it is already contentious, whether a punishable attempt of the commission of a crime exists in international criminal law. For cases concerning crimes other than genocide, chambers of the *ad hoc* tribunals have rejected this possibility.[534] Pursuant to the *ad hoc* tribunals' law, not even the attempt of committing a crime, apart from genocide, is punishable. As outlined above, it is argued that the criminalization of the attempt in customary international law was incorporated into the *ad hoc* statutes "only" through the inclusion of the modes of "planning" and "aiding and abetting in the planning and preparation" of the crime.[535]

In other words, the idea that the criminalization of the attempt bears importance in determining a mode's blameworthiness, as known from national legal systems, does not apply under the *ad hoc* tribunals. Thus, this line of thought cannot be considered as an argument for or against the role of ordering in the system of perpetration and participation.

5.3.2.4 The Necessity of a Special Intent

As shown, especially in multiple later judgments of the ICTY and ICTR, the chambers have required that the person ordering a crime possessed the specific intent of e.g.

---

[533] See above Sect. 5.1.3.

[534] *Akayesu*, 2 September 1998, para 473; *Krnolejac*, 15 March 2002, para 432 with Footnote 1292; agreeing Mettraux 2005, p. 293; Olásolo 2009, p. 30; see already Sect. 5.1.3.

[535] In this vein see: Ambos 2016, Article 25 mn. 48; Eser 2002, pp. 807–8; see already Sect. 5.1.3.

genocide or extermination as a crime against humanity.[536] The same is true for planning and instigating.[537] By contrast, responsibility for aiding and abetting does not require this specific intent.[538] The necessity of a special intent to commit genocide or extermination is considered to significantly elevate the seriousness of a person's participation in a crime and the length of the appropriate sentence accordingly.[539]

Consequently, the necessity of a special intent to incur liability for ordering, instigating, and planning a crime, speaks toward the same categorization in terms of seriousness as commission, which undoubtedly requires the *dolus specialis* of a crime.

5.3.2.5 Summary

This section shows certain parallels between ordering and forms of perpetration, especially indirect perpetration. These similarities especially lie in the necessity of the special intent of the crime and of exercising a strong influence over the recipients of the order. However, ordering is categorized as accessorial liability by the *ad hoc* tribunals. The combination of criteria, which heighten the seriousness of the participation in a crime by affixing the label of accessorial liability suggests exactly that: a highly blameworthy form of accessory liability.

5.3.3 *The Influence of Modes of Liability on Sentencing at the* Ad Hoc *Tribunals*

Sentencing at the *ad hoc* tribunals has been heavily criticised as inconsistent, disparate, and uncertain.[540] Empirical analysis, however, has shown a certain degree of consistency in the sentencing practice.[541]

The impact of modes of liability on sentencing is crucial in determining whether the tribunals could and should regard ordering, planning, and instigating as adequate forms to capture the behaviour of high- and mid-level actors. Findings on the relation between the form of responsibility and the length of sentences allow conclusions on

---

536 Cf. Sect. 5.1.1.4.

537 See above Sect. 5.1.1.4.

538 See only *Krstić*, 19 April 2004, para 140; in the following para 141, the appeals chamber also bases its rejection of the necessity of a special intent for aiding and abetting on a comparison of several national legal systems. The German system is named as a system in which an aider and abettor does not need to show specific intent. However, contrary to what is argued for international criminal law, German criminal law requires no special intent from an instigator either. For details on the irrelevance of a special intent for aiding and abetting see *supra* Sect. 5.1.1.4.

539 For details see *supra* Sect. 5.3.3.

540 Ambos 2014, p. 268 with extensive references in Footnote 166.

541 Holá et al. 2012, pp. 549–50; Meernik and King 2003, p. 747; see also D'Ascoli 2011, p. 260; Sloane 2007, p. 733; for further references see Ambos 2014, pp. 268–70 with respective footnotes.

the blameworthiness associated with these forms and on a potential hierarchy between them to be drawn.

5.3.3.1 Basic Rules on Sentencing in the Statutes

Pursuant to Articles 23 and 24 of the ICTR and ICTY statutes respectively, the tribunals must consider the "gravity of the offence" and the "individual circumstances of the convicted person".[542] However, when considering aggravating circumstances ("individual circumstances"), the prohibition of double counting must be observed. No factor that has been considered within the definition of the offence can be considered as an aggravating circumstance. This concept only applies to aggravating individual circumstances and does not extend to the gravity of the offence. This means that in describing the gravity of the offence, factors that played a role when determining crimes and responsibility can be considered.[543] Additionally, factors considered in the gravity of the offence cannot be considered as aggravating circumstances and *vice versa.*[544]

It is seemingly common sense amongst the chambers of the *ad hoc* tribunals that a position of authority or influence or the abuse of such a position should lead to a longer sentence.[545] Empirical studies also confirm that such a link exists between a leadership position and the length of sentences.[546]

The tribunals' view on the influence of modes of liability on the sentence is clear in theory: the gravity of the offence is defined *inter alia* by the "form and degree of participation" of the convicted.[547] It is submitted that form and degree refer to

---

542 Drumbl 2016, p. 431; Holá et al. 2012, p. 541; Mettraux 2005, p. 347.

543 Ambos 2014, p. 288; i.e., the authority of the actor, which had to be proven as a requirement for ordering, could also be considered to determine the gravity of the offence.

544 Ibid., p. 288; ICTY, *Prosecutor v. Miroslav Deronjić*, 20 July 2005, IT-02-61-A, para 106; *D. Milošević*, 12 November 2009, para 309.

545 Boas et al. 2007, pp. 413–4 with Footnote 176; Drumbl 2016, p. 434; Mettraux 2005, pp. 350, 353–4; for an extensive list of ICTY and ICTR jurisprudence see Epik 2017, pp. 349–50 with Footnote 201 and 389 with fn. 329, 330; see also the more recent judgments in *Nyiramasuhuko et al.*, 14 December 2015, paras 3353, 3359; *Đorđević*, 27 January 2014, paras 937–40; *Karemera et al.*, 29 September 2014, para 682; *Karadžić*, 24 March 2016, paras 6035, 6052; *Mladić*, 22 November 2017, para 5193.

546 Holá 2012, pp. 13, 16; Meernik and King 2003, pp. 747–8; Meernik 2011, pp. 596, 601–2; see also Ewald 2010, pp. 395–402.

547 *Kupreškić et al.*, 14 January 2000, para 852; ICTY, *Prosecutor v. Zlatko Aleksovski*, 24 March 2000, IT-95-14/1-A, para 182; ICTY, *Prosecutor v. Zejnil Delalić et. al.*, 20 Febuary 2001, IT-96-21-A, para 731; *Krnolejac*, 15 March 2002, para 522; *Ntakirutimana* 21 February 2003, para 883; *Naletilić*, 31 March 2003, para 740; *Blaskić*, 29 July 2004, para 683; *Kajelijeli*, 1 December 2003, para 963; *Galić*, 30 November 2006, para 409; *Milutinović et al.*, 26 February 2009, para 1147; *Kalimanzira*, 20 October 2010, paras 226-7; *Đorđević*, 23 February 2011, para 2207; *Ntawukulilyayo*, 14 December 2011, para 244; *Karemera*, 2 February 2012, para 1721; *Stanišić and Župljanin*, 27 March 2013, para 892; *Karadžić*, 24 March 2016, para 6031; *Mladić*, 22 November 2017, para 5185; Cryer et al. 2019, p. 470; Drumbl 2016, p. 431; Holá et al. 2012, p. 541; Holá 2012, p. 13; Mettraux 2005, pp. 347–8.

two different aspects in this phrase. The degree of participation refers to the factual conduct of the accused, whereas the form of participation can validly be read as referring to the mode of liability which is fulfilled through the convict's conduct.[548]

In contrast to this, the meaning of modes of responsibility for sentencing has been questioned in some instances. The *Krnolejac* trial chamber stated that "[c]ategorising offenders may be of some assistance, but the particular category selected cannot affect the maximum sentence which may be imposed, and it does not compel the length of sentences which will be appropriate in the particular case".[549] However, such general statements against an influence of modes of liability on sentencing are scarce.

All in all, the influence of modes of liability on sentencing remains obscure. Only some principles concerning the relation between responsibility and length of sentence developed in *ad hoc* jurisprudence.

5.3.3.2 Principles and Tendencies in the Relation Between Forms of Liability and Sentencing

The first principle relates to aiding and abetting in the system of modes of liability under the *ad hoc* tribunals' statutes. A substantial amount of chambers found that "principal perpetration warrants a higher sentence than aiding and abetting".[550] The *Semanza* appeals chamber added that a higher sentence should be imposed on a person who ordered extermination, than on an aider and abettor.[551] The appeals chamber found Laurent Semanza guilty of ordering genocide and extermination as a crime against humanity.[552] Consequently, the appeals chamber raised Semanza's sentence for his involvement in the respective crimes from 15 to 25 years.[553] A

[548] Damgaard 2008, pp. 245–6.

[549] *Krnolejac*, 15 March 2002, para 77; in the same vein *Milutinović*, 21 May 2003, Separate Opinion of Judge David Hunt, para 31. See also Book 2011, pp. 129–30.

[550] *Kajelijeli*, 1 December 2003, para 963; *Vasiljević*, 25 February 2004, para 182; *Krstić*, 19 April 2004, para 268 (referring to the relation between aiding and abetting and co-perpetration); *Semanza*, 20 May 2005, para 388; *Gacumbitsi*, 7 July 2006, para 201; *Simić*, 28 November 2006, para 265 (referring to participation in a JCE and aiding and abetting); ICTR, *Emmanuel Ndindabahizi vs. the Prosecutor*, 16 January 2007, ICTR-01-71-A, para 122; ICTY, *Prosecutor v. Vidoje Blagojević and Dragan Jokić*, 9 May 2007, IT-02-60-A, para 334; *Nchamihigo*, 12 November 2008, para 388; *Kalimanzira*, 22 June 2009, para 744; *Karemera*, 2 February 2012, para 1720; *Nyiramasuhuko et al.*, 14 December 2015, para 3424. According to Ohlin, van Sliedregt and Weigend, the same relation between JCE and aiding and abetting can be found in the law of the SCSL, see Ohlin et al. 2013, p. 742.

[551] *Semanza*, 20 May 2005, para 388; see also paras 2-3 of the Separate Opinion of Judge Shahabudeen and Judge Güney in which they state that Semanza, having been found guilty of ordering genocide, was a perpetrator of genocide and would have deserved a life sentence. See also Boas et al. 2007, pp. 411–12.

[552] For the trial chamber's findings and conviction of aiding and abetting see *Semanza*, 15 May 2003, paras 435–6, 465, 553; for the appeals chamber see *Semanza*, 20 May 2005, para 364.

[553] *Semanza*, 20 May 2005, para 389. As the remainder of the trial chamber's determination of sentence was left intact, Laurent Semanza was sentenced to 34 ½ years of imprisonment (see ibid., paras 380, 395, 398–9, sentence in IV. Disposition; Boas et al. 2007, p. 412).

similar tendency can be seen in the appeals judgments in *Ntawukulilyayo*, in which the chamber contrasted ordering and aiding and abetting:

> The reversal of Ntawukulilyayo's conviction for ordering removes the only direct form of responsibility by which he was found to have participated in the Kabuye hill killings. The Appeals Chamber notes that aiding and abetting is a mode of responsibility which has generally warranted lower sentences than forms of direct participation such as commission or ordering.[554]

The chamber in *Nyiramasuhuko* considered this accordingly when they ruled that "aiding and abetting is a form of responsibility that has generally warranted lower sentences than forms of direct participation such as committing and ordering".[555] This has been reiterated by the appeals chamber in *Mrksić et al.*, extending the statement to planning and instigating as well.[556]

Given that planning and instigating require a similar causal nexus and the same mental element as ordering,[557] these modes of liability are also likely to lead to a higher sentence *vis-à-vis* the one imposed for aiding and abetting.[558]

The second principle concerns the relationship between JCE and aiding and abetting. The latter is usually considered less grave.[559]

Some chambers also held that hands-on commission could entail a lower sentence than participation in a JCE.[560] There is furthermore empirical evidence that, where hands-on-perpetration coincided with another form of participation of a high-ranking person, the combination would lead to a higher sentence than "leadership-involvement" alone would have.[561]

Chambers of the ICTR frequently reiterated another, third, principle of sentencing: a life sentence is usually reserved for those who planned or ordered crimes, and those who participated with particular zeal or sadism.[562]

In addition, other observations on the relationship between modes of liability and sentencing can be made.

---

[554] *Ntawukulilyayo*, 14 December 2011, para 244.

[555] *Nyiramasuhuko et al.*, 14 December 2015, para 3424.

[556] ICTY, *Prosecutor v. Mile Mrkšić and Veselin Šljivančanin*, 5 May 2009, ICTY-95-13/1-A, para 407; Ohlin et al. 2013, p. 741.

[557] For elements of instigating see Boas et al. 2007, pp. 358–9, 363; Mettraux 2005, pp. 281–2; for planning see Boas et al. 2007, pp. 354–8. See already Sect. 5.1.1.3.

[558] See also Boas et al. 2007, p. 412.

[559] See the description by ibid., pp. 409–10 with judgments in Footnote 148.

[560] Holá 2012, p. 14; *Prosecutor v. Milorad Krnojelac*, 17 September 2003, para 75; *Krajišnik*, 27 September 2006, para 1158, stating that the fact that the convicted was no principal offender (he was convicted for participating in a JCE), did not lessen his responsibility.

[561] D'Ascoli 2011, pp. 153, 259–60.

[562] *Musema*, 16 November 2001, para 383; *Ntakirutimana* 21 February 2003, para 884; *Ndindabahizi*, 15 July 2004, para 500; *Gacumbitsi*, 7 July 2006, para 206, reaching this conclusion without literally reiterating the principle; *Karera*, 7 December 2007, para 583; *Bagosora et al.*, 18 December 2008, para 2270; *Kanyarukiga*, 1 November 2010, para 684; *Karemera*, 2 February 2012, para 1720; Holá 2012, p. 14.

Chambers sometimes pointed to the necessity of a special intent (where required for the relevant crime) to explain the severity of sentences. The appeals chamber in *Krnolejac* and *Brđanin* indicated that participation in a JCE was more serious than aiding and abetting. It reasoned that for the former, the actor had to share the intent of the principal offender, whilst this was not necessary for the aider and abettor.[563] In *Krstić*, the appeals chamber substituted a conviction of committing genocide (by participating in a JCE), with one of aiding and abetting genocide because the convicted had lacked the necessary genocidal intent.[564] The chamber reduced Krstić's sentence, explaining that the lack of genocidal intent significantly diminished his responsibility.[565] This rationale corresponds with the principle that aiding and abetting generally warrants lower sentences, as it does not require the accused to have the special intent of a crime.

When fulfilled alone, superior responsibility tended to lead to lower sentences.[566]

The prohibition of double counting of factors in sentencing comes into play when a person who abused their authority is convicted for ordering.[567] However, according to the appeals chamber, there is a difference between a person abusing their authority and influence, and them using their influence to order the commission of a crime. Consequently, this would not fall under the prohibition of double consideration.[568]

Concerning responsibility for planning, the appeals chamber in *Kanyarukiga* explicitly stated that planning would not constitute a less grave responsibility than the (hands-on) commission of the crime.[569]

5.3.3.3 Summary and Conclusion

Modes of liability were regularly mentioned and evaluated when determining sentences. However, it remains unclear how decisive their influence was on sentencing.

The tribunals seemingly differentiate between more and less active or relevant forms of perpetration and participation within Articles 6 (1) and 7 (1) of the Statutes.

---

[563] *Prosecutor v. Milorad Krnojelac*, 17 September 2003, para 75. See also *Brđanin*, 1 September 2004, paras 272–4.

[564] *Krstić*, 19 April 2004, para 134; Boas et al. 2007, pp. 408–9.

[565] *Krstić*, 19 April 2004, para 268.

[566] This view is expressed by the trial chamber in ICTY, *Prosecutor v. Enver Hadžihasanović and Amir Kubura*, 15 March 2006, IT-01-47-T, para 2076; speaking of an "even greater flexibility" in imposing sentences: *Orić*, 30 June 2006, para 724; Holá et al. 2012, pp. 544, 547.

[567] This is different to the aforementioned consideration of superior responsibility as an aggravating factor in sentencing. However, both could naturally fall together, as can be seen in the appeal by Pauline Nyiramasuhuko in *Nyiramasuhuko et al.*, 14 December 2015, paras 3353–4, 3359.

[568] *Karemera et al.*, 29 September 2014, para 680-3; the same was possibly given in *Nyiramasuhuko*, 24 June 2011, para 6207; *Nyiramasuhuko et al.*, 14 December 2015, para 3359; see with regards to this Drumbl 2016, pp. 434–5, stating that Nyiramasuhuko's abuse of a superior position was considered, as opposed to her mere status as a superior.

[569] ICTR, *Gaspard Kanyarukiga v. The Prosecutor*, 8 May 2012, ICTR-02-78-A, paras 277, 281.

As the less active form, aiding and abetting (usually described as indirect responsibility) warrants lower sentences than the other modes of liability. In comparison, commission (including through a Joint Criminal Enterprise), planning, instigating, and ordering (often described as direct responsibility) are thought to lead to higher sentences.[570]

In practice, however, to date, the mode of liability has not been found to significantly influence the length of sentences.[571] Perhaps because of this practical disregard of modes of liability in sentencing, it remains unclear whether commission (also via JCE) warrants longer sentences than ordering, planning or instigating. The fact that the tribunals usually only delineate the chosen direct mode from aiding and abetting, supports the view that the different modes of direct participation do not warrant different sentence lengths. This is also supported by the finding that planning, ordering, and instigating require the special intent of the actor to the same extent as commission does.

It can therefore be concluded that the tribunals consider the modes of liability in different categories: Aiding and abetting warrants lower sentences as a more inactive (indirect) mode of liability. The other, more active modes of liability, i.e., commission (including JCE), ordering, planning, and instigating warrant higher sentences. Within the latter group, no differentiation exists in principle. This finding speaks in favour of a hierarchy of forms of responsibility, albeit one, which does not distinguish between commission and accessorial forms of liability, but between commission, ordering, planning, and instigating as direct modes and aiding and abetting as an indirect mode of responsibility.

5.3.4 *Legal Concurrences and Choice of Modes of Liability*

The issue of legal concurrences can be crucial when exploring a system and hierarchy of forms of responsibility. If chambers must choose between different heads of liability, this can enable conclusions on the existence of a hierarchy between these modes. If a conduct fulfils two modes of liability, but one always takes precedence over the other, this indicates a hierarchy. If, on the other hand, a conduct fulfils two modes of liability, but whether one or the other takes precedence depends on the circumstances of the case, there can be no hierarchy between these modes.

Instead, one might speak of a phenomenological, or associative choice of modes of liability.[572] If two or more modes of liability coexist in the judgment to attribute responsibility for a single conduct, this only enables limited logical conclusions on

[570] Boas et al. 2007, p. 413; Holá 2012, p. 14. On the terminology of direct and indirect forms of responsibility, see Sect. 5.3.1. *supra*.

[571] D'Ascoli 2011, pp. 259–60. Holá et al. stipulated that the modes of liability could "augment" or "lessen" the gravity of the crime, but do not count modes of liability among the factors which they found relevant either, cf. Holá et al. 2012, pp. 544 and 546–7, where modes of liability are not found to be among the significant predictors.

[572] Cf. Werle and Jessberger 2020, mn. 863.

a hierarchy as apparently no need exists to determine the precedence of any of these modes. Nevertheless, in this latter case, the choice of a mode of responsibility may still shed light on the relation between them. This can be the case if the ruling chamber does not convict under all the modes fulfilled by the accused's conduct, but rather only chooses two, instead of say, three fulfilled modes of liability.

The *ad hoc* tribunals' chambers frequently chose to convict under one form of responsibility or another. In such cases, many chambers based their choice on what they found to be the "appropriate" form of responsibility.[573] The definition of this term remains unclear, although it has been invoked above that the expressive or descriptive value of modes may play a role in such a choice.

Some commentators submitted that, when determining the appropriate form of responsibility, the tribunals have partially applied a normative approach (i.e. one based on a hierarchy of modes), and partially relied on a phenomenological associative approach (i.e. one based on the modes' literal description of the actor's conduct).[574] It has also been suggested that concurrences at the *ad hoc* tribunals would always grant precedence to commission over ordering, instigation and planning, which would establish a hierarchy.[575] The latter conclusion makes sense if one assumes that in a differentiated system of perpetration and participation, commission must always act as the single most blameworthy form of responsibility. However, the responsibility forms in a differentiated system might also be distinguished from each other based on phenomenological or empirical considerations. Such a system may be implied where a judgment confirms principal liability alongside forms of accessory liability, and subsequently raises the question which of those forms would be appropriate. Such a judgment could rely on phenomenological considerations as it would not automatically grant precedence to principal liability.[576]

Another categorization of modes of responsibility has been proposed above. Pursuant to this, forms of direct responsibility (commission, ordering, planning, instigating) are considered equally blameworthy, with all of them being considered more serious than aiding and abetting.[577] The approach to concurrences in certain judgments can justifiably be interpreted as following this distinct approach which would have to rely on both normative and empirical considerations to decide on the most appropriate mode of liability.

The following section analyses judgments grouped according to the conclusions that can be drawn from them concerning the system of perpetration and participation that may underlie the *ad hoc* tribunals' jurisprudence.

---

573 *Krstić*, 2 August 2001, para 602; *Krajišnik*, 27 September 2006, para 877; *Milutinović et al.*, 26 February 2009, para 77; *Krajišnik*, 17 March 2009, para 652; *Đorđević*, 27 January 2014, para 831; Werle and Jessberger 2020, mn. 863. Also note the formulation of "best reflecting the conduct" of the accused in *Nahimana et al.*, 28 November 2007, para 483; *Đorđević*, 23 February 2011, para 2194; see also the description as "characterizing" conduct in *Stakić*, 31 July 2003, para 468; *Ndindabahizi*, 16 January 2007, para 123.

574 Werle and Jessberger 2020, mn. 863; see also the analysis in Burghardt 2008, pp. 377–9.

575 Schabas 2006, p. 296.

576 Burghardt 2008, pp. 377–9.

577 See the foregoing Sects. 5.3.1–5.3.3.

5.3.4.1 Convictions Under All Fulfilled Heads of Responsibility Without Any Possible Conclusions

In a first group of judgments, the accused were convicted under all heads of liability that the chamber found fulfilled. This does not allow any conclusions as to a relationship between the modes to be drawn. In *Kayishema and Ruzindana*, the chamber found one of the accused guilty of *"instigating, ordering, committing or otherwise aiding and abetting in the planning and preparation and execution of genocide"*.[578] The view that several forms of responsibility could be entered concurrently was shared by several other chambers. The trial chambers in *Đorđević, Ndindabahizi, Musema* and *Akayesu* convicted the accused based on different heads of responsibility.[579] The appeals chamber in *Ndindabahizi* confirmed this view.[580]

5.3.4.2 Judgments that Imply a Hierarchy With "Committing" Being the Most Serious Form

Some trial chamber judgments of the ICTY explicitly took the view that, where the same conduct would lead to a conviction for planning or ordering and committing a crime, the accused could only be convicted of the latter.[581] Commission thus took precedence over planning and ordering on principle. Some of these judgments also confirmed that, where planning and ordering would have been fulfilled in addition to commission, this could be regarded as aggravating circumstances.[582] These judgments imply a hierarchy between forms of responsibility in which committing a crime is the most blameworthy form.[583]

---

[578] ICTR, *The Prosecutor v. Clément Kayishema and Obed Ruzindana*, 21 May 1999, ICTR-95-1-T, para 554, see also paras 558, 568.

[579] *Akayesu*, 2 September 1998, para 692; *Musema*, 27 January 2000, paras 891, 897, 903, 908, 912, 922, 936, 949; *Ndindabahizi*, 15 July 2004, para 485; *Đorđević*, 23 February 2011, para 2194; Burghardt 2008, pp. 377–8.

[580] *Ndindabahizi*, 16 January 2007, paras 121–3. The chamber rejects the idea of convictions under *alternative* modes of liability but affirms that a conviction would be possible under several heads of responsibility if they are unequivocally identified and put into relation to the respective conduct of the accused.

[581] *Kordić and Čerkez*, 26 February 2001, para 386; *Stakić*, 31 July 2003, paras 443, 445; *Brđanin*, 1 September 2004, para 268; *Milošević*, 12 December 2007, para 956.

[582] *Brđanin*, 19 March 2004, para 268; *Milošević*, 12 December 2007, para 956.

[583] See Burghardt 2008, p. 378.

5.3.4.3 Judgments Open to Interpretation: The Appeals Chambers' Rulings in *Karemera and Ngirumpatse, Đorđević, Dragomir Milošević* and *Kamuhanda*

The appeals chamber in *Đorđević* decided that, in this specific case, a conviction for committing and aiding and abetting the same crime, based on the same conduct, was not warranted. It therefore reversed the appellant's conviction under aiding and abetting,[584] implying a hierarchy between the two forms. Something similar can be observed in the appeals judgments against *Kamuhanda, Dragomir Milošević* and *Karemera and Ngirumpatse.*

The concurrent trial chamber convictions of Jean de Dieu Kamuhanda under ordering and aiding and abetting were substituted by the appeals chamber for one of ordering alone.[585] This can be interpreted as being based on a hierarchy between these forms, pursuant to which ordering takes precedence.[586]

However, some commentators suggested that the judgment did not establish such a principle.[587] Rather, it decided that—in the specific case—the conduct of the accused was most appropriately described by ordering alone, even though a concurrent conviction for aiding and abetting would—in general—have been possible.[588] The same interpretation would be valid for the appeals judgments in *Dragomir Milošević* and in *Karemera and Ngirumpatse.* Just as in *Kamuhanda*, the appeals chamber substituted Dragomir Milošević's conviction for planning and ordering with one of ordering alone, because it found that "responsibility for ordering … fully encompasse[d] his criminal conduct and d[id] not warrant a separate conviction for planning the same crimes."[589] The appeals chamber in *Karemera and Ngirumpatse* followed the same logic. It found that responsibility for commission (via JCE) fully encompassed the accused's criminal conduct, crushing their concurrent conviction for aiding and abetting.[590] This reading suggests that in the relevant cases one mode of liability fully encompassed the criminal conduct, rendering a conviction under the others redundant,[591] without implying that this would automatically happen in other cases.

---

[584] *Đorđević*, 27 January 2014, paras 824–834. See in this regard Schabas 2006, p. 296.

[585] *Kamuhanda*, 19 September 2005, para 77.

[586] Burghardt 2008, p. 378; Judge Wolfgang Schomburg apparently endorsed this view in his Separate Opinion in *Kamuhanda*, 19 September 2005, paras 386–9; the statement of the trial chamber in *Orić*, 30 June 2006, para 269, which quotes the *Kamuhanda* appeals judgments may also be understood in this way.

[587] See *Kamuhanda*, 19 September 2005, Separate Opinion of Presiding Judge Theodor Meron, para 366; Separate and Partially Dissention Opinion of Judge Mohamed Shahabuddeen, para 402; Separate Opinion of Judge Inés Weinberg de Roca on Paragraph 77 of the Judgment, para 417.

[588] For this interpretation see Boas et al. 2007, pp. 389–90, citing the separate opinions from the foregoing footnote.

[589] *D. Milošević*, 12 November 2009, paras 274, 333.

[590] *Karemera et al.*, 29 September 2014, para 448.

[591] *Kamuhanda*, 19 September 2005, para 77; *D. Milošević*, 12 November 2009, paras 274, 333; *Đorđević*, 27 January 2014, paras 829-34; *Karemera et al.*, 29 September 2014, para 448.

The *Kamuhanda* appeals judgment can provide further clarification. The appeals chamber determined that Kamuhanda's presence at a parish compound, his statement that the armed persons around him should get to "work" and his authority had aided and abetted the killings and thus the crime of genocide.[592] It then affirmed responsibility for ordering based on the same facts. Considering this complete overlap of underlying facts, the chamber discarded responsibility for aiding and abetting because ordering "fully encapsulate[d]" the criminal conduct.[593] As the conviction of Kamuhanda for ordering and aiding and abetting rested on the same acts, the mode of ordering was deemed sufficient to adjudicate the wrong perpetrated by the accused. The same reasoning underlies the other judgments cited above.[594]

It is tempting to interpret these judgments as establishing a hierarchy between certain modes of liability. However, they can also be explained based on a phenomenological approach. The *Kamuhanda* and *Dragomir Milošević* judgments opted for ordering instead of aiding and abetting and planning, respectively. In *Kamuhanda*, the accused *inter alia* told a group of armed men to get to "work", which they understood as an order to kill Tutsi and the chamber evaluated it as ordering.[595] In *Dragomir Milošević*, it was inferred from the circumstances that the accused had ordered the shelling of Sarajevo, because he had been the military commander of the respective forces with tight control over their operational actions, especially the deployment of artillery.[596] Due to their central position of authority in the respective situation in both cases, a phenomenological view could equally lead to the conclusion that ordering was the better description of the accused's responsibility. That they also aided and abetted or planned the crimes through the same conduct, was perhaps seen as a less fitting description of what they had done. The same can be said of the *Đorđević* and the *Karemera and Ngirumpatse* judgments. From a phenomenological perspective, the conduct of a person who significantly contributes to a criminal enterprise with others, is perhaps better described as participation in a JCE than as aiding and abetting as JCE reflects the joint efforts of the participants.

Therefore, it is possible to interpret these judgments as not establishing a hierarchy of modes of responsibility, as their choices could have also been determined by phenomenological, associative considerations.

Additionally, these judgments can also be reconciled with the interpretation that no hierarchy exists between commission, ordering, planning, and instigating. When establishing the precedence of commission (including JCE), instigating, ordering, or planning in these cases, it could be understood that chambers relied on a vague concept of appropriateness, closely connected to the specific case, and thus to phenomenological considerations. This can be seen in the case of Dragomir Milošević, where the chamber decided that ordering would better describe his

592 *Kamuhanda*, 19 September 2005, paras 71–2.

593 Ibid., paras 73–7.

594 *D. Milošević*, 12 November 2009, para 274; *Karemera et al.*, 29 September 2014, para 448; *Đorđević*, 27 January 2014, paras 829–834.

595 *Kamuhanda*, 19 September 2005, paras 71, 74–6.

596 *D. Milošević*, 12 November 2009, paras 272–274.

conduct than planning. Hence, the judgments establish no specific hierarchy between these four forms of responsibility. However, where the precedence of any of these four modes was established over aiding and abetting, this could be due to the fact that aiding and abetting was considered a lesser form of responsibility. Consequently, these judgments would establish both, a normative and a phenomenological choice of modes of liability. Nonetheless, it is conceded that this is only one of three possible interpretations.

5.3.4.4 Judgments That May Imply a Phenomenological Approach or a Hierarchy in Which Commission is Not Considered More Blameworthy Than Certain Other Forms

As outlined above, a judgment in which ordering or planning, for example, take precedence over commission, can be interpreted as establishing a purely phenomenological associative approach for the entire system of perpetration and participation. However, it may also imply that only between those two modes, there is no hierarchical relationship, but instead principle phenomenological choice applies, while these two modes may still be in a hierarchical relation to others.

The trial chamber in *Milutinović et al.* stated that a conviction could only be based on one single form of responsibility.[597] The chamber rejected the automatic precedence of commission over ordering, planning, and instigating. It took the view that, where commission and another form under Article 7 (1) of the statute were established, a chamber had to "identify the most appropriate form of liability".[598]

The trial chamber in *Renzaho* convicted the accused under the heads of ordering and aiding and abetting on two occasions. In both instances, it affirmed that a conviction for commission (by participating in a JCE) would have been possible as well, but that it had opted for the conviction under ordering and aiding and abetting.[599]

This could obviously be a choice based exclusively on associative or descriptive considerations and thus speak to a phenomenological approach. However, the chamber assured that no harsher punishment would have followed a conviction for committing the crime.[600] This illustrates that the chamber considered whether commission would take precedence based on hierarchical considerations, ultimately denying this, however, and giving precedence to ordering and aiding and abetting.

This could be described as an approach pursuant to which, one of the direct forms of liability (commission, ordering, planning, instigating) must be chosen. In this case, the choice was ordering. As no hierarchy between commission and ordering exists following this reading, the choice must have been based on other considerations of "appropriateness". It is conceivable that the expressive (phenomenological) value was decisive.

---

[597] *Milutinović et al.*, 26 February 2009, para 77.

[598] Ibid., para 77.

[599] *Renzaho*, 14 July 2009, paras 766 with Footnote 857, 770 with Footnote 858.

[600] Ibid., paras 766 with Footnote 857, 770 with Footnote 858.

However, the question remains why aiding and abetting was confirmed along with ordering for the same conduct of the accused Tharcisse Renzaho. This cannot be explained through the latter interpretation which would imply a hierarchy between ordering and aiding and abetting. Instead, this supports a phenomenological approach, under which ordering and aiding and abetting were chosen as the best descriptors of the way the accused contributed to the crimes in question.[601]

5.3.4.5 Summary

The tribunals' jurisprudence on the legal concurrences of forms of responsibility is incoherent. Whether a person can be convicted under different heads of responsibility for the same conduct is contentious. It has been affirmed in principle and in practice by some judgments. Other judgments have not followed this. The analysed judgments neither enable a clear conclusion on matters of concurrences, nor on the guiding principle—normative or phenomenological—used to differentiate between modes of liability.

The findings, in themselves, enable different conclusions on a system of perpetration and participation in the law of the *ad hoc* tribunals. Unfortunately, by being completely opposite to and irreconcilable with each other, they do not enable one convincing interpretation.

5.3.5 *Excursion: The ICTR Appeals Chamber's Approach Opposed to the Preceding Findings*

The appeals chamber of the ICTR has in later judgments shown a tendency to adjudicate criminal conduct as "committing" a crime whenever possible, without relying on the figure of JCE. This was done in *Gacumbitsi, Seromba, Munyakazi, Kalimanzira* and *Nyiramasuhuko*. The chamber held that if the accused's action "was as much an integral part of genocide as were the killings which it enabled", they should be liable for committing genocide.[602] This seemingly displays a tendency of the appeals chamber to introduce a hierarchy of forms of responsibility with commission being the most blameworthy form.[603] The *Gacumbitsi* judgment encourages a relatively clear distinction in seriousness between commission on the one hand, and ordering

---

[601] This part of the judgment would allow the grouping of it into the category of Sect. 5.3.4.1 as well.

[602] *Gacumbitsi*, 7 July 2006, para 60; *Seromba*, 12 March 2008, para 161; *Munyakazi*, 5 July 2010, para 430; *Kalimanzira*, 20 October 2010, para 219; *Nyiramasuhuko et al.*, 14 December 2015, para 3322.

[603] van Sliedregt 2012, pp. 80–1; Zorzi Giustiani 2008, pp. 798–9.

and instigating on the other.[604] In this vein, in his separate opinion in *Gacumbitsi,* Judge Shahabuddeen explained that a person being such an integral part of a crime "not only order[s] or instigate[s] but actually participate[s] in the "commission" of the crime".[605] These judgments stand in direct contrast to and are irreconcilable with the proposed common denominator reading, as they do not recognize any form of accessory liability as being as blameworthy as commission.

It must be kept in mind though, that the chambers usually only applied this concept to the commission of genocide.[606] This restricts the value of this line of judgments for the overall interpretation, because it runs contrary to the usual approach of the tribunals of applying forms of responsibility in the same fashion to all crimes.[607]

Apart from this, the decisions can be criticised from different angles. It has been remarked that the "integral part" formula does not enable a reasonable distinction of commission liability from forms of accessory liability.[608] Furthermore, whilst stating that "commission" would not be limited to the physical commission, the chambers completely ignore the existence of the doctrine of JCE. This doctrine has been the approach to perpetration liability for contributions other than hands-on commission and no guidance is provided on how these two concepts of non-physical commission are meant to work together or be delineated from each other.[609] In some of the judgments, the chambers expressly relied on German jurisprudence for indirect perpetration.[610] However, as Judge Liu points out, through their appeals chamber, the *ad hoc* tribunals had previously rejected that the notion of indirect perpetration was part of customary international criminal law.[611] In this vein, it can also be criticised that the decision lacks precise sources besides hinting at the *Eichmann* and IMT judgments.[612] As previously stated, it is impossible to meaningfully read a legal doctrine of indirect perpetration into the *Eichmann* and post-World War II judgments.[613]

Additionally, these judgements stand in outright contradiction to other appeals chamber judgments from the same period. The appeals chamber in *Ntawukulilyayo*

---

[604] "The appellant did not simply 'order' or 'plan' genocide from a distance and leave it to others to ensure that his orders and plans were carried out; nor did he merely "instigate" the killings", *Gacumbitsi*, 7 July 2006, para 61.

[605] Ibid., Separate Opinion of Judge Shahabuddeen, para 22.

[606] So far, only the *Seromba* judgment applied this interpretation of commission to another crime other than genocide, and this was readily criticized by Judge Liu, see *Seromba*, 12 March 2008, Dissenting Opinion of Judge Liu, para 2.

[607] Boas et al. 2007, p. 117.

[608] Zorzi Giustiani 2008, p. 797. This is of little surprise given the reliance of the Seromba appeals chamber on the German *Mauerschützen* case concerning the political bureau (see *Seromba*, 12 March 2008, para 389). On the vague objective requirements of the German jurisprudence for indirect perpetration through an organisation see, Chap. 2, Sect. 2.3.2.3.

[609] *Seromba*, 12 March 2008, Dissenting Opinion of Judge Liu, para 6.

[610] Ibid., para 389; *Gacumbitsi*, 7 July 2006, para 42 with Footnote 62.

[611] *Seromba*, 12 March 2008, Dissenting Opinion of Judge Liu, paras 9–10.

[612] Boas et al. 2007, p. 117.

[613] See Chap. 3, Sect. 3.3.1.2 and Chap. 4, Sect. 4.3.3.

categorized ordering as a form of "direct participation", stressing this form's heightened blameworthiness deliberately.[614] The initial *Gacumbitsi* judgment stressed factors such as the presence of the accused at the crime scene and his participation in the selection of victims, and went on to state that the accused "did not simply 'order' or 'plan' genocide from a distance."[615] However, this is in complete contradiction to the guiding principle in the *Eichmann* case. It significantly diverges from the findings which have shaped the debate on leadership liability in international criminal law. As reiterated time and again, increasing distance plays absolutely no role for the responsibility of a decision maker or architect of international crimes. Therefore, the presence at the crime scene and the influence over specific criminal incidents cannot serve to establish heightened blameworthiness.

This line of judgments stands in contradiction to the common interpretation that may be applied to many ICTY and ICTR judgments. However, its reasoning is unconvincing for the abovementioned reasons. It is especially submitted that these judgments are too few and their reasoning not corroborated by jurisprudence from the same chambers during the same period. These judgments therefore do not establish a coherent doctrine or opinion concerning the general mode of committing a crime and its relation to other modes. They stand out as doctrinally incoherent offshoots.

5.3.6 Conclusion on the Role and Position of Ordering in a System of Perpetration and Participation at the Ad Hoc *Tribunals*

The *ad hoc* tribunals' jurisprudence on forms of responsibility and its interpretation is contentious. The analysis above suggests that aiding and abetting was usually considered less serious than the other accessorial modes of liability,[616] while the position of ordering, planning, and instigating within the system is contentious.

As shown, the tribunals expressed a range of ideas and considerations on the mode of ordering and the system of perpetration and participation. Some points directly mirror the respective chamber's view on how the modes of liability should be interpreted. Others indicate features of the forms of responsibility suggesting a different interpretation to the two traditional views (normative differential and unitary) on the system and the categorisation of responsibility forms within it.

614 *Ntawukulilyayo*, 14 December 2011, para 244.

615 *Gacumbitsi*, 7 July 2006, paras 60–1.

616 Boas et al. 2007, p. 412; Burghardt 2008, pp. 304–6; Olásolo 2009, p. 135.

5.3.6.1 Summary of Observations

Summed up, these observations and their respective indications are the following:

- Terminology: Commission, ordering, planning, and instigating are often described as direct responsibility in contrast to aiding and abetting which is called indirect responsibility.[617] This suggests that no different level of blameworthiness applies to commission, ordering, planning, and instigating.
- Legal requirements: The *mens rea* of the ordering actor (and potentially that of the planner and instigator) must comprise the special intent of a crime, where the crime so requires.[618] This requirement suggests that commission (including JCE), and thus also, ordering, planning, and instigating, is more serious. Aiding and abetting does not require the special intent of a crime. In this regard, no difference in seriousness exists between commission, ordering, planning, and instigating.
- Sentencing: In principle, no gradation applies between commission, ordering, planning, and instigating, whilst all these forms are considered more serious than aiding and abetting and command responsibility.[619] This finding supports the view that no difference in seriousness applies between committing, ordering, planning, and instigating a crime.
- Concurrences: Some chambers treat commission, ordering, instigating, and planning as equal, and would not let commission take precedence over the others. Other judgments, however, did the exact opposite.[620] Therefore, no conclusions are possible based on the evaluation of the concurrences practice. Yet, many judgments are reconcilable with the view that a differently structured hierarchy exists between modes of liability.

5.3.6.2 An Alternative Interpretation of the System of Perpetration and Participation Under the *Ad Hoc* Tribunals' Laws

To a certain extent, the observations of this section contradict both of the common interpretations of the system of perpetration and participation in *ad hoc* jurisprudence. Neither a normative-differential approach with a strict hierarchy of blameworthiness between principal and accessory liability, nor a phenomenological approach (be it unitary or differential) without any hierarchy, seem to exist. Instead, an interpretation of multiple judgments is possible, in which ordering, planning, and instigating qualify as direct, yet accessory liability. This reading is possible if one accepts that

[617] See above at Sect. 5.3.1.; see also the exceptional judgment in *Nchamihigo*, 12 November 2008, para 388 where the chamber described the accused, who had been convicted for ordering, instigating, and aiding and abetting as a "principal perpetrator".

[618] See Sects. 5.1.1.4 and 5.3.3.

[619] See Sect. 5.3.3.

[620] See Sect. 5.3.4.

one term (direct liability) describes the seriousness of a crime, whilst the other (accessory liability[621]) refers to the technicality of requiring the commission of a crime by another. Consequently, commission, ordering, planning, and instigating a crime can lead to direct responsibility, a term which implies a higher seriousness or blameworthiness than indirect responsibility (aiding and abetting, complicity in genocide). In contrast to commission, responsibility for ordering, planning, and instigating will still be regarded accessorial, i.e., derivative liability (implying the necessity of the commission of a crime by another).

Consequently, Articles 6 (1) and 7 (1) of the statutes can be read as applying a hierarchy between forms of responsibility, albeit a different one than previously formulated. The most serious forms of participation in a crime are commission, ordering, planning, and instigating. Aiding and abetting and complicity in genocide are considered less serious. Of the most serious modes of liability only commission qualifies as primary responsibility, whereas ordering, planning, and instigating are derivative, accessorial liability and share this feature with aiding and abetting, as well as complicity in genocide.

The consequence that the same potential blameworthiness is ascribed to persons who committed, ordered, planned, or instigated a crime, corresponds with the finding that these forms require the necessary *dolus specialis* to incur liability for crimes like genocide and persecution. This corresponds with the findings that no difference exists in principle between the appropriate sentencing lengths for commission, ordering, planning, and instigating, while aiding and abetting is perceived as warranting lower sentences and requires no special intent.

In terms of legal concurrences and under the assumption that one form of responsibility must take precedence over the rest, the choice between commission, ordering, planning, and instigating must use a parameter other than a hierarchy of seriousness. The choice can be based on phenomenological considerations, as apparently happened in some judgments.

This interpretation of the role of modes of liability within the system of perpetration and participation is based on what can be referred to as the common denominators of the—otherwise often contradictory—*ad hoc* jurisprudence on modes of responsibility.

5.3.6.3 A Confrontation of the Alternative Interpretation with Prominent Opinions from Literature

One must acknowledge that some judgments support one of the two traditional classifications of the modes of responsibility. This is especially true for those that aim to interpret the statutes as including a strict hierarchical system of perpetration and participation.

---

[621] ICTY and ICTR also frequently use the term of accomplice liability, which is avoided for terminological coherence in this thesis and referred to with the term "accessory" liability.

The interpretation in favour of a hierarchical differentiated system of perpetration and participation pursuant to Article 6 (1) ICTR and Article 7 (1) ICTY Statute, as supported by some commentators, reveals a somewhat narrow approach to the issue. The same is true of the opposite view. It seems that only these two systems are considered as possibilities in interpreting the *ad hoc* statutes. Alternative interpretations deviating from what is commonly known in various national legal systems, are apparently not considered.[622] This narrow view may mirror a tendency to simplify matters in comparative law. Such simplification may generally be necessary but can evidently also lead to oversimplification. One should be mindful, for example, that the German system of perpetration and participation does not explicitly recognize a hierarchy of blameworthiness with commission at the top, but instead provides for the same punishment for perpetrators and instigators.[623]

An example of such an approach can be found with Olásolo, who narrowly interprets ordering as a form of accomplice, and therefore less blameworthy, liability while preferring JCE and indirect perpetration as the concepts of choice in dealing with high-level criminality.[624] When discussing the *ad hoc* jurisprudence, his interpretation is mostly based on the recognition of participation in a JCE as a form of commission, i.e. as giving rise to primary responsibility.[625] It has been questioned, whether his interpretation of ordering takes sufficient notice of certain details in jurisprudence.[626] Furthermore, the interpretation applies the narrow view that any form of primary responsibility automatically implies a higher blameworthiness than forms of accessory liability. Consequently, where possible, any form of commission is to be preferred over ordering. This is based almost exclusively on two points. Firstly, the perception that participation in a JCE is more blameworthy than aiding and abetting and consequently more serious than other forms of accessorial liability. Secondly, the questionable finding that no special intent would be necessary for ordering crimes.[627] Both assumptions have been proven to be unfounded in *ad hoc*

---

[622] See e.g., Judge Schomburg, who, in his separate opinion in the *Gacumbitsi* appeals judgment, elaborates on unitary and differentiated systems of perpetration, concluding that "as the Tribunals' jurisprudence favours a distinction between principal and accessory (Täterschaft und Teilnahme) for the determination of individual criminal responsibility, it must also accept the consequences which follow from this approach. It is impossible to make a difference in terms of substantive law between planning, instigating, ordering, committing or aiding and abetting, without acknowledging that, in principle, each of those modes warrants distinction on the sentencing level as well. The difference in individual criminal responsibility must be mirrored in the sentence", see *Gacumbitsi*, 7 July 2006, Separate Opinion of Judge Schomburg on the Criminal Responsibility of the Appellant for Committing Genocide, para 6 [footnotes omitted]. As seen in Chap. 3, this statement was driven by Judge Schomburg's conviction that the statutes of the ICTY and ICTR should be interpreted closer to the German understanding of perpetration and participation, see Chap. 3, Sect. 3.3.1.2.

[623] Cp. Chap. 2, Sect. 2.2.5 (referring to Roxin who indeed favours such a hierarchy) but note the criticism on this, and the possibility of reading the German system very differently in Chap. 8, Sect. 8.1.5.

[624] Olásolo 2009, pp. 25, 135 with Footnote 238, 139–40.

[625] Ibid., pp. 20–26.

[626] Cf. Sect. 5.1.1.4.

[627] Olásolo 2009, pp. 139–40.

jurisprudence. No rule stipulates that the commission of a crime is more blameworthy than its ordering, planning, or instigating.[628] Of course, aiding and abetting is almost unanimously regarded to be less serious, however, the relation between the other forms is precisely what has not been sufficiently considered. As demonstrated, particularly the special intent requirement is one of the factors leading to an equivalent seriousness between commission and ordering.[629] Hence, the view expressed by Olásolo cannot be sustained as a general interpretation of the system of perpetration and participation in the law of the *ad hoc* tribunals.

Chambers and individual judges have also stated that the statutes of the ICTY and ICTR establish a formal hierarchy of modes of liability, with commission at the top.[630] In a separate opinion, Judge Shahabuddeen expressly stated that the convicted had "not only 'ordered' or 'instigated' but actually participated in the 'commission' of the crime".[631] Whilst it is not contested that such a reading of Articles 6 (1) and 7 (1) of the statutes is generally possible, it has been shown that this view is not convincing. This is particularly so given the legal requirements, range of possible application and expressive value of the mode of ordering and (as far as considered) planning and instigating. The only remaining difference following the interpretation proposed in this book is that ordering, planning, and instigating are accessorial liability. However, it seems questionable that derivativeness of responsibility alone is an indicator for blameworthiness or for the expressive value of a mode of liability.

Other scholars and judges have warned against applying a hierarchy of blameworthiness to the forms of responsibility of the *ad hoc* tribunals.[632] This view is often interconnected with opinions on the scope of commission, i.e., on JCE or the expanded view on commission. This is due to the fact that the aspiration to convict someone for committing a crime rather than, e.g., instigating or aiding and abetting it, logically entails the discussion about whether this is necessary to reflect the accused's responsibility and guilt.[633]

It is difficult to conclude that no differentiation in seriousness and consequently punishment is attached to different forms of responsibility at all. Aiding and abetting is commonly referred to as warranting lower sentences. Yet, when it comes to commission, ordering, planning, and instigating—direct forms of liability in the language of many chambers—one can say that the jurisprudence has not generally established a hierarchy between them, neither in terms of concurrences, nor of sentencing lengths.

---

[628] Cf. Sect. 5.3.3.

[629] See Sect. 5.1.1.4.

[630] See especially above at Sects. 5.3.4.2. and 5.3.5.

[631] *Gacumbitsi*, 7 July 2006, Separate Opinion of Judge Shahabuddeen, para 22.

[632] *Milutinović*, 21 May 2003, Separate Opinion of Judge David Hunt on Challenge by Ojdanić to Jurisdiction Joint Criminal Enterprise, para 31; Boas et al. 2007, pp. 413–4, 422–3; Zorzi Giustiani 2008, pp. 798–9.

[633] See the critical discussion by Judge Liu in *Seromba*, 12 March 2008, paras 6–18; see also *Gacumbitsi*, 7 July 2006, Partially Dissenting Opinion of Judge Güney, paras 3, 6–7, who criticizes the expansion of the term commission, although without elaborating on the question of an implied hierarchy.

As pointed out above, some commentators take the view that ordering (not planning or instigating), is more closely related to the concept of indirect perpetration or agency.[634] This interpretation is based on the necessary vertical power structures[635] or the contention that the physical perpetrators do not have to act with any relevant *mens rea*.[636] Given that the authority requirement must make the recipient of an order feel "compelled" to act, this could sound convincing. This would place the mode of ordering in the proximity of what is understood as indirect perpetration.[637] Additionally, at least one chamber shared the view that ordering should be regarded as principal/primary liability.[638] However, in light of the findings above, it seems that there is little to be done about ordering being considered accessorial liability in the general jurisprudence of the *ad hoc* statutes.[639]

Thus, the way in which ordering is applied by the *ad hoc* tribunals does not resemble the requirements of indirect perpetration.[640]

Finally, Burghardt submits that the jurisprudence differentiates between primary and secondary liability, establishing a hierarchy of blameworthiness, yet not clarifying the categorization of certain forms of responsibility within this hierarchy.[641] In light of the submitted, this can be opposed to a certain extent. Some forms of liability have frequently been referred to as accessory liability in the sense of derivative liability yet were not considered less blameworthy than primary responsibility.

The foregoing argumentation illustrates that the proposed understanding of the modes of responsibility helps overcome some of the issues of interpreting *ad hoc* jurisprudence. It can reconcile some judgments that are usually interpreted as being contrary to each other. This interpretation can therefore outline a system of perpetration and participation based on common ground in much of the *ad hoc* tribunals' jurisprudence.

This can serve as a basis for the further analysis of forms of responsibility, as well as for the assessment of ordering as an appropriate mode to deal with high- and mid-level decision makers and architects of crimes.

---

[634] See above Sect. 5.1.2; Ambos 2004, p. 569; Badar 2013, p. 335.

[635] Ambos 2004, p. 569.

[636] Badar 2013, p. 335.

[637] See Sect. 5.1.1.2 for the authority requirement, see also on the ICC's requirement in this regard Chap. 3, Sect. 3.1.2.3.

[638] *Nchamihigo*, 12 November 2008, para 388, see already Sect. 5.3.1.

[639] See Sects. 5.1.2. and 5.3.1.

[640] However, one should keep in mind that the question of ordering as accessorial liability or a form of indirect perpetration is deeply intertwined with the unsettled issue of the "accessorial object". As mentioned, it has been argued by Vogel that only the objective element of the crime would be the accessorial object on international criminal law (see Vogel 2002, pp. 424–5). If that was true, the difference between indirect perpetration and ordering as an accessorial mode of liability would become increasingly blurred.

[641] Burghardt 2008, pp. 303–8.

5.4 Summary and Conclusion

Under the law of the *ad hoc* tribunals, ordering requires the exercise of a—however informal—position of authority over another, which compels the other to commit a crime. The authority requirement can apply to the relation between mid-level actors and their subordinates, as well as to persons on the highest level of a hierarchy. The ordered crime must be committed and the ordering actor must fulfil the *mens rea* requirement of the crime, including the special intent.

In concert with planning and instigating, ordering provides for a scope of criminalization which is almost equally broad to the one provided by JCE.[642] The application of these forms of responsibility would have the considerable advantage that they would describe the actor as someone who had used authority to set the crime in motion (ordering), who came up with central ideas or schemes behind the mass atrocities (planning), and/or who had planted the criminal ideas in the other actor's heads (instigating).

Such a use of ordering, as seen in a few judgments, would not lead to lower sentences and would not be generally regarded as a label of lower blameworthiness.

It is possible to read the *ad hoc* tribunals' jurisprudence as establishing a hierarchy of seriousness which separates committing, ordering, instigating, and planning (first tier, direct forms of responsibility) from aiding and abetting and complicity in genocide (second tier, indirect forms of responsibility) and command responsibility (third tier). Within the first tier, only committing is regarded non-derivative, primary responsibility, whilst the others are derivative/accessorial liability. These terms, however, carry no implication as to the blameworthiness of the actor but indicate legal technicalities, i.e., the necessity of the commission of a crime by another.

Therefore, the use of ordering (in concert with planning and instigating) in the practice of the ICTY and ICTR falls short of its potential. Its role is unnecessarily decreased by the reliance on the broad and unspecific concept of JCE. Instead, in conjunction with planning and instigating ordering could be applied to mark the criminal conduct of persons in the highest echelons of power, without carrying a lower sentence or other implications of a lower culpability. In this regard, we can see many parallels between the theory of ordering liability underlying post-WWII jurisprudence and that of the ICTY and ICTR. However, there are also certain differences, concerning the lower practical frequency with which this mode is used in the *ad hoc* tribunals, and the issue of architects of crimes, which cannot be grasped by

642 It has been acknowledged that certain contributions that could be recognized under a JCE would only qualify as aiding and abetting or, in extreme cases, even fall outside of this scope and remain under impunity. However, such conduct will be extremely scarce. The advantage of the developed common denominator enables the attribution of the highest degree of responsibility to persons who are most intimately involved with international crimes by committing, ordering, planning, or instigating them. See above Sect. 5.2.4.3.

the law of the *ad hoc* tribunals on ordering. Concerning decision makers of international crimes, however, ordering a crime would have been a viable tool to deal with leadership criminality under the ICTY and ICTR Statutes.

References

Ambos K (2004) Der Allgemeine Teil des Völkerstrafrechts. Duncker & Humblot, Berlin

Ambos K (2007) Joint Criminal Enterprise and Command Responsibility. Journal of International Criminal Justice 5:159–183

Ambos K (2014) Treatise on International Criminal Law - Volume II: The Crimes and Sentencing. Oxford University Press, Oxford

Ambos K (2016) Art. 25. In: The Rome Statute of the International Criminal Court - A Commentary. C.H. Beck/Hart/Nomos, Munich

Ambos K (2018) Internationales Strafrecht. C. H. Beck, Munich

Ambos K, Bock S (2016) Individual Criminal Responsibility. In: De Brouwer A-M, Smeulers A (eds) The Elgar Companion to the International Criminal Tribunal for Rwanda. Edward Elgar Publishing, Cheltenham, 202–231

Badar ME (2006) "Just Convict Everyone!"—Joint Perpetration: From Tadić to Stakić and Back Again. International Criminal Law Review 6:293–302

Badar ME (2013) The Concept of Mens Rea in International Criminal Law - The Case for a Unified Approach. Hart Publishing, Oxford

Bantekas I (2002) Principles of direct and superior responsibility in International Humanitarian Law. Manchester University Press, Manchester

Boas G, Bischoff JL, Reid NL (2007) Forms of Responsibility in International Criminal Law. Cambridge University Press, Cambridge

Book JP (2011) Appeal and Sentence in International Criminal Law. BWV Berliner Wissenschafts-Verlag, Berlin

Burghardt B (2008) Die Vorgesetztenverantwortlichkeit im völkerrechtlichen Straftatsystem. BWV Berliner Wissenschafts-Verlag, Berlin

Cassesse A (2004) Black Letter Lawyering v. Constructive Interpretation. Journal of International Criminal Justice 2:265–274

Cassesse A (2007) The Proper Limits of Individual Criminal Responsibility under the Doctrine of Joint Criminal Enterprise. Journal of International Criminal Justice 5:109-133

Cryer R (2004) General Principles of Liability in International Criminal Law. In: McGoldrick D, Rowe p. (eds) The Permament International Criminal Court—Legal and Policy Issues. Hart Publishing, Oxford, 233–262

Cryer R, Robinson D, Vasiliev S (2019) An Introduction to International Criminal Law and Procedure. Cambridge University Press, Cambridge

Cryer R, Friman H, Robinson D, Wilmshurst E (2016) An Introduction to International Criminal Law and Procedure. Cambridge University Press, Cambridge

D'Ascoli S (2011) Sentencing in International Criminal Law. Hart Publishing, Oxford

Damgaard C (2008) Individual Criminal Responsibility for Core International Crimes—Selected Pertinent Issues. Springer, Berlin

Danner AM, Martinez JS (2005) Guilty Associations: Joint Criminal Enterprise, Command Responsibility, and the Development of International Criminal Law. California Law Review 93:75–166

Del Ponte C (2006) Investigation and Prosecution of Large-scale Crimes at the International Level—The Experience of the ICTY. Journal of International Criminal Justice 4:539–558

Drumbl M (2016) Sentencing and Penalties. In: De Brouwer A-M, Smeulers A (eds) The Elgar Companion to the International Criminal Tribunal for Rwanda. Edward Elgar Publishing, Cheltenham, 422–443

Epik A (2017) Die Strafzumessung bei Taten nach dem Völkerstrafgesetzbuch. Mohr Siebeck, Tübingen

Eser A (2002) Individual Criminal Responsibility. In: Cassesse A, Gaeta P, Jones JRWD (eds) The Rome Statute of the International Criminal Court—A Commentary. Oxford University Press, Oxford, 767–823

Ewald U (2010) 'Predictably Irrational'—International Sentencing and its Discourse against the Backdrop of Preliminary Empirical Findings on the ICTY Sentencing Practices. ICLR 10:365–402

Finnin S (2012) Elements of Accessorial Modes of Liability—Article 25 (3) (b) and (c) of the Rome Statute of the International Criminal Court. Martinus Nijhoff Publishers, Leiden

Goy B (2012) Individual Criminal Responsibility before the International Criminal Court—A Comparison with the Ad Hoc Tribunals. International Criminal Law Review 12:1–70

Gustafson K (2007) The Requirement of an "Express Agreement" for Joint Criminal Enterprise Liability. Journal of International Criminal Justice 5:134-158

Haan V (2005) The Development of the Concept of Joint Criminal Enterprise at the International Criminal Tribunal for the Former Yugoslavia. International Criminal Law Review 5:167–201

Heine G, Weisser B (2019) § 27. In: Schönke/Schröder-StGB. C.H. Beck, Munich

Holá B (2012) Sentencing of International Crimes at the ICTY and ICTR. Amsterdam Law Forum 3–24

Holá B, Bijleveld C, Smeulers A (2012) Consistency of international sentencing: ICTY and ICTR case study. European Journal of Criminology 9:539–552

Jain N (2014) Perpetrators and Accessories in International Criminal Law—Individual Modes of Responsibility for Collective Crimes. Hart Publishing, Oxford

Jordash W (2013) Joint Criminal Enterprise Liability: Result Orientated Justice. In: Schabas W, McDermott Y, Hayes N (eds) The Ashgate Research Companion to International Criminal Law. Ashgate Publishing Limited, Farnham, 133-161

Meernik J (2011) Sentencing Rationales and Judicial Decision Making at the International Criminal Tribunals. Social Science Quarterly 92:588-608

Meernik J, King K (2003) The Sentencing Determinants of the International Criminal Tribunal for the Former Yugoslavia: An Empirical and Doctrinal Analysis. Leiden Journal of International Law 16:717–750

Mettraux G (2001) Current Developments. International Criminal Law Review 1:261–284

Mettraux G (2005) International Crimes and the ad hoc Tribunals. Oxford University Press, Oxford

Ohlin JD (2007) Three Conceptual Problems with the Doctrine of Joint Criminal Enterprise. Journal of International Criminal Justice 5:69–90

Ohlin JD (2015) Co-Perpetration: German Dogmatik or German Invasion? In: Stahn C (ed) The Law and Practice of the International Criminal Court. Oxford University Press, Oxford, 517–537

Ohlin JD, van Sliedregt E, Weigend T (2013) Assessing the Control-Theory. Leiden Journal of International Law 26:725–746

Olásolo H (2009) The Criminal Responsibility of Senior Political and Military Leaders as Principals to International Crimes. Hart Publishing, Portland

Olásolo H, Carnero Rojo E (2015) Forms of Accessorial Liability under Article 25(3)(b) and (c). In: Stahn C (ed) The Law and Practice of the International Criminal Court. Oxford University Press, Oxford, 557–591

Osiel M (2005) The Banality of Good: Aligning Incentives against Mass Atrocity. Columbia Law Review 105:1751–1862

Piacente N (2004) Importance of the Joint Criminal Enterprise Doctrine for the ICTY Prosecutorial Policy. Journal of International Criminal Justice 2:446–454

Satzger H (2018) International and European Criminal Law. C.H. Beck, Munich

Schabas WA (2016) The International Criminal Court—A Commentary on the Rome Statute. Oxford University Press, Oxford

Schabas WA (2006) The UN International Criminal Tribunals—The former Yugoslavia, Rwanda and Sierra Leone. Cambridge University Press, Cambridge

Sloane RD (2007) Sentencing for the 'Crime of Crimes'. Journal of International Criminal Justice 5:713-734

Steer C (2017) Translating Guilt—Identifying Leadership Liability for Mass Atrocity Crimes. T.M.C. Asser Press, The Hague

Stewart JG (2012) The End of "Modes of Liability" for International Crimes. Leiden Journal of International Law 25:165–219

van der Wilt H (2007) Joint Criminal Enterprise—Possibilities and Limitations. Journal of International Criminal Justice 5:91–108

van Sliedregt E (2007) Joint Criminal Enterprise as a Pathway to Convicting Individuals for Genocide. Journal of International Criminal Justice 5:184-207

van Sliedregt E (2012) Individual Criminal Responsibility in International Criminal Law. Oxford University Press, Oxford

van Sliedregt E (2015) Perpetration and Participation in Article 25(3). In: Stahn C (ed) The Law and Practice of the International Criminal Court. Oxford University Press, Oxford, 499–516

Ventura MJ (2019) Ordering. In: de Hemptinne J, Roth R, van Sliedregt E (eds) Modes of Liability in International Criminal Law. Cambridge University Press, Cambridge, 284–306

Vogel J (2002) Individuelle Verantwortlichkeit im Völkerstrafrecht. Zeitschrift für die gesamte Strafrechtswissenschaft 114:403–436

Werle G, Jessberger F (2020) Principles of International Criminal Law. Oxford University Press, Oxford

Zorzi Giustiani F (2008) Stretching the Boundaries of Commission Liability. Journal of International Criminal Justice 6:783–799

Chapter 6
Responsibility for Ordering Under Article 25 (3) (b) of the Rome Statute

Contents

Abstract This chapter analyses the ICC's jurisprudence on ordering liability in detail. It finds that the ICC in its decisions on ordering does not deviate much from the customary international criminal law as defined by the ICTY and ICTR as far as legal requirements are concerned. Where differences can be found, this chapter outlines and evaluates them. It finds that the narrower causal nexus requirement of ICC jurisprudence is appropriate but criticises the tendency to treat ordering, soliciting and inducing as one common mode of liability. It is shown that ordering liability was thought of as a proper mode of responsibility for high-level leaders in the early days of the ICC but was soon replaced through indirect perpetration liability. An analysis of the facts considered by the ICC to prove the requirements of ordering liability suggests that it could be used instead of indirect perpetration in many instances as the court recurs to the same facts to prove the requirements of both forms of responsibility. This result leads to the effect of ordering responsibility

J. Block, *Reconciling Responsibility with Reality*, International Criminal Justice Series 33, https://doi.org/10.1007/978-94-6265-607-9_6

not playing any significant role in the current practice of the ICC, which is criticised in this chapter.

Keywords International Criminal Court · Ordering · Authority · Accessory liability · Hierarchy of blameworthiness · Special intent · Attempt to order

6.1 Conceptualization of Ordering Under Article 25 (3) (a) Rome Statute

The Rome Statute of the International Criminal Court encompasses ordering as a form of liability in Article 25 (3) (b) Rome Statute.

The Statute in Article 25 (3) (b) reads:

> In accordance with this statute, a person shall be criminally responsible and liable for punishment for a crime within the jurisdiction of the Court if that person: …
>
> b. Orders, solicits or induces the commission of such a crime which in fact occurs or is attempted[.]

The ICC has issued arrest warrants and decisions on the confirmation of charges based on ordering in multiple cases.[1] However, convictions in which the accused's conduct involved a hierarchical or influential position relied mostly on the mode of indirect (co-)perpetration.[2] So far, none of the accused have been convicted for ordering a crime.

This section explores the precise shape of ordering responsibility under Article 25 (3) (b) Rome Statute, and together with the findings of the two previous chapters lays the foundations to ascertain if and how ordering under the Rome Statute can be properly used to adjudicate high-level criminal responsibility in international criminal law.

---

[1] ICC, *The Prosecutor v. Raska Lukwiya*, Issuance of a Warrant of Arrest, 8 July 2005, ICC-02/04, para 30; ICC, *The Prosecutor v. Okot Odhiambo*, Issuance of a Warrant of Arrest, 8 July 2005, ICC-02/04, para 32; ICC, *The Prosecutor v. Dominic Ongwen*, Issuance of a Warrant of Arrest, 8 July 2005, ICC-02/04, para 30; ICC, *The Prosecutor v. Vincent Otti*, Issuance of a Warrant of Arrest, 8 July 2005, ICC-02/04, para 42; ICC, *The Prosecutor v. Joseph Kony*, Issuance of a Warrant of Arrest, 27 September 2005, 02/04-01/05, para 42; ICC, *The Prosecutor v. Germain Katanga and Mathieu Ngudjolo Chui*, Confirmation of Charges, 30 September 2008, ICC-01/04-01/07, para 36; ICC, *The Prosecutor v. Sylvestre Mudacumura*, Issuance of a Warrant of Arrest, 13 July 2012, ICC-01/04-01/12, para 76; ICC, *The Prosecutor v. Bosco Ntaganda*, Confirmation of Charges, 9 June 2014, ICC-01/04-02/06, para 97; ICC, *The Prosecutor v. Laurent Gbagbo*, Confirmation of Charges, 12 June 2014, ICC-02/11-01/11, para 278; ICC, *The Prosecutor v. Charles Blé Goudé*, Confirmation of Charges, 11 December 2014, ICC-02/011-02/11, para 194; ICC, *The Prosecutor v. Dominic Ongwen*, Confirmation of charges, 23 March 2016, ICC-02/04-01/15, para 36, 145; ICC, *The Prosecutor v. Mahmoud Mustafa Busayf Al-Werfalli*, Warrant of Arrest, 15 August 2017, ICC-01/11-01/717, para 28; ICC, *The Prosecutor v. Patrice-Edouard Ngaïssona and Alfred Yekatom*, Document Containing the Charges, 18 September 2019, ICC-01/14-01/18, para 190–1.

[2] Cf. e.g., the cases discussed in Chap. 3, Sect. 3.1.2.

As seen above, Article 25 (3) (b) of the Rome Statute lists three forms of contributions to a crime: ordering, soliciting, and inducing. This list stands opposed to the forms of commission of a crime (a), aiding, abetting and otherwise assisting in a crime (c) and contributing in another way to a crime committed by a group of persons (d).

This structure has led Pre-Trial Chamber I to conclude that the three forms of *littera* (b) describe "in essence one broader category of instigating".[3] The chambers in *Bemba et al.* only partially adopted this categorization and sorted soliciting and inducing into the more comprehensive category of instigation.[4] Regardless, it is a common view to regard ordering as closely related to instigating.[5] At times, this leads to a complete disregard of the different variations of Article 25 (3) (b) in statements about the *littera's* scope.[6] Thus far, some chambers of the ICC have identified the fact that a "person prompts another to commit a crime" as the common feature of the three forms in *littera* (b).[7] In the view of the chambers, the difference between ordering and instigation is defined by the authority criterion, which is only required for the former.[8]

The chamber in the *Bemba et al.* trial judgment described the role of ordering within these three forms as being the "strongest form of influence over another person".[9]

Given the structure of *littera* (b), the apparent wish of the chambers to establish a common basis for the modes of liability in Article 25 (3) (b) Rome Statute in these statements is understandable. However, considering the weight and importance of the exercise of authority, it is highly questionable whether the categorization into the same group as instigation is prudent. It is unconvincing to summarize the ordering and instigating of a crime as conduct, characterized by the "prompting" of another person to commit a crime, whereas indirect perpetration through an organised apparatus of power is not placed into this category.

The *Gbagbo* Decision on the Confirmation of Charges provides a good example of this unwarranted mingling of modes of liability. After affirming that Gbagbo

---

[3] *Gbagbo*, 12 June 2014, para 243; *Blé Goudé*, 11 December 2014, para 159.

[4] ICC, *The Prosecutor v. Jean-Pierre Bemba et al.*, Confirmation of Charges, 11 November 2014, ICC-01/05-01/13, para 34; ICC, *The Prosecutor v. Jean-Pierre Bemba Gombo et al.*, Trial Judgment, 19 October 2016, ICC-01/05-01/13, para 73.

[5] For this view in literature see e.g. Goy 2012, p. 54; Werle 2007, p. 967; Ventura describes ordering in general as "a very close relative of" or "aggravated" instigating, see Ventura 2019, p. 284.

[6] Cf. ICC, *The Prosecutor v. Bosco Ntaganda*, Appeals Judgment, 30 March 2021, ICC-01/04-02/06-A A2, Separate Opinion of Judge Luz del Carmen Ibáñez Carranza, paras 278 et seq. in which the existence of ordering was apparently completely forgotten.

[7] *Gbagbo*, 12 June 2014, para 243; *Ongwen*, 23 March 2016, para 42; ICC, *The Prosecutor v. Ahmad Al Faqi Al Mahdi*, Decision on the Confirmation of Charges, 24 March 2016, ICC-01/12-01/15, para 25; ICC, *The Prosecutor v. Al Hassan Ag Abdoul Aziz Ag Mohamed Ag Mahmoud*, Issuance of a Warrant of Arrest, 22 May 2018, ICC-01/12-01/18, para 183; in the same vein Ambos 2018, § 7 mn. 44.

[8] *Blé Goudé*, 11 December 2014, para 159; *Bemba et al.*, 19 October 2016, para 77; *Al Hassan*, 22 May 2018, para 184.

[9] *Bemba et al.*, 19 October 2016, para 77; *Al Hassan*, 22 May 2018, para 184.

had authority over the perpetrators, the Pre-Trial Chamber stated that there were substantial grounds to believe that he "instructed or otherwise instigated" his forces to carry out actions which led to crimes. According to the chamber his "instructions or instigation" had a direct effect on the commission of the crimes and found that he had meant to "instruct or instigate".[10] The chamber described several instances of orders given and other, more general conduct of the accused. These included orders, which he was believed to have given to the Ivorian armed forces to attack a suburb of Abidjan with heavy weapons.[11] The description of such events with the terms "instructed or otherwise instigated" is unfortunate, as if the chamber did not wish to state clearly whether Gbagbo held authority over the perpetrators. This concerns an important aspect of the charges because the accused's exercise of authority over others constitutes a crucial part of their wrongdoing. From the actor's perspective, there is a difference between the decision to commit a crime being generated by compelling authority or by other factors, which may be less influential, controllable, and predictable. Mixing ordering, soliciting, and inducing ignores this difference and thus, ignores authority as one of the most relevant factors in the ascription of guilt in international criminal law.[12]

No trial chamber to date has relied on the broad categorisation of ordering, inducing, and soliciting under one category for a conviction. Considering the foregoing, it is to be hoped that it will remain this way.

6.2 Legal Requirements

The ICC case law on ordering is limited and thus, so are the possible conclusions to be drawn from it. Scholars have often relied on the canon of—apparently—established rules on ordering from the *ad hoc* tribunals to interpret Article 25 (3) (b) Rome Statute.[13] However, such a transfer of an interpretation warrants caution, given that the Rome Statute, as an international treaty, can depart from customary law. Additionally, one should not forget that ordering has been a neglected form of responsibility, playing a much smaller role in practice than it could. Therefore, transferring what is often considered the predominant view on ordering runs the risk of obscuring certain details in the customary law sources, especially in the jurisprudence of the *ad hoc* tribunals.

[10] *Gbagbo*, 12 June 2014, para 244.

[11] Ibid., para 246.

[12] The Confirmation of Charges Decision in Al-Hassan is similar in this regard, as only soliciting and inducing are charged, but the chamber nevertheless mentions the accused's authority, see 181 *et seq.*, 187–8.

[13] See e.g. the analysis by Finnin 2012, pp. 43 et seq.; Olásolo and Carnero Rojo 2015, pp. 556 et seq.

6.2.1 Conduct Element: Giving an Order

Under Article 25 (3) (b) Rome Statute, a person may incur liability for ordering a crime, if he or she "instructs another person in any form" to commit a crime or the attempt of such a crime, or to carry out an act which results in the commission or attempt of a crime.[14]

The order does not have to be given to the physical perpetrator directly but can go through intermediaries.[15]

It has been asserted that an order need not be given in writing or any other form.[16] This description is omnipresent in the *ad hoc* tribunals' jurisprudence and must be equally true under the Rome Statute. The case law of the ICC supports this view with several instances of non-written, informal instructions charged as orders.[17]

The arrest warrants against the members of the Lord's Resistance Army mention the possibility of multiple persons being responsible for ordering a crime together. They state that the respective accused "together with other persons [...] ordered or induced the commission of crimes".[18] However, the competent chamber did not elaborate, leaving the requirements for "joint ordering" obscure.

Most instances of ordering at the ICC are found in conduct that can be described as that of giving "direct instructions". The confirmation of charges decisions in *Mudacumura, Ntaganda, Gbagbo* and *Blé Goudé* mostly relied on the (suspected) issuance of such instructions.

The content of such orders varied. For example, Laurent Gbagbo was believed to have issued orders that referred to certain operational goals. The content of these instructions would not *per se* constitute the commission of an international crime, but it would lead to the commission of crimes in a foreseeable manner.[19] On the contrary, in the cases of Sylvestre Mudacumura and Bosco Ntaganda, the instructions given

---

[14] *Mudacumura*, 13 July 2012, para 63; *Ntaganda*, 9 June 2014, para 145; *Gbagbo*, 12 June 2014, para 244; ICC, *The Prosecutor v. Laurent Gbagbo and Charles Blé Goudé*, Reasons for oral decision of 15 January 2019 on the Requête de la Défense de Laurent Gbagbo afin qu'un jugement d'acquittement portant sur toutes les charges soit prononcé en faveur de Laurent Gbagbo et que sa mise en liberté immédiate soit ordonnée, and on the Blé Goudé Defence no case to answer motion, 16 July 2019, ICC-02/11-01/15, para 1966; Ambos 2016, Article 25 mn. 22.

[15] *Mudacumura*, 13 July 2012, para 63.

[16] Olásolo and Carnero Rojo 2015, p. 563; Ventura 2019, p. 294.

[17] *Ntaganda*, 9 June 2014, para 111, 148; *Blé Goudé*, 11 December 2014, paras 27–9, 162.

[18] *Kony*, 27 September 2005, para 42; *Lukwiya*, 8 July 2005, para 30; *Odhiambo*, 8 July 2005, para 32; *Ongwen*, 8 July 2005, para 30; *Otti*, 8 July 2005, para 42; Goy 2012, p. 54. See also ICC, *The Prosecutor v. Mathieu Ndgudjolo Chui*, Trial Judgment, 18 December 2012, ICC-01/04-02/12, Concurring Opinion of Judge Christine Van den Wyngaert, para 62.

[19] Laurent Gbagbo was believed to have issued instructions to prevent a demonstration and to regain control over the quarter of Abobo (Abidjan, Côte d'Ivoire) in several meetings with the top-level commanders of the Ivorian security forces. In both cases, he was thought to have stressed that all kind of means could be used, see *Gbagbo*, 12 June 2014, paras 24, 246 (demonstration), 154–5, 173–5, 246 (attack on Abobo). As stated previously, it is unfortunate that the chamber in these instances remarked that the accused had "instructed or otherwise instigated" certain crimes, leaving it open whether his authority extended over the recipients of these instructions in the specific instances.

by the accused specifically aimed at unlawful acts, such as killing civilians, pillaging and destroying civilian property or rape and sexual enslavement.[20] Therefore, it can be concluded that orders can take the form of specific instructions or more general directives or guidelines.[21] This is in line with post-World War II and *ad hoc* jurisprudence on the matter. It also follows from these observations that orders do not have to be blatantly illegal but can simply refer to goals or conduct that will lead to the commission of crimes.[22]

As the *Mudacumura* confirmation decision shows, the approval of orders prepared by subordinates also qualifies for a conviction under ordering.[23]

The *Gbagbo and Blé Goudé* acquittal decision can be read as establishing that the order must be addressed to an identifiable group of persons. The chamber denied ordering responsibility for Charles Blé Goudé because the recipients of his alleged instructions were not identified and pursuant to the chamber, his words would have had different effects on different groups of the alleged perpetrators (involving police officers but also local youth groups).[24]

In the view of many authors, an order cannot be given by omission,[25] and so far, jurisprudence has not indicated anything to the contrary.

The decisions on *Gbagbo* and *Blé Goudé* furthermore show how the eventual categorization of conduct as either ordering or instigating, logically depends on the authority of the actor.[26] Given that orders in the sense of Article 25 (3) (b) do not have to have a certain form, the same conduct can qualify as one of these two modes of responsibility.

Some orders stand out as public statements, directly addressed at the people who would later physically perpetrate the crime. In *Ntaganda*, the accused told soldiers under his command at a parade to kill and harm civilians and rape and enslave women in the upcoming attack.[27] Charles Blé Goudé was accused of having ordered (or instigated) youth organizations in the Yopougon quarter of Abidjan by publicly telling them to go back to their neighbourhoods and report every "stranger". This

[20] *Mudacumura*, 13 July 2012, para 65 (suspected to have approved orders to pillage civilian property and to attack villages of Mianga and Busurungi); *Ntaganda*, 9 June 2014, paras 111–2, 114–5, 148 (suspected to have ordered the commission of crimes during two attacks, including by telling troops under his authority to "shoot everybody and appropriate everything, including women").

[21] See also Finnin 2012, p. 45; Olásolo and Carnero Rojo 2015, p. 562.

[22] See e.g. *Gbagbo and Blé Goudé*, 16 July 2019, Annex B, paras 1971–3.

[23] *Mudacumura*, 13 July 2012, para 65 repeatedly refers to the accused's approval of certain orders such as: an order to pillage civilian property, orders for two specific attacks on villages and other military field operations in general.

[24] See *Gbagbo and Blé Goudé*, 16 July 2019, Annex B, para 2008 (the statement of course bears relevance for the determination of the accused's authority over the recipients as well). See in the same vein, but based on *ad hoc* jurisprudence: Olásolo and Carnero Rojo 2015, p. 562.

[25] Cryer et al. 2019, p. 360; Olásolo and Carnero Rojo 2015, p. 563.

[26] See the respective formulations "instructed or otherwise instigated" at *Gbagbo*, 12 June 2014, para 246; *Blé Goudé*, 11 December 2014, para 161. See also the list of requirements in *Gbagbo and Blé Goudé*, 16 July 2019, Annex B, paras 1966-7 which only differ in the existence of authority, and of course the action verbs of ordering, soliciting, and inducing.

[27] *Ntaganda*, 9 June 2014, paras 111, 148.

statement referred to perceived supporters of the accused's political opponent and was believed by the chamber to have been perceived as an order to attack such individuals.[28]

It has been argued that it must be possible to prove the existence of orders through circumstantial evidence.[29] This is possible under the law of the ICTY and ICTR and should be adhered to in ICC practice as well.[30] The proceedings against Charles Blé Goudé have already shown an attempt to use such inferences. The pre-trial chamber inferred from certain video footage that the accused had instructed the audience of his speech to engage in violence. The trial chamber rejected this allegation but at no point argued that an inference from circumstance would be impossible. Rather, the circumstances in the *Blé Goudé* case were found to be too ambiguous to conclude that only an order of the accused could have led to the following crimes.[31]

Overall, ICC jurisprudence, to date, allows only limited conclusions on the conduct element of ordering and there are few suggestions that it would deviate from rules established by the *ad hoc* tribunals. An interpretation of the conduct element of ordering close to customary international law seems reasonable, as the *ad hoc* tribunals have established a detailed canon of rules, which has sparked no essential criticism so far.

6.2.2 Position of Authority

In line with *ad hoc* jurisprudence and the larger proportion of the precedents of post-World War II jurisprudence, ordering under Article 25 (3) (b) Rome Statute requires that the ordering person be in a position of authority in relation to the physical perpetrator.[32]

The authority requirement has been described as the "very cornerstone" of ordering liability.[33] This proves particularly true in light of the judicial trend to condense ordering, soliciting, and inducing into a broader category of "prompting

[28] *Blé Goudé*, 11 December 2014, paras 27–9, 162.

[29] Olásolo and Carnero Rojo 2015, p. 563.

[30] Where an unquestionable authority of an actor over the physical perpetrators exists and these perpetrators commit large-scale crimes according to a repeating pattern, the existence of an instruction can be a logical conclusion. Of course, the existence of other (intermediary) actors with authority must be considered.

[31] *Gbagbo and Blé Goudé*, 16 July 2019, Annex B, paras 1986–2002. It also remained unclear whether the perpetrators of the subsequent crimes had even listened to or been told about the accused's speech.

[32] *Mudacumura*, 13 July 2012, para 63; *Ntaganda*, 9 June 2014, para 145; *Gbagbo*, 12 June 2014, paras 244; *Blé Goudé*, 11 December 2014, para 160; *Bemba et al.*, 19 October 2016, para 77; *Al Hassan*, 22 May 2018, para 184; *Gbagbo and Blé Goudé*, 16 July 2019, Annex B, para 1966.

[33] Ventura 2019, p. 299.

another to commit a crime", as authority is the one important requirement making a difference *vis-à-vis* instigation.[34]

6.2.2.1 The Necessary Shape of Authority

At first glance, it is surprising and unhelpful that the trial chamber in *Bemba et al.* adopted the formulation of a "superior-subordinate relationship" when elaborating on the authority requirement, even quoting related case law from the ICTR and ECCC.[35] Interestingly, none of these quoted judgments implies the necessity of such a superior-subordinate relationship. On the contrary, the Duch Trial Judgment of the ECCC explicitly rejects this narrower requirement.[36] It would therefore be wrong to assert that the trial chamber wanted to revise this settled matter.[37] The correct standard for the position of the ordering actor is a "position of authority".

Consequently, authority as required by Article 25 (3) (b) first alternative is broader than the superior-subordinate relationship as required by Article 28 Rome Statute.[38]

In *Blé Goudé,* the pre-trial chamber describes the shape of authority by stating that the accused had the capacity to compel the conduct of a group of people who were among the physical perpetrators of the crime.[39] It thus seems that the ICC is following the example set by customary law in this regard.

Finnin argues against this interpretation and demands that authority should have a higher threshold. She believes that the broader authority criterion is "incredibly broad and flexible", which would lead to many cases being grasped by ordering that should rather be categorized under soliciting or inducing.[40] Instead, she demands that orders should be binding and consequently enforceable. This would be the case where a type of disciplinary regime is in place to ensure compliance with orders.[41]

---

[34] For the further course of this thesis, it will be distinguished between ordering and instigation, the latter being the umbrella term for soliciting and inducing. The latter two are hardly distinguishable through any relevant requirement. This use does not endorse the abovementioned approach of certain chambers to speak of "instruction or instigation" but simply serves as an easier terminological distinction between ordering and the other two forms of *littera* (b).

[35] *Bemba et al.*, 19 October 2016, para 77.

[36] See ECCC, *Duch Trial Judgment*, Judgment, No. 001/18-07-2007/ECCC/TC, para 527; the other cited judgments are: ICTR, *Siméon Nchamihigo v. the Prosecutor*, 18 March 2010, ICTR-2001-63-A, para 188; ICTR, *Théoneste Bagosora et al. v. The Prosecutor*, 14 December 2011, ICTR-98-41-A, para 277.

[37] In the same vein against a superior-subordinate relationship: Olásolo and Carnero Rojo 2015, pp 561–2; Ventura 2019, p. 287; some authors use "de-facto superior-subordinate relationship" as a synonym for authority, see Ambos 2016, Article 25 mn. 22; Werle and Jessberger 2020, mn. 617; Schabas, however, still describes the case law on the matter as "divided", see Schabas 2016, p. 574. Cp. the discussion *supra* at Chap. 5, Sect. 5.1.1.2.

[38] Goy 2012, p. 54.

[39] *Blé Goudé*, 11 December 2014, para 160; Eser 2002a, p. 796 ("bound by obedience"); Goy 2012, p. 54; Heller 2011, p. 607.

[40] Finnin 2012, pp 56–8.

[41] Ibid., pp 56–7.

This view is unconvincing in light of customary international law and the experiences at the *ad hoc* tribunals. Uniformity of international criminal law is helpful in many instances and, despite the Rome Statute being a treaty and therefore being capable of deviating from customary law, should not be abandoned if the law in question has proven senseful.

As discussed above, a narrow "superior-subordinate" requirement for ordering has—in essence—not been applied by the *ad hoc* tribunals. In fact, a broad understanding of the necessary position of the ordering person towards the recipient has always been required.[42] Furthermore, several cases before the *ad hoc* tribunals have shown that authority over perpetrators may stem from various factors, amongst which a formal or enforceable hierarchy is only one. Cases like *Gacumbitsi* or *Semanza* at the ICTR terrifyingly exemplify how a person in a traditionally influential position—without any formal disciplinary means at their disposal—can tip the balance and thus effectively decide over the commission of a crime. This would have been true for the accusations levied against the accused in the *Blé Goudé* case if the allegations could have been proven.[43] Charles Blé Goudé was believed to have had authority over youth organisations that supported then-president Laurent Gbagbo. Allegedly, he had gained the capability to mobilise the youth organizations through continuous presence and inflammatory speeches at rallies. He was said to have created a state of alert among the youth in which they would be at his disposal. In this state he publicly instructed the members of the youth organizations to await his orders in the near future. Furthermore, Blé Goudé was believed to have created a sense of threat among these youth groups, which led to a perceived need of self-defence.[44] When tensions in Abidjan rose, he allegedly mobilised these youth groups at public meetings and sent them to "defend" their neighbourhoods. As a result, they allegedly erected roadblocks and killed civilians whom they perceived to be supporters of the political opponent.[45]

Together with the earlier ICTR cases, this shows that if people feel compelled to act according to a person's instructions, whether such an instruction is enforceable may be irrelevant, especially for the victims. Authority over groups of people is therefore a dangerous tool, regardless of the formalization and sanctioning regimens in place.

Soliciting or inducing are no adequate labels for these situations as they do not require the strong, compelling influence of the actor over the group.[46] On the other hand, ordering does require this, if the authority requirement is broadly defined. Thus, the broad interpretation of authority accurately mirrors the wrongdoing of the actor.

---

[42] See Chap. 5, Sect. 5.1.1.2.

[43] Charles Blé Goudé was acquitted on all charges, see *Gbagbo and Blé Goudé*, 16 July 2019, para 28.

[44] *Blé Goudé*, 11 December 2014, paras 75, 93–9; 160.

[45] Ibid., paras 27–9. Note that Charles Blé Goudé's responsibility for certain crimes which he had allegedly ordered was rejected by the trial chamber, cp. *Gbagbo and Blé Goudé*, 16 July 2019, Annex B, paras 1983, 2008, 2016.

[46] See for the opposite view Finnin 2012, p. 56.

By using authority to compel others to commit a crime, the actor creates a higher risk that the crime will be committed, as opposed to someone who does not exert such influence (and could thus be an instigator). However, this risk does not depend on the availability of disciplinary measures but on the factual pressure exerted on the perpetrator, or any sense of compulsion felt by them.

Authority does not have to be exercised directly over the physical perpetrators but can exist in the form of chain authority. This means that a chain of authority is necessary, but also sufficient where the order passes through different levels of a hierarchy. In this regard, the trial chamber in *Gbagbo and Blé Goudé* questioned whether one of the accused would have been able to exercise authority over certain youth groups, irrespective of the will of the leaders of these groups.[47] This shows that two ways of exercising authority within a hierarchy are possible: an actor can either exercise authority directly over the physical perpetrators or over the intermediary, who then exercises authority over the executioners of the crime. This finding is in line with the presumptions about chain authority at the *ad hoc* tribunals.[48]

It is noteworthy that the group or affiliation of the specific perpetrators must be identified. This again corresponds with *ad hoc* jurisprudence and is necessary to determine whether authority was exercised over the actual perpetrators.[49]

Another question arises regarding the consistency of the authority. It has been asserted that ICTY and ICTR law requires only temporary authority over the perpetrator.[50] Cases before the ICC have not yet dealt with such situations. Therefore, there is no indication of whether the ICC would follow the *ad hoc* tribunals' broad notion of authority or whether it would require a more stable position in which authority not only extends to the specific order. The examples from Rwanda show that people in such a position can play a decisive role in situations on the verge of violence—if they instruct their community to engage in violence, their calls will often be heard. This decisive role may speak in favour of including not only informal and social but also temporary authority in this requirement.

6.2.2.2 Factors Establishing Authority, Especially Control Over the Perpetrator or Organisation

When it comes to the question of authority over the perpetrators, the factors mentioned in the relevant decisions are the hierarchy and degree of organisation,[51] the position of the actor within the organization and the actor's "control" over the perpetrators.

---

[47] *Gbagbo and Blé Goudé*, 16 July 2019, Annex B, para 1970.

[48] See Chap. 5, Sect. 5.1.1.2.

[49] *Gbagbo and Blé Goudé*, 16 July 2019, Annex B, para 2008.

[50] See Chap. 5, Sect. 5.1.1.2.

[51] *Ongwen*, 8 July 2005, paras 7–8, 16, 30; *Mudacumura*, 13 July 2012, para 64; see also *Gbagbo*, 12 June 2014, para 245: "control … through the official state hierarchy".

Sylvestre Mudacumura's *FDLR*, for example, was described as a "large, well organised organisation which has a clear hierarchical structure".[52]

The actor's position within the organisation is also frequently mentioned. For example, Sylvestre Mudacumura is described as the "top military commander" of the *FDLR*.[53] In the same vein, Bosco Ntganda was described as occupying "a high-ranking position" and having "significant responsibility" within the *UPC/FPLC*.[54] Similar descriptions can also be found in *Ongwen*, *Al Hassan* and the *Katanga and Chui* decision on the confirmation of charges.[55]

These first two criteria can be found again when chambers evaluate the most prominent factor in authority: the "control" over the perpetrators and/or the organisation. The concept of control, within the sense of "enabling the controlling person to decide whether and how a specific crime will be committed", has been deconstructed in Chap. 3 as far as decision makers in mass atrocities are concerned.[56] However, the way in which a notion of "control" over the physical perpetrators is invoked by the chambers of the ICC to establish authority and thus ordering liability, is an important indicator for the shape of the authority criterion and for later comparisons.

Control is mentioned in the *Mudacumura*, *Gbagbo* and *Blé Goudé* decisions.[57]

In *Mudacumura*, the pre-trial chamber described the accused's role as such that he had "control over his forces and authority over recruiting, promoting, removing and disciplining them". His dominance and control comprised the ability to prevent them from demobilisation, to authorise their marriage and to control the information they received from the outside world.[58]

In the confirmation of charges against Laurent Gbagbo, to underline its finding that Gbagbo had exerted authority over the perpetrators of the alleged crimes, the chamber stated that he and his inner circle allegedly exercised control over the Ivorian defence forces (*FDS, Forces de Défense et de Sécurité*). He also controlled militias and mercenaries through their *de facto* integration into the *FDS* and—in some cases—through personal links with the militias' leaders and by providing them with weapons and financial support. In addition, the chamber determined that the accused had the ability to reorganise the forces who remained loyal to him after defections and that he had close ties with Charles Blé Goudé who had allegedly played a major role in mobilising and directing the pro-Gbagbo youth.[59] Both of the latter statements

[52] *Mudacumura*, 13 July 2012, para 64.

[53] Ibid., para 64.

[54] *Ntaganda*, 9 June 2014, para 147.

[55] *Ongwen*, 8 July 2005, para 16; *Katanga and Chui*, 30 September 2008, para 470; *Al Hassan*, 22 May 2018, para 187. Note that Al Hassan's responsibility is apparently only treated as that of inducing or soliciting, although the chamber remarked on his authority.

[56] See Chap. 3, Sect. 3.3.3.

[57] *Mudacumura*, 13 July 2012, para 64; *Gbagbo*, 12 June 2014, para 245; in *Blé Goudé*, 11 December 2014, para 160 the term control is not mentioned, but the chamber speaks of the accused's capacity to define the activities of the group of perpetrators.

[58] *Mudacumura*, 13 July 2012, para 64.

[59] *Gbagbo*, 12 June 2014, para 245.

describe the accused's capability of determining the actions of others and thus amount to some concept of control as well.

The same idea on control can be found in *Blé Goudé*, where the chamber found that the accused had the capacity to define the mobilisation of the youth organisation and, through this, could compel their conduct, leading to him having authority over the perpetrators. He was also believed to have been able to compel the conduct of militias.[60] However, Blé Goudé's alleged authority over youth organisations differed from the assumption of control in other cases. He allegedly forged ties with different youth organisations and their leaders. His capacity to "define their mobilisation" allegedly stemmed from him being publicly known and the impact of his words on the youth groups. It was thought that he then created a sense of threat and necessity of self-defence in public events and called upon the youth groups via television to meet at a specific location the following day. There, he supposedly gave them instructions in a public speech that led to the commission of crimes.[61] This method of exercising control differs from the one exercised through a disciplinary regime in a military-style hierarchy. However, both types have in common that the actor can influence the conduct of others and thus trigger a violent course of events.[62]

In the *Ntaganda* confirmation of charges one can also identify a notion of control. The pre-trial chamber determined that the accused "ensured that breaches of the disciplinary rules" were punished. The consequence of such behaviour was control over the *UPC/FPLC* troops through the disciplinary regime.[63]

It is not surprising that the chambers in many of these cases relied on the same findings when elaborating on the control over an organisation necessary for indirect perpetration through an organization.[64]

Finally, the congruence of facts used to prove the nominally different requirements of ordering and indirect perpetration through an organization becomes overtly clear in *Ntaganda*. The chamber elaborates on the accused's authority and then points to its own determination of Ntaganda's control in the context of indirect perpetration.[65]

---

[60] *Blé Goudé*, 11 December 2014, para 160.

[61] Ibid., paras 27–9, 162.

[62] To reiterate, this is not to be confounded with a decision over the eventual commission of specific crimes, which simply does not rest with an instructing leader, see Chap. 3, Sect. 3.3.3.

[63] *Ntaganda*, 9 June 2014, para 147. Bosco Ntaganda's insistence on discipline is one of the facts establishing his control over the organization as an indirect perpetrator, see para 120.

[64] For a summary of these, see Chap. 3, Sect. 3.1.2.1. See in particular: *Blé Goudé*, 11 December 2014, paras 149–51, stressing the accused's control over the *FDS*, mercenaries and militias; *Gbagbo*, 12 June 2014, para 234, describing the organised and hierarchical state apparatus and consequent command over the *FDS*, the authority of the accused within it, his ability to reorganise his forces and the link to the militias; *Ntaganda*, 9 June 2014, para 120, describing *inter alia* his position and insistence on discipline; *Katanga and Chui*, 30 September 2008, paras 470, 540–1, describing the position of the accused in connection with both modes of liability. This even holds true for Blé Goudé's alleged control over youth groups, cf. *Blé Goudé*, 11 December 2014, para 151. See already above at Chap. 3, Sects. 3.1.2.1 and 3.1.2.2.

[65] *Ntaganda*, 9 June 2014, para 147 with fn. 599. Fn. 599 hints to para 120 where the chamber determines whether Ntaganda had control over an organized apparatus of power.

As previously illustrated, chambers equally relied on the "authority" of actors within their organised groups to prove their "control" over these organisations when establishing the facts for indirect perpetration through an apparatus of power.[66]

Hence, it can be concluded that, in determining the position of authority, the ICC's chambers mostly rely on the same facts and factors, which they use to establish the objective criteria of indirect perpetration through an organization. For now, this allows the conclusion that when the criterion of "control over an organisation" in the mode of indirect perpetration is affirmed, authority over the perpetrators will usually be given as well.[67]

This would probably not be true where authority stems from purely social or traditional factors, however, due to the lack of such incidents having come before the ICC, this remains indeterminable. As previously criticised, the attempt of the pre-trial chamber in the situation in Côte d'Ivoire makes it conceivable that chambers would attempt to establish not only ordering authority, but also an apparatus of power even in such informal situations. Such an attempt would critically overburden the latter concept.

6.2.2.3 Factual Positions of the Accused/Wanted Individual Under Ordering

Persons indicted under Article 25 (3) (b) Rome Statute for ordering a crime occupied different positions within state's hierarchies and within non-state armed groups.

Laurent Gbagbo was president of Côte d'Ivoire and, despite having lost the presidential elections, retained many presidential powers during the time in which he allegedly ordered crimes in the post-election violence.[68] Charles Blé Goudé was Minister for Youth, Vocational Training and Employment in Gbagbo's government. However, the functions he exercised were connected to his non-formalized, public work with youth groups where he stirred notions of threat, "self-defence" and violence.[69]

Besides the indicted, the remaining persons associated with ordering by the ICC, at least within their arrest warrants, were military decision makers within non-state armed groups.

[66] See Chap. 3, Sect. 3.1.2.1.

[67] In the same vein: *Chui*, 18 December 2012, Concurring Opinion of Judge Christine Van den Wyngaert, para 56.

[68] *Gbagbo*, 12 June 2014, paras 78–85. Note that the trial chamber in its acquittal decision did not question Gbagbo's authority over the armed forces during the relevant period. The chamber noted that in this period, he still occupied the role of president, and exercised the according level of authority over the state forces (*Gbagbo and Blé Goudé*, 16 July 2019, Annex B, para 1970).

[69] See *Gbagbo*, 12 June 2014, para 51 on the role of Charles Blé Goudé, as well as *Blé Goudé*, 11 December 2014, para 75.

This was true in *Mudacumura, Ntaganda, Katanga and Chui* (Eastern Congo), *Kony, Lukwiya, Odhiambo, Ongwen* and *Otti* (Uganda) and with regards to Alfred Yekatom (Central African Republic).[70]

The range of positions held by those who stand or stood accused under the head of ordering thus varies in the practice of the ICC. With a former president, a person with potential influence over a great territory and a vast number of subordinates has been indicted. In terms of the nature of the relationship between ordering individual and physical perpetrators, Blé Goudé stands out with his supposed informal influence over youth groups in certain parts of Abidjan, Côte d'Ivoire. The other persons listed above can be described as leaders or high-ranking commanders of non-state armed groups. They occupied or were believed to have occupied the highest (Joseph Kony, Germain Katanga), or one of the highest posts (Sylvestre Mudacumura, Bosco Ntaganda, Dominic Ongwen, Alfred Yekatom) in formalized non-state hierarchies. Virtually all their organizations are believed to have rested on efficient (often military style) structures of command and control, with hierarchies and often disciplinary measures.[71] The similar circumstances of those indicted does not lead to a narrower framing of the authority criterion, as the specific way in which authority is exercised can and does vary with each respective situation. Moreover, it is the various types of position, including the informal one attributed to Charles Blé Goudé, which should be acknowledged. Through this, ICC practice confirms a broad understanding of authority.

More importantly, most allegations contained charges of indirect perpetration under Article 25 (3) (a) and ordering under lit. (b) in the alternative.[72] This overlap is congruent with the findings of the last section on authority and "control": the modes

[70] Katanga and Chui were indicted as chiefs of two armed groups and charged with commanding an attack involving up to a thousand fighters on behalf of Katanga's organization, see *Katanga and Chui*, 30 September 2008, paras 36, 540–1, 545. Mudacumura was wanted as the "top military commander" of an armed group in the Kivu provinces in eastern Congo, see *Mudacumura*, 13 July 2012, para 64. Ntaganda was deputy chief of staff—the third highest rank—within an armed non-state organization, which comprised "numerous" fighters organized in "sectors, brigades, battalions…" see *Ntaganda*, 9 June 2014, paras 14–5, 17. Kony was the chief of the LRA in Uganda, see *Kony*, 27 September 2005, para 7; Otti was the LRA's vice-chairman and second in command, see *Otti*, 8 July 2005, paras 8–9; Lukwiya was the LRA's army commander, see *Lukwiya*, 8 July 2005, para 8; Odhiambo was deputy army commander of the LRA, see *Odhiambo*, 8 July 2005, para 9; Ongwen was one of four brigade commanders and member of the Control Altar together with the afore-mentioned, see *Ongwen*, 8 July 2005, paras 8-9, *Ongwen*, 23 March 2016, para 12. Yekatom headed a military styled group of approximately 3000 men in a part of the Central African Republic, see *Ngaïssona and Yekatom*, 18 September 2019, paras 21–2, ICC, *The Prosecutor v. Alfred Yekatom and Patrice-Edouard Ngaïssona*, 5 May 2020, ICC-01/14-01/18, para 65.

[71] *Mudacumura*, 13 July 2012, paras 24, 64; on Bosco Ntaganda's armed group see *Ntaganda*, 9 June 2014, paras 15–8; on the armed groups allegedly headed by Katanga and Ngudjolo Chui see *Katanga and Chui*, 30 September 2008, paras 543–4; on the Lord's Resistance Army in Uganda see *Kony*, 27 September 2005, paras 7–9, *Ongwen*, 23 March 2016, paras 56–8; on the Anti-Balaka in the Central African Republic see *Ngaïssona and Yekatom*, 18 September 2019, paras 21–22 (Yekatom's group), 62–89 (the Anti-Balaka in general).

[72] *Katanga and Chui*, 30 September 2008, paras 33, 36; *Ntaganda*, 9 June 2014, para 97; *Gbagbo*, 12 June 2014, para 278; *Blé Goudé*, 11 December 2014, para 194; *Ongwen*, 23 March 2016, counts of charges following paras 39, 56 and 65; *Ngaïssona and Yekatom*, 18 September 2019, paras 628,

of indirect perpetration through an organisation and ordering share many features as far as their requirements are concerned.

Considering the broad authority requirement, some authors state that ordering not only encompasses the conduct of military commanders, but also commanders of unconventional forces and political party leaders.[73] Naturally, this determination is accurate and will often be the case as formalized hierarchies remain a reliable provider of power, i.e., of influence over others. However, the mode of ordering does not limit liability to any specific role or position. The above mentioned *Blé Goudé* case and the cases of Rwandan *bourgmestres* before the ICTR underline the importance of this point: even without any formalized position within an organization or party, a person can enjoy powerful influence over others, which can then be used to spark violence.

6.3 Summary: Authority as a Broad but Accurate Requirement

Given the flexible authority criterion, the factual basis to establish authority is unsurprisingly broad, equally grasping influence through formal hierarchies and over informal groups or crowds. Consequently, the factual positions of those indicted under ordering vary, as does the type of influence they exert over the physical perpetrators. The flexibility or "broadness" of the authority requirement is what makes it accurate and well-suited for international criminal law, as it ties the actor's responsibility to their decision-making power over others. A person who can compel others to engage in violent conduct will often be in the powerful position to decisively influence whether a situation escalates into the wide-spread commission of mass atrocities, the specific incidents of which will be out of the leader's influence, or whether a situation remains comparatively calm, avoiding the large-scale commission of crimes.

630 on the alleged responsibility of Alfred Yekatom; Sylvestre Mudacumura had been accused under indirect co-perpetration and ordering, but—failing to establish reasonable grounds to believe in a common plan within his group—the arrest warrant only affirmed charges for ordering, see *Mudacumura*, 13 July 2012, paras 62, 76. The arrest warrant for Joseph Kony from 2005 is based solely on allegations of ordering crimes, see *Kony*, 27 September 2005, counts following para 42.

[73] Olásolo and Carnero Rojo 2015, p. 562.

6.3.1 *Causal Nexus: A Direct Effect on the Commission of the Crime*

ICC chambers took the stance that the effect an order must have on the commission or attempt must be a "direct effect" on the commission of the crime.[74] This formulation differs from the "direct and substantial effect" that was required by the *ad hoc* tribunals.[75]

Two interpretations regarding the causal nexus criterion and its history at the *ad hoc* tribunals are possible: either the ICC interprets the Rome Statute's rules on causality stricter than those under the *ad hoc* tribunals, or the formulation changed slightly while the material law remained the same.

When outlining the "direct effect" requirement, the pre-trial chamber in *Mudacumura* quoted two ICTR judgments, opening the respective footnote with the words "*but see*". The quoted appeal judgments from the ICTR used the usual "direct and substantial contribution" formula adopted by the *ad hoc* tribunals.[76] This indicates a deliberate departure of the chamber from the former requirement of a direct and substantial contribution.

Given the perceived similarity between ordering, soliciting, and inducing, it seems logical that chambers of the ICC would require the same causal nexus criterion—a direct effect on the commission or attempt—for all modes of Article 25 (3) (b).[77] Jurisprudence on soliciting and inducing can therefore prove helpful in this regard.

Under this premise, the explanation of a "direct effect" by the *Bemba et al.* trial chamber is particularly striking:

> Lastly, the Chamber must establish that the 'soliciting' or 'inducing' has had a direct effect on the commission or attempted commission of the offence. This means that the conduct of the accessory needs to have a causal effect on the offence. This approach seems warranted as the instigator, the intellectual author, without whom the offence would not have been committed, or not in this form, prompts the commission of the offence. Even if the physical perpetrator were already pondering on committing the offence in general, the instigator must have generated the final determination to commit the concrete offence. If the physical perpetrator, on the other hand, is already determined to commit the offence (*omni modo facturus*) then

[74] *Mudacumura*, 13 July 2012, para 63; *Ntaganda*, 9 June 2014, para 145; *Gbagbo*, 12 June 2014, para 244; *Gbagbo and Blé Goudé*, 16 July 2019, Annex B, para 1966. For this view in literature see Ambos 2016, Article 25 mn. 23; Olásolo and Carnero Rojo 2015, p. 564; Ventura 2019, p. 287.

[75] See Chap. 5, Sect. 5.1.1.3.

[76] ICTR, *The Prosecutor v. Clément Kayishema and Obed Ruzindana*, 1 June 2001, ICTR-95-1-A, para 186; ICTR, *The Prosecutor v. Jean de Dieu Kamuhanda*, 19 September 2005, ICTR-99-54A-A, para 75; quoted in *Mudacumura*, 13 July 2012, para 63 with fn. 132.

[77] On the similar treatment of these modes of liability see already above at Sect. 6.1, see also *Ntaganda*, 9 June 2014, paras 145 (ordering), 153 (inducing); *Gbagbo*, 12 June 2014, para 244, 247 ("instruction", referring to ordering "or instigation"); *Bemba et al.*, 19 October 2016, para 81 (soliciting, inducing); *Al Hassan*, 22 May 2018, para 185 (soliciting and inducing).

the contribution of the instigator does not have a direct effect on the commission of the offence.[78]

The appeals chamber in *Bemba et al.* seemingly repeated this ruling, emphasising that a "causal relationship" between the act of instigation and the crime has to be given in the sense that the instigator "prompted the principal perpetrator" to commit the crime.[79] Pre-trial chamber I also adopted this requirement in the *Al Hassan* decision on the issuance of a warrant of arrest.[80]

This narrow interpretation is new to international criminal law. As demonstrated above, a strict causal nexus between the order and the commission of the crime was not part of the *ad hoc* tribunals' law on ordering.[81] However, the parallel treatment of the modes of Article 25 (3) (b) Rome Statute, and the statement of the pre-trial chamber in *Mudacumura* lead to the conclusion that the chambers require a strict causality criterion for ordering.

Chambers of the ICC usually rely on evidence implying that: (1) the accused had possessed authority, (2) he had ordered/instructed a certain behaviour and (3) the crimes instructed had been carried out or the ordered conduct had taken place and had led to the crimes.[82] These instances also imply a rather strict causal relation between the order and the commission of the crime.

Therefore, it appears that the ICC has indeed departed from the lower threshold required by the *ad hoc* tribunals in which the order does not have to be a causal condition in the strict sense. Instead, under the Rome Statute, ordering (and soliciting and inducing) requires an order which generated the perpetrators decision to act and was therefore *conditio sine qua non* for the crime. The prosecution thus must prove that the crime in question would not have been committed or would not have been committed in this specific form, but for the order.[83]

The application of this narrow requirement should be welcomed, despite departing from customary law.[84] Considering that the mode of planning a crime was not incorporated into the Rome Statute, one could argue that this interpretation of the causal nexus unnecessarily narrows the scope of responsibility for ordering. However, as shown and endorsed above, the authority criterion should be interpreted as requiring the capacity to compel the physical perpetrator to commit the crime. With this in mind, many preparatory or supportive instructions that do not address perpetrators of the

---

[78] *Bemba et al.*, 19 October 2016, para 81; footnotes omitted, italics in original. The chamber quotes the *Mudacumura* Arrest Warrant decision and the *Ntaganda*, Decision on the Confirmation of Charges.

[79] ICC, *The Prosecutor v. Jean-Pierre Bemba et al.*, Appeals Judgment, 8 March 2018, ICC-01/05-01/13 A A2 A3 A4 A5, para 848.

[80] *Al Hassan*, 22 May 2018, para 185.

[81] See Chap. 5, Sect. 5.1.1.3.

[82] See e.g. *Mudacumura*, 13 July 2012, para 66; *Ntaganda*, 9 June 2014, para 149; *Gbagbo*, 12 June 2014, para 247; *Blé Goudé*, 11 December 2014, paras 161–2.

[83] But see for a different view Olásolo and Carnero Rojo 2015, p. 264; O'Keefe 2015, p. 188; Ventura 2019, mn. 25, who all base their analysis on *ad hoc* jurisprudence.

[84] For the opposite view see Finnin 2012, p. 146.

crime cannot qualify as ordering anyways. Thus, a narrow causal nexus requirement aligns with the authority criterion above and highlights the seriousness of ordering.

6.3.2 *Mental Element*

Questions regarding the necessary *mens rea* for ordering under the Rome Statute concern two separate issues: the general mental element standard under the ICC's law for ordering (Sect. 6.2.4.1)[85] and the necessity of a special intent for the ordering person (Sect. 6.2.4.2).

6.3.2.1 General *Mens Rea* Standard

As the general rule on *mens rea,* Article 30 Rome Statute applies to responsibility for ordering.[86] This means that the ordering person must act with intent and knowledge. Pursuant to Article 30 (2) (a) the actor who orders a crime must have the intent to engage in the conduct, i.e., to give an order.[87] Furthermore, they must mean to cause the consequence or at least be aware that the crime will be committed due to the order in the ordinary course of events.[88] As discussed earlier, the "ordinary course of events" standard implies that the consequence will occur with virtual certainty, a standard which is stricter than that of *dolus eventualis.*[89]

Under the *ad hoc* tribunals, the awareness of a "substantial likelihood" suffices to fulfil the necessary *mens rea* of ordering.[90] The concept of substantial likelihood implies a lower degree of probability and risk than the virtual certainty requirement. The latter implies that "the consequence will follow, barring an unforeseen or unexpected intervention that prevent this occurrence".[91] Consequently, intent for ordering is understood to be narrower under the Rome Statute than under the law of the *ad hoc* tribunals.[92]

---

[85] For the general rules on the mental element under Article 30 Rome Statute, see Chap. 3, Sect. 3.1.2.5.

[86] Goy 2012, p. 55; Olásolo and Carnero Rojo 2015, p. 564; Pigaroff and Robinson 2016, Article 30 mn. 6.

[87] *Gbagbo*, 12 June 2014, para 244; *Blé Goudé*, 11 December 2014, para 164; *Gbagbo and Blé Goudé*, 16 July 2019, Annex B, para 1966; Ventura 2019, p. 302.

[88] *Mudacumura*, 13 July 2012, paras 63, 67; *Ntaganda*, 9 June 2014, para 145; *Gbagbo*, 12 June 2014, para 244; *Blé Goudé*, 11 December 2014, para 164; Olásolo and Carnero Rojo 2015, p. 565; Ventura 2019, p. 302.

[89] See Chap. 3, Sect. 3.1.2.5.

[90] See Chap. 5, Sect. 5.1.1.4.

[91] *Bemba et al.*, 19 October 2016, para 29.

[92] Ventura 2019, p. 302; but see the interpretation of Olásolo and Carnero Rojo 2015, p. 566.

Additionally, knowledge pursuant to Article 30 (3) means that the ordering person needs to be aware of the necessary circumstances.[93] This means that the ordering person must be aware of the direct effect (causal nexus) the order will have on the commission of the crime.[94] It is logical to assume that the ordering person must also be aware of their authority over the perpetrators. This results from the other *mens rea* requirements. If an actor means to give an order, in awareness of the fact that this will have a direct effect on the commission of the crime, this implies that they are also aware of their influence on the perpetrator.[95] Additionally, it would be inconsistent to require *mens rea* for all criteria of a liability form, such as intent and knowledge regarding the order and its effect, but not for the central authority requirement, which is a circumstantial element of ordering.[96] Hence, an ordering person must be aware of their position of authority (as a circumstance) in virtue of Article 30 (3) Rome Statute.[97]

In sum, under Article 25 (3) (b), 30 Rome Statute, a person giving an order must mean to give that order in awareness of their position of authority and the direct, causal effect the order will have on the commission of the crime. Therefore, they must be aware that the crime will be committed with virtual certainty.

6.3.2.2 Necessity to Fulfil a Special Intent

A central issue is the question of whether the special intent or *dolus specialis* for crimes like genocide or persecution as a crime against humanity,[98] is necessary to incur responsibility for ordering under Article 25 (3) (b) Rome Statute. This is contentious in academic literature.[99]

---

[93] Regarding the circumstances of the crimes, i.e. context elements, see *Mudacumura*, 13 July 2012, para 67 (awareness of armed conflict); *Blé Goudé*, 11 December 2014, para 164 (awareness of widespread and systematic nature of attacks that would ensue). Article 30 (3) also mentions awareness of the consequences, but this has no autonomous meaning in addition to the rule of Article 30 (2) (b), see Pigaroff and Robinson 2016, Article 30 mn. 30.

[94] See for the awareness of the causal nexus: *Mudacumura*, 13 July 2012, para 67; *Gbagbo*, 12 June 2014, para 244 ("was aware that those crimes would be committed ... as a consequence of his instruction or instigation"); the same wording can be found in *Blé Goudé*, 11 December 2014, 164; see also Olásolo and Carnero Rojo 2015, p. 567; of the opposite opinion Finnin 2012, pp 195–7.

[95] However, it is technically conceivable that a person orders an act with the necessary intent and awareness of the subsequent ordinary course of events, but simultaneously does not consider their authority as a causal factor, instead relying on the assumption that the instruction will only induce or solicit the commission of the crime by another.

[96] Finnin 2012, pp 58, 189.

[97] In the same vein ibid., pp 189, 212; Olásolo and Carnero Rojo 2015, p. 567.

[98] For a more comprehensive list of special intent crimes under the Rome Statute, see Finnin 2012, p. 183.

[99] Against such an intent: Goy 2012, p. 55; Olásolo and Carnero Rojo 2015, p. 565; Werle 2007, p. 968; Werle and Jessberger 2020, mn. 619; in favour of an intent requirement for ordering: Ambos 2013, p. 163 (who sees ordering as a form of perpetration); Clark 2008, p. 547; note that Eser 2002b, p. 797 does not reject the necessity of the special intent of certain crimes for the instigator/ordering

Commentators against a special intent requirement for ordering and instigating usually base their opinion on the assumption that ordering is a secondary form of responsibility.[100] However, it is questionable whether the categorization as accessorial liability must or should lead to rejecting this requirement for all or some forms of accessorial liability. It would make sense if the system of perpetration and participation relied on normative criteria and strictly differentiated between the more blameworthy principal and the less blameworthy accessory. However, given the findings on the blameworthiness of ordering, planning, and instigating under the law of the *ad hoc* tribunals, it is debatable whether such a system is and should be established under the Rome Statute.

As to the state of international customary law, it has been shown above that ordering a crime under the law of the *ad hoc* tribunals requires the ordering person to fulfil the special intent of the crime.[101]

The ICC case law on this matter is very limited. Some decisions addressing special intent crimes do not allow a conclusion on this issue, as the question of special intent is treated separately from single modes of responsibility or is not treated specifically at all.[102] The confirmation of charges in *Gbagbo* and *Blé Goudé* seemingly establish that special intent is only necessary for the commission of the crime in virtue of Article 25 (3) (a). Both elaborate on the necessary *mens rea* for indirect co-perpetration and for ordering. For the former, the decisions explicitly state that, regarding the crime of persecution, the accused "intended the discriminatory use of violence" against the supporters of the political opponent.[103] By contrast, when considering the necessary mental element for ordering, the chamber stated that the accused knew that the civilians targeted would be those who supported the political opponent.[104]

Considering the observations on *ad hoc* jurisprudence, including the high blameworthiness associated with special intent, it would be preferable for the ICC not to adopt the pre-trial chamber's approach in the *Gbagbo* and *Blé Goudé* cases. Up to this point, the observations on ordering support it being a form of responsibility that captures the conduct of decision makers with substantial influence over the unfolding

person but rather acknowledges that Article 25 (3) (b) has no own mental element that goes beyond Article 30.

[100] Goy 2012, p. 55; according to Werle it gives the form of liability the "correct weight within a differentiated participation model" if ordering does not require a special intent, see Werle 2007, p. 968.

[101] See Chap. 5, Sect. 5.1.1.4.

[102] In *Mudacumura*, 13 July 2012, the crimes of torture and pillaging are charged, which require a special intent, but no findings as to such intent of the accused are made. In *Ngaïssona and Yekatom*, persecution and pillaging are charged and the necessary intent is addressed, but without being brought in connection with any of the charged modes of liability, see *Ngaïssona and Yekatom*, 18 September 2019, paras 238, 261. The same is true in *Ongwen*, 23 March 2016, Disposition: The Charges Confirmed, from part "4. Attack on Pajule camp of internally displaced persons on or about 10 October 2003 (Counts 1–10)" on.

[103] *Gbagbo*, 12 June 2014, para 236; *Blé Goudé*, 11 December 2014, para 154.

[104] *Gbagbo*, 12 June 2014, para 249; *Blé Goudé*, 11 December 2014, para 164.

of crimes. As such, they should be required to demonstrate the necessary intent as their conduct sets the commission of the relevant crimes in motion.

6.3.3 Commission or Attempted Commission of the Crime

Pursuant to Article 25 (3) (b) to (d) Rome Statute, the enumerated modes of liability are only fulfilled if the crime to which they are related is committed or attempted. Consequently, the crime which was ordered, or should occur due to the order in the ordinary course of events, must at least have been attempted.[105] Regarding the order of an attempted crime, Article 25 (3) (b) is broader than its equivalent at the *ad hoc* tribunals. This is the logical consequence of the Rome Statute recognizing the punishable attempt of the commission of crime in Article 25 (3) (f).[106] Accordingly, if an order to commit a crime is given and the perpetrators attempt to comply, the ordering person can incur liability for ordering the attempted commission, despite the order not being carried out and the crime ultimately not being committed.

Whether the attempt to order the commission of a crime is or should be seen as criminalized under the Rome Statute will be discussed below.

6.4 Application of Ordering to High-Level Decision Makers Before the ICC

The requirements of ordering do not differ greatly from those familiar from the *ad hoc* jurisprudence. Differences between ICC and *ad hoc* jurisprudence exist as far as the necessary causal nexus, the mental element and the attempt are concerned. In the former two aspects, ordering under the Rome Statute proves narrower, and in the latter, it is broader than the law of the *ad hoc* tribunals.

These differences notwithstanding, it can be suspected that, given the generally parallel requirements and observations on the scope of ordering under the *ad hoc* tribunals and in post-World War II jurisprudence, ordering can equally be applied to high-level decision maker cases before the ICC.[107] This presumption is backed by several decisions in which ordering was the responsibility form of choice of the prosecution or chamber at some point. In these decisions, ordering and indirect perpetration through an organisation were swapped during the proceedings, apparently

---

105 Satzger 2018, mn. 51; Schabas 2016, p. 574; Werle and Jessberger 2020, mn. 659; Ventura 2019, p. 299.

106 See Ventura 2019, pp 299–300.

107 As observed above, the conduct of architects of crimes who do not give instructions to the physical perpetrators will often not qualify as ordering. This has been the case under the *ad hoc* tribunals' law and will also apply under the Rome Statute, especially given the stricter causal nexus requirement. See Sect. 6.2.3.

without any differences in the underlying facts (see below Sect. 6.3.1). Furthermore, facilitated by the parallels between their respective requirements, one can analyse cases originally treated under indirect (co-)perpetration under the requirements of ordering (see below Sect. 6.3.2).

As only the commission of large-scale crimes has thus far triggered ICC action, the analysis presupposes that international crimes were in fact attempted or committed.[108] It furthermore implies that the necessary causal nexus between the instructions issued by the accused and the crimes existed. It is submitted that, where an instruction to commit a crime qualifies as a "substantial contribution" to a common plan (indirect co-perpetration) or as the necessary conduct element of indirect perpetration, this instruction will also have the necessary "direct effect on the commission of the crime" (ordering).

6.4.1 Replacement of Ordering and Indirect Perpetration With Each Other

In a range of cases, ICC jurisprudence establishes that ordering can be applied to high-level decision makers of international crimes. It does so by charging the respective accused with indirect (co-)perpetration and ordering for the same conduct and by relying on the same evidence to substantiate these charges.

The arrest warrants against the leadership of the Lord's Resistance Army and the consequent proceedings against Dominic Ongwen serve as one example for this. All of the wanted members of the so-called "control altar" of the LRA were originally wanted for ordering the crimes which were attributed to them, while indirect (co-) perpetration did not yet exist and was not included in the arrest warrants.[109] In the pre-trial proceedings against Dominic Ongwen, indirect (co-)perpetration and ordering were charged simultaneously for many crimes.[110] The decision on the confirmation of charges consequently does not differentiate explicitly between the evidence for one or the other mode of liability. Instead, it lists the facts that can equally serve to find Ongwen responsible for indirect perpetration or ordering. This method is applied explicitly by the chamber, which includes indirect perpetration, indirect co-perpetration, ordering, contribution to a group crime and command responsibility in its list of "common elements of modes of liability".[111] The chamber determines that

[108] Consequently, the necessary accessorial object, as required by the jurisprudence, is also assumed. For ordering as accessorial liability and the scope of this see below at Sect. 6.4.1.

[109] *Lukwiya*, 8 July 2005, para 30; *Odhiambo*, 8 July 2005, para 32; *Ongwen*, 8 July 2005, para 30; *Otti*, 8 July 2005, para 42; *Kony*, 27 September 2005, para 42.

[110] See *Ongwen*, 23 March 2016, paras 36, 38, 42.

[111] Ibid., para 9.

Ongwen's subordinates were "conditioned by, and under threat of, physical punishment". In the view of the chamber, the violent disciplinary system guaranteed adherence to rules and orders.[112] Additionally, the chamber asserted with an obvious nod to command responsibility that Ongwen had "command and control" or "authority and control" and the power to issue orders, including those to engage or disengage troops in hostilities.[113] His position as a commander holding various ranks and positions over the relevant period is also mentioned.[114] The chamber consequently found reasonable grounds to believe that Ongwen was responsible as an indirect (co-)perpetrator, for ordering or for command responsibility in many instances.[115] However, the following trial chamber decision only rested on findings of Ongwen being an indirect co- and indirect perpetrator, while it described many of the relevant acts of the accused as ordering.[116]

In the *Katanga and Chui* case, the prosecution originally charged the accused with ordering the crimes in question.[117] This was amended with the arrest warrant decisions and changed into a charge of indirect co-perpetration.[118] This alone shows that a substantial overlap of ordering and indirect (co-)perpetration exists, which allowed the pre-trial chamber a simple re-characterisation of facts.

The pre-trial chamber in *Gbagbo* and *Blé Goudé* confirmed the charges for both of the indicted, based on indirect co-perpetration and ordering.[119] The determination of the respective position and influence for both modes of responsibility relied on the same circumstances and mostly on the same conduct as well. Laurent Gbagbo's control over a hierarchical apparatus of power was affirmed, based on the same facts which also supported his position of authority. These included the hierarchies in place over state forces and separate militias and mercenaries, the provision of materiel and finances to the latter and their organisational structures and loyalty.[120] Concerning the *actus reus*, the same effect can be observed. The chamber determined that Gbagbo had contributed in a coordinated manner (indirect co-perpetration) and

---

[112] Ibid., p. 72 para 11.

[113] Ibid., p. 73 para 13.

[114] Ibid., p. 73 para 12.

[115] Ibid., p. 80 para 39, Nos. 11–23; p. 84 para 52 Nos. 24–36; p. 88 para 65 Nos. 37–49; p. 101 para 124 Nos. 61–68; p. 103 para 131 Nos. 69–70.

[116] ICC, *The Prosecutor v. Dominic Ongwen*, Trial Judgment, 4 February 2021, ICC-02/04-01/15, paras 2862, 2913, 2916, 2963, 3010, 3093, 3110.

[117] Cf. ICC, *The Prosecutor v. Germain Katanga*, Arrest Warrant Decision, 6 July 2007, ICC-01/04-01/07, para 54; ICC, *The Prosecutor v. Matthieu Ngudjolo Chui*, Arrest Warrant Decision, 6 July 2007, ICC-01/04-02/07, para 55.

[118] The pre-trial chamber in the respective arrest warrant decisions pointed to the perceived difference between ordering as an accessorial mode of liability and commission. It then re-characterized the charges into commission or ordering in the alternative, see *Katanga*, 6 July 2007, paras 54, 60; *Chui*, 6 July 2007, paras 55, 60; see also *Katanga and Chui*, 30 September 2008, paras 469–70; Steer 2017, p. 302; van Sliedregt and Yanev 2019, mn. 55 with fn. 186–7.

[119] *Gbagbo*, 12 June 2014, paras 241, 251; *Blé Goudé*, 11 December 2014, paras 158, 166.

[120] *Gbagbo*, 12 June 2014, paras 233–4 (concerning indirect co-perpetration), 245 (concerning ordering).

ordered the crimes by issuing instructions which led to attacks on civilians, but also by mobilising youth groups and militias for his cause and emphasising his plans to stay in power.[121]

The same mostly holds true for Charles Blé Goudé whose control (exercised together with others) and authority were allegedly based on his capability to mobilise the youth groups, as well as his personal ties with, and support lent to militia leaders.[122] His alleged mobilisation of the youth groups counted as a contribution to the common plan[123] and a relevant instruction for ordering.[124] The elaborations of the chamber differ slightly regarding the criminal conduct: the accused's contribution to the common plan is *inter alia* seen in his recruiting, training, equipping and financing of militias.[125] His ordering is *inter alia* evidenced through instructions he gave to a specific leader of a group to participate in the violent suppression of a demonstration.[126] In this regard, the chamber's statement that Blé Goudé was "not the ultimate decision maker" is a precise description.[127] Given that the accused's contributions were important to the overall campaign, one could describe him as an architect, or organiser as far as these supportive acts are concerned.

The charges against Bosco Ntaganda were initially confirmed under the heads of indirect co-perpetration and ordering.[128] The bulk of the findings referred to the same behaviour and circumstances and mostly the same crimes were deemed attributable to Ntaganda.[129] A discrepancy can be identified, where Ntaganda's acts amounted to purely organisational conduct and to acts amounting to the crime of conscripting and enlisting children under the age of 15.[130] This finding is in line with those made in the case of Blé Goudé, discussed above.

In the case of Sylvestre Mudacumura, the pre-trial chamber rejected Mudacumura's responsibility for indirect co-perpetration because no common plan could be established.[131] However, it confirmed his responsibility for ordering.[132] In doing

---

[121] Ibid., paras 232, 246.

[122] *Blé Goudé*, 11 December 2014, paras 151–2 (control), 160 (authority).

[123] It is submitted that given Blé Goudé's alleged personal role as a leadership figure, the chamber would also have affirmed him being an indirect perpetrator who controlled the youth groups as his organisation. In this case, it would have relied on the same conduct as for ordering, instead of the broader view that it subsequently took to substantiate the contribution requirement of indirect co-perpetration.

[124] *Blé Goudé*, 11 December 2014, paras 142, 161–2.

[125] Ibid., para 142.

[126] Ibid., para 161.

[127] Ibid., para 142.

[128] *Ntaganda*, 9 June 2014, paras 101–21, 135; 145–52.

[129] Ibid., paras 109–115 (contribution to common plan), 119–20 (control over a hierarchical organisation), 148 (conduct qualifying as ordering), 149 (authority).

[130] See e.g. Ibid., paras 110 (provision of weapons, securing additional troops), 113 (assuming a coordinating role before an attack), 116–7 (conscription and enlistment of children under the age of 15).

[131] *Mudacumura*, 13 July 2012, para 62.

[132] Ibid., para 69.

so, it elaborated on Mudacumura's position as the top military commander of the Congolese/Rwandan rebel group *FDLR* and the group's distinguishing feature as a large, well-organised organisation with a clear hierarchy. The chamber explicitly stated that Mudacumura had "control over his forces and over recruiting, promoting, removing and disciplining them". It also stated that "compliance with Mr. Mudacumura's orders was required".[133] These findings would have unequivocally carried a conviction under indirect perpetration through an organisation as well, had this mode been charged alone and not in conjunction with co-perpetration.[134] The relevant conduct was identified as consisting of several general orders issued by Mudacumura, instructing his subordinates to create a humanitarian catastrophe and to engage in pillaging. Additionally, the chamber found that any field operation had to be approved by Mudacumura.[135]

6.4.2 *Qualification of Decision Makers Under Ordering in ICC Cases*

In other decisions or entire cases, ordering does not play a role, i.e., was not included in the charges. For these cases, it is worth exploring whether responsibility for ordering the crimes could have reasonably been charged.

As in earlier sections, this analysis must rely on findings which chambers made when examining indirect (co-)perpetration. It can be expected, however, that the findings should be useful in determining liability for ordering due to its similarity to indirect perpetration through an organisation.

6.4.2.1 Position of Authority

As stated above, the authority criterion is often proven through the same evidence as indirect perpetration through an organisation, i.e., control over an organisation.[136]

Under this presumption, it is probable that authority could be affirmed for the indicted in many cases in which the ICC applies indirect perpetration through an organisation.

In *Al Gaddafi*, the pre-trail chamber affirmed the role, position, and importance of the three wanted persons: Muammar Al Gaddafi, Saif Al Islam Gaddafi, and Abdullah Al Senussi. The finding that they exercised comprehensive influence over the respective branches of the state apparatus that were subordinate to them was affirmed for all three. The chamber found reasonable grounds to believe that members of the state apparatus would act according to their instructions. It was found that every

---

[133] Ibid., para 64.

[134] See Chap. 3, Sect. 3.4.

[135] *Mudacumura*, 13 July 2012, para 65.

[136] See above Sect. 6.2.2.2.

level of the apparatus could be instructed directly by the accused, the instructions were binding and their implementation obligatory. In the security forces, strict and intensive military training were enforced, and it was believed that each individual feared the other.[137]

According to the findings of the pre-trial chamber, in the situation in Sudan, Omar Al Bashir exercised control over the state apparatus. He allegedly controlled local and state security committees, which were subordinate to him.[138] The chamber affirmed reasonable grounds to believe that Al Bashir was "in full control of all branches" of the state of Sudan and as *de jure* and *de facto* president played an essential role.[139] In the same situation, Abdel Raheem is wanted over charges which rest on his "*de jure* authority" and "*de facto* power over security bodies" in the region of Darfur, Sudan. Raheem served as the president's special representative for Darfur and Minister of the Interior, and as such exercised authority over several branches of the security forces.[140]

Bosco Ntaganda,[141] who was indicted *inter alia* for ordering crimes, was finally convicted as an indirect co-perpetrator. The trial chamber's findings included the fact that he had been one of the highest authorities within the *UPC/FPLC*.[142] His position included having competence over operations and organisation.[143] His orders were "respected and executed" and both military operations in which the crimes in question were committed, were "executed in line with the orders issued".[144] Furthermore, the chambers elaborated on the brutal disciplinary methods of the *UPC/FPLC*.[145] They led to complete obedience from the organisation's fighters.[146] Additionally, it was found that Ntaganda "inspired fear over the troops…".[147]

According to the pre-trial chamber, William Ruto, one of the accused in connection with the post-election violence in Kenya, held a position at the very top of a criminal network, from which he could control this organisation. His orders would be carried out, which was "ensured" through a double mechanism of payment and

---

[137] ICC, *The Prosecutor v. Muammar Mohammed Abu Minyar Gaddafi, Saif Al-Islam Gaddafi and Abdullah Al-Senussi*, Arrest Warrant Decision, 27 June 2011, ICC-01/11, paras 72–5, 84–6.

[138] ICC, *The Prosecutor v. Omar Hassan Ahmad Al Bashir*, Issuance of a Warrant of Arrest, 4 March 2009, ICC-02/05-01/09, paras 216–20.

[139] Ibid., paras 221–2.

[140] ICC, *The Prosecutor v. Abdel Raheem Muhammad Hussein*, Arrest Warrant Decision, 1 March 2012, ICC-02/05-01/12, para 31.

[141] For a more detailed analysis of the possibility to convict Ntaganda for ordering crimes see Block 2022, pp. 723 et seq. The analysis therein draws from the findings of this thesis.

[142] ICC, *The Prosecutor v. Bosco Ntaganda*, Trial Judgment, 8 July 2019, ICC-01/04-02/06, para 814.

[143] Ibid., para 827.

[144] Ibid., para 816.

[145] Ibid., para 817.

[146] Ibid., para 819.

[147] Ibid., para 828.

punishment.[148] Francis Muthaura, another accused in the same situation, was found to have gained control over the violent *Mungiki* sect through an agreement with the sect's leader.[149] Within the sect, violent punishment regimens led to comprehensive obedience by the members.[150]

The pre-trial chamber found that Simone Gbagbo acted as the "*alter ego*" of Laurent Gbagbo, making state decisions and being close to other members of Gbagbo's alleged leadership gang. As such, she was allegedly able to instruct the pro-Gbagbo forces to commit crimes.[151]

In all these examples, chambers elaborated extensively on the power and influence of the respective actors over others. This mostly happened when exploring the requirements of indirect perpetration through an organisation.[152] However, there can be no doubt that whenever a person's control over an organisation is affirmed, this will automatically lead to them being able to issue compelling instructions and thus having authority over the perpetrators of the crime. This means that an indirect perpetrator who relies on an organisation will always qualify as a person who can be liable for ordering as well.

6.4.2.2 Actus Reus: The Accused Must Have Given an Order

Where instructions are given orally and are not documented, the *actus reus* of ordering may sometimes be the most difficult to prove. However, chambers of the ICC have found sufficient evidence of direct instructions to convict an accused or at least confirm charges in many cases. Furthermore, the existence of an instruction can be inferred from circumstantial evidence.[153] It must be remembered that on the one hand, charges brought under indirect perpetration through an organisation (or indirect co-perpetration) are often vague regarding the specific conduct of the accused. On the other hand, indirect perpetration through an organisation also contains a conduct element, and many cases before the ICC, with charges of indirect (co-)perpetration relied on the assumption of conduct that consisted of direct instructions.[154]

In the *Al Gaddafi* arrest warrant decision, the chamber explicitly mentioned several acts of the wanted people. Muammar Al Gaddafi was *inter alia*, believed to have instructed the chief of the security apparatus, Al Senussi, to supress the protests

---

[148] ICC, *The Prosecutor v. William Samoei Ruto, Henry Kiprono Kosgey and Joshua Arap Sang*, Confirmation of Charges, 23 January 2012, ICC-01/09-01/11, paras 316–7.

[149] ICC, *The Prosecutor v. Francis Kirimi Muthaura, Uhuru Muigai Kenyatta and Mohammed Hussein Ali*, Confirmation of Charges, 23 January 2012, ICC-01/09-02/11, para 408.

[150] Ibid., 208–13, 408.

[151] ICC, *The Prosecutor v. Simone Gbagbo*, Arrest Warrant Decision, 2 March 2012, ICC-02/11-01/12.

[152] Cf. Sect. 6.2.2.2.

[153] See Sect. 6.2.1.

[154] See, Chap. 3, Sect. 3.1.2.5.

against the regime in Benghazi.[155] Al Senussi, in turn, allegedly commanded his troops to crack down, directly instructing them to attack protesters. In one instance, he supposedly gave direct orders to shoot civilians.[156] Saif Al Islam Gaddafi purportedly used his authority and power to implement the plan of suppressing the civilian population, ordering the mobilisation of troops and the imprisonment and elimination of political dissidents.[157]

In *Al Bashir*, the pre-trial chamber alleged that the indicted had used his control to ensure the implementation of the common plan.[158] In this case, an inference as to the existence of certain instructions would have been necessary and possible. Given the large-scale commission of crimes, based on the same pattern and the alleged tight control of Al Bashir over the state apparatus, it can be reasonably inferred that he must have given instructions concerning the violent campaign against the Fur, Masalit and Zaghawa in Darfur. Bashir's special representative Abdel Raheem allegedly coordinated the campaign in Darfur on a regional level and issued orders to the notorious *Janjaweed* militia when they participated in operations with government forces.[159]

Bosco Ntaganda gave the final order for the troops of the *UPC/FPLC* to advance and commence the attack during which many of the crimes in question were committed.[160] The previous night, he explained the next day's attack to some of the troops in more "specific terms". He told them to "kill and appropriate everything", which meant to murder civilians of the Lendu ethnicity and loot their property.[161] Ntaganda was the overall commander of the subsequent attack, he gave orders to troops and received their reports.[162] The orders included direct instructions, referring to which objects should be targeted by heavy weapons.[163] His orders referred to "the Lendu" and did not distinguish between civilians and fighters.[164] A second operation, which also led to crimes attributed to Ntaganda, was also commanded by him directly.[165] In a later operation, Ntaganda ordered some of his fighters to fire at fleeing civilians with a grenade launcher.[166] He also ordered the shooting of two prisoners.[167] All this was summarized by the chamber as a "direct order to kill

155 *Gaddafi et al.*, 27 June 2011, para 79.
156 Ibid., para 87.
157 Ibid., para 80.
158 *Al Bashir*, 4 March 2009, para 220.
159 *Abdel Raheem*, 1 March 2012, paras 24–6.
160 *Ntaganda*, 8 July 2019, paras 485, 840.
161 Ibid., paras 415, 484, 841.
162 Ibid., paras 842, 844.
163 Ibid., para 843.
164 Ibid., para 845.
165 Ibid., para 846.
166 Ibid., para 848.
167 Ibid., para 849.

civilians and loot", and as an "active role as an operational commander, identifying targets".[168]

In the situation in Kenya, the accused Muthaura was found by the pre-trial chamber to have "expressly directed the *Mungiki* to commit crimes", and to have "issued instructions to a series of mid-level perpetrators in order to secure the perpetration of the crimes as planned".[169]

According to the pre-trial chamber, William Ruto led the discussions within the leadership of his network and personally devised the plan to commit crimes after the election crisis. Allegedly, he personally gave instructions concerning the crimes to be committed, identifying the victims who should be killed, the property that should be looted, etc.[170]

Simone Gbagbo was believed to have instructed pro-Gbagbo forces to commit crimes, *inter alia* by specifying the measures to quell anti-government protests.[171]

These examples demonstrate how central parts of the conduct of many accused before the ICC can be grasped by ordering. This is essentially because, among the various acts, there often seem to be very direct instructions, addressed to the physical perpetrators of crimes. However, where a person's conduct fulfils organisational, supportive functions, such as the provision of materiel and finances, training or the enlisting and mobilisation of physical perpetrators, i.e., where a person is an architect rather than a decision maker, this conduct does not qualify as giving an order. This is in line with the findings on the limitations of ordering under the *ad hoc* tribunals.[172]

6.4.2.3 Mental Element

Concerning the mental element, the similarity of indirect perpetration through an organisation and ordering again enables certain findings.

The pre-trial chamber in *Al Gaddafi* affirmed that all three accused intended to bring about the commission of crimes, knew about the widespread and systematic nature of the attack and of their own role within the state as well as their power to "control their subordinates".[173]

In *Abdel Raheem*, the pre-trial chamber elaborated on the alleged *mens rea* of the indicted. It found that, to the same extent as his alleged co-perpetrators (including Al Bashir), Raheem was aware that the plan would lead to the commission of crimes and of the circumstances enabling control, i.e., of the joint exercise of control over the state apparatus.[174]

---

[168] Ibid., para 855.

[169] *Muthaura et. al.*, 23 January 2012, para 413.

[170] *Ruto et al.*, 23 January 2012, paras 309–10.

[171] *Simone Gbagbo*, 2 March 2012, para 32.

[172] See Chap. 5, Sect. 5.2.4.2.

[173] *Gaddafi et al.*, 27 June 2011, paras 81, 88.

[174] *Abdel Raheem*, 1 March 2012, para 37.

In *Ntaganda*, the trial chamber affirmed that the accused had intended the crimes to be committed and that this would occur pursuant to his orders.[175] Ntaganda was also aware of his powers and intended to use them accordingly.[176]

In the case against *Ruto et al.*, the chamber equally affirmed that the accused William Ruto knew of the circumstances enabling "joint control", which resulted in his influence over the criminal network and power and authority over its members.[177] In the same way, Francis Muthaura's knowledge of his own role was affirmed by the pre-trial chamber in *Muthaura et al.*[178]

Simone Gbagbo was also believed to have been aware of the circumstances enabling her to issue instructions to pro-Gbagbo forces and to have acted with the requisite intent regarding the commission of the crime.[179]

As far as the mental element is concerned, no difference can be spotted between ordering and indirect (co-)perpetration. Given that the actor must be aware of their position and this position will establish authority as soon as it establishes control over an organisation, the awareness of these circumstances is largely identical. The intent regarding one's own actions is also the same, as long as it refers to conduct that qualifies as both a relevant act under indirect (co-)perpetration and ordering.

6.4.3 Influence on Specific Crimes, Temporal and Spatial Extent and Position

The applicability of ordering to all relevant cases before the ICC that have been treated under indirect (co-)perpetration, shows that no significant difference exists between the cases encompassed by the two forms. This is true for the influence on specific crimes, the actors' temporal and spatial distance to the crime and the resulting crimes' extent in time and space. Likewise, no difference in terms of the actors' positions can be identified thus far.

These findings are in line with those concerning the *ad hoc* tribunals and the cases before them, which were treated under ordering and participation in a JCE.

6.4.4 Conclusion: The Applicability of Ordering to Decision Maker Cases Before the ICC

The observations of this section show that ordering can generally be applied to the same cases, the same actors, and the same conduct as indirect perpetration through an

[175] *Ntaganda*, 8 July 2019, paras 1171, 1188, 1198.
[176] Ibid., paras 1174–5.
[177] *Ruto et al.*, 23 January 2012, para 333.
[178] *Muthaura et. al.*, 23 January 2012, para 419.
[179] *Simone Gbagbo*, 2 March 2012, para 35.

organisation. The only difference emerges when the scope of ordering is compared to indirect co-perpetration. Due to the breadth of possible *actus rei* under this doctrine, it grasps supportive, organisational, and coordinating conduct that does not fall under the objective element of ordering. This is comparable to the difference between ordering and JCE under the *ad hoc* tribunals' jurisprudence. The Rome Statute does not contain a mode of planning a crime, which can be regarded as a major disadvantage precisely because of the potential applicability of this mode to architects of crimes.[180] However, it does include aiding and abetting and the contribution to a group crime in Article 25 (3) (c) and (d). These modes of liability will usually be fulfilled, where a person's conduct qualifies as a contribution to a common plan under indirect co-perpetration.

Nevertheless, the foregoing cases indicate that participants in large-scale violence before the ICC were often involved directly with the issuance of criminal orders. In other words: the high- and mid-level actors before the ICC so far were hardly ever purely architects of crimes. They were often decision makers and, as such, their behaviour could be adjudicated under the head of ordering a crime.

6.5 The Relation of Ordering and Other Forms of Responsibility Under the Rome Statute

To determine the role of ordering under the jurisprudence of the ICC and to assess whether it can serve as an appropriate tool to adjudicate the wrongdoing of high- and mid-level decision makers, the position of this mode of liability *vis-à-vis* the other forms of participation in the statute is of great importance.

6.5.1 Ordering in a Differentiated System of Perpetration and Participation

The categorization of ordering into a system of liability (differentiated or unitary) is the basis to assess the mode's relation to other forms of responsibility (Sect. 6.4.1.1). Apart from the general categorisation, it must also be determined what "accessorial" means, i.e., what is required as an accessorial object (Sect. 6.4.1.2).

6.5.1.1 The Categorization of Ordering as Accessorial Responsibility

The ICC interprets the Rome Statute as establishing a differentiated system of perpetration and participation, which distinguishes between principal and accessory

---

[180] See in a similar vein *Chui*, 18 December 2012, Concurring Opinion of Judge Christine Van den Wyngaert, para 15.

liability.[181] The wording of Article 25 (3) (b), (c) and (d) support this, as they require that the crime be committed or at least attempted. The necessity of another committing or attempting to commit the crime is the typical starting point for the determination of accessorial liability.[182] The structure of Article 25 (3) with its different letters seems to support this view as well.[183] This distinction between autonomous liability for principals and derivative liability for accessories is inherent to the ICC's interpretation.[184] Accordingly, this distinction between perpetration and participation in Article 25 (3) Rome Statute has garnered much support in academia.[185]

The ICC's jurisprudence on the categorization of ordering within this system is clear: ordering under Article 25 (3) (b) Rome Statute is seen as a form of accessorial liability.[186]

The overall interpretation of the system has not gone without criticism from dissenting judges and scholars alike.[187] Especially the categorization of ordering as accessory liability has sparked criticism. In Ambos' view, ordering constitutes a form of indirect perpetration ("through another person") and is thus principal liability.[188] Vest does not believe that ordering must be categorized as accessorial liability and stresses that it should have been introduced as a form of perpetration.[189] Heller criticises that categorizing ordering as accessorial liability fails to reflect that the violation

---

[181] See already Chap. 3, Sect. 3.1.1.

[182] Cryer et al. 2019, p. 360; on the different notions of accessorial liability see Ambos 2004, pp 616-8, who explains that the distinction between derivative and autonomous liability is inherent not only to continental, but also to Anglo-American systems of perpetration and participation.

[183] Burghardt 2010, p. 91; Werle 2007, pp 956–7; Werle and Burghardt 2010, p. 851.

[184] ICC, *The Prosecutor v. Thomas Lubanga Dyilo*, Appeals Judgment, 1 December 2014, ICC-01/04-01/06 A 5, para 998; ICC, *The Prosecutor v. Germain Katanga*, Trial Judgment, 7 March 2014, ICC 01/04-01/07, para 1385; on the exact requirement of the accessorial nature, see further below.

[185] Burghardt 2010, p. 91; Olásolo 2009, p. 26; Werle and Jessberger 2020, mn. 614–16, 659; apparently also Satzger 2018, § 13 mn. 51; critical: Safferling 2011, § 5 mn. 70; see on the tendency towards differentiated systems in international criminal law van Sliedregt 2012, pp 73–4.

[186] ICC, *The Prosecutor v. Thomas Lubanga*, Confirmation of Charges, 29 Januaryy 2007, ICC-01/04-01/06, para 320; *Katanga and Chui*, 30 September 2008, paras 467, 470; *Mudacumura*, 13 July 2012, para 63; *Katanga*, 7 March 2014, para 1383; *Bemba et al.*, 19 October 2016, para 73. See also Goy 2012, p. 55; Olásolo and Carnero Rojo 2015, p. 557; Sato 2012, pp 295, 299; van Sliedregt 2012, p. 108; Ventura 2019, p. 284; Werle 2007, p. 957; Office WCR 2010, 54.

[187] See the Separate Opinion of Judge Adrian Fulford in ICC, *The Prosecutor v. Thomas Lubanga Dyilo*, Trial Judgment, 14 March 2012, ICC-01/04-01/06, paras 6–7; Concurring Opinion of Judge Christine Van den Wyngaert in *Chui*, 18 December 2012, paras 14, 21; see also Lanza 2021, p. 145 (functional unitary system); Rastan 2009, pp 267–8; Stewart 2012, pp 207, 218; Ambos interprets Article 25 (3) Rome Statute as a unitary model in a functional sense (German *"funktionales Einheitstätersystem"*) in Ambos 2016, Article 25 mn. 2; an early vote for a unitary perpetration model can be found with Eser 2002a, pp 787–8.

[188] See only: Ambos 2016, Article 25 mn. 22; Ambos 2018, § 7 mn. 45; see also Eser 2002a, pp 787, 797 who agrees that ordering should be seen as indirect perpetration, and therefore advocates that the inclusion of ordering in the statute was perhaps superfluous. In the same vein Yanev 2018, p. 468.

[189] Vest 2011, pp 364–5.

of law by an ordering person is twofold: they violate the duty to control their subordinates and misuse their power to ensure the crime is committed.[190] Rastan questions why a superior who orders the commission of a crime should not be held liable as a principal of the crime.[191] Many of these objections to categorizing ordering as accessory liability build on the heightened seriousness of giving orders that lead to crimes.[192] These opinions therefore touch upon the question of blameworthiness. They seemingly imply that a differentiated system leads to a hierarchy of blameworthiness between modes of liability that would downgrade the seriousness of ordering. However, this is not necessarily the case. For the purposes of this chapter, the categorisation of modes into principal, i.e., autonomous, and accessorial, derivative forms of liability is explored, without indicating a gradation in seriousness.

Under this premise, it seems established that the ICC treats ordering as accessorial liability.

6.5.1.2 The Accessorial Object in ICC Jurisprudence

The categorization as accessorial, derivative liability means that the responsibility for ordering, as well as of the other modes, is dependent on the commission of the crime by another. However, this does not determine how far this derivativeness extends. It must be questioned, what is required by Article 25 (3) (b)–(d) to establish that a crime "in fact occurs or is attempted"?

It is questionable whether this means that the perpetrator of the crime must be punishable for its commission. It could suffice that they only fulfil the *actus reus* of the crime, or that they also acted with the necessary *mens rea*. Vogel suggested that customary international criminal law only recognizes the former alternative in what he calls "very limited" accessorial liability.[193] However, it has been submitted above that the law under the *ad hoc* tribunals shows a tendency to require the *actus reus* and *mens rea* of the crime be established.[194]

Academic literature on the Rome Statute often only considers two possible types of accessorial liability. According to a strict approach, the principal must be punishable, i.e. have fulfilled the *actus reus* and *mens rea*, without any defence in their favour.[195] The limited or partially derivative approach distinguishes between justifications and excuses within the defence and rejects liability if the principal was justified, but affirms it if they were "only" excused.[196] The limited approach can be found

---

[190] Heller 2011, p. 607.

[191] Rastan 2009, pp 267–8.

[192] Cf. also the criticism by Judge Morrison in *Ntaganda*, 30 March 2021, Separate opinion of Judge Howard Morrison on Mr. Ntaganda's appeal, paras 9–10.

[193] Vogel 2002, pp 425, 427, 434. See also Gropengießer and Kreicker 2003, p. 286 (speaking of a "loosened understanding of accessory liability", translation by the author).

[194] See Chap. 5, Sect. 5.1.2.

[195] Finnin 2012, pp 102–6; Fletcher 2000, pp 641–2.

[196] Finnin 2012, pp 106–12; Fletcher 2000, p. 642.

in many differential national legal systems.[197] In comparison to these approaches, Vogel's aforementioned observation is somewhat novel, although it has garnered academic support.[198] It is inherent to international criminal trials that the *mens rea* of the physical perpetrators can only be assumed—to an even greater extent than that of the indicted officials—because they do not stand trial themselves and their identities remain unknown. Consequently, it seems possible that the notion of accessorial liability in international criminal law does not require the dependence on the commission *strictu sensu* of a crime, but rather only the factual dependence of the act being committed by another.[199]

However, ICC jurisprudence shows a tendency to require the commission or attempted commission of the crime in the sense that objective and subjective elements are the prerequisite for accessorial liability.[200] The trial chamber in *Katanga* elaborated on the issue when determining Katanga's responsibility under Article 25 (3) (d) Rome Statute. Regarding the requirement that a crime within the jurisdiction of the court had to be committed, the chamber stated that "both the objective and subjective elements specific to the crime(s) and their contextual elements must be established".[201] It continued to state that for all crimes relevant in the case, principal liability of natural persons had to be established in contrast to liability of "the group". Consequently, the trial chamber ascertained that each crime had to be "intentionally committed by one or more persons".[202] Whilst the *Katanga* judgment is the most unequivocal in this regard, it is not the only evidence of this view. Many of the decisions in which accessorial modes of liability were charged elaborate on the intent of the physical perpetrators.[203] Whether the physical perpetrators must display the necessary *dolus specialis* to allow accessory liability to arise for others, remains mostly undiscussed by ICC jurisprudence. The *Katanga* trial chamber elaborated on the necessity of the physical perpetrators of the crime of pillaging to act with the necessary intent.[204] As examined earlier, requiring such special intent for the

[197] Ambos 2004, p. 618 with fn. 444 with further sources on comparative law.

[198] Ibid., 618; Ambos 2018, § 7 mn. 40; Gropengießer and Kreicker 2003, p. 286.

[199] In the Anglo-American legal system e.g., derivative liability only refers to the factual dependence of acts of participation on a crime, see Ambos 2004, pp 616–8.

[200] In the same vein see Goy 2012, p. 10.

[201] *Katanga*, 7 March 2014, para 1622.

[202] Ibid., para 1623.

[203] Such is the case in *Katanga and Chui*, 30 September 2008, paras 281, 302, 306, 323, 325, 336, 397, 426, 435, 443; *Gbagbo*, 12 June 2014, paras 201 (referring to the perpetrator's intent in case of an attempted crime), 204–5; *Blé Goudé*, 11 December 2014, paras 121, 122–3; ICC, *The Prosecutor v. Jean-Pierre Bemba Gombo*, Trial Judgment, 21 March 2016, ICC-01/05-01/08, paras 629, 637, 647, 694–5.

[204] *Katanga*, 7 March 2014, paras 913, 952. Katanga was charged primarily as an indirect perpetrator at this point, and therefore no questions of accessorial objects arose for him. The fact that the chamber considers the *dolus specialis* of the executioners of the crimes anyways, however, can be seen as a sign that it would have done so in any case and that a lack of such intent would become relevant for potential accessories.

physical executioners would also be in line with certain judgements from the *ad hoc* tribunals' jurisprudence.[205]

Considering this, it is realistic that accessorial liability under the Rome Statute requires the physical actors to act with all necessary mental elements, including special intent.

The interpretation of accessorial liability reaffirms the tendency of the *ad hoc* tribunals.

For purposes of the Rome Statute, there is therefore little in support of the notion of a very broad accessorial liability in international criminal law. Instead, it seems highly probable that the physical perpetrators must fulfil the *actus reus* and *mens rea* of the crime to allow accessorial liability to arise under the jurisprudence of the ICC. Potential defences of these perpetrators have not been discussed. Thus, no conclusion is possible on whether the concept of accessorial liability might be even narrower, expecting the perpetrators not to have defences as well.[206]

6.5.1.3 Conclusion

For now, it suffices to acknowledge that the ICC interprets Article 25 (3) Rome Statute as applying a differentiated model, which distinguishes between principals and accessories. Ordering is considered by the court to be a form of accessorial liability. Responsibility for ordering therefore requires the objective and subjective elements of the crime to be fulfilled by the physical perpetrator.

This approach to accessorial liability can have the lamentable effect of limiting the possible scope of ordering to the crimes fulfilled by the perpetrators even where a crime requires a special intent to be given. This means that, e.g., no ordering of genocide or persecution as a crime against humanity would be possible, where the physical perpetrators do not act with the necessary genocidal or discriminatory intent, even though the ordering person might be driven by such an ulterior motive. The ICC has not yet ruled on such cases, but *ad hoc* precedents show that it is not unthinkable that, even where the physical perpetrators are unknown, their special intent could be denied.[207]

The distinction into principals and accessories does not pre-determine the conclusion on whether accessorial modes of liability must be considered less blameworthy than principal responsibility. As discussed, this has not been the case in most of the *ad hoc* jurisprudence and the issue is therefore examined separately.[208]

---

[205] See, Chap. 5, Sect. 5.1.2.

[206] See for an overview of the common approaches to the accessorial object Finnin 2012, pp 101–14.

[207] See ICTR, *Prosecutor v. Bagosora et al.*, 18 December 2008, ICTR-98-41-T, paras 2119 and 2121–2, where the chamber denied the genocidal intent of the physical perpetrators.

[208] For the analysis of ICC jurisprudence in this regard see below at Sect. 6.4.3.4. For the preferable interpretation in line with *ad hoc* jurisprudence see Chap. 7, Sect. 7.2.4.

6.5.2 *The Attempt to Order a Crime*

If only the attempt to commit a crime is punishable, while the attempt to e.g., order, induce or instigate is not, this obviously leads to a limitation of criminalized conduct for accessorial liability in comparison to principal liability.

The attempt to commit a crime is punishable according to Article 25 (3) (f) Rome Statute. At first glance, the rule seems to criminalize the attempt of the *commission* of a crime in the same sense as Article 25 (3) (a).[209] However, Article 25 (3) (f) is not necessarily meant to be read as being exclusive, because the term commission is used differently throughout Article 25.

The ICC has not yet had to answer this question, but the trial chamber in *Lubanga* expressed the view that attempt pursuant to Article 25 (3) (f) only applies to commission, as provided for in *littera* (a).[210] Academic literature describes the situation as unclear.[211]

Requiring the attempt or commission of the crime, Article 25 (3) (b) does not *a priori* preclude an attempt to order also being punishable. Systematically, *litterae* (b) to (d) enumerate the modes of participation in a fulfilled or attempted crime but contain no statement as to the criminalization of their own respective attempt. This is reinforced by the criminalization of the attempt not being part of the description of commission under lit. (a) but being found separately in lit. (f).[212]

Ambos advocates for a twofold answer to the question, proposing that the attempt to "instigate" should be punishable, whilst that of the other accessorial forms under Article 25 (3) should not.[213] As the statute does not address attempts of secondary modes of liability, he argues that the question should be resolved based on normative considerations. He contends that "forms of instigation" are inherently more serious than forms of assistance under lit. (c) and (d). Additionally, he states that instigation can be compared to the inchoate incitement to genocide: "If an attempted incitement, directed towards an unidentified and uncontrolled group of potential perpetrators, is punishable, the same should apply to an attempted instigation a fortiori given that it influences identifiable persons and thus affects more directly the decision to commit the main offence."[214]

---

[209] This is argued in *Lubanga*, 29 January 2007, para 998; Herzig 2013, p. 198; Werle and Burghardt 2014, p. 857; Wirth 2012, p. 979.

[210] *Lubanga*, 14 March 2012, para 998. The chamber connects this with the statement that perpetration "must require more than accessory liability".

[211] Werle and Jessberger 2020, mn. 807.

[212] Ambos draws attention to the fact that Article 25 (3) (b)–(d) surprisingly does not answer the question of whether the attempt to participate in a crime is punishable, see Ambos 2013, p. 257; Ambos 2004, p. 747.

[213] Ambos 2013, p. 258.

[214] Ibid., p. 258; incitement to genocide is an inchoate offence, see Cryer et al. 2019, p. 362; Schabas 2016, p. 582.

Notwithstanding Ambos' different categorisation of ordering,[215] his reasoning seems particularly true for this mode of liability, which requires the exercise of authority in addition to addressing an identifiable group of people.[216]

The identical conduct element of ordering and indirect perpetration through an organisation also speaks in favour of a criminalization of attempted ordering. The attempted indirect commission is unquestionably punishable under *littera* (f). As discussed, the conduct underlying both modes is very similar, requiring the actor to instruct others to commit crimes.[217] In light of this, attempted ordering appears equally proximate and dangerous to the commission of the crime as attempted indirect commission.

The attempt to order a crime should thus be regarded punishable under the Rome Statute, but, in view of the jurisprudence, it is questionable whether this view is shared by the court. For the ICC, a reason to affirm a punishable attempt only for commission under Article 25 (3) (a) could lie in its perception of a hierarchy of blameworthiness between modes of liability.

6.5.3 *A Hierarchy of Blameworthiness and the Expected Influence of Ordering on Sentencing*

Despite the choice of a differential model of perpetration and participation leading to criticism, the ICC's jurisprudence is relatively unequivocal in this regard. It is of paramount importance to determine what degree of blameworthiness is ascribed to the mode of ordering. This section outlines the opinions of chambers and judges at the ICC as can be identified in decisions and separate opinions (Sect. 6.4.3.1), in the practice on concurrent convictions (Sect. 6.4.3.2) and in sentencing (Sect. 6.4.3.3). This section thereby provides the final piece in the analysis of ordering in relation to other modes of liability.

---

215 In Ambos' view, ordering is a form of indirect perpetration, see Ambos 2013, p. 163. His statements on "instigation" might therefore not include ordering. However, in his view, this makes no difference with regard to the punishable attempt of ordering, because the attempt of all forms of perpetration is punishable pursuant to Article 25 (3) (f).

216 Ambos concedes that the uncontrollable nature of public incitement can be seen as the reason for it also being punishable as an inchoate crime (see ibid., p. 258). The direct addressing of a specific group of perpetrators over whom the speaker has authority can be seen as equally dangerous, given that the influence over the addressees is much stronger.

217 See Chap. 3, Sect. 3.1.2.5 and Sect. 6.2.1.

6.5.3.1 The Jurisprudence of the ICC

As presented in detail earlier, the majority view of the chambers at the ICC establishes a hierarchy of blameworthiness between forms of responsibility in Article 25 (3) (a) to (d).[218]

According to this majority view, it must be assumed that ordering is deemed less blameworthy than commission liability under Article 25 (3) (a) Rome Statute. Whether ordering is deemed more or equally serious as participation under *litterae* (c) and (d) remains unclear. This downgrading of ordering in comparison to forms of commission liability is contrary to the findings extrapolated from the *ad hoc* tribunals' overall jurisprudence.

Certain incidents in ICC practice raise the suspicion that this view on ordering was also not established in the early years of the court's existence.

In the 2005 arrest warrant against Joseph Kony, the chamber apparently did not take the view that a hierarchy reigned between the modes of *littera* (a) and ordering. Kony, as top leader of the LRA, was indicted on a broad range of charges which all relied on ordering as the relevant mode of liability.[219] The arrest warrant decision is much older than the *Lubanga* trial chamber decision, which established the control over the crime approach. However, given that the issue of a hierarchy of blameworthiness is well-known in international criminal law, it is unlikely that the arrest warrant decision only applied ordering because there was nothing better at hand. Instead, the *Kony* decision implies that ordering can be the most suitable form of responsibility for high-level criminality without implying a hierarchy of blameworthiness. The same was true for the arrest warrant decisions by Pre-Trial Chamber II for the leaders of the LRA, i.e., the decisions concerning the *Lukwiya, Odhimabo, Ongwen* and *Otti* arrest warrants.[220]

The charges against Germain Katanga and Mathieu Ngdujolo Chui were also based on ordering and only changed into indirect co-perpetration later during the proceedings.[221]

All the accused were wanted and charged as the most responsible, highest-ranking individuals in their cases. The fact that they were initially wanted or indicted under ordering illustrates that, in the early years of the court, ordering was not considered less blameworthy, but rather considered an appropriate mode for leadership liability and thus necessarily one of the most serious forms of participation.

The separate opinion of Judge Van den Wyngaert points in a similar direction. She explains that, in her view, there are no reasons why a distinction between principals and accessories must lead to a hierarchy of blameworthiness. She substantiates this

---

[218] See Chap. 3, Sect. 3.1.4.

[219] *Kony*, 27 September 2005, para 42 see counts 1, 4–33.

[220] *Lukwiya*, 8 July 2005, para 30, counts 6–8 (being all counts); *Odhiambo*, 8 July 2005, para 32, counts 10–19 (being all counts); *Ongwen*, 8 July 2005, para 30, counts 27–33 (being all counts); *Otti*, 8 July 2005, para 42, counts 1, 4–33 (count 3 as the only other ground for the decision to rest on, refers to inducing the commission of war crimes).

[221] See *Katanga*, 6 July 2007, paras 54, 60; *Chui*, 6 July 2007, paras 55, 61; Steer 2017, p. 307; van Sliedregt and Yanev 2019, mn. 55.

by pointing out how ordering or inducing are often at least as reprehensible as the physical perpetration, and that this is independent of whether one categorizes ordering as indirect perpetration or derivative responsibility.[222] The criticism also includes her observation that, in the context of international crimes, aiding and abetting could be as blameworthy as perpetration.[223]

These points notwithstanding, the majority view of the ICC's chambers is different in theory and leads to ordering being treated as a less blameworthy form of responsibility in comparison to commission.

6.5.3.2 Concurrences: Precedence of Principal Liability Under ICC Jurisprudence

The chambers of the ICC have mostly chosen an approach that gives perpetration precedence over participation. In the *Lubanga* confirmation of charges decision, the chamber explained that the procedural question of whether accessorial modes of liability could be considered would become moot if the chamber found substantial grounds to believe in the accused's liability as a perpetrator.[224] In the *Lubanga* trial judgment, the chamber did not explain its decision as clearly but also "limit(ed) its analysis" to Lubanga's responsibility as a co-perpetrator.[225] The trial chamber in *Al Mahdi* decided that, as the responsibility of the accused as a co-perpetrator was affirmed, there was no need to make any further findings on modes of accessorial liability.[226] In *Ntaganda*, the trial chamber found it neither necessary nor appropriate to reach findings on the other charged modes of liability after affirming indirect co-perpetration of the accused.[227] The trial chamber in *Ongwen* took the same stance.[228]

At some points, chambers or judges consider the possibility that an accused's conduct can fulfil more than one mode of liability.[229] However, with the exception of the separate opinion of Judge Fulford, these statements do not seem to rule out the predominance of perpetration over forms of accessorial liability in the chambers' views. This is especially evident in *Al Mahdi* and *Ntaganda*. In the latter, the chamber acknowledges said possibility, but in the same paragraph mentions that this would be inappropriate in light of the accused's principal liability.[230] In *Al Mahdi*, the statement refers to two types of perpetration and addresses this immediately after determining that no inquiries into accessorial liability will be made, due to the positive findings on

---

[222] *Chui*, 18 December 2012, Concurring Opinion of Judge Christine van den Wyngaert, paras 22–3.

[223] Ibid., Concurring Opinion of Judge Christine van den Wyngaert, paras 24–5.

[224] *Lubanga*, 29 January 2007, para 321.

[225] *Lubanga*, 14 March 2012, para 978.

[226] *Al Mahdi*, 24 March 2016, para 58.

[227] *Ntaganda*, 8 July 2019, para 1200.

[228] *Ongwen*, 4 February 2021, para 2791.

[229] *Lubanga*, 14 March 2012, Separate Opinion of Judge Adrian Fulford, para 7; *Bemba*, 21 March 2016, para 174; *Al Mahdi*, 24 March 2016, para 59.

[230] *Ntaganda*, 8 July 2019, para 1200.

perpetration.[231] By contrast, Judge Fulford clearly stated that, in his view, the modes under Article 25 (3) (a) to (d) are not mutually exclusive and rejected the notion of perpetrator liability taking precedence.[232]

The issue has received little attention in academic literature, perhaps because it is mostly seen as a logical conclusion of the choice of system. If one advocates for a differentiated system, based on a normative hierarchy of blameworthiness with principal liability as the single summit of seriousness, the precedence of perpetration over participation will appear as a logical conclusion. In this vein, Werle and Jessberger promote a predominance of perpetration over participation based on their view that Article 25 (3) Rome Statute establishes a hierarchy of blameworthiness.[233] In light of the abovementioned judgments, it seems that these authors are in line with the majority view at the ICC.

This contemporary jurisprudence on concurrences implies that, wherever perpetration can be affirmed, no findings on ordering or any other accessorial mode will be made. This choice of modes of responsibility where concurrences arise is tantamount to a normative view. Under a phenomenological, naturalistic approach, ordering or any other mode of accessorial liability would take precedence over commission, where it better described the blameworthy conduct. However, such an approach is not taken by the ICC.

Thus, if any form of perpetration can be affirmed for the conduct of the accused, accessorial modes of liability, such as ordering, will not play a greater role in the judgment. They will either not be charged at all or discarded after the chamber has affirmed the principal responsibility of the accused. Given that indirect perpetration through an organisation is based on an unconvincing and illusory notion of control and indirect co-perpetration potentially accumulates exceedingly different types of conduct under one head of responsibility, it is doubtful that this approach is advisable.[234]

6.5.3.3 The Influence of Modes of Liability on Sentencing at the ICC

Finally, it can be asked whether a conviction under perpetration also leads to a higher sentence. To date, the ICC has convicted very few people, making it difficult to determine the general role of modes of liability in sentencing.

Article 78 (1) Rome Statute stipulates that, in determining the sentence, the court should consider "such factors as the gravity of the crime and the individual circumstances of the convicted person".

---

[231] *Al Mahdi*, 24 March 2016, 58–9.

[232] *Lubanga*, 14 March 2012, Separate Opinion of Judge Adrian Fulford, para 7.

[233] Werle and Jessberger 2020, mn. 616–17, they acknowledge that the *ad hoc* jurisprudence has been divided over this matter (see already Chap. 5, Sect. 5.3.4).

[234] The latter especially comes to mind when looking at the comparable tendency with JCE under the ICTY and ICTR, see Chap. 5, Sect. 5.2.4.

The trial chambers in *Al Mahdi* and *Ntaganda* expressed the view that the head of responsibility under which the respective accused were convicted was relevant for the determination of their guilt.[235] In both judgments, the chambers mentioned the mode of liability under which the convicted were found guilty.[236] They did not elaborate any further on the respective modes of liability and their impact on sentencing. However, the *Ntaganda* chamber stated that the constitutive elements of the crime and modes of liability would be used to assess the gravity *"in abstracto"*.[237] Thus, the lack of further elaborations on the role of modes of liability may be explained with these chambers' view that Article 25 (3) implies a hierarchy in which commission pursuant to lit. (a) is the most serious form of liability.[238] As they convicted the accused as perpetrators, they perhaps saw no further need to elaborate on the (implied) consequence of a heightened blameworthiness and sentence. The chamber in *Ntaganda* also emphasized that it saw *no* hierarchy between the different forms of commission within Article 25 (3) (a) Rome Statute.[239]

Other chambers took the opposite view and considered the modes of liability irrelevant in determining the length of the sentence. In the view of the *Katanga* trial chamber, the differentiation in Article 25 (3) does not "in any way amount to a hierarchy of blameworthiness, let alone prescribe, even by implication, a scale of punishments".[240] The trial chamber in *Bemba* rejected the idea that responsibility under Article 28 Rome Statute would entail an inherently lower or higher blameworthiness than responsibility under Article 25 (3).[241] The quoted rejection of a hierarchy between Article 25 (3) and Article 28 must imply that the chamber also does not recognize a hierarchy within Article 25 (3) itself.[242] In the *Lubanga* judgment, besides mentioning the mode of liability under which Thomas Lubanga was convicted, the chamber remained mostly silent in the course of sentencing.[243]

The approach taken in assessing the gravity of crimes can be aligned with the chambers' view on the question of a hierarchy of blameworthiness in modes of responsibility. As shown in the *Ntaganda* sentencing decision, a chamber can endorse

[235] *Al Mahdi*, 24 March 2016, para 107, where it states that sentencing in other cases was based on other circumstances, "including the applicable modes of liability and sources of law"; *Ntaganda*, 8 July 2019, paras 11, 16.

[236] *Al Mahdi*, 24 March 2016, para 107; *Ntaganda*, 8 July 2019, para 11.

[237] *Ntaganda*, 8 July 2019, para 11.

[238] *Al Mahdi*, 24 March 2016, para 58; the *Ntaganda* trial chamber is less explicit in this regard but refrains from findings on accessorial modes of liability because it confirmed the charges based on principal liability, see *Ntaganda*, 8 July 2019, para 1200.

[239] *Ntaganda*, 8 July 2019, para 15.

[240] *Katanga*, 23 May 2014, para 61.

[241] *Bemba*, 21 March 2016, para 16.

[242] The sentencing decision on Article 28 Rome Statute reads: "It is not, inherently, a hierarchically lower or higher mode of liability in terms of gravity than commission of a crime under Article 25 (3) (a), or any other mode of liability identified in Article 25 (3) (b) to (e)"; see ibid., para 16. The chamber thus levels the degree of blameworthiness of all mentioned modes of liability, leaving little room to interpret this as implying *any* kind of hierarchy.

[243] *Lubanga*, 14 March 2012, para 52.

a two-step gravity assessment, where the first step considers *inter alia* the mode of liability *in abstracto,* thereby determining the length of sentence through this mode of liability.[244]

Alternatively, a chamber, like the trial chamber in *Katanga,* can advance a single-step *in concreto* assessment of the personal conduct, rejecting a hierarchy of modes of liability.[245]

Different authors endorsed the view that forms of responsibility should play a role in sentencing.[246]

In summary, it can be observed that the current stance of sentencing jurisprudence mirrors the respective chambers' view on the hierarchy of blameworthiness. However, the limited number of sentencing decisions and the absence of elaborations therein do not enable conclusions on any specific view of the chambers, which would exceed their statements on the hierarchy question. Therefore, it can be concluded that where a chamber endorses a hierarchy of blameworthiness, it also takes this hierarchy into account in sentencing. This is a coherent application of the doctrine.

6.5.3.4 Conclusion: Ordering as a Less Blameworthy Form of Responsibility Under the Current Majority Opinion at the ICC

The foregoing has shown that the majority opinion on Article 25 (3) (a) to (d) Rome Statute assigns a lower seriousness to the mode of ordering a crime. Notwithstanding the capability of ordering to capture the wrongdoing of high-level decision makers, it is regarded as less blameworthy and secondary to perpetration. In theory, this form of responsibility leads to lower sentences than forms of perpetration.

This is contrary to the conclusions drawn in the two previous chapters: jurisprudence in post-World War II trials and at the *ad hoc* tribunals established ordering as a form of highly blameworthy involvement in crimes. Despite the often-conflicting concepts, already in post-World War II jurisprudence, but especially at the ICTY and ICTR, ordering can be identified as an accessorial yet grave form of participation that does not convey less blameworthiness than commission liability. The ICC's majority approach on the issue runs contrary to this historic role of ordering.

---

[244] *Ntaganda,* 8 July 2019, para 11.

[245] *Katanga,* 23 May 2014, para 61.

[246] D'Ascoli 2011, p. 322; Melloh 2010, pp 504–5 who bases his conclusion *inter alia* on the assumption that perpetration and participation would entail different kinds of blameworthiness.

6.6 Conclusion: Ordering Is Suitable but Downgraded in Practice

Despite its suitability to describe and adjudicate their conduct, ordering is not primarily applied to cases of high- and mid-level decision makers at the ICC. Its role is therefore diminished in the ICC's current practice, and it seems questionable whether it serves any relevant purpose at all. This is problematic and unsettling.

Since the trial against Adolf Eichmann, it has been reiterated time and again that where systemic crime is perpetrated on a large scale through organisations or groups of people, the responsibility of persons higher up the hierarchy will usually overshoot that of the individual physical perpetrators. The current interpretation of ordering as a less blameworthy form of responsibility stands in sharp contrast to this "mantra" of international criminal law. A person who orders the commission of a crime is—through their authority—higher up the (formal, informal, or purely situational) hierarchy than the physical perpetrator. Nevertheless, the current interpretation assigns them a lower level of blameworthiness. This is true in all cases, as authority over the physical perpetrator is a necessary requirement of ordering a crime.

Such a diminished role of the mode of ordering does not correspond to its historic development, which has been outlined in the previous chapters. Additionally, doubts arise regarding what conduct is meant to fall under ordering at all. Indeed, it has been shown that control over an organisation and authority are often proven through the same circumstances, just as control over an organisation and almost automatic compliance overlap as requirements within the mode of indirect perpetration through an organisation.

It must therefore be explored whether there is a separate field of application for ordering and indirect perpetration through an organisation. The potential application of ordering to cases of high-level decision makers, as outlined above, calls the existence of a separate field into doubt. If no such field of application can be identified, it must be evaluated whether it is helpful or useful and therefore desirable to apply indirect perpetration instead of ordering, or whether ordering should be the form of responsibility applied to cases of leadership criminality before the ICC.

References

Ambos K (2004) Der Allgemeine Teil des Völkerstrafrechts. Duncker & Humblot, Berlin

Ambos K (2013) Treatise on International Criminal Law—Volume I: Foundations and General Part. Oxford University Press, Oxford

Ambos K (2016) Art. 25. In: Ambos K (ed) The Rome Statute of the International Criminal Court—A Commentary. C.H. Beck/Hart/Nomos, Munich

Ambos K (2018) Internationales Strafrecht. C. H. Beck, Munich

Block J (2022) Ordering as an Alternative to Indirect Co-Perpetration—Observations on the Ntaganda Case. Journal of International Criminal Justice 20:717–735

Burghardt B (2010) Modes of Participation and their Role in a General Concept of Crimes under International Law. In: Burchard C, Triffterer O, Vogel J (eds) The Review Conference and the Future of the International Criminal Court—Proceedings of the First AIDP Symposium for Young Penalists in Tübingen, Germany, co-organized by the AIDP YP Committee. Kluwer Law International, Alphen aan den Rijn, 81–98

Clark RS (2008) Drafting a General Part to a Penal Code: Some Thoughts Inspired by the Negotiations on the Rome Statute of the International Criminal Court and by the Court's First Substantive Law Discussion in the Lubanga Dyilo Confirmation Proceedings. Criminal Law Forum 19:519–552

Cryer R, Robinson D, Vasiliev S (2019) An Introduction to International Criminal Law and Procedure. Cambridge University Press, Cambridge

D'Ascoli S (2011) Sentencing in International Criminal Law. Hart Publishing, Oxford

Eser A (2002a) Individual Criminal Responsibility. In: Cassesse A, Gaeta P, Jones JRWD (eds) The Rome Statute of the International Criminal Court—A Commentary. Oxford University Press, Oxford, 767–823

Eser A (2002b) Mental Elements—Mistake of Fact and Mistake of Law. In: Cassesse A, Gaeta P, Jones JRWD (eds) The Rome Statute of the International Criminal Court: A Commentary. Oxford University Press, Oxford, 889–948

Finnin S (2012) Elements of Accessorial Modes of Liability—Article 25 (3) (b) and (c) of the Rome Statute of the International Criminal Court. Martinus Nijhoff Publishers, Leiden

Fletcher GP (2000) Rethinking Criminal Law. Oxford University Press, Oxford

Goy B (2012) Individual Criminal Responsibility before the International Criminal Court—A Comparison with the Ad Hoc Tribunals. International Criminal Law Review 12:1–70

Gropengießer H, Kreicker H (2003) Nationale Strafverfolgung völkerrechtlicher Verbrechen/National Prosecution of International Crimes 1—Deutschland. edition iuscrim, 21–452

Heller KJ (2011) The Rome Statute of the International Criminal Court. In: Heller KJ, Dubber MD (eds) The Handbook of Comparative Criminal Law. Stanford University Press, Stanford, 593–634

Herzig A (2013) Die Tatherrschaftslehre in der Rechtsprechung des Internationalen Strafgerichtshofs. Zeitschrift für internationale Strafrechtsdogmatik 189-200

Lanza G (2021) Indirect Perpetration and Organisationsherrschaftslehre. Duncker & Humblot, Berlin

Melloh F (2010) Einheitliche Strafzumessung in den Rechtsquellen des ICC-Statuts. Duncker & Humblot, Berlin

O'Keefe R (2015) International Criminal Law. Oxford University Press, Oxford

Office WCR (2010) Modes of Liability and the Mental Element—Analyzing the Early Jurisprudence of the International Criminal Court

Olásolo H (2009) The Criminal Responsibility of Senior Political and Military Leaders as Principals to International Crimes. Hart Publishing, Portland

Olásolo H, Carnero Rojo E (2015) Forms of Accessorial Liability under Article 25(3)(b) and (c). In: Stahn C (ed) The Law and Practice of the International Criminal Court. Oxford University Press, Oxford, 557–591

Pigaroff DK, Robinson D (2016) Art. 30. In: The Rome Statute of the International Criminal Court—A Commentary. C.H. Beck/Hart/Nomos, Munich

Rastan R (2009) Review of ICC Jurisprudence 2008. Northwestern Journal of International Human Rights 7:261–298

Safferling C (2011) Internationales Strafrecht. Springer-Verlag, Heidelberg

Sato H (2012) International Criminal Responsibility Concerning 'Control over an Organization' and Command Responsibility *Lato Sensu*. International Criminal Law Review 12:293–300

Satzger H (2018) International and European Criminal Law. C.H. Beck, Munich

Schabas (2016) The International Criminal Court—A Commentary on the Rome Statute. Oxford University Press, Oxford

Steer C (2017) Translating Guilt—Identifying Leadership Liability for Mass Atrocity Crimes. T.M.C. Asser Press, The Hague

Stewart JG (2012) The End of "Modes of Liability" for International Crimes. Leiden Journal of International Law 25:165–219

van Sliedregt E (2012) Individual Criminal Responsibility in International Criminal Law. Oxford University Press, Oxford

van Sliedregt E, Yanev L (2019) Co-Perpetration Based on Joint Control over the Crime. In: de Hemptinne J, Roth R, van Sliedregt E (eds) Modes of Liability in International Criminal Law. Cambridge University Press, Cambridge, 85–120

Ventura MJ (2019) Ordering. In: de Hemptinne J, Roth R, van Sliedregt E (eds) Modes of Liability in International Criminal Law. Cambridge University Press, Cambridge, 284–306

Vest H (2011) Völkerrechtsverbrecher verfolgen - Ein abgestuftes Mehrebenensystem systemischer Tatherrschaft. Stämpfli Verlag AG, Bern

Vogel J (2002) Individuelle Verantwortlichkeit im Völkerstrafrecht. Zeitschrift für die gesamte Strafrechtswissenschaft 114:403–436

Werle G (2007) Individual Criminal Responsibility in Art. 25 ICC Statute. Journal of International Criminal Justice 5:953–975

Werle G, Burghardt B (2010) Die mittelbare Mittäterschaft - Fortentwicklung deutscher Strafrechtsdogmatik im Völkerstrafrecht? In: Bloy R (ed) Gerechte Strafe und legitimes Strafrecht - Festschrift für Manfred Maiwald zum 75 Geburtstag. Duncker & Humblot, Berlin, 849–864

Werle G, Burghardt B (2014) Täterschaft und Teilnahme im Statut des Internationalen Strafgerichtshofs. Festschrift für Kristian Kühl zum 70 Geburtstag. C.H. Beck, Munich, 851–866

Werle G, Jessberger F (2020) Principles of International Criminal Law. Oxford University Press, Oxford

Wirth S (2012) Co-Perpetration in the Lubanga Judgment. Journal of International Criminal Justice 10:971–995

Yanev L (2018) Theories of Co-Perpetration in International Criminal law. Brill Nijhoff, Leiden

Part III
Comparison, Evaluation and Conclusion

Ordering is not applied to cases of high- and mid-level decision-makers in practice and instead indirect perpetration through an organisation is considered the more appropriate approach. Considering this, this final part compares the findings regarding the two forms of responsibility to illustrate the extent to which they differ, if at all. It will be evaluated whether the different categorization and the ICC's clear preference for indirect perpetration through an organisation are coherent (Chap. 7). Based on this comparison and evaluation, a more convincing approach to dealing with decision-makers of mass atrocities by the ICC is then outlined (Chap. 8).

Chapter 7
Comparison and Evaluation

Contents

Abstract This chapter compares indirect perpetration through an organisation and ordering under the law of the Rome Statute, taking the findings of the foregoing chapters into account. The comparison takes note of the criticism formulated earlier on indirect perpetration through an organisation as well as the features of ordering liability. It concludes that no meaningful distinction between indirect perpetration and ordering is possible. This is due to the nearly complete overlap of the legal requirements of both forms of responsibility. It also follows from the fact that the notions control over the crime and authority of an ordering person describe the same kind of influence of the leader behind the crime. The chapter then explores whether compelling reasons speak in favour of applying indirect perpetration through an organisation instead of ordering and finds that no such reasons exist. No sentencing rules indicate that commission liability should be punished more severely than ordering liability. The concepts of expressive justice and fair labelling do not favour an application of indirect perpetration through an organisation on leadership figures either, as the doctrine provides no intelligible description of the wrongdoing of such persons, whilst responsibility for ordering provides such a description. It is

J. Block, *Reconciling Responsibility with Reality*, International Criminal Justice Series 33, https://doi.org/10.1007/978-94-6265-607-9_7

therefore concluded that responsibility for ordering crimes should be applied on decision makers of international crimes instead of indirect perpetration through an organisation.

Keywords Indirect perpetration through an organisation · Ordering · Sentencing · Hierarchy of blameworthiness · Fair labelling · Expressive justice · Accessorial liability

7.1 Comparison of Indirect Perpetration Through an Organisation and Ordering

If a meaningful difference between the two modes' legal requirements and their scope of criminalization of specific conduct exists, this could be a convincing reason to rely on the use of indirect perpetration through an organisation instead of ordering. Another reason may lie in the categorization of the two forms of responsibility within the system of perpetration and participation of Art. 25 (3) Rome Statute. This concerns the conception of these modes as principal and secondary responsibility respectively. It also concerns the question of whether the forms should be read as establishing a hierarchy of blameworthiness.

This chapter approaches the issue in a two-step manner. First, the forms of responsibility are compared in all relevant aspects (Sect. 7.1). Based on the outcome of this comparison, the chapter then evaluates the categorisation of the two modes as a "more" and a "less" blameworthy form of responsibility (Sect. 7.2).

As a general guideline for the comparison, this chapter will consider that an interpretation of Art. 25 (3) should lead to a meaningful use of both forms of liability, the commission through another person and the ordering of a crime. Where an overlap exists that marginalises the scope of application of one of the forms, one must determine the reasons and whether they are represented in the majority opinion's interpretation of the overall system. Should this be the case, this system must be questioned critically as well.

To provide a comprehensive comparison, this section compares the two modes of liability in terms of their historic development (Sect. 7.1.1), their legal requirements (Sect. 7.1.2), the underlying notion of control and the alleged lack thereof in cases of ordering (Sect. 7.1.3), the cases grasped by them (Sect. 7.1.4) and the evidence available to prove them (Sect. 7.1.5). Lastly, whether a meaningful difference can be identified by ways of this comparison will be summarized (Sect. 7.1.6).

7.1.1 Historic Development

Roxin in his initial writings on indirect perpetration through an organization acknowledges that national criminal law "did not expect" cases of large scale international crimes and that the appropriate assessment of such cases would "hardly be possible as long as we have no effective super-national criminal law".[1] In connection thereto, Roxin later states that "the question [of responsibility for mass atrocities; *comment by the author*]... is difficult to answer with the traditional arsenal of concepts in our doctrine of participation".[2] However, is this true for the development of international criminal law since its dawn in the aftermath of World War II? Or has international criminal law produced forms of liability that allow the suitable attribution of responsibility, at least in the form of ordering a crime?

A look into the development of both forms of responsibility as they have been displayed here, sheds light on this issue.

Ambos' assertion that the doctrine of indirect perpetration through an organisation can be read into the *Justice* case,[3] is questionable.[4] The same is true for the Eichmann case, which has occasionally been mentioned as an early application of the doctrine.[5] These cases contain factual descriptions of dynamics which the respective tribunal and court found relevant, but they do not rely on legal doctrine and develop no legal requirements.[6]

Therefore, the more accurate description is that indirect perpetration through an organization was first devised by Claus Roxin in 1963. It is based on indirect perpetration, a form that is traditionally used to attribute responsibility to persons who make use of a physical perpetrator who is not him- or herself criminally responsible. The doctrine developed into the leading academic approach to cases of mass atrocities in German law and was imported into some other jurisdictions as well.[7] The German BGH adopted a form of the doctrine in the 1990s after rejecting it for decades in cases where it could have served to adjudicate former Nazi officers and other decision makers.[8] Roxin's doctrine operates from a crime-centred perspective and is not based on a systemic model of imputation. This may be the reason why other German scholars later proposed another, more systemic, theoretical groundwork for

---

[1] Roxin 2011, pp 194–5.

[2] Ibid., pp. 195–6.

[3] Ambos 2018, § 7 mn. 25.

[4] As discussed in Chap. 3, Sect. 3.3.1.2 and Chap. 4, Sects. 4.3.2 and 4.3.3, the jurisprudence of the U.S. military tribunals considers systemic, collective aspects of responsibility, but it does not construct an approach resembling the doctrine of indirect perpetration through an organisation or the underlying control theory.

[5] For criticism on this view see Chap. 3, Sect. 3.3.1.2. In favour Ambos 2018, § 7 mn. 25; critical also Kress 2006, p 306.

[6] See Chap. 3, Sect. 3.3.1.2 and Chap. 4, Sects. 4.3.2 and 4.3.3.

[7] Chap. 2, Sects. 2.2.2 and 2.2.6. For the use in other national legal systems see the evaluation in Chap. 3, Sect. 3.3.1.2.

[8] See Chap. 2, Sect. 2.3.

the theory. However, their approach leads to the question of whether "acting through another" would still be the correct legal provision under which this systemic responsibility could be categorized, or whether a new provision would be necessary.[9] Just as the traditional doctrine, the ICC's theory builds on a narrow, crime-focused notion of control without explicit or relevant systemic elements.[10] Given Claus Roxin's abovementioned statements on the limitations of national criminal law, one could wonder why Art. 25 (3) (a) Rome Statute was even designed in such close resemblance to the German provision in section 25 para. 1, 2. Alternative GCC and did not receive more attention in the drafting process.

Put somewhat harshly, it could be concluded that the ICC adopted a doctrine that emanated in national criminal law as a makeshift solution, where—according to the doctrine's inventor—no proper legal characterisation of participation in mass atrocities was explicitly provided for by the law.[11]

Thus, it can be said that the doctrine developed as a national approach to mass atrocities in Germany and some Spanish speaking legal systems. It should also be remembered that the real driving force in Germany's jurisprudence was the—highly contentious—policy to apply the doctrine to crimes committed in business enterprises.[12] Additionally, we have seen that some—German-driven—attempts to establish a form of the doctrine at the ICTY and ICTR were made, whilst most chambers of these tribunals preferred another form of liability for leadership criminality.

The Rome Statute arguably invites its interpretation in light of the control theory and applying indirect perpetration through an organization based on Art. 25 (3) (a). On this basis, the ICC now upholds the theory.

This development, from a make-shift solution based on insufficient national law provisions to an approach institutionalized only at the latest international criminal tribunal, hardly qualifies as a natural or well-founded development of an international instrument for the adjudication of high-level leadership criminality.

Responsibility for ordering was first included in Art. 2 para. 2 CCL 10 and served for the adjudication of many former Nazi officials in the Nuremberg subsequent trials. In these circumstances, the mode was *inter alia* applied to the commission of crimes in the ambit of military occupation, including the infamous *Einsatzgruppen* and their hundreds of thousands of murders. At that time, the approach to forms of responsibility, as far as they could be distinguished, was that ordering was treated as one of the more direct and blameworthy forms.[13]

---

[9] See Chap. 2, Sect. 2.4.

[10] See Chap. 3, Sects. 3.1.3 and 3.2.3.

[11] Roxin in his initial writings took the view that the traditional forms of responsibility, known in national criminal law, could not serve for cases of mass atrocities, which inspired him to develop the theory of indirect perpetration through an organisation (Roxin 2019, p 280). Roxin today considers his own theory, which is necessarily based on the same limited possibilities of the national legal system, as the correct approach for international criminal law (see ibid., Chpt. 12 mn. 365, 369 (referring to the organisations typically found in international criminal law cases)).

[12] See Chap. 2, Sect. 2.3.2.2.

[13] See Chap. 4, Sect. 4.6.

Responsibility for ordering certain crimes was introduced into the Geneva Conventions, where it was stipulated that military commanders who committed or ordered the commission of grave breaches of the conventions must be punished.[14] It thus found its way into international humanitarian law as an international obligation of states to criminalize certain behaviour.[15]

The ILC Draft Penal Code of Crimes against the Peace and Security of Mankind previsioned the express criminalization of ordering.[16]

In their provisions on individual criminal responsibility, the statutes of the ICTY and ICTR contained responsibility for ordering, which the *ad hoc* tribunals made ample use of for both high- and mid-level decision makers of international crimes. Despite the tribunals' preference for JCE, it can be observed that ordering was generally perceived to embody a high level of blameworthiness.[17] Responsibility for ordering as a form of responsibility can also be found in the statute of the SCSL.[18] It is not surprising that responsibility for ordering was then included in Art. 25 (3) Rome Statute.[19] Consequently criminal responsibility for ordering a crime is part of customary international law.[20]

At the ICC, ordering was considered the appropriate mode of liability for decision makers of international crimes in the early days of its work.[21]

The authority of the person giving the order has been one central aspect of the mode of liability since the jurisprudence of the Nuremberg subsequent trials. There, the mode required that the actor "add his authoritative weight" to the order (or drafted it).[22] Later the mode developed to require the "compelling authority" of the ordering person over the physical perpetrators.[23]

The development of the two forms therefore differs significantly. One is derived from a national legal doctrine; it constitutes a make-shift solution for cases that are not typically targeted by national criminal law and has no relevant predecessors in international criminal law. The other approach emerged in the ambit and for the adjudication of international crimes and was subsequently embodied in all relevant provisions in this field of law.

---

[14] Cryer 2004, p 244.

[15] See Art. 49 GA I, Art. 50, GA II, Art. 129 I GA III, Art. 146 I GA IV; Bantekas 2002, p 50; see already the Introduction in Part II.

[16] Cf. ILC Draft Code of Crimes against the Peace and Security of Mankind, Article 2 (3) (b). See on this Vest 2002, p 234–4 with fn. 44; Vest 2014, p 304.

[17] See Chap. 5, Sect. 5.3.6.

[18] Cf. Art. 6 (1) of the Statute of the Special Court for Sierra Leone.

[19] The inclusion of ordering has been interpreted by Cryer as a rejection of the model of indirect perpetration through an organisation, see Cryer 2004, p 243.

[20] Ambos 2018, § 7 mn. 45; Werle and Jessberger 2020, mn. 665. In this vein also Finnin 2012, p 44; Olásolo and Carnero Rojo 2015, p 560.

[21] See Chap. 6, Sect. 6.3.1.

[22] See Chap. 4, Sect. 4.2.3.

[23] See Chap. 5, Sect. 5.1.1.2 and Chap. 6, Sect. 6.2.2.

As illustrated in this book, both modes of liability share their focus on decision makers of international crimes and fail to grasp the conduct of architects of crimes that participate in purely planning and organisational functions.[24]

As far as decision makers behind international crimes are concerned, it can thus be concluded that indirect perpetration through an organisation is perhaps the best available alternative in the ambit of some national jurisdictions.[25] However, on the level of international criminal law it is rivalled by the older, well-established form of responsibility for ordering.

Based on this historical analysis, it must be asked to which extent the two forms overlap or whether there is a meaningful difference between the two. Only in the latter case, is a senseful development of international law doctrine under the Rome Statute possible with the application of both modes of liability. In case of a complete or nearly complete overlap, the doctrine under the Rome Statute should be changed to provide for a reasonable application of Art. 25 (3) (a) and (b), provided there are no other convincing reasons to maintain a preference of one of the modes. If no such reasons can be identified, the necessity of indirect perpetration through an organisation, as a relatively recent import from national law, must be questioned. This is especially true, given the history and development of ordering as a form of responsibility known to many international criminal law regulations.

7.1.2 Legal Requirements

Responsibility for indirect perpetration through an organisation and for ordering crimes arises from a differently structured set of requirements. In ordering, only the "position of authority" refers to the circumstances under which an instruction must be given. Indirect perpetration through an organisation is based on three objective circumstantial prerequisites that supposedly lead to control over the crime: "Control over an organisation", which is built in the form of an "organised and hierarchical apparatus of power" and in which "the commission of crimes is secured because the orders of the accused are complied with almost automatically". These requirements overlap to a certain degree.[26] The comparison of these criteria splits them into two

[24] This cannot be said about ordering under CCL 10 under which being involved in the drafting of orders (i.e., planning of the subsequent crimes), without possessing authority to issue such orders is sufficient, see Chap. 4, Sect. 4.2.3.2. Apart from this, indirect perpetration through an organisation (in its traditional German version and as applied by the ICC) and ordering are only applied to people who instruct or otherwise make the physical perpetrators of crimes act (cf. Chap. 2, Sects. 2.2.6 and 2.6.1; Chap. 3, Sect. 3.1.5; Chap. 5, Sects. 5.2.4.2 and 5.2.4.4; Chap. 6, Sects. 6.2.2.4 and 6.3.4). It has been observed that purely acting as the architect of a crime may be connected to the size and bureaucratic foundation of organisations because many situations before the ICC do not produce evidence on individuals acting purely as planners or organisers, as they usually also hold power to instruct the commission of crimes and use it (see Chap. 3, Sect. 3.4, Chap. 6, Sect. 6.3).

[25] In this vein see ICC, *The Prosecutor v. Thomas Lubanga Dyilo*, Trial Judgment, 14 March 2012, ICC-01/04-01/06, Separate Opinion of Judge Adrian Fulford, para 10.

[26] Chap. 3, Sect. 3.1.2.5.

categories that are distinguishable in both forms, although they overlap as well: The position of the actor (Sect. 7.1.2.1) and the mechanisms that become causal for the crime (Sect. 7.1.2.3). In between them, the conduct element must be compared as well (Sect. 7.1.2.2).

7.1.2.1 The Position of the Actor

An indirect perpetrator who acts through an organisation must be in a position of "control over the organisation".[27] So far, only a limited core of relevant aspects has been established. Control over an organisation means that the actor can steer a part of the organisation. To be able to do so, the ICC usually expects them to hold a position of power, command, or authority in relation to the members of the (part of the) organisation. The term "authority"[28] plays a central role within the relevant elaborations but is not further defined in the jurisprudence. There are many factual indicators which range from the existence of military hierarchies and communication chains to disciplinary measures and even the provision of weapons and finances. Based on the also necessary notion of control over the crime and almost automatic compliance with orders, it became evident that only control over a part of the organisation, whose members directly perpetrate crimes, suffices. The ability to steer a merely logistical or otherwise organisational unit of a large apparatus cannot suffice. Control and directing part of the organisation need not amount to a comprehensive say in the physical perpetrators' actions. The capability to steer them into the commission of the crimes suffices and the indirect perpetrator must not be in a position to stop the physical perpetrators once they have started engaging in them.[29]

A person who orders the commission of a crime must hold a "position of authority" over the physical perpetrators.[30] This authority must amount to a type of pressure under which the physical perpetrators feel compelled to act. As discussed, in establishing this compelling authority, chambers of the ICC mostly investigate hierarchies, the position of the actor within such hierarchies and their "control"[31]. The latter can be described as a consequence of the former two. Meaning that where a person occupies a relevant position within a hierarchy, they will have control over the physical perpetrators in the form of authority. However, authority can also be exercised where clear hierarchies are absent and a person's recognition as a leader establishes their control over the physical perpetrators.[32] Therefore, authority essentially means a form of influence over the physical perpetrators that makes the recipients feel compelled to act.

---

[27] See Chap. 3, Sect. 3.1.2.1.

[28] Not to be confounded *a limine* with the legal concept of authority under ordering liability.

[29] See Chap. 3, Sects. 3.1.2.1 and 3.1.2.5.

[30] See Chap. 6, Sect. 6.2.2.

[31] Not to be confounded *a limine* with the legal concept of "control over an organisation" or "control over the crime" in indirect perpetration.

[32] See Chap. 6, Sect. 6.2.2.3.

It has been outlined that the two criteria, control over an organisation and authority, overlap substantially and the foregoing confrontation of the two requirements proves this. This is no secret and not seen critically. One chamber even used internal references in its findings on authority and simply pointed to its own findings on the accused's control over an organisation to substantiate that the accused had authority over the perpetrators.[33]

Chambers also apply matching terminology to describe the contents of the two requirements. In the ambit of control over an organisation, the authority over the members of the organisation is often referred to. When elaborating on the authority requirement, chambers often test how far the person controls the organisation and therefore its members.

This necessarily leads to the question where the difference between the two requirements lies, or rather whether there is any difference to begin with. The answer to this can only lie in the necessity of an "organisation" in indirect perpetration. The requirement that the indirect perpetrator must be in a position to control "an organisation", is closely linked to the "organised and hierarchical apparatus" criterion. By contrast, the authority requirement of ordering is not connected to an organisation but can extend over one or many other persons, irrespective of their organisational circumstances. Despite authority mostly being proven through hierarchies and structures within organisations in practice, this does not rule out cases in which authority is exercised through social or personal ties not constituting an organised and hierarchical apparatus of power. The historic precedent of such authority can be found in the ICTR's cases of *bourgmestres*. These pertained to persons with limited powers over government forces (which would qualify as a part of an organisation) but with considerable influence over their communities based on their superior social and traditional standing.[34]

So far, no such cases have come before the ICC, and it is noteworthy that Rwandan *bourgmestres* hardly qualified as high-level decision makers, instead ranging on the lower end of influential characters. However, the factors that are believed to justify the attribution of responsibility for steering a group of people into criminal action are manifold. Some may be found only within organised structures, others—such as personal, social influence—may not. However, the resulting power of the individual is the same. It is the influence exerted over other people that makes them feel compelled to commit the crime. Where it is given, such influence warrants no distinction between the factors that lead to it.

Therefore, the somewhat broader scope of authority is a reasonable description of the actor's influence over others and a better choice to capture this influence than the narrower "control over an organisation".

---

[33] ICC, *The Prosecutor v. Bosco Ntaganda*, Confirmation of Charges, 9 June 2014, ICC-01/04-02/06, para 147 with fn. 599. Fn. 599 hints to para 120 where the chamber determines whether Ntaganda had control over an organized apparatus of power.

[34] See Chap. 5, Sect. 5.1.1.2.

Apart from this, the requirements of control over an organisation and position of authority overlap completely. There is hardly a case imaginable, where one criterion could be given, while the other would be denied.

7.1.2.2 The Conduct Element

It has been criticised that indirect perpetration through an organisation seemingly lacks an explicit conduct element. Consequentially, it is critiqued that this form of responsibility only asks whether a person possesses, not whether they also exercise control over an organisation. However, it has been concluded that, given the narrow control criterion of the ICC and considering the relevant jurisprudence, direct instructions are necessary to trigger indirect perpetration through an organisation. Logically, such instructions can pass through intermediaries within the organisation. Whether the conduct of the indirect perpetrator must contain the instruction to commit crimes, or whether lawful directives that can be executed in a criminal way suffice seems unclear.[35]

To incur liability for ordering crimes, a person must give an order. This may take the form of more general instructions or directives but must be neither written nor explicit. The order can pass through intermediaries, and it is possible to issue an order jointly with other persons.[36] The order does not have to be blatantly illegal.[37]

Furthermore, the conduct within both forms of responsibility must be causal in the sense of a "but for" condition (*conditio sine qua non*) for the commission of the crimes.[38]

The conduct element of ordering and the necessary acts that will give rise to indirect perpetration through an organisation are very alike. Indeed, the uncertainty whether instructions for lawful conduct can trigger responsibility seems to be the only remarkable difference between the two.

7.1.2.3 The Mechanisms That Lead to the Commission of the Crime

Ordering and indirect perpetration through an organisation focus on the dynamic or mechanism that leads to the commission of the crime in different ways. With indirect perpetration, almost automatic compliance with the actor's orders given in a hierarchical and organised apparatus of power must lead to the commission of the crimes). With ordering, it is the authority of the ordering person that compels

[35] See Chap. 3, Sect. 3.1.2.5.

[36] The possibility of joint ordering can play a role in cases where one of the traditional approaches to indirect co-perpetration—the joint control of several persons in one committee over one organisation—is given. In such situations, any direct instruction issued jointly by two or more persons, could qualify as joint ordering if the remaining necessary criteria are given.

[37] See Chap. 6, Sect. 6.2.1.

[38] See Chap. 3, Sect. 3.1.2.5, and Chap. 6, Sect. 6.2.1.

the physical perpetrators to commit the crime. In both forms of responsibility, the mechanisms, when triggered through the conduct of the actor, must be a causal factor for the commission of the crime.[39]

Almost Automatic Compliance in a Hierarchical and Organised Apparatus of Power

To incur liability as an indirect perpetrator through the use of an organisation, this organisation must be shaped as a hierarchical and organised power structure. Within it, the orders of the indirect perpetrator must be complied with almost automatically.

Despite uncertainties as to the criterion's actual scope, it has been shown that certain features of an organisation are often required to establish a hierarchical and organised apparatus of power. True to the wording of the requirement, these often include: organisational structures in different units and branches, a hierarchy between different vertical layers of the organisation and communication channels between these layers.[40] Such organisational structures may be difficult to prove, but most certainly exist in the ambit of asymmetrical conflicts in which international crimes often come before the ICC.[41]

At its core, the requirement of almost automatic compliance relies on some factors that are often considered together: fungibility of the perpetrators, strict and violent training and/or disciplinary regimens. At times payment mechanisms have been mentioned as well. Apart from this, jurisprudence reveals no further tangible features of the criterion. Sometimes, it is combined with the requirement of an organised and hierarchical apparatus, with the ruling chamber leaving unspecified which of the organisation's features would lead to almost automatic compliance.[42]

Authority That Compels the Physical Perpetrator to Commit the Crime

The authority criterion requires the physical perpetrators to feel compelled to commit the crime when they are instructed to do so. Authority could be defined as the influence under which the physical perpetrator prefers to obey and repress their own inhibitions, doubts, and reservations due to the negative consequences they expect if they defy the order. Compelling authority does not mean that a pressure amounting to duress is required. The fear of mere social disadvantages, loss of reputation etc. should suffice.[43] Furthermore, it does not mean that the ordering actor must exert this compelling authority directly over the physical perpetrators. Rather, they can give compelling instructions to one person who in turn has authority over the executioners. This has been referred to as "chain authority" throughout the course of this book. Compelling authority can stem from different factors, including formal hierarchies

---

[39] This means causality in a strict sense where the act of the indirect perpetrator or ordering person is *conditio sine qua non* for the commission of the crimes; see Chap. 3, Sect. 3.1.2.5, Chap. 6, Sect. 6.2.3.

[40] See Chap. 3, Sect. 3.1.2.2.

[41] See Chap. 3, Sect. 3.3.2.1.

[42] See Chap. 3, Sect. 3.1.2.3.

[43] For some more detailed thoughts on the definition of authority cf. Block 2022, p 719.

or social-traditional norms. In practice, the ICC relies on the same indicators that it also uses to establish the criteria of indirect perpetration through an organisation. One of which is the position and influence of the accused, which would serve to prove control over an organisation and automatic compliance with orders.[44]

Comparison

The fact that the ICC often relies on the same facts when establishing authority and almost automatic compliance/the existence of a hierarchical apparatus of power has been pointed out repeatedly. But is this based on evidentiary convenience or do no differences truly exist between these criteria?

To begin with, authority and the prerequisites of indirect perpetration do not differ in terms of the level or degree of influence that must be exercised over the physical perpetrators. For both indirect perpetration and ordering, the physical actor can act under a certain pressure which is found in the authority and almost automatic compliance requirements. This pressure does not have to amount to a state where the physical actor would potentially be excused under duress. This is one of the central points of indirect perpetration through an organisation as a version of the perpetrator behind the perpetrator. If the coercive element is strong enough to constitute duress felt by the executioner of a crime, indirect perpetration through an organisation is nevertheless possible.[45] Due to the obscure scope of accessory liability in international criminal law, it is unclear whether ordering could still be affirmed where the physical perpetrator is coerced and therefore excused. Given the practice of the ICC, this question seems to be of a theoretical nature, as neither in ordering nor in indirect perpetration through an organisation has it been deemed relevant to inquire into the potential defences of the physical perpetrators thus far.[46]

Fungibility, as one of the factors used to establish almost automatic compliance is, by itself, not part of the authority requirement. In contrast to indoctrination and strict disciplinary regimens, fungibility could be seen as entirely independent from the physical perpetrator's will. However, we have also seen how the ICC establishes authority based on the structures of an organised and hierarchical apparatus of power. Of course, it is conceivable that a chamber could confirm indirect perpetration based on fungibility, whilst denying the authority requirement of ordering. However, it is highly questionable what an apparatus would look like if it fulfilled the two necessary requirements for indirect perpetration through an organisation, whilst simultaneously not granting compelling authority to the indirect perpetrator.[47]

---

[44] See Chap. 6, Sect. 6.2.2.

[45] ICC, *The Prosecutor v. Germain Katanga*, Trial Judgment, 7 March 2014, ICC-01/04-01/07, para 1404.

[46] This could be interpreted as establishing that the defence of the physical perpetrator is irrelevant for the accessorial object, but it may also simply be a practical consequence of not knowing and being able to question the physical perpetrators.

[47] Without referring to the mode of ordering, even Roxin has acknowledged that a certain form of authority exists in the organisations which he envisages in his theories. See Roxin 2019, p 278; Roxin 2011, p 204 ("Rather, the essential factor is that, in their crimes, members act not on their own initiative and contrary to the goals of their group, but as organs of [the] leadership whose

The violent and strict training regimens that are often referred to by the ICC amount directly, and without question, to the same standard as the authority requirement. Menacingly strict disciplinary regimes or the indoctrination of child soldiers through violent and strict training regimes have exactly that one effect: superiors enjoy the influence to compel the recipients of their instructions to act.

German scholars voiced certain thoughts on the relevant mechanisms within indirect perpetration through an organisation that can equally be found in the authority requirement of ordering.[48] Schlösser proposes redefining the form of control/domination that emanates from organised power structures as the "social domination" of the crime. He reaches this conclusion by observing the social pressure on the members of organisations that leads to their conformity with the organisation's goals.[49] Schünemann identified the "system of violence" in which there is an implicit threat of violent punishment for non-compliance as a relevant mechanism in indirect perpetration through an organisation.[50] The proposal by Schmidhäuser, although written years previously, refers to situations which are easily imaginable in circumstances like those of the Rwandan Genocide. It suggests widening indirect perpetration through an organisation to include situations where a person delivers the victims to a group of potential perpetrators.[51]

These suggestions all refer to indirect perpetration in the traditional German approach and to the relevant mechanism that should be required by this theory. However, they also show how scholars often identify factors they deem relevant for indirect perpetration that are also covered by the authority requirement in the mode of ordering. Schlösser even defines the social pressure which he relies on as authority.[52] What Schlösser describes is aptly grasped by the description of the authority requirement, i.e., a kind of influence over the physical perpetrator that makes them feel compelled to act. The same is true for the implicit threat of violence which Schünemann recognizes as the most relevant point. The cases referred to by Schmidhäuser were addressed by the *ad hoc* tribunals under ordering, where people like *bourgmestres* exercised their social, informal authority over a crowd.[53]

Finally, academic literature apparently has little choice but to frequently realize that authority exercised by a person is the vital part and the consequence of those factors described in indirect perpetration through an organisation.[54]

---

authority they recognize", addition in parenthesis by the author). In this regard, one must remember that fungibility expects that, eventually, someone will carry out the instruction. If this person felt compelled to comply with the instruction, authority would also be affirmed.

[48] See Chap. 2, Sect. 2.2.3.7.

[49] Schlösser 2004, pp 206-8.

[50] Schünemann 2006, p 412.

[51] Schmidhäuser 1982, Chpt. 10 mn. 95.

[52] See Schlösser 2004, p 205, who bases his definition of authority as social hegemony or power (*soziale Herrschaft*) on the writings of Max Weber.

[53] See Chap. 5, Sect. 5.1.1.2.

[54] Kiss 2019, mn. 11. Concerning Kiss' reliance on the control criterion to distinguish between indirect perpetration and ordering, see below at Sect. 7.1.3.

The foregoing considerations imply that the authority requirement of ordering will always be given where a person qualifies as an indirect perpetrator. The next question is therefore whether authority is broader than that and describes dynamics that will not fall under the criteria of automatic compliance within an organisation.

Ultimately, one must reach the same conclusion as in the assessment of the actor's necessary position: wherever authority is exercised through something other than organisational features, the criterion is broader than those of indirect perpetration through an organisation. This applies to cases in which the instructing person evidently enjoyed great social, traditional, or personal-relational influence over others. One could speak of "less formalized" relations of authority. The above-mentioned cases of *bourgmestres* in the Rwandan genocide serve as the most impressive example of such authority. These examples may be expressed in a more abstract form if one were to speak of elders or chiefs of communities in societies in which people adhere to the word of persons in traditional leadership roles.[55] Such roles could also be exercised by religious leaders whose words and actions bear enormous influence on their community, despite such communities not being ordered and structured like organisations.

Personal relationships in which a person is highly dependent on another and will therefore act according to the other person's words can potentially also establish authority of one person over another. Such relations between two individuals have not gained importance so far where ordering was applied in international criminal law. Whether ordering could be applied, instead of inducing or soliciting, is a relevant theoretical issue, nevertheless. Under a strict construction of the authority requirement, such individual relationships would qualify as ordering, whilst the mechanisms of perpetration through an organisation would be denied.

Additionally, it can be suspected that certain dynamics exist within organisations that could be described as authority, which would not qualify as ensuring almost automatic compliance with orders. However, given the broad and flexible approach taken by chambers to the differentiation between organisational structures and automatic compliance, it is highly doubtful that the existence of an organisation would be confirmed and the almost automatic compliance with orders denied, while the authority requirement is affirmed. Consider e.g., a person who runs a branch of an apparatus as their personal fiefdom in which all subordinates feel compelled to comply with instructions, but this is based on joint beliefs or personal advantages and not on strict disciplinary regimens. Is it realistic that the ICC would deny that the leader's orders were "complied with almost automatically" in such a case because no priorly-established factors of this criterion existed in the organisation? This is doubtful. Instead, the chamber might expand the notion of almost automatic compliance. After all, this requirement was established in a broad manner by the ICC to allow encompassing the dynamics within many different organisations.

---

[55] See in this regard how the chamber in Ruto partially based its findings of control on the position of the accused William Ruto as an "elder" of the perpetrators' community, cf. ICC, *The Prosecutor v. William Samoei Ruto, Henry Kiprono Kosgey and Joshua Arap Sang*, Confirmation of Charges, 23 January 2012, ICC-01/09-01/11, para 329–30.

As discussed previously, the ICC's jurisprudence on what qualifies as an organisation seems indefinite, and the criterion's scope seems vague. This vagueness significantly limits the difference between the mechanisms of the two forms of responsibility. If the existence of an organisation is easily affirmed, more persons qualifying under ordering will also qualify under indirect perpetration.

With these considerations in mind, it can be concluded that where no organisation exists to provide for the relationship between the instructing person and the perpetrators, the instructor may still exercise authority in certain constellations and may therefore be liable for ordering crimes.[56] Wherever an organisation exists, and a person enjoys authority as well, almost automatic compliance with orders will likely also be affirmed.[57]

The difference between the mechanisms that lead to the instructions of indirect perpetrators and ordering actors being carried out therefore lies in the organisational circumstances. Giving an order with authority is broader because authority can be exercised outside of organisational structures, whereas indirect perpetration through an organisation logically requires an organisation. In practice, however, the ICC has not seen any case in which a group of perpetrators would not have qualified as an organisation but authority in ordering would have been affirmed. Some cases before the ICTR, however, provide us with insight on cases where, despite the lack of an organisation, persons may enjoy authority over others that becomes relevant for the commission of mass atrocities.

7.1.2.4 The Mental Element

The general *mens rea* requirement under the Rome Statute is stipulated in Art. 30 Rome Statute, and as such applies to indirect perpetration and ordering alike.[58]

According to Art. 30 (2) (a) this means that the actor must mean to engage in their conduct. This refers to the objective conduct element. Consequently, the actor must mean to give an instruction, order, directive, or any other kind of request for both forms of responsibility.[59]

---

[56] This has also been identified by Olásolo 2009, p 141. Olásolo also identifies a second and third scenario based on Roxin's doctrine. As he points out, ordering would be broader than Roxin's traditional approach where authority exists over members of an organisation that does not act detached from the law or where the organisation's members are not fungible (see ibid., pp 141–2). This is correct but not applicable before the ICC, as examined in Chap. 3 and the comparison above. Therefore, under the current doctrine only the case of ordering where no indirect perpetration through an organisation applies is conceivable.

[57] Admittedly it is imaginable that this will be different in the exceptional case of authority extending over one individual member of an organisation. Given the organisational, collective focus of indirect perpetration through an organisation and the mechanisms of the apparatus, such an individual relationship may not be seen as establishing "almost automatic compliance".

[58] See Chap. 3, Sect. 3.1.2.4 and Chap. 6, Sect. 6.2.4.1.

[59] Cf. the findings on the similar conduct element above at Sect. 7.1.2.2.

Regarding the subsequent commission of crimes, the ordering person and the indirect perpetrator must intend to cause the crime's commission or be aware that the crimes will be committed in the ordinary course of events, i.e., with virtual certainty.[60]

The actor must furthermore have knowledge regarding the circumstances. This is where most of the relevant objective elements have their subjective point of reference. An indirect perpetrator must know of the circumstances that establish the organisation, their control over it and those facts that lead to almost automatic compliance with the orders. An ordering person must know those circumstances that establish their authority.[61] As previously mentioned, the objective elements hardly differ in this regard, although at times authority can be broader than the mechanisms of indirect perpetration (automatic compliance within an organisation). The objective point of reference is broader, and consequently, an ordering actor can be required to be aware of a wider range of factors relating e.g., to personal relations, traditional roles, and the consequent weight of their word.

Finally, as a form of commission, indirect perpetration requires the necessary specific intent where the relevant crimes demand such an intent.[62] Certain chambers of the ICC have denied the necessity of such an intent for an ordering actor, a conclusion that could be connected to the form's categorization as accessory liability. It has been submitted that this reasoning should not be followed, as it would contradict a considerable part of *ad hoc* jurisprudence and—more importantly—undermine the gravity that is otherwise inherent to the ordering of international crimes.[63] Should trial chambers and the appeals chamber of the ICC decide not to require such *dolus specialis* for ordering, this would result in a major difference between the two forms of responsibility.

7.1.2.5 Conclusion: Almost Complete Overlap of Legal Requirements

This section has shown that the legal requirements of indirect perpetration through an organisation and ordering overlap almost completely. This significant overlap leads to the question of whether the two forms can be meaningfully distinguished from each other. Such a distinction is necessary because, as discussed previously, the current interpretation of the Rome Statute through the ICC implies a meaningful difference between commission liability and forms of accessorial liability. If it is possible to identify a reason for such distinction, the complete overlap as far as the scope of indirect perpetration is concerned is unproblematic. At least for differential normative systems of perpetration and participation it is not untypical that the conduct grasped by narrower forms of perpetration is also completely encompassed by forms

[60] Cf. Chap. 3, Sect. 3.1.2.4 and Chap. 6, Sect. 6.2.4.1.

[61] Chap. 3, Sect. 3.1.2.4 and Chap. 6, Sect. 6.2.4.1.

[62] Chap. 3, Sect. 3.1.2.4.

[63] Chap. 6, Sect. 6.2.4.2.

of accessory liability.[64] The ICC currently interprets Art. 25 (3) Rome Statute as establishing such a system. However, this leads to a difference in blameworthiness. To justify such a legal difference, forms of responsibility must differ based on a tangible normative distinction criterion. This criterion in the view of the ICC is the notion of control over the crime.

7.1.3 "Control" versus No Control

Control has generally been defined as the capability of deciding whether and how a crime is committed. Like every form of commission under the control theory, indirect perpetration requires or must lead to control over the crime. Ordering, as an accessorial form of liability does not require and is not expected to establish control over the crime.[65]

Consequently, the difference between indirect perpetration through an organisation and ordering is described in jurisprudence and literature by hinting to the fact that an indirect perpetrator would have control, whilst an ordering person does not.[66] This is sometimes bolstered by stating that an ordering person cannot be certain that their orders will be carried out, whereas an indirect perpetrator has this certainty.[67] In the same vein, Werle and Burghardt state that cases of ordering exist, in which no control of the ordering person is given, especially where the ordering person him- or herself is also a recipient of orders.[68]

But what is control within the meaning of indirect perpetration through an organisation? Is control—as supposedly exercised by an indirect perpetrator controlling an organisation—a specific form of influence that can be distinguished from other forms of influence? That would be necessary to enable a meaningful distinction in the way that has been proposed by the ICC and a significant number of scholars. Only if control over the crime represents an influence distinguishable from other forms of influence, can it justify attributing a higher level of responsibility and blameworthiness. If control is merely an intangible concept tied to the specific requirements of

[64] Consider the fact that a contribution to joint perpetration by providing significant assistance during the execution stage will additionally qualify as aiding and abetting in many national legal systems.

[65] See on the role of the control criterion Chap. 3, Sect. 3.1.3. In this section, it was rejected that the ICC would apply a concept of "diminishing" control from Art. 25 (3) (a) to (d). Instead, control should be an all or nothing concept in which perpetrators have control and accessories do not.

[66] ICC, *The Prosecutor v. Germain Katanga and Mathieu Ngudjolo Chui*, Confirmation of Charges, 30 September 2008, ICC-01/04-01/07, para 517; ICC, *The Prosecutor v. Dominic Ongwen*, Trial Judgment, 4 February 2021, ICC-02/04-01/15, para 2783; ICC, *The Prosecutor v. Bosco Ntaganda*, Appeals Judgment, 30 March 2021, ICC-01/04-02/06-A A2, Separate Opinion of Judge Luz del Carmen Ibáñez Carranza, para 283, with broader reference to the difference between perpetration and instigation; Jessberger and Geneuss 2008, p 865; Kiss 2019, mn. 11; Olásolo 2009, p 141; Ventura 2019, mn. 10, 42. In a similar vein see Lanza 2021, p 57.

[67] Kiss 2019, mn. 11; Olásolo 2009, p 141.

[68] Werle and Burghardt 2014a, p 864.

indirect perpetration through an organisation without independent meaning, it cannot serve as a distinction criterion.

The latter view has been gradually confirmed through this book. As illustrated earlier, the concept of control is illusory and a misguided description of the influence of decision makers behind mass atrocities. The concept of control over the crime pretends that a decision maker in an organisation can determine whether and how a specific crime is committed. However, mass atrocities are shaped by numerous decisions on many different levels and, as far as the specific crime is concerned, the decisions by low- and mid-level actors overrule the more general decisions of the supposed indirect perpetrator. Given the temporal and spatial distance of high-level leaders to the crimes, it is simply wrong to believe that they can decide whether the specific crime—e.g., the murder of a civilian—will be committed. This decision lies with other people. Mid-level actors can decide to exclude certain potential victims from their plans or prioritize their means to commit the crime in a way that spares certain persons. Depending on the situation, a low-level executioner can decide not to act and thereby enable the successful hiding or escape of a potential victim.[69] Therefore, what the ICC refers to as control is an illusion.[70]

Consequently, one could rephrase the description of what is now called control in indirect perpetration to read: Control is the power or influence of a person who decides that crimes (of a certain type) will be committed by members of the organisation when following their instructions and barring the occurrence of unforeseen events.[71] Consequently, control in ICC jurisprudence is only the (theoretically unconvincing) description of a type of influence assigned to a person who fulfils the requirements of indirect perpetration through an organisation. That description would have to be rephrased in the proposed way to come anywhere close to reality.

Following this proposed description of the substance of the control criterion, distinguishing between indirect perpetration and ordering becomes impossible.

It has been established how the requirements of indirect perpetration through an organisation and ordering are vastly the same. More importantly, there is no case in which the criteria of the former would be fulfilled whilst those of the latter would be denied.

This has a lot to do with two points. Despite its seeming reference to collective structures, indirect perpetration through an organisation expects a direct involvement of the perpetrator in instructing the crime. Ordering requires compelling authority and can therefore hardly be meaningfully distinguished from the mechanisms that are understood to ensure automatic compliance within an organisation.

In other words, the above-mentioned description of what control in indirect perpetration means at the ICC also describes the mode of ordering (when exercised in an

[69] See Chap. 3, Sect. 3.3.3.

[70] Note again that this refers to the narrow, crime-centred approach to control. As seen in Chap. 2, one can also justify perpetrator liability with a systemic approach to indirect commission in which the specific crime is less of a focus (Chap. 2, Sect. 2.4). This reasoning, however, is not applied by the ICC (Chap. 3, Sect. 3.2.3).

[71] See Chap. 3, Sects. 3.1.3 and 3.2.3.

organisation). An indirect perpetrator/ordering person decides that crimes of a certain type will be committed by members of the organisation, barring the occurrence of an unforeseen event.

This is where the arguments in favour of indirect perpetration through an organisation fail. There is no way to distinguish between ordering and indirect perpetration based on a notion of control. Likewise, there are no cases within hierarchical and organised power structures in which a person would fulfil the authority requirement *vis-à-vis* subordinates but would not qualify as an indirect perpetrator. This is especially true where higher levels of decision makers exist because both indirect perpetration and ordering function for all levels of actors who exercise the necessary influence.

Naturally, ordering is broader than this as it does not necessitate an organisation, but that is irrelevant. Chapter 3 highlighted how the organisation will often play a role in the large-scale planning and execution of crimes, but it does not change the limited influence of the person in the background over specific crimes. Consequently, if the influence of indirect perpetrators and ordering persons is the same, with only the grasped circumstances being somewhat broader, this does not lead to a meaningful distinction.

This means that in the ICC's doctrinal theory, ordering and indirect perpetration through an organisation stand in direct contrast to each other as one leads to and requires control, and the other does not. However, in practice, there is no such difference.[72] The statement that an indirect perpetrator has control whereas an ordering actor does not, is a hollow phrase. It lacks tangible principles as to how this supposed "control" differs from the influence of a person giving orders with authority over the perpetrators. It can be regarded as the blind import of national law doctrine, in complete disregard of the explicit form of ordering.

This finding supports a conviction that has been tangible in the chapters of this book and the truth of which is now impossible to deny: The authority of the person who orders a crime makes the ordering of a crime especially blameworthy. This is based on the same considerations that underlie the doctrine of indirect perpetration through an organisation.[73]

---

[72] This was suspected earlier by certain authors, see Ambos 2016, Art. 25 mn. 22; Eser 2002, p 797; Yanev 2018, pp 468–70 (arguing that military superiors who order crimes always control their subordinates, which approaches the issue from the opposite side). See also the similar opinion voiced by Judge Morrison in *Ntaganda*, 30 March 2021, Separate opinion of Judge Howard Morrison on Mr. Ntaganda's appeal, para 9.

[73] See similarly: Cryer 2004, pp 246–7; Rastan 2009, p 268; Eser implies the same in Eser 2002, p 797. See also *Ntaganda*, 30 March 2021, Separate opinion of Judge Howard Morrison on Mr. Ntaganda's appeal, para 7.

7.1.4 Encompassed Cases

Ordering crimes under Art. 25 (3) (b) Rome Statute is perfectly applicable to the cases of high- and mid-level decision makers of international crimes. The application of this mode is not restricted to actors on the middle levels of organisations but applies to the highest echelons of power.[74] This is consistent with findings from post-World War II trials and the *ad hoc* tribunals' jurisprudence.[75]

Architects of crimes whose conduct is restricted to a planning or organisational capacity and whose instructions do not directly address the physical perpetrators and their task to commit the crime cannot qualify as "ordering" a crime under *littera* (b).[76] This also holds true for indirect perpetration through an organisation.[77]

In terms of situations and the relevant *modus operandi* of crimes, there is also no difference between the two modes of liability. There are no ways to trigger the commission of mass atrocities that would lead to responsibility solely under indirect perpetration through an organisation but not under ordering. This is the consequence of the overlapping criteria of both forms which rely on identical facts. This has been demonstrated *inter alia* in the previous chapter on ordering.[78] Throughout the history of both modes of responsibility, they have been applied to a broad array of cases of mass atrocities. The early application of ordering was centred around the commission of crimes through military or military-style organisations like the *Wehrmacht* and parts of the Nazi SS.[79] However, this did not shape the application of ordering under the *ad hoc* tribunals which used it to adjudicate different kinds of conduct on different levels of state hierarchies, concerning administrative directives and military orders alike.[80] Indirect perpetration in German theory was affirmed for members of the highest echelons of the GDR state apparatus, but would have been equally applied to commanders who ordered the shooting of refugees at the border.[81] From the perspective of the traditional academic doctrine, any position can lead to responsibility for indirect perpetration through an organisation, as no restriction is placed on the position of the actor.[82] This parallel history of cases that potentially fall under both forms of responsibility culminates in ICC jurisprudence, which does not provide for any distinction criterion between the two forms of responsibility and is based on a set of overlapping legal requirements.[83]

---

74 See Chap. 6, Sect. 6.3.4.

75 See Chap. 4, Sects. 4.2.3.1, 4.2.3.2, 4.6 and Chap. 5, 5.2.3.

76 See Chap. 6, Sects. 6.2.2.4 and 6.3.4.

77 See Chap. 3, Sects. 3.2.1.5, 3.1.5 and 3.4.

78 See Chap. 6, Sect. 6.3.

79 See Chap. 4, Sect. 4.6.

80 See Chap. 5, Sect. 5.1.1.2.

81 See Chap. 2, Sect. 2.3.2.1.

82 See Chap. 2, Sect. 2.2.3.3.

83 See Sect. 7.1.2.

The broader authority requirement additionally allows for other situations to be adjudicated under ordering. However, thus far such a situation has not come before the ICC.[84]

Thus, ordering covers all potential cases of indirect perpetration through an organisation and additional ones where the latter mode would fail due to the absence of organisational structures.

7.1.5 Evidence

It has been described how both modes of liability can be proven, partly through direct and partly through indirect evidence. It has also been shown that where both modes are charged, the evidence considered is usually the same.[85]

The logical conclusion from the foregoing comparison is that authority can be proven through a broader variety of facts because the prosecution does not necessarily have to prove the existence of an organisation and its hierarchical structures.[86]

However, given the central role of organisation-related evidence in proving authority in earlier decisions, it is questionable whether evidence to prove only the authority requirement can be attained more easily. Additionally, the effective way in which organisational structures can lead to authority over its members raises the question of whether the underlying facts will often be different from what we have seen so far. As outlined in the criticism in Chap. 3, mass atrocities often rely on organisational structures and authority for ordering will often stem from such structures in practice.

---

[84] The case against Charles Blé Goudé and his alleged control and authority over youth groups comes to mind as a potential ICC example of a lacking organisation. The pre-trial chamber affirmed control and authority over the youth groups on behalf of Blé Goudé in the confirmation of charges (ICC, *The Prosecutor v. Charles Blé Goudé*, Confirmation of Charges, 11 December 2014, ICC-02/011-02/11, paras 151, 160). Given the pre-trial chamber's statement that such youth groups lacked a clear hierarchy but that they recognized Blé Goudé as their leader, one could have expected authority to be affirmed and the existence of an organisation denied. This would have led to a precedent case in ICC jurisprudence in which only ordering would have been affirmed. However, this did not come to pass. Instead, the trial chamber acquitted Blé Goudé and denied the charges under both heads of liability (see ICC, *The Prosecutor v. Laurent Gbagbo and Charles Blé Goudé*, Reasons for oral decision of 15 January 2019 on the Requête de la Défense de Laurent Gbagbo afin qu'un jugement d'acquittement portant sur toutes les charges soit prononcé en faveur de Laurent Gbagbo et que sa mise en liberté immédiate soit ordonnée, and on the Blé Goudé Defence no case to answer motion, 16 July 2019, ICC-02/11-01/15, Annex B, paras 1942, 1970, 1983). This may also show how the concept of organised power structure is treated so broadly that the potential room for application of ordering shrinks even further.

[85] See Chap. 3, Sects. 3.2.2.1–3.2.2.4 and Chap. 6, Sect. 6.2.2.2.

[86] In the *Katanga* judgment, it was precisely the lack of evidence on the organisational structures and the superior position and competences of the accused within these structures that prohibited the finding of Katanga's responsibility as an indirect co-perpetrator (cf. *Katanga*, 7 March 2014, paras 1419-21; van Sliedregt 2015, p 514).

Therefore, it will generally not be easier to obtain evidence for one form of responsibility.

7.1.6 Conclusion

The extensive overlap of indirect perpetration through an organisation with ordering leads to the conclusion that perpetration through an organisation is technically unnecessary for the adjudication of the conduct of leaders who order the commission of large-scale crimes.[87] Responsibility for ordering is explicitly embodied in the Rome Statute. Indirect perpetration through an organisation in turn is interpreted into the law based on a textual interpretation which is far from compelling.[88]

However, ordering a crime is a broader form of responsibility meaning that there remain some cases to apply it even under a coherent application of the doctrine of perpetration by ways of control over an organisation. This scope of application has so far gained no practical importance under the ICC's jurisprudence, but cases at the ICTR have shown that such situations are conceivable.

At this point it is necessary to put the foregoing observations in the right perspective. Some scholars assert that, if ordering and indirect perpetration would overlap completely and entirely, then "ordering would be redundant".[89] This conclusion confuses the interpretational situations of the two forms of responsibility and the premises set by the Rome Statute. Ordering, as well as indirect perpetration in the form of the perpetrator behind the perpetrator, are explicitly laid down in the Statute. In conformity with Article 31 (1) of the Vienna Convention on the Law of Treaties (VCLT), these provisions must be interpreted in a way that allows for their ordinary meaning.[90] This is where the above-mentioned interpretation goes astray:[91] it is possible to find an ordinary meaning for the term perpetrator behind the perpetrator without applying the theory of perpetration through an organisation. The latter doctrine is not necessary to make sense of Art. 25 (3) (a).[92] However, it is hardly possible to find another ordinary meaning for the term of ordering a crime which is explicitly provided for in Art. 25 (3) (b). This does not change even if, as Art. 31 (1) VCLT suggests, one does not rely on a "layman's" understanding of the terms, but takes the perspective of "a person reasonably informed on the subject matter

87 Weigend 2011a, pp 101-2; Weigend 2015, pp 551–2.

88 See the criticism in Chap. 3, Sect. 3.3.

89 Kiss 2019, mn. 44 with fn. 118; Ventura 2019, mn. 42.

90 This means that the "regular, normal or customary" meaning of the terms employed by an international treaty must be found, cf. Dörr 2012, Article 31 General rule of interpretation mn. 41.

91 For a similar reasoning see Yanev 2018, p 470, asserting that the existence of ordering questions the adherence to the control theory and not necessarily *vice versa*.

92 For examples of other cases of the perpetrator behind the perpetrator see Chap. 3, Sect. 3.2.1.

of the treaty".[93] Ordering has an unequivocal shape in the history of international criminal law and, in the legal ambit of the Rome Statute, the term implies responsibility for instructing subordinates to commit crimes, which is not true for the term of "commission through another".[94]

Considering this overlap, the criticism of the control theory, and especially indirect perpetration through an organisation and its internal logic gains even more weight. Its import may have created more problems than it solves and, in comparison to the equally capable mode of ordering, this speaks strongly against the doctrine.[95]

Additionally, we have seen that the underlying factual dynamics as described by the requirements of ordering and indirect perpetration amount to the same kind of influence over the physical perpetrators. This not only renders the distinction criterion of control useless, but also leads to the necessary conclusion that a person who orders a crime is especially blameworthy, just as it is assumed for indirect perpetration.

This last point is connected to the question of a hierarchy of blameworthiness, and again, one must not confound the premise given by the Rome Statute with what one wishes to see in it. The Rome Statute does not explicitly or unequivocally establish such a hierarchy. Therefore, the overlap of indirect perpetration through an organisation and ordering does not imply that ordering is rendered redundant. It would only imply this if ordering was definitively categorized as less blameworthy within the statute. Instead, the findings on the impossible distinction between the two forms raise doubts regarding the interpretation that forms of commission are meant to be more blameworthy than modes of accessory liability. Consequently, any overlap of the two modes of responsibility leads to the necessity of justification for the doctrine of indirect perpetration through an organisation.

As its application leaves room for an independent application of ordering, it must be further examined whether there are convincing reasons to adhere to the doctrine of indirect perpetration through an organisation. Should this not be the case, the doctrine of perpetration through an organisation based on control over the crime would have to be dispensed with due to the foregoing findings. Notwithstanding the criticism, the use of the doctrine of perpetration through an organisation may still be necessary and desirable if other reasons beside its unconvincing notion of control speak in favour of it. Such a reason could lie in an explicit or implicit categorisation of indirect perpetration as a more serious form of liability than ordering. This is not clearly stipulated by the Rome Statute and would therefore have to be interpreted into it.

[93] On the issue of perspective for the ordinary meaning, see Dörr 2012, Article 31 General rule of interpretation.

[94] As previously discussed, the terms of commission through another, regardless of that other's responsibility, entails different possibilities of legal interpretations, i.e., different varieties of the perpetrator behind the perpetrator. Concerning ordering: covering *bourgmestre* cases as seen in ICTR jurisprudence, which would provide for non-organisational authority exercised by the ordering actor, can hardly be thought to be the ordinary meaning of Art. 25 (3) (b) Rome Statute. In comparison to all other instances in which ordering can be affirmed, such cases seem very rare, have yet to come before the ICC and do not correspond to the "regular, normal or customary" meaning of "ordering".

[95] See also Rastan 2009, p 267; Weigend 2015, pp 552–3.

7.2 Evaluation: The Nature of Responsibility and the Blameworthiness of Indirect Perpetration and Ordering

Interpreting indirect commission in the manner of the doctrine of control over an organisation is no necessity. There is no conduct, situation or differing form of influence which would not be grasped by ordering and would therefore call for the broad interpretation of indirect perpetration. A similar situation exists in the German legal system, as discussed in Chap. 2.

However, as examined previously, the conception of the doctrine in Germany is linked to two interpretative arguments, both of which are connected to the overall system of perpetration and participation. These two points are also considered in the international debate:

- The forms of responsibility that come to mind instead of indirect perpetration through an organisation (instigation in German law, ordering under the Rome Statute) are accessorial liability and therefore depend on the commission of a crime by another.
- Instigation and ordering are considered less blameworthy by courts and scholars whereas indirect perpetration is considered to properly express the high degree of blameworthiness of decision makers behind international crimes.

These two points are assessed below.

7.2.1 Principal versus Accessorial Liability Under the Rome Statute

As exemplified above, the ICC and many scholars interpret Art. 25 (3) (a) to (d) as establishing a differentiation system of perpetration and participation. Forms of commission under Art. 25 (3) (a), which include indirect perpetration through an organisation, are considered principal, perpetrator liability. All other forms of responsibility of Art. 25, including ordering a crime, are considered accessorial liability. The latter is derivative of the commission of a crime by another person.[96]

The accessorial object of this derivative liability consists of the entirety of the offence, i.e., the perpetrators must fulfil the objective elements and act with the necessary subjective intent. This seems to include the specific intent of crimes that demand *dolus specialis*, such as genocide and persecution (a crime against humanity).[97] Another issue concerns the question of whether the physical perpetrators must be criminally liable to provide for a sufficient accessorial object. Based on certain civil

[96] See Chap. 6, Sect. 6.4.1.

[97] See Chap. 6, Sect. 6.4.1.1.

law legal systems, it has been proposed to split the Rome Statute's defences into justifications and excuses, with only the latter enabling accessorial liability. For example, this would mean that where a person acts in self-defence (a "justification"), no accessorial liability would be possible. A person acting under duress (an "excuse") would allow responsibility for accessories for their crime.[98] However, given that the Rome Statute does not acknowledge such a distinction, it is possible and more realistic to consider defences either completely or not at all when defining the accessorial object. This would mean that the "commission of a crime" as the point of reference in Art. 25 (3) (b) to (d) could be denied or affirmed if the physical perpetrators had or had no defence available to them.[99] This issue cannot be explored further in this book. For the further comparison, it will be assumed that the physical perpetrators of mass atrocities will usually not have defences at their disposal.

Not all scholars share the approach of reading a differentiated model into Art. 25 (3) (a) to (d) of the Rome Statute.[100] Eser explains that the wording of Article 25 (3) does not necessarily imply a differentiation system.[101] He is more inclined towards a unitary model for the interpretation of Art. 25 (3) as it leads to less dependency on the principal when ascertaining the responsibility of participants.[102] This makes sense in light of the foregoing speculations about the accessorial object. Stewart equally argues for a unitary system. He points out that the considerations on blameworthiness which many commentators connect with a differentiation model can still be considered in sentencing, even if a unitary model is applied.[103] Ambos takes the view that the model is a functional unitary one, which can be found in the systems of Austria and Sweden.[104]

A unitary system would also circumvent the problem that, under the current interpretation, it is possible for the special intent of an accessory to be irrelevant. Their ordering, instigation, or aiding can only qualify as a participation in the special intent crime, if the physical perpetrators act with such intent as well.

However, as Aksenova has pointed out, one can also consider the material requirements of accessorial liability as a safeguard for the proper construction of a link between the accused and the physical perpetrator, as a positive effect of a differentiated model.[105]

---

[98] For a detailed explanation of the approaches, one in which defences are considered as one category, the other splitting them into two categories, see Finnin 2012, pp 101–18.

[99] Vogel did not expect defences to rule out accessory liability in international criminal law, see Vogel 2002, pp 424–5; he pointed out that this tendency could be seen in ICTR, *Prosecutor v. Jean-Paul Akayesu*, 2 September 1998, ICTR-96-4-T, para 531. Burghardt's findings confirm this view in Burghardt 2008, p 307 with decisions in fn. 1026.

[100] See in addition to the sources quoted below: Kress 1999, p 9.

[101] Eser 2002, p 788. He acknowledges that the structure of Art. 25 (3) Rome Statute speaks in favour of a differentiated model.

[102] Ibid., pp 787–8.

[103] Stewart 2012, pp 206–9.

[104] Ambos 2013, p 146; Ambos 2018, § 7 mn. 13. See also Lanza 2021, p 145.

[105] See Aksenova 2016, pp 171–2.

Various scholars argue that ordering should be read, or should have been embodied in the Rome Statute as principal liability.[106] Several provisions in which ordering can be found indicate an equation of ordering and commission.[107] In Vest's view, this means that categorizing ordering as accessory liability was not compelling, and establishing ordering as principal liability in the Rome Statute would have allowed for an elegant solution of the issue of leadership criminality.[108] Ambos hints to the similarity of the underlying situations of ordering and indirect perpetration and therefore argues, that ordering in Art. 25 (3) (b) must be considered principal liability.[109] Cryer underlines how certain historic precedents allowed for a conviction of attempted ordering, which he reads as an indicator for the status of ordering as principal liability in its historic use.[110]

A historic and text-based interpretation of ordering under the Rome Statute does not entirely support these views. The *ad hoc* tribunals for the former Yugoslavia and Rwanda conceptualised ordering as accessorial liability.[111] The same can be found for ordering under CCL 10, although with the due remark that a doctrinally relevant distinction between principal and accessorial liability was not established by the Nuremberg Military Tribunals.[112]

If one were to acknowledge that a differentiation system is embodied in Art. 25 (3) Rome Statute, the article's structure seems to imply that ordering is accessorial liability. Under this premise, one would usually only consider the wording of *littera* (a) (commission) to imply non-derivative perpetrator liability. The history and thus uniformity of international criminal law speak in favour of categorising ordering as accessorial liability, as does the structure of Art. 25 (3). This interpretation will be referred to in the following.

However, one must remember that a differentiated system does not necessarily entail a hierarchy of blameworthiness between its forms of responsibility.[113] Where

---

106 Cryer 2004, pp 243–7; Ambos 2016, Art. 25, Art. 25 mn. 22; Vest 2011, pp 364–5; Vest 2014, p 304, who however argues in the latter source that "perpetration through another" would be the correct denomination.

107 See Introduction to Part II. These provisions describe the persons committing a certain international crime through terminology such as "commits or orders to commit". Article 2 ICTY Statute, Article 4 ICTR Statute, Article 3 SCSL Statute. Such formulations can also be found in the Geneva Convention's articles on criminal responsibility, see Art. 49 GA I, Art. 50, GA II, Art. 129 I GA III, Art. 146 I GA IV. Vest also points to Art. 19 of the ILC's Draft Code from 1991 that regulated responsibility for genocide for cases in which an individual "commits or orders the commission" of genocide (A/46/10 Report of the International Law Commission on the Work of its forty-third session, p. 101); Vest 2011, p 365.

108 Ibid., 365.

109 Ambos 2016, Art. 25 mn. 22; Ambos 2018, § 7 mn. 45.

110 Cryer 2004, pp 243–4; Cryer et al. 2019, p 360.

111 See Chap. 5, Sect. 5.1.2.

112 See Chap. 4, Sect. 4.1.

113 See the observations on the relation between forms of responsibility under the law of the *ad hoc* tribunals in Chap. 5, Sect. 5.3.6. On the general possibilities to differentiate between principal and accessory liability with or without a normative gradation between modes of liability see van Sliedregt 2012, pp 71–3; van Sliedregt 2015, pp 502–3 (non-normative approach), 508 (normative

it does, one may speak of a normative differentiated model, although this does not necessarily imply that only non-derivative forms of commission/principal/perpetrator liability would be characterized as the gravest form of involvement. As seen earlier, the German provision on instigation, an undisputedly accessorial, derivative mode of liability, leads to the same punishment as perpetration.[114]

Another way of differentiating between forms of responsibility is the empirical, naturalistic, or phenomenological approach, in which it is not the label of perpetrator or participant that decides which form is the correct one to describe the actor's conduct. Instead, it is the description of the conduct through the mode of liability that is relevant.[115]

As outlined earlier, the ICC and many commentators adhere to the former of these two differentiation approaches and read Art. 25 (3) (a) as establishing a hierarchy of blameworthiness with commission as the single most blameworthy form of involvement. But what are the arguments in favour of such a hierarchy?

7.2.2 The Majority Approach: Ordering as a Less Blameworthy Form of Responsibility in Comparison to Forms of Commission

Most of the chambers of the ICC interpret the forms of responsibility in Art. 25 (3) as being arranged in a hierarchy of seriousness. In this hierarchy, forms of commission under *littera* (a) are considered the most blameworthy forms of involvement in a crime. It is not entirely clear whether the forms of participation in *litterae* (b) to (d) are ranked in a hierarchy of blameworthiness as well, although this seems probable. Consequently, ordering, inducing, and soliciting (*lit.* (b)) would be the next lower level of blameworthiness, followed by aiding and abetting (c) and finally the participation in or contribution to a group crime (d).[116]

approach); Vogel 2002, pp 406–9 (general approaches to naturalistic and normative distinction between participants in crimes), 422 (observations on international criminal law practice).

[114] See Chap. 2, Sect. 2.2.5.

[115] See Burghardt 2008, pp 303–8 on the different naturalistic and normative views taken in *ad hoc* jurisprudence; van Sliedregt 2012, pp 71–2; van Sliedregt 2015, pp 502–3 (empirical "complicity approach"); Vogel 2002, pp 406–9, 422.

[116] See Chap. 3, Sect. 3.1.4. The degradation of blameworthiness through all *litterae* of Art. 25 (3) is only implied by some judgments but can be considered the most prominent interpretational assistance in literature.

This interpretation is supported by many scholars.[117] However, many others oppose it, often proposing alternatives.[118]

Concerning the relation of ordering and indirect perpetration, the system thus establishes that the former is less serious than the latter.[119] This leads to the paradoxical effect that the historic development and the legal requirements of ordering speak in favour of applying it to high- and mid-level decision makers,[120] however, the lower mark of blameworthiness that is associated with it, and the consequent sentencing principles seemingly stand against this.

Therefore, the reasons for interpreting Art. 25 (3) Rome Statute as establishing a hierarchy of blameworthiness between ordering and forms of commission must be analysed and questioned. One of the forms of responsibility on which the ICC relies most in practice, indirect perpetration through an organisation, is imported from the German, Spanish and certain Latin American legal systems. The flaws and shortcomings of this doctrine have been imported as well, some of which may be used as arguments against a hierarchy of blameworthiness.

7.2.3 *Critical Analysis of Arguments in Favour of a Hierarchy of Blameworthiness*

Chambers of the ICC have been silent on their reasons for adopting a hierarchy of blameworthiness, and at least one trial chamber has rejected such a hierarchy. Supportive scholarly literature, however, has produced a range of arguments which must be evaluated.

---

117 Burghardt 2010, pp 91–3; Goy 2012, pp 1, 10; Olásolo 2009, p 27 (who takes the view that Art. 25 (3) contains an implicit principle of mitigation of sentences for accessories); Steer 2017, pp 377–80; Werle 2007, pp 953, 957; Werle and Burghardt 2014a, pp 855–61; Werle and Burghardt 2014b, pp 315–8; Werle and Jessberger 2020, mn. 616–17. Van Sliedregt acknowledges the expressive value of the normative approach but, to prevent over-reliance on the mode of commission, demands the limiting of the effect of the normative approach to Art. 25 (3) (a), see van Sliedregt 2012, p 81. Vest is of the view that a certain distinction is necessary, but would only see an *indication* of blameworthiness in the difference between principal and accessory, see Vest 2014, pp 308–9.

118 In favour of a unitary model: Rastan 2009, p 269; Stewart 2012, pp 207, 218; tending to interpret Art. 25 (3) as a unitary approach: Eser 2002, pp 787–8; Kress 1999, p 9; against a hierarchy of blameworthiness also Aksenova 2016, pp 167, 177; Gil Gil and Maculan 2015, pp 362-4; Militello 2007, p 949; Sadat and Jolly 2014, p 785; van Sliedregt 2015, p 500. Critical of the (in its view still too limited) extent of perpetrator liability see Office WCR 2010, 57 ff.; Ambos 2018, § 7 mn. 13, sees a "functional unitary model" in Art. 25 (3), but recognizes a hierarchy between the different forms of perpetration, see below.

119 Chap. 6, Sects. 6.4.3 and 6.5.

120 Cf. the legal requirements and potential applicability of ordering as portrayed in Chap. 6, Sects. 6.2 and 6.3.

7.2.3.1 The Wording of Article 25 (3) Rome Statute

Werle, Jessberger and Burghardt suggest that the wording and structure of Art. 25 (3) not only imply a differentiated, but also a normative model of perpetration and participation.[121] This argument is deeply linked to the control over the crime theory. If commission through another is possible through a guilty agent, as Art. 25 (3) (a) stipulates, the empirical or naturalistic view cannot be used to distinguish between perpetration (as hands on commission) and participation. Under such a naturalistic view, whoever acts through an agent—especially a guilty one—would usually qualify as an accessory.[122]

However, while the wording and structure of Art. 25 (3) may speak against a purely empirical, naturalistic, or phenomenological differentiation model, it does not logically imply the interpretation given to the provision by the above-mentioned scholars. Other sources from academic literature indicate that the control criterion could be used to define forms of commission, without importing the hierarchy of blameworthiness it is usually attached to.[123] Additionally, the wording of *littera* (a) indeed implies that a form of indirect perpetration is previsioned in which the criminal responsibility of the physical perpetrator cannot be the decisive factor.[124] However, other cases of perpetrators behind a perpetrator exist.[125] Therefore, although the autonomy principle is indeed rejected by the statute, neither the control theory nor indirect perpetration through an organisation are necessarily endorsed by Art. 25 (3).[126]

This means other interpretational approaches next to the control theory are possible which would not result in the hierarchy being read into Art. 25 (3). Additionally, even if the control theory is followed in general, it does not necessarily lead to the application of perpetration through an organisation. Instead, other cases of the perpetrator behind the perpetrator can be subsumed under *littera* (a), which are not construed to convey a higher blameworthiness but rather to display a discrepancy in knowledge between the physical and indirect perpetrator.[127]

The wording of Art. 25 (3) can therefore be interpreted in a way in which it is not tailored to only grasp the most blameworthy forms of participation in a crime.

---

[121] Burghardt 2010, pp 91–2; Werle and Burghardt 2014a, pp 856–7; Werle and Jessberger 2020, mn. 616–17.

[122] Burghardt 2010, pp 91–2. Werle and Burghardt 2014a, pp 856–7.

[123] In this vein see van Sliedregt 2012, p 88; van Sliedregt 2015, p 515.

[124] See Chap. 3, Sect. 3.1.2 and 3.1.2.1.

[125] See Chap. 2, Sect. 2.2.3; Chap. 3, Sect. 3.1.2 and 3.1.2.1.

[126] See Aksenova 2016, p 168; Weigend 2011a, p 105 (speaking of "several options" to interpret "committing through another").

[127] Chap. 2, Sect. 2.2.3; Chap. 3, Sect. 3.1.2 and 3.1.2.1. The cases that have been listed include that of a gradual mistake of fact (the physical perpetrator has the necessary mental element but errs in terms of the gravity of their conduct as far as the violated legal assets are concerned).

7.2.3.2 The Limited Criminalization of Attempt in Art. 25 (3) (f) Rome Statute

A chamber of the ICC and some authors have held that a normative distinction between commission and the other forms of liability is expressed through the criminalisation in Art. 25 (3) (f) of the attempt of solely the former.[128] However, this reading of *littera* (f) is not necessarily compelling, due to the different meanings of "commission" within Art. 25 Rome Statute. Under this premise, the recognition of a criminalized attempt to order the commission of crimes was advocated for earlier.[129]

Additionally, even if it is accepted that attempted participation is not criminalized under Art. 25 (3) Rome Statute, this does not strictly speak in favour of a hierarchy. German academic debate has produced another potential argument for not criminalizing or mitigating the punishment of attempted participation. Acts of participation often take place at an earlier point in time than attempted commission. This holds true if we compare the attempt to instigate or aid another with the attempted physical commission of a crime.[130] It does not hold true for the conduct elements of indirect perpetration through an organisation and ordering, as they are the same.[131] However, such ponderations should be considered if one accepts a limited attempt provision, and from this, tries to draw conclusions regarding a hierarchy of blameworthiness.

7.2.3.3 Does Accessory Liability Constitute a Lesser Wrong per se Due to the Derivative Nature of its Responsibility?

Kiss advances that accessory liability would entail a lower responsibility than principal perpetration because of its derivative nature. He asserts that "accessories are responsible for their own wrong" and that "[p]articipants are *not* to be attributed and convicted for the 'crime committed' but for their own lawbreaking, consisting of a contribution to the principal's commission of the crime." This latter part is also described by him with the statement "principals and accessories do not infringe the same prohibitive norm".[132] The second of these assertions cannot be sustained. It

---

[128] ICC, *The Prosecutor v. Thomas Lubanga*, Confirmation of Charges, 29 January 2007, ICC-01/04-01/06, para 998; Herzig 2013, p 198; Werle and Burghardt 2014a, p 857; Wirth 2012, p 979.

[129] See the arguments listed in Chap. 6, Sect. 6.4.2; in favour of attempted ordering see also Ambos 2013, p 258.

[130] A person who only attempts to instigate could fail to generate the other person's decision to commit the crime. Such an attempt therefore happens during a stage of communication which can lie way ahead of the crime that the instigator wants to be committed. The attempt to commit a crime requires a substantial step be taken. This will be the case where the legally protected assets are already in danger (see Ambos 2018, § 7 mn. 69). This will often be at a later point in time than the attempted instigation. This explanation of the non-criminalization of an attempted instigation has been developed by Herzberg 2000, pp 49–51.

[131] See Sect. 7.1.2.2.

[132] Kiss 2019, mn. 37, footnotes omitted, emphasis in original; see also mn. 8 with fn. 15.

may be true that, as Kiss argues, forms of liability are "*extensions of liability*",[133] but that does not mean that the prohibitive norm, violated by accessories, is a different one than that violated by principals.[134]

Under the jurisprudence of the *ad hoc* tribunals, accessories are punishable because they participate in the crime, not because of some other, independent wrong connected to their conduct. This is reflected by the fact that a participant is still guilty of the crime, as the verdicts of numerous decisions of the ICTY and ICTR demonstrate. The *ad hoc* tribunals convict the accused for being "guilty of" a crime and only subsequently name the form of responsibility.[135]

The ICC resorts to the same manner of wording in its verdicts. Participants are found guilty of the crime, not of another wrong or individual form of "participation in war crimes".

Consider e.g., the conviction of Germain Katanga under Art. 25 (3) (d) Rome Statute. The relevant part of his conviction reads:

> Guilty, under article 25 (3) (d) of the Statute, as an accessory to the crimes committed on 24 February 2003 of:
>
> – Murder as a crime against humanity under article 7(1)(a) of the Statute;
> – Murder as a war crime under article 8(2)(c)(i) of the Statute; ...[136]

Evidently, the form of liability is mentioned in this finding, as it should be when a chamber differentiates between forms of liability, nevertheless, the accused is still "guilty... of: Murder". Consequently, the ICC is in line with *ad hoc* jurisprudence in this regard. All ICC convictions thus far have followed this example.[137]

---

[133] Ibid., mn. 37 with fn. 87, italics in the original.

[134] If this were the case, it would have to be questioned why indirect and co-perpetration do not constitute extensions of liability. Beginning with the description of the criminal conduct in the provisions on the respective crimes, it is usually only hands-on commission that emerges as the "natural" way of committing the crime. From this perspective, despite giving rise to principal liability, acting through another is an extension of the statutory liability for the crime.

[135] See e.g. *Akayesu*, 2 September 1998, 8. Verdict; ICTY, *Prosecutor v. Radoslav Brđanin*, 1 September 2004, IT-99-36-T, para 1152; ICTR, *Prosecutor v. Bagosora et al.*, 18 December 2008, ICTR-98-41-T, para 2258; ICTR, *Prosecutor v. Tharcisse Renzaho*, 14 July 2009, ICTR-97-31-T, para 812; ICTR, *The Prosecutor v. Pauline Nyiramasuhuko et al.*, 24 June 2011, ICTR-98-42-T, para 6186 all of which contain findings of responsibility under modes of secondary participation; see also Stewart 2012, p 168.

[136] *Katanga*, 7 March 2014, XII. Disposition.

[137] See *Lubanga*, 14 March 2012, para 1358; ICC, *The Prosecutor v. Jean-Pierre Bemba Gombo*, Trial Judgment, 21 March 2016, ICC-01/05-01/08, para 752; ICC, *The Prosecutor v. Jean-Pierre Bemba Gombo et al.*, Trial Judgment, 19 October 2016, ICC-01/05-01/13, VII. Verdict; ICC, *The Prosecutor v. Bosco Ntaganda*, Trial Judgment, 8 July 2019, ICC-01/04-02/06, XII. Disposition. Most of the guilty verdicts are based on a form of Art. 25 (3) (a), but some findings rely on accessorial modes of liability. The *modus* in which guilt is displayed in the verdicts shows that there is no difference regarding what the convict is guilty of; perpetrators and accessories are guilty of the crime.

In accordance with this, Judge Christine Van den Wyngaert took the stance that the differentiation between principals and accessories in Art. 25 (3) Rome Statute does not imply a gradation in blameworthiness.[138]

This theory on the wrong of participation in a crime has been recognized and debated in international criminal law, but there is nothing to suggest that international criminal legal practice leads to any other conclusion.[139]

From a comparative perspective, it is worth mentioning that the German legal system takes the same stance on the wrongdoing of the act of the secondary participant. An accessory participates in the crime committed by another, and therefore becomes liable for their participation in the crime and its wrongfulness.[140] The same is true for the common law of England where principals and secondary parties are not only equated through the Accessories and Abettors Act of 1861,[141] but where secondary liability does not constitute a wrong *per se* but the wrong is derived from the participation in the crime of another.[142]

Kiss' statement regarding the fact that an accessory is responsible for their own wrong is true in German criminal law and may be the case in international criminal law as well. However, this does not mean that his idea of an "own wrong", in the sense of a wrong that is separate from the wrong of the crime, is also true. Instead, the common statement that a participant commits an own wrong, wishes to illustrate that their wrongdoing is not fully dependent on the principal and their wrong. Under German law, if the principal is excused (e.g., under duress or due to mental illness), this will not bar the accessory's liability. In this regard, their instigation or aiding constitutes an individual wrong.[143]

It can thus be observed that the initially mentioned statements do not describe the view of the ICC, the *ad hoc* tribunals or scholarly literature. An accessory to the crime violates the same prohibitive norm as the principal: both are guilty of the crime. Therefore, the fact that accessory liability is derived from principal liability does not *per se* result in a lower blameworthiness.

---

138 ICC, *The Prosecutor v. Mathieu Ndgudjolo Chui*, Trial Judgment, 18 December 2012, ICC-01/04-02/12, Concurring Opinion of Judge Christine Van den Wyngaert, para 22. She also hints to the 50 years sentence that Charles Taylor received based on a conviction for aiding and abetting certain crimes in para 26.

139 See e.g. the remarks by Stewart 2012, p 168 with further references in fn. 9.

140 Heine and Weisser 2019, Vor §§ 25ff. mn. 15–17; German academia overwhelmingly rejects the idea that participation in a crime would be an independent form of offence, see at mn. 19.

141 Simester et al. 2019, p 225; see also Jain 2014, pp 155–6.

142 Simester et al. 2019, p 236; see also Jain 2014, p 156.

143 The corresponding theory in German law is called *Theorie vom akzessorischen Rechtsgutangriff* (roughly: theory of the accessorial violation of the legal asset). According to it, there is a dependency of the wrong of the secondary party because it requires a legally relevant violation of the law by another. However, through their action, the accessory commits an own violation/attack on the legally protected asset (see Heine and Weisser 2019, Vor §§ 25ff. mn. 16). It is this latter point that shows how an accessory is blamed for the wrong of (their participation in) the crime and not a violation of another prohibitive norm.

7.2.3.4 The Influence of Forms of Liability on Sentencing

If forms of responsibility under the Rome Statute necessarily led to a differing gradation of sentences, this rule would constitute a compelling statement by the drafters of the statute in favour of a hierarchy between the respective forms.

As previously discussed, the German criminal code contains an obligatory mitigation of sentence for aiders and abettors.[144] Consequently, the German discussion around a hierarchy of blameworthiness is only focused on the existence or non-existence of a hierarchy between forms of commission and instigation, both of which receive the same sentence.[145]

Such a situation does not exist under the rules of the Rome Statute Art. 78 contains no provision on whether modes of liability should play a role in sentencing.[146]

Rule 145 (1) (c) RPE stipulates that the "degree of participation of the convicted person" shall be considered by the competent chamber when determining the sentence.[147] This rule can be interpreted as being in favour of a hierarchy of blameworthiness, if the "degree of participation" is read as "form" or "mode" of participation.[148] However, such a reading is far from compulsive. It has been pointed out that both Art. 78 and its associated Rule 145 RPE refer to the sentencing stage, which speaks against them referring to the question of modes of liability.[149]

In the *Ntaganda* sentencing decision, the trial chamber decided to take the degree of the accused's participation into account in its *in concreto* assessment of the gravity

---

[144] See Chap. 2, Sect. 2.2.5.

[145] See Chap. 2, Sect. 2.2.5; in general on sentencing and forms of responsibility in Germany see Weigend 2011b, pp 265–6. A hierarchy of blameworthiness is rejected e.g. by Herzberg, 2000, 49 ("Instigation … encompasses the same quantitative wrong", translation by the author); Herzberg ZIS 2009, 579; Hruschka, ZStW 110, 608; Joecks 2017, § 25 mn. 159–60; Krey and Nuys 2009, pp 212–3, 222–3.

[146] Instead, Art. 78 Rome Statute refers to the gravity of the crimes and the individual circumstances of the convict. None of these terms is associated with the head of responsibility under which guilt was imputed, see e.g. Khan 2016, Article 78 mn. 15–16; Ohlin 2022, p 249.

[147] Rule 145 RPE—Determination of sentence

(1) In determination of the sentence pursuant to article 78, paragraph 1, the Court shall:

(c) In addition to the factors mentioned in article 7, paragraph 1, give consideration *inter alia*, to the extent of the damage caused, especially the harm caused to the victims and their families, the nature of the unlawful behaviour and the means employed to execute the crime; the degree of participation; the degree of intent; the circumstances of manner, time and location; the age, educational social and economic condition of the convicted person.

[148] Olásolo 2009, p 27; Office WCR 2010, 58; Zorzi Giustiani 2009, p 441. See in a similar vein: Vest 2014, pp 307–8; Weigend 2015, p 552. For an explanation see also Damgaard 2008, pp 245–6 with fn. 444.

[149] Sadat and Jolly 2014, p 783. Also see the rejection of a hierarchy by Khan 2016, Article 78 mn. 16; Ohlin 2022, p 249.

of the crimes.[150] As discussed above, the *in concreto* assessment concerns personal conduct and does not refer to abstract modes of liability, which would be considered if a chamber makes an *in abstracto* evaluation. Furthermore, as portrayed earlier, the case law of the *ad hoc* tribunals took the stance that the gravity of the offence would *inter alia* be defined by the "form and degree of participation".[151] The relevant term to explain the role of forms of responsibility in sentencing must have been the *form* of participation. Therefore, in the language of the *ad hoc* tribunals, the *degree* of participation describes the actual manner of conduct of the accused, whereas the *form* of participation refers to the respective mode of liability.[152]

In contrast to *ad hoc* jurisprudence, Rule 145 (1) (c) RPE only refers to the "degree of participation". The practice of the *ad hoc* tribunals was already (partly) existent when the RPE were adopted by the Assembly of States Parties during its first session in 2002. Therefore, it seems unlikely that the wording of Rule 145 (1) (c) RPE was intended to include forms of responsibility. Had this been the intention, it could have been phrased in accordance with the *ad hoc* jurisprudence.

These points advocate against forms of participation playing a role in sentencing.[153]

Regardless, even if the degree of participation clause in Rule 145 (1) (c) RPE refers to modes of liability, the rule does not establish which of the modes should lead to which consequence in sentencing. Accordingly, the rule would still not speak in favour of the specific hierarchy proposed by most of the chambers of the ICC and the supportive academia. Instead, it could equally be interpreted as proposed earlier for the system at the *ad hoc* tribunals. In ICTY and ICTR jurisprudence, only aiding and abetting are considered less blameworthy than commission, planning, ordering, and instigating.[154] Such an interpretation would also be possible if one accepted that forms of participation must be taken into account in sentencing according to Rule 145 (1) (c) RPE, which makes no remark as to *how* modes of liability would have to be taken into account.

Such a hierarchy (in which commission and certain accessorial forms of responsibility are equally blameworthy), and its expression through sentencing rules is also

---

[150] *Ntaganda*, 8 July 2019, para 34–5, at para 11 the chamber pointed out that modes of liability must be considered in the *in abstracto* assessment. Thus, while arguing in favour of a hierarchy of blameworthiness, the chamber also stated that "degree of participation" would not refer to modes of liability.

[151] See Chap. 5, Sect. 5.3.3.

[152] See also Damgaard 2008, p 246 with fn. 444.

[153] In a similar vein: Guilfoyle 2011, p 268; van Sliedregt 2015, pp 510–11; *Ntaganda*, 30 March 2021, Partly concurring opinion of Judge Chile Eboe-Osuji, paras 42, 48.

[154] See Chap. 5, Sect. 5.3.6.

one possible interpretation of the German national system[155] and can also be found in other national legal systems.[156]

7.2.3.5 Fair Labelling and the Expressive Value of a Hierarchy of Blameworthiness

The previous subsections indicate that there are no compelling reasons to interpret Art. 25 (3) Rome Statute in the sense of a decreasing gradation of seriousness from *littera* (a) to (d). Consequently, the decision to adapt this hierarchy through the control theory is a policy choice of the chambers of the ICC.[157]

The last, but far from least reason that may speak in favour of the doctrine can be identified as its alleged expressive value. This refers to the supposed capability of the control theory and indirect perpetration through an organisation to appropriately describe the grave responsibility of decision makers behind international crimes.

The Groundwork for the Expressive Value Argument

Many commentators in international criminal law acknowledge how the expressive value or function of a conviction under the head of indirect perpetration through an organisation speaks in favour of this doctrine.[158] This is usually directly connected to notions of the principle of fair labelling.[159] However, these concepts are not among those traditionally cited as the purposes of criminal punishment and therefore require a closer look.[160]

---

[155] This is effectively argued by supporters of the *Anstiftungslösung* ("instigation solution") for decision makers of crimes in the German debate. Due to instigation pursuant to Section 26 GCC receiving no mitigation of punishment, it is argued that the German criminal law system does not acknowledge any distinction in blameworthiness between perpetration and instigation. This is held by: Díaz y García Conlledo 2017, pp 719–20; Herzberg 2000, pp 48–51; Herzberg 2009, p 580; Hruschka 1998, pp 607–8; Joecks 2017, § 25 mn. 159–60; Krey and Nuys 2009, pp 213, 222–3; Noltenius 2003, p 322; Renzikowski 1997, p 91; Rotsch 2000, p 561; Schild 2017, § 26 mn. 4; Zazcyk 1996, p 414; see also Puppe 2013, p 530, who highlights that in such cases, the full sentencing range of Section 26 GCC, i.e. of punishing the instigator as a perpetrator, should be used.

[156] In France, instigation is punished as perpetration and the instigator is at times seen as more blameworthy than the physical perpetrator because they presumably do not even have the courage to get their own hands dirty, see Weisser 2011, p 95. Spain and a range of Latin American criminal law systems recognize forms of "qualified participation" that receive the same punishment as perpetrators, see Maculan 2013, p 83.

[157] See also Steer 2017, p 307.

[158] *Ntaganda*, 30 March 2021, Separate opinion of Judge Luz del Carmen Ibáñez Carranza, para 224; Ohlin et al. 2013, p 725; Steer 2017, pp 380–3; van Sliedregt 2015, p 511; van Sliedregt 2012, p 81; Weigend 2015, p 552; See also Guilfoyle 2011, p 255 et seq.

[159] *Ntaganda*, 30 March 2021, Separate opinion of Judge Luz del Carmen Ibáñez Carranza, para 224; Guilfoyle 2011, pp 255, 260; Steer 2017, pp 380–1; van Sliedregt 2015, p 511.

[160] On the traditional theories of goals of punishment see e.g. Neubacher 2006, pp 967–9; Neubacher 2020, pp 25–9. However, on the gaining importance of expressive theories of punishment in international criminal law see Demko 2020, p 176 with further sources in fn. 2.

When referring to forms of responsibility,[161] fair labelling aims to ensure that the label of responsibility applied to a participant in a crime accurately describes their specific involvement.[162] The accuracy of this description includes the wrongfulness and severity of the involvement, which makes forms of responsibility an important tool in distinguishing between different forms of wrongdoing.[163] It has been stated that descriptive labels should be intelligible on a standalone basis, i.e. without relying on labels that are only understandable if their definition is known to the reader.[164] The scope of fair labelling is sometimes also defined as describing the offending behaviour to the public and differentiating that behaviour for the purposes of those working within the criminal justice system.[165]

Fair labelling in turn seems to relate to expressive justice, at least on the stage of international criminal law.[166] van Sliedregt describes the underlying rationale and connection between fair labelling and expressive justice and the majority opinion's conclusion on the hierarchy of blameworthiness as follows:

> Value is attached to fair labelling and the idea that international criminal justice is tasked with expressing a narrative. Fair labelling accounts for the advance of the normative approach to criminal participation and the desire to adhere to the distinction between those who are culpable as principals and those who are culpable as accessories. Stigmatization through principal status is important bearing in mind the denunciatory and educational function of punishment. Making clear who masterminded crimes by referring to him/her as a 'principal' who 'commits' crimes is important in communicating to victims and the international community as a whole who was the 'real' culprit.[167]

The narrative and expressive functions of punishment or, in a broader sense, criminal prosecution of international crimes is explored by an increasing number of

[161] The principle of fair labelling is usually and primarily debated with reference to substantive crimes, see e.g. Ashworth 2009, pp 78-80; Chalmers and Leverick 2008, p 217 et seq.; Simester et al. 2019, pp 32–3. However, as the debate shows, there is a strong tendency to value its concepts and ponderations with reference to the use and purpose of forms of liability in international criminal law.

[162] Granik 2015, p 990; Steer 2017, p 380.

[163] Chalmers and Leverick 2008, p 242; Steer 2017, pp 380–1. This corresponds to the principle of fair labelling when applied to substantive offences. In this regard, its purpose has been described as follows: "The law must make clear what sort of criminal each offender is-what the conviction is *for*." See Simester et al. 2019, p 33, italics in the original. See also Ashworth 2009, pp 78–80.

[164] Chalmers and Leverick 2008, p 222; Stewart 2014, p 334 (referring explicitly to forms of responsibility).

[165] Ashworth 2009, p 78; Chalmers and Leverick 2008, p 246.

[166] See e.g. Ohlin 2011, p 751 (speaking of "...the expressive role of properly declaring the international community's precise condemnation of the criminal activity..."); Stewart 2014, pp 334–5 connects the descriptive and expressive capabilities that play a role under fair labelling with the expressive potential of international criminal law. This connection between the two concepts is compelling because fair labels must be precise descriptions and, therefore, automatically lead to an appropriate expression of the actor's culpability.

[167] van Sliedregt 2015, p 511.

authors.[168] It is seldom directly connected to forms of liability, but such a connection follows from the general perspective of this theoretical approach to the *raisons d'être* of international criminal justice. As van Sliedregt describes, theories explored under the head of "expressive punishment" or "expressive justice" acknowledge a storytelling, narrative function of international criminal tribunals, as well as the function of expressing a denunciatory, stigmatising message about the people involved in international crimes.[169] Other authors describe the function of expressive justice as the communication of the historic truth, which also encompasses the public marking or labelling of acts as wrongful and the individualisation of responsibility in collective contexts.[170] Forms of responsibility with their descriptive reference to the actor's conduct naturally play an important role in this context.

The discussion about indirect perpetration through an organisation in German academia has always referred to these thoughts, albeit in vague and undefined terms.[171] Instead of references to fair labelling and expressive justice, the German national debate is rife with statements referring to the suitability of indirect perpetration through an organisation to "properly" or "adequately" express the wrongdoing of leaders behind international crimes.[172] These kind of references to the necessary "adequacy" of modes of liability can also be found in the debate in international criminal law.[173] Judge Howard Morrison pointedly described one aspect underlying these considerations by stating that:

> It is important that a criminal court produce judgments that can be understood by affected communities in terms of why the person is being held accountable for the crimes committed. It is also critical that the person him or herself can fully understand why he or she is charged with certain acts and why his or her acts attract criminal responsibility.[174]

This groundwork for fair labelling and expressive justice is recognized as a convincing argument in favour of indirect perpetration through an organisation and

[168] Demko 2020, p 176 et seq.; Drumbl 2007, pp 173–80; Sloane 2007, p 39–94; Wringe 2010, pp 119–33; extensively see Werkmeister 2015, p 272 et seq.

[169] van Sliedregt 2015, p 511. See also Steer 2017, pp 381–2. See also on the "disapproval function" of assigning responsibility for international crimes Demko 2020, p 188.

[170] See Werkmeister 2015, pp 286 et seq. (communication of historic truth in general), 293–4 (public labelling as wrongful conduct), 294–5 (individualisation of responsibility). See already on the aim of historic documentation Neubacher 2006, p 969.

[171] In the same vein Dubber and Hörnle 2014, p 323 ("There seems to be an intuition that this needs to be decided as a matter of fair labelling"). The use of vague terms instead of reference to the discussed principles may be due to the focus of national criminal law on individual perpetrators and single crimes in which theories of expressive justice and fair labelling have played a minor role thus far.

[172] See Chap. 2, Sect. 2.2.5. See also *Ntaganda*, 30 March 2021, Partly concurring opinion of Judge Chile Eboe-Osuji, para 36 describing Roxin's original approach as a "fair-labelling strategy".

[173] Ibid., Separate opinion of Judge Luz del Carmen Ibáñez Carranza, para 297; Separate opinion of Judge Howard Morrison on Mr Ntaganda's appeal paras 3, 14, 27; Cf. the analysis by Guilfoyle 2011, pp 255, 285.

[174] *Ntaganda*, 30 March 2021, Separate opinion of Judge Howard Morrison on Mr Ntaganda's appeal para 27.

a hierarchy of blameworthiness throughout international and German academia.[175] Therefore, despite the notions of expressive justice and fair labelling bearing some uncertainties as to their doctrinal role, it must be acknowledged that they have long played and continue to play an important role in the issue of leadership criminality.

This being said, it must be questioned whether fair labelling and the quest for expressive justice are compelling reasons for an interpretation of Art. 25 (3) Rome Statute in the sense of the majority approach at the ICC. Do the labels of commission liability and indirect perpetration through an organisation serve these purposes? Do they reliably convey to the international community, the victims, the participants in the crimes and other relevant groups that the individuals convicted under these labels are those who bear the highest responsibility?

Two Observations on Hierarchies of Blameworthiness and Their Expressive Function

As a basis for exploring the questions posed above, two observations must be made concerning the connection between hierarchies of blameworthiness and their expressive functions.

Firstly, exploring the expressive value of forms of responsibility as a reason for a hierarchy requires distinguishing reasons from consequences.

It is occasionally submitted that because of the higher blameworthiness of certain modes of liability, only their application to leadership figures behind mass atrocities would lead to the appropriate expression of their wrongdoing and to fair labelling.[176]

This argument can only be valid where the provisions unequivocally establish a system of perpetration and participation in which certain forms are unquestionably associated with lower responsibility. The most relevant indicators are provisions on facultative or obligatory mitigation of sentence and provisions of mitigated and limited punishment for attempts.[177] Another pointer would be the wording of a provision that only allows one interpretation, i.e., that chooses a particular system. As discussed above, none of these indicators exist in the Rome Statute.[178]

Under this premise, every argument relying on the heightened blameworthiness of commission necessarily becomes circular. One cannot establish the elevated blameworthiness of commission by pointing to its expressive value, which is based on its

175 This applies even to sceptics of the doctrines, such as van Sliedregt 2015, p 511; Weigend 2015, p 552. The same is true in the German debate, see e.g. Rotsch 2000, p 561, who, despite the manifold opposition to the figure, suspected that it would not lose its popularity within courts due to the "political explosiveness" of the involved cases. He referred to the trials of former officials of the German Democratic Republic in the Federal Republic of Germany. See also Krey and Nuys 2009, p 212 (speaking of a "legitimate concern").

176 Cf. Chap. 2, Sect. 2.2.5, observe how Roxin deduces the importance of the "central figure" not only directly from the wording but also concludes that the wording must lead to higher sentences only for perpetrators, despite the regulation of instigation to the contrary.

177 For the role of sentencing structures in fair labelling see Chalmers and Leverick 2008, p 243.

178 In German criminal law, a hierarchy can be deduced from the obligatory mitigation of sentence for the aider and abettor (Section 27 para 2 GCC). However, this does not allow conclusions on the relation between commission and instigation.

elevated blameworthiness. Where a legal regulation on the degrees of seriousness of forms of responsibility is missing, such a seriousness as a tool of fair labelling must follow from another factor. This observation leads us to a second point.

This second point is the linguistic, terminological dimension of fair labelling and modes of liability.

First and foremost, this means that where the law does not unequivocally prevision a hierarchical gradation of forms of responsibility, fair labelling and expressive justice become mostly a linguistic issue. Without clear and unequivocal guidance by the law, the choice of terms for the modes of liability becomes even more crucial for fair labelling. This is all the truer, given that the addressees of these theories are not only and primarily, lawyers. Instead, fair labelling and expressive justice aim to convey the appropriate message of the actor's wrongdoing to the international community and to the victims of international crimes. In other words, if the principle of fair labelling must "ensure that the label applicable to each offender accurately describes the wrongfulness and severity of his or her specific involvement",[179] but the law makes no statement concerning this severity, such a conclusion must be derived from the employed language itself.

Under this premise, the descriptive, terminological precision of modes of liability plays an outstanding role.[180] This descriptive precision is challenged by common knowledge and understanding, given that different people interpret terms differently. This becomes increasingly problematic in the ambit of international criminal law. The law is enforced through the ICC under the Rome Statute and concerns situations in many different countries. It will therefore necessarily be described and communicated in different languages. Thus, issues of translation may arise. Terms can be translated in different ways and every translation bears the potential of conveying something slightly different to the reader or listener of the other language. In this regard, precise descriptive terms may have advantages in comparison to broad abstract terms. It is conceivable that more precise descriptions can be translated more aptly, whereas broad abstract terms can potentially lead to more misunderstandings during their translation.

The linguistic precision of modes of liability must therefore be one of the guiding aspects in the further analysis. The forms of indirect perpetration through an organisation (and, underlying this, the commission of a crime) and ordering a crime must be analysed under this perspective.

---

[179] Steer 2017, p 380.

[180] It should be remembered that Claus Roxin's work with its reliance on the "central figure" (*Zentralgestalt*) and the terms of "committing", "instigating" and "aiding", which he found in the German criminal system, decisively shaped his reasoning for the doctrines of domination of the crime and indirect perpetration through an organisation. In describing the perpetrator as the central figure, he explicitly recurs to what he believes is the common understanding of a *Täter* (a perpetrator) in the German language; see Chap. 2, Sect. 2.2.2. The precision of the employed terminology is recognized e.g. by ibid., pp 381–2 and Weigend 2015, p 552, although these authors' evaluation of terminological precision is shaped more by the legal implications than the considerations that will be outlined in the following.

The Expressive Value of Indirect Perpetration Through an Organisation

Many scholars acknowledge the expressive value of indirect perpetration through an organisation. This is true for the international criminal law debate[181] but is also common—in less clear terms—in the German debate.[182]

Thoughts on the capability of perpetration/commission liability to properly express the wrongdoing of influential persons behind international crimes were already voiced by the Jerusalem District Court[183] and reign in Roxin's conception of the doctrines.[184] The ICC's chambers do not rely openly on such a view, instead mostly mentioning other reasons to justify their interpretation of Art. 25 (3) Rome Statute.[185] However, the doctrine's capability to contribute to "proper labelling" of the accused's responsibility was addressed by the appeals chamber in its *Lubanga* decision.[186] It was also heavily relied upon in the separate opinion of Judge del Carmen Ibáñez Carranza on the *Ntaganda* appeals judgment.[187] Furthermore, as briefly discussed in Chap. 3, it seems that the ICC follows teleological and policy considerations, primarily aiming at the adjudication of high-level decision makers and architects in its overall choice of a system.[188] It can therefore be suspected that this view on the high expressive value of the doctrine is shared by chambers of the ICC.

The belief in the expressive value of the form of indirect perpetration through an organisation is closely connected to the law's wording that such a person commits a crime through another. The label that a decision maker behind an international crime "committed" a war crime or genocide is perceived to best describe their central responsibility.

---

181 Burghardt 2010, pp 91–2; Kiss 2019, mn. 34–6; Lanza 2021, p 248; Minkova 2021, p 238 (although being sceptic about the mode's value to describe the relationship between the perpetrators); Ohlin 2022, p 252; Steer 2017, pp 378, 382; van Sliedregt 2015, p at 511; van Sliedregt 2012, p 81; Weigend 2015, p 552; Werle and Burghardt 2014a, pp 858–9 (hinting *inter alia* to the particularities of international crimes as forms of collective violence); in a similar vein see Jain 2014, p 135; Olásolo 2009, p 142.

182 Cf. Chap. 2, Sects. 2.2.5 and 2.5. Admittedly, the points of reference for German scholars are different because their object of comparison to indirect perpetration through an organisation is instigation, not ordering. That the precise wording of the German *Anstiftung* (instigation) is one of the reasons why scholars feel reluctant to accept this as a suitable mode of liability for leadership criminality was suspected earlier, see Hruschka 1998, p 608. Hruschka outlined that things would perhaps have developed differently if the German mode would still be called "*intellektueller Urheber*" (intellectual author) as it was in the 19th century.

183 District Court of Jerusalem, *Judgment Against Karl Adolf Eichmann—Unofficial Translation*, 40/61, mo. 197.

184 See Chap. 2, Sect. 2.2.5.

185 See Chap. 3, Sect. 3.3.1 on the arguments employed by the ICC in the conception of the doctrine.

186 ICC, *The Prosecutor v. Thomas Lubanga Dyilo*, Appeals Judgment, 1 December 2014, ICC-01/04-01/06 A 5, para 462.

187 *Ntaganda*, 30 March 2021, Separate Opinion of Judge Luz del Carmen Ibáñez Carranza, paras 224, 297, 314; Kiss 2019, mn. 34.

188 See Chap. 3, Sect. 3.3.1.3.

This book has outlined a range of issues pertaining to the theory of indirect perpetration through an organisation, some of which raise doubts as to the expressive worth of the doctrine.

Starting with the legal-technical dimension of the concept, it has been established that the doctrine is contentious, not only in German national law but even more so on the stage of international criminal law. The latter is even more understandable than the former, given the different legal backgrounds of scholars and practitioners in this field. However, more importantly, uncertainties and confusion reign within the application and scholarly description of the doctrine in international criminal law. As previously seen, even the concept and role of "control" within the doctrine are contentious and are sometimes used in different ways.[189] Additionally, no clear guideline as to the difference between indirect perpetration and indirect co-perpetration is discernible, given that in a number of cases one doctrine was applied where the other would have seemingly fit better.[190] It has been submitted that it is the technical complexity of the doctrine which leads to such uncertainties. Guilfoyle even argues that the doctrine would display the physical executioners as less responsible because—technically speaking—the law puts them in a situation comparable to that of innocent agents.[191] Although this was not intended by the scholars who conceived the doctrine, Guilfoyle's perception should serve as a reminder of a central problem: even among legal scholars, it is far from clear how the control theory and indirect perpetration through an organisation should work and what they convey about the persons involved at different stages of the crime. It is highly questionable whether such a doctrine can be expected to contribute greatly to fair labelling and expressive justice when it is not interpreted and understood uniformly by the lawyers employing and developing it. Stewart described this in honest terms when he stated:

> In fact, I suspect that, like me, many senior practitioners within this discipline also struggle with the concept…[192]

The next point concerns the stylistic and textual presentation of responsibility for crimes in ICC judgments. As mentioned, convictions under the Rome Statute are logically convictions for being guilty of a crime, not a form of responsibility. This can read, for example as:

> **GUILTY** of murder as a crime against humanity (Article 7(1)(a) of the Statute), as a direct perpetrator under Art. 25 (3)(a) of the Statute…[193]

With regards to the expressive value of the term indirect perpetration, some authors have argued that the worth of employing the doctrine lies in labelling those mainly responsible as "*genocidaires*" instead of persons who, e.g., assist a *genocidaire*.[194]

---

[189] See Chap. 3, Sect. 3.4.

[190] See Chap. 3, Sect. 3.4.

[191] Guilfoyle 2011, pp 265–6, 275, 276.

[192] Stewart 2014, pp 334–5.

[193] *Ntaganda*, 8 July 2019, VII. Disposition.

[194] Steer 2017, p 378.

However, we can see that this is not how ICC judgments function in practice, and it is submitted here that this practice is for the better. Instead of the personal labelling of the convict as a "*genocidaire*" or war criminal, the ICC's verdicts convict individuals for being guilty of a crime and display the convict's responsibility in descriptive terms. The convict does not assume the personal attribute of *being* a war criminal, but instead they are guilty of a crime *as* a direct perpetrator, instigator etc. This difference, marginal (and perhaps unintentional) as it may be, shows that the convict is still a human being, although one who has assumed great guilt through their participation in serious crimes. However, this preferable way in which ICC judgments list and describe the convict's guilt and form of responsibility, leads to doubts concerning the expressive value of forms such as indirect perpetration through an organisation.

The ability of such a verdict to understandably describe the enormous responsibility of a decision maker and leader of a criminal organisation is questionable.

First, the judgments' disposition will not contain the full name of the doctrine because "through an organisation" is not considered part of the legal denomination of the mode of liability. Instead, the person will be convicted as an "indirect perpetrator". The role of the organisation does not appear in the disposition.[195] Equally irrelevant is the term "principal", which usually does not appear in verdicts.[196]

The worth of the term "indirect perpetrator" is an issue of its own. There is no doubt that for scholars who affirm the expressive value of labelling, the label of "indirect perpetrator" and the underlying term of committing a crime, carry a descriptive weight, tantamount to assigning the main responsibility for a crime. However, the descriptive value of the form of responsibility is doubted by many other scholars, equally skilled in questions of systems of imputation of responsibility.

When the focus shifts from legal academics and practitioners to laypersons, the expressive value of the doctrine becomes even more questionable.

The Oxford Dictionary defines perpetration as "the act of committing a crime or doing something wrong or evil". To commit is defined as "to do something wrong or illegal". These terms contain very little description of how and under which circumstances a person committed the wrong or evil. Perhaps the most useful definition of "indirect" is "not done directly; done through somebody/something else". Therefore, the linguistic descriptive possibilities of "indirect perpetration" amount to the

[195] Even if it did, its descriptive value for a lay person would be doubtful. The term principal may always play a role in the judgment itself, but that concerns the storytelling, narrative function of the judgment. A function that can also be fulfilled under the application of other modes of liability because the organisational framework of mass atrocities will always play a role in international criminal judgments, regardless of the charged forms of responsibility.

[196] At best, "principal" will be associated with the adjectives "most important" or "main". This could have a certain value, although the descriptive value of the terms "perpetrator" or "perpetration" will be questioned below. Regardless, such a use would potentially lead to the kind of confusion that scholars sometimes associate with the doctrine. What if several high-level participants are convicted as "principals" of the same crimes? Due to the conceivable expressive value of the term, the reader would have to assume that all of them were the "main" or "most important" actor behind the crime. Additionally, a physical perpetrator who only committed a single crime will also be a "principal". Thus, while the category "principal" might have some potential for fair labelling, it is not too promising in the quest for intelligible expressive justice.

statement that someone "did something wrong or illegal, not directly but through somebody else".

Based on this, it is highly questionable whether the label "indirect perpetration" bears much descriptive value for judicial lay persons at all. It can be assumed that the term is instead perceived for what it is: a legal technical term which is immediately associated by lay persons with the legal profession and the expectation that the underlying considerations are legal technicalities.[197] This may be somewhat less true for the term "commission", which could be associated with a close connection between the actor and the crime. However, it seems questionable whether the statement "Person A committed war crimes" actually bears a heightened descriptive value for the addressees of the judgment. This is especially true, given that Person B, who was the hands-on perpetrator of war crimes, would equally be described with the words "committed war crimes".[198] Regarding this latter point, Guilfoyle's abovementioned criticism may prove accurate.

In general, it seems that the terms of perpetration and, to a lesser extent, commission do not carry a noteworthy descriptive value when it comes to identifying the seriousness of contributions to mass atrocities. The additions of "indirect" perpetration and commission "through another" provide no assistance. In both cases, it is conceivable that a person unfamiliar with the legal intricacies will have little to no accurate associations when reading or listening to such formulations.[199] The term "indirect" may further complicate matters, as it could be understood by a lay person as a limitation to the leader's influence or responsibility.[200]

Additionally, one should not forget that the terms of indirect perpetration and commission through another must be translated into the languages of affected communities. A task which will often complicate matters because the terms are

---

[197] In the same vein, see Stewart 2014, pp 334–5. Also note that the term "perpetration" is employed nowhere in the statute, potentially further obstructing any meaningful association by a lay person trying to make sense of a judgment that relies on such terminology.

[198] This issue is inherent to all approaches to indirect perpetration through an organisation. Cf. on this Orozco López 2021, p 239.

[199] In this regard, Stewart points out how, when reporting on the ICC's charges against Laurent Gbagbo, the BBC had to place the term "indirect co-perpetration" in quotation marks. Stewart remarks that the accused and the victims from Côte d'Ivoire would have problems making sense of this term, see Stewart 2014, p 334; referring to https://www.bbc.com/news/world-africa-15960254. Accessed 6 April 2023. A similar example can be found in an article by the Guardian about the acquittal of Gbagbo and Blé Goudé in 2019. In it, the journalist referred to the charges by stating that they "included ordering murder and gang-rape" and did not recur to the term of indirect co-perpetration, see https://www.theguardian.com/world/2019/jan/15/ex-ivory-coast-president-laurent-gbagbo-acquitted-at-icc. Accessed 6 April 2023. Similar considerations have also been raised by Judge Christine Van den Wyngaert when she doubted that anyone in or outside of the D.R. Congo could have known about the "elaborate and peculiar" form of indirect co-perpetration or the control theory, see *Chui*, 18 December 2012, Concurring Opinion of Judge Christine Van den Wyngaert, para 20 (note, however, that her criticism focuses more on the accused and his possible prior knowledge of the form of responsibility).

[200] This concern was voiced by William Schabas at the online event "International Criminal Responsibility: Current Challenges and Future Perspectives", hosted by the British Institute for International and Comparative Law on 12 May 2021.

rather abstract and already connected to a range of legal systems and their use within them.

From the linguistic viewpoint, the descriptive value of indirect perpetration through an organisation is therefore questionable.

Moreover, it was highlighted in Chap. 3 how the scope of positions, influence and conduct that can lead to responsibility as an indirect perpetrator based on control over an organisation is relatively undefined.[201] Additionally, the analysis of the JCE doctrine and its comparison to ordering under *ad hoc* jurisprudence has demonstrated how certain doctrines can blur the descriptive capabilities of forms of responsibility, where different contributions fall under the same head of liability.[202] Given that the margins of indirect perpetration through an organisation are not entirely defined, this form runs the same risk. In contrast to the JCE doctrine, it does not acknowledge various contributions as necessary conduct.[203] However, the terminology itself—indirect perpetration through an organisation—does not clearly explain that it was the actor's power and influence over the members of the criminal organisation that led to the commission of crimes because they gave a relevant instruction.

As far as the descriptive value of this form of responsibility is concerned, the terminology of indirect perpetration seems of little help. It does not, by itself, imply any of the form's requirements. It also does not expressly mention or identify the conduct of the actor, despite there being identifiable behaviour leading to the commission of crimes: the order, given by the indirect perpetrator to the members of their organisation.[204]

The Expressive Value of Ordering a Crime

Under the interpretation of Art. 25 (3) Rome Statute, which is followed here, ordering a crime is a form of "accessory" liability, which must be taken into account. As the last ordinary meaning of "accessory", the Oxford Dictionary defines "a person who helps somebody to commit a crime or who knows about it and protects the person from the police". If understood as reflecting the widespread common association of the word "accessory", this definition could cast a doubt over the expressive value of all forms of accessory liability. However, as outlined regarding the term "principal", it is a reasonable practice not to use it in verdicts. As far as expressive justice is concerned, the terms principal and accessory do not contribute much value because they contain no information on the specific wrongdoing for which responsibility is attributed.

---

[201] See Chap. 3, Sects. 3.1.2.1–3.1.2.3 and 3.3.2.

[202] See Chap. 5, Sect. 5.2.4.1.

[203] However, this problem may arise with the combined mode of indirect co-perpetration, under which any sufficiently important contribution can lead to responsibility. Note on this the criticism by Morrison *Ntaganda*, 30 March 2021, Separate opinion of Judge Howard Morrison on Mr. Ntaganda's appeal, para 28, who states that through the different legal technicalities of the doctrine, the link between the actor and the crime might even appear weaker than it was; see also para 41, which speaks of "mislabelling facts".

[204] On the seldom discussed conduct element of indirect perpetration through an organisation, see Chap. 3, Sect. 3.1.2.5.

Consequently, while the terms could potentially play a role in expressing and categorizing the degree of the actor's wrongdoing, it is a laudable practice that they do not. They would only serve as a limited, two-fold categorisation, the associative capacity of which can be questioned for the term "accessory".

This leaves the term "ordering" to be analysed for its expressive value. The Oxford Dictionary defines an order (in the relevant context) as "something that somebody is told to do by somebody in authority". Another common definition for an order is "an authoritative command or instruction". Notwithstanding the manifold uses of the verb "to order" in the English language, there is a good chance that a person who reads that somebody is,

> **GUILTY** of murder as a crime against humanity (Article 7(1)(a) of the Statute), for ordering the crime under Art. 25 (3)(b) of the Statute…

will immediately have certain ideas about the wrongdoing of the convict. A certain authority of the person who gives the order is an inherent part of the linguistic concept of "ordering something". Therefore, even lay persons who read or hear such a verdict will associate something with it that is very close to the legal concept. More importantly, the reader also has the chance to immediately understand the wrongfulness of the conduct for which responsibility is attributed to the convict. They told somebody to commit a serious crime while invoking their authority over them. The gravity of this is understandable to any reader because the invocation of authority will—for many—be inherent in the word "order". Additionally, most people will immediately associate the term with the social-psychological, and perhaps legal-disciplinary character that an "order" has. One does not have to be a soldier to realise that it is difficult to reject an "order", and that the person giving such orders therefore assumes a grave responsibility if these orders directly lead to or even explicitly instruct the commission of crimes.

The descriptive potential of the mode of "ordering" may have been one of the reasons for including the form in Art. 2 para. 2 CCL 10, and for its subsequent use as one of the more blameworthy forms of participation under this provision.[205]

Later, the intuitive association of a certain seriousness or blameworthiness with the terminology of someone "ordering the commission of a crime" may have inspired the drafters of several international criminal and humanitarian law provisions. As seen earlier, the Geneva Conventions, the ILC Draft Code and the statutes of the ICTR and ICTY seemingly equated the commission of crimes with the ordering of crimes in specific provisions.[206] These wordings did not make it into the interpretation of the forms of responsibility under the respective statutes.[207] However, they serve as a reminder that "ordering" is not only a technically obvious term in the military context of early international humanitarian law, but also a precise description of the type of influence exercised by persons in positions of power. Based on this descriptive value, it is a logical conclusion to apply a form of responsibility that is denominated

---

205 Cf. Chap. 4, Sect. 4.6.

206 See Introduction to Part II and Sect. 7.1.1.

207 See Chap. 5.

"ordering a crime" to leadership responsibility.[208] The same consideration apparently influenced early arrest warrant decisions and prosecution documents which relied on ordering as the relevant mode of liability under which alleged high-level criminals were charged.[209]

The establishment of the control theory and indirect perpetration through an organisation pushed the early acknowledgment of the expressive value of ordering aside and led to the marginalisation of this mode of liability. Since then, ordering has been compared to indirect perpetration through an organisation, and statements concerning the relation between the two modes have often been imported from German national law.[210]

German academic literature does not explicitly recognize or rely on expressive value and fair labelling considerations. However, such thoughts have always played a role in the history of indirect perpetration through an organisation in Germany.

The Jerusalem District Court stated that known forms of liability in national criminal law could not describe Adolf Eichmann's involvement in the crimes and therefore chose to convict him as a perpetrator.[211] A similar statement can be found in Roxin's original writings on the matter.[212] Proceeding from this, Roxin developed his notion of indirect perpetration through an organisation and was met with much support. Apart from certain arguments concerning the system of perpetration and participation in German criminal law, the traditional German solution always hinged on the impression that the other pertinent mode of liability could not properly express the wrongdoing of the Eichmanns and Himmlers of Nazi Germany, and of course, of Hitler. In the opinion of many commentators, it would not do those mainly responsible justice to label them as "instigators" pursuant to Section 26 GCC.[213] Even some scholars who oppose indirect perpetration through an organisation have recognized that convicting high-level leaders of mass atrocities under the alternative of "*Anstiftung*" (instigation) could contribute to general unease due to its wording.[214] Many scholars believe that instigation is shaped by certain features, such as the necessity of the instigator having to search for and convince a physical perpetrator, or the final decision over the commission of the crime having to be left to the physical

[208] As previously mentioned, other authors have endorsed assigning more significance to the form of ordering a crime, acknowledging its existence in international criminal law and its potential, see e.g. Vest 2014, p 304; Vest 2011, p 365, stating that the approach to "committing or ordering the commission" would have allowed for an elegant solution to the issue of leadership criminality. See also Cryer 2004, pp 244–7.

[209] See Chap. 6, Sect. 6.3.1.

[210] See above Sect. 7.1.3.

[211] *Judgment Against Adolf Eichmann*, No. 197.

[212] Roxin 2019, p 280.

[213] See only Roxin 2011, pp 198–9; Ambos 2004, pp 593–4. Cf. also Chap. 2, Sect. 2.2.5.

[214] Krey and Nuys 2009, p 212 (calling this a "legitimate concern"); Hruschka 1998, p at 608 suggests that a different wording for instigation may change this wide-spread unease to use instigation in such cases.

perpetrator. None of this would apply to typical situations of indirect perpetration through an organisation, or so it is asserted.[215]

It has been demonstrated that these legal arguments cannot be sustained. As far as they concern the suggested difference between instigation and indirect perpetration, they convey an incorrect impression of the indirect perpetrator's influence over the specific situations.[216] Under the theories of fair labelling and expressive justice, such arguments can be pertinent where they refer to a deficiency of a form of responsibility in expressing the wrongfulness of certain conduct.

However, for the purposes of this book, it is irrelevant whether instigation could be considered to properly express the details of the wrongdoing of a leader behind an international crime. The focus of this book is the form of ordering a crime in international criminal law.

Responsibility for ordering a crime does not exist in German criminal law and has therefore never been the standard to which the (alleged) expressive value of indirect perpetration has been compared.[217] The question must therefore be whether the reservations which have been voiced in the German academic debate concerning the expressive value of instigation would still be valid when referring to ordering?

This seems very unlikely considering the descriptive value of the term ordering. It is conceivable that people will associate a less decisive, or at least a very personal form of influence over the physical perpetrator with the term instigation. It is far from unthinkable to picture an instigator as someone with malign intent, but without any other powers, who relies on persuasion and manipulation to, after many attempts and different argumentative or manipulative approaches, finally talks someone else into committing a crime. There is no doubt that the descriptive value of instigation would then be limited and unfit for decision makers of international crimes. This is not what the mode of ordering conveys in terms of its descriptive label. Instead, with its linguistic (and legal) implication of the use of authority to command others, ordering a crime creates exactly the kind of label, which many commentators in the German debate determine to be missing with instigation. Namely, that the person in the background has superiority (authority), leading to a considerable amount of psychological pressure on the physical perpetrator, thus resulting in the ordered person acting as they are told.

Admittedly, ordering does not necessarily imply the disposition of the ordering actor over a larger number of potential perpetrators, nor does it imply that the crime

---

[215] Roxin 2019, Chpt. 12 mn. 400; see also for the alleged "certainty" Roxin 2003, § 25 mn. 114 (but see on this concept's invalidity Chap. 3, Sect. 3.3.2.3. Schroeder asserts that within such an organisation, there is little restraining force keeping the physical perpetrator from committing the crime, which would be different with typical situations of instigation (Schroeder 1995, p 178). Ambos comes to similar conclusions based on such arguments and rejects *instigation* as a viable alternative for international criminal law (Ambos 2004, pp 593–4).

[216] See Chap. 4, Sects. 4.3.2. and 4.3.3.

[217] Note that, when arguing for a systemic view on indirect perpetration through an organisation in international criminal law, Ambos still compares this form to instigation, cf. Ambos 2004, pp 593–4.

will be committed with any certainty. However, this is irrelevant. First, because fungibility is irrelevant for the commission of specific crimes, and certainty is no suitable or reasonable criterion to describe the influence of the person in the background. Second, because from a linguistic viewpoint, indirect perpetration does not convey this either.

Reservations concerning instigation as a solution for decision maker criminality in mass atrocities may have some justification,[218] but they fail when confronted with the terminology of the mode of ordering a crime.

It is suggested that a precise term like ordering also bears much potential for unequivocal translations. The Rome Statute in its official translations, for example, speaks of "*ordener*" (Spanish), "*ordonner*" (French), "*anordnen*" (German) "*ordenar*" (Portuguese). These translations have a common stem and are likely to raise associations comparable to those described above with a view to the English wording. That this will be true for translations into other languages, such as those of the affected communities, can only be assumed here. However, given that every society in the world is probably familiar with relationships between superiors and subordinates, such an assumption is not too fanciful. Likewise, the difficulty of rejecting a person's instruction, if that person acts with authority, is most likely also known to every human society. Therefore, it can be assumed that most languages will provide for a precise and evocative translation of the term "ordering".

This intuitive association with the term ordering cannot even be ignored by chambers of the ICC. Decisions like the trial chamber judgment against Dominic Ongwen show, how it is natural to resort to the (non-technical) term of ordering, when describing the conduct of the accused, despite categorizing it under another form of responsibility.[219]

It can therefore be concluded that the form of responsibility of "ordering" is highly suitable to convey an impression, a label of the wrongdoing of decision makers who use their authority over others to make them commit crimes.

Conclusion

If the law must reflect who the real culprit is, it must resort to clear and unequivocal terms. This goal is better accomplished by using the term "ordering" than through the use of "indirect perpetration" or "commission through another". Ordering provides for a pictorial, easily accessible description of the actor's conduct and of their implied

---

[218] In this regard, Judge Fulford's separate opinion in the Lubanga trial judgment comes to mind, in which he states that "particular domestic considerations" made the doctrine of indirect perpetration through an organisation necessary in Germany (see *Lubanga*, 14 March 2012, Separate Opinion of Judge Adrian Fulford, para 10). There is some truth in this argument concerning the expressive value and label of instigation. In contrast to the form of ordering as available under the Rome Statute, instigation may indeed lack the possibility of adequately describing and conveying the blameworthiness of the actor.

[219] Cf. the descriptions of the acts of the accused in *Ongwen*, 4 February 2021, paras 2862, 2913, 2916, 2963, 3010, 3093, 3110.

authority. Indirect perpetration and commission through another convey an impression of complex legal technicalities but not of the most blameworthy focal point of a leader's conduct.

Therefore, contrary to what is asserted by the majority approach in international criminal law, fair labelling and expressive value do not speak in favour of a hierarchy of blameworthiness with forms of commission liability at the top.

7.2.4 No Reasons for a Hierarchy of Blameworthiness as Applied by the Majority Opinion

Based on the foregoing, it must be concluded that there are no compelling arguments leading to the interpretation of Art. 25 (3) as establishing a strict hierarchy of seriousness from *lit.* (a) to (d). In particular, there is no reason to believe that only the forms of commission are the most blameworthy types of participation. Instead, liability for ordering a crime should be given the same status as one of the highly blameworthy forms of responsibility.

7.3 Preliminary Conclusion

Indirect perpetration through an organisation developed as a makeshift solution in German national criminal law to deal with decision makers of mass atrocities in a system of perpetration and participation that was originally made to adjudicate individual crimes in everyday criminality. By contrast, ordering developed as a mode of liability, specifically designed for the ambit of international criminal law, and was applied to high- and mid-level decision makers in this ambit.

The comparison of indirect perpetration through an organisation and ordering further shows a complete overlap of both forms as far as the legal requirements of indirect perpetration through an organisation are concerned. There is no conceivable case under indirect perpetration through an organisation that would not be covered by ordering. Ordering, in turn, is slightly broader, but only to a limited practical relevance. Where this broader scope becomes relevant, there is no doubt that the ordering person's conduct is as dangerous and reprehensible as that of the typical leader of a criminal organisation.[220] It has been further established, that there is no difference between the influence of an indirect perpetrator who controls an organisation and thus, supposedly, controls the commission of the crime and a person who orders the commission of crimes. Control over the crime, as it is interpreted by the ICC, is an illusion and the actual influence that is exercised by an "indirect perpetrator through

[220] See above Sect. 7.1.2.

an organisation" is tantamount to the authority exercised by a person who orders the commission of crimes.[221]

Furthermore, as has been outlined above, the Rome Statute does not envisage a hierarchy of blameworthiness in Art. 25 (3) Rome Statute that would treat commission liability under *lit.* (a) as the single most blameworthy form of responsibility. No compelling legal reasons for such a hierarchy can be deduced from the law of the Statute. The principles of fair labelling and expressive justice contradict such a hierarchy. Under such considerations, ordering a crime bears the greater potential to adequately convey and describe the wrongdoing of decision makers in the ambit of international criminal law.

Consequently, indirect perpetration through an organisation is an unnecessary import into the interpretation of the Rome Statute, because of the explicit criminalization of ordering a crime under Art. 25 (3) (b).

References

Aksenova M (2016) Complicity in International Criminal Law. Hart Publishing, Oxford

Ambos K (2004) Der Allgemeine Teil des Völkerstrafrechts. Duncker & Humblot, Berlin

Ambos K (2013) Treatise on International Criminal Law—Volume I: Foundations and General Part. Oxford University Press, Oxford

Ambos K (2016) Art. 25. In: The Rome Statute of the International Criminal Court—A Commentary. C.H. Beck/Hart/Nomos, Munich

Ambos K (2018) Internationales Strafrecht. C. H. Beck, Munich

Ashworth A (2009) Principles of Criminal Law. Oxford University Press, Oxford

Bantekas I (2002) Principles of direct and superior responsibility in International Humanitarian Law. Manchester University Press, Manchester

Block J (2022) Ordering as an Alternative to Indirect Co-Perpetration—Observations on the Ntaganda Case. Journal of International Criminal Justice 20:717–735

Burghardt B (2008) Die Vorgesetztenverantwortlichkeit im völkerrechtlichen Straftatsystem. BWV Berliner Wissenschafts-Verlag, Berlin

Burghardt B (2010) Modes of Participation and their Role in a General Concept of Crimes under International Law. In: Burchard C, Triffterer O, Vogel J (eds) The Review Conference and the Future of the International Criminal Court—Proceedings of the First AIDP Symposium for Young Penalists in Tübingen, Germany, co-organized by the AIDP YP Committee. Kluwer Law International, Alphen aan den Rijn, 81–98

Chalmers J, Leverick F (2008) Fair Labelling in Criminal Law. The Modern Law Review 71:217–246

Cryer R (2004) General Principles of Liability in International Criminal Law. In: McGoldrick D, Rowe P (eds) The Permanent International Criminal Court—Legal and Policy Issues. Hart Publishing, Oxford, 233–262

Cryer R, Robinson D, Vasiliev S (2019) An Introduction to International Criminal Law and Procedure. Cambridge University Press, Cambridge

Damgaard C (2008) Individual Criminal Responsibility for Core International Crimes—Selected Pertinent Issues. Springer, Berlin

Demko D (2020) An Expressive Theory of International Punishment for International Crimes. In: Jessberger F, Geneuss J (eds) Why Punish Perpetrators of Mass Atrocities. Cambridge University Press, Cambridge, 176–195

[221] See above Sect. 7.1.3.

Díaz y García Conlledo M (2017) Das Handeln im Rahmen eines organisatorischen Machtapparates: Täterschaft oder Teilnahme? Goltdammer's Archiv 711–720
Dörr O (2012) Article 31 General rule of interpretation. In: Vienna Convention on the Law of Treaties—A Commentary. Springer, Heidelberg
Drumbl M (2007) Atrocity, Punishment, and International Law. Cambridge University Press, Cambridge
Dubber MD, Hörnle T (2014) Criminal Law—A Comparative Approach. Oxford University Press, Oxford
Eser A (2002) Individual Criminal Responsibility. In: Cassesse A, Gaeta P, Jones JRWD (eds) The Rome Statute of the International Criminal Court—A Commentary. Oxford University Press, Oxford, 767–823
Finnin S (2012) Elements of Accessorial Modes of Liability—Article 25 (3) (b) and (c) of the Rome Statute of the International Criminal Court. Martinus Nijhoff Publishers, Leiden
Gil Gil AG, Maculan E (2015) Current Trends in the Definition of 'Perpetrator' by the International Criminal Court: From the Decision on the Confirmation of Charges in the *Lubanga* case to the *Katanga* judgment. Leiden Journal of International Law 28:349–371
Goy B (2012) Individual Criminal Responsibility before the International Criminal Court—A Comparison with the Ad Hoc Tribunals. International Criminal Law Review 12:1–70
Granik M (2015) Indirect Perpetration Theory: A Defence. Leiden Journal of International Law 28:977–992
Guilfoyle D (2011) Responsibility for Collective Atrocities: Fair Labelling and Approaches to Commission in International Criminal Law. Current Legal Problems 64:255–286
Heine G, Weisser B (2019) Vor §§ 25ff. In: Schönke/Schröder-StGB. C.H. Beck Munich
Herzberg RD (2000) Mittelbare Täterschaft und Anstiftung in formalen Organisationen. In: Amelung K (ed) Individuelle Verantwortung und Beteiligungsverhältnisse bei Straftaten in bürokratischen Organisationen des Staates, der Wirtschaft und der Gesellschaft. Pro Universitate, Sinzheim, 33–53
Herzberg RD (2009) Das Fujimori-Urteil: Zur Beteiligung des Befehlsgebers an den Verbrechen seines Machtapparates. Zeitschrift für internationale Strafrechtsdogmatik 11:576–580
Herzig A (2013) Die Tatherrschaftslehre in der Rechtsprechung des Internationalen Strafgerichtshofs. Zeitschrift für internationale Strafrechtsdogmatik 189–200
Hruschka J (1998) Regreßverbot, Anstiftungsbegriff und die Konsequenzen. Zeistschrift für die gesamte Strafrechtswissenschaft 110:581–639
Jain N (2014) Perpetrators and Accessories in International Criminal Law—Individual Modes of Responsibility for Collective Crimes. Hart Publishing, Oxford
Jessberger F, Geneuss J (2008) On the Application of a Theory of Indirect Perpetration in *Al Bashir*. Journal of International Criminal Justice 6:853–869
Joecks W (2017) § 25. In: Münchner Kommentar zum Strafgesetzbuch: StGB, Band I §§ 1–37. C.H. Beck Munich
Khan KA (2016) Article 78. In: The Rome Statute of the International Criminal Court—A Commentary. C.H. Beck, Munich
Kiss A (2019) Indirect Commission. In: de Hemptinne J, Roth R, van Sliedregt E (eds) Modes of Liability in International Criminal Law. Cambridge University Press, Cambridge, 30–57
Kress C (1999) Die Kristallisation eines Allgemeinen Teil des Völkerstrafrechts: Die Allgemeinen Prinzipien des Strafrechts im Statut des Internationalen Strafgerichtshofs. Humanitäres Völkerrecht—Journal of International Law of Peace and Armed Conflict (HuV—JILPAC) 12:4–10
Kress C (2006) Claus Roxin's Lehre von der Organisationsherrschaft und das Völkerstrafrecht. Goltdammer's Archiv 304–310
Krey V, Nuys M (2009) Der Täter hinter dem Täter—oder die Liebe der Strafrechtler zum Glasperlenspiel. In: Böse M, Sternberg-Lieben D (eds) Grundlagen des Straf- und Strafverfahrensrechts: Festschrift für Knut Amelung zum 70 Geburtstag. Duncker & Humblot, Berlin, 203–223
Lanza G (2021) Indirect Perpetration and Organisationsherrschaftslehre. Duncker & Humblot, Berlin

Maculan E (2013) La fertilización cruzada jurisprudencial y los modelos de responsabilidad—Acordes y desacuerdos en la jurisprudencia latinoamericana. In: Gil Gil A, Maculan E (eds) Intervención Delictiva y Derecho Penal Internacional—Reglas de atribución de la responsabilidad en crímenes internacionales. Dykinson, Madrid, 207–233
Militello V (2007) The Personal Nature of Individual Criminal Responsibility and the ICC Statute. Journal of International Criminal Justice 5:941–952
Minkova LG (2021) Expressing what? The stigmatization of the defendant and the ICC's institutional interests in the Ongwen case. Leiden Journal of International Law 34:223–245
Neubacher F (2006) Strafzwecke und Völkerstrafrecht. Neue Juristische Wochenschrift 966–970
Neubacher F (2020) Criminology of International Crimes. In: Jessberger F, Geneuss J (eds) Why Punish Perpetrators of Mass Atrocities? Cambridge University Press, Cambridge, 25–44
Noltenius B (2003) Kriterien der Abgrenzung von Anstiftung und mittelbarer Täterschaft Europäischer Verlag der Wissenschaften, Frankfurt am Main
Office WCR (2010) Modes of Liability and the Mental Element—Analyzing the Early Jurisprudence of the International Criminal Court
Ohlin JD (2011) Joint Intentions to Commit International Crimes. Chicago Journal of International Law 11:693–753
Ohlin JD (2022) The Hierarchy of Blameworthiness. In: Jessberger F, Vormbaum M, Burghardt B (eds) Strafrecht und Systemunrecht. Mohr Siebeck, Tübingen, 247–256
Ohlin JD, van Sliedregt E, Weigend T (2013) Assessing the Control-Theory. Leiden Journal of International Law 26:725–746
Olásolo H (2009) The Criminal Responsibility of Senior Political and Military Leaders as Principals to International Crimes. Hart Publishing, Portland
Olásolo H, Carnero Rojo E (2015) Forms of Accessorial Liability under Article 25(3)(b) and (c). In: Stahn C (ed) The Law and Practice of the International Criminal Court. Oxford University Press, Oxford, 557–591
Orozco López HD (2021) Roxins mittelbare Täterschaft kraft organisatorischer Machtapparate—Eine kritische Analyse. Zeitschrift für internationale Strafrechtsdogmatik 233–248
Puppe I (2013) Die Architektur der Beteiligungsformen. Goltdammer's Archiv 514–536
Rastan R (2009) Review of ICC Jurisprudence 2008. Northwestern Journal of International Human Rights 7:261–298
Renzikowski J (1997) Restriktiver Täterbegriff und fahrlässige Beteiligung. Mohr Siebeck, Tübingen
Rotsch T (2000) Tatherrschaft kraft Organisationsherrschaft? Zeitschrift für die gesamte Strafrechtswissenschaft 112:518–562
Roxin C (2003) Strafrecht Allgemeiner Teil Band II Besondere Erscheinungsformen der Straftat. C. H. Beck, Munich
Roxin C (2011) Crimes as Part of Organized Power Structures. Journal of International Criminal Justice 9:191–205
Roxin C (2019) Täterschaft und Tatherrschaft. De Gruyter, Berlin
Sadat L, Jolly J (2014) Seven Canons of ICC Treaty Interpretation: Making Sense of Article 25's Rorschach Blot. Leiden Journal of International Law 27:755–788
Schild W (2017) § 26. In: Nomos Kommentar Strafgesetzbuch. Nomos, Baden-Baden
Schlösser J (2004) Soziale Tatherrschaft—Ein Beitrag zur Frage der Täterschaft in organisatorischen Machtapparaten. Duncker & Humblot, Berlin
Schmidhäuser E (1982) Strafrecht Allgemeiner Teil. J. C. B. Mohr (Paul Siebeck), Tübingen
Schroeder F-C (1995) Der Sprung des Täters hinter dem Täter aus der Theorie in die Praxis. Juristische Rundschau 177–180
Schünemann B (2006) Die Rechtsfigur des "Täters hinter dem Täter" und das Prinzip der Tatherrschaftsstufen. In: Hoyer A, Müller HE, Pawlik M, Wolter J (eds) Festschrift für Friedrich-Christian Schroeder zum 70 Geburtstag. C.F. Müller, Heidelberg, 401–413
Simester AP, Spencer JR, Stark F, Sullivan GR, Virgo GJ (2019) Simester and Sullivan's Criminal Law—Theory and Doctrine. Hart Publishing, Oxford

Sloane RD (2007) The Expressive Capacity of International Punishment: The Limits of the National Law Analogy and the Potential of International Criminal Law. Stanford Journal of International Law 43:39–94

Steer C (2017) Translating Guilt—Identifying Leadership Liability for Mass Atrocity Crimes. T.M.C. Asser Press, The Hague

Stewart JG (2012) The End of "Modes of Liability" for International Crimes. Leiden Journal of International Law 25:165–219

Stewart JG (2014) Ten Reasons for Adopting a Universal Concept of Participation. In: van Sliedregt E, Vasiliev S (eds) Pluralism in International Criminal Law. Oxford University Press, Oxford, 320–341

van Sliedregt E (2012) Individual Criminal Responsibility in International Criminal Law. Oxford University Press, Oxford

van Sliedregt E (2015) Perpetration and Participation in Article 25(3). In: Stahn C (ed) The Law and Practice of the International Criminal Court. Oxford University Press, Oxford, 499–516

Ventura MJ (2019) Ordering. In: de Hemptinne J, Roth R, van Sliedregt E (eds) Modes of Liability in International Criminal Law. Cambridge University Press, Cambridge, 284–306

Vest H (2002) Genozid durch organisatorische Machtapparate. Nomos, Baden-Baden

Vest H (2011) Völkerrechtsverbrecher verfolgen—Ein abgestuftes Mehrebenensystem systemischer Tatherrschaft. Stämpfli Verlag AG, Bern

Vest H (2014) Problems of Participation—Unitarian, Differentiated Approach, or Something Else? Journal of International Criminal Justice 12:295–309

Vogel J (2002) Individuelle Verantwortlichkeit im Völkerstrafrecht. Zeitschrift für die gesamte Strafrechtswissenschaft 114:403–436

Weigend T (2011a) Perpetration through an Organization—The Unexpected Career of a German Legal Concept. Journal of International Criminal Justice 9:91–111

Weigend T (2011b) Germany. In: Heller J, Dubber MD (eds) The Handbook of Comparative Criminal Law. Stanford University Press, Stanford, 252–287

Weigend T (2015) Indirect Perpetration. In: Stahn C (ed) The Law and Practice of the International Criminal Court. Oxford University Press, Oxford, 538–556

Weisser B (2011) Täterschaft in Europa. Mohr Siebeck, Tübingen

Werkmeister A (2015) Straftheorien im Völkerstrafrecht. Nomos, Baden-Baden

Werle G (2007) Individual Criminal Responsibility in Art. 25 ICC Statute. Journal of International Criminal Justice 5:953–975

Werle G, Burghardt B (2014a) Täterschaft und Teilnahme im Statut des Internationalen Strafgerichtshofs. Festschrift für Kristian Kühl zum 70 Geburtstag. C.H. Beck, Munich, 851–866

Werle G, Burghardt B (2014b) Establishing Degrees of Responsibility: Modes of Participation in Article 25 of the ICC Statute. In: van Sliedregt E, Vasiliev S (eds) Pluralism in International Criminal Law. Oxford University Press, Oxford, 301–319

Werle G, Jessberger F (2020) Principles of International Criminal Law. Oxford University Press, Oxford

Wirth S (2012) Co-Perpetration in the Lubanga Judgment. Journal of International Criminal Justice 10:971–995

Wringe B (2010) War Crimes and Expressive Theories of Punishment: Communication or Denunciation. Res Publica 16:119–133

Yanev L (2018) Theories of Co-Perpetration in International Criminal law. Brill Nijhoff, Leiden

Zazcyk R (1996) Die "Tatherrschaft Kraft organisatorischer Machtapparate" und der BGH. Goltdammer's Archiv 411–415

Zorzi Giustiani F (2009) The Responsibility of Accomplices in the Case-Law of the Ad Hoc Tribunals. Criminal Law Forum 417–445

Other Documents

District Court of Jerusalem, *Judgment Against Karl Adolf Eichmann—Unofficial Translation*, 40/61

Chapter 8
Conclusion: The Responsibility of Decision Makers for Ordering the Commission of International Crimes

Contents

Abstract Based on the outcome of the foregoing chapter, this chapter summarizes the reasons for applying ordering liability instead of indirect perpetration through an organisation to decision makers of international crimes. It states that the historic development and uniformity of international criminal law, the expressive value and the form's concise legal requirements are among the reasons to apply it in practice. The chapter then analyses what an interpretation of the Rome Statute could look like if ordering liability were applied to decision makers of international crimes. Under such an approach, indirect (co)perpetration through an organisation becomes unnecessary and accessorial modes of liability gain importance. Indirect perpetration still plays a role as a form of fall-back liability. Finally, the chapter provides some thoughts on

J. Block, *Reconciling Responsibility with Reality*, International Criminal Justice Series 33, https://doi.org/10.1007/978-94-6265-607-9_8

what future systems of perpetration and participation in international criminal law could look like. It is suggested that descriptive forms of responsibility based on direct linkage principles such as ordering and planning should play a greater role due to their precise description of the actor's wrongdoing and their potential contribution to fair labelling and expressive justice.

Keywords Ordering · Indirect perpetration through an organisation · Accessorial liability · Fair labelling · Expressive justice · Hierarchy of blameworthiness · Accessorial object · Direct linkage principle

8.1 Reasons in Favour of Ordering Being the Suitable Mode of Liability for High- and Mid-level Decision Makers

With indirect perpetration through an organisation being an unconvincing and unnecessary concept, responsibility for ordering crimes must be considered the most suitable method of adjudicating the conduct of decision makers of mass atrocities.

Different aspects in favour of the practical and theoretical preference for ordering a crime, as one of the most blameworthy forms of participation in crime, have been identified in this book.

Responsibility for ordering a crime under Article 25 (3)(b) Rome Statute is considered accessory liability in this context and as equally blameworthy as principal liability for commission. The advantages of applying ordering to decision makers of international crimes will be summarized below, considering the findings of earlier chapters and the foregoing comparison.

8.1.1 History and Uniformity: An Inherently International Concept for One of the Most Relevant Forms of Leadership Conduct in Mass Atrocities

As a form of liability, ordering has a special history in international criminal law. The Nuremberg and Tokyo Charters excluded; it is accounted for in the most relevant provisions on individual criminal liability in international criminal law.[1]

This history leads different authors to assert that ordering should be considered principal liability, sometimes describing it as a form of "indirect perpetration".[2] Others lament that ordering was ignored by the drafters as a chance to elegantly provide for leadership criminality under the Rome Statute.[3]

---

[1] See Introduction to Part II.

[2] Ambos 2016, Article 25 mn. 22; Cryer 2004, pp. 244–7.

[3] Vest 2011, p. 364.

However, the categorization of ordering as accessorial liability does not automatically imply an unsuitability for leadership criminality. The historic use of ordering by the Nuremberg Military Trials, as well as at the ICTY and ICTR leads to an interpretation of ordering as a highly blameworthy concept of international criminal responsibility. Its historic use also illustrates that it has always been perceived as a fitting tool to adjudicate high- and mid-level decision makers of international crimes. Whilst this use has never been unchallenged, ordering was nevertheless always considered a suitable form of responsibility for leadership criminality. It therefore constitutes a uniformity in the otherwise divided international law on individual responsibility for leadership conduct.

Under this historic impression, one could assume that the provision for ordering liability in Article 25 (3)(b) Rome Statute was meant to exclude other approaches to leadership liability.[4] It is conceivable that some delegations to the Rome Conference would have expected ordering to fulfil this role. However, as the first international court, the ICC adopted an approach that explicitly degrades ordering into a form of second tier, less blameworthy liability. Paradoxically, this approach is based on the import of a national legal doctrine that emerged precisely because the respective legal system supposedly did not contain any other suitable possibility to adjudicate the wrongdoing of decision makers of mass atrocities.

This import is accompanied by the conviction of some practitioners and scholars that the underlying rationale and *Dogmatik* of the German model would be especially well-suited to the adjudication of decision makers (and architects) of international crimes. It has even been asserted that the successful export of the German doctrine must be based on the theories being “either theoretically convincing, pragmatically useful, or both”.[5] However, none of this is convincing as far as the doctrine of indirect perpetration through an organisation and the underlying rationale of control are concerned. It has been found that the factual, crime-centred concept of control, as applied by the ICC, ignores relevant dynamics of mass atrocities, especially the influence of mid- and low-level participants.[6] Various legal requirements of the doctrine also call for considerable criticism.[7] The doctrine does not promote the gathering of evidence, nor is it easily comprehensible to legal practitioners from different legal systems. Consequently, it has no special practical value.

The ICC’s reliance on indirect perpetration through an organisation and the control criterion is therefore a questionable import of national criminal legal theory.

The history and uniformity of international criminal law speak in favour of adjudicating decision makers of international crimes under the head of ordering the commission of crimes.

---

[4] In this vein Cryer 2004, p. 243.

[5] Ohlin 2015, p. 537. Note that Ohlin refers to co-perpetration in the quoted chapter but explores the control theory and its overall capability as a basis for a convincing model.

[6] See Chap. 3, Sect. 3.3.3.

[7] See Chap. 3, Sect. 3.3.2.

8.1.2 Practice Cases and Their Description: Ordering as a Comprehensive, Intuitive and Suitable Label

To convict a person of being responsible for "ordering the commission" of a crime, has been described above as a precise description and valuable label for the committed wrongdoing.[8] The chapters of this book have outlined, that one can distinguish between decision makers and architects of crimes to differentiate between two types of high- and mid-level contributions to mass atrocities. Both forms of conduct are highly and equally reprehensible. This stems from the interdependence of these figures: if a decision maker is dependent on an architect to enable and facilitate large-scale crimes or these crimes would not have been conceived but for the architect's drafting of the relevant plans, both actors deserve the highest possible label of blameworthiness.

The scope of this book was initially defined as exploring "leadership responsibility", comparing indirect perpetration through an organisation and ordering. Both forms of liability proved to be exclusively applicable to decision makers of international crimes. However, at certain points in time (ordering at U.S. Military Tribunals in Nuremberg), or under certain theoretical conceptions (the systemic approach to perpetration through an organisation), they were or could be considered to encompass the conduct of architects of crimes as well. The objects of comparison therefore seemingly narrowed the scope of this book, but this limitation proved not to be much of a restraint. Although most cases at the ICC are charged under the combined mode of indirect co-perpetration, the analysed decisions usually identify a plethora of acts of the accused that qualify as direct decision making.[9]

Thus, the architect—the planner and organiser—who does not give the direct instruction for the crime is currently of less importance in the practice of the ICC. The high- and mid-level perpetrators that are specifically targeted by the court usually make the relevant decisions that lead to the commission of crimes. In the future cases may arise before the ICC in which organisations with a high division of labour and architects in decisive roles play an important role. However, for the current doctrinal challenges, the narrowed scope of the comparison is less relevant than it may seem.

Based on this and in connection with the overview of cases before the Nuremberg Military Courts and the ICTY and ICTR, a clear picture of decision makers in international criminal law arises. They can be in the highest echelons of power, occupy lower positions that are more connected with socio-traditional influence or any position in between. They trigger the commission of crimes through general directives, guidelines, or instructions at one end of the spectrum, and very specific orders at the other. Their influence over others varies and stretches from the power derived from official and effective state structures over strict disciplinary regimens

---

[8] See Chap. 7, Sect. 7.2.3.5.

[9] The rigid adherence to the doctrine of indirect co-perpetration is barely understandable, given that the less complex form of indirect perpetration through an organisation would work well, and no attribution of the acts of co-perpetrators is usually necessary in these cases. Cf. also Chap. 6, Sect. 6.3.1.

and indoctrinations to traditionally recognized social constructs. Several of these factors can be at interplay but they all have the same effect on the people carrying out the crime: they feel compelled to do so by the higher authority which tells them to act.

The attempts of international tribunals and the ICC to develop collective or systemic forms of responsibility[10] are understandable and laudable given the collective nature of mass atrocities. However, when decision makers of international crimes are concerned, it is often possible to identify certain commands they gave, which qualify as direct instructions to commit crimes. In cases in which such orders can be identified and proven, the reliance on more complex, systemic forms of liability is misguided. Neither the concept of JCE nor that of indirect perpetration carries a specific descriptive value for individuals not familiar with the intricacies of the law. Ordering in turn does, and it applies to many relevant cases of high-level international criminals.

When considering this, the import of indirect perpetration through an organisation again seems ill-founded. The expressive value and fair labelling of high-level decision makers have always been one of the driving forces behind this German doctrine. However, if fair labelling and expressive justice are sought, then why do courts resort to the imprecise technical term of indirect perpetration through an organisation when a form of responsibility exists that precisely describes the reprehensible conduct of the accused in easily understandable terms?

Considering the foregoing, it is unconvincing to resort to any other mode of liability than ordering, where cases are shaped by a leader's instructions to commit crimes.

Ordering poses a comprehensive, intuitive, and suitable mode of liability that covers all forms of highly reprehensible exertion of influence over physical perpetrators of crimes.

8.1.3 The Legal Requirements: Ordering as the More Precise Form of Responsibility

The authority criterion of ordering a crime is a more suitable, more precise, and simultaneously more flexible criterion than those of indirect perpetration through an organisation. It refers precisely to the relevant relation between the ordering person and the physical perpetrators of the crime, i.e., the superiority of the ordering person based on the effect that the recipients of the order feel compelled to adhere to their instructions.

---

[10] Cf. on the systemic approach to indirect perpetration through an organisation in Chap. 2, Sect. 2.4, on the categorisation of JCE as a collectivist approach based on indirect linkage principles see Chap. 5, Sect. 5.2.4. Indirect perpetration through an organisation in the way it is applied by the ICC cannot be seen as such a systemic model given its reliance on crime specific control (cf. Chap. 3, Sects. 3.1.2.3 and 3.2.3).

In contrast to what some scholars invoke, nothing in this form of responsibility would suggest its application to mid-level actors. Instead, the fact that authority can be exercised as "chain authority" leads to its applicability to persons in the highest echelons of power.[11] Simultaneously, the criteria of ordering are slightly broader than those of indirect perpetration. Through this, they enable the adjudication of cases that—despite not involving organised power structures—contain an equally high influence of a person over others, which can tip the point and trigger massive violence, if misused. If a person enjoys such influence (be it in formalized hierarchies or based on informal or even socio-cultural relations), its exertion is what constitutes the reprehensible conduct, and it is not dependent on the existence of an organisation. To reiterate the quote from the introduction, if a person cries "Havoc!" and lets slip the dogs of war, it does not matter where their influence comes from. What matters is that people listen to this cry and consequently wreak havoc.

Ordering is therefore slightly broader than indirect perpetration through an organisation, but through its authority requirement captures the relevant point of decision maker liability. Its broadness in comparison to perpetration through an organisation does not diminish the essence of this form of responsibility. Instead, it extends the liability for the highly reprehensible use of compelling influence over others to the rare situations in which no organisational structures are involved in creating such an influence.

8.1.4 The Overall System: Ordering Within the Correct Hierarchy of Blameworthiness

Ordering must be considered one of the forms of liability that contains the highest level of blameworthiness for such a participation in a crime. This does not conform with the current interpretation of Article 25 (3) Rome Statute, as advanced by most chambers at the ICC and many scholars. However, it is the only reasonable categorisation of ordering, considering the essence of this form of responsibility and the nature of participation in international crimes.

One of the unquestionable truths of individual responsibility for international crimes is that responsibility often increases the farther a person is removed from the scene because the actor's influence on the overall criminal context rises.[12]

Due to its authority requirement, ordering necessarily implies such an increase in distance and responsibility compared to the physical perpetrator. Due to their authority, the ordering actors are always higher up the hierarchy than the physical perpetrator.

[11] See Chap. 6, Sect. 6.2.2.1.

[12] District Court of Jerusalem, *Judgment Against Karl Adolf Eichmann - Unofficial Translation*, 40/61, No. 197.

Moreover, the heightened responsibility ascribed to decision makers and architects of international crimes does not stem from the number of crimes committed because of their acts. Such a quantitative consideration would not be connected to the form of responsibility but gain relevance in sentencing. Instead, it is the power to influence the outcome of situations that is decisive. In the case of decision makers, their influence over physical perpetrators leads to the commission of crimes. Such influence is necessarily given where a person is found responsible for ordering a crime. The question arises why such a person would be considered less blameworthy than the executioner, if the latter does not enjoy heightened influence, but the former does?

Under these findings, it is absurd to treat forms of commission as more blameworthy than ordering.[13]

Categorizing ordering as an accessorial, but one of the most blameworthy forms of responsibility would therefore avoid a contradiction and enable a relevant application of this form of liability.

Some authors criticise Article 25 (3)(b) Rome Statute as a missed chance to codify ordering as principal liability.[14] By not doing so, the provision is faulted for missing the central blameworthiness of the conduct of giving criminal orders.[15]

As the legal characterisation of one of the most relevant and serious types of participation in international crimes, there is no argument against structuring ordering as principal liability in a differentiated system of perpetration and participation, or any ("strict" or functional) unitary system. However, the interpretation of ordering as accessorial liability has been prevalent in the history of international criminal law, and the ICC's interpretation of that aspect contributes to uniformity of law. Furthermore, accessory liability for remote actors can also fulfil certain restrictive functions, especially when compared to broad "collective" forms of participation like JCE or indirect co-perpetration.[16] Accessorial forms of responsibility can lead to more precise charges because certain acts and circumstances must be identified more specifically than what is demanded by the sometimes-vague requirements of broad notions of perpetration. This in turn, can lead to fairer proceedings.[17] Therefore it should not be considered problematic that ordering is interpreted as accessorial liability under the Rome Statute.

---

13 Concerning the specific form of ordering, we can find such a consideration in the ILC's 1996 Draft Code of Crimes against the Peace and Security of Mankind, Commentary to Article 2, No. (8) in which the ILC states that "The superior who orders the commission of a crime is in some respects more culpable than the subordinate who merely carries out the order...".

14 Cryer 2004, p. 247; Vest 2011, p. 365.

15 Cryer 2004, p. 245.

16 Aksenova 2016, pp. 171–2.

17 Ibid., 172–3.

8.1.5 The Comparative Perspective: Leadership Liability as a Highly Blameworthy but Differently Regulated and Approached Issue in National Legal Systems

From a comparative perspective, it is no novelty for an accessorial form of responsibility to be considered among the most serious forms of involvement in a crime.

In German criminal law, the most prominent alternative approach to leadership criminality is the so-called *Anstiftungslösung* ("instigation solution"). It is based on various considerations, some of which have played a role in the analysis of liability forms in this book.[18] From a technical perspective, there is nothing in German criminal law which would hinder the application of instigation to leadership figures involved in mass atrocities. Instigation can take the form of "chain instigation" (*Kettenanstiftung*) which would allow the conviction of a person at the apex of an organisation as an instigator if their instruction travelled through various tiers of a hierarchy.[19] One of the central aspects of this approach lies in the equal punishment of instigation under the German GCC.

Where a form of responsibility is not provided with a mitigation of sentence, but instead provides that the convicted shall be "punished as a perpetrator", the law envisions no differentiation in seriousness between perpetration and the respective form of participation.[20]

One can therefore argue that the hierarchy of blameworthiness which supporters of indirect perpetration through an organisation invoke as one pillar of their theoretical groundwork, does not exist in this form in German law. Consequently, instigation would be the correct and suitable form to be applied to decision makers of large scale crimes.[21] On the other hand, it must also be recognized that the expressive and descriptive capability of the term instigation (*Anstiftung*) is of limited value for leadership criminality.[22] Regardless,[23] even within the system which devised indirect perpetration through an organisation, it is far from inconceivable that an accessorial

---

[18] The rejection of certainty as a possible distinction criterion between perpetration and participation (see Chap. 3, Sect. 3.3.2.3) is often employed when advocating for instigation. In this context, it is argued that—under the right circumstances—an instigator can be equally sure that their instigation will lead to a successful commission of the crime; see e.g. Herzberg 2009, p. 578; Renzikowski 1997, p. 89, "probability does not lead to perpetration" (translation by the author).

[19] Schild 2017, § 26 mn. 4; see also Heine and Weisser 2019, § 25 mn. 28; Weisser 2012, pp. 227–8.

[20] Herzberg, 2000, 49 ("Instigation … encompasses the same quantitative wrong", translation by the author); Herzberg 2009, 579; Hruschka 1998, p. 608; Joecks 2017, § 25 mn. 159–60; Krey and Nuys 2009, pp. 212–3, 222–3. See also Weigend 2015, p. 538 with fn. 1.

[21] This view is taken inter alia by: Herzberg 2000, p. 48 et seq.; Herzberg 2009, p. 579; Hruschka 1998, p. 606; Noltenius 2003, p. 322; Orozco López 2021, p. 247; Renzikowski 1997, p. 91; Rotsch 2000, pp. 561–2; Zazcyk 1996, p. 414.

[22] See already Chap. 7, Sect. 7.2.3.5.

[23] The limited descriptive value of "instigation" cannot be ignored, and German law differs considerably from the Rome Statute and its use of "ordering" in this regard.

form of liability is considered equally blameworthy to commission, and is therefore applicable to leadership criminality.

According to Maculan, a comparable situation exists in the criminal codes of Spain, Peru, Colombia and Argentina, which recognize qualified forms of accessory liability that are explicitly vested with the same punishment as perpetration.[24] Under French law, instigation as accessorial liability is often considered more blameworthy than commission. The reasoning being that the instigator cannot even muster the courage to commit the crime him- or herself.[25] A similar observation has been made concerning the U.S. Code of Laws of the United States of America, where the punishment of accessories is explicitly drawn level with that of perpetrators.[26] The English Accessories and Abettors Act of 1861 equally envisions the same punishment for perpetrators and accessories.[27] Eboe-Osuji interprets the latter two acts as examples of a development in many legal systems.[28] According to Eboe-Osuji, other systems which do not recognize an elevated position of principal perpetrators, in one way or another, are Australia, Canada, Ireland, Malta, New Zealand and Nigeria.[29] According to van Sliedregt, in dealing with crimes committed in World War II, Dutch law also developed a notion of accessory liability that does not recognize any mitigation of punishment and could thus be applied to contributors of such crimes on different hierarchical levels.[30]

According to Weigend, equal punishment of instigators and perpetrators is also known to the Polish Penal Code.[31]

Other national approaches simply use other categorisations or denominations of responsibility forms that are regarded as the correct and most blameworthy approach

---

[24] Maculan 2013, p. 83. Cf. fn. 47–50 for provisions in the respective criminal statutes. The same observation is made by Eboe-Osuji, see ICC, *The Prosecutor v. Bosco Ntaganda*, Appeals Judgment, 30 March 2021, ICC-01/04-02/06-A A2, Partly concurring opinion of Judge Chile Eboe-Osuji, para 41; by Morrison, see ibid., Separate opinion of Judge Howard Morrison on Mr. Ntaganda's appeal, para 10 with fn. 11 and Díaz y García Conlledo 2017, p. 719.

[25] Weisser 2011, p. 95. The same punishment for instigators has also been underlined by Van den Wyngaert (see ICC, *The Prosecutor v. Mathieu Ndgudjolo Chui*, Trial Judgment, 18 December 2012, ICC-01/04-02/12, Concurring Opinion of Judge Christine Van den Wyngaert, para 27 with fn. 39); *Ntaganda*, 30 March 2021, Partly concurring opinion of Judge Chile Eboe-Osuji, para 53; see ibid., Separate opinion of Judge Howard Morrison on Mr. Ntaganda's appeal, para 10 with fn. 11; Weigend 2015, p. 538 with fn. 1.

[26] 18. U.S. Code § 2 (a); see *Chui*, 18 December 2012, Concurring Opinion of Judge Christine Van den Wyngaert, para 27 with fn. 39; Ohlin 2015, p. 519.

[27] Simester et al. 2019, p. 225.

[28] *Ntaganda*, 30 March 2021, Partly concurring opinion of Judge Chile Eboe-Osuji, para 50. Note that in his view such acts lead to a system in which everyone is "a party" to a crime, which he describes as monistic systems in para 53. However, it is submitted here, that by analysing the wording of the respective regulations, one would have to examine in detail whether these systems rely entirely on unitary/monistic systems or rather "only" reject hierarchies of blameworthiness between perpetration and participation.

[29] Ibid. Partly concurring opinion of Judge Chile Eboe-Osuji, para 52.

[30] Van Sliedregt 2015, p. 503 with fn. 27.

[31] Weigend 2015, p. 538 with fn. 1; see *Ntaganda*, 30 March 2021, Separate opinion of Judge Howard Morrison on Mr. Ntaganda's appeal, para 10 with fn. 11.

to leadership responsibility within their system. According to Schroeder, the law of the Soviet Union contained the highly blameworthy form of "organiser" of a crime. This mode worked without reliance on the distinction between principals and accessories.[32] Portuguese criminal law recognizes the highly blameworthy form of instigation as a form of principal liability.[33]

These, necessarily limited, examples show that the proposed solution of ordering as a highly blameworthy form of accessory liability is far from being a novelty or specialty. Indeed, when focussing on indirect perpetration through an organisation, it has been found that many European jurisdictions have no need for such complex theories, given their different approaches to perpetration and participation.[34]

Reference was made earlier to a study of the German *Max-Plank-Institut* for international and foreign criminal law on the punishment of leaders for their involvement in crimes in different jurisdictions worldwide. Its findings confirm that national legal systems only agree on the functional outcome, i.e., the qualification of leaders of criminal groups as highly responsible participants without using the same doctrinal approaches.[35]

This excursion allows the conclusion that the proposed application of ordering within the ambit of Article 25 (3)(b) Rome Statute is neither untypical nor unknown to national legal systems.

8.1.6 Conclusion

Ordering is the correct form of responsibility to be applied to high and mid-level decision makers of international crimes. It was introduced and developed as an inherently international mode of liability, tailored around one typical form of leadership involvement in international crimes: the issuance of an instruction, guideline, directive or simply, an order. It is perfectly capable of fulfilling this task and should be applied accordingly.

[32] Schroeder 1965, p 167.

[33] For an extensive description, see de Figueiredo Dias 2013, 633 et seq.

[34] Weisser 2011, pp 296–9.

[35] See Chap. 3, Sect. 3.3.1.2; for an overview of the conclusion of the study see at https://csl.mpg.de/en/research/projects/general-legal-principles-of-international-criminal-law-on-the-criminal-liability-of-leaders-of-criminal-groups-and-netwo/ (last accessed on 25 May 2021).

8.2 Consequences of the Proposed Approach

If the advice in the conclusion of this comparison is heeded, the ICC will start convicting decision makers of international crimes for ordering the crimes pursuant to Article 25 (3)(b) Rome Statute, but what consequences will result from such an approach?

It should be kept in mind that the ICC cases that were examined in this book contained charges of indirect perpetration or indirect co-perpetration. This notwithstanding, in many cases, it was possible—in accordance with the findings of the relevant decisions—to identify conduct and circumstances that would have also served to confirm responsibility for ordering at the respective procedural stage of the trial. Together with the analyses of cases in post-World War II and the *ad hoc* tribunals' jurisprudence, this led to the conclusion that instructions issued with authority by high-level actors are often identifiable, rendering the respective approach to this conduct one of the most relevant. The consequences of the application of ordering in such cases must be observed under this premise.

8.2.1 The Overall Hierarchy of Blameworthiness in the System of Article 25 (3)(a) to (d) Rome Statute

It has been submitted that ordering must be interpreted as equally blameworthy to forms of commission under *lit.* (a) of Article 25 (3) Rome Statute. This leads to the question of the overall relation of *litterae* (a) to (d) under the Rome Statute. It is not this books' primary aim to contribute arguments against or in favour of a unitary or a normative differentiated model. This has been done before and in much detail.[36] As also explored, the question of a hierarchy of blameworthiness can be answered by recurring to a differently structured approach, where some forms of (principal or accessorial) liability are considered more serious than others. Considering the jurisprudence of the U.S. military tribunals in Nuremberg[37] and of the *ad hoc* tribunals,[38] as well as the conclusions on the appropriate role of ordering, one can therefore conclude that a gradation of seriousness should be read between *litterae* (b) and (c) of Article 25 (3) Rome Statute. This would render commission, ordering, soliciting and inducing the more blameworthy forms of involvement, whereas aiding

---

[36] See in favour of a unitary model e.g. Stewart 2012, pp. 165 et seq.; also expressing a tendency in favour Eser 2002, p. 788; detailed accounts of arguments in favour of a differentiated normative system: Burghardt 2010, pp. 91–3; Werle and Burghardt 2014, pp. 301–319. See also the proposal to try a combination of the features of different models by van Sliedregt and Weisser 2022, p. 632.

[37] The Nuremberg subsequent trials did not clearly distinguish between principals and accessories. However, the trials indicated that "principals" and those "accessories" who order a crime count among the more (and equally) blameworthy participants in crime. See on this Chap. 4, Sects. 4.4, 4.5 and 4.6.

[38] See Chap. 5, Sect. 5.3.6.

and abetting (c) and the contribution to a crime committed by a group of persons with a common purpose (d) would be considered less serious.[39] Simultaneously, the difference between forms of perpetration under *littera* (a) and those of participation under *litterae* (b) to (d) could be found in the accessorial nature of the latter forms. Ordering, soliciting, and inducing would be considered highly blameworthy forms of accessory liability.

Considering the role of "authority" in determining the seriousness of ordering, which is not required for soliciting and inducing, the equal seriousness of these modes can be called into question. It has not been the focus of this book to inquire into the role, influence, and subsequent blameworthiness of instigators. However, the structure of Article 25 (3)(b) may imply an equal seriousness, as the assignment of different degrees of blameworthiness to the forms regulated therein may not have been intended.

Due to their lack of authority, a person who solicits or induces must often exert a greater effort, as they may have to convince the perpetrators to do their bidding. Meanwhile, an ordering actor can simply rely on their authority. On the other hand, once the instigation is successful, the influence of a soliciting and inducing individual is grave and serious. Therefore, it could be seen as equally consequential and blameworthy as ordering and commission.[40] *Ad hoc* jurisprudence speaks to an equal categorisation of ordering and instigation in terms of blameworthiness.[41] Given the ICC's focus on high- and mid-level perpetrators, coupled with the fact that, due to the dynamics and nature of mass atrocities, these individuals usually rely on their authority over the perpetrators, soliciting and inducing play a minor role in practice. However, where these modes are relevant, they could also prove to be highly reprehensible, even in comparison to ordering. Imagine Politician A slowly convincing (instigating) General B with various arguments to order his troops to commit crimes. Would A truly be less blameworthy than B?

Based on this, it is conceivable to view all forms of participation under *lit.* (b) as equally blameworthy and serious to commission. However, as this is partially due to the structure of Article 25 (3) and the difference in authority is not to be disregarded, it should be scrutinized more closely.

Whether aiding and abetting should receive a mitigation of sentence is contentious in literature and remains mostly obscure within ICC jurisprudence. As stated earlier with reference to ordering, chambers that are in favour of a hierarchy of blameworthiness conform to the view that forms of accessorial liability deserve a lesser sentence

---

[39] Concerning the relation between perpetration and ordering, this opportunity has been briefly mentioned for the Rome Statute by Vest 2014, p. 304.

[40] This is one of the arguments raised by supporters in favour of applying instigation instead of indirect perpetration through an organisation in Germany. They explain that when generating the perpetrator's decision to act, an instigator does not necessarily face more hurdles than an indirect perpetrator with an organisation, depending on the executioner's state of mind. Additionally, certain national legal systems explicitly or arguably treat instigation as blameworthy as commission liability, which also speaks in favour of such a categorisation under *lit.* (b) of the Rome Statute (see above Sect. 8.1.5).

[41] See Chap. 5, Sect. 5.3.6.

when all other factors considered are equal. The same stance is logically taken by supporters of a general hierarchy in Article 25 (3) Rome Statute.[42] The Katanga trial chamber took a different stance,[43] which is shared by Judges Adrian Fulford and Christine Van den Wyngaert.[44] Jurisprudence of the *Ad hoc* tribunals, however, also suggests the principle of sentence mitigation for aiding and abetting.[45] Some scholars hint to the fact that not all forms of contributing to mass atrocities can be anticipated, which would speak in favour of not categorising all forms of liability in normative terms.[46] This is a valuable point considering the difficulties of identifying contributions to and their importance for the unfolding of mass atrocities. However, under the principles of fair labelling and expressive justice, it is questionable whether such an approach is advisable. The ordinary meaning of the term "aiding and abetting", which will be the label for the actor, seems to imply a lesser importance to the realisation of the crime.[47] The same can be said about Article 25 (3)(d). Pursuant to this interpretation, it is advisable to indeed treat the modes under I and (d) as less blameworthy than those under (a) and (b).[48] The flexibility of sentencing ranges under the Rome Statute still provides for the possibility of severe sentences for aiders and abettors and contributors to common purpose crimes, as even in such a hierarchy, forms of liability will only be one factor to consider in sentencing.[49]

---

[42] See Chap. 6, Sect. 6.4.3.3.

[43] ICC, *The Prosecutor v. Germain Katanga*, Trial Judgment, 7 March 2014, ICC-01/04-01/07, para 1386.

[44] ICC, *The Prosecutor v. Thomas Lubanga Dyilo*, Trial Judgment, 14 March 2012, ICC-01/04-01/06, Separate Opinion of Judge Adrian Fulford, paras 8–9; *Chui*, 18 December 2012, Concurring Opinion of Judge Christine Van den Wyngaert, para 24.

[45] See Chap. 5, Sect. 5.3.3. But see van Sliedregt 2015, pp. 513–4, against a mitigation for aiding and abetting, and arguing that the characteristic as a "form of lesser liability" only concerns the comparison to JCE.

[46] See Ohlin 2015, p. 531; van Sliedregt 2015, p. 513.

[47] A definition for aiding, proposed by the Oxford Dictionary reads, "to help someone or something to do something, especially by making it easier". To abet is defined as, "to help or encourage somebody to do something wrong". As an idiom, "aid and abet" is defined as "to help somebody to do something illegal or wrong".

[48] For opposed suggestions that value the collective dimension of criminals see e.g., *Ntaganda*, 30 March 2021, Partly concurring opinion of Judge Chile Eboe-Osuji, paras 47, 55, 66–7 and ibid., Separate opinion of Judge Howard Morrison on Mr. Ntaganda's appeal, paras 36–7.

[49] The possibility of severe sentences for aiders and abettors has e.g. been pointed out in *Chui*, 18 December 2012, Concurring Opinion of Judge Christine Van den Wyngaert, para 26 (with a hint to the 50 years sentence against Charles Taylor passed by the SCSL). In contrast to the position taken here, Judge Van den Wyngaert does not endorse any hierarchy of blameworthiness (see para 27).

8.2.2 *The Role of Indirect (Co-)Perpetration Through an Organisation*

Indirect perpetration through an organisation should be dispensed with as an unconvincing and unnecessary doctrine under the Rome Statute and responsibility for ordering should be applied in the relevant cases.[50] Given that the requirement of at least one co-perpetrator exercising control over the crime through their organisation would be inapplicable, this would effectively also eradicate indirect co-perpetration through an organisation. In some cases, this would make little difference in terms of the actor's culpability because they often exercise authority and can thus qualify under ordering. This is even more so, given the fact that the possibility of joint ordering has been recognized by the ICC, albeit not yet discussed in detail.[51] Therefore, there will be few cases which currently lead to highly blameworthy responsibility under indirect co-perpetration, yet will only fulfil *litterae* I or (d) in the future. However, such cases may exist, and where they arise, the lack of the form of "planning", as known from the ICTY and ICTR Statutes, becomes evident.[52] This is a potential lacuna. Nevertheless, this does not outweigh the advantages of discarding flawed doctrines and applying other, more precise, and better-founded approaches.

8.2.3 *The Distinction Between Forms of Perpetration and Participation*

Discarding the doctrines of indirect perpetration through an organisation and indirect co-perpetration (where indirect perpetration is committed through an organisation), leads to the next issue: what behaviour are the forms of commission meant to grasp under this approach, and how are they distinguished from forms of participation?

The described preference for the application of ordering a crime does not necessarily mean that the control theory should be abolished completely.[53] The theory was not the focus of this book, apart from where it is necessarily connected to indirect perpetration through an organisation. Other forms of control as devised in the theory could be more convincing than the specific notion of control connected with indirect perpetration through an organisation.

---

[50] In a similar vein on the preferable path to abolishing indirect perpetration through an organisation see van Sliedregt 2015, p. 514. See also Vest 2014, p. 304 suggesting a similar outcome ("It might be easier to apply the mode of *ordering as a form of instigation equating to perpetration.*" Italics in the original).

[51] See Chap. 6, Sect. 6.2.1.

[52] See already *Chui*, 18 December 2012, Concurring Opinion of Judge Christine Van den Wyngaert, paras 28–9.

[53] Although this is a possible conclusion. See in this vein Yanev 2018, p. 470 for whom the existence of ordering discredits the court's implementation of the control theory.

Article 25 (3)(a) Rome Statute recognizes the commission through another, criminally liable, executioner. Therefore, other cases of the perpetrator behind the perpetrator could be acknowledged, while only the specific doctrine of indirect perpetration through an organisation must be abolished. Valuable cases of perpetrators behind perpetrators could be provided for where the background actor deceives the physical perpetrator about damage that is likely to be caused by the executioner's acts.[54] Next to this, indirect perpetration can play a role, where the person in the background exerts pressure that amounts to duress or deceives the executioners in a way which leads them to act without the necessary intent.[55] The use of child soldiers could be an important field of application of indirect perpetration, if the mode is applied as described. Regardless of the fact that the ICC has no practical jurisdiction over child soldiers,[56] their use could constitute an act of indirect perpetration by the respective commander, if practice and theory should determine their non-liability.[57]

The latter two proposals again concern the question of the accessorial object. They would only make sense where the lack of criminal liability on the part of the executioner disables accessory liability. This issue has been touched upon before and cannot be elaborated here.

The notion of control as concerning joint perpetration has not been discussed, and therefore, no analysis or suggestions will be provided.[58] As previously stated, indirect co-perpetration will no longer function as a theory because the link to the executioners, the indirect perpetration through the organisation, is abolished. One could consider transmitting the findings on the lack of control of decision makers who are far removed from the crime onto co-perpetration. This would raise the question whether a co-perpetrator cannot be present at the scene but contribute through acts of planning and preparation. Their ability to influence the "whether and how" of the commission of the specific crime could seem questionable.[59]

Concerning the distinction between forms of liability within the respective groups of *litterae* (a) and (b) on the one hand, and (c) and (d) on the other, naturalistic or empirical aspects must decide, due to the lack of hierarchies within the groups. Considering the foregoing findings, this means that where a person orders responsibly acting subordinates to commit crimes, this will constitute ordering. If the physical perpetrators are deceived or coerced in a manner that leads to them not fulfilling the

---

54 This would amount to the category of a so-called "gradual mistake of fact", see Chap. 2, Sect. 2.2.3. This is conceivable, e.g., where the use of certain types of weapons is instructed and the physical actors do not know about the true potential of these weapons, which could apply to weapons of mass destruction, certain types of ammunition etc.

55 See also Weigend 2011, pp. 109–10; Weigend 2015, pp. 554–6 who votes for such a narrower and more traditional understanding of indirect perpetration in the statute. In a similar vein see the ponderations by Vest 2014, p. 304.

56 See Article 26 Rome Statute, "Exclusion of jurisdiction over persons under eighteen".

57 Whether child soldiers are generally excused from criminal liability is contentious, see for an overview Fagan et al. 2016, pp. 259–61; McQueen 2018, pp. 112–21.

58 However, note that proposals for non-control-based approaches to joint perpetration exist, see e.g. Yanev 2018, pp. 588 et seq. See also Ohlin 2015, pp. 531 et seq.

59 Cp. the analysis in Chap. 3, Sect. 3.3.3.

mens rea or having a defence, this qualifies as indirect perpetration. The same is true for cases of gradual mistakes of fact of the executioner and other non-organisational cases of the perpetrator behind the perpetrator. Finally, indirect perpetration could apply where the executioners do not possess the necessary special intent of certain crimes, yet the indirect perpetrator does.

8.2.4 Accessorial Object and Executioners Without Special Intent

As previously discussed, accessorial liability under the jurisprudence of the *ad hoc* tribunals and at the ICC expects physical perpetrators, not only to fulfil the objective elements of a crime, but to act with the necessary intent and knowledge. In the jurisprudence, this seemingly extends over the specific or special intent (*dolus specialis*), where such is necessary for the crime.[60]

Under the approach advocated for above, this leads to the effect that ordering genocide or persecution as a crime against humanity etc. is impossible where the physical perpetrators lack the necessary intent. In practice, this will seldom pose a problem, given that the special intent has thus far only been denied in rather untypical situations.[61]

In such cases, indirect perpetration can serve as a form of fall-back liability. This problem could also be remedied by conceptualizing ordering as perpetration liability or limiting the accessorial object to the *actus reus*.[62] In both cases, it would become irrelevant to what extent the physical perpetrators acted intentionally. However, both options would contradict earlier international criminal law jurisprudence on ordering and would be less compatible with the structural distinction between Article 25 (3)(a) and (b). This structural distinction is adhered to here and, as proposed, serves to distinguish between principal and secondary liability.

National criminal law also possesses remedies for the unpleasant effect discussed in this section.[63] In German criminal law, certain elements inherent to certain offences do not have to be fulfilled by the physical perpetrators when determining the liability

---

[60] See Chap. 5, Sect. 5.1.2 and Chap. 6, Sect. 6.4.1.2.

[61] In ICTR, *Prosecutor v. Bagosora et al.*, 18 December 2008, ICTR-98-41-T, para 2121 an ICTR trial chamber denied the responsibility for genocide for the specific incident of the killing of members of the opposition. The chamber did not find it proven that these men were murdered with the necessary genocidal intent. However, the chamber might have found it equally difficult, albeit perhaps possible, to prove such an intent for the accused himself if that had been necessary. For the large scale murder of Tutsis, the chamber affirmed the genocidal intent of both physical perpetrators and the accused (see e.g. ibid., paras 2126, 2135, 2138–9). This shows that such cases are untypical and will be scarce in practice.

[62] The first is *inter alia* proposed by Ambos (Ambos 2016, Article 25 mn. 22), the second has been suspected by Vogel (Vogel 2002, pp. 425, 427, 434).

[63] See on the general possibilities of convicting principals and accessories of different offences: Du Bois-Pedain 2019, pp. 117–9.

of accessories. According to the overwhelming opinion in academic literature, this is the case, for example, where an instigator, driven by greed, tells another to murder someone and the physical perpetrator does not act out of such greed. In this situation, only the instigator would be punishable for "murder under specific aggravating circumstances" (greed), while the hands-on killer would only qualify for "murder". Despite the accessorial object in both the *actus reus* and *mens rea* only being the crime of murder, the specific state of mind of the instigator results in him being punishable for another, more serious crime.[64] A similar, albeit differently reasoned outcome is apparently possible in England, where jurisprudence has developed to convict accessories guilty of more serious offences than the perpetrators.[65] This excursion shows that a change of jurisprudence in this regard is also conceivable.

In summary, the doctrine's potential outcome is unsatisfying in cases where the physical perpetrators lack the necessary special intent, but the ordering person possesses such intent. However, we have also seen that such cases will probably be rare in practice, and that indirect perpetration can provide for a classic fall-back liability. Under the current provision of Article 25 (3) Rome Statute, this is probably preferable to adjusting international jurisprudence that is, to some extent, established.

8.2.5 *Type of Model: Individual, Direct Linkage Rather Than Systemic, Indirect Linkage*

Responsibility for ordering a crime is based on a concept of direct linkage between the crime and the actor. Even though several layers of a hierarchy may act as intermediaries, this form of responsibility ultimately requires proof that the accused issued a decree, guideline, directive, order, or other instruction that, under their authority, led to the commission of the specific crime.[66]

As previously seen, the requirements and underlying concept of indirect perpetration through an organisation in the way it is applied by the ICC, do not significantly

[64] This is the consequence of Section 28 GCC, which reads:

"Special personal characteristics

(2) If the law provides that special personal characteristics aggravate, mitigate or rule out punishment, then this applies only to that party to the offence (offender or participant) in whom they are present."

The "greed" element of aggravated murder is interpreted as falling under this provision, and that it is therefore a personal characteristic that elevates the offence of murder to murder under specific aggravating circumstances. The view that this effect applies to the crimes of murder and aggravated murder is rejected by German jurisprudence but affirmed by the overwhelming majority in academia, see Eser and Sternberg-Lieben 2019, Vorbemerkungen zu den §§ 211 ff. mn. 3-6; Du Bois-Pedain 2019, p. 118.

[65] Du Bois-Pedain 2019, pp. 118–9.

[66] Chap. 6, Sect. 6.2.

differ from this. Consequently, perpetration through an organisation in its current interpretation at the ICC is also based on a link that is direct, albeit flawed.[67]

In this regard, the proposed primary reliance on the mode of ordering does not change much. However, by leading to the inapplicability of indirect co-perpetration, a change is effected at another point. Undoubtedly, this can potentially lead to a down-grading of some participants to aiders and abettors, which would be unwarranted. However, despite their outspoken reliance on indirect co-perpetration, cases at the ICC have often produced reasonable grounds to believe that direct orders were given by the accused. Where this was not the case, it was often the entire narrative of an apparatus of power and the actor's role in it that collapsed during trial, not merely a lack of evidence of direct instructions. Under this impression, the reliance on a direct linkage model, such as ordering, does not seem to be overly detrimental. In light of fair labelling and expressive justice, it can have an increasingly positive effect. It is difficult to comprehend why a court would primarily resort to technocratic, systemic solutions with little expressive and descriptive value (indirect perpetration) when it can also convict under a head of liability with a high expressive value (ordering).

One could conclude from the observations made in this book that forms of direct linkage which were specifically created to deal with mass atrocities—such as ordering and planning—can provide for suitable solutions to the dilemma of attributing individual responsibility for specific acts in a collective context.[68] This is true for a broad range of conduct, which will typically be identifiable in cases of mass atrocities. Forms of responsibility like ordering and planning probably emerged as an instinctive reaction to mass atrocities, and the problem of attributing individual responsibility. They thus represent a natural approach to the issue, and as such, have been and still are open to international criminal law. Forms such as ordering a crime can create a natural balance between the individual and collective nature of mass atrocities when attributing liability. By denominating and specifying the type of necessary conduct and circumstances, such forms restrict the imputation of responsibility to measurable and identifiable contributions, i.e., to the planning or ordering of a crime.[69] Simultaneously, the linguistic denomination and legal requirements of such forms convey a sense of the collective nature of mass atrocities by themselves. By requiring authority and the issuance of an order, for example, they embody the typical systemic surroundings of mass atrocities, without which the forms themselves make little sense. This systemic reference of ordering, and arguably planning, vests them with the potential to be applied to many high-level and mid-level participants in mass atrocities without

[67] Cp. Chap. 3, Sects. 3.1.3 and 3.2.3. See also Chap. 7, Sect. 7.1.3.

[68] This dilemma has been *inter alia* described by Heine 2000, p. 926. He states: "In dealing with systemic wrong, our criminal law gets into a basic conflict: the principle of individual responsibility limits the liability of a person for systemic, social reasons. In contrast to this, a system of collective liability … demands responsibility of the individual for the wrong of a system."

[69] It is submitted that this is the opposite of what has been described by Morrison as the weakening effect of the descriptions provided by complex legal findings under the theories of indirect (co-) perpetration; See *Ntaganda*, 30 March 2021, Separate opinion of Judge Howard Morrison on Mr. Ntaganda's appeal, para 28.

the necessity of justifying the reliance on systemic, indirect linkage principles.[70] In so far, they are truly international forms of responsibility.[71]

8.2.6 *Conclusion*

This section has shown that sense can be made of the interpretation proposed earlier, in which ordering under Article 25 (3)(b) Rome Statute replaces indirect perpetration through an organisation as the approach to dealing with decision makers of international crimes. Not all solutions of the overall system seem completely satisfactory, as they are based on a provision that does not provide for a coherent, uncontradictory doctrine. Therefore, the last section outlines some thoughts on what a future system of perpetration and participation in international criminal law should consider, based on the observations of this book.

8.3 Thoughts on Future Provisions on Forms of Responsibility in International Criminal Law

The observations on identifiable high-level contributions to mass atrocities, and their precise labelling through forms such as ordering and planning simultaneously question and confirm what courts and scholars have always identified as one of the main problems of responsibility attribution in international criminal law.

The Jerusalem District Court and Claus Roxin explained that the involvement of important leaders and organisers in international crimes defy the known categories of perpetration and participation.[72] This statement was certainly understandable as far as forms of direct linkage that are widely known in national criminal law, such as traditional concepts of commission, instigation and aiding and abetting are concerned. This led to the comprehensible effect of the development of broader notions of liability, often based on notions of perpetration. However, certain forms of responsibility that had concurrently developed in international criminal law seemingly defy this reasoning by referring to factual dynamics, inherent to mass atrocities, while still offering direct linkage imputation of responsibility for specific crimes. Ordering

---

[70] In this sense, ordering in the form, which is proposed here, can naturally refer to any of the three tiers of mass atrocities as identified by Vest (cp. Vest 2014, pp. 417–34, also note the charts at pp. 436–7). However, it is suggested here that wherever a decision directly steers the physical perpetrators into the commission of the crime, ordering is the correct form of liability to apply under Article 25 (3) Rome Statute. Vest's Model recognizes the use of different forms of responsibility in this regard, but rejects the application of ordering (see Vest 2011, pp. 432–3 with fn. 239; Vest 2002, p. 243).

[71] See Stewart 2014, pp. 334–5 calling for the development of one coherent international notion of individual criminal responsibility for mass atrocities.

[72] *Judgment Against Adolf Eichmann*, No. 197; Roxin 2019, p. 280.

and planning are such forms responsibility. It is advisable that future systems of perpetration and participation in international criminal law take this development into account.

First and foremost, this means that, where they are created anew, such provisions should not align themselves too closely to forms of responsibility known from national legal systems. Instead, modes of participation that bear a high descriptive value, and can therefore serve for fair labelling and expressive justice whilst avoiding complex legal technicalities, should be the focus.[73]

Ordering and planning should play a role in this regard. The high value of a form that refers to the planning of mass atrocities was recognized in early provisions and then seemingly dropped and ignored in favour of more technical approaches, such as JCE and indirect co-perpetration.[74]

However, future provisions do not have to content themselves with merely including ordering and planning. Comparable to how these two forms identify relevant contributions to mass atrocities that can be made at different stages of preparation and execution, and on different tiers of a hierarchy, other ways of contributing to mass atrocities can be identified and explicitly criminalized in a form of participation.

Article 8*bis* (1) in connection with Article 25 (3)*bis* Rome Statute show an example of how a provision can list in detail the relevant contributions to a large criminally relevant operation. This is true for the crime of aggression as criminalized in Article 8*bis*, but these relevant contributions could equally be identified where campaigns of mass atrocities are carried out by state forces or non-state actors. Article 8*bis* (1) lists "planning, preparation, initiation or execution" as the relevant contributions to a crime of aggression. Article 25 (3)*bis* limits the liability for the crime of aggression to political and arguably military leaders in the highest echelons of a state apparatus. However, this is due to the special characteristics of this crime and is of no importance here.[75]

The relevant novelty of Article 8*bis* (1) is the identification of contributions to the criminal operation, in this case, the act of aggression. All four types of relevant conduct have been defined in scholarly literature.[76] An act of aggression that qualifies under Article 8*bis* will necessarily involve a military operation of a state with a larger number of people, and the operation itself must be in contradiction to the rules of the UN Charter.[77] Under this premise it is comprehensible that there is no "hands on" commission of aggression, as a single soldier can hardly commit what would qualify

---

[73] In a similar vein: Stewart 2014, pp. 334–5.

[74] Note again *Chui*, 18 December 2012, Concurring Opinion of Judge Christine Van den Wyngaert, para 15 on the lamentable fact that the form of planning was ignored by the drafters of the Rome Statute.

[75] Ambos 2016, Article 25 mn. 54.

[76] Zimmermann and Freiburg 2016, Article 8bis mn. 23–32. See also Clark 2017, pp. 567 et seq.

[77] Zimmermann and Freiburg 2016, Article 8bis mn. 46–9 (on the necessary violation of the UN Charter through a state action) mn. 63–4 (on the necessary scale, i.e., involvement of the military operation).

as a stately act of aggression by him- or herself.[78] This is different with genocide, war crimes and crimes against humanity, where a single physically harmful act can constitute such a crime.

However, if the legal aspect is disregarded, the factual difference between the crimes in terms of the surrounding circumstances is marginal to non-existent. It is precisely at the core of the debate about modes of liability that all international crimes are usually committed as mass atrocities which involve planning, organisation, and an oversight over larger groups of physical perpetrators.

The contributions to the crime of aggression identified in Article 8*bis* (1) Rome Statute are possible examples of identifiable ways to contribute to any operation leading to mass atrocities, and can therefore, together with ordering and planning, serve as a pool of examples for future provisions.[79] A future provision could stipulate that the "planning, ordering, preparing, initiating or executing" of an international crime leads to individual criminal liability for this crime. Of course, it would be necessary to inquire more broadly and deeply into typically relevant contributions in the higher and mid-level echelons of criminal organisations.

Regardless, such an approach would bear a high descriptive value. It would contribute more directly to the fair labelling of participants in mass atrocities. The expressive function of international criminal law will benefit from judgments specifying that President A "planned and ordered" the genocide in country X, General B "prepared and ordered" the brutal attacks on the ethnic minorities in Region Y, Desk Officer C "planned and prepared" the genocide through the acquisition and distribution of forbidden chemical agents and cluster bombs and Colonel D "prepared, initiated and ordered" the destruction of Village Z and the widespread murder and deportation of its inhabitants.

By outlining which forms of contribution are deemed serious and grave enough to warrant listing in the provision, such a definitive list of contributions would also express the drafters' normative viewpoint.

Next to such descriptive modes of liability, the role of systemic, indirect linkage models would have to be reconsidered under this approach. Systemic modes of liability, in the sense of the German systemic approach to perpetration through an organisation, could complement the criminalization of a wide range of typical conduct. Next to the detailed listing of relevant contributions to the criminal operations, the role of systemic forms of responsibility, such as the establishment and maintenance of the underlying apparatus, may lose some of its relevance. Certain acts with a distant but important function in the context of the crimes, may fall under one of the modes of a descriptive list of direct linkage responsibility. However, there will still be plenty of personnel, including members of the highest political and military ranks, that remain uninvolved in the criminal campaigns, but support the system

[78] This is connected to the purpose of the crime of aggression: it protects states from the use of force by other states and does not address individual rights as protected assets, see ibid., mn. 33.

[79] Note the difference of this suggestion to the current Art.8*bis* which is a provision on a crime and the relevant criminal conduct, not on modes of liability and must therefore be read in conjunction with Article 25 (3) Rome Statute. On the issue of bringing the conduct words of Article 8*bis* and Article 25 (3) together see Clark 2017, pp. 575 et seq.

through the vital roles they fulfil for its overall functioning. For such cases, systemic forms of responsibility can play an important role. For situations in which the scope of the crimes is limited in terms of geography and involved organisations, there will probably be fewer people who play a vital role for the organisation's functioning without becoming directly involved in the planning, preparation, and ordering of crimes. However, even in such a scenario, this is possible. For instance, it is plausible that a leading member of the political branch of a non-state organisation can support such a movement without contributing to crimes directly.

It is conceivable that the terms "perpetrator" and "commission" would not play a role in either the descriptive or the systemic category. Such a system could be structured as a differentiated one, in which the physical perpetrators constitute the necessary basis for other forms of attribution but are not considered especially blameworthy. "Perpetration" and "commission" would describe the hands-on commission of crimes. However, such a system could also use these terms differently. A provision could state that those who order, plan, etc. a crime and those who contribute to the system behind the crime are considered perpetrators who commit the crime. Such a provision would establish a functional unitary system, in which no derivative liability exists, but different forms of perpetration can establish different degrees of blameworthiness.

The more traditional forms of participation such as aiding and abetting, and instigation should still be found in future provisions.

It has been advocated by some authors that a three-tier view on mass atrocities should be established, in which every tier would correspond to a different hierarchical level of involved actors. The three levels from top to bottom would be the leadership, the organisational and the execution level. The first level concerns all crimes committed based on the leadership's role in conceiving and organising such crimes. The second level leads to the attribution of responsibility for all crimes organised and executed within a certain range of competence and the third level corresponds to the single criminal incident.[80] Vest has proposed that on all three levels, perpetration and participation must be possible.[81]

Vest's approach is also linked to the concept of *Gesamttat* ("overall crime"),[82] according to which participation in a crime of a mass atrocity can be established in various steps, which take the typical collective circumstances into account. As described in Chap. 2, under the concept of the overall crime, the accused contributes to the overall criminal context through their act, and out of this context, the crime

---

[80] Vest 2011, pp. 409–10, 417–26; Vest 2014, p. 309. Agreeing: Ambos 2013, pp. 177–9.

[81] Cf. Vest 2011, pp. 417–8 (execution level), 419–25 (organisation level and the special case of concentration camps), 425–34 (leadership level). Note that Vest takes the view that ordering as a form of accessory liability would be unsuitable, based on the well-known arguments of supposedly limited expressive functions (ibid., pp. 432–3 with fn. 239). According to Vest, however, a conceptualisation of ordering as principal liability, especially within the conduct description of substantive crimes would have served as a valuable solution, see ibid., p. 365; Vest 2002, pp. 243–4.

[82] The term has been shaped, albeit with a focus on different situations by Dencker 1996, p. The translation of *Gesamttat* as overall crime can be found in Vest 2014, p. 309.

is committed by another person.[83] This shifts the issue of causality from the link between the act and the consequence, to the connection between the overall criminal context and the consequence.[84] One can therefore speak of a model of imputation based on an indirect linkage principle.[85]

To some extent, the reference to the overall plan or crime—as opposed to the individual crimes—has been inherent to the adjudication of mass atrocity contributions from the beginning, even where differentiated forms of responsibility existed.[86] It was submitted above, that precise forms of responsibility, which identify and describe the actor's contribution, contain a "systemic reference" by referring to conduct typical for the collective dynamics behind mass atrocities and, in their specificity, make little sense as forms of participation outside of large-scale crimes. Provisions that embody both specific and systemic forms of liability work well with the concepts of the overall crime. Whilst the specific forms require a link to criminal incidents, this link can take the form of orders, plans, guidelines or a pattern of vitally supportive conduct, such as the large-scale acquisition of weaponry, provisions etc. One could say that they require a direct link, but this link can be shaped by the patterns, procedures, and regulations of the collective through which it is channelled. Thus, these forms can naturally lead to criminal responsibility on the higher levels of the overall context. With their systemic reference, these highly descriptive forms indicate the shaping conduct of an influential character within the overall context. They should therefore be relied upon, wherever possible.

The systemic forms that should accompany the more direct and descriptive forms of participation, would be styled more after the indirect linkage idea of the overall crime concept. They will naturally refer to the higher contextual tiers of the overall crime and to conduct which does not establish a direct link.

Another question would concern the general system of perpetration and participation in a future provision. It has been briefly mentioned above that for the ideas discussed here, both a differentiated system (based on derivative liability) or a functional unitary system (with different forms of non-derivative liability) could serve. The overall discussion concerning systems, as referred to in this book, often equates a system with a certain hierarchy of blameworthiness.

We have seen that a traditional or strict unitary system still garners considerable support in academic literature. However, under the impression that—aside from doctrinal coherency—fair labelling and expressive justice play the most important

83 Marxen 1998, pp. 231–2; Vest 2011, p. 400.

84 Marxen 1998, p. 233; Vest 2011, p. 400.

85 Note again the quote by Marxen: "A link between the acting individual and the criminal consequence must still exist, but it does not have to be a direct link" (Marxen 1998, p. 233, translation by the author). See on direct and indirect linkage principles van Sliedregt 2012, pp. 181–2. The novelty of Vest's approach in this context, is the outlining of the three different levels as described above. His concept allows the construction of an "overall criminal context" for one or several specific crimes (execution stage), a wider spatial and temporal context of a pattern (organisational level) and the overall national criminal context (leadership level), see for this synthesis Vest 2011, pp. 400–1, also regard the graphs at pp. 436–7.

86 See e.g. *Judgment Against Adolf Eichmann*, No 197, referring to *the* crime of the Holocaust.

role for the future development of perpetration and participation in international criminal law, a strict unitary system without any hierarchy of blameworthiness should be rejected. Instead, future provisions should contain clear mitigation rules for certain forms of participation, including aiding and abetting. Next to highly differentiated forms of organisational, preparatory and executive contributions, the normative decision should determine that other contributions that do not amount to any of these forms, carry a lower blameworthiness.[87] This would also correspond to the system's goal of describing and expressing the wrongdoing of the actor in precise terms.

Whether all the proposed descriptive and systemic forms of participation would lead to unmitigated punishment would have to be scrutinized. It seems logical that most will grasp the conduct of decision makers and architects who shape and enable the subsequent crimes, and who should therefore not enjoy a reduction of sentencing.

As speculated earlier, the future system could therefore work as a functional unitary system[88] or a differentiated system with very limited accessory liability. An explicit and detailed regulation on the attribution of responsibility in international criminal law does not have to stick to the categories that emerge from a comparative view on national systems. Consequently, the denomination of the system is largely irrelevant. However, it should bear certain features that remedy some of the points criticised earlier as unsatisfying.

This means that a future system should allocate little importance to the *mens rea* of the physical perpetrators when assessing the liability of decision makers and architects of international crimes. Whether they acted with sufficient knowledge of the circumstances to establish their own liability, should not make a difference for the persons who plan, organise, and order the commission of such crimes. Furthermore, their state of mind will hardly ever be determinable in practice.

As far as a *dolus specialis* is necessary, the system should pay no regard to the physical perpetrators. The relevant *dolus specialis* of international crimes lies with those individuals primarily responsible for planning, organising and ordering genocide, persecution, etc.[89]

Defences available to the physical perpetrators must be equally irrelevant for the people in the background. It will often be indeterminable whether a person acted

---

[87] Some authors reject such a mitigation *inter alia* based on the potential plethora of highly blameworthy contributions to mass atrocities (see e.g. Ohlin 2015, p. 531), a concern that should be remedied if a rule on liability contains several specified forms of direct participation (ordering, planning, etc.) and systemic forms of responsibility.

[88] Note that the term "unitary system" is often used in the debate around a hierarchy of blameworthiness as implying the opposite of such a hierarchy. However, nothing would impede a system of perpetration limiting itself to original forms of principal liability whilst recognizing that some are more blameworthy than others. Cf. Ambos' interpretation of Article 25 (3) Rome Statute as a functional unitary system which implies different degrees of responsibility at Ambos 2013, pp. 145–8.

[89] Based on such an observation, different authors take the view that at least for the physical perpetrators of genocide, the "special intent" should indeed be equated with the lower threshold of knowledge of the circumstances that shape the genocidal attack. See e.g. Kress 2018, VStGB § 6 mn. 82, 88; Vest 2001, pp. 485–6; van der Wilt 2006, pp. 241 et seq. (with an overview regarding the debate).

under pressure that already amounted to duress or whether it was "only" socio-psychological pressure that made the perpetrator act.

These points naturally follow from the evolving concept of the "overall crime" and its collective context. While the specific perpetrators of a single crime may be acting without the necessary *mens rea* or have certain defences, this will not change the overall criminal context. Large scale crimes against humanity, war crimes and genocide are not brought about by leaders unknowingly, and they are never done in self-defence. Consequently, factors which could play a role for the individual actors on the ground should not influence the liability of those on the higher levels of responsibility.

Under these circumstances, a form of indirect perpetration becomes irrelevant, or at least bears minimal importance for the bulk of relevant cases. Instead, if a person instructs others over whom they have authority, this person will be liable for ordering the subsequent crimes, irrespective of the knowledge, special intent, pressure, or deception under which the executors act. This would also be welcome from the perspective of fair labelling and expressive justice. The term indirect perpetrator will always be less of a comprehensible label than terms such as ordering, planning, and other precise descriptors.

Whether and to what extent the attempt, especially of the descriptive and systemic forms of participation, should be punishable would have to be decided. Attention would have to be paid to the fact that many of the descriptive and systemic forms of liability trigger responsibility at an early point in time where the danger for the protected legal assets will still be rather abstract. In an analogy to the current provision in Article 25 (3)(f) Rome Statute, it would perhaps be possible to define an attempt of the overall crime. Participation could then be punishable as attempted ordering or attempted initiation of a crime, where the steps taken by the accused represent substantial steps towards the commencement of the overall situation.

The denomination of such a system, whether one would call it functionally unitary or differentiated with a very limited accessorial object may be of less importance than one might think. This is especially the case because the system should also explicitly envisage mitigated and unmitigated punishment.

Of course, this does not rule out the use of specific denominations for the overall system. For example, it could explicitly state that persons falling under the central descriptive forms or the systemic forms would be "perpetrators", whereas aiders and abettors would be "accessories". To avoid any terminological misunderstandings, one could rely on a functional unitary approach, in which the terminology of principals and accessories is avoided and different perpetrators (ordering perpetrators, planning perpetrators, aiding perpetrators) explicitly receive different punishments.

This section provided a necessarily rough outline of cornerstones for a future model of liability for international crimes. Some of the thoughts may sound radical but seem warranted considering the findings of the book. It has been established that as far as individual responsibility is concerned, the import of national legal doctrines has misguided the development of international criminal law. At the same time, a parallel, but often neglected group of concepts with high descriptive value emerged that can serve as examples for the development of a future system of individual criminal responsibility. It is to be hoped that the approach outlined in this final chapter will be followed to enable the emergence of truly international modes of liability. Modes that serve the interests not only of the legal elite of some national legal systems, but also of the victims and the international community by clearly and understandably describing the wrongs committed by decision makers and architects of international crimes.

References

Aksenova M (2016) Complicity in International Criminal Law. Hart Publishing, Oxford

Ambos K (2013) Treatise on International Criminal Law - Volume I: Foundations and General Part. Oxford University Press, Oxford

Ambos K (2016) Art. 25. In: The Rome Statute of the International Criminal Court - A Commentary. C.H. Beck/Hart/Nomos, Munich

Burghardt B (2010) Modes of Participation and their Role in a General Concept of Crimes under International Law. In: Burchard C, Triffterer O, Vogel J (eds) The Review Conference and the Future of the International Criminal Court - Proceedings of the First AIDP Symposium for Young Penalists in Tübingen, Germany, co-organized by the AIDP YP Committee. Kluwer Law International, Alphen aan den Rijn, 81–98

Clark RS (2017) Individual Conduct. In: Kreß C, Barriga S (eds) The Crime of Aggression - A Commentary. Cambridge University Press, Cambridge, 565–589

Cryer R (2004) General Principles of Liability in International Criminal Law. In: McGoldrick D, Rowe P (eds) The Permanent International Criminal Court - Legal and Policy Issues. Hart Publishing, Oxford, 233–262

de Figueiredo Dias J (2013) Täterschaftliche Anstiftung - Zur Vereinbarkeit des Konzepts mit der Lehre von der Tatherrschaft. In: Freund G, Murmann U, Bloy R, Perron W (eds) Grundlagen und Dogmatik des gesamten Strafrechtssystems: Festschrift für Wolfgang Frisch zum 70 Geburtstag. Duncker & Humblot, Berlin, 633–652

Dencker F (1996) Kausalität und Gesamttat. Duncker & Humblot, Berlin

Díaz y García Conlledo M (2017) Das Handeln im Rahmen eines organisatorischen Machtapparates: Täterschaft oder Teilnahme? Goltdammer's Archiv 711–720

Du Bois-Pedain A (2019) Participation in Crime. In: Ambos K, Duff A, Roberts J, Weigend T, Heinze A (eds) Core Concepts in Criminal Law and Criminal Justice - Volume I. Cambridge University Press, Cambridge, 94–134

Eser A (2002) Individual Criminal Responsibility. In: Cassesse A, Gaeta P, Jones JRWD (eds) The Rome Statute of the International Criminal Court - A Commentary. Oxford University Press, Oxford, 767–823

Eser A, Sternberg-Lieben D (2019) Vorbemerkungen zu den §§ 211 ff. In: Schönke/Schröder-StGB. C.H. Beck, Munich

Fagan T, Hirstein W, Sifferd K (2016) Child Soldiers, Executive Functions, and Culpability. International Criminal Law Review 16:258–286

Heine G (2000) Täterschaft und Teilnahme in staatlichen Machtapparaten - NS- und DDR-Unrecht im Vergleich der Rechtsprechung. Juristenzeitung 920–926

Heine G, Weisser B (2019) § 25. In: Schönke/Schröder-StGB. C.H. Beck, Munich

Herzberg RD (2000) Mittelbare Täterschaft und Anstiftung in formalen Organisationen. In: Amelung K (ed) Individuelle Verantwortung und Beteiligungsverhältnisse bei Straftaten in bürokratischen Organisationen des Staates, der Wirtschaft und der Gesellschaft. Pro Universitate, Sinzheim, 33–53

Herzberg RD (2009) Das Fujimori-Urteil: Zur Beteiligung des Befehlsgebers an den Verbrechen seines Machtapparates. Zeitschrift für internationale Strafrechtsdogmatik 11:576–580

Hruschka J (1998) Regreßverbot, Anstiftungsbegriff und die Konsequenzen. Zeistschrift für die gesamte Strafrechtswissenschaft 110:581–639

Joecks W (2017) § 25. In: Münchner Kommentar zum Strafgesetzbuch: StGB, Band I §§ 1–37. C.H. Beck, Munich

Kress C (2018) VStGB § 6. In: Münchener Kommentar Strafgesetzbuch - Nebenstrafrecht III Völkerstrafgesetzbuch. C.H. Beck, Munich

Krey V, Nuys M (2009) Der Täter hinter dem Täter - oder die Liebe der Strafrechtler zum Glasperlenspiel. In: Böse M, Sternberg-Lieben D (eds) Grundlagen des Straf- und Strafverfahrensrechts: Festschrift für Knut Amelung zum 70 Geburtstag. Duncker & Humblot, Berlin, 203–223

Maculan E (2013) La fertilización cruzada jurisprudencial y los modelos de responsabilidad - Acordes y desacuerdos en la jurisprudencia latinoamericana. In: Gil Gil A, Maculan E (eds) Intervención Delictiva y Derecho Penal Internacional - Reglas de atribución de la responsabilidad en crímenes internacionales. Dykinson, Madrid, 207–233

Marxen K (1998) Beteiligung an schwerem systematischen Unrecht - Bemerkungen zu einer Völkerstrafrechtlichen Straftatlehre. In: Lüderssen K (ed) Aufgeklärte Kriminalpolitik oder Kampf gegen das Böse? - Band III: Makrodelinquenz. Nomos, Baden-Baden, 220–236

McQueen A (2018) Falling Through the Gap: The Culpability of Child Soldiers Under International Criminal Law. Notre Dame Law Review Online 91:100–127

Noltenius B (2003) Kriterien der Abgrenzung von Anstiftung und mittelbarer Täterschaft. Europäischer Verlag der Wissenschaften, Frankfurt am Main

Ohlin JD (2015) Co-Perpetration: German Dogmatik or German Invasion? In: Stahn C (ed) The Law and Practice of the International Criminal Court. Oxford University Press, Oxford, 517–537

Orozco López HD (2021) Roxins mittelbare Täterschaft kraft organisatorischer Machtapparate - Eine kritische Analyse. Zeitschrift für internationale Strafrechtsdogmatik 233–248

Renzikowski J (1997) Restriktiver Täterbegriff und fahrlässige Beteiligung. Mohr Siebeck, Tübingen

Rotsch T (2000) Tatherrschaft kraft Organisationsherrschaft? Zeitschrift für die gesamte Strafrechtswissenschaft 112:518–562

Roxin C (2019) Täterschaft und Tatherrschaft. De Gruyter, Berlin

Schild W (2017) § 26. In: Nomos Kommentar Strafgesetzbuch. Nomos, Baden-Baden

Schroeder F-C (1965) Der Täter hinter dem Täter: Ein Beitrag zur Lehre von der mittelbaren Täterschaft. Duncker & Humblot, Berlin

Simester AP, Spencer JR, Stark F, Sullivan GR, Virgo GJ (2019) Simester and Sullivan's Criminal Law - Theory and Doctrine. Hart Publishing, Oxford

Stewart JG (2012) The End of "Modes of Liability" for International Crimes. Leiden Journal of International Law 25:165–219

Stewart JG (2014) Ten Reasons for Adopting a Universal Concept of Participation. In: van Sliedregt E, Vasiliev S (eds) Pluralism in International Criminal Law. Oxford University Press, Oxford, 320–341

van der Wilt H (2006) Genocide, Complicity in Genocide and International v. Domestic Jurisdiction. Journal of International Criminal Justice 4:239–257

van Sliedregt E (2012) Individual Criminal Responsibility in International Criminal Law. Oxford University Press, Oxford

van Sliedregt E (2015) Perpetration and Participation in Article 25(3). In: Stahn C (ed) The Law and Practice of the International Criminal Court. Oxford University Press, Oxford, 499–516

van Sliedregt E, Weisser B (2022) The Ntaganda Case and Individual Criminal Liability at the ICC - Foreword. Journal of International Criminal Justice 20:627–635

Vest H (2001) Humanitätsverbrechen - Herausforderung für das Individualstrafrecht? Zeitschrift für die gesamte Strafrechtswissenschaft 113:457–498

Vest H (2002) Genozid durch organisatorische Machtapparate. Nomos, Baden-Baden

Vest H (2011) Völkerrechtsverbrecher verfolgen - Ein abgestuftes Mehrebenensystem systemischer Tatherrschaft. Stämpfli Verlag AG, Bern
Vest H (2014) Problems of Participation - Unitarian, Differentiated Approach, or Something Else? Journal of International Criminal Justice 12:295–309
Vogel J (2002) Individuelle Verantwortlichkeit im Völkerstrafrecht. Zeitschrift für die gesamte Strafrechtswissenschaft 114:403–436
Weigend T (2011) Perpetration through an Organization - The Unexpected Career of a German Legal Concept. Journal of International Criminal Justice 9:91–111
Weigend T (2015) Indirect Perpetration. In: Stahn C (ed) The Law and Practice of the International Criminal Court. Oxford University Press, Oxford, 538–556
Weisser B (2011) Täterschaft in Europa. Mohr Siebeck, Tübingen
Weisser B (2012) Zur umweltstrafrechtlichen Verantwortlichkeit von Leitungspersonen in Unternehmen. In: Hecker B, Hendler R, Proelss A, Reiff P (eds) Verantwortlichkeit und Haftung für Umweltschäden - 28 Trierer Kolloquium zum Umwelt- und Technikrecht vom 6 bis 7 September 2012. Erich Schmidt Verlag, Berlin, 215–236
Werle G, Burghardt B (2014) Täterschaft und Teilnahme im Statut des Internationalen Strafgerichtshofs. Festschrift für Kristian Kühl zum 70 Geburtstag. C.H. Beck, Munich, 851–866
Yanev L (2018) Theories of Co-Perpetration in International Criminal law. Brill Nijhoff, Leiden
Zazcyk R (1996) Die „Tatherrschaft Kraft organisatorischer Machtapparate" und der BGH. Goltdammer's Archiv 411–415
Zimmermann A, Freiburg E (2016) Article 8bis. In: The Rome Statute of the International Criminal Court - A Commentary. C.H. Beck, Munich

Other Documents

District Court of Jerusalem, *Judgment Against Karl Adolf Eichmann - Unofficial Translation*, 40/61

Table of Cases

Documents on Cases of the U.S. Military Tribunals and Other Post-World War II Jurisprudence

Law Reports of Trials of War Criminals Vol. IV, 1948

Law Reports of Trials of War Criminals Vol. V, 1948

Law Reports of Trials of War Criminals Vol. XI, 1948

Law Reports of Trials of War Criminals Vol. XV, 1948

Trials of War Criminals Before the Nuernberg Military Tribunals Under Control Council Law No. 10, Vol. II, U.S. Government Printing Service 1950

Trials of War Criminals Before the Nuernberg Military Tribunals Under Control Council Law No. 10, Vol. III, U.S. Government Printing Service 1950

Trials of War Criminals Before the Nuernberg Military Tribunals Under Control Council Law No. 10, Vol. IV, U.S. Government Printing Service 1950

Trials of War Criminals Before the Nuernberg Military Tribunals Under Control Council Law No. 10, Vol. IX, U.S. Government Printing Service 1950

Trials of War Criminals Before the Nuernberg Military Tribunals Under Control Council Law No. 10, Vol. V, U.S. Government Printing Service 1950

Trials of War Criminals Before the Nuernberg Military Tribunals Under Control Council Law No. 10, Vol. VI, U.S. Government Printing Service 1950

Trials of War Criminals Before the Nuernberg Military Tribunals Under Control Council Law No. 10, Vol. VIII, U.S. Government Printing Service 1950

Trials of War Criminals Before the Nuernberg Military Tribunals Under Control Council Law No. 10, Vol. XI, U.S. Government Printing Service 1950

Trials of War Criminals Before the Nuernberg Military Tribunals Under Control Council Law No. 10, Vol. XIV, U.S. Government Printing Service 1950

Cases before the Federal Court of Justice of Germany

German Federal Court of Justice, Judgment, 15.09.1988, in: Neue Juristische Wochenschrift, 1989, 912

German Federal Court of Justice, Judgment, 03.11.1992, in: Neue Juristische Wochenschrift, 1993, 141

J. Block, *Reconciling Responsibility with Reality*, International Criminal Justice Series 33, https://doi.org/10.1007/978-94-6265-607-9

German Federal Court of Justice, Judgment, 25.03.1993, in: Neue Juristische Wochenschrift, 1993, 1932

German Federal Court of Justice, Judgment, 18.01.1994, in: Neue Juristische Wochenschrift, 1994, 2237

German Federal Court of Justice, Judgment, 19.04.1994, in: Neue Juristische Wochenschrift, 1994, 2240

German Federal Court of Justice, Judgment, 20.10.1993, in: Neue Juristische Wochenschrift, 1994, 267

German Federal Court of Justice, Judgment, 26.7.1994, in: Neue Juristische Wochenschrift, 1994, 2703

German Federal Court of Justice, Judgment, 26.07.1994, in: Neue Juristische Wochenschrift, 1994, 2708

German Federal Court of Justice, Judgment, 03.11.1994, in: Neue Juristische Wochenschrift, 1995, 1564

German Federal Court of Justice, Judgment, 04.03.1996, in: Neue Juristische Wochenschrift, 1996, 2042

German Federal Court of Justice, Judgment, 06.06.1997, in: Neue Zeitschrift für Strafrecht, 1997, 544

German Federal Court of Justice, Judgment, 23.10.1996, in: Neue Juristische Wochenschrift, 1997, 951

German Federal Court of Justice, Judgment, 11.12.1997, in: Neue Juristische Wochenschrift, 1998, 767

German Federal Court of Justice, Judgment, 08.11.1999, in: Neue Juristische Wochenschrift, 2000, 443

German Federal Court of Justice, Decision, 07.07.2001, in: Neue Juristische Wochenschrift, 2001, 3060

German Federal Court of Justice, Judgment, 08.03.2001, in: Neue Juristische Wochenschrift, 2001, 2409

German Federal Court of Justice, Judgment, 06.11.2002, in: Neue Juristische Wochenschrift, 2003, 522

German Federal Court of Justice, Decision, 26.08.2003, in: Neue Juristische Wochenschrift, 2004, 375

German Federal Court of Justice, Decision, 02.11.2007, in: Neue Zeitschrift für Strafrecht, 2008, 89

German Federal Court of Justice, Decision, 29.07.2009, in: Neue Zeitschrift für Strafrecht, 2010, 103

German Federal Court of Justice, Judgment, 22.04.2014, in: Neue Zeitschrift für Strafrecht, 2014, 459

German Federal Court of Justice, Decision, 20.09.2016, in: Neue Juristische Wochenschrift, 2017, 498

Cases before the International Criminal Tribunals for the Former Yugoslavia and for Rwanda and before the Special Court for Sierra Leone

ICTY, *Prosecutor v. Ivica Rajić*, Rule 61 Decision, 13 September 1996, IT-95-12-R61

ICTY, *Prosecutor v. Duško Tadić*, 7 May 1997, IT-94-1-T

ICTR, *The Prosecutor v. Jean Kambanda, Indictment* 28 October 1997, ICTR-97-23-DP

ICTR, *Prosecutor v. Jean-Paul Akayesu*, 2 September 1998, ICTR-96-4-T

ICTR, *The Prosecutor vs. Jean Kambanda*, 4 September 1998, ICTR-97-23-S

ICTY, *Prosecutor v. Zejnil Delalić et al.*, 16 November 1998, IT-96-21-T

ICTR, *The Prosecutor v. Clément Kayishema and Obed Ruzindana*, 21 May 1999, ICTR-95-1-T

ICTY, *Prosecutor v. Duško Tadić*, 15 July 1999, IT-94-1-A

ICTR, *Prosecutor v. Georges Anderson Nderubumwe Rutaganda*, 6 December 1999, ICTR-96-3-T

ICTY, *Prosecutor v. Kupreškić et al.*, 14 January 2000, IT-95-16-T

ICTR, *The Prosecutor v. Alfred Musema*, Trial Decision, 27 January 2000, ICTR-96-13-A

ICTY, *Prosecutor v. Tihomir Blaskić*, 3 March 2000, IT-95-14-T

ICTY, *Prosecutor v. Zlatko Aleksovski*, 24 March 2000, IT-95-14/1-A

ICTY, *Prosecutor v. Zejnil Delalić et. al.*, 20 February 2001, IT-96-21-A

ICTY, *Prosecutor v. Dario Kordić and Mario Čerkez*, 26 February 2001, IT-95-14/2-T

ICTR, *The Prosecutor v. Clément Kayishema and Obed Ruzindana*, 1 June 2001, ICTR-95-1-A

ICTR, *Prosecutor v. Ignace Bagilishema*, 7 June 2001, ICTR-95-1A-T

ICTR, *The Prosecutor v. Protais Zigiranyirazo—Indictment*, Indictment, 20 July 2001, ICTR-01-73-T

ICTY, *Prosecutor v. Radislav Krstić*, 2 August 2001, IT-98-33-T

ICTY, *Prosecutor v. Slobodan Milošević, Second amended Indictment "Kosovo"*, 16 October 2001, IT-99-37-PT

ICTY, *Prosecutor v. Miroslav Kvočka et al.*, 2 November 2001, IT-98-30/1-T

ICTR, *Alfred Musema vs. The Prosecutor*, 16 November 2001, ICTR-96-13-A

ICTY, *Prosecutor vs. Milorad Krnojelac*, 15 March 2002, IT-97-25-T

ICTR, *The Prosecutor vs. Ignace Bagilishema*, 3 July 2002, ICTR-95-1A-A

ICTY, *Prosecutor v. Slobodan Milošević, Amended indictment "Bosnia and Herzegovina"*, 22 November 2002, IT-02-54-T

ICTR, *The Prosecutor v. Elizaphan and Gérard Ntakirutimana* 21 February 2003, ICTR-96-10 and ICTR-96-17-T

ICTY, *Prosecutor v. Mladen Naletilić and Vinko Martinović*, 31 March 2003, IT-98-34-T

ICTR, *Prosecutor v. Laurent Semanza*, 15 May 2003, ICTR-97-20-T

ICTY, *Prosecutor v. Milan Milutinović et al.*, Decision on Ojdanić's Motion Challenging Jurisdiction—Joint Criminal Enterprise, 21 May 2003, IT-99-37-AR72

ICTY, *Prosecutor v. Milomir Stakić*, 31 July 2003, IT-97-24-T

ICTY, *Prosecutor v. Milorad Krnojelac*, 17 September 2003, IT-97-25-A

ICTR, *Prosecutor v. Juvénal Kajelijeli*, 1 December 2003, ICTR-98-44A-T

ICTR, *The Prosecutor v. Ferdinand Nahimana et al.*, 3 December 2003, ICTR-99-52-T

ICTY, *Prosecutor v. Stanislav Galić*, 5 December 2003, IT-98-29-T

ICTR, *The Prosecutor v. Jean de Dieu Kamuhanda*, 22 January 2004, ICTR-95-54A-T

ICTR, *Prosecutor v. André Ntagerura et al.*, 25 February 2004, ICTR-99-46-T

ICTY, *Prosecutor v. Mitar Vasiljević*, 25 February 2004, IT-98-32-A

ICTY, *Prosecutor v. Radoslav Brđanin*, Decision on Interlocutory Appeal, 19 March 2004, IT-99-36-A

ICTY, *Prosecutor v. Radislav Krstić*, 19 April 2004, IT-98-33-A

ICTR, *Prosecutor v. Sylvestre Gacumbitsi*, 17 June 2004, ICTR-2001-64-T

ICTR, *The Prosecutor vs. Emmanuel Ndindabahizi*, 15 July 2004, ICTR-2001-71-I

ICTY, *Prosecutor v. Slobodan Milošević, Second amended Indictment "Croatia"*, 28 July 2004, IT-02-54-T

ICTY, *Prosecutor v. Tihomir Blaskić*, 29 July 2004, IT-95-14-A

ICTY, *Prosecutor v. Radoslav Brđanin*, 1 September 2004, IT-99-36-T

ICTY, *Prosecutor v. Dario Kordić and Mario Čerkez*, 17 December 2004, IT-95-14/2-A

ICTY, *Prosecutor v. Pavle Strugar*, 31 January 2005, IT-01-42-T

ICTY, *Prosecutor v. Miroslav Kvočka et al.*, 28 February 2005, IT-98-30/1-A

ICTR, *Prosecutor v. Laurent Semanza*, 20 May 2005, ICTR-97-20-A

ICTR, *Juvénal Kajelijeli vs. The Prosecutor*, 23 May 2005, ICTR-98-44A-A

ICTY, *Prosecutor v. Miroslav Deronjić*, 20 July 2005, IT-02-61-A

ICTR, *The Prosecutor v. Jean de Dieu Kamuhanda*, 19 September 2005, ICTR-99-54A-A

ICTY, *Prosecutor vs. Fatmir Limaj et al.*, 30 November 2005, IT-03-66-T

ICTR, *The Prosecutor v. Aloys Simba*, 13 December 2005, ICTR-01-76-T

ICTY, *Prosecutor v. Enver Hadžihasanović and Amir Kubura*, 15 March 2006, IT-01-47-T

ICTY, *Prosecutor v. Milomir Stakić*, 22 March 2006, IT-97-24-A

ICTR, *Édouard Karemera et al. v. The Prosecutor*, Decision on Jurisdictional Appeals—Joint Criminal Enterprise, 12 April 2006, ICTR-98-44-AR72.5—ICTR-98-44-AR72.6

ICTY, *Prosecutor v. Naser Orić*, 30 June 2006, IT-03-68-T

ICTR, *The Prosecutor v. André Ntagerura, Emmanuel Bagambiki and Samuel Imanishimwe*, 7 July 2006, ICTR-99-46-A

ICTR, *Sylvestre Gacumbitsi v. The Prosecutor*, 7 July 2006, ICTR-2001-64-A

ICTR, *Prosecutor v. Tharcisse Muvunyi*, 12 September 2006, ICTR-2000-55A-T

ICTY, *Prosecutor v. Momčilo Krajišnik*, 27 September 2006, IT-00-39-T

ICTR, *Aloys Simba v. The Prosecutor*, 27 November 2007, ICTR-01-76-A

ICTY, *Prosecutor v. Blagoje Simić*, 28 November 2006, IT-95-9-A

ICTY, *Prosecutor v. Stanislav Galić*, 30 November 2006, IT-98-29-A

ICTR, *The Prosecutor vs. Athanase Seromba*, 13 December 2006, ICTR-2001-66-1

ICTR, *Emmanuel Ndindabahizi vs. the Prosecutor*, 16 January 2007, ICTR-01-71-A

ICTY, *Prosecutor v. Radoslav Brđanin*, 3 April 2007, IT-99-36-A

ICTY, *Prosecutor v. Vidoje Blagojević and Dragan Jokić*, 9 May 2007, IT-02-60-A

ICTY, *Prosecutor v. Milan Martić*, 12 June 2007, IT-95-11-T

SCSL, *Prosecutor against Brima, Kamara, Kanu*, 20 June 2007, SCSL-04-16-T

SCSL, *Prosecutor against Moinina Fofana et al.*, 2 August 2007, SCSL-04-14-T

ICTY, *Prosecutor v. Fatmir Limaj , Haradin Bala, Isak Musliu*, Appeals Judgment, 27 September 2007, IT-03-66-A

ICTY, *Prosecutor v. Mile Mrkšić et al.*, 27 September 2007, IT-95-13/1-T

ICTR, *Ferdinand Nahimana et al. v. The Prosecutor*, 28 November 2007, ICTR-99-52-A

ICTR, *The Prosecutor v. François Karera*, 7 December 2007, ICTR-01-74-T

ICTY, *Prosecutor v. Dragomir Milošević*, 12 December 2007, IT-98-29/1-T

SCSL, *Prosecutor against Alex Tamba Brima et al.*, 22 February 2008, SCSL-2004-16-A

ICTR, *The Prosecutor v. Athanase Seromba*, 12 March 2008, ICTR-2001-66-A

ICTY, *Prosecutor v. Ljube Boškoski and Johan Tarčulovski*, 10 July 2008, IT-04-82-T

ICTY, *Prosecutor v. Milan Martić*, 8 October 2008, IT-95-11-A

ICTR, *The Prosecutor vs. Siméon Nchamihigo*, 12 November 2008, ICTR-01-63-T

ICTR, *Prosecutor v. Bagosora et al.*, 18 December 2008, ICTR-98-41-T

ICTY, *Prosecutor v. Milan Milutinović et al.*, 26 February 2009, IT-05-87-T

ICTY, *Prosecutor v. Momčilo Krajišnik*, 17 March 2009, IT-00-39-A

ICTY, *Prosecutor v. Mile Mrkšić and Veselin Šljivančanin*, 5 May 2009, ICTY-95-13/1-A

ICTR, *The Prosecutor v. Callixte Kalimanzira*, 22 June 2009, ICTR-05-88-T

ICTR, *Prosecutor v. Tharcisse Renzaho*, 14 July 2009, ICTR-97-31-T

ICTY, *Prosecutor v. Dragomir Milošević*, 12 November 2009, IT-98-29/1-A

ICTR, *Siméon Nchamihigo v. the Prosecutor*, 18 March 2010, ICTR-2001-63-A

ICTY, *Prosecutor v. Ljube Boškoski and Johan Tarčulovski*, 19 May 2010, IT-04-82-A

ICTY, *Prosecutor v. Vujadin Popović et al.*, 10 June 2010, IT-05-88-T

ICTR, *Prosecutor v. Yussuf Munyakazi*, 5 July 2010, ICTR-97-36A-T

ICTR, *The Prosecutor vs. Dominique Ntawukulilyayo*, 3 August 2010, ICTR-05-82-T

ICTR, *Prosecutor v. Callixte Kalimanzira*, 20 October 2010, ICTR-05-88-A

ICTR, *Prosecutor v. Gaspard Kanyarukiga*, 1 November 2010, ICTR-2002-78-T

ICTY, *Prosecutor v. Vlastimir Đorđević*, 23 February 2011, IT-05-87/1-T

ICTR, *Tharcisse Renzaho v. The Prosecutor*, 1 April 2011, ICTR-97-31-A

ICTY, *Prosecutor v. Ante Gotovina et al.*, 15 April 2011, IT-06-90-T

ICTR, *The Prosecutor v. Pauline Nyiramasuhuko et al.*, 24 June 2011, ICTR-98-42-T

ICTR, *The Prosecutor v. Yussuf Munyakazi*, 28 September 2011, ICTR-97-36A-A

ICTR, *The Prosecutor v. Casimir Bizimungu et al.*, 30 September 2011, ICTR-99-50-T

ICTR, *Dominique Ntawukulilyayo v. The Prosecutor*, 14 December 2011, ICTR-05-82-A

ICTR, *Théoneste Bagosora et al. v. The Prosecutor*, 14 December 2011, ICTR-98-41-A

ICTR, *The Prosecutor v. Grégoire Ndahimana*, 30 December 2011, ICTR-01-68-T

ICTR, *Prosecutor v. Édouard Karemera et al.*, 2 February 2012, ICTR-98-44-T

ICTR, *Gaspard Kanyarukiga v. The Prosecutor*, 8 May 2012, ICTR-02-78-A

SCSL, *Prosecutor v. Charles Ghankay Taylor*, 18 May 2012, SCSL-03-01-T

SCSL, *Prosecutor v. Charles Ghankay Taylor, Sentencing Judgment*, 30 May 2012, SCSL-03-01-T

ICTY, *Prosecutor v. Ramush Haradinaj et al.*, 29 November 2012, IT-04-84bis-T

ICTY, *Prosecutor v. Zdravko Tolimir*, 12 December 2012, IT-05-88/2-T

ICTR, *The Prosecutor v. Augustin Ngirabatware*, 20 December 2012, ICTR-99-54-T

ICTY, *Prosecutor v. Mićo Stanišić and Stojan Župljanin*, 27 March 2013, IT-08-91-T

ICTY, *Prosecutor v. Jovica Stanišić and Franko Simatović*, 30 May 2013, IT-03-69-T

ICTY, *Prosecutor v. Vlastimir Đorđević*, 27 January 2014, IT-05-87/1-A

ICTR, *Édouard Karemera et al. v. The Prosecutor*, 29 September 2014, ICTR-98-44-A

ICTR, *The Prosecutor v. Pauline Nyiramasuhuko et al.*, 14 December 2015, ICTR-98-42-A

ICTY, *Prosecutor v. Radovan Karadžić*, 24 March 2016, IT-95-5/18-T

ICTY, *Prosecutor v. Ratko Mladić*, 22 November 2017, IT-09-92-T

MICT, *Prosecutor vs. Radovan Karadžić*, 20 March 2019, MICT-13-55-A

Cases before the ICC

ICC, *The Prosecutor v. Dominic Ongwen*, Issuance of a Warrant of Arrest, 8 July 2005, ICC-02/04

ICC, *The Prosecutor v. Okot Odhiambo*, Issuance of a Warrant of Arrest, 8 July 2005, ICC-02/04

ICC, *The Prosecutor v. Raska Lukwiya*, Issuance of a Warrant of Arrest, 8 July 2005, ICC-02/04

ICC, *The Prosecutor v. Vincent Otti*, Issuance of a Warrant of Arrest, 8 July 2005, ICC-02/04

ICC, *The Prosecutor v. Joseph Kony*, Issuance of a Warrant of Arrest, 27 September 2005, 02/04-01/05

ICC, *The Prosecutor v. Thomas Lubanga*, Confirmation of Charges, 29 January 2007, ICC-01/04-01/06

ICC, *The Prosecutor v. Germain Katanga*, Arrest Warrant Decision, 6 July 2007, ICC-01/04-01/07

ICC, *The Prosecutor v. Matthieu Ngudjolo Chui*, Arrest Warrant Decision, 6 July 2007, ICC-01/04-02/07

ICC, *The Prosecutor v. Jean-Pierre Bemba et al.*, Confirmation of Charges, 11 November 2014, ICC-01/05-01/13

ICC, *The Prosecutor v. Thomas Lubanga Dyilo*, Appeals Judgment, 1 December 2014, ICC-01/04-01/06 A 5

ICC, *The Prosecutor v. Charles Blé Goudé*, Confirmation of Charges, 11 December 2014, ICC-02/011-02/11

ICC, *The Prosecutor v. Dominic Ongwen*, Confirmation of charges, 23 March 2016, ICC-02/04-01/15

ICC, *The Prosecutor v. Jean-Pierre Bemba Gombo*, Sentencing Decision, 21 June 2016, ICC-01/05-01/08

ICC, *The Prosecutor v. Ahmad Al Faqi Al Mahdi*, Trial Judgment, 27 September 2016, ICC-01/12-01/15

ICC, *The Prosecutor v. Jean-Pierre Bemba Gombo et al.*, Trial Judgment, 19 October 2016, ICC-01/05-01/13

ICC, *The Prosecutor v. Mahmoud Mustafa Busayf Al-Werfalli*, Warrant of Arrest, 15 August 2017, ICC-01/11-01/717

ICC, *The Prosecutor v. Jean-Pierre Bemba et al.*, Appeals Judgment, 8 March 2018, ICC-01/05-01/13 A A2 A3 A4 A5

ICC, *The Prosecutor v. Jean-Pierre Bemba Gombo et al.*, Judgment on Sentencing Appeal, 8 March 2018, ICC-01/05-01/13 A6 A7 A8 A9

ICC, *The Prosecutor v. Al Hassan Ag Abdoul Aziz Ag Mohamed Ag Mahmoud*, Issuance of a Warrant of Arrest, 22 May 2018, ICC-01/12-01/18

ICC, *The Prosecutor v. Bosco Ntaganda*, Trial Judgment, 8 July 2019, ICC-01/04-02/06

ICC, *The Prosecutor v. Laurent Gbagbo and Charles Blé Goudé*, Reasons for oral decision of 15 January 2019 on the Requête de la Défense de Laurent Gbagbo afin qu'un jugement d'acquittement portant sur toutes les charges soit prononcé en faveur de Laurent Gbagbo et que sa mise en liberté immédiate soit ordonnée, and on the Blé Goudé Defence no case to answer motion, 16 July 2019, ICC-02/11-01/15

ICC, *The Prosecutor v. Patrice-Edouard Ngaïssona and Alfred Yekatom*, Document Containing the Charges, 18 September 2019, ICC-01/14-01/18

ICC, *The Prosecutor v. Alfred Yekatom and Patrice-Edouard Ngaïssona*, 5 May 2020, ICC-01/14-01/18

ICC, *The Prosecutor v. Dominic Ongwen*, Trial Judgment, 4 February 2021, ICC-02/04-01/15

ICC, *The Prosecutor v. Bosco Ntaganda*, Appeals Judgment, 30 March 2021, ICC-01/04-02/06-A A2

Other Cases

District Court of Jerusalem, *Judgment Against Karl Adolf Eichmann—Unofficial Translation*, 40/61

ECCC, *Decision on the Appeals against the Co-Investigating Judges Order on Joint Criminal Enterprise (JCE)*, 20 May 2010, 002/19-09-2007-ECCC/OCIJ

ECCC, *Duch Trial Judgment*, Judgment, No. 001/18-07-2007/ECCC/TC

Index

J. Block, *Reconciling Responsibility with Reality*, International Criminal Justice Series 33, https://doi.org/10.1007/978-94-6265-607-9